A Unique Sufi Interpretation

DECODING
THE
QURAN

AHMED HULUSI

A Unique Sufi Interpretation

DECODING
THE
QURAN

AHMED HULUSI

www.ahmedhulusi.org/en/

Translated by ALIYA ATALAY

Translator's Note

"I am the city of knowledge and Ali is its gate; so whoever desires knowledge,

let him enter the gate."

(Muhammad saw)

"The secret of the Quran is in al-Fatiha, the secret of al-Fatiha is in the Basmalah,

and the secret of the Basmalah is in the letter B (ب).

And I am the POINT beneath the 'B' (ب)!"

(Ali ra)

When Hadhrat Ali (ra) made this statement he was probably not referring to a cryptograph. Nor was he presenting a code or a cypher in the literal sense. He was, however, shedding light on a paramount code – the encodement of existence.

By positing that the entire Quran is contained in a single letter, and depicting himself as a point comprising it, Hadhrat Ali (ra) effectively alludes to what modern science has come to theorize as the 'holographic universe.' In other words, the whole is contained in the part; each and every iota of existence potentially contains the whole, and what we label as the 'whole', or the 'outside world', is our hologram. That is, we live in the virtual projection of our own perceptions and beliefs, which consequently nullifies the concept of 'other', thus endorsing the non-duality of existence.

So, if the universe is contained in the Quran, and the Quran is contained in the 'point', we, every single one of us, are encrypted 'points' of micro universes, containing within us the infinite vastness of endless potentiality.

It is this principle upon which Ahmed Hulusi establishes his interpretation of the Quran, drawing the attention to the self and the Self rather than things or god/s 'out there.' Taking special note of words that begin with the letter B, he construes their meanings introspectively, directing the reader to turn inward for their rendition.

Although the masculine pronoun 'He' was unavoidable, it is needless to say 'Allah' – the infinite consciousness beyond all preconceived and preconditioned ideas – transcendentally and indubitably surpasses any gender or form. As such, it is important to keep in mind that 'Allah' is a name that encompasses all the Names, qualities and attributes – the manifest and the unmanifest – pertaining to existence and nonexistence.

Though some key words such as Rabb and Rasul have been used in their original form, as no English counterpart adequately captures their meanings, I have devised a glossary (included at the end) explaining what they mean according to Ahmed Hulusi, in hope of aiding their correct understanding.

When Ahmed Hulusi shared with me a copy of his Turkish Quran four years ago at a 'coincidental' meeting, my first response was to ask him if there was an English version, to which he answered, "Perhaps you will translate it!" At the time, I had no such intentions or any involvement in literary translations, so I laughed his comment off. Two years later, fate had me translating his book, The Observing One. Since then I have had the honor of translating five of his books, followed by Decoding the Quran, which took just over a year to complete. I am unable to express my gratitude enough to have had the blessed opportunity to work on such a unique interpretation of the Quran with such a fabulous team, especially Guner Turkmen and Onder Tuncay, whose exceptional support has been invaluable to the completion of this project.

As I write this note on this revered night of Ramadan, I ask that you forgive me for any inadequacies and/or mistakes I may have made, for all imperfections pertain to me, while it is the countenance of the eternal One who is perfect.

May the key of the letter B unlock our selves to our Selves…

"Indeed, when He wills a thing, His command is 'B'e… and it is!" (36:82)

Aliya Atalay
Sydney, 2013

CONTENTS

Introductory Information To Understanding The Quran.................... 1

An Important Note About Understanding 'Decoding The Quran'........................ 10

Decoding The Quran.............................. 12

An Essential Message........................... 24

The Exalted, Magnificent And Perfect Qualities Of The Names Of Allah (Al-Asma Ul-Husna).... 26

1. Al-Fatiha............................... 53

2. Al-Baqarah............................ 55

3. Ali-Imran............................. 96

4. An-Nisa.............................. 120

5. Al-Ma'idah........................... 142

6. Al-An'am.............................158

7. Al-A'raf..............................177

8. Al-Anfal.............................200

9. At-Tawbah..............................209

10. Yunus.................................225

11. Hud....................................238

12. Yusuf.................................251

13. Ra'd...................................263

14. Ibrahim..............................270

15. Al-Hijr...............................276

16. An-Nahl.............................283

17. Al-Isra...............................296

18. Al-Kahf..............................308

19. Maryam..............................319

20. Ta-Ha................................327

21. Al-Anbiya...........................339

22. Al-Hajj..............................348

23. Al-Mu'minun.......................357

24. An-Nur..............................366

25. Al-Furqan..........................374

26. Ash-Shu'ara.......................382

27. An-Naml............................395

28. Al-Qasas...........................404

29. Al-Ankabut........................413

30. Ar-Rum.............................421

31. Luqman.............................427

32. As-Sajda............................431

33. Al-Ahzab............................435

34. As-Saba.............................443

35. Fatir..................................449

36. Ya-Sin... 455
37. As-Saffat... 461
38. Saad.. 471
39. Az-Zumar... 478
40. Al-Mu'min.. 486
41. Fussilat... 495
42. Ash-Shura.. 501
43. Az-Zukhruf.. 507
44. Ad-Dukhan.. 514
45. Al-Jathiya.. 518
46. Al-Ahqaf... 522
47. Muhammad.. 527
48. Al-Fath.. 531
49. Hujurat.. 535
50. Qaf... 538
51. Adh-Dhariyat....................................... 542
52. At-Tur... 546
53. An-Najm.. 550
54. Al-Qamar... 554
55. Ar-Rahman... 558
56. Al-Waqi'a... 564
57. Al-Hadid.. 570
58. Al-Mujadila... 575
59. Al-Hashr.. 579
60. Al-Mumtahina...................................... 583
61. As-Saff.. 586

62. Al-Jumu'a..............................588

63. Al-Munafiqun.........................590

64. At-Taghabun.........................592

65. At-Talaq.............................594

66. At-Tahrim...........................597

67. Al-Mulk.............................599

68. Al-Qalam............................602

69. Al-Haqqa............................606

70. Al-Ma'arij..........................609

71. Nuh.................................612

72. Al-Jinn.............................615

73. Al-Muzammil........................618

74. Al-Muddathir.......................621

75. Al-Qiyama..........................625

76. Al-Insan...........................628

77. Al-Mursalat........................631

78. An-Naba............................634

79. An-Nazi'at.........................637

80. Abasa..............................640

81. At-Takwir..........................642

82. Al-Infitar.........................644

83. Al-Mutaffifin......................646

84. Al-Inshiqaq........................648

85. Al-Buruj...........................650

86. At-Tariq...........................652

87. Al-A'la............................653

88. Al-Ghashiya.................................... 655

89. Al-Fajr.. 657

90. Al-Balad...................................... 659

91. As-Shams..................................... 661

92. Al-Lail....................................... 663

93. Ad-Dhuha..................................... 665

94. Ash-Sharh.................................... 666

95. At-Tin.. 667

96. Al-Alaq....................................... 668

97. Al-Qadr...................................... 670

98. Al-Bayyina................................... 671

99. Al-Zalzala.................................... 672

100. Al-Adiyat................................... 673

101. Al-Qaria.................................... 674

102. Al-Takathur................................ 675

103. Al-Asr...................................... 676

104. Al-Humaza..................................677

105. Al-Fil...................................... 678

106. Quraysh....................................679

107. Al-Ma'un.................................... 680

108. Al-Kawthar.................................681

109. Al-Kafirun.................................682

110. An-Nasr....................................683

111. Al-Masad.................................... 684

112. Al-Ikhlas...................................685

113. Al-Falaq.................................... 686

114. An-Nas...687
About The Author..689
Glossary..691

INTRODUCTORY INFORMATION TO UNDERSTANDING THE QURAN

The original script of this work you've picked up to **READ** is not a book comprising *the orders and commands of a God up in the heavens, who apparently revealed it to his postman-prophet on earth*!

It is the **Knowledge of the Reality** and the **System** (*sunnatullah* [denotes the laws and order of Allah, that is, the mechanics of the System and the laws that govern the manifested worlds]) *disclosed* by the *Rabb* of the worlds (the source of the infinite meanings of the Names), from the dimensional depths to the consciousness of **Rasulullah** (the locus of Allah's knowledge, i.e. the focal point of the cosmos through which divine knowledge is expressed and disseminated), through the act of **revelation** (*irsal*)!

Let it be emphasized from the outset that...

This book is neither a translation nor an interpretation of the Quran. It can never replace the Quran! It is merely an attempt to share one or two aspects of the multi-layered meanings of the Quran!

This book is only a window looking at the Quran through the viewpoint endowed to Allah's servant, Ahmed Hulusi. Indeed, it is a reflection of only a part of the scene observed from this window!

The foundation of the viewpoint from this window is in accord with the following example:

When both eyes of a person are healthy and functional, the view is whole and clear. Those who don't have a full vision wear glasses or lenses. The **Quran** is like a lens bestowed by **Allah** so that one can obtain a clear and healthy vision of the two truths; the **Book of the Universe**, and the **System** (*sunnatullah*), to **READ** them correctly.

In order to see the **Reality** as clear and one, we need the glasses of foresight (*basirah*) and knowledge, whereby the letter **B** comprises one lens, and the knowledge of the Absolute Self-sufficient One (*al-Ahad-us-Samad*) constitutes the other lens.

The former lens is the very first letter of the Quran; the letter **B**. Its meaning is revealed in Muhammad's (saw) words **"The part is the same as the whole!"** which I have explained in consonance with the **Holographic Reality** in my book *The Observing One*. Every point perceived as a part or a unit in existence, contains the entire *al-Asma* (the Names) with their complete potentiality.

The latter lens, that is, the knowledge of the Absolute Self-Sufficient One, has been embedded at the end of the **Quran**, in the chapter *al-Ikhlas* (literally means 'sincerity' in English, and is the name of the last and also the shortest chapter of the Quran). It is the accentuation that the One denoted by the name **Allah** is **One** (*Ahad*) and **Absolute Self-Sufficient** (*Samad*). It is *HU*! There is no 'other' than *HU*! *As-Samad* connotes '**Absolute Self-Sufficient ONEness to and from which nothing can be added or taken away.**'

If these two truths do not yield one view, **the soul of the Quran and the message it aims to give** can never be perceived correctly; the *reality* of the 'God up in the heavens and the prophet on earth' will never be known.

Indeed, this book endeavors to aid the reader to evaluate the signs of the Quran in the light of the One denoted by the name Allah, as the Absolute Self-Sufficient One.

As far as we are aware, there are no other works to the likes of this book. Many works have been produced conveying somewhat depthless and perhaps historical narrations of the Quran, rather than reflecting its actual message and soul. Most of these works employ such obscure language that it is no wonder many readers find it distasteful to read. Pedantic attempts to remain faithful to 'word-for-word' translations have reduced this **timeless literary masterpiece** into the misunderstood puzzle of our day.

Moreover, as you will see while reading it, this **literary masterpiece** frequently employs **various examples and metaphors** to explain the many truths contained within it, urging the reader to contemplate on their meanings... Sadly, however, the limited comprehension of the majority has taken these Quranic metaphors **literally** and rendered them as **laws**, fortifying their belief in a heavenly God, his messenger on earth and a heavenly book containing his decrees.

I am of the belief that if the essential idea can be duly reflected to the reader, people will have an exceedingly different approach and understanding of this supreme **knowledge**.

Due to this, before you start to **READ** it, I would like to share the principal message and some of the concepts of this **book – knowledge** according to my understanding.

The essential objective of the Quran is to aid the people to understand and get to know **the One denoted by** the name **Allah**, and to safeguard them against the God notion that leads to **duality** (*shirq*).

While believing in an external God, no matter how far and beyond in space He may be, is an explicit advocacy of duality (*shirq*), fostering ideas that there are 'other' beings with power in existence aside or apart from Allah (including one's ego) is an implicit promotion of duality.

The **knowledge** (Book) that has descended to address **humanity** forewarns its evaluators with these words:

"**Those who support 'duality'** (fragmenting existence; assuming there is a God *AND* there is everything *ELSE*) **are contaminated!**"

"**Those who have not cleansed themselves of the contamination** (of duality; the idea that there is a God and there is *also* me) **shall not touch it** (the knowledge – Quran... for they cannot understand it!)"

"**Indeed, duality** (assuming the existence of 'others' that are 'apart' from the One denoted by name Allah) **is a grave atrocity!**"

"**Duality is the only offence that Allah will definitely not forgive; everything else may be forgiven if He wishes to!**"

Those who want to be free of **duality** are encouraged to believe in the One denoted by the name Allah.

The Quran explains the two stages of believing in Allah as:

A) **To believe in Allah** (including faith in Allah with duality)

B) **To believe in Allah in accord with the meaning of the letter 'B'.**

The former elucidates the need to cleanse from the **explicit** notion of **duality** resulting from the illusion of an **external God**.

The latter, entails the pure belief that is free of even **implicit duality** which is the covert tendency of doing *shirq* by **equating one's ego or assumed self to one's *Rabb*** (the *al-Asma*, i.e. the reality of the Names that constitute one's essential reality).

Let us see how the paramount **knowledge of reality** revealed through **Sufism** (*tasawwuf*), to which many people scoff at, explains the misconception of **implicit duality** and how this topic is covered in the **Quran:**

This is directly from Hamdi Yazir's translation (the international Sahih translation has been used here). Notice that the verse isn't addressing the past, but it is talking directly to Rasulullah Muhammad (saw) about the faith of the people around him at that time:

"That is from the news of the unseen which We reveal, [O Muhammad], to you. And you were not with them when they put together their plan while they conspired.

And most of the people, although you strive [for it], are not believers.

And you do not ask of them for it any payment. It is not except a reminder to the worlds.

And how many a sign within the heavens and earth do they pass over while they, therefrom, are turning away.

And most of them believe not in Allah except while they associate others with Him." (Quran 12:102-107)

Now, let's remember the very important verse and warning that made me write the book *Mind and Faith* - Chapter 4 (*Nisa*): 136 is revealed to Muhammad (saw) and is in reference to the believers around him:

'O you who have believed; *Aminu B'illahi'* That is, **'O you have believed, believe in Allah in accord with the meaning of the B sign.'**

What does this mean?

It means: **Among all the worlds that are constituted by the meanings of the names of Allah, your reality, existence, and being also comprise the Names of Allah. Your** *Rabb*, **your very Reality is the** *al-Asma* **(the Names). Therefore, neither you nor anything else around you is anything other than the manifestations of these Names. So do not be of those who fail to see this non-dual reality, and who give a separate existence to things** (like God) **they believe is 'other' than Allah. Such duality will only result in burning, both in this life and the next.**

However, the eighth verse of the 2nd Chapter (*Baqarah*) asserts the inability of the masses to conceive such truths as their manifestation (as the composition of the Names) is not as intellectuals:

"And of the people are some who say, 'We believe in Allah (in accord with the meaning of the B sign) **and the Last Day,' but they are not believers** (in accord with the meaning of the B sign)."

Hence, dismissing the eminent meaning entailed by the letter **B** simply as 'implicit duality' and not giving it the attention it deserves, has inevitable spawned the '*God up in the heavens, and me on earth*' misconception, resulting at the point it has come to today.

Whereas...

The invalidity of duality has been made evident right from the very first letter; the letter **B**, of the first verse (chapter) called the '*Basmalah*.' This truth, concealed by many Quran scholars due to the conditionings they receive throughout their training, was first made apparent by Hadhrat **Ali** approximately 1400 years ago.

Hadhrat Ali, the zenith of sainthood, pointed to this truth, considered to be a secret in his time, with his words:

"The secret of the Quran is in al-Fatiha (the opening chapter), the secret of al-Fatiha is in the B-ismillah, and the secret of the B-ismillah is in the letter B (ب). I am the POINT beneath the 'B' (ب)!"

This truth to which Hadhrat **Ali** was pointing, plays a key role in the Quran as a symbol of warning, initially encountered as the letter **B**, the first letter of the first verse '*B-ismillah*', and then throughout the whole Quran.

The late Hamdi Yazir, in his *Interpretation of the Quran*; Ahmed Avni Konuk, in his construal of the *Fusus-al Hikam* (*The Bezels of Wisdom* by Ibn Arabi) and Abdulaziz Majdi Tolun, in his commentary on *Insan-i Kamil* (*The Perfect Man*) have all given adequate warnings about this truth.

I, too, to the best of my capability, tried to evaluate the verses of this divine book in the light of this truth; taking into special consideration where the letter **B** has been used and what meaning it entails in this particular position.

The verse '*B-ismillah*' emphasizes the importance of **READ**ing the **Quran** with the awareness of the meanings implied by the letter **B**. The letter **B** points to the reality that, all joy or grief that is experienced by one, result from one's own inner reality, in accordance to the meanings projected from one's essence. The letter **B** tells us that one's experience of heaven or hell **is the direct result of one's actions**; that is, what manifests through one is based on the **Names** that are inherent within them. Thus '*B-ismillah*' is repeated at the beginning of every chapter, reminding us of this truth.

According to my understanding, '*B-ismillahirrahmanirrahim*' is a chapter in itself.

It is impossible to understand the **Quran**, without first comprehending the purpose, indicated by the Absolute Reality the name

Allah denotes, which is based on the Quran itself, and the teachings of the most magnificent human to have ever lived on earth, **Muhammad Mustapha** (saw).

If this purpose is not recognized, the wrong approaches will be taken towards the Quran; as if it were a history book, a good virtue book, a social order book, or a book containing the knowledge of the universe, etc.

Whereas, the most prominent truth that stands out to the **READer** who has no prejudice or preconditions, are the **hints that enable one to abandon the dual view**, and the teachings of the ways in which the consciousness can be cleansed towards this reality. Humans, because of the way they have been created, are immortal beings! **They only taste death** and, by constantly experiencing new realms of existence (*ba'th*), they go on to live an eternal life!

Death is the Doomsday of the person, where the veil of the body is lifted and the person observes their own reality, and then begins to live the consequences of how much they were able to use this reality during their earthly life. As you **READ** you will see the various depictions of this throughout the book.

Hence...

Humans must know and understand their own reality and live their life accordingly, so they can use the **potential** arising from their **Reality** and earn **heavenly** life... that is, of course, if their **Rabb (the Names that comprise their essence)** has enabled them to! The act of turning towards one's Rabb, should not be an external turn, but an internal one towards one's own Reality, which is what praying (*salat*) is – an inward turn towards one's own essence.

At this point we must take heed of the following:

According to my understanding (and as I tried to elucidate in my book *Renew Yourself* the structure I refer to as the 'universe within universes', in respect of its reality, is a **multidimensional single frame picture**, or, a **'singular holographic knowledge – an ocean of energy'** with all its dimensions. The whole of this ocean is contained in each of its drops. It is the quantum potential! As **Rasulullah** (saw) declared with his words: **"The part mirrors the whole!"**

As I have tried to explain in detail in my book *Muhammad's Allah* there is no **'other'** (concept, content, or form) in existence that can be likened or equated in any way to the One denoted by the name **ALLAH**.

Due to this reality, all enlightened beings extending from the contemplation and observation chain of Hadhrat Ali and Hadhrat **Abu Bakr**, who was referenced in the Quran as **'the second of the two'** have all confirmed the same reality: **"There is only Allah, and nothing else!"** This is why observing and evaluating His universal perfection (*hamd*) **belongs** only to **Allah**! As there is no other, Allah is the evaluator of Himself!

Duality is an invalid and **illusory** notion!

Mankind arrives at this erroneous judgment with their **illusions**, becoming veiled (*kufr*) to the **true Unity behind the misperception of multiplicity**! Consequently, people live their lives believing themselves to be **only the material body** which will eventually die and be cast away to nonexistence or they assume the existence of an exterior God, whether up in the heavens of within the self (*shirq*)!

Whereas according to the **people of Allah**, who base their views on the **Quran** and **Rasulullah**, the core of the matter is:

'HU,' other than whom nothing exists, observes His knowledge, with His knowledge, i.e. the **properties** (quantum potential) **denoted by the Beautiful Names** (*al-Asma al-Husna*), **in His knowledge** (the dimension of knowledge)... This act of observing has neither beginning nor end. **HU** is beyond being conditioned or limited by what He observes (i.e. HU is *Ghani* from the worlds.)

Hence, **all the worlds and everything they comprise**, which were all once **nonexistent** have become **existent** with the qualities of the **Names**, via this act of **observing**!

All things in the conceptual world are like the manifestations of the various compositions of the **Names of Allah**, shortly referred to as **the Names** (*al-Asma*). Just like how the approximately 100 hundred atoms comprise the whole of the material world with all its countless forms and beings.

Perhaps we can even say, the timeless, non-local quantum potential is **observing** itself from the point of view of the Names. Hadhrat **Ali's** WARNING, **"Knowledge was a single point, but the ignorant have multiplied it"** denotes the reality that the **quantum potential** is a single **point**, which manifests into the perceived according to the perceiver, whereby these perceivers are the **ignorant**.

Albeit the **Beautiful Names** have generally been taught to be 99 in the broad sense, in respect of their details they are infinite.

All perceivable and non-perceivable things are made up of these **qualities that are denoted by the Names** (of Allah); hence, this act of creation has been referred to as '**the *Rabb* of the Worlds.**' The word '*Rabb*' is the **Name-composition** that constitutes the perceived individual.

The phrase '*b-izni Rabb*' which literally means 'with the permission of *Rabb*' refers to the **suitability of the Name-composition to that particular situation.**

The phrase '*b-iznillah*' which means 'with the permission of Allah' can denote either of two meanings, depending on its context. That is, it either refers to the **suitability and appropriateness of the Name-composition to the purpose of creation of the worlds**, or **the suitability of the Name-composition to the purpose of the individual's existence.** As there is no 'other' *Uluhiyyah* but the **ONE**.

Due to this **ONEness**, the **Quran** emphasizes the concept of **consequence** (*jaza*) and reinforces that all individuals will live the **consequences** of the behaviors that result from them. This is why there is a reiteration of the fact that '**each will live the consequences of his or her actions, for there is no God that oppresses and punishes**' throughout the Quran.

The meaning of '**all individuals will be given their due rights**' means, whatever is necessary for the fulfillment of the individual's **purpose of existence** will be given accordingly.

Taqwa is generally understood as **protection** or '**to be protected from the wrath of Allah.**' What this alludes to in fact is the protection one should take to avoid engaging in the behaviors that may result in the unfavorable expressions of the Names with which they have been created, as everyone will inevitably live the consequences of their own doings.

As I said, the **Quran** is not literally a written book sent down from God above to his postman-prophet on earth via certain intermediary beings. **It is the KNOWLEDGE of the Reality and the System (*sunnatullah*), revealed (dimensionally) to his consciousness, from his *Rabb*, that is, the Names comprising his essential reality.**

In the view of the enlightened ones the Quran is a 'confirmation' in the appearance of a 'proposal.'

The BOOK alludes to the KNOWLEDGE pertaining to the Reality and the System (*sunnatullah*).

In terms of being the **Knowledge of Reality** it reveals the **Reality** of everything, both perceivable and unperceivable. In terms of being the

Knowledge of the System (*sunnatullah*) it explains **the mechanics of the System and the Order of the dimensions in which individual beings will forever reside**.

A **human** is a **vicegerent** on earth. This can be understood both as the planet and as the body. For human is beyond a mere body, and once a human leaves the body, an indefinite continual of existence will go on through various forms of resurrections (*ba'th*).

All of the proposals that are made to humans are aimed at enabling them to know their true selves in the light of their Reality and to live the requirements of this, discovering and using their intrinsic qualities. All of the prohibitions, on the other hand, are essentially to prevent humans from being deluded into thinking they are their physical body, and hence, squandering the potential given to them on egoistic, bodily pleasures that will have no meaning after they taste death. As their current potential has been given to discover their Reality and attain the beauty of both this life and the next.

If this work aids in a better evaluation of the **Quran**, I confess my inability to duly give thanks for such a blessing. My works are the compulsory requirement of my servanthood. Success is only with Allah's favor and blessing! I also apologize for my inadequacies and mistakes. For it is impossible for a servant to deservedly evaluate the words of Allah!

AHMED HULUSI
25 October 2008
North Carolina, USA

AN IMPORTANT NOTE ABOUT UNDERSTANDING 'DECODING THE QURAN'

The Quran is the **knowledge** (book) revealed by the *presence of Allah*. No words or literal concepts pertaining to the 'presence of Allah' can be valid. Perhaps we may refer to the original of the Quran as being written in the language of **Allah**. For, if (as the Arab polytheists claimed) Muhammad (saw) had written the Quran, then we could have said the Quran has been originally written in the Arabic language!

Whereas the Quran, originally in the language of Allah, was *revealed* by the angel Gabriel, to Muhammad (saw), in his own language, Arabic, so that the people of that region can understand its message.

The Quran refers to this truth with the verse:

"And We disclosed every Rasul with the language of his people so they may explain clearly to them... Allah sends astray whom He wills and guides whom He wills... And He is the Aziz, the Hakim." (Quran 14:4)

As the Quran, **originally in the language of Allah**, has been revealed in the very rich language of Arabic, it exposes different levels of knowledge to different levels of understanding. Each verse, in respect of the metaphors and allegories it contains, signifies a various number of meanings.

Due to this profound depth contained in the original Quran that has been revealed to us in Arabic, it is impossible to duly and comprehensively translate (and interpret) this magnificent book into another language!

All translations and interpretations are limited by the knowledge and understanding of the translator's vocabulary. Hence, all such works are like excerpts from this magnificent source of knowledge.

At this point I'd like to draw your attention to an important detail.

Many Sufi scholars, also considered to be 'Saints', from Haji Baktash Waliyy to Muhyiddin ibn al-Arabi, spoke **flawless Arabic** and arrived at the same understanding based on the knowledge they gained from the Quran... On the other hand, followers of orders such as **Wahhabism**, who consider Muhyiddin ibn al-Arabi and the Sufi tradition to be blasphemous, *also* possess an **immaculate understanding of the Arabic language** and arrive at their judgment based on the *same* Quran.

Think about it!

How did the eminent scholars and saints, who had profound knowledge of the Arabic language, such as Abdul Qadir Jilani, Imam Ghazali, Sheikh Naqshbandi, Abdul Karim al-Jili, Syed Ahmad Rufai and Imam Rabbani, understand and apply the Quran? And how others, who also speak perfect Arabic and who claim these saints are **blasphemous** (*kafir*), have arrived at *their* understanding of *a God, who apparently has hands and feet, who sits on a throne in heaven, and sends books down to Earth to guide humanity*!?

Sadly, many of the current translations of the Quran, especially the English ones, have been translated based on this latter understanding, while only a *rare few* works have been done in the light of the former approach.

This *Key to the Quran* may perhaps be considered more as a **figurative interpretation**. As far as I am aware it is the first of its kind in Turkey. It can never be considered to contain all of the meanings of the Quran. According to my observation, it may only be considered as reflecting only one of the many facets of this noble book. Another construal could have also been done, if it was desired, exposing other facets of the Quran.

Due to this reason, NO translation or interpretation of the Quran could be referred to as the 'Turkish Quran' or the 'English Quran'. One should read these books with the awareness that they are only vehicles to help one understand the Quran.

DECODING THE QURAN

The world has entered the Age of Aquarius declaring: **The time for renewal is upon us!**

Heeding this announcement, I too have renewed my outlook on the Quran, and have begun to approach it with a totally new understanding!

The warning in this **miraculous Book of Knowledge, "You say you follow in the footsteps of your forefathers, but what if your forefathers were on the wrong path?"** compelled me to re-evaluate the Quran from the very beginning with a completely new outlook.

Religion has become contaminated with outdated interpretations of the past and degenerated with stories from the corrupted version of the Old Testament, further reducing and simplifying it for the masses to understand. I knew beyond doubt that the reality of religion could only be reached through the correct understanding of the Quran.

So, on the 15th night of the month of Ramadan, I commenced my mission to decipher and share this knowledge with my brothers and sisters. I thoroughly studied the Quran in light of the well heeded guidance of eminent saints and scholars, such as Abdul Qadir Jilani, Muhyiddin ibn al-Arabi, Imam Rabbani, Ahmad Rufai, and Imam Ghazali (may Allah's peace and blessing be upon them all). Thankfully, committing 15-18 hours a day, I was able to complete my study in 120 days. Thus emerged the understanding of the **Quranic verses** in respect of the meaning of the letter **B**.

Since the Quran addresses **the whole of humanity throughout all ages as guidance to the truth**, this particular construal has been done in the light of the realities of today, the modern age.

It is an explanation of why certain incidents that took place thousands of years ago, the details of which are unknown, have been narrated time and time again reaching us today, and possibly even the generations to come.

Most importantly, it employs a holistic approach to the seemingly disconnected events, laws, edicts and *commands of God,* **integrating** this miraculous **knowledge,** to define just *how* and *why* it is a concern to **humans**.

Let us now delineate our findings, some of which have been included in our work.

The Quran has come to man to inform them of the reality of their essence and what they will be faced with in the future, so they can observe certain practices and abstain from others accordingly.

What is the reality of **a human being**? Why did the Quran come to **remind – invoke** (*dhikr*) mankind of their reality?

The answers to these questions, along with how **man** should understand the One denoted by the name **Allah**, are the most important and prominent topics covered in the Quran.

Let me approach this with the method of the Quran and explain with a parable. Think of a baby who is placed in a car at the time of birth and is brought up in this car until he is 40 years of age, never once leaving the vehicle. Until he is 40 years old he is consistently programmed with the conditioning *"you are this vehicle"*, such that by this age he has absolute and doubtless belief in it. Imagine now, he is told, at the age of 40: **"You are not this vehicle, you are a human being, get out of this vehicle and be free!"** But alas! He has come to see the steering wheel, the gearstick, and the gas and brake pedals as his very organs! How, at this point, can he be 'reminded' of the reality that he is not this vehicle, but that he is a 'human being' who can live independently of this vehicle?

He must first believe in what is being told, and then he must follow the instructions that are given to him so he can be emancipated...

As I have tried to explain with this simple example, **Humans** are beings with pure universal **consciousness** who have opened their eyes in an **earthly** body, operated by an individual **consciousness**!

Their self, the **consciousness** that is the **Universal Intellect** (*Aql-i kull*), has become veiled during the course their life, and **human beings** began to think they are merely the decomposable biological body they occupy.

Thus it became imperative to *remind* **them** of their reality! That is, that they are not the decomposable biological body in which they are temporarily residing, but an ethereal being! A being that will **change dimensions, level by level**, *realizing its angelic properties* (Quran 84:19) with which it will experience the realm of Paradise!

This is why Rasuls were manifested to remind (warn) *earthlings* of their **human** qualities. So that, **humans**, aware of their essential reality, can prepare themselves accordingly for the infinite existence awaiting them after their biological bodies return to the earth.

As for those who lack **human** qualities, they will deny their reality (*kafir*) and live their lives driven by their earthly and bodily desires, deprived of the expressions of pure consciousness. Consequently, they will continue their indefinite existence **fully aware** in the state described as **Hell**.

Everything that has emerged from **nothingness** into this realm of multiplicity derives its **existence** from, and functions with the **Names of Allah**. As such, in respect of pure **consciousness**, **humans** who become aware of and live according to this reality are termed **vicegerents**.

The Quran refers to such blessed souls as the **'living'** and **'seeing'** ones. While contrarily, those who fail to recognize or deny their reality, are referred to as the **'non-living'** and **'blind'** ones. Humans who recognize and live accordingly to their reality, possess **angelic** properties in terms of the essence of pure **consciousness**. **Such humans are essentially comprised of the properties denoted by Allah's names.** As they manifest the meanings of these Names, in ways befitting true humans, the state referred to as **heaven** occurs. In other words, heaven is not an abode for *mere earthlings*, but a state of life for **humans** whose **angelic** qualities can become manifest. I earnestly hope this point is understood well.

All examples and events that are narrated in the Quran are for the sole purpose of enabling **humans** to remember their essential reality, to *know* themselves, and hence to make better use of their current lives.

One of the most important things that deserves attention in regards to the style of the Quran is:

Everything, that is, **the heavens, the earth and everything in between**, is formed by the properties known as the **Names of Allah**. Hence, all perceivable and unperceivable things are invoking (calling upon) the One denoted by the Name Allah, by means of their life and function. Therefore, everything, with its natural disposition, is in a state of **servitude to the qualities of the Names** that comprise its existence, i.e. to Allah.

Due to this, the word 'WE' is used frequently in the Quran, emphasizing the reality that just as **the 'meaning' aspect of creation has been created with the Names the 'action' aspect of creation also comes about with the properties of the Names.**

Thus, by saying 'WE', the actions arising from the seeming multiplicities are actually being referred to their rightful owner.

'The *Rabb* of the Worlds' (*Rabbul Alameen*) refers both to the existence comprised of the Names and the actual Names comprising it.

This being the case, the structural properties of the pre-eternal Names and their expressions, i.e. the cosmos, are in no other state but that of absolute servitude to Allah. Creation is in a constant act of invoking and remembering Allah, displaying Allah's knowledge and power, at all times. Allah informing mankind about this reality is nothing other than a confirmation. This is why Allah says 'WE' when referring to the Names.

This being said, in order to prevent one from conditioning or limiting Him with these meanings, the warning that **His Absolute Essence** (*dhat*) **is 'beyond and free** (*Ghani*) **from the worlds'** is frequently made. Nothing in existence can be likened to or define His Absolute Essence.

This also means, **His 'governance of the worlds' is through the paths of each of His Names, whether these Names manifest under the name of astrology, or as the known and unknown life forms within the cosmos; whether one calls it consciousness, or forms of consciousness, invisible beings, or heaven and hell, all dimensions of existence are various ways of His governance.**

As for the real meaning of polytheism or **duality** (*shirq*): one who fails to recognize the One denoted by the name Allah in all that is implicit and explicit (within the self and in the outer world) **as the manifestations of the Names** is defined as a polytheist or a dualist in the Quran. In other words, assuming a separate and equal existence to the manifestations of Allah's Names is an act of fragmenting the Oneness of reality, and hence an act of advocating duality (*shirq*). (The original word that is used in the Quran is min dooni Allahi which means 'as equal' or 'equivalent to' referring to an existence that is 'other' than Allah. Whereas, Allah affirms that no other form of existence can be found outside of Allah as Allah encompasses the whole of existence. Thus, negating any possibility of the equivalence of other gods, lords, etc, the Quran uses the word min dooni Allahi.) That is to say, it is an act of committing *shirq* (assuming a separate existence) with the Names, to the Names.

As can be understood from above, Allah, who in respect of **His Absolute Essence** is **free from concepts such as duality and non-duality**, defines *shirq* to be a failure to recognize the true nature of existence. That is, when one fails to see that everything in manifestation is essentially comprised of the Names, one is assuming an equivalent existence to the Names, and this goes against the reality of non-duality. Hence, such a person falls short of truly understanding Allah and goes on living in an illusory world in his imagination.

Denial (*kufr*) on the other hand, rests upon the false belief that none is governing the individualized consciousness other than itself. Restricting the infinite consciousness to an individualized manifestation by calling it

'I' is a grave insult and limitation to the infinite qualities of the Names, which cannot be confined to a mere physical body. Such an attempt is termed denial (*kufr*) and is said to be going against the infinite qualities of the Reality of the Self, at least in terms of **faith**. Continual attempts in this way eventually lead one to confine the Self to the physical body alone, paving the path to pursuing a life of bodily pleasures, and adopting the view that **death** is *extinction* rather than a change of abode.

Hypocrisy is the lowest and densest state of the bodily life. A hypocrite (*munafiq*) is one who chooses not only to deny the Reality but also to take advantage of the believers for material benefits by *imitating* them! While even a dog approaches his owner for food with true sincerity and loyalty, a hypocrite lacks genuine intent and approaches others only with vested interests. The result upon realizing the truth of the matter is indefinite burning and no compensation.

Faith (*iman*) is the realization of consciousness, through the intellect, i.e. through analysis of various data, that beyond the seeming reality of forms and concepts lies infinity and it is this infinity that must be sought after. It is to know the 'I'ness as consciousness, which cannot be confined into a material form, and to strive in this path. The hadith **"He who lives by '*La ilaha illallah*' ("There is no God. There is only Allah.") will assuredly enter Heaven"** points to this truth. This is applicable for those who have not encountered a Rasul. Those who have encountered a Rasul, whether by person or by teaching, are bound to believe in the **Rabb of the Worlds** (the source of the infinite meanings of the Names), or **Allah,** in accordance to the teachings of the Rasul, by having faith in the Rasul.

I say "having faith in the Rasul" because by appearance a Rasul is also an earthling with a physical body, there is no apparent difference between a Rasul and other humans. Yet the difference lies in that a Rasul is the articulation of the Reality, which cannot be seen with the physical eyes but initially experienced only through having faith.

The Quran explains **faith in the One denoted by the name Allah** as being in two stages. The first stage pertains to an 'external' creator beyond the reach of individual consciousness, that is, a creator or 'the dimension of the Names' comprising infinite and illimitable qualities. This is the faith shared by the majority of believers, and in terms of its proceeds, enables one to live a life bearing a paradisiacal state of existence. The second stage applies to believers with a truly enlightened heart and who have reached the essence of faith. This is the faith implied by the letter **B**, which points to the truth that the reality of the **Self** is the qualities of the **Names**, and these qualities are and forever will manifest themselves. Hence, it calls the believer to awaken to the reality that through his own acts he is at all times invoking and serving Allah, and as such, observing and evaluating the universal perfection of Allah on worldly forms *(Hamd)* manifested by the name *al-Waliyy* **in his own being** *(b-Hamdihi)*.

'To believe in the angels' means to have 'faith in the potentials' arising from the Names. In other words, **angels** signify the various potentials that arise during the process of the Names becoming activated from their dormant states. Since what has come to be known as the world of multiplicity essentially comprises individualized manifestations of various Names, the higher (subtler) state of everything in existence is **angelic** *(malakiyyah)*... The difference lies not in whether this is present or not, but in whether this reality is recognized or at least, believed in or not. One who accepts himself only as an earthling through individual consciousness and who lacks **faith** will have grave difficulty recognizing and accepting this truth.

'To believe in the Books-Knowledge' is to have faith in the **knowledge** of reality and the mechanics of the system - *sunnatullah* imparted by the Rasuls and Nabis via a process known as **revelation**, that being the dimensional transferal (emergence) of this knowledge through pure consciousness.

Rasuls are the enlightened ones who acquire the knowledge of the reality through pure consciousness (without the influence of their personal consciousness) from the Names and angelic potentials in their essence via **revelation** and who communicate these truths at the level of consciousness.

To believe in the **afterlife**, or an eternal life, is to know with conviction that the Self will not become extinct after losing its body during death, but that **death** is also an experiential reality. That is, when the physical-biological body is omitted a process called resurrection *(ba'th)* will take place, during which one will pass to another dimension of life with the **spirit body**, shared by other invisible beings and eventually continue its life in either of two dimensions known by various names.

When the letter **B** is used as a prefix to a word in regards to having faith, such as 'to believe in the hereafter' *(bil-akhira)* or afterlife, it points to the various stages of development the **Self** will indefinitely go through (Quran 84:19) in pursuit of self-actualization.

The concept of **'protection'** *(taqwa)* or **'to have fear of Allah'** is also generally misunderstood. Since the name Allah does not refer to an external God, the real reference is made to the Names and their governance. Allah created the worlds with the Names and governs it with the System known as *sunnatullah*. The one law that most absolutely applies here is that of the Name *al-Hasib* inherent in one's **'Name composition'**, whereby one's experience of their latter stage is a result of their former stage. Simply put, whatever behavior one has at any given time whether it is an action or a thought, one will inescapably live its consequence at some point in their life. This has been expressed as **'the One who is swift at reckoning'** (*Sari'ul-Hisab*) and **'the One who responds to wrongdoing with severe punishment'** (*Shadid al-Ikab*).

Therefore, living in a system with caution and prudence has been termed as 'fearing Allah' or as 'protection' (*taqwa*). Since **'*sunnatullah* = the system and mechanics of Allah'** is essentially the manifestation of the Names of Allah, it is not incorrect to refer to this as 'fear and protection from Allah' after all. As such, an act of ungratefulness to any being is an act of ungratefulness to Allah, and its consequence will be lived accordingly! This process is known as '*jaza*' (consequence). Hence, *jaza* is not really the result or punishment but the *automatic experience* of the *consequence* of an act.

The Quran invites its readers to contemplate through its innumerous parables and metaphors, all to remind (*dhikr*) humans of their own reality.

Unfortunately, due to the conditions of time and place, and the comprehension levels of the people, the examples that can be given are not many. Due to this, the limited number of objects that people do know of has been associated with various meanings over time, such that the same word has been used to refer to different things in different times, or to different specifications of the same thing. For example, while the Arabic word **'*sama*'** is seldom used to refer to the 'sky' or 'space' it is more commonly used in reference to the 'states of consciousness' or the 'intellectual activity in one's consciousness.' Another example is the word **'*ardh*'**. While infrequently used to refer to the earth, it is generally used to refer to the 'human body.' The human body is also denoted by other words such as **'*an'am*'** which means 'domestic animal' referring to the animalistic nature of mankind, i.e. eat, drink, sleep, sex etc., and **'*dabbah*'** which refers to the material and earthly make-up of the biological body. The word **'*shaytan*'** (Satan) has been used to connote mankind's tendency to reduce and limit their boundless consciousness, in respect of their essential Name composition, to the base bodily state. The word 'mountain' is also seldom used to denote what it actually means; while it is more commonly employed to imply the 'ego', the 'I' or 'I'ness. Also, when the word **'*ardh*'** is used in reference to the **'body'**, the word **'mountain'** is seen to denote the **'organs'** of the body. For example, the verse **'the mountains walk but you perceive them to be still'** indicates the constant activity and renewal of our interior organs, which seem to be fixed like the mountains on earth.

The word '*zawj*' is also used in various contexts to mean different things. While its most common usage is to mean **'partner in marriage'** it has also seen to be used in the context of consciousness implying the partner or **equivalent of consciousness and the body that will fall into disuse at some point**. In fact, the seventh verse of chapter 56, *al-Waqi'a*, states '*azwajan thalathah*' to mean **'three kinds'** not three wives!

If we evaluate the words of the Quran in a constricted literal sense and in reference to only one meaning, we will not only be doing grave injustice but also paving the pathway to the primitive belief that it is an obscure and inconceivable Godly book of commands!

Whereas the Quran is the articulation, through revelation, of the *Rabb* of the worlds (the source of the infinite meanings of the Names), giving us the knowledge about the system by which the implicit qualities of the Names manifest to create the explicit world. This is what **'religion'** is!

Man, in other words **'pure consciousness'**, is the *personified* Quran. Earthlings who believe themselves to be no more than their physical bodies have been called 'human beings' due to this universal consciousness present in their innermost essence. When units of consciousness (in earthly bodies) refuse to have faith in this, they are denying their innermost essence and reducing themselves to mere material existence. Hence, the Quran describes such people as **'they are like cattle, nay, they are even more astray (from being a human) in their way'** (Quran 25:44). In other words, only the animalistic appetites of their physical bodies drive their lives. They deny the magnificent and superior qualities of their own reality and function only with the stimuli of the neurons in their intestines (the second brain), thereby reducing their lives to the animal – bodily state.

As for the frequent narrations of the lives and examples of Rasuls and Nabis in the Quran... All of these are also **examples of possible intellectual or physical errors humankind are prone to and should be cautioned against**. Nevertheless, such incidents have been lived by every human population of every century in one way or another!

In regards to the creation of Adam, the Quran says: **'Indeed, the example of Jesus to Allah is like that of Adam'** (Quran 3:59). That is, in terms of his physical body, Adam was also born from a mother's womb. His body also went through all the common biological stages of development. This has been explained through various metaphors. Besides all of this, however, what is really meant by 'Adam' is a human who has **consciously** recognized and accepted **all of the meanings of the Names** and thus deserved the title **'vicegerent'**. This is what truly matters. All the rest are details and probably even unnecessary, as it doesn't really matter from where and how the material body, which will eventually decompose back into simple matter under the earth, came about. Certain symbols and metaphors have been employed to imply his biological aspect was created from the earth's atomic constituent, like all other earthlings, but his biological body is of no relevance to what is really being denoted by this name. **'Adam', is 'pure consciousness', formed from nothingness,** and composed of (*'ja'ala'* not *'khaleqa'*) the qualities of the Names and designated as a 'vicegerent' (*khalifa*) on earth. It is a shame that many fail to understand this reality and spend their lives arguing over the creation process of his mortal biological body!

The satanic being referred to as **'Iblis'** has an interesting story. Iblis, while essentially a Name composition comprised of angelic qualities, displays an inadequate expression of the Names *al-Waliyy, al-Mumin* and *al-Hadi*. Due to his own inadequacy, he fails to recognize how profoundly the Names are manifested on the creation of supreme form (*'ahsani takwim'*). Hence, he evaluates Adam according to his apparent qualities and fails to see his superiority in terms of the Names and their expressions. Moreover, he assumes that accepting the superiority of Adam over his own creation will mean denying his own reality, since he too is created with and from the Names, and thus he refrains from prostrating. Evidently, **it is impossible for one to evaluate a quality that he himself lacks.**

Eventually this leads to pure consciousness in the form of Adam approaching the forbidden tree, i.e. becoming restricted by the requisites of the bodily life. This is also an interesting anecdote. *Satan convinces Adam to the 'wrong' according to his own 'right',* imposing the idea: "You have been created with the reality of the Names, you cannot be restricted or conditioned by anything, you should do as you wish. If you don't eat from the forbidden tree, that is, if you don't live the requirements of the bodily life, you would be accepting limitation and thus denying your essential reality, thereby depriving yourself of immortality!"

Consequently, humanity at the level of the Inspiring Self (*nafs-i mulhima*), symbolized with the name Adam, becomes veiled from the **higher states of** pure **consciousness**, and falls to the bodily state of the Commanding Self (*nafs-i ammarah*), becoming conditioned by bodily needs. When this reaches the ultimate point of forgetting their own essence, the reminders and imparters of reality, i.e. Rasuls, become manifest, inviting mankind back to their essence, back to having **faith** in the higher states of **consciousness**.

When human beings, who are manifestations of Universal Pure Consciousness, begin to experience themselves as individualized conscious beings in this physical body, the struggle of this relationship with their 'partner' (body) and the battle to go back to their essential reality commences.

In short:

There are two types of consciousness. The first is the manifestation of the Names as a whole, to observe itself through the appearance of individualized compositions. This is the Universal Pure Consciousness. The second kind is the individual consciousness of each manifestation, formed by genetic inheritances, environmental conditionings and astrological influences. For the purpose of clarity in this book, we will refer to the second kind as 'consciousness' to avoid confusion. Consciousness is an output of the brain and hence confines itself to comprise only the body (humanoid). Consciousness uses the mind to evaluate ideas and to live accordingly. But the mind, pressured by the body's biological make-up, often malfunctions. As such, it is near impossible for the mind to find the reality all on its own. Furthermore, the mind makes judgments based on sensory perception. This is why the mind is invited to 'believe', to have **'faith'** in what lies beyond its area of perception. For, the reality 'beyond' matter encompasses matter.

While the stories of **Abraham** (saw) caution us from idolizing and deifying our exterior and interior faculties, i.e., the body and its components, the narrations about **Lot** (saw) give examples of the felonious lives led by those who were captives of their bodily demands and sexuality. In the case of **Moses** (saw) on the other hand, the emphasis is on the Pharaoh's claim to be God, warning us from the grave danger we may encounter in pursuit of getting to know our true selves.

When the fruit of reality manifests in one's consciousness, no matter how essentially true it may be to claim 'I am the Reality', it is ultimately only one compositional reflection of the infinite Names that compose one's essence! The whole of manifestation comprises the **compositional Name qualities**. Thus, even though by 'essence' everything obtains its life force from 'Allah' and everything is the 'Reality' **they are not the 'Rabb of the Worlds'** (the source of the infinite meanings of the Names), **that is, nothing that has become manifest in the apparent cosmos can be the 'source' and 'discloser' of the infinite and illimitable Names!** Nothing that has become manifest can be the 'Rabb' of other manifestations. Hence, the Pharaoh encountered what he did because of his ignorance to this truth. All those who aspire to attain and live the reality go through this perilous state, known in Sufism as the station of the Inspiring Self (*nafs-i mulhima*)! Resultantly, just when one is a step away from the reality, one becomes seized by the idea with which Satan infused Adam: "Do not restrict yourself! Do as you wish, become limitless!", and falls into the dense and base pit of the bodily state, the station of the Commanding Self (*nafs-i ammarah*). This is why the Quran repeatedly narrates the story of Moses (saw) and the Pharaoh.

The event known as **Doomsday** (*qiyamah*) points to the **various experiences of one's consciousness during the process of death**. The imminent doomsday is one's personal death. For, with death, an unchangeable state of existence known as the afterlife commences. The global doomsday has been awaited for approximately 1400 years now, whereas all that has been said in reference to Doomsday has direct pertinence to one's own death. While everyone has their own Savior (*Mahdi*), Antichrist (*Dajjal*) and Jesus (*Isa*), and is subject to the activities symbolized by these names throughout their whole lifetime, people ignorantly think 'Doomsday' is only a galactic event involving the end of our solar system or the world, supposedly to take place at some time predicted by some people!

Unfortunately, the inability to comprehend the life period of hundreds of millions of years at the galactic level, and the attempt to evaluate time based on the data received from one's untaught environment, and the primitive understanding of a God with a magic wand, had led humanity to adopt an improper understanding of the doomsday explained in the Quran.

As for **heaven and hell...** The Quran makes a clear statement **"heaven as a parable (representation, similitude)"** (Quran 52:20 and 47:15, 'Math'alul jannatillatiy') and thus makes it evident that all expositions of 'heaven' in the Quran are symbolic and metaphoric. It is quite challenging to both comprehend and talk about a state of existence in which the **'awakened' ones** will dwell, in congruence with the Power and other Name qualities they will be endowed with, and far from all bodily limitations. This is why **"Allah says: I have prepared for my pious servants that which no eye has ever seen, no ear has ever heard, and no human mind has ever conceived"**.(Bukhari Muslim and Tirmidhi.)

Hell is most certainly an atrocious state of existence, in terms of the physical body one will assume in that environment. According to our observation it will be sustained in the Sun. I wrote about this in detail in my book *The Mystery of Man* in 1985. On the other hand, hell in respect of consciousness, which has a stronger emphasis in the Quran, is a far more dreadful torment: When one dies they will realize they have been endowed with the **qualities and potentials of the Names**, and have been given the most perfect opportunity to discover and manifest these during their earthly life. In the case that they squandered this chance by indulging in the physicality of things rather than internal values, they will feel an inexplicably tremendous remorse knowing they no longer have a chance to compensate. This burning will be the greatest hellfire one can experience!

As for the hellish state of existence while still on earth, it is when the consciousness confines itself to a bodily state of existence and becomes attached to others and conditioned by value judgments.

There are many more notes to make but I guess I should not extend this introduction any further. If the *Rabb* of the Worlds (the source of the infinite meanings of the Names), wills, the doors of inspiration will be opened up to you also and you will have the delightful experience of READing the **living Quran** as it talks to you in person, and tells you about yourself.

Nevertheless, if you read this work, *Decoding The Quran*, in light of all that I have explained here, I believe you will hear it talking to you and feel the Quran living within your Self in a way that you have never experienced before.

If you question my concept... All I can say is, let us wait and see... Death is too near! If I am rightly guided, it is with the favor of Allah, and I am forever impotent from duly thanking Him. If this work is valid and legitimate, I don't know how those with differing opinions will react! This is my understanding of the Quran, how you take it is up to you!

If, in this work that I share with you without any material expectation in return, any humanly interference has occurred on my part besides my *Rabb*'s (the Names constituting my essence) guidance and inspiration, I earnestly apologize.

All success is from Allah, and any shortcoming or error is from the inadequacy of my individual consciousness.

Astaghfir'ullah wa atubu ilayh. (I ask for repentance (forgiveness, the covering of my shortcomings due to my human nature) from Allah. My repentance (return) is to HU alone.)

AHMED HULUSI
21 January 2009
North Carolina, USA

AN ESSENTIAL MESSAGE

Unfortunately, my interpretation of the Quran, which has been done in the light of the **Knowledge of the Reality**, has inadvertently led to some misunderstandings. One of these is the notion that everything begins and ends with man. Of course, in respect of man's essential reality, all that I have written are concepts that are shared by and agreed upon by all enlightened individuals.

However...

Mankind isn't the be-all and end-all.

We cannot deny that within the universe and galaxy in which we reside, in fact within our very solar system, exists countless different species of life forms, which our five-sense dependent science has not yet perceived, but which many unconditioned, objective people find very comprehensible.

The system mechanics that constitutes the make-up of a human being may very well be present in other species in the universe.

This truth is validated in the Quran!

Whether we take the example of **Abraham** (saw), **Lot** (saw) or even **Mary** (saw) we repeatedly encounter these beings mentioned as **'Rasuls'** throughout the Quran.

Moreover, I may very comfortably state that the angelic being referred to as **'Gabriel'** is not a product of imagination but a form of life unable to be fully perceived by our limited sense perception, while its images are a product of the data processing system in the brain. This applies to all beings referred to as angels!

I do not feel it is appropriate to say anything further regarding this topic at this stage, when the intrinsic mechanics of the brain are only just being discovered and reported in our modern world. But I must add one more note: If you believe in their sincerity and genuineness, many enlightened saints such as Abdul Karim al Jili and Muhyiddin ibn Arabi have made contact with these life forms. The following thought provoking verse also pertains to this truth:

"I have no knowledge of the discussions of the *Mala-i A'la* (the Exalted Assembly of angels)." (Quran 38:69)

There are many reports regarding certain species and their functions referred to as '*Mala-i A'la*' in Shah Waliyyullah Dahlawi's renowned book

Hujjatullah Baligha, translated into Turkish by the Theology Professor Hayreddin Karaman.

Rasulullah Muhammad's (saw) words: **"Befriend me with the *Rafiq-i A'la* (the Highest Company)"** also sheds light on this phenomenon!

Therefore...

One should not become so captivated with the inner dimension of things as to neglect their exterior-universal aspects.

Finally, as I had stressed in my book *Spirit, Man, Jinn* 40 years ago, let us be well aware and cautioned against the 'jinni activities' marketed today under the guise of being 'angelic.'

AHMED HULUSI
18 June 2010

THE EXALTED, MAGNIFICENT AND PERFECT QUALITIES OF THE NAMES OF ALLAH (*AL-ASMA UL-HUSNA*)

B'ismi-Allah ar-Rahman ar-Rahim... Allah, who created me with His Names (exalted, magnificent, and perfect qualities), is *Rahman* and *Rahim*!

Let us heed the fact that a **'name'** is only used as a **reference** to an object or quality. A name does not explain what it references in totality, but merely alludes to an identity, or an attribute of an identity. Sometimes, a name is used only to channel the attention to multiple qualities, without revealing anything about the identity.

In the case of the **Names of Allah**, let us contemplate the following: Are the Names of Allah *a collection of fancy titles of a God beyond*? Or, are they references made to the creational properties of Allah (which the senses and conditionings externalize!) with which the entire known cosmos and everything in it becomes manifest from **nothingness** into a shadow **existence**?

Once this reality is fully conceived and comprehended we may move on to the Names of Allah.

The Quran, which has been conveyed as a *Dhikr*, i.e. 'the remembrance of man's essential reality', is actually a disclosure of the Names to expound 'Uluhiyyah'. It is the **Totality of the Names** (all of the Names that have been imparted to us and that comprise our existence) that man has been endowed with and is invited to **remember**! Some of these have been disclosed in the Quran and some were revealed by the Rasul of Allah. One can never say that the names that refer to Allah are limited to only 99. Let us give an example... There are many names, such as *Rabb*, *Mawla*, *Kareeb* and *Hallaq*, that are mentioned in the Quran but are not included as part of the 99 Names. The name *Mureed*, which alludes to the attribute of **'will'** (i.e. He does as He wishes) mentioned in the verse '*yaf'alu ma yureed*', is also not included among the 99 Names. Contrarily, the names *Jalil*, *Wajid* and *Majid* are all included in the 99 Names but are not mentioned in the Quran. Thus, it would be a mistake to confine the Names of Allah to only 99, when the **Dimension of the Names** designates the infinite quantum potential, which involves the act of **observing in Allah's Knowledge**. Man is provided with these Names as a reminder of their own true essence. Perhaps once one remembers and lives accordingly to their essential reality, many more Names will be disclosed to them. Also, we may say **heaven** alludes to this truth too, while we may not even be aware of the Names that pertain to and compose the universes within universes of infinite existence!

The enlightened ones (*Ulul Albab*) have used the phrase **'the shadow existence'** to mean 'the things we perceive do not exist in and by themselves but they are compositions of Names that manifest **according to the perceiver'**.

In fact, even the phrase 'Name compositions' is metaphorical; it is only to adapt the dual view to the One reality. Absolute reality is the observing of the **'multidimensional single frame'** by the One who **'manifests Himself every moment in yet another wondrous way'**. (Quran 55:29) What we refer to as 'Name compositions' is only like one stroke of the paintbrush on this magnificent picture.

Due to having a **name** all perceivable things seemingly have a separate individual existence, whereas, because there is no God beyond, **what is really perceived as an existent object is essentially none other than the materialized Names (qualities) of Allah.**

This being said, the One denoted by the Names cannot be divided or fragmented into pieces, it is not composed of parts, it is even beyond concepts such as being 'absolute One', 'illimitable', 'infinite' and so on. It is '*Ahad-us-Samad*' (the Absolute Self-Sufficient One) and only mentioned this way in the Quran once! **Allah, HU, other than whom nothing exists**! This knowledge cannot be comprehended by the human mind unless it is revealed or divinely inspired and observed in one's consciousness! The mind, logic and judgment cannot survive here. He who attempts to intellectualize this reality will only be misguided. This reality is not open for debate! Any urge to do so will only reveal ignorance! This is the reality that pertains to Gabriel's words: **"If I take one more step I will burn"**!

It must be realized that the Names of Allah point to the quality of His knowledge, not His *mind*, as this is inconceivable. The **mind** is a function of the brain designed to create the world of multiplicity. Essentially, even the phrases 'the Universal Intellect' (*Aql-i kull*) and 'the First Intellect' (*Aql-i awwal*) are relative concepts and are used metaphorically to denote the system by which the attribute of **knowledge** is disclosed.

The Universal Intellect refers to the dimension of knowledge that is present within the depths of all beings, within one's essence. This is also the source of revelation.

The First Intellect, on the other hand, is a tailored phrase for the novice mind, to describe the dimension of knowledge present in the manifestation (*sh'an*) of the Names.

'The dimension of Acts' (*af'al*) is nothing but the disclosure of the Dimension of Names which 'manifests itself every moment in yet another wondrous way'! The material world as we know it is this quantal plane, though differences of perception have led to the assumption that it is a **different** dimension.

The observing One, the one being observed, the observation, are all ONE! 'The wine of paradise' alludes to this experience. One who is caught up in the perception of **multiplicity** has no chance but to engage in the chatter of this knowledge, without any experience of its reality.

As for the **Acts**, activities, multiplicity and what we perceive as the corporeal world... Existence belongs only to that which is denoted as the Dimension of Names.

'Observing knowledge in knowledge with knowledge' designates that the very disclosure of the Names is the act of **observing**. In this respect, all **forms** are created and observed in knowledge. Hence it has been said **'the worlds (or creation) have not even smelled the scent of existence yet'**. Here, the **part** is the observer, and the **whole** is the observed one!

The force (*kuwwa*) pertaining to the Names is referred to as **angels**, which, in essence, constitute the **reality of mankind**. One who becomes aware of their reality is said to have **'united with their *Rabb*'**! Once this state is reached, if it doesn't continue, the resulting pain has been narrated as an intense hellish suffering! This is the domain of **Power** (*Qudrah*) and the command **Be!** (*Kun*) originates from here; this is the dimension of **knowledge**, where the mind and its functions are completely obsolete! This is the essence of the land of **wisdom** (*hikmah*)! The **mind** can only watch the activities that take place in the land of wisdom, where only **consciousness** can actively participate!

The dimension of Acts (*af'al*) in comparison to this plane (the dimension of Power) is a totally **holographic** (shadow) state of existence. All the activities of the entire parallel and multiple universes and all their inhabitants, i.e. natural resources, plants, animals (humanoids) and the jinni, are **governed** by the *Mala-i A'la* (the Exalted Assembly of angels) in this plane, depending on the perception capability of the perceiver.

Rasuls and their successors, the saints, are like the vocal expressions of the *Mala-i A'la*, that is, the forces (potentials) of the Names, on earth! And all of this is part of the **observation** taking place in the **dimension of Knowledge**! The essence of **man**, in this sense, is **angelic** and he is invited to **remember his angelic nature and to live accordingly**. This is an in-depth and intricate topic... Those who are not acquainted with this knowledge may find my words regarding the **observation** taking place from various dimensions to be contradictory. However, the reality I experienced when I was 21 years of age in 1966, which I have penned in my book *Revelations*, has been verified time and time again throughout the 45 years that followed it, and I have shared it all without expecting any tangible or intangible return. The knowledge I share is not a pass-down to me, rather it is the direct blessing of Allah for which I am eternally grateful! As such, there is no contradiction in my words. If it appears that way, it is probably due to the inability to make the correct connections, resulting from an inadequate database.

So, if this is the reality as I have observed, how should the topic of the **Names of Allah** be approached?

The Names of Allah are initially expressed through pure consciousness (revelation) without the interference of one's consciousness, which tries to evaluate them later. The Names are cosmic universal qualities (not in the galactic sense).

The Most Beautiful Names belong to Allah. The structural qualities they denote pertain to the Absolute Self-Sufficient One. The Names look to the quantum potential beyond time and place; the Names signify the **point**. As such, the Names and their meanings belong to Allah alone and are free from becoming conditioned by human concepts.

"Exalted (Subhan – beyond) **is Allah what they attribute to Him."** (Quran 23:91)

"And to Allah belongs the most Beautiful Names, so turn to Him through the meanings of His names. And leave the company of those who practice deviation (fall into duality) **concerning His Names. They will be recompensed for what they have been doing."** (Quran 7:180)

That is, leave the company of those who restrict the Names with their humanly values, and fail to recognize the reality of the Beautiful Names and who do not know Allah is respect of His *Akbariyyah*!

"And believes in (confirms) **the Most Beautiful** (Names) (to be his essential reality)**, we will ease him towards ease."** (Quran 92:6-7)

Even the consequence of **good** is related to the Names:

"For the doers of good (*ihsan*) **is the Beautiful** (Names) **and more** (pleasure). **No darkness** (egotism) **will cover their faces** (consciousness)**, nor derogation** (which results from deviating from one's essence). **Those are companions of Paradise; they will abide therein eternally."** (Quran 10:26)

Allah's Absolute Essence (*dhat*) cannot be likened to anything in existence. With His greatness (*Akbariyyah*) He is free from becoming limited or conditioned by His creation or the attributes denoted by His Names, which constitute one point amongst infinite others. In other words, what is referred to as the **Dimension of Names** is like a multidimensional holographic single frame. And, despite the fact that it is perceived as the **realm of multiplicity**, this realm of activity is essentially a unified field of existence created with the compositional qualities in His knowledge.

To summarize before going further...

The qualities and attributes that we have come to acquire through revelation as the Names of Allah (singular in nature) are the very structural compositions that manifest the totality of all the universal dimensions, from nothingness into this shadow (holographic) existence. This reality, of which earthly vicegerency aspires to become aware, is far beyond the reach of the cruel and ignorant.

The Dimension of Names is the 'exalted, magnificent, and perfect attributes and qualities' with all its sub-dimensions and inner-existence!

Let us now ponder on the world perceived by humanity... and then **"raise our gaze to the heavens and observe"** as the Quran states, without dogmatic views and bigotry, with the understanding of universality formed by proficient knowledge!

What value does a world based on our miniscule perception have in comparison to the magnificence, glory and perfection of the universe?

I hope, in the light of this understanding, we can approach the **Names of Allah** with the awareness that their revelation depends on the purging of the individual consciousness (based on its limited perception and conception of the Book of Knowledge) and that **their effects pertain to the whole of the cosmos**, constantly manifesting new meanings and expressions.

I would also like to take this opportunity to express one of my concerns. I do not feel the knowledge I shared through previous articles has been correctly understood. Let me restate that the meanings, qualities and attributes denoted by the **Names of Allah are only one point among infinite others in the sight of Allah**. Also, the quantum potential expressed as the **Reality of Muhammad** or the **Angel named Spirit** is not only pre- and post-eternal, but it is also the reality I refer to as the 'multi-dimensional single frame' picture! Because this has not been well understood, Allah is still perceived *as the one God out there*! Whereas the whole **observation** and all that has been articulated pertain only to a **point**: Allah is just Allah, Allah is *Akbar*! *Subhanahu min tanzihiy* (HU is beyond comparability)!

Please be aware that what I write and share with you can never be taken as the final conclusion; in fact, it can only be an introduction! It is not possible to openly disclose through publication matters that are deeper than this. Anyway, the people of this path will recognize that even what we have already shared are things that have never been shared in this much detail and this openly before. This is a very sensitive topic as the reader may very easily fall into the misconception of either an external God or worse, confine the reality to his Pharaoh-like 'I'ness and animalistic bodily self!

I tried to shed some light on the topic of the Names (*al-Asma*). Let us now take a look at the qualities and attributes denoted by these exalted, magnificent and perfect Names (*al-Husna*)... As much as simple words allow of course...

THE TRIGGER SYSTEM

All of the qualities and attributes pertaining to the Names are entirely present at every point of existence! However, depending on the desired manifestation, some attributes gain precedence over others, like the channels in an equalizer, to make up the specific formation. Also, qualities denoted by **certain Names naturally and automatically trigger the expressions of certain other Names**, in order to generate a new manifestation. This system is known as '*sunnatullah*' and entails the **universal laws of Allah** (or the laws of nature as those with limited perceptive ability would say) and the mechanics of His system.

This is a glorious mechanism beyond description; all beings from pre-eternity to post-eternity subsist with all their inter and inner dimensions and perceivable units within this system!

All **thoughts** and **activities** projecting from consciousness, whether through the universe or a single person's world, are all formed within and according to this system.

In short, we may refer to this mechanism, where qualities of Names trigger one another, as the **trigger system**.

As I warned above, consider the entire universality of existence (which is ONE by essence) as the plane of manifestation of these Names. The trigger system applies to every instance of perception by a perceiver in every plane of existence within this universality. Since the entire sequence of certain qualities triggering other qualities is a *known*, it is said that the pre- and post-eternal knowledge of everything that has and will happen at all times is present in Allah's knowledge!

The following verses and the Name *Hasib* allude to this trigger system:

"...Whether you show what is within your consciousness (your thoughts) **or conceal it, Allah will bring you to account for it with the Name *Hasib*..."** (Quran 2:284)

"Whoever does an iota's weight of good will see it." (Quran 99:7)

Evidently, the consequence of an action or thought is inevitably experienced within this system. **This is why every thought or action of gratitude or ungratefulness we may have output in the past would have most definitely caught up with us, or is bound to in the future.** If one seriously contemplates on this many doors will open and secrets will reveal themselves. The **mystery of fate** is also pertinent to this mechanism!

Let us now follow these signpost-like Names to discover the secret lands they point to:

ALLAH

ALLAH... Such a name... It points to *Uluhiyyah*!

Uluhiyyah encompasses two realities. HU which denotes **Absolute Essence** (*dhat*) and the realm of infinite points in which every single point is formed by the act of **observing knowledge through knowledge**. This act of observing is such that each point signifies an individual composition of Names.

By respect of His absolute essence, Allah is **other than**, but in terms of His Names, Allah is the **same as** the **engendered existence** (*sh'ay*) yet nevertheless **far and beyond** (*Ghani*) **from the worlds and any similitude!** This is why Allah, who created the engendered existence (*sh'ay*) and the acts with His Names, uses the plural pronoun 'We' in the Quran. For, in essence, the engendered existence (everything in creation) is none other than Allah! Please note that by engendered existence (*sh'ay*) we are referring to the Dimension of Names that constitute existence. One can ponder and contemplate the essence of creation and existence, but **one cannot contemplate the Absolute Essence of Allah.** It is inconceivable and inappropriate; indeed, it is absolutely impossible! This is because one that has been created with the expressions of Allah's Names cannot fully comprehend the Absolute Essence of Allah! Even if this knowledge is revealed by **divine inspiration** – which is impossible – it is inconceivable. This is why it is said 'the path of such pursuit ends in nothingness'.

HU

HU'Allahulladhiy la ilaha illa HU!

Whether via revelation or through consciousness, HU is the inner essence of the reality of everything that is perceived... To such extent that, as the reflection of *Akbariyyah*, first **awe** then **nothingness** is experienced and, as such, the Reality of Hu can never be attained! **Sight cannot reach HU!** HU denotes absolute obscurity and incomprehension! As a matter of fact, all names, including Allah are mentioned in connection with HU in the Quran!

"HU ALLAH is AHAD."

"HU is RAHMAN and RAHIM."

"HU is AWWAL, AKHIR, ZAHIR and BATIN."

"HU is ALIY and AZIM."

"HU is SAMI and BASIR."

And also the last three verses of Chapter *al-Hashr*...

It is also important to note that using HU as a prefix to other Names is first to establish incomparability *(tanzih)* and then to denote similarity *(tashbih)* in reference to the given Name. This should be remembered at all times.

AR-RAHMAN

Ar-Rahman signifies the materialization of the essence of every iota with Allah's Names in His knowledge. In modern terms, it designates the quantum potential. It is the potential of the source of the entire creation. It is the name of the **Dimension of Names**! All things obtain their **existence** at the level of **knowledge and will** with the attributes denoted by this name.

As signified by the verses *"ar-Rahmanu ala'l arsh'istiwa"* (Quran 20:5) and *"ar-Rahman Allamal Quran, Khalekal Insan, Allamul bayan"* (Quran 55:1-4). *Rahman* is the reality that manifests in **consciousness**! The 'mercy' is in the act of 'manifesting it into existence.'

The narration of Muhammad (saw) that **'Allah created Adam in the image of *Rahman***' means the knowledge aspect of man reflects the qualities of *Rahman*, i.e. the qualities of the Names.

The essence (*dhat*) of man is also related to the name *Rahman*. As such, the polytheists are not able to comprehend the notion of prostrating to *Rahman* (Quran 25:60) and Satan (the mind, illusion) rebels against *Rahman* (Quran 19:44). These verses indicate the manifestation of the essence of 'Man'.

AR-RAHIM

Ar-Rahim is the Name that brings the infinite qualities of *ar-Rahman* into engendered existence. In this sense, it is the 'observation' of the potential. *Ar-Rahim* observes itself through the forms of existence, by guiding the conscious beings to the awareness that their lives and their essential reality are comprised of and governed by the Names.

"...And is ever He, *Rahim* to those who believe in their essential reality" (Quran 33:43).

Ar-Rahim is the source of the plane of existence referred to as 'heaven'.

Ar-Rahim is the producer of the angelic state.

AL-MALEEK

The Sovereign One, who manifests His Names as he wishes and governs them in the world of acts as He pleases. The one who has providence over all things.

"Subhan is He in whose hand (governance) **is the Malakut** (the force of the Names) **of all things, and to Him you will be returned** (the illusory self – ego will come to an end and the Absolute Reality will be discerned). (Quran 36:83)

The Sovereign One who has no partners!

He who is blessed with this awareness will find himself only in absolute submission to *al-Maleek*! Objection and rebellion will cease. *Al-Maleek* is the foremost quality pertinent to the phenomenon known as its manifestations through a continuum (*arsh-i istiwa*).

"Whatever is in the heavens and whatever is on the earth glorify (tasbih, with their unique dispositions) **Allah, *the Maleek, the Quddus,***

the Aziz, the Hakim (to manifest whatever meanings He desires)**."** (Quran 62:1)

AL-QUDDUS

The One who is free and beyond being defined, conditioned and limited by His manifest qualities and concepts! Albeit the engendered existence is the disclosure of His Names, He is pure and beyond from becoming defined and limited by them!

AS-SALAM

One who enables a state of peace by emancipating individuals from the conditions of nature and bodily life and endows the experience of 'certainty' (*yakeen*). One who facilitates the comprehension of Islam for the believers, and enables the heavenly state of existence called '*Dar'us-Salam*' (the explicit manifestation of our implicit potentials). (Quran 36:58)

This name is triggered by the name *ar-Rahim*:

"'Salam,' a word from a 'Rahim' Rabb shall reach them (they will experience the manifestation of the Name Salam) **!"**

AL-MU'MIN

The One who enables the awareness that He, by respect of His Names, is beyond what is perceived. This awareness reflects upon us as **'faith'** (*iman*). All believers, including Rasuls and angels, have their faith rested upon this awareness, which frees the mind from the enslavement of illusion. While illusion can deter the mind, which uses comparison to operate, it becomes powerless and ineffective in the sight of faith.

The inherent quality of the Name *al-Mu'min* manifests itself directly from Awareness in one's consciousness, thereby rendering obsolete the effect of illusion.

AL-MUHAYMIN

The One who maintains and protects the manifestations of His Names with His own system (*al-Hafidhu war-Rakiybu ala kulli shay*)!

Al-Muhaymin also designates the One who safeguards and protects (the trust).

The root word of *al-Muhaymin* is *amanah* (trust), mentioned in the Quran as the trust from which the heavens, the earth and the mountains refrained, but which 'Man' (the twin brother of the Quran) accepted. Essentially, it indicates the consciousness pertaining to the knowledge of the Names, symbolized as the angel 'SPIRIT', which is then passed on to Man, the vicegerent on earth. That is, the 'trust' signifies living with the awareness that your essence is comprised of the Names. This works in conjunction with the name *al-Mu'min*. The angel (force) named SPIRIT also possesses a form since it is also a manifestation, and as such, it is *Hayy* and *Qayyum* due to the perfection of its 'faith' in the infinite qualities of the Names.

AL-AZIZ

The One who, with His unchallengeable might, disposes as He wishes. The One whose will to do as He likes, nothing can oppose. This name works in parallel with the name *Rabb*. The *Rabb* attribute carries out the demands of the Aziz attribute!

AL-JABBAR

The One whose will is compelling. The corporeal worlds (engendered existence) are compelled to comply with His demands! There is no room for refusal. This *'jabr'* (compelling) quality will inevitably express itself and apply its laws through the essence of beings.

AL-MUTAKABBIR

The One to whom the word 'I' exclusively belongs. **Absolute 'I'ness** belongs only to Him. Whoever, with the word 'I', accredits a portion of this Absolute 'I'ness to himself, thereby concealing the 'I'ness comprising his essence and fortifying his own relative 'I'ness, will pay its consequence with 'burning' (suffering). Majesty (Absolute 'I'ness) is His attribute alone.

AL-KHALIQ

The ONE Absolute Creator! The One who brings individuals into the existence from nothingness, with His Names! Everything *al-Khaliq* creates has a purpose to fulfill, and according to this unique purpose, possesses a natural predisposition and character. Hence it has been said:**"characterize yourselves with the character of Allah"** (Tahallaku biakhlakillah) to mean:Live in accordance with the awareness that you are comprised of the structural qualities of the Names of Allah!

AL-BARI

The One who fashions all of creation (from micro to macro) with unique functions and designs yet all in conformity with the whole, like the harmonious functioning of all the different organs in the body!

AL-MUSAWWIR

The fashioner of forms. The One who exhibits 'meanings' as 'forms' and devises the mechanism in the perceiver to perceive them.

AL-GAFFAR

The One who, as requisites of divine power or wisdom, 'conceals' the inadequacies of those who recognize their shortcomings and wish to be freed from their consequences. The One who forgives.

AL-QAHHAR

The One who executes the effects of His Name '*Wahid*' and renders invalid the seeming existence of the relative 'I'ness.

AL-WAHHAB

The One who bestows and gives unrequitedly to those He wishes, oblivious of deservedness.

AR-RAZZAQ

The One who provides all necessary nutrition for the survival of any unit of manifestation regardless of its plane of existence.

AL-FATTAH

The One who generates expansion within individuals. The One who enables the recognition and observation of Reality, and hence, that there is no inadequacy, impairment, or mistake in the engendered existence. The One who expands one's vision and activity, and enables their proper usage. The One who enables the recognition and use of the unrecognized (overseen).

AL-ALEEM

The One who, with the quality of His knowledge, infinitely knows everything in every dimension with all its facets.

AL-QABID

The One who exercises His verdict by retaining the essence of an individual's Name reality. The One who restrains and enforces withdrawnness.

AL-BASIT

The One who opens and expands; the One who enables dimensional and in-depth sight.

AL-KHAFID

The One who abases. The One who capacitates a state of existence which is far from reality. The creator of the *'asfali safileen'* (the lower state of existence). The former of the vision of **'multiplicity'** to conceal the reality.

AR-RAFI

The One who exalts. The one who elevates conscious beings to higher states of existence; to enable the realization and observation of their essential reality.

AL-MU'IZZ

The Giver of Honor. The One who bestows honor to whom he wishes and holds them in esteem over others.

AL-MUDHILL

The One who exposes dishonor in some and degrades below others. The One who deprives from honorable qualities and compels to humiliation with the veil of 'I'ness (ego).

AS-SAMI

The One who perceives His manifestations at every instance. The One who enables awareness and comprehension.

This name triggers the Name *al-Basir*.

AL-BASIR

The One who is constantly observing His manifestations and evaluating their outputs.

AL-HAKAM

The Absolute Judge whose judgment (verdict) is irresistibly applied.

AL-ADL

The One who provides each of His manifestations their due right in consonance with **their creation program**. The One who is absolutely free from unjustness or tyranny.

AL-LATIF

The One who is subtly present in the depths of every manifestation. The One whose favors are plentiful.

AL-HABIR

The One who is aware of the manifestations of His Names at all times. The One who allows his manifestations to discern the level of their comprehension via their outputs.

AL-HALIM

The One who refrains from giving sudden (impulsive) reactions to events, but rather evaluates all situations in respect of their purpose of manifestation.

AL-AZIM

The magnificent glory beyond any manifestation's capacity of comprehension.

AL-GHAFUR

The One who's Mercy should never be doubted or given up on. The One who enables necessary cleansing and triggers the name *Rahim* to bestow blessings.

ASH-SHAKUR

The One who allows the proper use of His bestowals in order that He may increase them. The One who enables the due evaluation of resources such that more can be attained. This name triggers the name *al-Karim*. If this name is not activated in one's life, one will be obstructed from a connection with Allah and not able to duly use his resources, turning his attention to other things and hence becoming veiled from the blessings of Allah. This leads to 'ungratefulness', which is defined as the inability to adequately evaluate and use blessings. Eventually this results in total deprivation.

AL-ALIY

The Highest (or the Sublime). The sublime One who observes existence from the point of reality (essence).

AL-KABIR

The magnitude of the worlds He created with His Names are incomprehensible.

AL-HAFIZ

The One who provides all requirements to preserve and maintain existence.

AL-MUQEET

The One who facilitates the expression of the Name *al-Hafiz* by providing the necessary material and spiritual platform for it.

AL-HASIB

The One who maintains individuality by holding them to account of their behavioral output through the mechanics of 'consequence'

In doing so, an indefinite flow of formation is established.

AL-JALIL

The One who, with His magnificent comprehensiveness and perfection, is the sultan of the world of acts.

AL-KARIM

The exceedingly generous and bountiful One who bestows His bounties even upon those who deny His existence. The ability to READ (*iqra*) is only possible through the activation of this Name, which lies dormant within the essence of every individual.

AR-RAQIB

The One who watches over and keeps under control the manifestations of His Names, with His names, at all times.

AL-MUJIB

The One who unequivocally responds to all who turn towards Him (in prayer and invocation) and provides their needs.

AL-WASI

The All-embracing. The One who embraces the whole of existence with the expressions of His Names.

AL-HAKIM

The One whose power of knowledge appears under the guise of 'causes', hence creating causality and leading to the perception of multiplicity.

AL-WADUD

The creator of attraction. The creator of unconditional and unrequited love. The essence within every beloved!

AL-MAJEED

The One whose majestic glory is evident through His magnificent manifestations!

AL-BAITH

The One who constantly transforms new dimensions of existence. As a requisite of the mechanism denoted by the verse **"Everything in the heavens and earth asks from Him; at every instance HU** (the Absolute Essence of Existence) **manifests Himself in yet another way! "**(Quran 55:29), *al-Baith* continually creates new experiences.

The expression of this name in respect to humanity is depicted in '*amantu*'(Comprises the six fundamentals of belief in Islam. It consists of belief in Allah, His angels, His books, His Rasuls, Doomsday [life after death] and destiny [*qadar*], that all good and evil are from Allah.) as 'to believe in life (resurrection) after death' (*bath'u badal mawt*) and the verse **"That you will certainly change dimensions and transform into bodies befitting those dimensions!"**.(Quran 84:19)

We said *ba'th* (resurrection) is to **taste** death and to commence a new state of life after death... However, resurrection is also possible here on earth in this plane of existence. Like the resurrections of *wilayah* (sainthood), *nubuwwah* (prophethood), and *risalah* (the personification of Allah's knowledge)! As all of these stations comprise new states of life.

To give an example, we may say *ba'th* is like the germination of a seed to sprout its plant, or 'give shoot to new life'. Similarly, life emerges from **death** (dormant inactive potential). In relation to the new state of existence, the previous state is considered as a 'grave' (*qabir*).

"That Hour (death) **will definitely come – there is no doubt about it. And Allah will definitely resurrect the beings** (individual forms of consciousness) **in their graves** (bodies) (to continue their lives through new bodies)!" (Quran 22:7)

ASH-SHAHID

The One who witnesses His existence through His own existence. The One who observes the disclosure of His Names and witnesses His manifestations! The enforcer of the reality that there is no other observer but Himself.

AL-HAQQ

The absolute and unequivocal reality! The source and essence of every function in manifestation!

AL-WAKIL

The One who provides the means for self-actualization. The One who advocates and protects those who place their trust in Him, providing them with the most auspicious outcomes. He who believes in the potential of the name *al-Wakil* in his own essence, will have confirmed his faith in all the Names (all his potentials). The source of the mystery of **vicegerency** lies in this Name!

AL-QAWWI

The One who transforms His power into the enabling potential for the manifestation of existence (hence comprising the force of the whole of existence).

The One who forms the angelic state.

AL-MATIN

The One who sustains the world of acts, the steadfast, the creator of robustness and stability, the provider of strength and resistance!

AL-WALIYY

The One who guides and enables an individual to discover their reality and to live their life in accordance to their essence. It is the source of *risalah* (personification of Allah's knowledge) and *nubuwwah* (prophethood), which comprise the pinnacle states of sainthood (*wilayah*). It is the dispatcher of the perfected qualities comprising the highest point of sainthood, *risalah*, and the state one beneath that, *nubuwwah*. While the expression of *nubuwwah* is indefinitely functional, the expression of *nubuwwah* applies only to earthly life. A *Nabi* continues to live at the same state of perfection after death, but his explicit role as a *Nabi* is no longer active. On the other hand, due to its inherent saintly qualities, *risalah* continues infinitely (as it does with saints).

AL-HAMID

The One who observes and evaluates His universal perfection on worldly forms manifested by His Name *al-Waliyy*.

Hamd belongs only to Him.

AL-MUHSI

The creator of the 'forms' (micro to macro) comprising the seeming multiplicities, each equipped with unique qualities and attributes, within UNITY.

AL-MUBDI

The One who originates the whole of creation in the corporeal worlds, all with exclusive and unique qualities.

AL-MU'ID

The One who restores life to those who turn back to their essence.

AL-MUHYI

The One who enlivens and enlightens! The One who enables the continuation of the individual's life through the application of knowledge and the observation of one's essential reality.

AL-MUMIT

The One who enables a 'taste' (experience) of death. The One who allows a transition between one state of existence to another.

AL-HAYY

The source of names! The One who gives life to the Names and manifests them. The source of universal energy, the essence of energy!

AL-QAYYUM

The One who renders Himself existent with His own attributes, without the need of anything. Everything in existence subsists with *al-Qayyum*.

AL-WAJID

The One whose qualities and attributes are unfailingly abundant. The manifest One. The One, from which nothing lessens, despite the abundance of His manifestations.

AL-MAJID

The magnificent and glorious One with unrestricted, infinite generosity and endowment (benevolence).

AL-WAHID

The One and only! 'ONE'ness far beyond any concept of multiplicity. The ONE, that isn't composed of (or can be broken into) parts (as in pantheism). The 'ONE'ness that renders duality obsolete! The 'ONE'ness that no mind or intellect can fully comprehend!

AS-SAMAD

The Pure Whole One! Free from the concept of multiplicity! Not formed of adjoining parts. Far from conceptualization and limitation. The self-sufficient One, in need of nothing!

An authentic hadith narrates: "*As-Samad* **is such that it bears no space or emptiness within it** (all, whole, one)."

AL-QADIR

The One who creates (discloses, manifests) and observes His knowledge with His power without depending on causality. The One who is absolutely boundless!

AL-MUQTADIR

The Determiner. The absolute possessor of all power pertaining to creation, governance, and disposition.

AL-MUQADDIM

The One who expedites (or prioritizes) the manifestation of Names according to their purpose of creation.

AL-MU'AKHKHIR

The One who delays manifestation in consonance with His name *al-Hakim*.

AL-AWWAL

The first and initial state of existence, the essential Name.

AL-AKHIR

The infinitely subsequent One, to all creation.

AZ-ZAHIR

The self-evident One, the explicit, unequivocal and perceivable manifestation.

AL-BATIN

The unperceivable reality within the perceivable manifestation! The source of the unknown (*Awwal, Akhir, Zahir, Batin, HU!*)

AL-WALI

The One who governs according to His own verdict.

AL- MUTA'ALI

The limitless, boundless Supreme One, whose supremacy encompasses everything! The One whose reality can never be duly reflected by any engendered, conceptualized existence. The One who is beyond being limited by any mind or intellect.

AL-BARR

The One who eases the actualization of individual temperaments and natural dispositions.

AT-TAWWAB

The One who guides individuals to their essence by enabling them to perceive and comprehend the reality. The One who allows individuals to repent, that is, to abandon their misdoings and to compensate for any harm that may have been caused. The activation of this Name triggers the name *Rahim*, and thus benevolence and beauty is experienced.

AL-MUNTAQIM

The One who makes individuals live the consequences of their actions that impede in the realization of their essence. To 'avenge' (*zuntiqam*) is to make one 'pay the price' i.e. face the consequence of their doings without exception or pity. Allah is beyond being bound by concepts such as revenge. When used in conjunction with 'severe in retribution' (*Shadid al-Iqab*) (Quran 59:4), *al-Muntaqim* denotes the force that most severely avenges individuals for failing to recognize their essence, by making them live out the consequences of their own obstructive actions in a most severe and intense way.

AL-AFUW

The One who forgives all offences except for 'duality' (*shirq*); the failure to recognize the reality of non-duality prevents the activation of the name *al-Afuw*. Note that to forgive an offence does not mean to compensate the losses of the past, for in the system of *sunnatullah* there is no compensation of the past!

AR-RA'UF

The compassionate and pitying One who protects individuals who turn to Him from all kinds of behavior which may cause harm or trouble to them.

AL-MAALIK'UL-MULK

The One who governs His Sovereignty as He wishes without having to give account to any individual.

"Say, 'Allah, the sovereign of all sovereignty... You give sovereignty to whom You will and You take sovereignty away from whom you will. You honor whom You will and You abase whom You will. In Your hand is all good. Certainly, you are Qadir over all things.'" (Quran 3:26)

DHUL-JALALI WAL-IKRAM

The One who makes individuals experience their 'nothingness' by enabling them to comprehend the reality that they were created from 'naught' and then bestowing them 'Eternity' by allowing them to observe the manifestations of the Names comprising their essence.

AL-MUQSIT

The One who applies justice, as the requirement of His *Uluhiyya*, by endowing every individual their due, based on their unique creation purpose.

AL-JAMI

The One who observes the whole of existence as a multi-dimensional single frame in His Knowledge. The One who gathers creation according to the purpose and function of their creation.

AL-GHANI

The One who is beyond being labeled and limited by the manifestations of His Names, as He is Great (Akbar) and beyond all concepts. The One who is infinitely abundant with His Names.

AL-MUGHNI

The One who enriches individuals and raises them above others in wealth and emancipates them. The One who enriches with His own riches. The One who grants the beauty of infinity (*baqa*) which results from '*fakr*' (nothingness).

"And did We not find you poor (faqr, in nothingness) **and made you rich** (with infinity – baqa, i.e.)**?** (Did we not make you a servant of the Ghani? Did we not enrich and emancipate you?)" (Quran 93:8)

"And indeed, it is HU who enriches and deprives." (Quran 53:48)

AL-MANI

The One who prevents those from attaining things they do not deserve!

AD-DARR

The One who afflicts individuals with various distressing situations (sickness, suffering, trouble) in order to make them turn to Himself!

AN-NAFI

The One who prompts individuals to engage in good thoughts and actions to aid them towards beneficent and auspicious outcomes.

AN-NUR

The Knowledge that is the source and essence of everything! The essence of everything is *Nur*, everything is comprised of knowledge. Life subsists with knowledge. Those with knowledge are the ever-living ones (*Hayy*), while those who lack knowledge are like living dead.

AL-HADI

The guide to the truth. The One who allows individuals to live according to their reality. The articulator of the truth. The guide to reality.

AL-BADEE

The incomparable beauty and the originator of beautiful manifestation! The One who originates innumerable manifestations, all with unique and exclusive qualities, and without any example, pattern, specimen etc.

AL-BAQI

The Everlasting. The One who exists beyond the concept of time.

AL-WARITH

The One who manifests under various names and forms in order to inherit and protect the possessions of those who abandon all their belongings to undergo true transformation. When one form is exhausted, He continues His existence with another form.

AR-RASHID

The guider to the right path. The One who allows individuals, who recognize their essential reality, to experience the maturity of this recognition!

AS-SABUR

"And if Allah were to hold responsible the people for their wrongdoings and enforce the consequences upon them at once, He would not have left upon the earth any creature (DABBAH, i.e. earthling, in human 'form' – not human)**, but He defers them until a specified time. And when their time comes, they can neither fall behind it nor precede it by even an hour."** (Quran 16:61)

The One who waits for each individual to execute his creation program before rendering effective the consequences of their actions. Allowing the tyranny of the tyrant to take place, i.e. activating the Name *as-Sabur*, is so that both the oppressor and the oppressed can duly carry out their functions before facing the consequences in full effect. Greater calamity forces the creation of increased cruelty.

A FINAL REMINDER

Obviously the meanings of the Names of Allah cannot be confined to such a narrow scope. This is why I refrained from going into this topic for many years. For I know it is impossible to duly cover the comprehensiveness of this topic. However, my own experience of the reflections of this knowledge has compelled me to cover this topic to some extent. I ask Allah's forgiveness. Many books have been written in this field. I only touched upon it based on my understanding today and in a way that is easy to remember. Perhaps I have unveiled only the tip of the iceberg!

SubhanAllahu amma yasifun! (Quran 23:91)

I feel I need to reiterate the importance of the following point before concluding this topic:

Everything that I have shared with you here must be observed and experienced within one's consciousness, after becoming cleansed from the restraints of the illusory identity ('I'ness) and the density of the bodily state of existence. **If this cleansing involves the automated repetitions of certain words and phrases without experiential confirmation, the results will be no different from a computer running a program, and hence, ineffective.** Sufism is a way of life! Those who narrate and repeat the words of others (hence gossip!) squander their lives, finding solace in Satan's adorned and embellished games!

The evidence of having attained the reality of this knowledge is the end of suffering! That is, if you are no longer bothered or troubled by anything or anyone, if no situation or person can upset you anymore, it means this knowledge has become your reality! **As long as one is bound by value judgments attached to conditionings and lives his life centered around emotions and behaviors resulting from these, his life will continue and mature as an 'earthling' (not a human) and be subject to 'causality', both here and in the afterlife.**

Knowledge is for application. So, let us begin with the application of: 'knowledge that is not applied is a weight on one's shoulders!'

Let us ask ourselves at the end of each day:

"Am I ready to embark on a 'one-way' journey tonight in my sleep?"

"Are worldly matters still bothering me and causing me to suffer? Or am I living my servitude in peace and happiness?"

If your answer is 'Yes', glad tidings to you my friend! If it is 'No', then many tasks await you tomorrow! In this case, when you wake up in the morning, ask yourself "What must I do today in order to go to bed in total peace and happiness tonight?"

Glory be to the One who allows us to live our days with the awareness that everything we own will perish...

Wassalam...

A special thank you to the honorable imam of Istanbul Kanlica Mosque, Hasan Guler Hodja, a venerable scholar and an exemplary man of knowledge, for sharing his valuable insight with me and for assisting me with '*Decoding The Quran*'.

AHMED HULUSI
03 February 2009
North Carolina, USA

1

AL-FATIHA

I seek refuge in the protective forces of the Names of Allah comprising my Essence from impulses generated by the accursed and rejected (rajim) Satan, which, as a result of preconditioning, causes our sense of illusion to perceive the existent as non-existent and the non-existent as existent, thereby making man believe he is an independent being and body outside the Names of Allah, directing man to the idea of an external deity-God in the heavens.

1. By the one who is denoted by the name Allah (who created my being with His Names in accord with the meaning of the letter 'B'), **the Rahman, the Rahim.**

2. Hamd (the evaluation of the corporeal worlds created with His Names, as He wills) **belongs to Allah, the Rabb** (the absolute source of the infinite meanings of the Names) **of the worlds** (the universe created within the brain of every individual)

3. The Rahman (the quality with which He forms the dimension of Names; the Quantum Potential)**, the Rahim** (the quality with which He continually creates the engendered existence with the meanings of the Names)

4. The Maleek (the Sovereign One, who manifests His Names as he wishes and governs them in the world of acts as He pleases. The One who has providence over all things) **or the Maalik** (the Absolute Owner) **of the eternal period governed by the decrees of religion** (sunnatullah).

5. You alone we serve, and from You alone we seek the continual manifestation of your Names (By manifesting the meanings of Your Beautiful Names we, as the whole of creation, are in a state of natural servitude to You, and we seek guidance to attain and maintain this awareness at all times)

6. Enable the realization that leads to our innermost essential reality (sirat al-mustaqeem)

7. The path of those upon whom You have bestowed favor (those who believe in the Names of Allah as comprising their essential self and experience the awareness of their force) **not of those who have evoked Your wrath** (who have failed to the see the reality of their selves and the corporeal worlds and who have become conditioned with their ego-identities) **nor of those who are astray** (from the Reality and the understanding of the One denoted by the name Allah, the al-Wahid-ul Ahad-as-Samad, and who thus associate partners with Allah [shirq; duality]).

2

AL-BAQARAH

By the one who is denoted by the name Allah (who created my being with His Names in accord with the meaning of the letter 'B'), the Rahman, the Rahim.

1. Alif Lam Meem.

2. This is the Knowledge (Book) of the reality and sunnatullah (the mechanics of the system of Allah), about which there is absolutely no doubt; it is the source of comprehension for those who seek protection.

3. Who believe in the reality (that their being comprises of the compositions of the Names of Allah) unknown to them (beyond their perception), and who establish prayer (who experience the meaning of salat alongside performing its physical actions) and who spend unrequitedly from both the physical and spiritual sustenance of life that We have provided for them for the sake of Allah.

4. And who believe in what has been revealed to you from your essence (from the depths of your essence to your consciousness) and what was revealed before you, and who, of their eternal life to come, are certain (in complete submission as a result of an absolute comprehension).

5. They are in a state of HUDA (comprehension of the reality) from their Rabb (the Name composition comprising their essence) and it is they who are successful.

6. Indeed, for those who deny (cover) the reality, it is all the same whether you warn them or do not warn them – they will not believe.

7. Allah has set a seal upon their brain's perception of the reality; their insight is veiled. They have deserved great suffering as the consequence of their actions.

8. And of the people are some who say, "We believe in Allah in accord with the meaning of the letter B (with the belief that the Names of Allah comprise their being) and the life to come (that they will

forever live the consequences of their deeds)" **but, in fact, their faith is not in line with this reality!**

9. They think (that by saying "we believe in accord with the meaning of the letter 'B'") **they can deceive Allah** (their essential reality) **and the believers, but they deceive only themselves, yet they are unaware of it!**

10. Their consciousness is not capable of healthy thought (they are unable to perceive the reality), **and Allah has increased this. They will incur a painful suffering for denying their reality.**

11. And when it is said to them, "Do not cause corruption (do not live contrary to your purpose of existence) **on the earth** (and your bodies)," **they say, "We are but reformers** (we use things justly and appropriately)."

12. Most assuredly, it is they who are the corrupters (perverting things out of place), **but they are not conscious of it.**

13. And when it is said to them, "Believe as the believers have believed," they say, "Should we believe as the foolish (the limited in intellect; those who live recklessly without thinking) **have believed?" Most definitely, it is they who are the foolish** (limited in intellect and unable to contemplate) **but they do not realize, they can not comprehend!**

14. And when they are with the believers, they say, "We believe – we accept"; but when they are alone with their devils/evil ones (the corrupters and deluders of their illusion) **they say, "Indeed, we are with you; we were only mocking them."**

15. (But) **it is they who Allah mocks** (for their incessant failure to comprehend Allah as their essential reality) **and leaves them in their transgression as a result of their blindness** (lack of insight).

16. Those are the ones who have bought fallacy (incapacity to recognize their reality) **in exchange for the truth that comprises their essence. Their transaction has brought them no profit, nor will it lead them to the truth!**

17. Their example is like someone who kindles a fire that illuminates their surrounding, yet because the Nur (light of knowledge) **from their essence does not shine through, Allah leaves them in darkness; they can no longer see!**

18. Deaf (unable to perceive), **dumb** (unable to articulate the reality) **and blind** (unable to grasp the obvious truth); **they cannot return to their essential reality!**

19. Or, it is as if they are in a rainstorm (of thoughts) **from the sky** (the domain of the intellect/intellectual activity), **within which is darkness** (the unknown), **thunder** (the clashing of rights and wrongs) **and lightning** (a sudden insight into the knowledge of the reality)! **They block their ears to the thunder from fear of death** (in fear of losing their constructed identities or ego in the face of the reality). **Allah is the Mu'id** (the All-Encompassing One) **who also comprises** (and encompasses) **the existence of the deniers of the truth.**

20. The lightning (the light of the reality) **almost seizes their sight** (their perception based on what they see). **Every time it lights** (the way) **for them, they progress a few steps with the light of the reality; but when the light is gone they are left in darkness. And if Allah had willed, He would have lessened the manifestation of His Names Sami and Basir on them. Indeed, Allah is Qadir over all things.**

21. O mankind, consciously serve (become conscious of your servitude to) **your Rabb** (the Names comprising your essence), **the creator of you and those before you, so that you may be of the protected ones.**

22. He made the earth (body) **a bed** (vehicle), **the sky** (consciousness – brain) **a place of living and revealed** (disclosed) **from the sky** (from the depths of consciousness) **rain** (knowledge) **and provided thereby sustenance of life** (both mental and bodily). **So do not fall into duality** (shirq) **by assuming the existence of an external deity-god!**

23. And if you are in doubt about what We disclosed to Our Servant (that which was revealed to his consciousness from his essential reality – the Dimension of Names) **then produce a surah the like thereof! If you are truthful** (true to your word) **call upon your witnesses other than** (the Uluhiyya denoted by the name) **Allah.**

Note: The word 'other' here is translated from the Arabic word 'doon' which connotes the impossibility of anything that can be likened to the One referenced as 'Allah'; hence any imagined god/s can only be 'other' (doon) than Allah and they can in no way be likened to or differed from or compared to the Absolute Reality called Allah. Any form of existence referenced by the word 'doon' also obtains its life force from the compositional qualities denoted by the Names of Allah, yet its existence can in no way be compared or held equal to Allah. Thus, any idea or thought an individual infers about the One denoted by the name Allah can never define Him in respect of His Absolute Reality. The verse 'laysa kamithlihi shay'a' – nothing can be likened to Him – in following chapters attenuates the fact that no concept can come close to defining the One referenced as Allah. All of this is designated by the word 'doon'. Since there is no word in English that duly captures the meaning of 'doon' I have no choice but to use the word 'other'.

24. But if you can't do this – and you will never be able to – then fear the fire, whose fuel is men and stones (forms of consciousness as men and stones; individual consciousness materialized into form in accord with that domain of existence – Allah knows best!)**, for that fire will burn the deniers of the reality!**

25. And give the good news to those who believe and engage in deeds to experience the reality, that for them there will be Paradises (the constant formation of knowledge in the state of observing the manifestations of Allah's Names) **beneath which rivers flow. As they are provided with this provision** (observation)**, they will say, "This is similar to that which we tasted before." And it is similar to that which they tasted before. They will abide therein eternally with their partners** (The word 'zawj' is also used in various contexts to mean different things. While its most common usage is to mean 'partner in marriage', it has also been used in the context of consciousness implying the partner or equivalent of consciousness and the body that will fall into disuse at some point. In fact, the seventh verse of chapter 56, al-Waqi'ah, states 'azwajan thalathah' to mean 'three kinds' not three wives!) **purified from the filth of shirq** (duality).

26. Indeed, Allah will not hesitate to use the example of a mosquito wing, or even a smaller item. And those who fulfill the requisites of their faith know that this is the Truth originating from their Rabb. But as for those who deny this truth, (without contemplating upon the examples that are provided) **they say, "What did Allah mean with this example?" This parable leads many astray** (due to the incapacity of their creational program – natural disposition [fitrah]) **and some, it directs to the truth** (to the realization of their essence). (With this parable) **Allah misleads no other than those who have lost their purity** (who have become veiled from the truth)!

27. Those who break the covenant of Allah (the requirements of manifesting the qualities of the Names and the potential to live at this level of awareness) **after coming to the world** (identifying with the illusory corporeal existence). **Who fragment that which has been ordered to be unified** (the observation of the reality of the Names) **and cause corruption** (squander their lives in pursuit of bodily desires – the impulses coming from the second brain in the stomach – the commands of the carnal self) **on earth** (their bodily life). **It is verily those who are the losers.**

28. How can you deny that the Names of Allah comprise your essence (in accord with the meaning of the letter B) **when you were lifeless** (unaware of your essential reality) **and He brought you to life** (with the knowledge He disclosed to you)**; again He will cause you to die** (from the state of thinking you are only the body), **and again He will bring you to life** (purify you from confining your existence to your body and enable you to live in a state of consciousness)**... eventually you will see your reality.**

29. It is HU (HU/He should be contemplated upon in multidimensional depth!) **who created for you all of that which is on the earth** (all of the qualities and functions of your body). **Then He turned to your consciousness** (brain) **and arranged it into seven realms** (seven levels of comprehension, seven stages of the self). **He is knowing of all things as He creates everything from Himself** (He comprises the essence of all manifestations).

30. And when your Rabb said to the angels (angels here are personifications of the qualities of the Names comprising one's body, hence the addressee here is you)**, "I will make upon the earth** (the body) **a vicegerent** (conscious beings who will live with the awareness of the Names)**." They said, "Will You make one who causes corruption and sheds blood therein, while we declare Your hamd** (evaluate your existence that you have manifested through us) **and engage in your tasbih** (are in service to Your will, which in every instant manifests in a different state) **and sanctify You** (hold you above and beyond all inadequacies)**?" Allah said, "Indeed, I am Aleem** (All-Knowing) **of that which you do not know."**

31. And He taught (programmed) **Adam** (the name 'Adam' in the Quran references every single human, who in reality is nonexistent and has been created from a state of nothingness through the manifestation of a composition of Names) **all of the Names** (all knowledge pertaining to the Names and their manifestation). **Then said to the angels, "Explain the** (qualities of the) **Names of** (Adam's) **existence, if you insist on your claim."**

32. (Unable to make this evaluation) **they** (the angels) **said, "Subhan, You are** (beyond being limited or conditioned by any of your constant creations)**! It is not possible for us to have any knowledge except that which You manifest through us! Undoubtedly, you are the Aleem**

(possessor of absolute knowledge) **and the Hakim** (the One who manifests this systematically)."

33. (He addressed), **"O Adam** (vicegerent who has been brought into existence from nothingness with the qualities of the Names), **inform them of the reality of the Names comprising your existence."** When **Adam informed them of the meanings of** (Allah's) **Names** (comprising his being, that is, when these qualities became manifest through him), **Allah made them realize, "Did I not tell you that I know the unknown** (the secrets and qualities that have not yet become manifest) **of the heavens** (state of consciousness) **and the earth** (the body). **And I know what you conceal and what you reveal!"**

34. **And when We said to the angels, "Prostrate before Adam** (the manifestation of Names who has come into existence from nonexistence; the Dimension of Names)"; **they all prostrated, except for Iblis. He refused out of arrogance – the magnanimity of his ego** (he realized his own essential reality comprised the qualities of the Names but failed to realize that the very same reality comprises the essence of all beings other than him) **and became of the deniers of the reality.**

35. **And We said, "O Adam, dwell, you and the one with whom you share your condition and life** (your wife, your body) **in the state of Paradise. Live however you will with the blessings of this dimension but do not approach this tree** (never fall into the misconception that your existence is confined to the body), **lest you suffer."**

36. **But Satan** (the assumption that they are only the body) **caused them to slip from** (the state of consciousness) **that they were in. And We said, "Descend as enemies** (of spirit and body) **to one another. You** (and your descendants) **will live upon the earth** (with the conditions of bodily life) **and benefit from it for some time."**

37. **Then Adam** (be aware and never forget, Adam is you!) **received knowledge – words – from his Rabb** (the dimension of Names within his brain) **and repented** (this knowledge enabled him to realize his mistake). **His repentance was accepted. Indeed, HU is the accepting of repentance and the One who allows the experience of its pleasant results with His Rahimiyyah.**

38. **We said, go down, all of you, from there** (the state of consciousness in which you feel free from bodily restrictions – Paradise life). **And when My Huda** (guidance; Rasul [knowledge] enabling the realization and comprehension of your essential reality) **comes to you**

from Me, whoever follows My Huda – they will have no fear nor anything to cause them grief.

39. And those who disbelieve and deny Our signs – they will abide **in fire** (suffering) **eternally.**

40. O Children of Israel, remember My favor that I have bestowed upon you and fulfill My covenant upon you so that I will fulfill your covenant from Me (in regards to the vicegerency in your creation), **and be afraid of only Me.**

41. And believe in what I have revealed (Quran) **confirming that which is with you** (Torah). **Be not the first to deny this truth. And do not exchange My signs** (the manifestations of the Names in relation to the secret of the letter B) **in your essence, for a small price. Protect yourself from Me!**

42. And do not mix the truth (the reality) **with falsehood! You conceal the truth while you know it!**

43. And establish salat (turn to and experience your essence both inwardly and outwardly) **and give alms** (give unrequitedly from what has been given to you) **and bow** (ruku) **with those who bow** (feel the greatness of Allah's Names in your essence and experience [tasbih] them, and as you stand back up saying 'samiAllahu...' realize this is perceived by the Mu'id, your essential reality).

44. Do you advise people to experience the beauty formed by Allah's Names and neglect to experience this yourselves? Though you read the Book (the knowledge of the reality of existence), **will you still not use your reason?**

45. Be patient (by relying on the qualities of the Names in your essence); **seek help by turning to these qualities through prayer** (salat). **Indeed, except for those who are in awe of Allah, this is difficult for the ego.**

46. Those who are in awe are certain that (by realizing the illusory nature of their ego) **they will meet their Rabb** (the essential reality of their self; the Names) **and indeed they will return to Him.**

47. O Children of Israel, remember My favor (the knowledge) **that I have bestowed upon you and that I excelled you over many nations.**

48. Be aware and protect yourselves from the day when no one can pay any price for another, nor will intercession (for another) **be**

accepted (Once the biological brain ceases to exist the spiritual brain is unable to evaluate new data and hence cannot accept intercession, that is, it rejects the knowledge of the reality), **nor will compensation be taken to free them, nor will they be aided.**

49. (And recall that) **We had saved you from the family of Pharaoh, who was afflicting you with the worst torment, slaughtering your sons and keeping your females alive. You were in a great affliction from your Rabb.**

50. **By manifesting the forces of Allah's Names in your essence We had parted the sea and saved you and drowned the family of Pharaoh as they were looking on.**

51. **We had pledged forty nights to Moses, and during this period you had deified a calf as wrongdoers** (you had done injustice to yourselves by falling into duality as a result of denying your essential reality).

52. **After this incident We had forgiven you, that perhaps you would be grateful** (realize and evaluate).

53. **And recall when We gave Moses the Book** (the knowledge of the reality of existence) **and the Furqan** (the ability and knowledge to differentiate right from wrong) **so that you would turn to the truth.**

54. **Moses had said to his people, "O my people, indeed by taking a calf** (as a deity) **you have wronged yourselves** (your essence). **So repent** (for denying His existence in your essence and turning to external deifications) **to the Bari** (the One who exquisitely creates existence with His Names) **and kill your illusory selves** (ego). **In the sight of the Bari, doing this is beneficial for you. He will accept your repentance. Indeed, He is the Tawwab** (Accepting of Repentance) **and the giver of grace as a result of it** (when the person discerns his mistake and repents, the quality referenced by Tawwab prevents any possible negative outcome and reverses these effects, allowing for new realizations to take place)".

55. **And you had said, "O Moses, we will never believe you until we see Allah outright"; after which lightening** (the knowledge of the reality to eradicate your existence) **had struck you while you were looking on.**

56. **Then after you tasted death** (your nothingness and that the Wahid'ul Qahhar is the one and only existence) **We had revived your life with a new understanding, that perhaps you would evaluate this.**

57. And We shaded you with clouds (to veil you from the scorching truth and to maintain your humanly life) **and revealed to you** (from your essence to your consciousness) **manna** (the force of power in the Names of Allah comprising your essence) **and quails** (the ability to feel your spiritual aspect) **saying, "Eat from the pure things with which We have provided you." And they** (by not evaluating the knowledge of the reality) **did not do wrong to Us but they did wrong to themselves** (A concealed meaning has been provided here in addition to the literal meaning of the verse).

58. And recall when We said, "Enter this city (dimension) **and eat whatever you will** (from the blessings of this dimension) **and enter the gate prostrating** (in confession of your nonexistence and that only the Names of Allah exist) **and ask to be forgiven** (for identifying with your ego) **so that We will forgive your mistakes** (formed by your illusory self)... **We will increase** (our blessings) **to those** (the doers of good) **who unrequitedly share from what We have bestowed upon them."**

59. But those among them, who did wrong to themselves, changed the things that were said to them to things that were not said to them. Resultantly We disclosed from the sky (from the amygdala in their brains) **suspicion** (illusion; ideas that cause torment).

60. And recall when Moses prayed for water for his people, and We said, "Strike the stone with your staff (with the forces of the Names in your essence)**." And** (when he struck) **there gushed forth from it twelve springs. Every group of people knew their way** (their source of water). **We said: "Eat and drink from the provision of Allah, and do not go to extreme causing corruption on the earth."**

61. And recall when you said, "O Moses, we can not be content with one kind of food. Call upon your Rabb to bring forth for us from the earth its green herbs and its cucumbers and its garlic and its lentils and its onions!" Moses asked, "Do you want to exchange what is beneficial and superior for what is lesser and worthless? Then go down to the city and you will find what you have asked for." And so they were covered with humiliation and poverty and were stricken with wrath (were reduced to a state of existence based on externality). **That was because they covered and denied the signs** (the forces of the Names) **of Allah in their essence, and going against the reality** (giving in to their ego) **they killed the Nabis. As a result of their rebellion, they transgressed the limits and went too far.**

62. Indeed, among the believers (despite their dualistic view - concealed shirq)**, the Jews, the Christians and the Sabeans** (who deify and worship the stars) – **those who believe that the Names of Allah comprise their essential reality and in the life after, and who, engage in the necessary deeds for their salvation** (A state of emancipation from the conditions of nature and bodily life and the experience of 'certainty' [yakeen].) **– will be rewarded** (with the resulting forces) **in the sight of their Rabb** (their composition of Names.) **They will have nothing to fear, nor anything to grieve over!**

63. And recall when We took your covenant and We raised over you the Mount Sinai (a miracle of Moses). **Hold what We have given you** (the knowledge of the reality) **as a force and remember** (dhikr) **what is in it so that you may protected.**

64. But after this you turned away once again and went back to your old ways. If it were not for the bounty and grace of Allah upon you, you would surely have been among the losers.

65. Assuredly, you would know about those among you who disrespect the Sabbath and transgress the limits. We said to them, "Become apes (live as imitators who refuse to experience the results of their reality)**, despised."**

66. This was so it can be an exemplary punishment for those who were present (who experienced this event) **and their successors and a lesson for those who seek protection.**

67. And recall when Moses said to his people, "Allah commands you to slaughter a cow." They said, "Are you mocking us?" He said, "I seek refuge in Allah, my essential reality, from being among the ignorant (those who are veiled from the reality)**."**

68. They said, "Turn to your Rabb to make clear to us what exactly He wants (slaughtered)**." "Indeed He says 'It is a cow which is neither too old nor too young, but in between the two', so now do as you are commanded."**

69. (Unsatisfied with this answer, they went into further unnecessary detail and) **said, "Turn to your Rabb to inform us of its color." "Indeed He says, 'It is a yellow cow, bright in color – pleasing to the eye.'"**

70. (Further insisting) **they said, "Turn to your Rabb to make clear to us exactly the kind of cow He wants us to slaughter; for many cows fit this description? Allah willing, we will find the right cow..."**

71. **"He says, 'It is an unyoked cow neither trained to plow the earth nor to irrigate the field, a free cow with no spot on her!'"** They said, **"Now you have come with the truth."** So (with great difficulty they found a cow with such attributes and) **they slaughtered her** (but they paid a great price to find the only cow that met the criteria). **They were nearly going to be unsuccessful!**

72. **And recall when you killed a man and disputed over it, whereas Allah brings out that which you conceal!**

73. **So, We said, "Strike** (with the divine forces in your essence) **the dead with a part of** (the cow you slaughtered)." **Thus does Allah bring the dead to life. He shows you the signs** (of the forces in your essence) **so that you might use your reason** (evaluate).

74. **After this your hearts became hardened again, like stones or even harder** (unable to manifest the reality in your essence). **Whereas there are stones from which rivers burst forth, and there are some that split open and water gushes out... There are even stones that fall and roll out in of awe Allah... Verily Allah is never veiled from what you do** (as He forms your existence with His Names).

75. **Do you covet the hope, o believers, that they** (the Jews with this genetic past) **would believe you? Whereas a group of them used to hear the word of Allah** (Moses) **and understand them, then deliberately distort it** (pervert its meaning).

76. **When they meet those who believe, they say, "We have believed"; but when they are alone with one another, they say, "Do you talk to them about the truth Allah has disclosed to you so that they can use it as evidence against you? Do you not think?"**

77. **Do they not know that Allah knows what they conceal and what they disclose?**

78. **There are among them** (ummiyyiina) **people who have no knowledge of the Book** (knowledge of the reality), **other than what they assume** (based on their conditionings); **they live with their** (baseless) **conjectures.**

79. **So woe to those who write the knowledge with their own hands** (driven by their illusory selves), **then say, "This is from Allah,"** in **exchange for a small price! Woe to what they write with their hands and woe to what they earn in this way!**

80. And they say, "The fire won't burn us except for a certain amount of days." Say to them, "Have you taken a covenant from **Allah** (the Absolute Reality in your essence)? **For Allah will never break His covenant. Yet you make fabrications against Allah.**"

81. No! The truth is not as they assume! Whoever earns evil (through his thoughts or actions) **and his mistake encompasses him** (his system of thought blinds him from the truth) **those are the people of the fire** (suffering) **eternally.**

82. But those who believe and do righteous deeds (for their salvation, as a result of becoming aware of their reality) **– they are the people of Paradise and will abide therein eternally.**

83. And recall when We made a covenant with the Children of Israel "Do not assume the existence of, and worship an 'other,' other than Allah; give your parents their due right; do good to your relatives, orphans, and the needy; speak good words to people (words that direct them to the reality)**; and establish salat and give zakah** (their practice of salat and zakah was different to the Islamic way)**." Yet after this, except a few of you, you turned away** (from your word)**, and you still continue to do so.**

84. And recall when We took your word that you will not shed each other's blood or evict one another from your homes, and you had bore witness and consented to this.

85. Yet you are killing one another and evicting a group of your people from their homes. You unjustly unite against them as enemies. And if they come to you as captives, you ransom them and evict them (although this was forbidden to you)**. So, do you believe in part of the knowledge of the reality (Book) and disbelieve in part? The recompense for those who do so among you is disgrace in worldly life; and on the Day of Resurrection they will be subject to the severest of suffering. Allah as your essential reality, is not unaware of what you do.**

86. Those are the ones who have bought the life of this world (bodily desires and pleasures) **in exchange for the eternal life to come** (the inner reality)**. Their suffering will not be lightened, nor will they be aided!**

87. Indeed, We gave Moses the Knowledge of the Reality (Book) and then sent a succession of Rasuls from among you as reinforcement. And We gave Jesus, the son of Mary, clear proofs (states that clearly confirm the knowledge of the reality). **We supported him with the Pure Spirit** (the force We manifested through him). **But every time a Rasul came to you with truths that went against the desires of your illusory selves, in the name of exalting your egos you denied some of them and killed some.**

88. **And they said, "Our hearts** (perception) **are cocooned** (by our world – preventing us from experiencing our reality)**." No, in fact they had fallen far from** (became cursed by) **Allah for denying the reality. How limited is your faith!**

89. **And when they** (the Jews) **sought insight to have victory over the disbelievers, who denied religion, there came to them a Book from Allah confirming the knowledge that was already with them – and that which they awaited** (Muhammad saw) **came to them, but they refuted him! So they live in a state far from Allah** (the curse of Allah is upon the deniers of the absolute reality).

90. **How wretched it is that out of envy they deny a servant of Allah, whom Allah revealed from His grace** (from one's essence to his consciousness)**, and because of this denial they cover the absolute reality within the 'self'! Because of this they were subjected to wrath upon wrath** (they were reduced to an unconscious state of living, veiled from their essential reality). **And for those who deny the reality** (disbelievers) **there is a humiliating punishment.**

91. **And when it is said to them, "Believe in what Allah has revealed," they say, "We believe only in what is revealed to us" and they disbelieve what has been revealed to others. Whereas those revelations confirm that which is within them! Say, "If you really believed in the reality that was revealed to you, then why did you kill the Nabis of Allah?"**

92. **Moses had certainly come to you with clear proofs, manifested from his essential reality. Yet you took a calf as god and did wrong to your selves** (to your essence).

93. **And recall when We took your covenant and raised over you the Mount Sinai** (removed your sense of ego)**, saying "Perceive, experience and live the requirements of what We have given you with the forces comprising your essence." But they said "We perceive but we do not accept." Because of their disbelief their hearts absorbed the love of the calf** (corporeality – externality – ego)**. Say, "If you say you are believers, and this is the result of your faith, how wretched an outcome for you!"**

94. Say, "If the abode of the eternal life to come with Allah belongs only to you and not others, then you should wish for death if you are true to your word!"

95. But they will never wish for death, because of what they have put forth with their hands (their sins). And Allah, as their reality, knows who outputs wrong.

96. And you will surely find them to be of the most ambitious of people about the worldly life! Even more than those who live in **shirq** (duality; associating partners with Allah). Each one of them desires to live a thousand years! Whereas a long lifespan will not distance them from suffering. And Allah, as their essential reality, is **the Basir** (the evaluator of what they do).

97. Say, "Whoever is an enemy to Gabriel should know that it is he who has revealed (the Quran) to your consciousness, by the permission of Allah (B-iznillah; the suitability of the Name composition comprising his essence), confirming that which was before him and as guidance and good news for the believers."

98. Whoever is an enemy to Allah (the reality of Uluhiyyah) and the realm of angels (the manifestations of the Names of Allah in the worlds) and His Rasuls (those through whom the reality is disclosed) and Gabriel (the disclosure of the Knowledge of Allah) and Michael (the force that guides to and enables the attainment of both physical and spiritual sustenance) then indeed, Allah is an enemy to those who cover this reality!

99. And We have certainly given clear evidence to you, which no one can deny except those whose purity of origin has become corrupt (with conditionings).

100. Is it not so that every time they entered into an agreement some of them violated and disregarded it? No, in fact most of them do not believe!

101. When a Rasul from Allah came to them confirming that which was with them, a group of those who had been given the Book (knowledge) threw the Book of Allah (the knowledge of the reality and sunnatullah) behind their backs (because he wasn't a Jew), as if they did not know the truth.

102. They had also followed the devils (those who cause corruption by inciting the illusion) in regards to (denying) the sovereignty (administration) of Solomon (formed by his essential reality). It was not

Solomon who disbelieved (curtained from his reality), **but the devils who** (by following their illusions) **disbelieved** (denied the reality), **teaching people magic and that which was revealed to the two angels** (to Maleek) **at Babylon, Harut and Marut. But the two angels did not teach anything to anyone without saying, "We are but a trial, so do not become a disbeliever by covering that which is in your essence** (by resorting to external forces to practice magic)." **And yet they learned from them that which causes separation between a man and his wife. But they cannot harm anyone except with permission from Allah. They were learning what harms them and not what benefits them. Indeed, those who purchased it** (magic) **will have no benefit in the eternal Hereafter. If only they knew how wretched the thing for which they sold the reality of their essence is.**

103. If they had believed and protected themselves (from shirq; duality), **then the reward from Allah would have been far better. If only they knew.**

104. O you who have believed, say not (to Allah's Rasul), **"Ra'ina"** ('watch out for us': the Jews used this word with a particular accent and emphasis to mean 'foolish'; this warning was made due to this insulting behavior) **but say, "Unthurna" and listen. For the deniers of the truth there is a painful suffering.**

105. Neither the disbelievers of the People of the Book nor the dualists (those who assert existence to their egos or external objects; dualistic view) **wish that any good should be revealed to you from your Rabb** (the qualities of the Names within your essence). **But Allah selects for His grace whom He wills, by way of his essence. Allah is the D'hul Fadhlul Azeem** (possessor of great bounty).

106. If We annul a verse or cause it to be forgotten We bring forth a better one or one that is similar to it. Do you not know that Allah is the Qadir (the possessor of continual and infinite power) **over all things?**

107. Do you not know that to Allah belongs the dominion (as He controls all of it as He wills at all times) **of the heavens and the earth** (consciousness and matter – the realm of the body) **and that you can have no friend or helper besides Allah?**

108. Or do you intend to question your Rasul as Moses was questioned before? And whoever exchanges the faith in his essence with the denial of the absolute reality has certainly lost the right way.

109. Many of the People of the Book (those to whom the knowledge of the reality has been given) **wish they could turn you away from faith to disbelief, purely out of their envy, even though they openly perceive the reality. So pardon them and overlook their offences until the command of Allah is disclosed to you. Indeed, Allah is Qadir over all things.**

110. Establish your salat (duly turn towards Allah both internally and externally) **and give zakah** (unrequitedly share from what Allah has provided to you with those in need). **Whatever good you do, you will find it with Allah** (within the realm of the Names comprising the inner depths of your brain). **Indeed, Allah** (whose Names form your being) **is the Basir.**

111. And they say, "None will enter Paradise except one who is a Jew or a Christian." This is merely their imagination. Say, "Produce your proof, if you speak the truth!"

112. No (things are not as they fantasize them to be)! **Whoever feels that his essence** (face) **is for** (the manifestations of the Names of) **Allah, his reward is with his Rabb** (his essential reality). **They will have no fear, nor anything to give them grief.**

113. The Jews say "The Christians have no valid grounds" and the Christians say, "The Jews have no valid grounds," although they both supposedly **recite the Book** (the revealed knowledge)! **Yet this is what those who are ignorant of this knowledge say! Allah will judge between them over which they differ, in the period of doomsday.**

114. And who are more unjust than those who prevent the dhikr of Allah (the acknowledgment that we do not exist, only Allah exists) **from being mentioned in places of prostration** (the experience of one's nothingness in the sight of the reality of the Names) **and strive toward their destruction** (by deifying the ego of the pure hearts). **Such people should enter there in fear. For they will be disgraced in this world** (in sight of those who know the truth)**, and in the eternal life to come, great suffering awaits them...**

115. And to Allah belongs the east (the place of birth and origin) **and the west** (setting – disappearance – death). **So wherever you turn, there is the Face of Allah** (you are face to face with the manifestation of Allah's Names). **Indeed, Allah is all-Encompassing and Knowing.**

116. They said, "Allah has taken a son." Subhan (exalted) **is He! Rather, to Him belongs whatever is in the heavens and the earth. All things are obedient to Him.**

117. He is the Badee (the Originator of the heavens and the earth who makes things without any sample or like). **When He wills a thing, He only says to it "Be" and it is.**

118. Those who do not know (what the name Allah denotes) **say** (assuming Allah is a god in the heavens), **"Why does Allah not speak to us or send us a miracle?" Those before them spoke in the same way. Their viewpoints resemble each other** (as a result of mirror neurons – they have the same mentality). **We have clearly shown our verses** (the signs of the reality) **to those who want to duly evaluate them.**

119. Indeed, We disclosed you as the Truth, as a bringer of good tidings and a fore warner. You will not be asked about the attendants of Hell.

120. And never will the Jews or the Christians approve of you until you follow their understanding of religion. Say, "Indeed, Allah is the guide to the realization of your essence (one cannot be guided unless Allah guides)." **If you follow their imaginations or delusions after what has come to you of knowledge, you will have neither a friend nor a helper from Allah.**

121. Those to whom the Book (the knowledge of sunnatullah) **has been given duly recite and evaluate it. They are the believers in Hu. And whoever denies Hu – it is they who are the losers** (for they deny their own reality).

122. O children of Israel, remember My favor upon you (that I informed you of your innermost essential reality)**, and that I made you superior over various nations.**

123. And protect yourself from a time when no one can pay anything to save another. No ransom (compensation) **will be accepted from him, nor will any intercession** (Once the biological brain ceases to exist the spiritual brain is unable to evaluate new data and hence cannot accept intercession, that is, it rejects the knowledge of the reality) **benefit him, nor can they be aided!**

124. And recall when Abraham was tested by his Rabb (the Name composition comprising his being) **through certain beings** (remember his answers on the sun, the stars and the moon) **and he had duly**

presented his evaluations on these matters and had thus successfully fulfilled the trial. Then his Rabb said, "Indeed, I will make you a leader (one who is followed due to his knowledge) **for the people.**" (Abraham) said, "And of my descendants?" (Allah) said, "My covenant excludes the wrongdoers."

125. **And We made the House** (Kaaba – heart) **a secure refuge for the people. So take the station of Abraham** (the realization/actualization of the forces of the Names) **as a place of prayer** (a place where salat is experienced). **We told Abraham and Ishmael, "Maintain My House in a state of purity for those who perform tawaf and those who retreat there to experience their servitude and those who bow and prostrate** (in prayer)."

126. **And Abraham had said, "My Rabb, make this a secure place and provide its people, whoever of them believes in Allah** (as comprising their innermost essential reality) **and the life of the hereafter, with the fruits of their deeds"** (His Rabb) **said, "I will still grant provision to he who denies the reality for a little** (in this worldly life); **then I will subject him to the fire** (suffering)." **How wretched is this confrontation with the truth!**

127. **And when Abraham was raising the main walls of the House** (Kaaba – heart – the 7th state [heaven] of consciousness) **with Ishmael** (saying)**, "Our Rabb, accept** (this) **from us. Indeed You are** (as the essence of existence) **the Perceiving the Aleem."**

128. **Our Rabb, enable us to be in submission to You and from our descendants form a nation in submission to You. And show us our rites** (of the application of Hajj – pilgrimage) **and accept our repentance. Indeed, You are the Tawwab** (Accepting of Repentance), **the Rahim** (who enables the experience of its beauties).

129. **Our Rabb, disclose a Rasul** (establish a form that manifests a configuration of Names to reveal the reality) **within them, who will teach and make them recite Your verses** (the manifestations of your Names in the realms of existence) **and give them knowledge** (the Book) **and the system of manifestation** (wisdom) **and purify them. Indeed, You are the Aziz** (the Exalted in Might), **the Hakim** (the Wise).

130. **And who will turn away from the people of Abraham** (those who believe in the/their reality) **except the foolish who are ignorant of the qualities of the Names that compose their essence? Indeed, We have chosen Him in this world and purified him. In the eternal life**

to come he will be among those that live the results of having attained their reality.

131. When his Rabb said to him "Submit", he said "I have submitted to the Rabb of the worlds" (Abraham had been made aware of his submission to the Rabb of the worlds).

132. And Abraham (in line with this truth) bequeathed his sons, just like Jacob (who said), "O my sons, indeed Allah has chosen for you this religion (comprehension of the system), so do not die without the awareness of your submission to Allah" (Muslim means one who has reached the awareness of his absolute and definite submission to Allah).

133. Or were you witnesses when death approached Jacob? When he said to his sons, "To what will you be in servitude after me?" They said, "We are going to continue our servitude to your God and the God of your fathers, Abraham and Ishmael and Isaac – the One and Only (the totality of the Names comprising existence) for we are aware of our submission to Him."

134. That was a community that has passed on. To them is what they earned, and to you is what you earn. And you will not be called to account about their deeds.

135. They say, "Be Jews or Christians so that you will be rightly guided." Say, "Rather, we follow the Hanif people of Abraham (we share the same faith, without the concept of a deity-god, with the consciousness of non-duality), for he was not of the dualists."

136. Say, "We have believed in Allah (the innermost essential reality of all things) and what has been revealed to us and what has been revealed to Abraham and Ishmael and Isaac and Jacob and his descendants; and what was given to Moses and Jesus; and what was given to the Nabis from their Rabb. In this sense, we make no distinction between any of them. We are of those that are in submission to Him!"

137. So if they believe in Him in the same way as you believe in Him, then they will have found the path to the reality. But if they turn away, they will be left as fragmented and narrow minded. Allah will be sufficient for you against them. And HU is the Sami and the Aleem.

138. The hue of Allah! And what can be better than being colored with the hue of Allah? We are of those who are in servitude to Him!

139. Say, "Do you argue with us about Allah? He is our Rabb and your Rabb! Our deeds (and their consequences) are for us, and your deeds (and their consequences) are for you. We turn to Him in pureness of essence."

140. Or are you claiming that Abraham and Ishmael and Isaac and Jacob and his descendants were Jews or Christians? Say, "Are you more knowing or is Allah?" Who can be more unjust than one who conceals the testimony of Allah? Allah, as the innermost essential reality of your being, is not unaware of what you do.

141. That was a community that has passed on. (The consequence of) what they earned is theirs, and what you earn will be yours! You will not be called to account about what they used to do.

142. Among the people there are those with limited understanding and a wretched state of life, who say "What (excuse) has turned them away from their old qiblah (i.e. from Jerusalem to Kaaba)?" Say, "To Allah belongs the east and the west. He enables the realization that leads to one's innermost reality for whom he wills (sirat al-mustaqeem)."

143. And thus we have made you a witness over the people and the Rasul a witness (an observer of the disclosure of the Names) over you. You are a just community (based on fairness and rightness). We changed the qiblah (direction) that you used to face to distinguish those who follow the Rasul from those who turn away and go back. This is very difficult for those other than whom Allah has guided. And never will Allah let your faith be fruitless. Indeed Allah is the Ra'uf and the Rahim, manifesting from the essence of man.

144. We see the turning of your face (how you change from state to state in observation of the reality) towards heaven. (Based on 'So wherever you turn, there is the Face of Allah' why should one necessarily be bound to Jerusalem when one can turn to the Kaaba to which Abraham invited...) We will surely turn you to a qiblah with which you will be pleased. So turn your face (your observation of the Reality) toward al-Masjid al-Haram (Kaaba – absolute nothingness – the unknown – unmanifest). And wherever you are, turn your faces toward Him (align your consciousness with your essence). Indeed, those who have been given the Book (the knowledge of the reality and the sunnatullah) know well that it is the Truth from their Rabb. And Allah, as their innermost essential reality, is not unaware of what they do.

145. And if you were to bring all the verses to those who were given the Book (the knowledge that guides to the reality), **they will still not follow your qiblah! Nor will you be a follower of their qiblah.** (In fact) **they will not follow each other's qiblah either. So if you follow their desires** (ideas and wants formed by their conditionings) **after what has come to you of knowledge, indeed, you would surely be among the wrongdoers.**

146. Some of those to whom We have given (the Book) **Knowledge know Him, just as they know their own sons. But a group of them deliberately conceal the Truth.**

147. The Truth (the absolute and unequivocal reality) **is from your Rabb** (the output of the Name composition constituting one's brain) **so never be among the doubters** (of this truth).

148. For everyone has a face pertaining to Him. So race towards good work (strive to know your self, the qualities comprising your essential reality). **Wherever you may be, Allah, your essential reality, encompasses you. Indeed, Allah is Qadir over all things.**

149. So from wherever (whatever thought; outlook) **you set out from, turn your face** (observation) **toward al-Masjid al-Haram** (the state in which the annihilation of multiplicity is experienced; the essence of prostration), **and certainly, it is the truth from your Rabb. And Allah as your essence is not unaware of what you do.**

150. So from wherever (whatever thought; outlook) **you set out from, turn your face** (observation) **toward al-Masjid al-Haram** (the state in which the annihilation of multiplicity is experienced; the essence of prostration). **And wherever you may be, turn your face toward it so that the people will not have any argument against you. Though those among you who are incessant wrongdoers will be against you. So fear them not, but fear Me so that I may fulfill My favor upon you, that you may attain the realization of your innermost essential reality.**

151. We revealed a Rasul from within you (to disclose the reality), **reciting** (teaching) **to you Our verses** (signs pertaining to our reality within the core of all existence) **and purifying you and teaching you the Book** (of the reality and sunnatullah) **and wisdom** (the system and mechanics of creation) **and that which you do not know.**

152. So remember (dhikr) **Me** (contemplate)**; so that I will remember you. And be grateful to Me** (evaluate Me) **and do not deny Me** (do not deny that I comprise your essence and the essence of the entire existence).

153. O you, who have believed, seek help through patience (endurance) **that generates from your essence and through salat** (the observation resulting from you turning towards your innermost essential reality; the Names)**. Indeed, Allah is with the patient** (with His Name Sabur).

154. And do not say "They are dead" about those who are killed in the way of Allah (because they were believers and they strived for their faith)**. On the contrary, they are alive, though you lack the capacity to perceive it.**

155. And We will surely test you with objects of fear, hunger, diminution of wealth and lives (of those who are dear to you) **and the fruits of your labor. But give good tidings to the patient** (those who refrain from reacting and wait to see how things turn out)**.**

156. (They are those) **who, when a calamity strikes them, say, "We are for Allah** (we are a manifestation of Allah's Names)**, and to Him we will return** (we will eventually experience this reality)**."**

157. They are the ones upon whom are blessings (salawat) **from their Rabb** (the facilitation towards the realization of their innermost essential reality) **and grace** (the observation of the beautiful manifestations of the Names)**. And it is they who have found the truth.**

158. Indeed, as-Safa and al-Marwah are among the signs of Allah. So whoever visits the House (Kaaba) **with the intention of performing Hajj or Umrah – there is nothing wrong with performing tawaf between them** (as-Safa and al-Marwah)**. And whoever volunteers to do more in the name of good – indeed, Allah is the Shakur** (abundantly appreciative) **and the Aleem.**

159. After what we have clearly informed with the Book, whoever conceals the signs and the means to reach the reality, they will be cursed by Allah (fall far from the Reality of Allah) **and cursed by all those who are capable of cursing** (i.e. they will experience the consequences of falling separate from Allah, both internally and externally)**.**

160. Except those among them who repent (admit and comprehend their mistake and rigorously abstain from it) **and those who correct themselves** (abandon their wrongful environment) **and those who**

speak the truth. I am the Tawwab and the Rahim (I accept repentance and enable the experience of favorable outcomes as a result of it).

161. As for those who cover the truth (deny that the corporeal worlds and their very selves are the manifestations of the Names of Allah) and who die upon this understanding... Certainly upon them is the curse of Allah (the consequences of falling far from the Reality of Allah), the curse of the angels (the consequences of falling far from the forces of the Names comprising their essence) and the curse of the whole of humanity (the consequences of being veiled from the reality manifesting through others).

162. They will forever live the consequences of these curses. Their suffering will never be lessened, nor will they be given respite (to amend their wrongdoing).

163. That which you have come to accept as your God is One (the One and only! The incalculable 'ONE'ness far beyond any concept of multiplicity). There is no deity-god, only HU, the Rahman, the Rahim (HU has created everything from His grace and the qualities of His Names).

164. Undoubtedly, in the creation of the heavens and the earth (the states of consciousness and the body), the succession of night and day (the contrast of observing the inexistence of the worlds and how it takes on forms to appear existent), the ships that sail in the sea for the benefit of mankind (the individualized consciousness swimming in the divine ocean of knowledge); how Allah sent down water from the heavens to bring the earth back to life after its death (revealing knowledge from the states of consciousness to manifest 'life' from the body, which is unconscious of its reality) and how He disperses therein all animate beings (how all strength and power within all the organs in the body are formed with Allah); and in the directing of the winds (the recognition of the Names in one's consciousness) and the clouds that are at disposal between the heaven and the earth (the initiation of bodily forces within one's consciousness), there signs for those who think (for those who use their intellect)!

165. There are some who deify and worship things other than Allah, loving them with the love of Allah (as though they are loving Allah)! The believers, on the other hand, are conscious that their beloved is only Allah (they don't attribute existence to anything else). When those who (by denying the reality) do wrong (to themselves) see the suffering they accrue as a result of this, they will realize that the only force

active in the universe is the force of Allah, but alas, it will be too late... if only they could have realized this sooner... Allah is shadid al-adhab (the One who severely enforces the consequences to those who are persistent in their wrongdoing).

166. **When those who are followed see the suffering awaiting their followers, they will walk away and disown them. When the truth becomes apparent, the tie between them will be severed!**

167. **The followers** (of things other than Allah) **will say, "If only we were given a second chance to relive our lives so that we can disown those we followed just as they have disowned us." Thus will Allah show the consequence of their doings with painful remorse. The internal burning that arises from their remorse will not cease!**

168. **O mankind, eat from what is allowed and clean of the earth** (partake of things pertaining to the bodily dimension that will not veil you from your reality). **Do not follow the steps of Satan** (do not act on the impulses from the second brain in your gut). **Certainly, he is an evident enemy.**

169. **He** (Satan) **will only command you to think and do things that will strengthen your ego, to only live for the sake of unlawful bodily pleasures, and to make baseless judgments about Allah without any knowledge.**

170. **When they are told, "Believe in what Allah has revealed** (the knowledge that the Names of Allah comprise your being and the entire existence and the knowledge of sunnatullah)**, they say, "No, rather, we follow that which our fathers followed** (external deification)"**... What if their fathers were misguided and failed to comprehend the reality?**

171. **The state of those who deny the truth is like that of those who hear a calling, yet they do not understand what it means. For they are deaf** (in respect of their understanding)**, dumb** (unable to voice the Truth) **and blind** (unable to evaluate the obvious reality)**. They do not think!**

172. **O believers! Eat that which is pure and clean from what We have provided for you. And be grateful to Allah** (evaluate this) **if it is only Him you wish to serve.**

173. **He has only forbidden to you dead animals, blood, the flesh of swine, and that which has been slaughtered in the name of things other than Allah. But if you are forced out of need, there is no sin upon you to eat of these without doing harm to your self, without**

making lawful (what is unlawful) and transgressing the boundaries (consuming more than necessary). Certainly, Allah is the Ghafur and the Rahim.

174. Those who conceal what has been revealed by the Book (the knowledge of the reality and sunnatullah) and sell it (their reality) for a small price (worldly values), fill their internal (world) with none other than fire (suffering). During doomsday Allah will not speak to them nor purify them. And they will have a tragic suffering.

175. They are those who have bought misguidance (invested their beliefs in external deification) in exchange of "BILHUDA" (faith in their essential reality; the Names of Allah) and suffering, in exchange of forgiveness (resulting from faith in one's essence; the Names). How resilient to fire they must be!

176. Thus Allah has revealed the knowledge of reality and the sunnatullah in His knowledge, which He manifested as multiple universes (Book), as the Truth. Verily, those who argue against the Book (in regards to this knowledge and formation) have fallen far from the truth.

177. Turning (your faces or your consciousness) to the east or the west (the reality of existence OR the knowledge of the mechanics of the system) does not mean you are experiencing its reality (albirra). To experience the reality (albirra) is to believe in Allah in accord with the meaning of the letter B, and to believe in the life to come, the angels (the unperceivable forces of the Names of Allah constituting existence), the Book (the essence of existence and the sunnatullah), the Nabis, and who give from their possessions with the love of Allah to their relatives, orphans, those in need, travelers who are stranded (from their homes), and to free slaves, and who perform salat (duly turn introspectively to Allah) and who unrequitedly share a portion of what Allah has bestowed to them (zakah), and who stay true to their word, and who are resistant in the face of calamity, ailment and violence. Those are the devout and the protected ones.

178. O believers, retribution (equality based process) in cases of murder has been determined for you: the free for the one with freedom, the slave for the enslaved, and the female for the feminine one. If the murderer is (partly) remitted by the victim's brother (or successor) then this should be adhered to and (compensation) be paid. This is an alleviation and grace from your Rabb. Whoever transgresses his limits after this, he will have severe suffering.

179. There is for you, life in retribution. The intelligent ones who contemplate... So that you may be protected.

180. When death approaches one of you, if a good (wealth) is going to be left, a bequest should be made to the parents or relatives. This is a duty upon those who wish to be protected!

181. And whoever alters (does not comply with the bequest) **after hearing it, the fault is only upon the one who alters it. Certainly Allah is the Sami, the Aleem.**

182. But if one fears a mistake or a deliberate aberration from the bequeather and mediates (among the inheritors), there is no fault upon him. Most certainly, Allah is the Ghafur, the Rahim.

183. O believers, Siyam (fasting – the act of reducing corporeality to its lowest level and turning to one's essence) has been decreed upon you. That you may be protected!

184. This is for a certain number of days. But whoever among you is ill or traveling, then they can make up for the days they couldn't experience (fasting). Those whose health condition is not strong enough for fasting should feed someone in need (for each day they miss) as compensation. One who gives more than this will have greater benefit. Siyam (fasting – the act of reducing corporeality to its lowest level and turning to one's essence) is more beneficial for you (than paying compensation), if only you knew.**

185. The Quran, which enables the realization of the truth and delineates the difference between the right and the wrong, has been revealed in the month of Ramadan. Whoever among you is present in this month should fast (experience the essence of fasting at every level). And whoever is ill or traveling can make up for the days that are missed. (HU) wants to facilitate experiencing your essential reality through fasting, not cause you hardship. By completing the required amount of days (HU) wants you to feel and appreciate His Akbariyyah, to the degree of your experience of the reality.

186. So, if my servants ask you of ME, undoubtedly I am Qarib (as close as the limits of one's understanding; remember the verse 'I am closer to you than your jugular vein'!) **I respond to those who turn to me** (in prayer). **So let them respond to me and believe in me so that they experience their maturation.**

187. It has been made permissible for you to approach (unite with) your wives on the nights preceding fasting. You are their garments

and they are your garments (the most intimate person in one's worldly life.) **Allah knows that you have been unjust to yourselves** (by abstaining from sexual relations throughout the nights) **and accepted your repentance and forgave you. So approach them in accord with Allah's creed. Eat and drink until the day begins** (the break of twilight) **then experience Siyam** (fasting) **until the night. Do not approach your wives while you are in retreat in the masjids. These are the limitations Allah puts, so do not go near them. Thus, Allah explains His signs so that you may be protected.**

188. **Do not consume the goods between you in a manner that goes against the truth. And do not deliberately run to the rulers to unjustly consume the goods of others, even though you know otherwise.**

189. **They ask you about the phases of the moon** (the lunar calendar). **Say, "These** (determining the times of worship via the lunar calendar) **are the measurements for the benefit of people and for Hajj. Experiencing the essence of the reality** (albirra) **is not to enter houses from the back door** (the indirect route to the truth, but to enter from the front door, the direct and short way) **in order to be of the protected ones. Protect yourselves from Allah so that you may be enlightened.**

190. **And with those who fight to kill you, fight in the way of Allah** (defend your right to live). **Do not transgress. Indeed, Allah does not like the transgressors.**

191. **Kill them wherever you catch them** (in the cause of defending your right to live). **Expel them from where they have expelled you! Fitnah** (provocation) **is more severe** (a crime) **than killing** (a man). **Do not fight near the Masjid al-Haram unless they fight you there. But if they try to kill you, then kill them. Such is the recompense of those who deny the truth.**

192. **If they cease** (what they do) **then indeed Allah is the Ghafur and the Rahim.**

193. **Fight them until the fitnah** (the pressure to make you give up your faith) **is lifted and you are able to practice the religion of Allah as you like. If they cease** (pressuring and fighting)**, there is no hostility except against the wrongdoers.**

194. **The sacred month of one is as the sacred month of another, in respecting this, fairness must be observed. So, whoever transgresses**

their boundaries (during this period) **and attacks you, attack them back in the same proportion! Protect yourselves from Allah and know well that Allah is with those who are protected.**

195. Give unrequitedly (feesabilillah) **in the way of Allah** (to reach Allah) **and do not destroy yourselves** (by being stingy.) **And do good! Certainly, Allah loves the doers of good.**

196. Complete the Hajj and Umrah for Allah. If you are prevented (from this) **then make an offering** (qurban) **and do not shave your heads until your offering is slaughtered. And whoever among you is ill or has an affliction** (preventing him from Hajj)**, should compensate by fasting, charity or sacrifice. When you are in times of safety** (when the afflictions are lifted)**, whoever wants to experience and benefit from Umrah until Hajj, should offer a sacrifice that can afford with ease. And whoever cannot find** (such a sacrifice) **should fast three days during Hajj and seven days after return; ten days in total. This is for those whose family** (place of living) **is not in the area of al-Masjid al-Haram. And protect yourselves from disobeying Allah. And know well that Allah is severe in due retribution.**

197. Hajj is during well-known months. Whoever intends to undertake Hajj during those months should abstain from ill speech, inappropriate conduct and behavior, and from quarreling. Whatever good you do, Allah knows it. Take provisions, but indeed the best provision is taqwa (protecting yourself in the way of Allah from the inadequacies of your identity). **O you of understanding and deep contemplation, protect yourselves from Me** (from My retribution in case you do wrong)**!**

198. There is no blame upon you for seeking the bounty of your Rabb (during the period of Hajj). **Remember** (dhikr) **Allah when you are collectively returning from Arafat, and remember** (dhikr) **Allah at al-Mash'ar al-Haram** (Muzdalifah)**. Remember** (dhikr) **Him to the degree of your realization of your essential reality, for indeed, before this, you were among the astray.**

199. Then depart from the place where all the people depart and ask forgiveness of Allah (for your inadequacies)**. Certainly, Allah is the Ghafur and the Rahim.**

200. And when you complete the rites of your Hajj remember (dhikr) **Allah with a greater intensity than you did your fathers** (out of custom). **Among the people are some who say, "Our Rabb, give us in this world"... They have no share in the eternal life to come.**

201. **And some say, "Our Rabb, give us bounties** (the experience of the beauties of the Names) **in the world, and bounties** (the beauties of the Names in our essence) **in the eternal life to come; protect us from the fire** (of falling into separation).**"**

202. **They are the ones who will attain the results of what they have earned. Allah instantly puts into effect the consequences of one's actions.**

203. **And remember Allah** (say takbir) **in the appointed days** (the second, third and fourth days of the Qurban Eid). **There is no blame upon whoever completes tasks in two days and hastens to leave, and there is no blame upon whoever delays it. This is for the protected ones... Protect yourselves from Allah** (for you will certainly live the consequences of your actions) **and know well that in the end you will most certainly be gathered unto Him** (you will reside in a realm in which the Absolute Reality will become apparent; you will be evaluated by the qualities of the Names that comprise your essence).

204. **And among the people, there are some whose speech about the worldly life pleases you, and he holds Allah as witness to what is in his heart... yet he is the fiercest of your opponents.**

205. **When he goes away, he runs to cause corruption on the earth, to destroy the produce and the lineage of the people. Allah does not like corruption.**

206. **When it is said to him, "Protect yourself from Allah** (for you will be faced with the consequences of your deeds),**" his ego takes hold of him and drags him to wrongdoing. Hell will sort him out, what a wretched place of rest it is!**

207. **And of the people there are some who sacrifice themselves** (their constructed illusory identities; egos) **so that Allah will be pleased with them. And Allah manifests as the Ra'uf from the essence of his servants.**

208. **O you who have believed, enter the state of submission collectively, and do not follow the steps of Satan** (the idea that you are only the body) **for he is clearly your enemy.**

209. **If after you have been given this much clear proof you still deviate, know well that Allah is the Aziz** (He will subject you to the consequences of your deeds with His unchallengeable might) **and the Hakim.**

210. **Are they waiting for Allah to come to them with angels in canopies of clouds and settle their matters? And to Allah all formations are returned.**

211. **Ask the Children of Israel how many clear signs We have given them. Whoever changes the favor of Allah after it has come to him** (should know well that) **Allah is just and severe in recompense** (putting into effect the consequences of one's actions).

212. **Worldly life has been adorned and beautified for the disbelievers** (those who deny their inner reality turn to the fancy outer world)**! They ridicule the believers** (because of this). **Yet the protected believers will be above them on the Day of Resurrection. Allah gives provision** (both limited sustenance for the corporeal life and infinite life sustenance pertaining to the realization of one's inner reality and its benefits) **to whom He wills without account.**

213. **Mankind was once a single community. Then Allah revealed Nabis** (manifestations of the perfection of Nubuwwah from within them) **as bearers of good news and as warners. He revealed to them the Book** (the knowledge of the reality and sunnatullah) **in Truth, to judge between their disputes. Those to whom the Book was given disagreed with it out of jealousy, even after clear truths had come to them. Allah, by His will** (B-iznihi; the suitability of the Names comprising their being) **guided the believers to the truth about which the others disputed. Allah guides to a straight path** (enables the realization of one's innermost essential reality) **whom He wills.**

214. **Or did you think you will enter Paradise without being tried with the distressing trials of those before you? They were tried and shaken with such hardship and calamity that the Rasul and the believers with him exclaimed, "When will Allah's help come?" Undoubtedly, the help of Allah is near.**

215. **They ask you what and to whom they should unrequitedly give in the way of Allah. Say, "Whatever good you give should be for parents, relatives, orphans, the needy and travelers who are far from their homes. Whatever good you do, Allah** (as the creator of your actions with His Names) **is well aware.**

216. **Fighting has been ordained for you, even though you despise it. Perhaps you dislike a thing that is good for you and like a thing that is bad for you. Allah knows, but you know not.**

217. They ask you about fighting in the sacred month (the month in which fighting is prohibited). Say, "Fighting in that month is a grave matter! But preventing (people) from the path of Allah, denying one's essence and being ungrateful to the al-Masjid al-Haram by preventing people from entering therein and expelling them, is far graver in the sight of Allah! Fitnah (provocation) is worse than killing." If they could, they would fight you until you renounce your faith. And whoever among you turns away from his religious understanding and dies as a denier of the truth, all his good deeds will become worthless, both in this world and the eternal life to come. Those are the inhabitants of fire (suffering) and will forever abide therein.

218. Certainly, those who believe and migrate and strive in the way of Allah, look forward to Allah's grace. And Allah is the Ghafur and the Rahim.

219. They ask you about intoxicants and gambling. Say, "In both of them there is great harm and some benefit for people, but their harm is greater than their benefit." They ask you about how much they should spend in Allah's way, say, "Spend whatever is surplus to your needs!" Thus Allah gives you clear signs so that you may reflect upon them (their reasons).

220. (Contemplate) upon this world and the eternal life to come! They ask you about orphans. Say, "Improving their welfare is best. If you are living together with them, they are your brothers." Allah knows the corrupter from the reformer. Had Allah willed, He could have put you in difficulty. Indeed, Allah is the Aziz and the Hakim.

221. Do not marry (dualist) women who associate partners with Allah until they believe. A believing slave woman is definitely better than a (dualist) woman who associates partners with Allah, however pleasing she may seem to you (for beauty is not in the body but in the sharing of faith). Nor give believing women in marriage to (dualist) men who associate partners with Allah until they believe. A believing slave man is certainly better than a (dualist) man who associates partners with Allah, however pleasing he may seem to you. Such people (dualists) call you to the fire but Allah invites you (as much as the qualities of the Names comprising your essence allow) to Paradise and forgiveness. Allah makes clear His signs (of the reality) to people so they (these truths) are remembered.

222. They ask you about menstruation... Say, "It is a difficult time. Do not have sexual relations with women until they are clean (of bleeding). **And when they are cleansed you can approach them from where Allah has ordained". Allah loves those who turn from their wrongdoing and who repent much and cleanse themselves.**

223. **Your women are your fields** (to bear children). **So plant your fields as you like. Prepare your selves for the future and protect yourselves from Allah and know that you will meet Him** (become aware of, and experience, the reality of the Names comprising your essence). **Give good tidings to the believers!**

224. **Do not let the oaths you make in the name of Allah prevent you from doing good, seeking protection and making peace between people. Allah is the Sami, the Aleem.**

225. **Allah will not hold you responsible for any oaths you make unknowingly, but He will hold you responsible for what is intended in your hearts** (consciousness). **Allah is the Ghafur, the Halim.**

226. **For those who swear not to approach their wives, there is a waiting period of four months. If they revert from their word, indeed Allah is the Ghafur, the Rahim.**

227. **If they decide to divorce, undoubtedly Allah is the Sami, the Aleem** (He knows their intentions).

228. **Divorced women should wait for three menstrual cycles without getting married, to discern whether they are pregnant or not. If they believe that Allah comprises their innermost essential reality and have faith in the life to come, they have no right to hide what Allah creates in their wombs. If their husbands want to reconcile in this period, they are of higher priority than others. Just as wives have rights over their husbands, husbands also have rights over their wives, but the rights of men are one degree more** (as the flow is from man to woman). **Allah is the Aziz, the Hakim.**

229. **Divorce is twice. After this it can either be resumed or permanently released free. It is not lawful for you to take back anything you have given your wives** (due to divorce). **But if the wife and husband both find it difficult to observe the boundaries set by Allah, the wife has the right to request divorce by returning the things he has given her, and there is no blame upon her for doing this. These are the boundaries set by Allah so do not transgress them. Whoever transgresses the limits will only do wrong to themself.**

230. And after all this, if he divorces his wife again (for the third time) then she is not lawful to him until after she has married another man. And if she gets divorced from the latter husband there is no blame upon her and her former husband to remarry each other, if they believe they can keep to the boundaries of marriage within the limits of Allah. These are limits of Allah, which He makes clear to people who know (Allah).

231. And once you divorce your wives and they reach the end of the three-months waiting period, either retain them with kindness or release them by good means. Do not keep them attached to yourselves to cause them misery, and whoever does so will only do wrong to himself. Do not take the creeds of Allah lightly. And remember the favor of Allah upon you and the Book and Wisdom He revealed to you to advise you based on the letter B. Protect yourself from Allah and know well that Allah, as the essence of everything (in respect of the dimension of the Names) is aware of everything.

232. When you divorce your wives and they reach the end of the waiting period, do not prevent them from getting remarried, if they agree among themselves on mutual terms. This is an advice upon those who believe in Allah and the life to come. This is better (clean from humanly conditionings) and purer for you. Allah knows and you know not.

233. (Divorced) mothers can breastfeed their children for two whole years, (if the fathers) wish to complete the nursing period. During this time the father is responsible for their provision and clothing, according to custom. No one will be subject to more than his capacity. And no mother or father should be subject to harm because of their child. The same applies for the heir. If they mutually agree to wean the child before the end of the two years, there is no blame upon them. If you wish to have your children nursed (by a wet nurse), there is no blame upon you so long as you pay the required according to what is customary. Protect yourselves from Allah and know well that He (as the creator of all that you do) is the Basir.

234. If any of you die and leave widows, the widows should wait for four months and ten days (before they remarry). After this period, there is no blame upon them for what they do according to custom (getting married to someone else). Allah, as the former of your actions, is the Habir.

235. There is no blame upon you if you hint a proposal of marriage to (divorced or widowed) **women** (during their waiting period), **or** conceal it in your heart. Allah knows that you will be inclined towards them. **But do not bond in marriage with them until the end of the waiting period. Know that Allah knows what is in your consciousness, so heed Him. Know that Allah is the Ghafur, the Halim.**

236. There is no blame upon you if you divorce women when you have not yet slept with them or specified a dowry for them. But provide them (your ex-wives) with benefits according to your ability – those with greater financial means should provide according to their capacity; those with lesser financial means should provide according to custom to the best of his ability. This is an obligation upon the doers of good.

237. If you divorce them after specifying a dowry but before you sleep with them, give them half the specified dowry. Unless they or those in whose hand lies the marriage contract forgoes it. To give them the full amount (of the dowry) is closer to taqwa (Protecting yourself in the way of Allah from the inadequacies of your identity). Do not forget to treat each other with grace. Certainly Allah is the Basir (evaluates all that you do).

238. Maintain salat (prayer; turning to Allah) **with care,** (in particular) **the middle salat** (asr prayer – the constant experience of this in one's consciousness). **Live in full submission in the way of Allah.**

239. If you fear danger then you can (perform salat) **while on foot or riding... When you are in safety remember** (dhikr) **Allah according to the teachings of the one who has taught you that which you did not know** (contemplate upon the manifestations of the qualities of His Names on worldly forms).

240. Those who die and leave widows should make a bequest for them of one year's maintenance without them having to leave their homes. But if they choose to leave their homes, then you will not be held responsible for them as they have used their rights. Allah is the Aziz, the Hakim.

241. Divorced women have the right to receive provision according to custom; this is an obligation upon those with taqwa.

242. Thus Allah explains the laws of existence for you, so that you may use your reason.

243. Did you not see the thousands who abandoned their homes out of fear of death? Allah said to them 'Die' and then brought them back to life. Undoubtedly, Allah is bountiful to mankind, but most of them do not appreciate (the bounty that is provided).

244. Fight in the way of Allah and know well that Allah is the Sami and the Aleem.

245. Who will want to lend Allah a good loan and receive it back in manifold! It is Allah who constricts (contraction and restriction within the ego; the Qabid) and grants relief (opens, expands, spreads with the Names; the Basit)... To Him you will be returned!

246. Did you not see the group from the Children of Israel after the time of Moses, they had said to their Nabi, "Disclose for us a king (leader) and we will fight in the way of Allah." The Nabi asked, "What if war is prescribed for you and you refrain from fighting?"... They said, "Why shouldn't we fight in the way of Allah? Especially when we have been driven out of our homes and from our children!" But when war was prescribed upon them, except for a few of them, they turned away from fighting. Allah (as the One who created them with His Names) is Aleem (All Knowing) of the wrongdoers.

247. Their Nabi said to them, "Indeed Allah has disclosed Talut as a king for you." They said, "How can he have sovereignty over us when we are worthier of sovereignty than he and he has no abundance of wealth?" Their Nabi said, "Certainly Allah has chosen him over you and increased him in (depth of) knowledge and body." Allah gives (the administration of) His sovereignty to whom He wills. Allah is the Wasi, the Aleem.

248. Their Nabi told them, "Certainly, a sign of his sovereignty is that a coffin (heart; universal consciousness) will come to you in which there will be happiness (inner peace and tranquility) from your Rabb, and relics (knowledge) left behind by the family of Moses and Aaron. The angel (the forces of the Names in your essence) will bring it to you. Certainly there is a clear sign in this, if you are of the believers.

249. When Talut set out with his army, he said (to his soldiers), "Indeed Allah will test you with a river. Whoever drinks from it is not of me, whoever does not drink from it, is of me, except those who take but a handful from it"... Except a few of them, they all drank from it. When he and those with him crossed over to the other side of the river, they said, "We have no strength left to fight

Goliath and his soldiers." Those who knew (with certainty) **from their essence** (due to their faith) **that they will meet Allah said, "Many times a small group has overcome a large group with the permission of Allah (B-iznillah). Allah is with those who persevere."**

250. **When they faced Goliath and his army, they prayed, "Our Rabb, give us the force of perseverance, make firm our feet, do not let us slip and give us the power of victory over the deniers."**

251. **Then** (with the permission of Allah) **the Names comprising their essence, they defeated them. David killed Goliath and Allah gave him** (David) **sovereignty and wisdom and taught him what He willed** (programmed him with the Names from his essence). **If Allah had not repelled some by** (means of) **others, the earth would have become corrupt** (unlivable). **But the bounty of Allah is upon the worlds.**

252. **These are the signs of Allah... Which we tell you in Truth... You are indeed one of the revealed Rasuls.**

253. **Of those Rasuls, We endowed some more highly than others. There are some to whom Allah spoke and some He raised in degree. And We gave clear proofs to Jesus the son of Mary and supported him with the Pure Spirit** (divine forces). **If Allah had willed those succeeding them would not have killed each other after clear proofs reached them. But they differed in opinion, some believed and some denied. If Allah had willed they would not have killed each other... But Allah does as He wills.**

254. **O believers, spend** (give unrequitedly out of your faith) **from what We have provided to you, before there comes a day in which there is no exchange, no friendship and no intercession... The deniers of the reality – they are the wrongdoers** (they wrong themselves).

255. **Allah is HU! There is no God** (deity)**, only HU! The Hayy and the Qayyum** (the sole source of life and the One who forms all things in His Knowledge with the meanings of His Names – the One with whom everything subsists). **Neither drowsiness overtakes Him** (separation from the worlds even for a single instance) **nor sleep** (leaving creation to its own accord and withdrawing to His Self). **To Him belongs everything in the heavens and on earth** (the dimensions of knowledge and acts). **Who can intercede in His sight except by the permission of the forces that manifest from the Names in one's essence? He knows the dimension in which they live and the dimension they are unable to perceive... Nothing of His knowledge can be grasped if**

He does not will (allow via the suitability of the Names in one's essence). His throne (sovereignty and administration [Rububiyyah]) encompasses the heavens and the earth. It is not difficult for Him to preserve them. He is the Aliy (illimitably supreme) and the Azim (possessor of infinite might).

256. There is no compulsion in (acceptance of) the religion (the system and order of Allah; sunnatullah)! The reality has become apparent (in its most perfect state) and has become distinct from corrupted ideas. Whoever abandons Taghut (worshipping the forces that don't exist, but are assumed to exist through illusion) and believes in Allah (the Names that form his essence) indeed he has grasped a strong grip within his essence, that can never be broken. Allah is the Sami and the Aleem.

257. Allah is a friend (Waliyy) to the believers; He brings them out of darkness (ignorance of the reality) into Nur (seeing the reality with the light of knowledge). As for those who actively deny (the truth) their friend is Taghut (illusory ideas and forces) it brings them out of Nur into darkness. They are the people of fire (bound to suffer). They will reside therein (the condition of suffering) forever.

258. Did you not see he who argued with Abraham about his Rabb because Allah gave him sovereignty? When Abraham said, "My Rabb is the giver of life and the taker of life" he said, "I can give and take life too." When Abraham said, "Allah raises the sun from the east, go ahead and raise it from the west if you can," the denier (concealer of the reality) was confounded! Allah will not guide (enable the realization of the reality to) the people of wrongdoing.

259. (Did you not hear about the) one who passed by a town in which the buildings were in ruins and the people were dead, he thought, "How will Allah restore life here after this death?" Allah caused him to die at that instance and after a hundred years brought him back to life. "How long did you remain in that state?" He asked... The man answered, "One day or a part of it." Allah said, "No, a hundred years have passed... Look at your food and your drink, they have not rotted, but look at your donkey (how it has rotted and only a pile of bones remain)! We made you a sign, an example for the people... Look at how We raise the bones and cover them with flesh." When it became clear to him, he said, "I know with certainty that Allah is Qadir over all things!"

260. And recall when Abraham said, "My Rabb, show me how you give life to the dead". His Rabb said, "Have you not believed?"

(Abraham) said, "Yes, but for my heart to be satisfied (I want to witness it)..." "Take four types of birds and train them so they grow accustomed to you, then place each of them upon four different hilltops and call them to yourself. They will come running (flying) to you. Know that Allah is the Aziz, the Hakim."

261. The example of those who spend their wealth unrequitedly out of their faith in Allah is like a single wheat seed that grows seven spikes, in each spike a hundred grains. And Allah multiplies it even more for whom He wills. Allah is the Wasi and the Aleem.

262. Those who, out of their faith in Allah, unrequitedly spend their wealth on people, and who don't remind and taunt people with it later, will have special rewards in the sight of their Rabb (the compositions of Names constituting the essence of their being). They will have nothing to fear or grieve.

263. A kind word and to cover a fault is better than a charity followed by offence. Allah is the Ghani and the Halim.

264. O believers, do not cancel your charities by taunting and hurting people with it, as do those who spend their wealth only to be seen (to make a name) and do not believe in Allah and the eternal life to come with the meaning of the letter B. Their example is like a rock covered with some earth, and when it rains the earth is gone and the rock is left bare. They will gain nothing from what they earn. Allah does not guide (enable the realization of their essential reality) those who deny the truth.

265. But for those who spend their wealth for Allah's pleasure (the term 'Allah's pleasure' or 'for the pleasure of Allah' means to not let one's conditionings limit the manifestations of Allah's Names) or due to what they encounter within their own selves (the understanding that they are comprise the compositions of Names)... Their example is like a garden on a hilltop, when heavy rain falls on it, it gives double the produce. And if heavy rain does not fall, even a drizzle suffices. Allah is Basir over your actions.

266. Would any of you want to have a garden of date palms and grapevines underneath which rivers flow and in which various fruits grow, but when old age comes he has weak offspring? Then a whirlwind of fire destroys the garden... Allah gives these signs so that you reflect.

267. **O believers, give unrequitedly from what you have earned and from the clean things of what We have produced for you from the earth. Do not give in charity bad things that you will not take yourself. Know well that Allah is the Ghani, the Hamid.**

268. **Satan** (illusion – the fear of loss) **will scare you with poverty** (refraining you from giving unrequitedly) **and command you to do foul deeds and to be stingy! But Allah promises forgiveness from Him and bounty. Allah is the Wasi, the Aleem.**

269. **He gives wisdom** (the system by which the qualities of the Names are manifested) **to whom He wills, and whoever has been given wisdom has certainly been given much benefit. And none will discern this except those with intellect and deep contemplative skills.**

270. **Whatever you spend and whatever vows you make, Allah knows** (makes you live their outcome), **but the wrongdoers have no helper.**

271. **It is good if you give charity openly, but if you keep your charity a secret and give in private it is better for you. This will atone for your bad deeds. Allah is Habir** (All-Aware) **of what you do** (as He comprises your being).

272. **It is not your responsibility to make them find the right path** (realize the reality of their essence)**! Allah guides** (enables this realization) **to whom He wills** (as this entails the expression of the Name Hadi within one's essence, not some form of external guidance)**! Whatever you spend in charity it is for your own good, if you give for the sake of Allah** (knowing and seeing the face of Allah) **whatever good you give, it will be fully repaid to you and you will never be wronged.**

273. (Your unrequited giving) **is for the needy who have fully submitted themselves to the way of Allah without sparing any time to work for worldly sustenance. And because they refrain from asking, one who has no insight into their situation would think they are wealthy, but you will recognize them from their faces. They will never shamelessly ask for something from another. Thus, whatever good you give, surely Allah is Aleem of it.**

274. **Those who give from their wealth by night and by day, in secret and in the open, their reward is with their Rabb** (emerging from their essence and ready to manifest in their consciousness). **They have nothing to fear or grieve.**

275. **Those who commit usury will stand like those who have been possessed** (obsessed with delusive ideas) **by Satan** (jinni). **This is because they equate usury to trade. Whereas Allah has permitted trade and forbidden usury** (in trade one pays the value of the good, but with usury one pays exceedingly more than the money originally owed. Hence, usury is contrary to the idea of unrequited helping and giving). **So, whoever abandons usury after receiving admonition from his Rabb, his past belongs to him, his judgment will be with Allah. And whoever reverts to usury, they are the inmates of fire. They will abide therein eternally.**

276. **Allah destroys** (income from) **usury and increases** (the return of) **charity! Allah does not favor those who persist in their mistakes.**

277. **Those who believe and perform the necessary beneficial deeds, establish salat and give zakah will have special rewards with their Rabb. They will have nothing to fear or grieve.**

278. **O believers, abandon the excess from usury to be protected from Allah, if you are of the believers.**

279. **And if you don't do this, know that you will have waged war against Allah and His Rasul. If you recognize your mistake and abandon it for good you can earn your right to receive your principal.** (This way) **you won't wrong and you won't be wronged.**

280. **If** (the indebted) **is in financial hardship, then grant them respite until a time of ease. If you write it off as an act of charity, it will be better for you, if only you knew.**

281. **Protect yourselves from the day when you shall be returned to Allah. That is when every soul shall be paid in full what it has earned, and they will not be wronged.**

282. **O believers, when you contract a debt for a specified time, write it down. Let a just person among you write it. And let the one who knows how to write not refuse to write as Allah has taught him. Let the one who has the liability** (the indebted one) **dictate. Let him fear his Rabb, Allah, and not leave anything out. If the indebted one is of limited understanding or a child, let his guardian dictate. Let two men be witnesses. If there aren't two men, then let the witnesses be one man and two women, so if one of them forgets or errs, the other can remind. And let not the witnesses refuse when they are called upon. And do not be weary to write the debt, whether it is small or large, including its specified term. That is**

more appropriate and stronger in the sight of Allah and a more sound approach to prevent doubt in the future. Except when the transaction between you involves cash, then there is no blame upon you if you do not write it. And take witnesses even when you make a transaction. Let no scribe be harmed or any witness. For if you harm them, you would have harmed yourself. And be protected from Allah. Allah teaches you. Allah is Aleem over all things.

283. If you are traveling and cannot find a scribe, pledges may be taken in word. If you trust each other, let the trustee restore the pledge faithfully and let him fear his Rabb. Do not conceal what you have witnessed. Whoever conceals his testimony, indeed his heart is guilty (unable to reflect its essence; veiled from its reality). Allah knows what you do in the scope of the letter B.

284. Whatever is in the heavens and the earth belongs to Allah (to manifest His Names)... Whether you show what is within your consciousness (your thoughts) or conceal it, Allah will bring you to account for it with the quality of the Name Hasib. He will forgive (cover) whom he wills and cause suffering upon whom He wills. Allah is Qadir over all things.

285. "The Rasul (Muhammad saw) has believed in what was revealed (knowledge that emerged from the dimensional depths) to him (to his consciousness) from his Rabb (the qualities of the Names of Allah comprising his essential reality). And so have the believers! They have all believed (in line with the meaning denoted by the letter B) that the Names of Allah comprise their essence, and in the angels (the forces of the Names constituting their being), the Books (all revealed knowledge) and the Rasuls... They say, "We make no distinction between (the ways in which the knowledge of Allah was revealed to) His Rasuls... We have perceived and obeyed, we ask for your forgiveness our Rabb; our return is to You."

286. Allah will never hold anyone responsible for that which they have no capacity. What he earns (as a result of his good deeds) is for his self, and the consequences of (his bad deeds) is also for his self. Our Rabb, do not punish us if we forget or make a mistake. Our Rabb, do not place upon us heavy duties like the ones you placed on those before us. Our Rabb, do not place on us a burden we cannot bear. Pardon us, forgive us, have grace on us. You are our protector. Give us victory over those who cover the reality (disbelievers) and deny You.

3

ALI-IMRAN

By the one who is denoted by the name Allah (who created my being with His Names in accord with the meaning of the letter 'B'), **the Rahman, the Rahim.**

1. Alif Lam Meem

2. He is Allah; there is no god or godhood, only 'HU' (the Name HU denotes the Absolute Essence, which can never be conditioned or limited by the corporeal worlds and/or any concepts. It is usually followed by another Name to signify the quality that becomes manifest through HU, in regards to the relevant topic), **Hayy** (life itself) **and Qayyum** (everything finds life and subsists with HU).

3. He, as the very reality itself, revealed what is in your hands (disclosed in your consciousness), **the Book** (knowledge of the reality and sunnatullah) **confirming the Truth from the past. He had also revealed the Torah** (knowledge disclosed to Moses) **and the Bible** (knowledge disclosed to Jesus).

4. As HUDA for people (to guide them to the reality, to show them the right path). **He also revealed the Furqan** (the ability to distinguish right from wrong, the good from the bad). **Certainly, those who cover and deny the signs of Allah** (the manifestations of His Names) **will have severe suffering. Allah is the Aziz, the Zuntaqim** (enforces the consequences of actions without any sympathy).

5. Allah! Nothing in the heavens (the dimension of consciousness – angelic realm – the quantal dimension; the essence of matter) **and the earth** (dimension of matter – the body – the earth) **is hidden from Him** (because He comprises the essence of everything with His Names. Concepts such as hidden or apparent apply only to 'things' or thingness)!

6. It is HU who shapes (forms, programs) **you in the womb** (mother's womb – in Arabic rahim; the productive mechanism within your essence: rahimiyyah) **as He wishes. There is no god, only HU, the Aziz, the Hakim.**

7. It is HU who has revealed to you the **KNOWLEDGE** (Book). **Some of its signs are clear** (open and net commands) **and comprise the basis – foundation of the knowledge** (Book) **– and some of it is allegorical** (metaphoric and symbolic expressions). **Those with deviation** (ulterior motives, distorted thoughts) **in their hearts, judge with the allegorical verses, interpreting them for the purpose of causing provocation. Only Allah knows their** (true and precise) **interpretation. Those who are grounded in knowledge** (deep contemplators) **say, "We believe, all of it is from our Rabb." And none can discern this except those who have reached the essence** (the intimates of reality through whom Allah hears, sees and speaks; ulul albab).

8. "Our Rabb, after giving us guidance (enabling us to recognize and discern the reality) **do not turn our consciousness** (back to the illusory identity – ego based existence), **and bestow your grace upon us from your Self** (ladun; the potential of the Names comprising my essence). **Most certainly you are the Wahhab."**

9. "Our Rabb, you will surely gather mankind in a period of whose coming there is no doubt. And never will Allah fail to fulfill His promise."

10. Certainly for the deniers neither their wealth nor their children will benefit them against what becomes manifest from Allah. They are fuel for fire.

11. (Their course) **is just like the dynasty of the Pharaoh and those who came before them.** (They had) **denied our signs** (the manifestations of the Names). **And Allah seized them in their error. Allah is severe in recompense** (severe in enforcing the due consequence of an offence; shadid al-iqab).

12. Say to the disbelievers (those who deny the reality), **"You shall be defeated and gathered in hell... How wretched a resting place!"**

13. The truth is there were signs for you and a lesson to be taken from the two groups who met in opposition. While one group was fighting for the cause of Allah, the others were deniers; (the believers) **saw with their own eyes that** (the deniers) **were twice their number. But Allah supports whom He wills with His aid. Certainly there is a great lesson in this for those with insight.**

14. Beautified for the people is the desire to indulge in the pleasures of women and children, heaped up sums of gold and silver, noble

horses and cattle. However these are but transitory pleasures of the world. But Allah... The most beauteous goal (to attain) is with Him.

15. Say, "Shall I tell you of something even better than all of this? For those who are protected in the sight of Allah there are Paradises underneath which rivers flow, they will reside therein eternally. There they will have pure spouses (this could also denote the spouse of consciousness; a perfect body free from any ailment) and the pleasure of Allah. Allah, as the essence of His servants, is the Basir.

16. They will say, "Our Rabb, we have indeed believed. Forgive us our faults and protect us from burning (suffering)."

17. (They are) the patient ones, loyal, content (in submission with the comprehension of their servitude), they give (to the needy) and ask for forgiveness for their inadequacies in the early morning (the process of awakening).

18. Allah knows with certainty that none exists other than He. He is HU, there is no other, only HU... And (so do) the forces (potentials) of His names (angels; compositions of qualities that manifest through the knowledge of reality) and those of knowledge (those who possess this knowledge also know, and thus testify to this reality) and maintain themselves in accord with this truth... There is no god, only HU, the Aziz, the Hakim.

19. Indeed, the religion (system and order) in the sight of Allah is Islam (the whole of creation is in a state of submission, whether conscious or unconscious of the qualities of the Names)! Those to whom a Book (knowledge) has been given, have fallen into division after this knowledge, because of jealousy and ambition. And whoever covers the existence of Allah in His signs (which are the manifestations of His Names) indeed Allah is swift in reckoning (Allah instantly puts into effect the consequences of one's actions; sari-ul-hisab).

20. If they argue with you say, "My face is in submission to Allah; so are those who follow me!" Ask those to whom the knowledge of reality and sunnatullah has been given and the illiterate ones (those who are unaware of this reality; the dualists), "Have you also accepted Islam?" If they submit they would have accepted the reality. But if they turn away, your duty is only to inform. Allah, as a result of His Names comprising His servants, is the Basir (evaluates).

21. As for those who deny the existence of Allah in His signs (the manifestations of His Names), and kill the Nabis against the will of

the Reality, and kill those who enjoin justice, give them the tidings of a severe suffering!

22. They are the ones whose deeds will be worthless both in this world and the eternal life to come. There will be no helpers for them.

23. Have you not seen those who were given a share of the revealed knowledge; they are invited to the revelation of Allah, that a judgment be made between them, but then some of them turn away and leave.

24. This is because they think, "The fire will not touch us except for numbered days." Their invented delusive belief is a betrayal to their religion.

25. So how will it (their state) be when we gather them together in a period that is sure to come, and the results of their deeds are given without any injustice!

26. Say, "Allah, the sovereign of all sovereignty... You give sovereignty to whom You will and You take sovereignty away from whom you will. You honor whom You will and You abase whom You will. In Your hand is all good. Certainly, you are Qadir over all things."

27. "You turn the night into day and turn the day into night. You bring the living out of the dead and the dead out of the living. You give provision (life sustenance) to whom You will without account."

28. Let not the believers abandon the believers and take the deniers of reality as their friends. Whoever does this severs his ties with Allah. This can only be done for protection. Allah warns you to be careful of Him. To Allah is your return!

29. Say, "Whether you conceal what is in your hearts or reveal it Allah (as its creator) knows it. He knows everything that is in the heavens and the earth (external and internal). Allah is Qadir over all things."

30. Each person will find before him everything he has done of good or evil on that day. He will wish there were a great distance between it and himself! Allah warns you to heed Him (for He will definitely make you experience the consequences of your actions). Allah is Ra'uf to his servants (from their essence).

31. Say, "If you love Allah follow me so that Allah will love you and forgive your faults. Allah is the Ghafur, the Rahim."

32. Say, "Obey Allah and the Rasul!"... If they turn away, then indeed Allah does not like the deniers of reality.

33. The truth is, Allah chose Adam, Noah, Abraham and his descendants, the family of Imran (in their time) over humans and purified them.

34. Descendants from each other, as a single lineage... Allah is the Sami, the Aleem.

35. Recall when Imran's wife said, "My Rabb, I have unconditionally pledged the child in my womb to You; accept it from me. Certainly You are the Sami, the Aleem."

36. And when she delivered (the child who she thought would be a boy) she said, "My Rabb, I have delivered a girl." Allah knew the female was not like the male (that a female could not perform in the same way as a male). "I have named her Mary. I seek protection from You for her and her lineage against the Satan, the expelled."

37. So her Rabb accepted her with cordiality and raised her like a precious flower. He put her in Zachariah's care. Every time Zachariah came to the temple he found her with new food. He asked her, "O Mary, where is this from?" (As a result of His grace it reached her through His servants). Indeed, Allah gives life sustenance (provision) to whom He wills, as He wills.

38. Thereupon Zachariah prayed to his Rabb, "My Rabb, grant me from Your ladun (the potential of the Names comprising my essence) a pure offspring. You are certainly the hearer of my prayer (perceiver of my introspection).

39. So when in the temple he was in a state of introspection with his Rabb, the angels said to him, "Allah gives you tidings of John, confirming a word (B-kalimah) from Allah (Jesus, the word of Allah, the manifestation of specific forces) and sayyid (the master/chief of forces) and chaste (in control of his ego), a righteous Nabi (living the Truth in his essence).

40. He said, "My Rabb, how can I have a son! I have reached old age and my wife is barren!" He said, "That may be (your case)... But Allah does as He wills!"

41. He (Zachariah) said, "My Rabb, grant me a sign". He said, "Your sign is that you will not be able to speak to people for three days except by gestures; so remember your Rabb much and experience the greatness of His glory in the morning and the evening."

42. And recall when the angels said to Mary, "O Mary, indeed Allah has purified (enabled you to experience your essence) and chosen you. He cleansed you (from the filth of duality) and chose you above all the women in the world (of your time)!"

43. "O Mary, be obedient to your Rabb (live in awe), prostrate (experience your inexistence in the sight of Allah's existence) and bow with those who bow (feel and acknowledge the Names that are manifest in your being)."

44. This knowledge is what we reveal of the unknown to you. And you were not with them when they drew lots as to which of them should be Mary's guardian. And you were not there when they were disputing with one another (regarding this).

45. When the angels said to Mary, "Allah gives tidings of a word from Him (B-kalimah; a servant to manifest His attributes) His name is the Messiah, Jesus, son of Mary. He is honored in this world (exalted in dignity) and the eternal life to come and is of the muqarriboon (lives in a state of qurbiyyah [manifests Names that are very specific to Allah due to his state of closeness] and an instrument for miracles)."

46. "He will speak to the people in the cradle and in maturity. He is of the righteous."

47. (Mary) asked, "My Rabb, how can I have a child when no man has touched me?" He said, "Just like that! Allah creates what He wills! When He decrees a matter, He only says 'BE' and it is."

48. He will teach (program – embed into existence) the Book (the knowledge of reality), Wisdom (the operation mechanism of the system and order formed by the Names of Allah in the worlds), the Torah (revelation – the knowledge revealed to Moses) and the Bible (the reality revealed as good news).

49. And He will send him as a Rasul to the children of Israel. (He) will say, "Indeed I have come to you from your Rabb bearing His signs in my essence. I will create out of clay a form of a bird for you and breathe into it (activate the forces of the Names within it) and it will become a bird with the permission of Allah (B-iznillah; with the will of Allah's Names to manifest in that particular form). I heal the blind and the leper, and give life to the dead with the permission of Allah (B-iznillah; in congruity with the forces of the Names comprising their essence). I also inform you (as Allah informs me) of what you eat and store in your houses. There is (an important) sign in this (regarding the power of your Rabb) for you, if you believe.

50. "And I come confirming what was before me (the original uncorrupted) of the Torah (revealed to Moses)... And to make lawful (halal) for you some of what was forbidden to you (through distortion). I have come to you with a sign – miracle from your Rabb. Protect yourselves from Allah and obey me."

51. "Allah (with His Names) is most certainly my Rabb and your Rabb! So become conscious of your servitude to Him and live accordingly. This is the straight path."

52. And when Jesus sensed their denial of the truth, he asked, "Who will help me in the way of Allah?" His disciples answered, "We are the helpers of Allah... We have believed in accord with the letter 'B' (that the essence of our being comprises the Names of Allah); witness this with your essence! We are in submission to Allah."

53. "Our Rabb, we have believed in what You have revealed (Jesus) from your reality (essence) and we have followed your Rasul, so register us among the witnesses (of the truth)."

54. They schemed, and received a scheme from Allah in response. Allah is the best of schemers. (In order to eliminate the discloser of the truth they resorted to secretly contriving against him, but through the very same method Allah overcame them, by making their schemes result against them.)

(The original word used here to denote scheme is 'makr.' Essentially, makr is the undertaking of an action, which separates one from Allah, yet the person is unaware of this and assumes he is not harmed by it so he continues to engage in it. Eventually he falls even further away from Allah, or the actualization of the forces of the Names within his essence, which is by far the greatest punishment one can incur.)

55. And recall when Allah had said, "I'm going to cause you to die (that is, they will not be able to assassinate you through their secret schemes, I will cause you to die when your time comes)... I'm going to raise you to myself (enable you to experience the supremacy of your essence); I'm going to purify you by removing you from among the deniers of the reality (disbelievers) and until Doomsday I'm going to

place those who follow you above those who deny the reality. In the end, your return is to Me. I will judge on matters over which you differed between each other."

56. "But as for those who deny the reality, I will subject them to severe suffering both in this world and the eternal life to come. And they will have no helpers."

57. And those who believed in 'their essential reality' and engaged in the necessary practices, the results of their work will be given to them in full. Allah does not like the wrongdoers!

58. This knowledge contains signs (pertaining to past events that are unknown to you) and wise remembrance (revealing the wisdom of those events).

59. "Indeed, the formation of Jesus in the sight of Allah is like that of Adam (if the formation of Jesus is like that of Adam, then the formation of Adam is like that of Jesus. This is the angle from which we should approach this topic). He created him from dust, then said to him 'Be' and he was (the creation of man by breathing the spirit [the activation of the forces of the Names] into that which is formed by dust – a molecular structure – is the same as breathing the spirit into a molecular structure formed in the mother's womb).

60. This is the Truth from your Rabb, so do not be of those who doubt!

61. Whoever disputes this reality after this knowledge has come to you, say, "Come, let us call our sons and your sons, our women and your women, ourselves and yourselves, and pray; may the wrath of Allah be upon those who lie about the reality."

62. Indeed, this is the truth of the matter. Godhood is an invalid concept; only Allah! In truth, Allah is HU, the Aziz, the Hakim.

63. If they turn away (from this truth), indeed Allah knows the corrupters (enforces the consequences of it).

64. Say, "O those to whom the knowledge of reality has come, let us come together on a common understanding, let us not consider servitude to anything other than Allah, let us not associate any partners (live in duality) to Allah, our essential reality; let not some of us deify (take as gods besides Allah) others of us (like Jesus)." If they turn away from this then say to them, "Bear witness that we are of those who have submitted to Allah."

65. O those to whom the knowledge of reality has come, why do you argue about Abraham? The Torah and the Bible were revealed after him (hence they narrated the situation). Do you not have the intellect to realize this?

66. (It is bad enough) you argue over things about which you have little knowledge, but why do you argue over things about which you have no knowledge? Whereas Allah knows, and you know not!

67. Abraham was neither a Jew nor a Christian... But he was of those (hanif) who did not believe in a god (external deity) and was aware that only Allah existed (the concept of oneness) and had submitted to Him (knew that Allah had absolute administration over their existence). His comprehension was free from duality!

68. Indeed, the closest ones to the truth with Abraham are those who follow his understanding, this Nabi (Muhammad saw) and those who believe in him. Allah is the Waliyy of the believers.

69. A group of those to whom the knowledge of reality has come, wanted to lead you astray, but they cannot lead anyone astray other than themselves. Yet they do not realize this.

70. O you to whom the knowledge of reality has come, even though you bear witness to the reality, why do you deny the existence of Allah in His signs (the manifestations of His Names)?

71. O you to whom the knowledge of reality has come, why do you hide the Truth within falsity and conceal the Truth while you repeatedly know of it?

72. A group of those to whom the knowledge of reality came said, "Go to the believers and tell them, 'we have believed in what has been revealed' then reject it at the end of the day (by saying you thought about it and realized it was not possible). Thus, maybe they too will (follow you and) abandon their way."

73. "Do not believe those who do not follow your religion!" Say, "Guidance is the guidance of Allah (involves the realization that the Names of Allah comprise one's being). Do you oppose because the like of what has been given to you is given to another, or because they are going to prevail over you (with what has been given to them) in the sight of your Rabb?" Say, "Most certainly, bounty is in the hands of Allah, He gives it to whom He wills. Allah is the Wasi, the Aleem."

74. "He specifies His grace (from whom He wills) to whom He wills! Allah is the Azim, the possessor of bounty."

75. Among the people to whom the knowledge of reality has been given is he who, if you entrust him with a great amount (of wealth), he will return it all to you as is. And among them is he who, if you entrust him with a single dinar (gold), he will not return it to you unless you constantly stand over him and demand it. (This is because of their thought) "The illiterate ones who are in opposition to us (who are ignorant of the reality) have no rights over us." They deliberately lie about Allah.

76. Indeed, he who stands by his word and protects himself, undoubtedly Allah loves those who are protected.

77. As for those who sell their covenant and promise to Allah for a small price; they have no share in the eternal life to come. Allah (not an external deity, the actualization of the forces of the Names within their essence) will not speak to them, look at them or purify them during the period of Doomsday. There is severe suffering for them.

78. There are some among them who talk by perverting the meaning (to mean something else) of the knowledge of reality, so that you think it is revealed knowledge. (Whereas) what they say is not revealed knowledge. They say, "It is from Allah," but it is not from Allah! They deliberately lie about Allah.

79. It is not possible that Allah should give a human the knowledge of the reality, authority and Nubuwwah, and he would say to the people, "Leave Allah and serve me!" On the contrary, he would say, "In compliance with the teachings of the knowledge of the reality and the practices you engage in, be of those who are conscious of their servitude to their Rabb."

80. He (the aforementioned one of knowledge) would not ask you to take the angels, or the Nabis as your Rabbs either. Why would he ask you to deny your reality after you have submitted to Allah?

81. And recall when Allah took the covenant of the Nabis, "I have given you from the knowledge of reality and Wisdom, from now on when a Rasul comes to you confirming what is with you, you shall believe in him completely and help him. Have you accepted and taken My heavy load upon yourselves?" They said, "We have accepted!" "Bear witness, as I too bear witness as your essential reality."

82. **Whoever turns away** (from this word), **they are the corrupted ones** (those whose beliefs are corrupt).

83. **While whatever is in the heavens and the earth** (the material and spiritual dimensions of the universe) **is willingly or unwillingly in a state of submission to Him, are they looking for something other than the religion of Allah** (Islam – the system and order created by Allah)? **(Yet) they will be made to return to Him.**

84. **Say, "We believe in Allah as the One who created our essence from His Names, and we believe in everything He revealed to us; and to Abraham, Ishmael, Isaac, Jacob and that which was revealed his descendants; to Moses and Jesus and in what was given to the Nabis from their Rabb. We do not make distinction among them. We have submitted to Him."**

85. **And whoever seeks a religion** (system and order) **other than Islam** (the consciousness of being in a state of submission) **his search will be ineffective! And he will be of the losers in the eternal life to come.**

86. **How will Allah guide people who deny the reality even after clear proofs come to them and they bear witness that the Rasul is the Truth! Allah does not guide the wrongdoing people.**

87. **The return of their deeds is the curse of Allah, the angels and the whole of mankind** (they have fallen separate from all of them).

88. **They will remain under these conditions forever. Their suffering will not be lightened and they will not be cared for.**

89. **Except if after this they** (acknowledge their mistake and) **repent and correct themselves** (amend their wrongdoings) **indeed Allah is the Ghafur, the Rahim.**

90. **But those who deny the reality and are persistent in their denial, their repentance will never be accepted. Indeed, they are the very people who have gone astray.**

91. **They deny the knowledge of reality and they die with this denial; even if they had a world of gold and offered it as ransom** (to save themselves) **it will never be accepted. Severe suffering awaits them and no one will help them.**

92. **"Never will you experience the essence of reality** (albirra) **until you unrequitedly give away that which you love. And whatever you**

give unrequitedly in the way of Allah, Allah (as its creator) knows it (and creates its return).

93. All food was lawful to the Children of Israel, except what Israel had made unlawful (forbade) to himself before the Torah was revealed. Say, "If you are loyal to your word bring the revelation (Torah) and read it!"

94. And whoever casts lies about Allah after this, they are the wrongdoers.

95. Say, "Allah has told the truth. So follow the people of Abraham (the religious understanding) as hanifs. He was not a dualist!"

96. The first house made for people was in Becca (the old name of Mecca), sacred for the worlds and a source of guidance.

97. In it there are clear signs and the station of Abraham. Whoever enters it will be in safety. Pilgrimage to the House (Kaaba, the abode of Allah in one's heart) is the right of Allah (the qualities of the Names in one's essence) upon all people who have the means to undertake it. But whoever denies (his ability to go even though he has the means to), indeed Allah is Ghani from the worlds.

98. Say, "O you to whom the knowledge of reality has come... While Allah witnesses all your deeds, why do you deny (or cover) the existence of Allah in His signs (the manifestations of His Names)?"

99. Say, "O you to whom the knowledge of reality has come... Even though you bore witness (to the reality) why do you avert the truth and turn the believers from the way of Allah? Allah is not unaware of your deeds."

100. O believers, if you follow some of those to whom the knowledge of reality has been given (who have gone astray afterwards), they will turn you back from belief to people of denial.

101. While the signs of Allah are displayed in front of you and there is a Rasul among you, how can you be of the deniers of the reality? Whoever (detaches himself from all else and) holds firmly onto Allah, the essence comprising his being, he has been guided to the straight path.

102. O believers... Protect yourselves duly from Allah (as He will definitely subject you to the consequences of your deeds) and die only as ones who have experienced submission.

103. Hold fast onto the rope of Allah (which leads to) **the reality of the Names in your being, all together, do not fall into separation. Remember the blessing of Allah upon you. Recall that you were enemies once, He brought you together by forming a mutual understanding in your consciousness; and due to this blessing that He manifested in you, you became brothers. You were near the edge of a fire pit; He saved you from that fire. Thus Allah explains his signs, so that you attain the reality.**

104. Let there be a community among you inviting you to good (the Truth), judging according to the Truth and reality, and advising you to walk away from things that are contrary to Religion. Those are the ones who will be emancipated.

105. Do not be like those who fall into division and separation after clear proofs have come to them. There is great suffering for them.

106. During that period, some faces (forms of consciousness) **will shine** (with the light of the Truth) **and some faces will darken** (with the darkness of the ego)... **Those with darkened faces** (will be told): **"You fell into denial after you believed! Experience the suffering brought forth by your being because of your denial of the reality."**

107. But those whose faces shine (as the result of their comprehension of their essence), **they will be in the grace of Allah... They will abide therein eternally.**

108. These are the signs of Allah, we make you recite them in Truth. Allah does not wish wrong upon the worlds.

109. Whatever is in the heavens and the earth, all of it belongs to Allah (they exist and subsist with His Names). **All will return to Allah** (a time will come when everything will see its essential reality, and those who fail to evaluate this will burn)**!**

110. You are the best community from among mankind. You judge with the Truth and reality, you advise abstinence from things that are contrary to religion, and you believe in Allah with the comprehension that your essence comprises the Names. Had those to whom the knowledge of reality was given (the People of the Book) **also believed, it would have been good for them. Some are people of faith, but the majority are deniers of the reality.**

111. (They) **can give you no harm other than torment. If they fight with you, they will turn their backs on you and flee. No help will be given afterwards.**

112. Their verdict is humiliation (belittlement) **wherever they are; they have been subject to the wrath of Allah and are bound to live in humiliation... Except those who hold firmly a rope from Allah** (the covenant 'You are our Rabb'; the realization that their essence is comprised of the Names) **and a rope from among man** (follow someone with this faith)! **For they were denying the existence of Allah in His signs** (the manifestations of His Names) **and killing the Nabis** (in compliance with their egos) **against the will of the Truth. This is because of their rebelliousness and transgression.**

113. They are not all the same. There is also a group among those to whom the knowledge of reality has been given who prostrate and read and evaluate the signs of Allah throughout the night.

114. They believe that the Names of Allah comprise the essence of their being and in the eternal life to come, they judge with the Truth and reality, they advise people against things that are contrary to Religion, and they hasten to (both material and spiritual) good. They are the righteous ones.

115. The good they do will never be denied. Allah, with the Names in the essence of the protected ones, is the Aleem.

116. As for those who deny the reality, neither their wealth nor their offspring can protect them against Allah. They are bound to burn eternally!

117. The example of what they spend in this servile material world (the lowest state of existence – worldly life) **is like a frosty wind that strikes and destroys the harvest of a people who wrong themselves. Allah has not wronged them, but it is they who wrong themselves.**

118. O believers... Do not befriend those other than your kind (those who are not of your faith and belief). (They) wait for an opportunity to harm you and seeing you in hardship makes them happy. Do you not see how their adversity overflows from their mouths! And what they conceal inside (their hearts) is even bigger. Thus, we clearly inform you of the necessary signs. Use your reason (evaluate).

119. You are such people (of belief) that (due to the reality you believe in) you like them. Whereas they do not like you (because you do not share their faith)! You believe in all of the knowledge of reality. When they see you they say, "We have believed"; but when they are left to themselves they bite their fingertips in rage. Say, "Perish in the fire of your rage!"... Most certainly Allah, as the very essence of your being with His Names, knows what you conceal within.

120. When a good thing happens to you, it grieves them; but, when an affliction befalls you, they rejoice. If you persevere and protect yourselves, their plot will never harm you. Most certainly, Allah encompasses what they do (without the concept of locality).

121. And remember when you left your family in the early morning to post the believers at their suitable stations for the battle. Allah is the Sami, the Aleem.

122. Then, two groups among you began to lose their courage. But Allah was their Waliyy. Let the believers place their trust in Allah (believe that the Name Wakil in their essence will fulfill its function).

123. (Truly) when you were in a weak and helpless state, Allah gave you victory at Badr. Then protect yourselves from Allah so you may be of the evaluators.

124. Remember when you told the believers, "Is it not sufficient for you that your Rabb reinforces you by the disclosure of three thousand angels?" (the manifestations of some of the forces of the Names through the believers to bring about courage and perseverance to struggle).

125. Yes... If you endure and protect yourselves, even if the enemy strikes you suddenly, your Rabb will reinforce you with five thousand angelic forces from the Names within your essence.

126. Allah did this as good tidings for you and to reassure you of the forces contained in your hearts (essence). Help is only from Allah, the Aziz and the Hakim.

127. And (Allah did this) to cut off (destroy) a part of the deniers of reality, and to make the other part turn back, abased.

128. It is not for you to judge; He will accept their repentance if He wills, or cause them suffering. For indeed, they are the wrongdoers.

129. Whatever is in the heavens and the earth belongs to Allah (they exist and subsist with His Names). He forgives whom He wills, and causes suffering to (enforces the consequences of the actions of) whom He wills. Allah is the Ghafur, the Rahim.

130. O believers, do not consume the doubled and multiplied return of usury (loansharking is forbidden)! Protect yourselves from Allah (for

He will definitely subject you to the consequences of your actions) **so you may be emancipated!**

131. Protect yourselves from the fire that is prepared for the deniers of reality.

132. Obey Allah and the Rasul so you may reach a state of grace.

133. Hasten to forgiveness from your Rabb (sourced from the composition of the Names in your essence) **and Paradise** (the abode of the actualization of the forces of Allah's Names), **which is as wide as the heavens** (the states of comprehension) **and the earth** (the platform of the forces)**... It has been prepared for the protected ones!**

134. They are the ones who give unrequitedly in the way of Allah during ease and hardship, they control their fury when they get angry, and they forgive people for their faults. Allah loves those who do good.

135. When they do something shameful or when they wrong themselves (by becoming veiled from Allah), **they think about Allah and ask for forgiveness for the wrong they have done. Who can forgive faults other than Allah! They are not persistent in their wrongdoing.**

136. The result (consequence) **of their actions is forgiveness from their Rabb and Paradises underneath which rivers flow. They will abide therein eternally. What an excellent reward it is for those who do useful deeds.**

137. Communities with lifestyles of their own have come and passed before you. Travel the earth (literally or by way of knowledge) **and see what has become of those who denied** (the reality).

138. This is an explanation (lesson) **for the people and guidance and advice for the protected ones.**

139. Do not weaken and do not grieve; you are the superior ones, if you are of the believers.

140. If you are touched by (the pain of a) **wound, a similar wound has touched other people as well. Such times recirculate among mankind. It is so that the believers can be known by Allah** (as the outcome of the manifestations of the Names in their essence) **and who bear witness to the reality at the expense of their own lives. Allah**

does not like those who do wrong (those who do not fulfill their duties to themselves and others).

141. (These events are so) **that Allah purifies the believers** (through these experiences) **and to destroy the coverers of the reality thereby.**

142. Or did you think you could enter (experience the state of) **Paradise before Allah makes evident who among you are the warriors** (those who struggle with perseverance and determination to live the reality) **and those who are patiently steadfast on this path!**

143. You had certainly wished for martyrdom without having to encounter death. Now you see it, but you keep looking on!

144. Muhammad is no other than the Rasul. Rasuls have come and gone before him too. If he dies or is killed now, will you turn back (from your faith and cause)**? And whoever turns back will not harm Allah! Allah will subject the grateful ones to the outcome of their gratefulness** (they will experience the results of their evaluation).

145. And it is not for one to die unless it complies with the unchanging program (kitaban muajjala) **formed by the Names of Allah in one's being** (B-iznillah)**! Whoever wants the blessings of this world, We will give in this world. And whoever wants the blessings of the eternal life to come, that is what We will give to him. We give the consequences** (outcomes) **of the grateful ones** (the product of their evaluation).

146. Many Nabis fought, even though in their company there were those who were experiencing their servitude to their Rabb. They did not slacken with the afflictions that befell them in the way of Allah, nor did they show weakness and succumb. Allah loves those who are steadfast during difficulty.

147. They had said, "Our Rabb, forgive our faults and the extreme ways in our affairs, give us resilience and patience, help us against the deniers of the reality, give us victory."

148. So Allah gave them the reward of this world and the most beauteous reward of the eternal life to come. Allah loves those who do good.

149. O believers, if you follow the disbelievers (the deniers and coverers of the reality) **they will turn you back on your heels and you will remain as losers.**

150. In truth, your protector is Allah! He renders victorious with His help.

151. We will cast fear into the hearts of those who deify (through duality) their egos (even though there is no such evidence) over the Names of Allah comprising their essence, and cover the absolute reality within. And their abode will be the fire... How wretched is the end of the wrongdoers!

152. Allah has indeed kept His word (at the battle of Uhud); you were about to destroy them with the force deriving from the Names of Allah in your essence (B-izniHi). But when Allah showed you that which you love (victory and spoils), you showed weakness and rebelled and quarreled against the command you were given. Some of you were after worldly things (so you abandoned your posts and ran after the spoils) and some of you were after eternal life (so you obeyed the command of the Rasul, persevered and became martyrs). Then Allah turned you back to show you your state. But Allah has forgiven you. Allah is full of bounty for those who believe.

153. Remember when the Rasul was calling you from behind, but you fled without looking at anyone. So Allah reprimanded you with distress upon distress, so that you don't grieve over your losses or remain with that which befell you (victory and spoils had escaped you and you had fallen into a state of shame). Allah, as the creator of your actions, is well aware of all things.

154. Then He revealed a sense of security to calm you after your distress. One group (the hypocrites and the two-faced) were worried about themselves (their interest). With ignorant assumptions they thought, "Did we have a say in this decision?" Say, "The judgment – decision – belongs completely to Allah!" They concealed within themselves what they didn't disclose. They said, "If we had a say in this decision we would not have been killed here." Say, "Even if you had stayed in your homes, those for whom death was written (programmed) would have, in any case, walked out of their homes and gone to the place of their death. Allah made you experience this to show you what is inside you (by outwardly revealing that which you conceal) and cleanse you from false ideas. Allah knows what is inside you, for the essence of your heart comprises His Names".

155. Those who fled when the two armies met in opposition did this because Satan (illusion) provoked the false ideas they had formed. But Allah has forgiven them. Allah is the Ghafur, the Halim.

156. O believers... **Do not be like those who deny the reality by saying, "Had they stayed by our side they would not have died or been killed" in regards to their brothers who go traveling the earth, or who go to battle. Allah formed this idea within them as a pain of longing. It is Allah who gives life and takes life away** (not the apparent causes)! **Allah is Basir of** (evaluates) **what you do** (as He is the essence and moreover the creator with His Names).

157. Indeed, **the forgiveness and grace you will obtain for being killed or dying in the way of Allah is better than what they accumulate** (in this world).

158. And indeed, if you die or are killed, to Allah you will be gathered (your evaluation will be by the Names of Allah that is your very essence).

159. With the grace Allah brought forth from your essence you were gentle with them. Had you been harsh and severe they would have scattered and left. Pardon them and ask for their forgiveness. Consult their opinions when making a decision regarding social matters. After a decision is made and put into practice, trust in Allah! Certainly, Allah loves those who place their trust in Him (have faith that the Name Wakil in their essence will fulfill its function).

160. If Allah helps you, nobody can be victorious over you. But if He leaves you to your own accord without help, who can be your helper! Let the believers place their trust only in Allah (their reality with His Names).

161. It is not possible for a Nabi to betray what is entrusted. Whoever betrays, he will come with his betrayal hung on his neck! After this, everyone will be given exactly what they earned (with their deeds) **they will not be wronged!**

162. Is one who pursues the pleasure of Allah (the forces of the Names within his essence) **like the one whose abode is hell, the place where Allah's anger is expressed? How wretched an end that is!**

163. They have different degrees in the sight of Allah (in terms of their knowledge, wisdom and understanding). **Allah is Basir of** (evaluates) **what you do** (for He is the essence and the creator of them with His Names).

164. Indeed Allah disclosed, as a blessing, a Rasul for the believers from within themselves (brought forth a Rasul from among their own kind) **he reads His signs; purifies them and teaches them the**

knowledge of reality and Wisdom (the system and order of all that is formed). (Whereas) previously they were in evident corruption!

165. When a (single) disaster struck you, although We had struck (the enemy) with one twice as great, you said, "Why and how did this come about?" Say, "It is the result of your ego." Indeed, Allah is the Qadir (the possessor of continual and infinite power) over all things.

166. What transpired at the battle of the two communities (the Battle of Uhud) was so that your essence, the Names of Allah, becomes apparent on the believers, and it becomes evident who each person (really) is.

167. (It was also so) that the hypocrites (two-faced) may be known. When they were told, "Come and fight or defend in the way of Allah," they said, "If we had known you were going to battle we would have come after you." That day, they were closer to the state of denial than the state of faith. They were not expressing their true thoughts! What were they trying to hide within when Allah knows the truth!

168. Those who did not go to battle said, in regards to their brothers, "If they had followed us they would not have been killed." Say, "If what you say is true, keep death away from yourselves if you can!"

169. And never think of those who have been killed in the way of Allah as dead. On the contrary, they are alive with their Rabb receiving provision (from the forces pertaining to their innermost essential reality).

170. They are happy with what Allah, as their essential reality, manifests as a bounty from their essence. They want to give the good news to those who stayed behind and did not join them – that there is neither fear nor grief for them.

171. They want to share the blessings and bounty of Allah upon them and bring good tidings that the deeds of the believers will not be left unrequited.

172. They responded to the call of Allah and the Rasul (even) after they were wounded, there is a great reward for the doers of good and the protected ones among them.

173. When they told them, "They have formed an army to fight with you, fear them," on the contrary, this news increased their faith, and

they said, "Allah is sufficient for us, and how excellent a Wakil He is!"

174. Due to their faith, they returned with the blessing and bounty of Allah, unharmed. They followed the pleasure of Allah. Allah, the Azim, is the possessor of bounty.

175. The Satan (who brought this news) can only frighten his own allies... Fear me (for you will face the consequences of your deeds based on the mechanics of the system; sunnatullah), not them, if you are of the believers.

176. Do not let the ones who compete in denying the reality upset you. Indeed, they cannot cause any harm to Allah. Allah does not will to give them any share in the eternal life to come (hence they are like this). There is great suffering for them.

177. As for those who buy denial in exchange of believing in their essential reality, they cannot cause any harm to Allah. There is severe burning (suffering) for them.

178. Those who live by denying the reality should not think that by extending their time We are doing them any good! We only extend it for them so they increase their faults (this is Allah's scheme for them). There is a humiliating suffering for them.

179. Allah will not leave the believers as they are. He will separate the clean from the impure. And Allah will not inform you of the unknown (Absolute Essence). But, Allah chooses from His Rasuls whom He wills (if He wants to inform you of what is unknown to you). So believe that the Names of Allah created you and all the worlds, and believe in the Rasuls (who have been revealed to inform you of this knowledge). If you believe and protect yourselves, you will reach a great reward.

180. Let not those who are stingy and withhold the provisions of Allah arising from the forces of the Names in their essence, as His bounty, think that this is good for them. On the contrary, it is bad! That which they withhold will be hung on their necks during the period of Doomsday! To Allah belongs the heritage (everything that forms with the forces of the Names) of the heavens and the earth. Allah is Habir of what you do (as their creator).

181. Indeed, Allah has perceived their word, "Certainly Allah is poor; we are wealthy." We will record their words and their killings of the

Nabis against the will of the Truth and tell them, "Taste the burning suffering!"

182. This is the consequence of what you did with your own hands. Allah does not unjustly punish His servants by manifesting on them what they did not deserve!

183. They (the Jews) had said, "Allah commanded us not to believe in any Rasul until he brings forth a sacrifice that fire will consume." Say, "Rasuls had come before me and they brought for you clear proofs and the things you want. If you are true to your word, why did you kill them?"

184. As they denied you, they have also denied the Rasuls that have come before you with clear proofs, divine and enlightening knowledge.

185. Every individual consciousness will taste death (life without a biological body will continue eternally). You will be rewarded in full for your deeds in the period of Doomsday (the period following your biological bodily life). Whoever is saved from burning (suffering) and put into (the state of) Paradise, he has indeed been liberated. The worldly life is nothing but a delusive pleasure (resulting in remorse).

186. You will surely be tested by your possessions and yourselves (egos). You will be abused by those to whom the knowledge of reality was given before you and the dualists. But if you endure and protect yourselves, (know that) this can only be achieved with determination.

187. And recall when Allah had taken a covenant from those to whom the knowledge of reality was given, "You must make it clear to the people and not hide it from them." But they left their covenant behind and exchanged it for a small price. How wretched an exchange!

188. Do not think highly of those who pride themselves with what they have done and love to be praised for what they haven't done! And do not think they will escape the suffering! Severe suffering awaits them.

189. To Allah belongs the kingdom of the heavens and the earth (for every "thing" or "thingness" in this scope is formed with the forces and meanings pertaining to His Names). Allah is Qadir over all things.

190. Indeed, there are signs in the creation of the heavens (from the perceivable realms to the quantal dimension) **and the earth** (all realms that are perceived as matter), **and the transformation of the night and the day** (why and how the night and day is formed and their periods, etc.) **for those who have reached the essence of reality** (ulul albab).

191. They (those who have attained the essence of the reality) **remember Allah while standing or sitting or** (lying) **on their sides and they contemplate the creation of the heavens and the earth** (depending on the day, the universe and its depths, or in terms of the brain, the place of the body and its attributes) **and say, "Our Rabb, You have not created these things for nothing! You are Subhan** (free from creating meaningless things; you are in a state of creating anew at every instant)! **Protect us from burning** (remorse for not being able to duly evaluate your manifestations)."

192. "Our Rabb, whoever You admit into fire, You have abased. No one can help (save) **those who do wrong to themselves!"**

193. "Our Rabb, we have indeed heard the one who said, 'Believe in your Rabb who has formed your essence with His Names' and we have believed him instantly. Our Rabb, forgive us our faults, erase our mistakes, let us come to You with Your servants who have united with You."

194. "Our Rabb, give us what You have pledged to Your Rasuls and do not humiliate us during the Doomsday period. Certainly, You never fail to fulfill Your oath."

195. Their Rabb responded to their prayer, "Never will I allow your deeds to be unrewarded, whether man or woman. You are all from each other (you have been created with the same qualities and hence bound by the same system). **As for those who have migrated, expelled from their homes, abused, fought, and killed in My cause, surely I will erase their faults. I will certainly admit them to Paradises underneath which rivers flow** (the state where one can achieve all his desires with a variety of knowledge that flows to his consciousness) **as a reward from Allah. The best of rewards are from Allah."**

196. Do not let the comfortable life (based on worldly – bodily pleasures) **of the deniers fool you...**

197. It is a temporary pleasure and satisfaction! In the end their abode will be hell (a place of suffering and burning in deep remorse of not having done the necessary practices). **How wretched a state and condition of life that is!**

198. **As for those who are protected from their Rabb, there are Paradises for them, underneath which rivers flow. They will abide therein eternally with what is revealed to them from Allah** (the forces that are revealed through dimensional emergence to their consciousness from the Names of Allah that comprise their essence). **The things in the sight of Allah are better for the abrar** (those who have reached Allah).

199. Certainly, there are some among those to whom the knowledge of reality has been given, who believe in their essence, the Names of Allah, and in what has been revealed to you, and to what has been revealed to them, in a state of awe towards Allah. They do not exchange the reality of Allah's existence in His signs for a small physical pleasure, which will veil them from this truth! They will have rewards from their Rabb (rewards that manifest from their own composition of Names). **Allah settles accounts instantly.**

200. O believers... Endure (the hardships you encounter) **and vie in patience with one another, be prepared for and in unity against the enemy and protect yourselves from Allah, so you may attain emancipation.**

Note: The meaning of the frequently used phrase "protect yourselves from Allah" according to us is: Since Allah is the constant creator of the consequences of all the thoughts and actions that you produce, if you do not wish to encounter unfavorable situations, avoid the actions and thoughts that lead to them, so you can be protected against the Hasib mechanism in your essence. Allah knows best!

4

AN-NISA

By the one who is denoted by the name Allah (who created my being with His Names in accord with the meaning of the letter 'B'), the Rahman, the Rahim.

1. O mankind, protect yourselves from your Rabb, who created you from a single self (there is only a single concept of 'self' inherent in the totality of all the brains. Depending on the different expressions of the brain this single self varies in attributes and becomes multiple 'selves,' i.e. constructed identities. The original self, however, remains as one, the primary I) and from it, its spouse (the bodily self) and produced from them many men and women and spread them (throughout the earth)! Protect yourselves from Allah (the Names comprising one's essential reality), in whose favor and in the favor of the Rahim (the reality of man formed by the dimension of Names) you ask of one another. For, Allah, with His Names, keeps you under His control (the Raqib) at all times.

2. Give the orphans their properties; do not exchange purity (of your essential reality) to filth (of the ego). Do not consume their properties by mixing them with your own. Indeed, that is a big crime.

3. If you do not have fear dealing justly with orphans (women), then marry those that are clean (of duality) two, or three, or four. But if you fear that you may not be just among them, then (suffice) with one or with what you have in your hands. (Do not live together out of wedlock.) This is the most suitable option to avoid injustice.

4. Give the dowry (marriage gift) to women with love. If they willingly and benevolently give a portion of it back to you, then accept it wholeheartedly.

5. Do not give or entrust your possessions that Allah gave to your management to the dissolute (limited in understanding, the unthinking). But provide for them from it, clothe them and give them beneficial advice.

6. Look out for and test the orphans until they reach a marriageable age. If you see that they are mature enough, then give their

properties back to them. **Do not hasten to consume their property by wasteful spending in fear that they will grow up and take ownership. Let the wealthy one be modest** (and refrain from consuming the properties of orphans) **and the needy one take only as much is customary** (without exceeding the boundary). **And let there be witnesses** (for the evaluation of your actions) **when you return their properties back to them. Sufficient for you is the quality of the Name Hasib from the Names of Allah that comprise your essence.**

7. There is a share for men of what parents and relatives leave behind (with death). **There is also a share for women of what parents and relatives leave behind, be it little or much, this is a share decreed by Allah.**

8. And if relatives, orphans and the needy (who aren't entitled for any share in an inheritance) **are present during the distribution, treat them with kindness and provide a small portion for them as well...**

9. Let them be concerned by Allah just as they would feel concern for their dependent children, if they were to leave them behind. Let them fear Allah and boldly speak the truth.

10. Indeed, those who consume the properties of the orphans are only filling their bellies with fire! A blazing fire is where they will end up.

11. Allah instructs you regarding your children as follows: The share of the male is twice that of the female... But if there are more than two females (children) **then leave for them two thirds of** (the estate); **if** (the heir) **is a single** (female), **then half of the estate is hers... If the testator leaves behind children** (as well as parents), **then for each parent one sixth of the estate should be given. If he has no children and his parents are his only inheritors,** (in this case) **the mother should be given one third and the father the remaining two thirds of the estate... If he leaves behind siblings, then the mother should be given one sixth of what remains after any bequest he may have made or any debt. You fathers and your sons... You cannot know which of them is more worthy of your estate.** (This is why these are) **an obligation from Allah... Indeed, Allah is the Aleem, the Hakim.**

12. (For the men) **half of what your wives leave** (inheritance) **if they have no child is yours; but, if they have a child, one fourth of what remains after any bequest they may have made and debt they may have had... If** (the men) **have no children, then one fourth of what you leave behind is for your wives, but if you have children then one**

eighth of what remains after your bequest (according to Hadith narrations by Bukhari and Muslim the bequest should not exceed one third) and debt... But if a man or woman leaves no ascendants or descendants, but has a brother or a sister, for each one is one sixth... If he has more (siblings) then they share one third of what remains after any bequest or debt... This (division) should not be detrimental... This is an ordinance from Allah... Allah is the Aleem, the Halim.

13. These are boundaries set by Allah. Whoever follows Allah and His Rasul, He will admit them into Paradises underneath which rivers flow. Now, that is a great liberation.

14. And whoever rebels against Allah and His Rasul and transgresses his limits, He will admit them to fire to abide there forever. A degrading suffering he will have.

15. Bring forth four witnesses against women who engage in harlotry. If they (all four of them) testify, confine them to their houses until death takes them, or until Allah opens another path for them (until they repent).

16. And if two men among you commit it, punish them. If they repent and correct themselves, then leave them to their own accord. For Allah is the Tawwab, the Rahim.

17. The type of repentance that is accepted by Allah is one made in regards to a mistake committed in ignorance. Those are the ones whose repentance Allah accepts. Allah is the Aleem, the Hakim.

18. There is no repentance for those who spend a lifetime in wrongdoing and at the time of death say "Now I repent!" And none for those who live in denial of the truth and repent in their last breath! We have prepared severe suffering for them.

19. O believers, it is forbidden for you to forcefully become heirs to women... Do not pressure them in order to take a portion of what you have given them (dowry)... Unless they openly (testified by witnesses) commit harlotry... Get on with them justly... Even if there is something you dislike about them, it may be that Allah has ordained much good in it.

20. If you want to leave one of your wives and take another in her stead, even if you have given them loads (of dowry) do not take it back (when separating). You cannot do this by blaming or slandering her!

21. How can you take it back after you have united with one another and you have given them your word (during marriage)?

22. Do not marry women who your fathers married. Except the past (except what has already occurred in the past). Undoubtedly this is immoral and hateful. Indeed, an awful custom!

23. It has been prohibited for you (to marry): Your mothers, daughters, sisters, aunts, the daughters of your brothers, the daughters of your sisters, your milk mothers who have nursed you, your sisters through nursing, the mothers of your wives, and your stepdaughters under your guardianship (who are born) of your wives with whom you have united. But if you have not united with the mothers of your stepdaughters, then there is no harm in you (marrying them)... And also prohibited for you are the wives of your sons who are from your loins, and to marry two sisters at the same time... Except what has already occurred in the past... Indeed, Allah is the Ghafur, the Rahim.

24. Married women, except whom you possess (as bondmaid), have also been prohibited. This is the decree of Allah upon you... And all others have been made lawful for you (to marry) by spending from your possessions, so that you refrain from adultery and live virtuously. To the women you marry and unite with, give their dowry in full. There is no harm in giving more than this if you mutually agree on it. Most certainly, Allah is the Aleem, the Hakim.

25. Those among you who don't have the means to marry believing free women, can marry believing girls in their possession... Allah (as your essential reality) is aware of your faith... You are from one another... Marry them with the permission of their owners. Give to them (their dowries) according to custom, on the condition they refrain from secret affairs and adultery, and live as chaste women... If they commit harlotry after you have united in marriage, then punish them with half of what free women (in this case) would be punished with... This (marrying bondmaids) is for him who fears doing wrong... Yet to be patient is better for you... Allah is the Ghafur, the Rahim.

26. Allah wants to make clear to you what you don't know, guide you to the good practices of those who came before you, and forgive you your faults. Allah is the Aleem, the Hakim.

27. **Allah wants to accept your repentance** (for your mistakes). **But those who follow their desires** (bodily temptations) **want you to go astray** (from the reality) **in corruption.**

28. **Allah wishes to lighten your burden. Man has been created weak.**

29. **O believers, do not wrongfully** (based on impermissible premises) **consume each other's wealth even if this is through a mutually agreed trade. Do not kill yourselves** (through wrongful deeds). **Indeed, Allah, as the creator of your being with His Names, is the Rahim.**

30. **Whoever does this by transgression and wrongfully, We will make him rest in Hell. This is easy for Allah.**

31. **If you avoid major mistakes** (duality, murder, etc.)**, We will cover your small mistakes and admit you to a place of abundance.**

32. **Do not foster jealousy toward those who Allah raises over others by what He provides for them from His bounty. Men will have the blessings of what they have earned; women will have the blessings of what they have earned. Ask for Allah's bounty. Most certainly, Allah is Aleem over all things** (as their essential reality).

33. **We have appointed heirs for what parents and relatives leave behind. Give their shares to those your oath binds. Allah is a witness to all things.**

34. **Men are protectors over women. Based on qualities Allah manifests from His bounty, some are superior to others; they give from their wealth unrequitedly. Righteous women are respectable and obedient toward their husbands. They guard their unknown with Allah's protection** (they do not unite with other men when alone). **Advise your spouses** (help them to recognize their mistakes)**, whom you suspect may be disobedient** (unable to carry the responsibilities of marriage), (if they resist to understand) **then forsake them in bed, and if this does not help either then strike them** (enough to offend them). **If they obey you then take no further action against them. Indeed, Allah is the Aliy, the Kabir.**

35. **If you fear dissension between them, assign an arbitrator from his family and an arbitrator from her family. If they desire reconciliation, Allah will enable it. Indeed Allah is the Aleem, the Habir.**

36. Serve Allah and do not associate partners (duality) to your essence with anything (do not deify or associate divinity to any form of existence)! Do good to you parents, relatives, orphans, the needy, close neighbors and far neighbors, your fellow traveler, those who are stranded, and those under your hand (in your possession). Indeed, Allah does not like those who are boastful and arrogant.

37. They are stingy and command stinginess upon others, and they hide what Allah gives to them from His bounty. We have prepared a degrading suffering for the deniers of the reality.

38. They spend their wealth as a means to boast, while they believe neither in Allah, the One who has created their essence with His Names, nor in the eternal life to come. Whoever is close to Satan, has indeed a terrible friend.

39. What would they have lost had they believed in Allah, the creator of their essence with His Names, and the eternal life to come, and given to others from what Allah has provided for them? Allah, as the One comprising their essence, is the Aleem.

40. Indeed, Allah does not do wrong to anyone, not even as much as an iota's weight! And if a good deed has been done, He multiplies it and provides a great reward from Himself (ladun; the potential of the Names comprising one's essence).

41. What will be their state when We bring forth a witness from within every community and hold you as a witness to them?

42. In that period, those who denied the reality and those who rebelled against the Rasul will wish to be swallowed by the earth. They will not be able to hide anything from Allah.

43. O believers, do not approach salat when you are not aware of what you do (in a drunken state) until you are conscious of what you are saying, or impure (after sexual intercourse) until you have performed whole body ablution, unless you are traveling. If you are sick or traveling, or come from the place of relieving yourselves (lavatory), or you have had sexual intercourse and you were not able to find water (to wash yourselves; ablution), then seek clean earth and wipe your faces and hands with it. Indeed, Allah is the Afuw, the Ghafur.

44. Do you not see those whom have been given a share of the knowledge of the reality? They buy corruption and want you to go astray from your path (of belief) as well.

45. Of course Allah, as their creator, knows those who are your enemies. Allah, the One who comprises your essence with His Names, is sufficient for you with His Name Waliyy and He will help you from your essence!

46. There are such among the Jews, who pervert the original meanings of the WORDS (they do not preserve the authenticity of the revelations)... They play with their tongues to form false concepts in regards to Religion and to mean: "We hear and we disobey", "Hear, but do not be heard" and "Raina – limited in understanding." If they had said, "We hear and we obey", "Hear" and "Unzurna – watch over us" it would have been better and more correct for them... But Allah has damned them due to their denial of their essential reality... Except for a very few of them, they do not believe.

47. O those to whom the knowledge of the reality has been given, before We erase your faces and turn them toward your backs (before we erase your knowledge and return you to your previous perversity), or curse you as We cursed the Sabbath-breakers, come and believe in that which We have revealed (the Quran) to confirm the knowledge of the reality that is already with you... The decree of Allah has been fulfilled.

48. Indeed, Allah does not forgive (apparent or discrete forms of) shirq (i.e. directly or indirectly assuming the existence of beings 'other' than Allah, whether external objects [apparent] or our own egos [discrete], thereby fragmenting the non-dual reality), but He forgives lesser sins other than this (ma doona – 'lesser sins' here connotes the perception that actions are initiated by the self/ego rather than by Allah), as He wills... And whoever associates partners to Allah, the essential reality of his being with His Beautiful Names (B'illahi), he would surely have made a tremendous mistake by slandering.

49. Do you not see those who consider themselves clean (the Christians and Jews who claim to be pure even though they are in a state of duality)? No (it is not as they think), Allah purifies whom He wills and they will not be wronged, not even as much as a thread in a date seed.

50. Look at how they lie and slander Allah! There cannot be a crime more evident than this!

51. Do you see those to whom a share of the knowledge of the reality has been given? They believe in Jibt (an idol assumed to

possess power) **and Taghut** (satanic forces) **and tell the deniers of the reality, "They are on a path more righteous than the believers."**

52. **They are the ones whom Allah cursed** (distanced from Himself). **And whoever Allah curses, there is no one to help him!**

53. **Or have they a share of sovereignty? Had that been the case they would not have even given as much as a date seed to the people.**

54. **Or are they unable to accept what Allah has given to them from His bounty and are envious? Indeed, we have given the knowledge of the reality and Wisdom** (knowledge of sunnatullah) **to the family of Abraham. We have given them a great sovereignty.**

55. **Some of them believed in what he had, and some denied. Sufficient is the fire of hell** (internal and external suffering) **for them.**

56. **Indeed, We will burn those who deny our signs** (the manifestation of the Names in their essence) **in the fire. So they may taste the suffering more, every time their skins are burnt** (due to their external attachments) **we will replace them with new skins** (externality). **Surely Allah is the Aziz, the Hakim.**

57. **As for those who believe and do as their faith requires, We will admit them to Paradises underneath which rivers flow. Forever they will abide therein. There they will have partners, purified** (from satanic traits). **We will place them in the shade of shades** (an environment far from any burning or discomforting condition).

58. **Indeed, Allah commands that you give the trusts to their rightful owners and that you judge between people justly** (giving everyone their due rights). **An excellent advice Allah gives you. Indeed, Allah is the Sami and the Basir.**

59. **O believers! Obey Allah and obey the Rasul, and those within you who are ulul amr** (have the authority to judge based on the knowledge of the reality and sunnatullah)... **When you fall into dispute concerning something – if you believe in Allah and the eternal life to come – turn that thing over to Allah and His Rasul... This is better and more appropriate an evaluation** (for correctly resolving the situation).

60. **Do you not see those who assume to believe in what has been revealed to you and revealed before you... even though they have been ordered to reject it, they wish to appoint Taghut as an**

arbitrator among themselves... Satan desires to lead them so astray that they can never turn back.

61. When they are told, "Come to what Allah has revealed and the Rasul," you will see the hypocrites turn away and distance themselves from you.

62. Yet when a calamity strikes them as a result of their actions they say, "B'illahi (by the reality of Allah) we intended nothing other than good and conciliation."

63. Those are the ones whom Allah knows what is in their hearts. Do not heed what they say, give them advice and notify them about the reality of their selves in a clear and apparent manner.

64. We have revealed every Rasul for them to be obeyed with the permission of Allah. Had they come to you after having wronged themselves and asked for forgiveness from Allah, and if the Rasul had asked for forgiveness on their behalf, they would surely have found Allah to be the Tawwab and the Rahim.

65. But that is not the case! By your Rabb, until they appoint you as an arbitrator for the conflicts between themselves, and comply with your judgment in full submission and without feeling any internal discomfort (objection), they would not have believed.

66. If We had written upon them "kill your selves" (be willing to die for the sake of Allah) or "leave your homes", except for a very few of them, they would not have done it. Had they followed the advice given to them, surely it would have been better and healthier for them.

67. Then We would surely have given them a great reward from Our ladun.

68. We would have guided them to the straight path.

69. Whoever obeys Allah and the Rasul, they will be companions of the Nabis, the loyal ones, the martyrs and the rightly guided ones, whom Allah has blessed. And excellent companions they are.

70. This bounty is from Allah. Sufficient is Allah for them, their essential reality with His Names.

71. O believers, be cautious, go to war in groups or altogether.

72. Indeed, there are some among you who linger behind. So if a disaster strikes you, he says, "Thank Allah I was not with them, Allah has favored me".

73. And if a favor (and success) from Allah reaches you, he says, "I wish I were with them so I could have had a share in their success," as if there were no cause for closeness between him and you.

74. Let those who are willing to give up their worldly life in exchange for the eternal life to come, fight in the way of Allah. And whoever fights and is killed or victorious in the way of Allah, We will give him a great reward.

75. What is the matter with you that you refrain from fighting for feeble men, women and children who cry, "Our Rabb, deliver us from this land of oppressors; grant us a patron and victory from Your Self (ladun)."

76. Believers fight in the way of Allah. As for those who deny the reality, they fight for the forces of Satan. Then fight the allies of Satan. Indeed, the trap of Satan is weak.

77. Did you not see those who were told, "Avoid bad things, establish salat, and pay alms"? But when fighting was ordained for them, alas, some of them were as terrified of people as the awe and fear they feel towards Allah, or even more... "Our Rabb, why did You ordain fighting for us; if only You had postponed it for a short time," they said... Say, "The pleasure of this world is little! The eternal life to come is better for the protected ones... You will not be wronged as much as a single date thread (i.e. in the slightest)."

78. Death will find you wherever you are. Even if you were within tall and sturdy towers... But if good comes to them, they say, "This is from Allah"; and if evil befalls them, they say, "This is from you." Say, "All of it is from Allah!" What is the matter with people that they do not try to understand the reality!

79. Whatever good comes to you it is from Allah, but whatever evil comes to you it is from your self (from complying with your conditioned beliefs including your alleged 'moral codes'). We have revealed you as a Rasul for the people. Sufficient is Allah, as your essence with His Names, as a Witness for you.

80. Whoever obeys the Rasul, obeys Allah in the reality! And whoever turns away (it is up to him), We have not revealed you (as a guard) over them.

81. "Aye" they say, yet as soon as you leave them, a group of them begin to contrive things against what you say during the night. Allah records their contrivances! Turn away from them and trust in Allah, refer your dealings to Him! Sufficient is Allah's Wakil quality in your essence, as an agent.

82. Do they not contemplate on the Quran in depth? If it were from a place other than Allah it would have been filled with many contradictions!

83. When they receive news regarding their safety or one that frightens them they hasten to spread it. Yet, if they had asked the Rasul or one with authority (ulul amr) they could have found out what the truth of the matter is. If it were not for Allah's bounty and grace upon you, except for a very few of you, most of you would have followed Satan (in this).

84. Fight in the way of Allah! You have no responsibility but to yourself! Encourage the believers, that perhaps Allah will weaken the might of the deniers of the reality. The might of Allah, and the consequences He enforces, are much more severe.

85. Whoever is a cause for good shall have a share of that good... And whoever is a cause for bad shall have a share in that bad... Allah is Muqeet over all things.

86. When someone greets you with a greeting greet him back with a more comprehensive greeting or one that is the like. Indeed Allah is Hasib over all things (enforces the consequences of all that becomes manifest).

87. Allah is HU; there is no god or godhood, only HU! He will bring you together in the period of Doomsday, of whose coming there is no doubt. And who can be more truthful in statement than Allah!

88. What is the matter with you that you were divided into two groups regarding the hypocrites, when Allah had made them fall back due to their misdeeds? Do you think you can guide those who Allah leads astray? Whoever Allah leads astray, you can no longer find a way for him.

89. They wish you would deny the reality as they do so that you can be alike... So do not take them as friends until they abandon oppression and wrongdoing... If they turn away (as enemies), then seize them and kill them wherever you find them... Do not take them as friends and helpers.

90. Except for those who take refuge with a community with whom you have a treaty, or who come to you with their hearts strained because they do not wish to fight you or their own people... If Allah had willed, He would set them upon you and they would have fought you... So if they leave you alone, do not fight you and offer you peace, then Allah does not allow you to harm them.

91. On the other hand, you will find that some want security from you and their own people... Every time they encounter a situation that is a cause for trial, they are taken aback... So if they do not stay away from you, offer you peace, and restrain their hands from you, then seize them and kill them wherever you catch them... And those, We have given you clear power over them.

92. It is not for a believer to kill another believer, except by mistake... And whoever kills a believer by mistake should free a believing slave and pay compensation to the family of the deceased, unless they give up (their rights to the killer)... If (the deceased) was a believer but from a people that is enemy to you, then (the killer) must free a believing slave... But if (the deceased) was from a people with whom you have a treaty, then (the killer) must pay compensation to the deceased's family and free a believing slave... And whoever is unable to find compensation must fast for two months consecutively, as repentance to Allah... Allah is the Aleem, the Hakim.

93. And whoever kills a believer intentionally, his recompense is hell wherein he will abide eternally. Allah has become angry with him, cursed him and prepared for him severe suffering.

94. O believers... When you go to war in the way of Allah, investigate well, and if one gives you a greeting (wants to make peace) do not say, "You are not a believer" aspiring for the goods of the worldly life... There are many spoils in the sight of Allah... You were like that yourself before, then Allah conferred His favor upon you... So research well... Indeed, Allah, as the creator of what you do, is the Habir.

95. Not equal are those who stay behind from war without a valid reason and those who fight in the way of Allah with their possessions and their lives (their sense of self)... Allah has raised the degree of those who struggle with their possessions and their lives over those who stay behind. Allah has given the best to all of them. But Allah has preferred those who strive in His cause over those who stay back, with a great reward.

96. Degrees, forgiveness and grace (He has given). **Allah is the Ghafur and the Rahim.**

97. Indeed, the angels told those who are in a state of doing wrong to themselves while they are taken by death, "In what condition were you? (Why were you in a state of doing wrong to yourselves?)"... **They said, "We were weak and helpless on earth"...** (The angels) **said, "Was Allah's earth not vast enough for you to migrate therein?"... Their refuge will be hell... What a wretched end!**

98. Except those who do not have the means to migrate – helpless men, women and children.

99. It is expected that Allah will pardon them. Allah is the Afuw, the Ghafur.

100. Whoever migrates (from a land in which he is oppressed) **in the way of Allah** (based on the verse 'flee to Allah'; migrate to your essential reality) **will find immense vastness on earth... Whoever leaves his home as a migrant to Allah and His Rasul** (with the reality disclosed by them) **and then dies on this way, his reward will be from Allah... Allah is the Ghafur, the Rahim.** (We have tried to highlight an inner meaning here alongside the obvious physical connotation of this verse.)

101. And when you are traveling throughout the land, there is no harm in shortening your salat (prayers) **if you fear the deniers of the reality may harm you. Indeed, those deniers or concealers of the reality are clear enemies to you.**

102. (My Rasul) **when you are among them** (but in an unsafe state) **and you lead them in prayer** (salat), **let a group of them stand in salat next to you while armed with their weapons... When they prostrate let the others stand in guard behind you... Then have the others come forward, who have not yet prayed, and let them pray with you... Let them take precautions and arms... The deniers of the reality wish for you to be negligent of your weapons and possessions so they may attack you suddenly. But if you are overtaken by rain or illness, there is no harm in leaving your arms...** (Though) **you should still take precautions... Indeed, Allah has prepared a degrading suffering for the deniers of the reality.**

103. When you have finished your salat (in an unsafe environment), **remember Allah while standing, sitting, or** (lying) **on your sides** (i.e. experience Him in your being at all times)**... When you feel satiated with the remembrance** (dhikr), **perform your salat** (duly experience the essence of salat with the sensitivity and receptivity incited by dhikr). **Indeed, the experience of salat at specific times has been inscribed upon the believers.**

104. Do not relent in the pursuit of the enemy... If you are suffering, they too are suffering just the same... Yet you can wish from Allah things that they cannot hope for... Allah is the Aleem, the Hakim.

105. Most certainly We have revealed the knowledge of the reality to you, so that you judge among the people by the Truth shown by Allah. Do not defend the traitors!

106. Ask for forgiveness from Allah. Indeed, Allah is the Ghafur, the Rahim.

107. Do not defend those who have betrayed themselves! Indeed, Allah does not like those who persist in betraying themselves.

108. (The two-faced hypocrites) **can hide from others but not from Allah! For He was present with them** (according to Sufism this denotes the unity of existence; that Allah creates every iota of existence with His Names) **when they were plotting during the night, things which He does not like. Allah is the Mu'id of what they do!**

109. You may defend them in the worldly life, but who will defend them during the period of Doomsday, and who will represent them?

110. Whoever commits a crime or wrongs himself (because of his ego, by assigning a separate existence to himself; duality) **then** (realizing his mistake) **repents to Allah, Allah is the Ghafur, the Rahim** (He forgives and enables the experience of the beauties from His grace)...

111. And whoever commits a crime, its consequence are for him alone (nobody else)! **Allah is the Aleem, the Hakim.**

112. Whoever does wrong or commits a crime and then blames an innocent person for it, he would indeed have committed open slander and a grave offence.

113. If it wasn't for the bounty of Allah upon you and the grace of HU, a group of them would surely have attempted to mislead you... But they only mislead themselves! They cannot cause you any harm! Allah revealed (from the dimension of Names to your consciousness) **the Book** (knowledge of the reality) **and Wisdom** (the knowledge of religion and sunnatullah) **to you, and taught you that which you did not know... The bounty of Allah upon you is great.**

114. There is no good in much of their private gatherings and interactions! Except those gatherings involving aid, benefit or reconciliation (and similar beneficial activities). Whoever does this seeking the pleasure of Allah, We will give him a great reward.

115. Whoever opposes the Rasul after the reality becomes clearly evident; We will abandon him in his path and lead him to hell in the end! What a wretched destination that is!

116. Allah will definitely not forgive shirq (duality) in regards to Him! But He forgives lesser faults other than this (offences lower than duality), for whom He wills... And whoever commits shirq (duality; assumes a separate existence independent of Him) to Allah (B'illahi), the creator of the entire existence with His Names, he has surely fallen into a corrupt belief far astray (from the reality)!

117. Those who turn to things other than Allah turn only to lifeless female deities in His stead, and hence they turn to none but the persistent malicious Satan (ego)!

118. Allah has cursed (Iblis)... For Iblis had said, "I will surely take from among Your servants a significant portion"...

119. "And I will surely mislead them, and I will arouse in them (sinful, bodily, empty) desires, and I will command them so they slit the ears of cattle (as sacrifice), and I will command them so they will alter the creation of Allah." And whoever deserts Allah and takes Satan (bodily temptations; ego) as master has certainly suffered a great loss.

120. Satan promises them and arouses false hope and desire in them. But Satan does not promise anything except delusion.

121. The destination of such people is hell (the state of suffering)! And they will have no way to escape it.

122. As for those who believe and live according to their faith (engaging in good deeds), We will admit them to Paradises underneath which rivers flow... They will reside therein eternally (as a result of the manifestation of the Names of Allah)... This is the promise of Allah in Truth! Is anyone more truthful than Allah?

123. (Sunnatullah – the system and order of Allah) is not according to your wishful thinking, nor the wishful thinking of those to whom the knowledge of the reality was given before you (and who failed to appraise it)! Whoever does wrong will live its consequences! (After

which) **he will not be able to find any protector or helper other than Allah!**

124. Whoever, as a believer, does a good deed, whether male or female, they will be admitted to Paradise, not an iota of their deeds will be lost.

125. Whose understanding of religion can be better than he who follows the people of Abraham as a doer of good (with the comprehension that his being is the manifestation of Allah's Names) **and in submission to Allah** (without the concept of a deity; with the consciousness of being in servitude to Allah alone) **and as a Hanif! Allah took Abraham as an intimate friend** (Halil; Abraham was blessed with the station of Hullet) (More information on this topic can be found in The Perfect Man by Abdulkareem Al-Jili).

126. Whatever is in the heavens and the earth is for Allah (for the manifestation of the meanings denoted by the Names). **Allah, as the creator of all things with His Names, is the Mu'id.**

127. They request a legal ruling concerning women... Say, "Allah already gives you a ruling about them!" It is already recited to you **how you do not give the rights decreed to the orphan girls and yet you desire to marry them, and how you need to be just to the children and the orphans... Whatever good you do, Allah is certainly Aleem of it** (for He is the creator of the good that you do).

128. If a woman fears ill-treatment from her husband or that he will forsake her, there is no fault in them seeking reconciliation... Reconciliation is best; the self (ego identities) **is prone to ambition... If you do good and protect yourselves, surely Allah is Habir of what you do** (as their creator).

129. No matter how hard you try you will never be able to treat your wives with equal fairness! (At least) **try not to neglect the others altogether while showing extra attention to one! If you be fair and protect yourselves, indeed Allah is the Ghafur, the Rahim.**

130. If (a husband and wife) **decide to separate, Allah will maintain them from His abundance, He will not leave them in need of each other. Allah is the Wasi, the Hakim.**

131. Whatever is in the heavens and the earth is for Allah (for the manifestation of the qualities denoted by the Most Beautiful Names)! **We advised you and those who came before you, "Protect yourselves from Allah"... If you deny the reality** (know that) **assuredly whatever**

is in the heavens and the earth is for Allah! Allah is the Ghani, the Hamid.

132. Whatever is in the heavens and the earth is for Allah (for the observation of the meanings denoted by the Most Beautiful Names)! Sufficient for you as Wakil is Allah, the One who created you with His Names.

133. O mankind, if He wills He can do away with you and bring others in your place! Allah has the power to do so!

134. Whoever desires the bounties of this world should know that both the bounties of this world and eternal life to come are from Allah. Allah is the Sami, the Basir.

135. O believers, be determined in the way of applying justice! Testify in the way of Allah even if this goes against your relatives or parents, whether rich or poor; for the right of Allah is higher than both! So do not follow your false conditionings to establish justice! If you distort the reality, certainly Allah, as the creator of your actions, is Habir.

136. O you who have believed, believe in Allah, and His Rasul, and in what He revealed to his Rasul (from the dimension of Names to his consciousness) and to those who came before you, in accord with the meaning signified by the letter B (Aminu B'illahi)... Whoever covers (denies) Allah, the creator of all with His Names, His angels (the forces which manifest the meanings of His Names), His Books (the knowledge of the reality He reveals), His Rasuls and the eternal life to come, has surely gone far astray in his faith.

137. Indeed, those who believe (first) then deny, then believe again (temporarily) and then deny (again) and increase in denial, Allah will neither forgive them nor give them direction.

138. Give tidings to the two-faced (hypocrites) of the severe suffering awaiting them!

139. Do those who leave the believers and befriend the deniers of the reality hope to find honor with them? Honor belongs entirely to Allah.

140. Revealed to you is this knowledge: Do not sit in an environment where the signs of Allah are denied or inappropriate things are spoken about them; until they change the subject! Otherwise, you will be just like them. (This verse should be evaluated

in the light of the scientific truth of 'mirror neurons.' This verse is clearly a miracle in respect of expressing a modern discovery almost 1500 years ago!) **Allah will bring the two-faced** (hypocrites) **and the deniers of the reality together in hell.**

141. **They watch to see what will become of you... If Allah gives you victory, they will say, "Were we not with you also?" If a success comes to the deniers, they say, "Have we not surpassed you, have we not protected you against the believers?" Allah will judge between you during the Doomsday period. Allah will not give the deniers of the reality a cause against the believers.**

142. **The hypocrites try to deceive Allah,** (whereas) **Allah turns the result of their deception against them! When they stand for prayer, they stand reluctantly, to show themselves to others, and they remember Allah very little.**

143. (The hypocrites) **waver between the two sides! Neither belonging to the people of faith, nor the deniers! And you can never find a way for those who Allah leads astray** (in faith)!

144. **O believers, do not leave the believers and befriend the deniers of the reality! Do you want to give Allah a strong case against yourself** (with this behavior)!

145. **Indeed the two-faced** (hypocrites) **are at the lowest depths of fire! And never will there be a helper for them!**

146. **Except those who** (realize their mistake and) **repent, fix their attitudes, cling to Allah with their essential reality, and purify their understanding of faith in the way of Allah... They are with the people of faith. And Allah will give the people of faith a great reward.**

147. **Why should Allah make you suffer you if you are grateful and believe! Allah is the Shakur, the Aleem.**

148. **Except by those who have been wronged, Allah does not like the utterance of offensive words! Allah is the Sami, the Aleem.**

149. **Whether you reveal or hide a good, or pardon a bad; Allah is the Afuw, the Qadir.**

150. **Those who deny Allah and His Rasuls, want to cause separation between Allah and His Rasuls. They say, "We believe in some of them and deny some." They want to adopt a position in**

between. (Another way to look at this is: They want to reject the reality and concept of 'revelation,' which is the manifestation of Allah's Names, and spread the concept of 'an external heavenly deity and His chosen prophet on earth' instead.)

151. They are the ones who completely deny the reality. We have prepared a degrading suffering for the deniers.

152. As for those who believe Allah's Names comprise the essence of all creation and in the (disclosure of) Rasuls, and who do not discriminate between them (in respect of their disclosure) Allah will give their rewards. Allah is the Ghafur, the Rahim.

153. The people of the book (the Jews) want you to bring down "a book from the heavens" for them... In truth, they had asked for something even greater from Moses... They had said, "Show us Allah outright," and the lightning struck them because of their wrongdoing... After clear proofs came to them, they took to worshiping a calf... We forgave even this and gave Moses an evident power.

154. We raised Mount Sinai over them so they keep their covenant, and told them, "Enter the gate in prostration." And We said, "Do not transgress the Sabbath" and took from them a solemn covenant.

155. We recompensed them for breaking their covenant, denying the existence of Allah in His signs (the manifestations of His Names), killing the Nabis against the will of the Truth and for saying "Our hearts are sealed" (our consciousness is cocooned). Indeed, We locked their understanding because of their denial! Except for a few of them, they will not believe!

156. For denying the reality and uttering a great slander against Mary!

157. And for saying, "We killed the Rasul of Allah, Jesus, the son of Mary"... In truth, they neither killed nor crucified him, but it was made to appear to them so (the crucified one). Those who argue about this are in doubt of it; they have no certain knowledge about it, they only talk with assumptions. What is certain is that Jesus was definitely not killed!

158. On the contrary, Allah raised him to Himself! Allah is the Aziz, the Hakim.

159. And there is no one who complied with the knowledge of the reality (in the past) who did not believe in him (his teachings) at the moment of death! He will be a witness against them during the Doomsday period.

160. We made many lawful bounties unlawful for them (the Jews), because of their wrongdoing and for preventing others from realizing their essential reality!

161. This (act of making things unlawful) was because they partook in usury even though it was forbidden to them and they unjustly consumed the property of others. And We have prepared severe suffering for those who persist in denying the reality.

162. Those among them who have attained depth in knowledge and the believers, believe in what was revealed to you as well as what was revealed before you. Those who perform their salat and give zakat and believe in Allah and the eternal life to come based on the meaning signified by the letter 'B'... We will give them a great reward.

163. We have revealed to you just as We had revealed to Noah and the Nabis after him... And We revealed to Abraham, Ishmael, Isaac, Jacob, the descendants, Jesus, Job, Jonah, Aaron and Solomon... We gave David the book of Psalms (Zabur; the knowledge of wisdom).

164. We have also revealed (to Rasuls) whose stories We have related to you or have not related to you... Allah spoke to Moses word by word.

165. We sent Rasuls as bringers of glad tidings and as warners so that mankind will have no argument against Allah after these Rasuls (the knowledge they provide)! Allah is the Aziz, the Hakim.

166. But Allah bears witness to that which He revealed to you, He has revealed it to you as the knowledge of HU. The angels (the forces pertaining to this revelation; Gabriel) also bear witness to this fact. Sufficient for you is Allah as a witness.

167. Those who deny the reality and prevent others from the way of Allah have gone far astray.

168. Indeed Allah will neither forgive nor open a path (of understanding) for those who deny the reality and who do wrong.

169. **Except for the path of hell** (the understanding that leads to a life of hell)**! They will abide therein eternally. This is easy for Allah.**

170. **O mankind, the Rasul has come to you from your Rabb in Truth! So believe in what is good for you! If you deny, know that whatever is in the heavens and the earth is for Allah** (for the manifestation of the qualities denoted by the Names of Allah). **Allah is the Aleem, the Hakim.**

171. **O those to whom the knowledge of the reality has come... Do not exceed the requirements of religion and transgress... Do not utter things that are not true about Allah... Jesus, the son of Mary, is only a Rasul of Allah and His Word... He has formed the manifestation of this quality through Mary, and he is a meaning** (spirit) **from Him** (His Beautiful Names)**... So believe in Allah, the essence of all things with His Names, and His Rasuls... And do not say "Three"** (the Father, the Son, the Spirit)**! End this; it is better for you... Allah is the One and Only** (the only One who has Uluhiyyah)**... HU is Subhan from the concept of having a child! Whatever is in the heavens and the earth is for Him... Sufficient for you is Allah as Wakil, your essential reality with His Names.**

172. **Neither the Messiah** (Jesus) **nor the great angels will disdain from being a servant to Allah! And whoever disdains from serving Him and is arrogant, He will gather them all unto Himself.**

173. **As for those who believe and fulfill the requirements of their faith, He is going to give their rewards in full and grant them more from His bounty... But those who disdain and are arrogant, He is going to punish them with a great suffering... And they will not be able to find a friend or a helper for themselves besides Allah.**

174. **O mankind! There has truly come to you a proof** (the articulation of the truth; Muhammad saw)**... We have revealed a clear Nur** (light of knowledge) **to you** (the Quran).

175. **"As for those who believe in Allah, the essence of everything, and hold fast unto Him as their essential reality – HU will admit them to grace** (rahmah) **and bounty** (the awareness of the qualities of the Names) **and guide them to Himself** (enable the observation of their innermost essence) **on the straight path** (sirat al-mustaqim)**."**

176. **They ask for an explanation – a judgment from you... Say, "Allah gives a ruling about one who has neither ascendants** (parents) **nor descendants** (children) **as heir: If a man dies and leaves no**

children but a sister, she will have half of what he has left... If a sister with no children dies, the brother will be the heir... If there are two sisters (of the deceased man) they will have two thirds of what he (their brother) left... If the siblings (the heirs) are brothers and sisters, then the male will have the share of two females"... Allah informs you so that you do not go astray... Allah is Aleem of all things, as their essential reality with His Names.

5

AL-MA'IDAH

By the one who is denoted by the name Allah (who created my being with His Names in accord with the meaning of the letter 'B'), the Rahman, the Rahim.

1. O believers, fulfill your contracts in full... Grazing livestock (sheep, cattle, goat, camel, etc.) has been made permissible for you with the condition that you do not consider hunting lawful animals for yourselves while you are in ihram, and except for that with which you have been informed... Indeed Allah ordains what He wills.

2. O believers! Do not disrespect the rites of Allah (the signs of Allah; that which evokes or causes to feel and perceive Allah) the sacred months, the sacrifices offered to the Baytullah, special sacrifices and to those who come to the Bayt in search of the bounty and the pleasure of their Rabb... You can hunt once you come out of ihram... Do not let your hatred towards a people who (previously) prevented you from entering the Masjid al-Haram lead you to transgress your boundaries... Help each other based on the essence of the reality (albirra) and taqwa (protecting yourself in the way of Allah from the inadequacies of your identity) not on wrongdoing and enmity... Protect yourselves from Allah (as He will enforce upon you the consequences of your actions). Certainly Allah is shadid-ul iqab (the Enforcer of the consequences of wrongdoings).

3. Prohibited to you is the flesh of dead animals, blood, the flesh of swine, and that which has been slaughtered in a name other than Allah. Also prohibited to you is the flesh of animals that are killed by strangling, or by beating, or in a fall, or skinned to death, or killed and partly eaten by a wild animal, or sacrificed on stone altars. Also, seeking fortune (in regards to the future) by divining arrows (or other fortune telling methods)! All of this is corruption. Those who deny the reality today have given up on invalidating your religion... So fear them not, but be in awe of Me. This day I have perfected for you your religion (your acquisition of religious knowledge) and completed My favor upon you and have approved for you Islam (complete submission to Allah) as (the understanding of) religion... Whoever is forced by severe hunger to eat of these may do

so, without assuming what is unlawful to be lawful... Indeed, Allah is the Ghafur, the Rahim.

4. They ask you what has been made permissible to them... Say, "All good and clean foods have been made permissible to you... And those caught by the hunting animals that you have trained in the way of Allah, so eat what they catch for you and speak the name of Allah upon them... Certainly Allah is (Shadid-ul Iqab: the Enforcer of the consequences of wrongdoings).

5. This day, all good and pure foods have been made permissible to you... The food of those to whom the knowledge of the reality has been given is permissible to you... And your food is permissible to them... And the chaste women from among the believers and those to whom the knowledge of the reality was given before you are permissible (in marriage) to you, with the condition that you give their due dowry, and they stay away from adultery and refrain from secret affairs... Whoever disregards the conditions and requirements of faith and denies the reality, all his work will become worthless and he will be among the losers in the eternal life to come.

6. O believers... When you rise to perform salat, wash your faces and your arms up to your elbows with water; wipe over your heads and wash your feet up to your ankles... If you are in a state of impurity (janabah) then wash your whole body... If you are ill or traveling or have been to the lavatory or if you have slept with women and you cannot find water, then seek clean earth and wipe your faces and hands with clean earth... Allah does not wish to make difficulty for you, but He wills to purify you and complete the favor of HU upon you; that you may be thankful (and evaluate).

7. Remember the favor of Allah upon you and the covenant with which He bound you when you said, "We hear and we obey"... Protect yourselves from Allah! Indeed Allah, as your essence with His Names, knows what is inside you.

8. O believers... Be steadfast in the way of Allah, and be just when you bear witness... Do not let your hatred for a people lead you to be unjust! Be just, this approach is nearer to protection... Protect yourselves from Allah! Indeed Allah (as their creator) is Habir of all your actions.

9. Allah has promised those who believe and live as their faiths require, "There is forgiveness and a great reward for them."

10. As for those who deny the reality and our signs (the manifestations of the Names) **they are the people of hell.**

11. O believers... Remember the favor of Allah upon you... Remember when a community wanted to lay their hands on you (harm you) **and He had pulled their hands away from you... Protect yourselves from Allah! Let the believers place their trust in Allah** (believe that the Name Wakil in their essence will fulfill its function).

12. Verily, Allah took a covenant from the Children of Israel... We rose among them twelve representatives... Allah had said, "I am indeed with you... If you perform salat, give zakah (alms)**, believe in the Rasuls and support them, and give Allah a good loan** (based on the emphasis 'I am indeed with you,' the loans you give to others are loans that are given to Allah)**, I will remove your wrongdoings and admit you to Paradises underneath which rivers flow... Whoever denies the reality after this has surely gone astray from the straight path."**

13. We have cursed them for breaking their covenant and hardened their hearts (locked their perception)**! They distort the meanings of words and have forgotten to take a share of the realities with which they have been cautioned. Except for a very few, you will see deceit from them... Forgive them and do not worry! Indeed, Allah loves the doers of good.**

14. And We had taken a covenant from those who say, "We are Christians!" They also forgot to take a share from what they were reminded of... So We caused among them animosity and hatred until the period of Doomsday... Allah will show them what they produce and do.

15. O those to whom the knowledge of the reality has been given... There has come to you Our Rasul who informs you of the many truths you conceal pertaining to the reality and who forgives most of you (for concealing it)**... Indeed, there has come to you a Nur from Allah and a Clear Book** (the clear knowledge of the sunnatullah).

16. Allah guides those who follow His pleasure (the faculty of realization within man's essence) **to the reality, with the qualities of the Names; the reality of Allah. Based on the appropriateness of their Name compositions, He will take them out of darkness to Nur, and guide them to a righteous life.**

17. Indeed, those who said, "Allah is the Messiah, the son of Mary" has denied the reality! Say, "Who has the power to prevent Allah if He chooses to destroy the Messiah, the son of Mary, his mother, and everyone else on earth?"... Everything in the heavens, the earth and in between is for Allah (for the manifestation and observation of the Names)! He creates what He wills! Allah is Qadir over all things.

18. The Jews and the Christians say, "We are the sons and the beloveds of Allah"... Say, "Then why does He punish you for your mistakes?"... No, you are also humans created by Him... He forgives whom He wills and abandons whom He wills to suffering... The dominion of the heavens, the earth and everything in between is for Allah... To Him is the return!

19. O those to whom the knowledge of the reality has been given... There has come to you a Rasul informing you of the truth, in a period of suspension between Rasuls... So that you don't say, "A bringer of tidings and a warner has not come to us"... Here is the bringer of tidings and warner... Allah is Qadir over all things.

20. Moses once said to his people, "My people, remember the favor of Allah upon you, He disclosed Nabis from within you and appointed you as rulers, He gave to you what He did not give to anyone else in the worlds (the knowledge pertaining to vicegerency upon earth)."

21. "My people, enter the Holy Land that Allah has assigned to you and do not turn back to the past, lest you turn back as losers."

22. They said, "O Moses, indeed a despot community lives there... Until they abandon this place we will not enter it... If they leave with their own will, then we will enter it."

23. Two men, upon whom Allah had bestowed His blessings, from the community they feared, said, "Enter upon them through the gate, for when you enter, you will prevail... If you are believers then place your trust in Allah (believe the Name Wakil in your essence will fulfill its function)."

24. They said, "O Moses, as long as they are there, we will never enter it... Go, you and your Rabb, and fight! Indeed we are sitting right here."

25. (Moses) said, "My Rabb... Indeed, my word has no bearing on anyone other than myself and my brother, so part us from the people (whose faith is) corrupt."

26. He said, "Indeed, that place has been forbidden for them. For forty years they will wander the earth confused... So do not grieve over those (whose faith is) corrupt."

27. Tell them the truth about the two sons of Adam... How they had both offered a sacrifice, where one was accepted and the other wasn't... (Cain, whose sacrifice was not accepted) said, "I will surely kill you"... (Abel, whose sacrifice was accepted) said, "Allah accepts only from the muttaqeen (those who live in line with their essential reality)."

28. "If you raise your hand to kill me, I promise I shall not raise my hand to kill you! For, I fear Allah, the Rabb of the worlds!"

29. "I want you to take on my sin and your own sin so you will be among the companions of the fire... This is the consequence of the wrongdoers!"

30. Finally, the ambition and jealousy driven by his ego made it easy for him (Cain) to kill his brother (Abel), so he killed him... Thus he became of the losers.

31. Then Allah disclosed a crow to him, grubbing the earth, showing him how to bury his brother's corpse... Cain said to himself, "Woe unto me! I am not even like this crow to know how to bury the corpse of my brother!" And he became of the regretful.

32. This is why we decreed upon the Children of Israel, "Whoever kills a person except (as retribution) for a (murdered) person or for spreading corruption in the land, it is as if he has killed the whole of mankind... And whoever saves a person's life, it is as if he has saved the whole of mankind..." Indeed, there has come to them our Rasuls as clear proofs; but after this most of them still squander on earth (do not evaluate what We have given them).

33. The retribution for those who fight with Allah and His Rasul, and strive to spread corruption on earth, is to be killed, or hung, or have their hands and feet cut crosswise, or to be prisoned. This is a disgrace for them in this world... And there is great suffering for them in the eternal life to come.

34. Except for those who repent before you seize them... Know well that Allah is the Ghafur, the Rahim.

35. O believers! Protect yourselves from Allah; ask for a cause to enable your closeness to Him and strive with determination on His path so that you may attain emancipation.

36. As for those who deny the reality, if they had everything on earth and twice as much again and offered it to ransom themselves from the suffering of the Doomsday period, it will never be accepted from them! A sad suffering awaits them.

37. They will want to escape the fire, but they will not be able to do so... Theirs shall be a perpetual suffering!

38. Cut off the hands of thieves, whether male or female, as an exemplary lesson from Allah for what they have done! Allah is the Aziz, the Hakim.

39. But whoever repents after his wrongdoing and corrects (his conduct) Allah will surely accept his repentance... Indeed Allah is the Ghafur, the Rahim.

40. Do you not know the (reality) sovereignty of the heavens and the earth is for Allah? He punishes whom He wills and rewards whom He wills! Allah is Qadir over all things.

41. O Rasul! Do not be grieved by those who say "We have believed" with their tongues while they have not believed with their hearts (consciously, by internalizing and experiencing its meaning) and who compete in denial... There are some among the Jews who listen to you to make lies, or as mediators on behalf of people who do not come to you... They pervert the meanings of the words and say, "If this be given to you, take it, but if not (if instead, a judgment is made based on Allah's laws) then stay away"... If Allah wills corruption for someone, you can no longer expect anything from Allah on his behalf... They are the ones whose hearts Allah does not wish to purify... There is disgrace for them in the world... And a severe suffering awaits them in the eternal life to come.

42. They constantly listen to lies and devour forbidden things... If they come to you, then judge between them, or turn away from them... If you turn away from them, they cannot give you any harm... But if you judge, then judge with justice... Indeed, Allah loves those who deal justly.

43. Why do they make you a judge when they have the Torah in which there is Allah's command? And yet they turn away from your judgment! They are not believers!

44. In truth, We have revealed the Torah, in which there is Nur and the knowledge of the reality... By it, the Nabis who have submitted, ruled the Jews, and so did the Rabbis (those occupied with the training of Jews according to the Torah) and the Priests (those with knowledge and wisdom) who were entrusted with the protection of the knowledge of the reality, and to which they were witnesses... So, do not fear man, fear Me! Do not sell the truths of which I inform you for a small gain. Those who do not judge by what Allah revealed, they are deniers of the reality!

45. We had decreed in it (the Torah), "A life for a life, an eye for an eye, a nose for a nose, an ear for an ear, a tooth for a tooth! And a wound for a wound..." But whoever forgives, this will expiate his past mistakes! And whoever does not judge in accordance with what Allah reveals, they are the wrongdoers.

46. We sent Jesus, the son of Mary, in the footsteps of them (the Nabis who had submitted) to confirm the knowledge from the Torah (as truth). And We gave him the Gospel, which contained Huda (the knowledge of the reality) and Nur, and confirmed what reached him from the Torah, as guidance and admonition for the protected ones.

47. Those who follow the Bible should judge with the creeds in the Bible revealed by Allah. Whoever does not judge with the creeds revealed by Allah, they are the corrupters!

48. We revealed to you a reality that confirms, protects, witnesses, rules over and encapsulates the Truth pertaining to the knowledge of the reality (sunnatullah) that came before you... So judge between them with what Allah has revealed... Do not leave what has come to you as the Truth and follow their empty fancies and desires... To each of you We prescribed a law (rules and conditions regarding lifestyle) and a method (a system based on fixed realities not subject to change with time). Had Allah willed, He would surely have made you a single community! But He wanted to try you with what He gave you (so you can see for yourself what you are)... So hasten to do good! To Allah you shall all return... He will inform you of the things you have been dividing and disputing over.

49. (This is what We have decreed upon you:) Judge between them with what Allah has revealed to you... Do not follow their (baseless) desires... Be cautious of falling into provocation about some of the things which Allah has revealed to you! If they turn away, know well that Allah wants to give them affliction due to some of their mistakes... Indeed, the majority of mankind is corrupted in faith.

50. Or do they want pagan laws (from the days of ignorance)? **Who is a better judge than Allah for people whose faith is firm?**

51. O believers... Do not befriend the Jews and the Christians... They are friends with one another... Whoever befriends them, he will indeed become one of them... Certainly, Allah will not guide the wrongdoers (He will not enable those who do wrong to themselves to experience the reality)!

52. You will see those devoid of healthy thought (the hypocrites) **saying, "We fear that things may turn against us" and hasten towards them** (the Jews and the Christians)... **Perhaps Allah will bring clarity or a verdict from Himself (HU) and they will become regretful over what they have been harboring within themselves.**

53. The believers say, "Are they the ones who solemnly swear with all their might and in the name of Allah to be with you?" Their deeds have become worthless; they have become losers.

54. O believers... Whoever among you renounces his faith (should know that) **Allah will bring** (in your stead) **a people who** (He) **will love, (and who) will love Him, who are humble toward the believers and honorable toward the deniers of the reality, who will fight in the way of Allah without fearing any condemnation from any condemner... That is the favor of Allah; He bestows it upon whom He wills.**

55. Your only Waliyy is Allah, the Rasul of HU, and the believers; they establish salat and give alms bowing down.

56. Whoever befriends Allah, the Rasul of HU, and the believers (should know) **the allies of Allah are the ones who will prevail!**

57. O believers... Do not befriend those who take your religion in ridicule and amusement among those to whom the knowledge of the reality has been given before you, nor those who deny the reality! Protect yourselves from Allah, if you are people of faith!

58. And when you call to prayer they take ridicule and make fun of it... This is because they are people who are unable to use their intellect.

59. Say, "O those to whom the knowledge of the reality has been given, do you resent us just because we have believed in Allah, our essential reality, to what has been revealed to us, and to what was revealed before us? The majority of you have gone astray!"

60. Say, "Shall I inform you of how wretched the consequences of your deeds are in the sight of Allah? They are those who Allah cursed and with whom He became angry! (Allah) changed them into followers of apes (those who live in imitation without reason), swine (those who live for their carnal pleasures) and Taghut (satan – illusions – impulses)! They are the ones whose dwellings are the most wretched and who have gone astray from the sound way!

61. When they come to you they say, "We have believed"... But in reality, they come to you in a state of denial and leave you in a state of denial... Allah, as the creator of their actions, knows better what they hide.

62. You will see most of them leaning towards offence against Allah and hastening to consume what has been forbidden... How wretched is what they do!

63. Why do the rabbis and the scholars (those with knowledge and wisdom) not prevent them from saying offensive things about Allah and from consuming what has been forbidden... How wretched is what they do and produce!

64. The Jews said, "The hands of Allah are tied"... Their claim became true about themselves; their hands were tied and they became cursed! On the contrary, both of Allah's hands are open; He continues to provide as He wills! Indeed, what has been revealed to you from your Rabb increases denial and transgression in most of them! We have cast between them animosity and hatred that will last until the Doomsday period! Whenever they kindled a fire of war, Allah extinguished it... (Yet still) they run to causing corruption on earth... Allah does not like those who run towards corrupting faith.

65. Had those, to whom the knowledge of the reality came, believed (evaluated this knowledge) and protected themselves (from shirq; duality) We would surely have erased their bad deeds and placed them in Paradises of Naim (a state in which the forces pertaining to Allah become manifest).

66. Had they evaluated and applied the requirements of the Torah, the Gospel, and what has been revealed to them from their Rabb, they would surely have enjoyed the blessings from above and below (spiritual and material provisions)! Among them are some who are on the just course (give everything its due right) but the majority of them are engaged in wretched deeds!

67. O (honorable) **Rasul... Announce that which has been revealed to you from your Rabb! If you do not, then you would not have conveyed the reality of HU! Allah protects you from the people... Indeed, Allah does not give guidance to people who deny the reality!**

68. **Say, "O those to whom the knowledge of the reality was given! You are not standing on any ground until you uphold** (apply directly to your life) **the Torah, the Gospel, and what has been revealed to you from your Rabb!" Indeed, that which has been revealed to you from your Rabb increases most of them in denial and transgression... So do not grieve over the people of denial!**

69. **Indeed, whoever among the Jews, the Sabeans and the Christians believes in Allah** (their very own Rabb and the Rabb of the worlds) **and in the eternal life to come and practices the requirements of this faith, there shall be no fear for them, nor shall they be grieved!**

70. **We had taken a covenant from the Children of Israel and disclosed for them Rasuls! But whenever a Rasul came to them with what their egos did not like, they denied some and killed some!**

71. **They thought there would be no harm in this; hence, they became blind** (to the reality) **and deaf** (to the call of the Truth)! **Then Allah accepted their repentance... But most of them became blind** (unable to evaluate the reality) **and deaf** (unable to perceive) **again! Allah** (as the creator of their deeds) **is Basir over what they do.**

72. **Certainly, those who said, "Allah is the Messiah, the son of Mary" have denied the reality...** (Whereas) **the Messiah had said, "O Children of Israel... Serve Allah, my Rabb and your Rabb... For whoever associates partners to Allah** (shirq; duality) **indeed Allah has made Paradise forbidden to him! His destination will be fire! There are no helpers for the wrongdoers!"**

73. **Indeed, those who said, "Allah is the third of the three" have become deniers of the reality! The concept of godhood is invalid; the possessor of Uluhiyyah is ONE! If they don't stop what they are saying, the deniers among them will surely live a painful suffering!**

74. **Are they still not going to repent to Allah and ask for forgiveness? Allah is the Ghafur, the Rahim.**

75. **Messiah, the son of Mary, is only a Rasul... Rasuls have come and gone before him! His mother was a woman of truth** (she had

witnessed the essential reality and testified to its existence without reservation)! **They both used to eat food** (they were human)! **Look at how We have informed them of the signs! Then look again, how they divert from the truth!**

76. **Say, "Do you serve those besides Allah, who neither give you harm, nor any benefit? Allah is HU, the Sami, and the Aleem.**

77. **Say, "O People of the Book... Do not exceed the limits and unjustly transgress the boundaries of your religion... Do not follow the empty delusions of a people who have diverted many from the right course in the past, and who have gone astray from the centerline!"**

78. **Those who deny the Truth from the Children of Israel have been cursed** (fell far from Allah) **by the tongue of David and Jesus, the son of Mary... This was because they rebelled and transgressed the boundary.**

79. **They did not prevent one another from the bad deeds that they did. How wretched were their deeds!**

80. **You will see the majority of them befriending those who deny the knowledge of the reality... How wretched is the eventuality prepared by their ego! The wrath of Allah is on them! They will be subject to suffering eternally.**

81. **Had they believed in Allah, the creator of their being with His Names, the Nabi** (Muhammad saw) **and what has been revealed to him, they would not have befriended them** (the deniers)**... But most of them are corrupted in faith.**

82. **Among man, you will indeed find the Jews and the dualists** (those engaged in shirq) **as the most severe in animosity towards the believers... And you will find the nearest of them in affection to the believers those who say, "We are Christians"... That is because among them** (Christians) **are men of deep knowledge and men who have renounced the world** (submitted themselves wholly to Allah)**, who have no arrogance.**

83. **And when they listen to that which has been revealed to the Rasul you will see their eyes overflowing with tears, for they recognize the knowledge revealed in the Truth... They say, "Our Rabb, we have believed... Write us down among the witnesses."**

84. "Why should we not believe in that which has come to us from Allah, our essence with His Names, and the Truth, when we have been longing for Him to admit us to the company of the righteous!"

85. And for this Allah rewarded them with Paradises underneath which rivers flow, where they will abide eternally... Such is the recompense for the doers of good! (The recompense/result/consequence of good is good).

86. But those who deny the knowledge of the reality and Our signs (the manifestations of the Names), they are the companions of hell!

87. O believers!... Do not forbid the pure provisions, which Allah made lawful to you, and do not transgress (by making unlawful what has been made lawful)! Indeed, Allah does not like the transgressors.

88. Eat of the lawful and good things Allah has provided for you... Protect yourselves from Allah, whom you believe is the essential reality of your being with His Names.

89. Allah will not hold you responsible for oaths you make thoughtlessly! But you are responsible for the oaths you make intentionally and consciously! The expiation for breaking an oath made consciously is feeding or clothing ten needy people, or freeing one slave! Whoever lacks the means to do this should fast for three days. This is the expiation for breaking your oaths! Keep your oaths... Thus does Allah explain His signs to you, so that you evaluate.

90. O believers... Intoxicants, gambling, objects of idolatry and divining arrows (fortune telling) are things of satanic abomination! Avoid them so that you may attain emancipation.

91. Satan seeks to sow animosity and hatred among you by means of intoxicants and gambling, and to keep you from the remembrance of Allah and from salat... Will you then desist?

92. Obey Allah, obey the Rasul and beware! If you turn away, know well (the responsibility) upon Our Rasul is only clear notification.

93. If those who believe and practice the requirements of their faith continue to protect themselves, they will reach (a higher state of) faith and engage in practices pertaining to it... Then, protecting themselves with this understanding they will reach an even higher understanding of faith... With this understanding and as a result of their faith they will protect themselves accordingly... Continuing to

protect themselves at this level of understanding will enable them to attain goodness (the station of observation)... **Allah loves the doers of good.**

94. **O believers... Allah will try you with something of the game that you hunt with your spears so that it may become evident who fears Him, their unknown** (which is unperceivable by them)! **And whoever transgresses after this, there is a painful suffering for him.**

95. **O believers... Do not hunt while you are in ihram** (attire worn by the pilgrim to represent a state he enters, where he refrains from worldly activities and turns wholeheartedly to Allah)... **Whoever intentionally kills game, the compensation is a sacrifice to be delivered to the Kaba, equivalent to the game that is killed, judged by two just men among you... Or in expiation, to feed the needy, or do the equivalent of that in fasting, so he may taste the consequence of his deeds... Allah has forgiven what is past... But whoever relapses, Allah will enforce the consequences of his deeds! Allah is the Aziz, the Zuntaqim** (severely enforces the consequences of an action).

96. **It has been made lawful for you to hunt and eat the fish of the sea as benefit for you and travelers... But forbidden to you is hunting on land while you are in ihram! Protect yourselves from Allah; unto Him you will be gathered.**

97. **Allah made the Kaba, the Sacred House, the Sacred Month, sacrificial animals and the garlands, a standing place for the people** (for the endurance and continuation of people's faith)... **This is so you know that Allah knows what is in the heavens** (the station of thought) **and the earth** (your body), **and that Allah is Aleem over all things.**

98. **Know that Allah will most certainly enforce the consequences of bad deeds, yet Allah is the Ghafur, the Rahim.**

99. **No more is the Rasul bound to do except provide the knowledge** (of the reality and its requisites). **Allah is aware of both that which you display and that which you conceal.**

100. **Say, "The impure and the pure are not equal in worth... Even though the majority of the impure may appear pleasing to you"... So then, o intelligent ones of deep contemplation who have attained the essence, protect yourselves from Allah so that you may attain emancipation.**

101. **O believers... Do not ask questions about things that you find unpleasant, when explained to you! If you ask such things while the**

Quran is being revealed, they will be explained to you! Allah has forgiven them... Allah is the Ghafur, the Halim.

102. A community before you asked such questions and then (unable to digest the answers) they became of the deniers.

103. Allah has not appointed (sacrifices known as) **bahirah, sai'bah or wasilah or ham** (these are fabricated traditions of some people). **But those who deny the knowledge of the reality are inventing falsehood about Allah! Most of them do not use their reason!**

104. When they are told, "Come to what Allah has revealed and to the Rasul," they say, "Sufficient for us is what we have acquired from our fathers"... Is that so even if their fathers knew nothing, nor were they guided to the realization of their essential reality?

105. O believers... You are responsible for yourselves! So long as you are aware of your essential reality, a misguided person (one who is devoid of the knowledge of his essential Self) cannot harm you! To Allah you will all return... He will show you the product of the things you do!

106. O believers... When death approaches one of you, two just witnesses should be present at the time of bequest... Or if you are traveling and death finds you, two witnesses are needed for you... If you have doubt (about their testimony), detain them after their prayer and let them swear by Allah, "We will not exchange our oath for any price, even if it should be a relative, and we will not conceal the testimony of Allah, for then we would be in fault."

107. But if it is found that these two were guilty of perjury in the past, let two others stand forth in their place and swear by Allah, "Indeed our testimony is truer than theirs for we have not transgressed, or we would have been of the wrongdoers."

108. This makes it more likely that people will bear true witness upon His face (in the name of Allah) and bring a solution to their (perjurers') fear that their testimony will be rejected after they bear witness... Protect yourselves from Allah and perceive! Allah does not guide people who are corrupt (in faith) to the reality!

109. When Allah gathers the Rasuls (he will ask them): "What was the response you received?" They will say, "We have no knowledge. Indeed, it is You who are the knower of the unknown."

110. Allah will say, "O Jesus, son of Mary! Remember my favor upon you and your mother... How I had vindicated you with the force of the Pure Spirit that had become manifest through your being... You spoke to people in the cradle and in maturity... I had taught you the Book, Wisdom, Torah and Gospel (I had disclosed this knowledge in your consciousness)... You designed from clay the form of a bird with my permission (B-iznihi) and breathed into it, then it became a bird with My permission (B-iznihi)! You healed the blind and the leper with My permission and brought the dead back to life with My permission... Remember that I restrained the Children of Israel from you! You came to them with obvious proofs, yet the deniers among them had said, "This is sheer magic!"

111. I revealed to the disciples, "Believe in Me and my Rasul (in light of the letter B)... They had said, "We have believed, bear witness that indeed we are Muslims."

112. The disciples had said, "O Jesus, son of Mary! Is your Rabb's power sufficient enough to reveal for us a ma'idah? (literally 'ma'idah' means a table with food; metaphorically it references the knowledge of the reality and gnosis... In other words, they were questioning Jesus' creational program, the specific configuration of Names comprising his essence, and whether it had such capacity.) Whereupon Jesus said, "Protect yourselves from Allah if you are true believers."

113. They said, "We want to eat from it (apply that knowledge) so our hearts can be satisfied (attain certainty in regards to what you teach us) and so we know what you explain to us is the (absolute) reality and be witnesses to it."

114. Jesus, son of Mary, said, "O Allah! Our Rabb... Reveal for us a ma'idah from heaven so it may be a feast and a proof from You, both for our past and for our future... Provide for us, for You are the best of providers."

115. Allah said, "Indeed I will reveal it for you... But whoever denies the reality after this, I will punish him in a way I have not punished anyone among the worlds!"

116. And Allah said, "O Jesus, son of Mary! Was it you that said to the people, 'Take me and my mother as deities besides Allah'?"... (Jesus) said, "Subhan, You are (I exonerate you)! How can it be possible for me to say something that is not true? Even if I had said it, You would have known it! You know what is within myself, but I know not what is within Your Self! Indeed, it is You, You alone, who is the Knower of the unknown!"

117. "I told them nothing other than what You commanded me: 'Attain the consciousness of servitude to Allah, who is both your Rabb and my Rabb'... I was a witness over them as long as I was among them... Then you made me die! You became Raqib over them! You are the witness over all things!"

118. "If You cause them suffering, indeed they are Your servants! If You forgive them, indeed it is You who are the Aziz, the Hakim."

119. Allah said, "This is the Day when the truthful will live the results of their truthfulness (their undoubted confirmation of the reality)! There are Paradises for them, underneath which rivers flow, in which they will abide eternally"... Allah is pleased with them, and they with Him... This is the great attainment!

120. The heavens, the earth and the existence of everything within them belongs to Allah (they are the manifestations of His Names)! He is Qadir over all things!

6

AL-AN'AM

By the one who is denoted by the name Allah (who created my being with His Names in accord with the meaning of the letter 'B'), the Rahman, the Rahim.

1. Hamd (the evaluation of the corporeal worlds created with His Names, as He wills) belongs to Allah, who has created the heavens and the earth, and formed the darkness (ignorance) and Nur (knowledge)... Those who incessantly deny the reality, equate (their illusory external gods) to their Rabb (the dimension of Names within their essence, and hence they live in duality)!

2. It is HU who has created you from water and clay, and decreed a span (specified time of bodily life)... The specified term of life is from Him... After all of this, you still have doubt.

3. Allah is HU, in the heavens and on earth... He knows what is in your essence and what you reveal! He knows what you are earning (with your deeds)!

4. No sign (revealed or apparent) from their Rabb comes to them, but they turn away from it!

5. And now they deny what has come to them in Truth! But the news of what they ridicule is going to reach them soon.

6. Did they not see how many generations We have destroyed before them... (Moreover) unlike you, We had established them upon the abundant regions of the earth, and sent the blessings of the heavens upon them and made the rivers flow beneath them... (Nevertheless) We destroyed them because of their faults! And after them, We brought forth another generation.

7. If We had sent down a (written) scripture to you, and they had touched it with their hands, the deniers of the knowledge of the reality would surely have said, "This is none other than obvious magic."

8. They said, "An angel (that we can see) **should have been sent down"... But if We had revealed an angel as such, the matter would have ended; no further time would have been given to them.**

9. If We had made Him (the Rasul of Allah saw) **an angel** (for you to see) **We would still have made him in the form of a man to make them fall into the same doubt-dilemma that they are in now** (whereupon they would have said, "he is just a man like us").

10. Indeed, many of Our Rasuls were also mocked before you! But those who mocked were enveloped by their own mockery!

11. Say, "Travel through the earth and see the end of the deniers (of the reality)."

12. Say, "To whom belongs the things in the heavens and the earth (forms which have come from a state of nothingness into 'relative' existence in order to manifest the meanings of the Names)?" **Say, "To Allah!" He has decreed His Grace** (the creation of the worlds based on His Rahman quality) **upon His Self. He will surely gather you in the period of Doomsday, about which there is no doubt! Those who have put themselves in loss will not believe!**

13. Whatever is in the night and the day is for Him! HU is the Sami, the Aleem.

14. Say, "Shall I befriend (by imagining one) **other than Allah, the creator** (and programmer of all things according to their specific functions) **of the heavens and the earth, who provides to maintain and subsist their existence, but who is Himself not in need of anything?"... Say, "I have been commanded to be the first of those who submit to Allah" and do not ever be of the dualists!**

15. Say, "Indeed, if I disobey my Rabb, I fear the suffering of the mighty Day (period)!"

16. He from whom (suffering) **is averted in that time, has definitely been blessed with Allah's grace! That is the clear liberation!**

17. If Allah subjects you to adversity, there is no one to remove it other than HU (in your essence)**... And if Allah subjects you to good, the endower of good is also HU, the One who is Qadir over all things.**

18. It is HU who is the subjugator over his servants (HU discloses Himself from within the depths of His manifestations to rule over His existence)! HU is the Hakim, the Habir.

19. Say, "What thing is greater in evidence?"... Say, "Allah is witness between me and you... This Quran was revealed to me so that I may warn you and whomever it reaches... Do you really testify that there are other gods besides Allah?"... Say, "I will not testify (to this)"... Say, "Uluhiyyah is ONE and indeed, I am free of your associations."

20. Those to whom We have given the knowledge of the reality know him (Muhammad saw) just like they know their own sons... Those who have lost their selves, they are not of the believers.

21. Who does more wrong than he who lies about Allah or His existence in His signs (the manifestations of His Names)? Most certainly, the wrongdoers (dualists) will not attain liberty.

22. The time when we gather them all together and ask the dualists, "Where are the partners you assumed existed besides Him now?"...

23. They can cause no more provocation other than saying, "By Allah, our Rabb, we were not of the dualists"!

24. Look at how they lie against their own selves and how the things they made up (deified in their imagination) have deserted them now.

25. And among them are some who hear you... But We have placed veils over their hearts (consciousness) and heaviness in their ears (comprehension) so they cannot perceive Him! No matter how many proofs they see, they will still not believe... Moreover, when the deniers of the reality who argue with you come to you, they will say, "This is nothing other than fairytales of the past."

26. They both prevent (others) from Him (the Rasul of Allah saw) and distance (themselves) from Him! They are only destroying their own selves, yet they can not perceive!

27. "If you could but see when they are confronted with the fire (suffering) how they will say 'Oh, if only we can go back (to our biological life on earth; as biological life is required to activate the forces within the brain) and not deny the signs of our Rabb (our intrinsic divine qualities and potential deriving from the Names that comprise our essential reality) and be among the believers'."

28. But that which they concealed before (the knowledge of the reality with which they had been endowed) **has now become apparent to them. And even if they were returned they would return to the things from which they had been forbidden, they are liars indeed.**

29. And they say, "There is none but our worldly life, and we will not be resurrected!" And they say, "There is none but our worldly life! Our lives will not continue!"

30. If you could but see when they will be made to stand before their Rabb (when they recognize and become aware of the potentials of the Names within their own reality). **He will say, "Is this not the reality?" They will say, "Yes, it is our Rabb." He will then say, "So now taste the agony as the consequence of denying the knowledge of the reality."**

31. Indeed, those who denied reuniting with Allah (the awareness of the truth that the essence of their being is comprised of the Names) **have become losers! When finally that hour** (the time to experience death) **suddenly came upon them, bearing their burdens on their backs, they said, "Woe unto us, for the practices we neglected and the deprivation we fell into thereby!" Be careful, wretched is** (the responsibility) **they bear!**

32. The life of your world (the lowest of the low; the world of conditionings) **is nothing but amusement and entertainment! The eternal life to come is surely better for the protected ones... Will you still not use your reason?**

33. We know what they say saddens you... But the truth is, those wrongdoers do not deny you, they deliberately deny the existence of Allah in His signs (the manifestations of His Names)!

34. And certainly Rasuls were also denied before you... But they endured their denial and torments until Our help came to them... And none can alter the words of Allah... Certainly, there has come to you some of what was revealed (to previous Rasuls).

35. If you find their rejection hard to bear then seek a tunnel into the ground or a ladder into the sky, if you can, and bring them a miracle (so they believe)! **Had Allah willed, He would have surely assembled them around the truth... So beware; don't be ignorant!**

36. Only those who can perceive will respond (to the invitation)! **As for the dead** (those who are devoid of knowledge), **Allah will resurrect**

them (enable them to realize their reality after they experience death) and to Him they will be returned.

37. They said, "Why doesn't he (the Rasul) reveal a sign from His Rabb!"... Say, "Allah is certainly Qadir to reveal a miracle... But most of them do not know."

38. "And there is no animate creature on (or within) the earth or bird that flies with two wings (knowledge and power) except (that they are) communities (formed with an order based on a specific system) like you! We have not neglected a single thing in the 'READ'able (Book) of the created existence!..." They shall all be gathered unto their Rabb.

39. Those who deny Our signs are the deaf (those who are unable to perceive their reality) and the dumb (those who are unable to acknowledge and admit the Truth) within darkness. Allah will lead astray whom He wills and keep whom He wills on the straight path!

40. Say, "Are you conscious of your state? If the wrath of Allah or that hour (promised event) comes to you, will you call upon one other than Allah? (Admit it) if you are truthful."

41. No, it is Him alone that you would call upon... And if He wills, He will reveal the truth of that which you call upon, and you will forget the things that you associate with Him!

42. Indeed, We have disclosed (Rasuls) to communities before you... And afflicted them with suffering and ailments so they may humble themselves and pray.

43. If only they had humbled themselves when Our wrath came to them! But their hearts hardened (their consciousness was locked) and Satan (their delusion) beautified their deeds to them.

44. When they forgot that which they had been reminded of (that they were created for Allah) We opened the doors of every (good worldly) thing to them... As they were rejoicing with what they were given, We seized them at once! Suddenly they lost all their hope and were left in despair!

45. Hence, the people who wronged (themselves) were eliminated! Hamd (the evaluation of the corporeal worlds created with His Names, as He wills) belongs to Allah!

46. Say, "Reflect, if Allah was to take away your sense of hearing (perception) and sight, and lock your hearts (consciousness), is there a god besides Allah that can give it back to you?" Look how We explain the signs in various ways, yet (despite this) they still turn away.

47. Say, "Have you ever considered if Allah's wrath was to come suddenly or openly, will any be destroyed other than the wrongdoers?"

48. We disclose the Rasuls only as bringers of glad tidings and as warners... So, whoever believes and reforms (their way) they will have no fear, nor will they grieve.

49. As for those who deny the realities of Our signs (the manifestations of the Names), they will taste suffering because of their corrupted beliefs!

50. Say, "I am not telling you I possess the keys to Allah's treasury... I do not know the unknown! Nor am I claiming to be an angel... I only follow what is revealed to me"... Say, "Can the blind and the seeing be equal? Do you still not reflect?"

51. And warn those who fear being gathered unto their Rabb (about what the Names in their essence will enforce upon them)... There is neither a Waliyy nor an intercessor for them other than He... Perhaps they will protect themselves.

52. Do not distance from yourself those who pray to their Rabb morning and evening seeking the face of (that which pertains to) HU... Neither you will be held responsible of the consequences of their deeds nor will they be held responsible for yours, so you do not need to distance them... (if you do this) you will have done wrong.

53. Hence we tried some with others, so they say, "Did Allah bestow upon these (needy ones with little income)?"... Does Allah not know best those who appreciate?

54. When those who believe in Our signs (the manifestations of Our Names) come to you, say to them, "Assalamu alaikum... Your Rabb has inscribed grace upon Himself! Whoever among you does wrong, then repents and corrects (his way), indeed, Allah is the Ghafur, the Rahim."

55. Thus We explain the signs so that the path of the faulty may become evident.

56. Say, "Indeed I have been forbidden to worship the deities you have taken besides Allah!"... Say, "I will never follow your empty fantasies! For then I will surely become corrupted and deviate from the way of the guided ones; those who realize their essential reality."

57. Say, "I am surely upon a clear sign from my Rabb, the truth which you have denied! What you seek to hasten (death) is not within my power... The judgment is for Allah alone! He informs of the Truth! He is the best distinguisher (of right and wrong)."

58. Say, "If that which you seek to hasten was within my power, this matter between us would have ended long ago!"... Allah knows best the wrongdoers.

59. The keys (knowledge) of the unknown (that which is unperceivable to you) are with HU! None knows them but HU"! He knows all things contained on land (manifest – perceivable) and in sea (the depths – knowledge)... No leaf falls without His knowledge (for all things are a manifestation of the Names of HU)... There is neither a single grain in the darkness of the earth, nor anything wet or dry, that is not recorded in a clear book (the book of the universe).

60. It is Him who makes you experience death (life without the awareness of the biological body) in the night ('Sleep is the brother of death' – Hadith) and knows what you do in the day... Then revives you in the day until a specified lifespan is fulfilled... Then you will be returned to Him... Then He will inform you of what you do (enable you to evaluate your life in terms of its essence).

61. HU is the subjugator over His servants (by means of disclosure from His multi-dimensional depths)! He reveals unto you protective (forces)... When finally the time of death comes to one of you, our Rasuls (forces, delegates) cause him to die! And they will not be late!

62. Then they will be returned unto Allah, their true protector... Know with certainty that the judgment is His, and He is the swiftest in taking account.

63. Say, "Who will save you when you humble yourselves and pray earnestly, 'If you save us from the darkness of the earth and the sea we will surely be of the thankful'?"

64. Say, "Allah will save you from that and from every distress... Yet you still associate others with Him!"

65. Say, "He has the power to disclose an affliction to you from above you (the sky – internal) or from beneath your feet (within the earth – external) or to fragment you into factions against each other, so you taste violence." Look how We diversify Our narration so you contemplate its depths and understand.

66. But your people denied it, while HU is the Truth! Say, "I am not your agent (you will have to face the consequences of not believing)!"

67. For every occurrence there is a pre-determined and specific time... You will know soon!

68. When you see those who engage in inappropriate talks regarding Our signs, turn away from them until they change the subject... If Satan makes you forget, then when you remember and become aware, do not continue to sit with the wrongdoers.

69. Those who are protected are not responsible for them... But they should remind them of the Truth nevertheless... Perhaps they will also protect themselves.

70. Leave those who have made their religion a hobby and a means for entertainment, who have been deceived by the worldly life, to their own accord. But remind them, lest a soul falls into destruction for what it has done! He will have neither a protector (Waliyy), nor an intercessor besides Allah... Even if he offers every ransom it will not be accepted from him! They are the ones who will be held as hostages as a result of what they have earned... There will be a scalding drink and great suffering for them for denying the knowledge of the reality.

71. Say, "Shall we pray to and call upon things other than Allah, who can give us no benefit or harm? Shall we go back to duality after Allah has guided us to the true path? Shall we be like the foolish one who devils seduces and pulls to the abyss while we have friends who say, "Come to us" and call us to a straight path?"... Say, "The guidance of Allah is this! We have been ordered to submit to Allah, the Rabb of the worlds."

72. And "Establish salat and protect yourselves from His wrath; to Him you will be gathered!"

73. HU has created the heavens and the earth in truth... Whenever He says, "Be", immediately it becomes... His word is the Truth! When the Horn is blown (to the body or the system – the manifestation occurs from the inside out) **the dominion is His! He knows the unknown and the witnessed... HU is the Hakim, the Habir.**

74. **And when Abraham said to his father Azar, "Do you take idols as deities? Indeed, I see you and your people in plain corruption."**

75. **Thus We gave Abraham the sight to observe the angelic realm** (the depths; the forces comprising the essence) **of the heavens and the earth to enable him to attain certainty** (to prevent him from becoming veiled from the reality of things by what he sees).

76. **When the night** (ignorance) **covered him, he saw a star** (became aware of his consciousness)**... He said, "This is my Rabb"... But when it set** (when he became inadequate in comprehending the reality) **he said, "I do not like those that set."**

77. **And when he saw the moon** (his emotional identity; his sense of self sourcing from his emotions) **he said, "This is my Rabb"... But when it set he said, "Indeed, if my Rabb had not guided me, I would surely have been among the astray."**

78. **And when he saw the sun** (his mind) **rising** (in hope it will enable him to experience the reality) **he said, "This is my Rabb, this is greater"... But when it set** (when he realized the inadequacy of his mind in discerning Allah) **he said, "O my people, indeed I am free from your associations."**

79. **"Certainly, I have turned my face** (my consciousness) **cleansed from the concept of a deity** (Hanif)**, toward the Fatir** (He who creates everything programmed according to its purpose) **who created the heavens and the earth, and I am not of the dualists."**

80. **His people opposed him and tried to authenticate** (the things they deified)**... (Abraham) said, "Are you arguing with me about Allah while He has guided me? I do not fear the things you associate with Him! Except what my Rabb wills** (harm can only reach me with the permission of my Rabb)**... My Rabb has encompassed everything with His knowledge... Do you still not think?"**

81. **"How can I fear the deities you associate with Allah when you don't fear associating them while He has not revealed any proof** (regarding their divinity)**?" So, which of the two ways deserves to be given more credence?**

82. Those who believe and who do not mix their faith with the wrong (concealed duality)... Security is their right... They are the ones who have found the right path!

83. This is the definite proof We have given to Abraham against his people. We raise to elevated degrees whom We will! Indeed, your Rabb is the Hakim, the Aleem.

84. And We gave to him (Abraham) Isaac and Jacob... All of them, We have guided (informed of the reality). And We guided Noah, and among his descendants, David, Soloman, Job, Joseph, Moses and Aaron... Thus We reward the doers of good.

85. And Zacharia, John, Jesus and Elias... All of them were of the righteous.

86. And Ishmael, Elisha, Jonah and Lot... We made them superior to all people (the worlds) (by enabling them to experience the mystery of vicegerency in their bodily life).

87. And some of their fathers, descendants and brothers! We have chosen them and led them to the right path.

88. This is Allah's guidance... He guides (enables the realization of the innermost reality of) whom he wills among His servants... If they had associated others with Allah (duality) then surely all of their earnings would have become vain.

89. They are the ones to whom We have given the Book (the knowledge of the reality and sunnatullah), Judgment and Nubuwwah... If they (the people) deny these things that We have given, We will entrust it to a people who will not deny any of it.

90. They are the ones who Allah has guided... So, follow their reality! Say, "I do not want a reward (for informing you)... it is only a reminder to people (the worlds)!"

91. And they did not duly appreciate Allah, by saying, "Allah has not revealed anything to any man" Say, "Who revealed the Book (knowledge) that Moses brought from his essence as Nur and protection for the people? You put it (knowledge) into parchments and show it, but you hide most of it... While much was taught to you, things neither you nor your fathers knew!"... Say: 'Allah' and let them amuse themselves in their empty discourse (their illusory world) in which they are absorbed."

92. This is a (Book) **We have revealed, blessed and confirmed those before it, to warn the Mother of Cities** (Mecca) **and those who live near her... Those who believe in the eternal life to come also believe in this knowledge... They are the ones who continue performing their salat** (prayers).

93. Who can do more wrong than one who lies about Allah or who says, "It has been revealed unto me" when nothing has been **revealed to him and who says, "I will reveal the like of what Allah has revealed"? If only you could see the wrongdoers when they live the intensity of death! The angels** (forces) **extend** (spread) **their hands and say, "Separate yourselves from your body** (world) **now as consciousness** (for you have tasted death, life without a body, and life continues)**! Today you will be punished with humiliation for the things you said about Allah not based on truth, and for being arrogant towards His signs."**

94. Indeed, you have come to Us as individuals, like how We created you the first time (with the awareness of your origin)**! You have left behind the illusions We conferred upon you... We do not see you with the intercessors you took, thinking they are partners** (of Allah)**... Indeed, the tie between you has been severed and everything you assumed existed has been lost!**

95. Indeed Allah is the cleaver that cracks and splits the seeds (creates forms of existence from the seeds of Names)**! He brings the living** (those who realize their infiniteness based on the Name Hayy) **from the dead** (those deprived of the knowledge of the reality)**... And the dead** (those who fail to leave their cocoon and fall into the state of the 'Inciting Self'; carnal state of existence) **from the living** (those who live with the knowledge of the reality, in the state of the 'Inspired Self')**! Thus is Allah! How you are turned** (from one state to another).

96. He tears away the darkness to bring forth the daylight! He has made the night for rest, and the Sun and the stars for measurement... This is the determination of the Aziz, the Aleem.

97. It is HU who forms the stars in the darkness of the night and the sea, so that you find guidance! We have indeed explained Our signs for a people who know.

98. HU has created you from a single soul (a single Self)**... and then a place of dwelling** (a place to know one's self, the formation of the world) **and then a container** (the body, a temporary place for safe keeping)... **We have indeed explained Our signs for a people of open understanding.** .

99. HU discloses water from the sky! With it We produce the growth of ALL THINGS! And from it We produced greenery... And from it grains arranged in layers... And clusters of dates hanging low from the sheath of the date palms... And We produce vineyards and olive groves and pomegranates, alike yet different! Look at its fruits when it yields and ripens... Indeed, there are signs in these for a people who believe.

100. Yet they attributed the jinn (invisible beings) **as partners onto Allah –** while He (Allah) **has created them** (the qualities they manifest comprise Allah's Names)! **Ignorantly they attributed sons and daughters unto Him! Subhan is He, above and beyond what they attribute!**

101. (He is) the **Badee** (the originator) **of the heavens and the earth! How can one free from the concept of companionship have a son! He created all! HU, as the creator of all with His Names, and by being present in their essence with His Names, knows them!**

102. Thus is your Rabb Allah! There is no god, only HU! The creator of all (not externally but from within dimensional depths)! **Become aware of your servitude to Him! He is Wakil over all things.**

103. Vision (sense perception) **perceives Him not but He perceives** (evaluates) **all that is visible.**

104. In truth, there has come to you proofs from your Rabb to be evaluated... Whoever evaluates them with insight it is for his own good, and whoever lacks insight it is his loss... I am not a guard over you!

105. Thus We explain Our signs in many ways, so they say, "You have learnt the requirements" and so We may make it clear for a people who know.

106. Follow what has been revealed to you from your Rabb! There is no god, only HU! Turn away from those with dualistic beliefs!

107. Had Allah willed, they would not have been dualists! We have not placed you as a guardian over them! Nor are you responsible for them (i.e. you are not their representative, and you are not charged with changing or guiding them).

108. Do not revile gods besides Allah... (In response to this) **they transgress the boundary and revile Allah out of their ignorance! Thus We made pleasing to every community their deeds... Then to their Rabb is their return... He will inform them of the meaning of all they did.**

109. **And they swear by Allah with all their might that they will believe if a miracle comes to them. Say, "Miracles are only with Allah"... Are you not aware that they will not believe even if a miracle came to them?**

110. **And thus We will lock their hearts** (the reflector of the Names to the consciousness – heart neurons) **and their eyes** (ability to perceive and evaluate) **just as they refused to believe before** (the miracle came)**! And We will leave them on their own in their transgression, wandering blindly!**

111. **If We had revealed angels to them and if the dead spoke to them and if We made them experience every stage of life after death** (life after the biological body ceases to exist) **they would still not believe, unless Allah should will... But most of them live in ignorance!**

112. **And thus We made enemies for every Nabi** (the informer of the eternal life) **- devils from among mankind** (those who confine their existence to their body alone and live in pursuit of their bodily pleasures) **and jinn... Some of them disclose decorative speech to others to deceive them! If your Rabb willed, they would not do that... So, leave them in that which they invent!**

113. **In order that the hearts** (the reflectors of the Names to the consciousness – neurons in the heart) **of those who do not believe in the eternal life to come, will incline toward it** (deception) **and delight in it, and hence continue doing what they are doing.**

114. **Shall I seek a judge other than Allah when He has revealed to you the knowledge of the reality and sunnatullah** (Book) **in detail? Those to whom We have given the Book know that it is revealed from their Rabb in Truth... Do not be of those who doubt!**

115. **The word of your Rabb has been confirmed and eventuated, as it deserves! None can alter his words... HU is the Sami, the Aleem!**

116. **If you follow the majority of those on earth they will mislead you from the way of Allah... They only follow their assumptions and talk without thinking!**

117. Indeed, your Rabb is HU! He knows best who goes astray! HU; the One who knows best those who experience the reality...

118. If you are of those who believe in His existence apparent in His signs (the manifestations of His Names) then eat of those things upon which the Name of Allah is mentioned!

119. Unless you are forced to out of need, why do you not eat the things upon which the name of Allah is uttered, when He has informed you in detail of the things He has prohibited to you? Indeed, most of them go astray (deviate the matter) ignorantly, with baseless ideas! Certainly, HU, your Rabb, knows best the transgressors.

120. In regards to the things Allah has forbidden, abandon both the apparent ones and the conceptual ones... Indeed, those who commit mistakes will definitely live the consequences of their actions.

121. Do not eat of the things upon which the name of Allah is not uttered. That is definitely corruption (of faith)! Indeed, the devils incite their friends to struggle with you... If you follow them, you will definitely be of the dualists.

122. Can the one who We enliven (with the knowledge of the reality) while he is dead and to whom We give the Nur of insight with which he can live among people be equal to the one who is left in darkness from which he can never escape? Thus the deeds of those who deny the knowledge of the reality have been made to seem pleasing to them.

123. Thus We have placed leaders (of crime) in every city as criminals so they conspire within... But they conspire against none but themselves, yet they are unaware!

124. When a proof comes to them, they say, "We will never believe until we are given like that which was given to the Rasuls of Allah"... Allah knows best where to manifest His reality! The criminals will be subject to debasement and severe suffering from Allah for what they used to conspire!

125. And whomsoever Allah wills the realization of his essential reality, He opens his breast (his innermost comprehension) to Islam (to the consciousness of his submission) and whomsoever He wills to lead astray, He makes his breast tight and constricted, as though he

were laboriously climbing into the sky! Thus Allah debases those who do not believe!

126. This is the straight path (as-sirat al-mustaqim) of your Rabb... We have indeed detailed the proofs to a people who can think and evaluate.

127. The abode of Salam (the state of existence pertaining to the meaning of the Name Salam) with their Rabb is for them! HU is their Waliyy because of what they used to do.

128. The Day when He will gather them together (and say), "O community of jinn, you have truly possessed (misled from reality) the vast majority of mankind." And their allies among mankind will say, "Our Rabb, we mutually benefited from each other, and we have now reached our term, which you appointed for us." He will say, "The Fire is your residence, wherein you will abide eternally, except for what Allah wills..." Indeed, your Rabb is the Hakim and the Aleem.

129. Thus We will make some of the wrongdoers friends with others as a result of what they used to do (they are companions to each other in the fire)!

130. "O communities of jinn and mankind, did there not come to you Rasuls from among you, relating to you My messages pointing to the reality and warning you of the coming of this Day?" They will say, "We bear witness against ourselves"; and the worldly life (they had conjured based on corporeality) had deluded them, and they will bear witness against themselves that they were deniers of the knowledge of the reality.

131. That is because your Rabb would not destroy communities of wrongdoers unless they have been informed through Rasuls.

132. Each of them has degrees according to their deeds... Your Rabb is not unaware of what they do.

133. Your Rabb is the Ghani and possessor of grace... If He wills He can do away with you and give vicegerency to whomsoever He wills after you... Just as He produced you from the descendants of another people!

134. Indeed, what you are promised is coming... You cannot cause Allah failure (to deliver His promise)!

135. Say, "O my people, do whatever you can! For I too will do (what I can)! Soon you will know whose worldly life will be at the end"... Indeed, the wrongdoers will not attain liberation.

136. They set aside for Allah a share in what He has created of crops and livestock. And with their assumptions, they said, "This is for Allah, and this is for whom we associate (with Allah)." However, what is for their associates does not reach Allah! But what is for Allah reaches those they associate... Wretched is their judgment!

137. And likewise, their partners (assumed gods) made the killing of children seem pleasing to the dualists to destroy them and bring confusion to their religion... Had Allah willed they would not have done so... So, leave them alone in what they invent.

138. They (those who take their traditional conditionings and value judgments as religious doctrine) said with assumption, "These animals and crops are untouchable... None can eat from them other than whom we will... The backs of these animals have been forbidden (one cannot ride them)"... Yet they slander against Him (Allah) and slaughter (some of) the animals without mentioning the name of Allah upon them! (Allah) will actualize the consequences of their slander upon them!

139. They said, "What is contained in the belly of this animal is only lawful for our men, it is forbidden to our women... But if it is born dead, then they (men and women) have equal share"... Allah will punish them for this slander... Indeed He is the Hakim, the Aleem.

140. Those who foolishly kill their children out of ignorance and forbid with slander the provision of Allah, which He has bestowed upon them, have indeed accrued a loss... They have indeed gone astray and are deprived of guidance.

141. HU builds trellised and untrellised gardens, dates, crops of various fruit, olives and pomegranates, similar and different... Eat of their fruit when it yields, and give its due (alms) on the day of its harvest... And do not squander, for He does not favor the squanderers.

142. And of the cattle there are some for carrying burdens and some for making beds (from its wool)... Eat of the provision Allah gives you (since He is the creator) and do not follow the ideas of Satan... He is indeed your obvious enemy.

143. There are eight pairs/mates: Two (pairs) of the sheep and two (pairs) of the goats... Say, is it the two males He has forbidden or the two females or that which the wombs of the two females contain?... Inform me with knowledge if you are truthful."

144. And two (pairs) of the camels, and two (pairs) of the cattle... Say, "Is it the two males He has forbidden or the two females or that which the wombs of the two females contain? Or were you witnesses when Allah advised you with this?"... Who does more wrong than one who ignorantly invents lies about Allah to mislead the people?... Indeed Allah does not guide the wrongdoing people.

145. Say, "I cannot find anything forbidden to one who eats from what has been revealed... Only the flesh of a dead animal, spilled blood, the flesh of swine – for indeed, it is impure – and that which has been slaughtered in the name of one other than Allah, with the hands of one with a corrupt faith... But whoever is forced to eat it (out of need) he may do so without assuming it to be lawful and without going to extreme..." Certainly, your Rabb is the Ghafur, the Rahim.

146. We have made all clawed animals forbidden to the Jews... We have also made forbidden to them the interior fat of cattle and sheep, except what extends to their backs or their entrails or is mixed up with a bone... We have punished them for transgressing... We are indeed truthful.

147. (My Rasul) if they have denied you, say, "Your Rabb is the Wasi, possessor of grace... His torment will not be held back from a people who do wrong."

148. The dualists will say, "Had Allah willed, neither us nor our fathers would have been dualists... and we would not have prohibited anything"... Likewise, those before them also denied, until they tasted Our punishment. Say, "Do you have a knowledge you can explain to us? You follow only assumption... You talk nonsense based on presumptions alone."

149. Say, "To Allah belongs the definite proof... If He had willed, he would surely have guided all of you."

150. Say, "Bring forward your witnesses who testify that Allah had prohibited this!"... And if they testify, do not testify with them... Do not follow the empty desires of those who deny Our signs

(manifestations of Names) **and the eternal life to come! They equate their deities to their Rabb.**

151. **Say, "Come, let me READ to you the things your Rabb has forbidden to you: Do not associate anything with Him... Do good to your parents... Do not kill your children out of poverty, We will provide for you and for them! Do not approach apparent** (alcohol, harlotry, etc.) **or hidden forms** (contemplating upon them) **of indecency... Do not kill the one who Allah has forbidden** (to be killed), **except by legal right** (like retribution)! (Allah) **makes this warning so that you use your reason!"**

152. **Do not approach the orphan's property until he reaches maturity, except for the purpose of administrating it in the best way... Make measurements and balances in full and with justice... We never charge anyone with that which is beyond his capacity. And when you speak, speak the truth, even if it concerns someone close to you! Fulfill your word to Allah! (Allah) makes this warning so that you use your reason!**

153. **This is my straight path, so follow it, do not follow other paths;** (otherwise) **they will divert you from His straight path... Thus Allah warns you so you may protect yourselves!**

154. **Then We gave Moses the knowledge of the reality and sunnatullah as guidance and grace, and to complete Our favor upon the doers of good and to clarify everything to them... So that they believe they will meet their Rabb.**

155. **This revelation is an abundant knowledge of the reality and sunnatullah! Follow it and adhere to it so you may receive grace.**

156. **So that you do not say, "Knowledge has only been revealed upon the two groups before us** (Jews and Christians); **we were unaware of what they read and evaluated"...**

157. **And so that you do not say, "If that Knowledge was revealed to us, we would surely have evaluated the guidance better than them"... Clear proofs, knowledge of the reality and grace have come to your from your Rabb... Who can do more wrong than one who denies the existence of Allah in His signs** (the manifestations of His Names) **and turns away from them! They will undergo the worst suffering as a result of turning away from Our signs!**

158. **Are they waiting for angels, or for their Rabb, or for the miracles of their Rabb to come to them in order to believe? The**

faith of he who had not believed before or whose faith did not benefit him (was not internalized) will be of no use when he sees the extraordinary signs of his Rabb! Say, "Wait, for we are also waiting."

159. Those who fragment the understanding of religion and form various sects, you shall have no business with them, my Rasul! Their account is left to Allah... They will be notified of the truth of what they used to do.

160. Whoever comes with one good, shall receive tenfold of what he brings... And whoever comes with one bad, will only receive the results of that one! They will not be wronged.

161. Say, "Indeed my Rabb has guided me to the straight path... To the religion in effect, the hanif people of Abraham... And he was not of the dualists.

162. Say, "Indeed my salat (prayer, introspection), my practices (to attain closeness to Allah), my life and everything I am to live through my death, is for Allah, the Rabb of the worlds (they are for the manifestation of the qualities pertaining to Allah's Names).

163. "The concept of duality cannot be conceived in regards to HU! I have been commanded thusly; I am the leader of those who experience submission!"

164. Say, "How can I think of a Rabb other than Allah when He is the Rabb of all! What each soul earns is for each soul... A criminal cannot take responsibility for the crime of another! Your return will be to your Rabb! He will inform you about the things over which you differ."

165. It is HU who appointed you vicegerents upon the earth (the body) and elevated some of you over others in degrees, to try you with (actualize) what He gave to you (the forces of the Names)... Indeed, your Rabb is sariul iqab (the One who enforces the consequences of actions without relenting)! He is the Ghafur, the Rahim.

7

AL-A'RAF

By the one who is denoted by the name Allah (who created my being with His Names in accord with the meaning of the letter 'B'), the Rahman, the Rahim.

1. Alif, Lam, Meem, Saad.

2. This Knowledge (Book) of the reality and sunnatullah that has been revealed to you, is for you to warn (the unbelievers) and to advise the believers (as to how and what to believe and what to practice)... So, let there be no more distress in you regarding this.

3. Follow what has been revealed to you from your Rabb... Do not follow allies (those who give external [information that leads you away from your divine reality] and internal [ego based, carnal information]) outside of your Rabb... How little you remember and contemplate in depth!

4. How many cities of people We have destroyed; Our torment came to them while they were sleeping at night or during the day.

5. When Our torment came to them, their exclamation was no other than, "We were indeed wrongdoers."

6. Most certainly We will ask both those to whom a Rasul has been sent and the Rasuls!

7. Surely We are going to reveal the truth of the matter! We are not unaware (of what transpires) (He is the Batin and the Zahir – The angelic forces comprising manifestation are derived from Our Names).

8. The evaluation (of everything that transpires) in that time is done in truth (based on the creeds of Allah)... Those whose scales (evaluations) weigh heavy, they are the ones who will overcome all obstacles and attain liberation.

9. And those whose scales (evaluations) weigh light, they are the ones who will have wronged Our signs and thus become losers.

10. Indeed We have established you upon the earth and produced blessings therein with which you sustain your livelihood. How little you evaluate!

11. In truth, We have created you and given you form. Then We said to the angels, "Prostrate to Adam (in respect of Adam being the manifestation of the totality of Allah's Names)"; so they all prostrated (realized their nothingness in the sight of the manifestation of Allah's Names), except for Iblis. He was not of those who prostrated (He was of the jinn; an ego-based existence).

12. (Allah) said, "What prevented you from prostrating when I commanded you?" (Iblis) said, "I am better than him. You created me from fire (radiation – a specific frequency based existence. Note that the word fire [naar] in this verse is the same as the word used in reference to hellfire. This is worth contemplating upon!) and created him from clay (matter)."

13. (Allah) said, "Descend from your rank, for this rank is not for arrogance and feeling superior over others! Go! Indeed, you have debased yourself."

14. (Iblis) said, "Reprieve me until the Day they are resurrected (after death)."

15. (Allah) said, "Indeed you are of those reprieved."

16. (Iblis) said, "Because You have led me astray, (yudhillu man yashau – based on the reality that He leads astray whom He wills), I shall most certainly sit on Your straight path (sirat al-mustaqim) to prevent them."

17. "Then I will come to them from before them (by provoking ambition in them and glorifying their sense of self [ego] to lead them to the denial of the Truth) and from behind them (by imposing delusive ideas in them and leading them to disguised forms of shirq [duality]) and on their right (by inspiring them to do 'good deeds' that will take them away from You) and on their left (by beautifying misdeeds and making the wrong appear as right)... And You will find most of them as ungrateful to You (unable to evaluate what You have given them)!"

18. (Allah) said, "Leave my rank; debased and distanced (from experiencing your reality)! Whoever follows you among them, I will surely fill hell with you all."

19. **"O Adam! Dwell, you and your spouse, in Paradise... Eat and drink from wherever you please, but do not approach this tree** (the body – the consequences of accepting yourself as the body)**... Lest you be among the wrongdoers.**

20. **Thereupon Satan whispered suspicions to them to make them aware of their ego and corporeality... He said, "The reason your Rabb forbids you from this tree** (experiencing your corporeality) **is so you do not become two angels** (in the realm of forces) **and live eternally!"**

21. **"And he swore to them, 'Indeed, I am from among the advisors'."**

22. **Thus he deceived them** (by imposing deluding thoughts, making them think they are the physical body; drawing their attention to their corporeality)**. And when they tasted that tree** (sex; the mechanism of reproduction) **they became aware of their corporeal-bodily selves! They began to cover themselves with the leaves of Paradise** (they tried to suppress their corporeality with the forces of the Names present in their essence)**... Their Rabb called to them, "Did I not forbid you from that tree and tell you that Satan is an obvious enemy to you?"**

23. **They said, "Our Rabb! We have wronged ourselves... If you do not forgive us and grace us we will surely be among the losers."**

24. (Allah) **said, "Descend** (to the constricted lower state of bodily existence from a life governed by pure forces) **as enemies to one another** (the duality of body and consciousness)**! And for you on the earth** (bodily state of existence) **is a set time of existence and a set period, in which you will receive your share of provisions.**

25. **He said, "You will live therein and die therein and from it** (the body) **you will be brought forth."**

26. **O Children of Adam... We have indeed disclosed to you clothing** (knowledge of the reality) **to cover your corporeality and as adornment** (treats from His bounty)**... The clothing for protection is surely the best... This is from the signs of Allah, perhaps they will think and take a lesson.**

27. **O Children of Adam! Do not let Satan** (your body) **tempt you into provocation like he removed your parents from Paradise by showing them their corporeality and thus stripping them of their clothes** (angelic forces)**! For, he and his helpers** (all satanic forces that serve the same function) **see you from a place where you do not see them... We**

have made the devils (corruptive forces – conditioned beliefs based on the five senses) **befriend the unbelievers.**

28. **Whenever they commit an indecency** (an action or thought leading to duality or to the denial of the reality) **they say, "We found our fathers doing it, and this is what Allah ordered us to do"... Say, "Allah certainly does not order indecency! Are you attributing to Allah things about which you have no knowledge?"**

29. **Say, "My Rabb has ordered for you to live justly; giving the due rights of all things... Set your faces** (experience the dissolution of your ego through submission) **in every masjid** (place of prostration) **and pray only to Him by specifying your understanding of religion to Him alone... You will return to Him in your initial state** (the state of Adam in Paradise).

30. **A group of you He guided and a group deserved to be in falsity! Indeed, they** (those who went astray) **had taken the devils** (the deviators) **as allies instead of Allah, and they consider themselves as rightly guided!**

31. **O Children of Adam, wear your adornment in every place of prostration... Eat and drink** (evaluate these) **but do not waste** (do not consume unnecessarily)**... For, He does not favor those who waste** (misuse the blessings they possess)!

32. **Say, "Who has prohibited the beautiful things and the clean – pure provisions that Allah has brought forth for His servants?"... Say, "They are for those who believe during the worldly life; and on Doomsday, it shall be theirs exclusively." Thus We detail Our signs for those with comprehension.**

33. **Say, "The truth is, my Rabb has only forbidden the following: Apparent and concealed indecencies, crime** (in the sight of Allah)**, oppression** (aspiring for the properties of others and desiring to seize it)**, associating things about which there is no proof of partnership, and saying things about Allah that you do not know."**

34. **And for all people a specified term** (lifespan) **is set. So when the end of their time has come, they can neither delay it by a single moment, nor can they hasten it.**

35. **O Children of Adam... When Rasuls come from among you to relate and explain Our signs to you, whoever protects and corrects himself will have no fear nor will they be grieved.**

36. Those who deny Our signs (the manifestations of the Names) **and who are arrogant toward them, they are the people of fire** (Naar, a specific wavelength, radiation)**! They will abide therein eternally.**

37. Who does more wrong than he who lies about Allah or denies His existence is His signs? They will attain their portion of the Book (the revealed knowledge)**... When finally our Rasuls come to them to take them in death, they will say, "Where are those you used to invoke besides Allah, those you assumed existed?"... They will say, "They are lost and gone" and will bear witness against themselves that they were deniers of the reality.**

38. (Allah) **will say, "Enter among those who had passed on before you of the jinni and mankind into the fire** (Naar, radiation, a searing environment of wavelengths)**"... Every time a new community enters, it will curse it's close ones with whom it shared the same belief! Finally, when all of them have entered, the latter group will say about the former groups, "Our Rabb... They are the one who corrupted us... So, give them double the suffering of fire** (radiation)**"... He will say, "For all of you there is double, but you do not know."**

39. The former ones will say to the latter ones, "You have no superiority over us... Taste the suffering brought by your own doings!"

40. Indeed, those who deny Our signs and are arrogant toward them, the gates of Heaven (the observation of the reality) **will not be opened for them, nor will they enter Paradise** (the state of experiencing the Names comprising their essence) **until a rob/camel enters through the eye of a needle** (i.e. never)**... Thus do We recompense the criminals!**

41. They will have a bed from Hell and coverings (curtains) **over them** (their consciousness)**... Thus do We recompense the wrongdoers.**

42. As for those who believed and performed the requirements of their faith... We do not charge anybody with what is beyond their capacity; they are the people of Paradise... They will abide therein eternally.

43. We have removed all forms of hatred and resentment from within them... Rivers flow beneath them... They will say, "That which has guided us here belongs to Allah, HAMD (the evaluation of

the corporeal worlds created with His Names, as He wills, belongs to
Allah)! **Had Allah not guided us, we could not have attained this...
Indeed, the Rasuls of Allah have come in Truth."**

44. The people of Paradise will call out to the people of the fire, **"We
have found what our Rabb promised us to be true... Have you found
what your Rabb promised you to be true?"... They said, "Yes."
Then an announcer among them will announce, "The curse of
Allah is upon the wrongdoers."**

45. (They are the ones) **who prevent you from the way of Allah and
who want to lead you astray... They are the ones who deny the
eternal life to come.**

46. There is a curtain between the two (Paradise and Hell)... **And on
A'raf** (the state of those who have believed in their essence, but have not
yet duly experienced its outcome) **are men who recognize each of them
by the marks on their faces... They will call out to the people of
Paradise, "Assalamu alaikum." They** (these men) **have not yet
entered Paradise, but they long for it.**

47. And when their eyes turn toward the people of fire (Naar,
radiation), **they will say, "Our Rabb! Do not place us with the
wrongdoers."**

48. The people of the A'raf (those who have believed in their essence
but have not yet duly experienced its outcome) **will call out to men** (of
hell) **whom they recognize by their mark, "Of no avail to you was
your wealth or your arrogance!"**

**49. "Are these the ones whom you swore that Allah will not embrace
with His grace?"** (Whereas now they are told): **"Enter Paradise! There
is no fear for you... And you will not be grieved!"**

50. The people of fire (Naar, radiation) **will call out to the people of
Paradise, "Pour upon us some of that water** (knowledge) **or from
whatever Allah has provided you** (the forces comprising heavenly
life)"... (They will be answered): **"Indeed Allah has made this
forbidden upon the deniers of the knowledge of the reality."**

51. They are those who have turned their religion (the knowledge of
the reality and the System; sunnatullah) **into an amusement and
entertainment, who have been deluded by the** (vile) **worldly life...
Just as they have forgotten the meeting of this day and consciously
denied Our signs, We will forget them today!**

52. And certainly We have brought them a source of information and detailed it based on knowledge, as a signpost to grace and guidance to a people who believe.

53. Do they wait only for its interpretation (its absolute meaning)? The time when its interpretation becomes manifest, those who forgot before will say, "Indeed the Rasuls of our Rabb have brought the Truth... Will there be any intercessors to intercede for us or could we be sent back so that we do differently to what we (previously) did!" They have indeed put themselves into loss, and realized the emptiness of what they assumed existed!

54. Indeed your Rabb is Allah, the One who created the heavens and the earth in six stages, then established Himself on the Throne (i.e. began to administer them as He pleased)... He covers the night with the cloth of the day, which rapidly follows the night... The sun, the moon, and the stars fulfill His command... Know without doubt that both creation and judgment belong to Him! Exalted is Allah, the Rabb of the worlds!

55. Pray to your Rabb beseechingly and genuinely... Indeed He does not like the transgressors.

56. And do not cause corruption on earth after its reformation... Pray to him with fear and with the belief that He will respond. Indeed, the grace of Allah is near the doers of good (the grace of Allah reaches you by the hand that delivers it).

57. It is HU who discloses the winds as good tidings before His grace... Until the winds carry the heavy clouds, We drive them to a dead land and disclose water from them and bring forth all types of fruit therein... Thus We bring forth the dead... Perhaps you will contemplate on what this means!

58. The vegetation of the clean and good land emerges with the permission (Bi-izni RabbiHI) of your Rabb... But from filth, nothing emerges other than what is useless... Thus We diversify the signs for a people who evaluate.

59. We had certainly revealed Noah to his people and he had said, "O my people, serve Allah... You have no deity besides Him... Indeed, I fear for you the punishment of a tremendous time."

60. The leaders in traditional opinion among his people said, "Indeed, we see you in clear error."

61. Noah said, "O my people... There is no error in my view... But I am a Rasul from the Rabb of the worlds."

62. "I convey the message of my Rabb to you... I talk in your favor (for) I know (with the bestowed knowledge) from Allah what you do not know."

63. "Are you surprised that your Rabb notifies you through a man among you, who He has charged to warn you, so that you may be protected and attain grace?"

64. But they denied him... So We saved him and those with him in the ship... And We drowned those who denied Our signs (manifestations of the Names)... Indeed, they were a people with no insight!

65. And to (the people of) Aad, their brother Hud... (He said) "O my people... serve Allah... you have no deity besides Him... Will you still not protect yourselves?"

66. The leaders among the disbelievers of his people said, "We see you in foolishness... and we presume you are a liar."

67. (Hud) said, "O my people... There is no foolishness in me... But I am a Rasul of the Rabb of the worlds."

68. "I convey to you the messages of my Rabb... I am a trustworthy advisor to you."

69. "Are you surprised that a man among you has been advised by your Rabb to warn you? Remember, think! He appointed you vicegerents after the people of Noah and increased you extensively in stature and provisions... Remember and evaluate the blessings of Allah so that you may be liberated."

70. They said, "Have you come to us so that we serve Allah, the ONE, and abandon what our fathers have worshipped? If you are speaking the truth, then bring us the thing with which you threaten us (so that we see it)!"

71. (Hud) said, "In truth, the hurricane of your Rabb's punishment and wrath (the state of duality) has already befallen you! Are you arguing with me about the unsubstantiated names you gave to the gods, you and your fathers, for which Allah has not revealed any evidence (in regards to their existence)? Then wait; indeed, I am with you among those who wait."

72. So we saved him and those with him by surrounding them with Our grace... And We uprooted those who denied our verses... They did not believe.

73. And to Thamud (We sent) their brother Salih... He said, "O my people! Serve Allah... You cannot have a deity besides Allah... Clear evidence has come to you from your Rabb... This female camel of Allah is a miracle for you! So leave her to eat on Allah's earth! Do not dare to ponder any harm upon her! Lest you fall into a painful punishment!"

74. "And remember when He made you vicegerents after Aad and established you upon the earth... You obtain palaces from it and carve its mountains to form homes for yourselves! Then remember and think about these blessings of Allah and do not cause transgression on the earth through corruption."

75. The leaders among the people (of Salih) who were arrogant said to the weaker believers among them, "Do you actually believe that Salih is disclosed by your Rabb?" They said, "We believe in what has been revealed through him (as though it has been revealed to us)."

76. The conceited arrogant ones said, "Indeed we are deniers of that which you believe."

77. Then they savagely slaughtered the female camel and were disobedient to the command of their Rabb, and they said, "O Salih... If you are of the Rasuls, then bring the punishment with which you threaten us."

78. A harsh earthquake seized them... They collapsed in their homes and died!

79. And he (Salih) turned away from them and said, "O my people... Indeed I have conveyed to you the message of my Rabb and advised you, but you do not like those who talk in your favor."

80. And remember when Lot said to his people, "Do you commit immoralities that no one before you in the world committed?"

81. "You leave women and sleep with men! No, you are a transgressing people!"

82. The answer of his people was only, "Evict them from your city... For they are men who are purified (from such things)."

83. So We saved him and his people... except his wife! She stayed behind and was of those who were caved-in!

84. We rained down upon them suffering (a volcanic eruption according to narration)! Have a look and see how these criminals ended up!

85. And We sent (disclosed) their brother Shuayb to Madyan. (He said): "O my people, serve Allah; you do not have a deity besides Allah... Clear evidence has come to you from your Rabb... So fulfill the measure and weight properly... Do not deprive people of their due... Do not cause corruption on the earth after its reformation... This is better for you, if you are believers."

86. "Do not intercept the path of people by threatening and preventing the believers from the way of Allah and wanting them to go astray! Have a think, you were few, He made you many... Have a look and see the end of the corrupters!"

87. "And if among you there is a group who believes in the reality I have brought and a group who does not believe, then be patient until Allah judges between us... He is the best of judges."

88. The leaders among the people (of Shuayb) who were arrogant said, "O Shuayb! Surely we will evict you and those who are with you from our city, or you must turn to the religion of our fathers"... (Shuayb said) "Even if we are unwilling?"

89. "We would surely have invented a lie against Allah if we turned to your ancestral religion after Allah has saved us from that baseless religious view... It is not possible for us to turn to it! Unless our Rabb, Allah so wills... Our Rabb has encompassed all things with His knowledge... We have placed our trust in Allah (we believe the Name Wakil in our essence will fulfill its function) Our Rabb, join us and our people upon the Truth... You are the best conqueror!"

90. The leaders among his people who denied the knowledge of the reality said, "If you follow Shuayb, you will surely be among the losers."

91. So the severe quake seized them... They were left fallen upon their knees in their homes.

92. Those who denied Shuayb were (perished) as though they had never resided there... Those who denied Shuayb became the losers.

93. (Upon this, Shuayb) **turned away from them and said, "O my people! Indeed, I had conveyed the message of my Rabb to you... I had advised you... But how can I grieve for people who deny the knowledge of the reality?"**

94. **And to whichever community We have revealed a Nabi We have surely seized its people with hardship and ailment** (to rid them of their egocentricity) **so they might turn** (to their essential reality) **with sincerity and humbleness.**

95. **Then We exchanged their hardship with good... When they reached comfort** (of possessions and offspring) **and prospered, they said, "Our fathers were also touched by hardship and ease** (so there is no lesson in this for us).**" So We seized them suddenly before they knew it!**

96. **If the people of those cities had believed and protected themselves, We would surely have opened blessings upon them from the heaven and the earth... But they denied! So We seized them with what they earned with their deeds!**

97. **Did the people of those cities feel secure from Our wrath coming to them one night while they were asleep?**

98. **Or did the people of those cities feel secure from Our wrath coming to them in the morning while they were at play?**

99. **(Or) were they secure from the plan of Allah** (that Allah will make them live the consequences of their deeds without them even realizing, and hence, thinking there is no consequence, they will continue to engage in their activities and sink further in failure)**! None can feel secure from the plan of Allah but the people who are in loss.**

100. **Have they, the inheritors of those who were destroyed, have** (still) **not realized the truth that if We will We could afflict them with calamities and lock their hearts** (consciousness) **so they will not be able to perceive!**

101. **So We successively relate to you the news of the dwellers of those places... Indeed, the Rasuls had surely come as clear proofs...** (But) **they did not believe** (in light of the letter B) **in what they previously denied** (religion)**... Thus Allah seals the hearts** (locks the consciousness) **of those who deny the knowledge of the reality.**

102. **And We did not find most of them devoted to their promise... We found the majority of them disobedient to the Truth.**

103. Then, after them, We disclosed Moses with Our proofs (manifestations of Names) to the Pharaoh and the leaders around him... But they did wrong (by not heeding the signs)... Look and see the end of the corrupters!

104. Moses said, "O Pharaoh! Indeed, I am a Rasul from the Rabb of the worlds."

105. "I am truly obligated to not speak about Allah except what is based on the Truth... I have indeed come to you as a clear sign from your Rabb... So, send the Children of Israel with me!"

106. (The Pharaoh said): "If you have come with a miracle, then bring it forth, if you are true to your word!"

107. (Upon this) Moses released his staff, and suddenly the staff appeared as a serpent!

108. And (Moses) drew out his hand, and suddenly (his hand) appeared as a bright white light!

109. The eminent ones (priests) among the people of Pharaoh said, "Indeed, this is a learned magician"...

110. "He wants to expel you from your land (status)"... (The Pharaoh asked) "What do you advise?"

111. They said, "Restrain him and his brother... Send heralds to the cities."

112. "Let them bring to you every learned magician."

113. And the magicians came to Pharaoh... They said, "If we prevail, there will indeed be a prize for us, will there not?"

114. (The Pharaoh said) "Yes"... "Indeed, you are going to be of the close ones to me."

115. (The magicians said) "O Moses... First you throw, then we will throw."

116. (Moses said) "You throw"... When they (the magicians) threw, they bewitched the eyes of the people and struck terror into them! They performed a great magic.

117. And We inspired to Moses, "Throw your staff"... And alas, it devoured their make-believe falsehood!

118. Thus the Truth was established and what they were doing was abolished.

119. They were overcome... They were debased!

120. The magicians fell down as though in prostration!

121. They said, "We have believed in the Rabb of the worlds..."

122. "The Rabb of Moses and Aaron!"

123. Pharaoh said, "Have you believed in Him without my permission? Surely this is a plot, which you devised and conspired, to drive the people out of the city... But you will soon see (the punishment)"

124. "I will indeed cut your hands and feet on alternate sides and then crucify you all."

125. (The magicians who had believed said) "Indeed, we will return to our Rabb."

126. "You are avenging us because we believed in the existence of our Rabb in His miracles (manifestations of His Names)... Our Rabb, give us the strength to persevere and let us die as those who have submitted to You."

127. The leaders among the people of Pharaoh said, "Will you leave Moses and his people so they cause corruption on the earth and abandon you and your gods?" (Pharaoh said) "We will kill their sons and keep their women alive... A devastating power we have over them."

128. Moses said to his people, "Seek help from Allah (the continual manifestation of the Names of Allah from your essence due to His Uluhiyyah; from the forces of the Names comprising your being) and have patience... Indeed, the earth belongs to Allah... He renders inheritors whom He wills among His servants... The future is for the protected ones!

129. (The people of Moses said) "We have been tortured before you came to us and after you have come to us"... (Moses said) "Perhaps your Rabb will destroy your enemy and appoint you vicegerents on earth (in their stead) and see how you will do."

130. We have certainly seized the people of Pharaoh with years of famine and deficiency in produce that perhaps they would reflect on its reason.

131. But when a good came to them they said, "This is our earning"... And when a bad came to them they saw it as an ill omen of Moses and those with him... Be careful, what they take as an ill omen is with Allah alone... But most of them cannot comprehend this!

132. And they said, "No matter what miracle you bring to bewitch us, we will not believe in you!"

133. So We sent upon them floods, locusts, lice, frogs and blood, as indicative signs! Yet they were arrogant and became a guilty community.

134. When suffering befell them, they said, "O Moses! Keep your word and pray to your Rabb... If you remove this suffering from us we will surely believe in you and we will send the Children of Israel with you."

135. But when We remove the suffering from them, until the specified term We have given them comes to an end, they will break their word at once!

136. Hence We have vehemently made them live the consequences of their deeds, and We drowned them in the sea for denying Our miracles and signs and for being heedless of them!

137. The people who had been scorned and oppressed, We made them the inheritors of the land, which We blessed with abundance, in the east and the west... The good word of your Rabb was fulfilled for the Children of Israel because of their patience. And We destroyed the things Pharaoh and his people were producing and what they were building!

138. We took the Children of Israel across the sea... They came upon a community of people who were worshipping their idols. They said, "O Moses... Make a god for us just like the gods they have" (Moses said) "Indeed, you are so ignorant!"

139. "Surely their faith and application will bring about destruction! What they are engaging in is worthless/vain."

140. "When he has chosen you (by informing you of the reality of vicegerency) over the worlds (mankind), shall I assume a god for you besides Allah?"

141. And (remember) We had saved you from the dynasty of the Pharaoh... (Remember how) they were afflicting you with the worst torment; they were killing your sons and keeping your women alive... And in that there was a great trial for you from your Rabb.

142. We pledged thirty nights to Moses... Then We added ten to it; thus the time appointed by his Rabb was completed to forty nights... Moses said to his brother Aaron, "Take my place among my people, reform, and do not follow those who want to incite provocation!"

143. When the period We appointed was complete, and his Rabb called out to him, (Moses) said to his Rabb, "My Rabb, show me Yourself, let me look at You!"... (His Rabb said) "Never can 'you' (with your illusory self – ego) see (comprehend) 'Me'... (Absolute Reality, Absolute 'I')... But look at the mountain (ego)... If the mountain remains in place after I reflect Myself, then you shall see Me!" When his Rabb reflected on the mountain (ego), He destroyed it... and Moses fell unconscious (freed from his self, I'ness, ego)! When he woke up, he said, "Subhan, You are (I exalt you)! I have repented to You... I am the first of the believers."

144. He said, "O Moses! Indeed, I have chosen you over the people with My messages and My words... So, take what I have given you and be among the grateful (those who benefit)!"

145. We wrote in detail for Moses on the tablets, about the things from which they should refrain, and the things they require for life... "Hold these firmly and order your people to properly apply and preserve them... I will show you the home of those who are disobedient (to these commands)."

146. I will hold away from my miraculous forces those who are arrogant on the earth without right, for whatever miracle they see, they will not believe! If they see the way of consciousness, they will not adopt it as a way... If they see the way of corruption, they will adopt it as a way... This is because they have denied Our signs (of the reality) and were heedless of them.

147. Those who have denied our signs (of the reality) and the meeting of the eternal life to come, their deeds have become vain... Are they not living solely the results of what they used to do?

148. And the people of Moses made, after him (after his departure to Mount Sinai) a bellowing calf, from their valuable ornaments... Did they not realize that the calf was neither able to talk to them, nor guide them to a path? They took it (as a deity) and became of the wrongdoers (they wronged themselves)!

149. When they thought about (what they were doing) and realized they had gone astray from the reality, they felt regret and said, "If our Rabb does not bestow His grace upon us and forgive us, surely we will be among the losers."

150. When Moses came back to his people, angry and grieved, he said, "What wretched things you did behind my back! Could you not have waited for the command of your Rabb?" Then he put down the tablets and held his brother by his head and pulled him toward himself... (Aaron said) "O son of my mother! Indeed, the people reckoned me weak and powerless and were nearly going to kill me... So, do not let the enemy rejoice and do not hold me equal with these wrongdoers!"

151. (Moses said) "My Rabb... Forgive me and my brother and include us into Your grace... You are the most Rahim of the Rahim (the One who manifests the infinite qualities of Your Names with Your grace)."

152. Indeed, those who took the calf (as god) will receive the wrath of their Rabb and debasement in the worldly life... Thus We recompense the slanderers.

153. But there are some who became regretful after their misdeeds and repented, and they believed... Indeed, your Rabb, thereafter, is the Ghafur, the Rahim.

154. When Moses' anger subsided he took the tablets... In that inscribed text, there is guidance (comprehension of the reality) and grace from their Rabb, for those who fear.

155. Moses chose seventy men among his people to go to the appointed place to repent... When a severe earthquake seized them, (Moses) said, "My Rabb... Had You willed, You could have destroyed both them and I (for covering the reality) before! Will You destroy us now for the actions of the foolish (limited in intellect)

among us? This is only your provocation (trial) with which You lead astray whom You will and guide whom You will... You are our Waliyy (guardian). Forgive us and bestow Your grace upon us... You are the best of forgivers."

156. "And decree good things for us both in this world and the eternal life to come... Indeed, we have turned to You"... He said, "I afflict whom I will with My wrath... My grace encompasses all things! I will decree it for those who protect themselves, who give alms, and who believe in the reality, in Our signs."

157. Those who follow the Rasul, the Ummi (unlettered) Nabi (whose natural disposition has not been corrupted and original purity is preserved) who has been stated in the Torah and the Gospel in their hands... He orders what is favorable (positive) according to Allah and forbids what is unfavorable (negative) he makes the clean things lawful and prohibits the filthy and ugly things, he relieves them of the heavy burdens on their backs and unshackles them from their chains (the ties preventing them from turning to Allah)... Those who believe in him, respect (support) him, help him and follow the Nur (Quran) that has been revealed to him, they are the ones who will attain liberation!

158. Say, "O people... I am indeed a Rasul of Allah who has come to you all... To HU belongs the sovereignty of the heavens and the earth! There is no god (deity) only HU! He gives life and causes death! So believe in Allah, whose Names comprise the essence of your being, and his Rasul, the Ummi (unlettered) Nabi, who believes in Allah, the essence of his self, and what He disclosed... Follow him so that you may be lead to the reality."

159. There is a group among the people of Moses who informs the reality based on the Truth, and as the requirement of living the reality, performs all things duly and justly!

160. We have divided them into twelve communities... And We inspired Moses, when his people asked for water from him, "Strike the stone with your staff (by integrating the staff with the forces within your essence)"... and there gushed forth twelve springs... Every group of people knew their way (their drinking place). And We shaded them with clouds and disclosed for them manna (power) and quails... (We said) "Eat from the clean and pure things with which We have provided you"... They did not do wrong to Us, but they wronged their own selves.

161. And (mention) when it was said to them, "Dwell in this city and eat from it wherever you will... Say, 'Forgive us' and enter through its gate by experiencing the meaning of prostration, so that We may forgive your mistakes... We will increase it even more for the doers of good."

162. Those among them who did wrong in deed, changed the words to a statement other than that which was said to them... This is why We sent down suffering from the sky as the consequence of their wrongdoing.

163. Ask them about the town by the sea!... How they had transgressed on Sabbath (by going fishing on a Saturday)... Because the fish increased in number and revealed themselves on Sabbath but disappeared on other days! We tried them like this because they were given to transgression.

164. And when a community among them said, "Why do you give advice to people who Allah will destroy or punish with a severe suffering?"... They said, "To be absolved from our responsibility in the sight of our Rabb; and so that perhaps they may protect themselves."

165. When they forgot the advice given to them, We saved those who tried to prevent wrongdoing, and seized the wrongdoers with a wretched suffering, because of the mistaken deeds they were doing.

166. And when they became arrogant and transgressed that which was forbidden, We said to them, "Become despised apes (creatures who live in imitation of one another, who cannot use their intellect)."

167. And your Rabb has declared, He will certainly manifest those who will inflict themselves with the worst torment until Doomsday... Indeed, your Rabb is Sari'ul Iqab (instantly forms the consequences of misdeeds)... Indeed, He is the Ghafur, the Rahim.

168. We have divided them into factions on the earth... There are some among them who are righteous (those who live according to the requirements of having faith in the reality)... And there are some among them who are of an inferior level... We have tried them with good and bad that perhaps they will turn to the reality.

169. And following them were new generations who inherited the knowledge of the reality... They were living to attain the wealth of this base worldly life and were claiming, "We will be forgiven anyhow." If they were offered an equal amount of worldly goods,

they would have taken that too... Was a covenant not taken from them that they would not say things about Allah not based on the Truth? Did they not take a lesson from it and study what is in it? The eternal life to come is better for the protected ones... Will you not use your reason?

170. As for those who adhere to the knowledge of the reality (Book) and perform salat (prayer; experience their essence), indeed, We will not leave those who are reformed and those who reform without a reward.

171. And (mention) when We had raised the mountain above them as if it was a canopy, and they thought it was going to fall upon them and destroy them... "Hold firmly what We have given you, reflect upon what is therein and remember it so that you may be protected."

172. And (mention) when your Rabb took from the children of Adam, from their loins (semen, genes), their descendants and made them testify to their own selves, asking them, "Am I not your Rabb?" and they said, "Yes, indeed we bear witness!" (Of this we remind you) – lest you say on the day of Resurrection, "We were cocooned (unaware of this knowledge) of this" (This refers to man being created upon the natural disposition of Islam).

173. And so that you don't say, "Our fathers lived only as dualists, and we are their descendants (the continuation of their genetic coding) so will You destroy us because of our fathers' denial of the Truth?" (i.e. This is an invalid excuse as everyone is created upon the natural disposition of Islam, but their understanding of religion derives from the environmental conditionings they receive).

174. Thus We explain in detail the proofs – signs – that perhaps they will return (to their essential reality).

175. Give them the news of the man to whom We have given Our signs, yet he detached himself from the knowledge and left it (forgot the reality and pursued a life based on ego-identity)... (Then) Satan (accepting one's self as only the body) made him a follower (of this belief, until finally) he became of the astray ones.

176. Had We willed, We would have elevated him with these signs... But (instead) he settled on earth (bodily life) and followed his baseless impulses! So, his example is like that of a dog: if you chase him he pants, if you leave him he pants... This is what the people who deny

Our signs look like! Relate this to them, perhaps they will contemplate upon it.

177. **How wretched is the state of people who deny Our signs** (manifestations of Names) **and** (hence) **do wrong to their selves!**

178. **Whoever is enabled by Allah to observe his innermost essential self, he is the one who reaches the reality! And whoever Allah leads astray, indeed they are the ones who are in loss.**

179. **Indeed, We have created and increased in number the majority of the jinn and mankind for the life of hell! They have hearts** (consciousness) **with which they cannot understand** (the reality), **they have eyes with which they cannot evaluate what they see, they have ears with which they cannot understand what they hear! They are like cattle** (an'am), **nay, they are even less conscious of the right way: it is they who are the truly heedless** (living in their cocoons)!

180. **And to Allah belongs the most beautiful Names** (the qualities denoted by those Names reference the One and the Absolutely Self-sufficient Allah, hence these Names and their meanings belong to Him alone and cannot be defined by human concepts. As noted in 23:91 "Exalted (Subhan) is Allah beyond what they attribute to Him"), **so turn to Him through the meanings of His Names. And leave the company of those who practice deviation** (fall into duality) **concerning His Names. They will be recompensed for what they have been doing.**

181. **And among those We created there is** (such) **a community, they guide to the reality by the Truth, and they give everything its due right!**

182. **We will progressively lead those who deny Our signs** (pertaining to the reality) **to destruction from where they do not know** (through a scheme).

183. **And I will give them time to do what they want... Indeed, My fine plan is firm.**

184. **Did they not give thought? There is no madness** (mindlessness) **in their companion! He is only a clear warner.**

185. **Did they not look into the angelic realms** (forces) **of the heavens and the earth, to anything Allah has created, and that perhaps their appointed time** (death) **has neared? So,** (if they do not take heed of this) **what statement will they believe in?**

186. Whoever Allah leads astray, there is no guide for him... He will leave them in their transgression, wandering blindly.

187. They ask you, "When will that hour arrive?"... Say, "Its knowledge is only with my Rabb... HU is the One who will reveal it when it is time! (Concepts such as time, place, object, and person cannot be conceived in regards to that reflection)... It weighs heavy on the heavens and the earth... It will come to you unexpectedly." They ask you as if you know it (through experience)... Say, "Its knowledge is with Allah alone... But the majority of the people do not know."

188. Say, "I cannot form any benefit or any harm for myself, other than what Allah wills... If I had known (the absolute) unknown, surely I would have multiplied all good and no harm would have touched me... I am merely a warner and a bringer of glad tidings for a people who believe."

189. HU created you from ONE single soul – I'ness (in the macro plan this is known as the Reality of Muhammad and the First Intellect, in the micro plan it is known as the human consciousness and the Grand Intellect) and from it, formed his partner (at the macro plan: the universe; at the micro plan: the brain) so that you dwell with her... And when he covered her (his partner) she loaded a light burden and carried it... When it got heavy, they both prayed to Allah, "Indeed, if You give us a righteous (child) we will surely be among the evaluators." (This verse can be understood both in terms of the formation of the worlds and the formation of humans).

190. But when He gave them a righteous (child) they associated partners with Him concerning what He gave them... Exalted is Allah above what they associate with Him.

191. Are they associating those who do not create anything when they themselves are created? (There is a reference in these two verses to the tendency of mankind to conceive natural events and creatures as deities/gods besides Allah.)

192. (The deities they associate with Allah) have neither the power to help them, nor themselves!

193. If you invite them to guidance (the realization of one's essential reality) they will not follow you... Whether you invite them or remain silent, it is all the same.

194. Those to which you turn besides Allah are merely servants like yourselves! If you are persistent (in your belief) call them and let them respond to you!

195. Do they have feet with which they walk, hands with which they hold, eyes with which they see, or ears with which they hear? Say, "Call your partners (that you associate with Allah) and conspire against me and give me no respite!"

196. Indeed, my Waliyy (guardian) is Allah, the One who has revealed the knowledge (Book) of the reality! He befriends the doers of good.

197. Those to whom you call upon (for help) besides Him, have neither the power to help you nor can they help themselves.

198. If you call them for guidance they will not hear... You will think they are looking at you but they will not see!

199. Be forgiving, judge with positive and useful things, and turn away from the ignorant!

200. If an impulse comes to you from Satan (if you are tempted towards bodily desires and curtained from your reality) immediately seek refuge in Allah (the forces of the Names comprising your essential reality)... For He is the Sami, the Aleem.

201. As for those who are protected, when an impulse touches them from Satan (those who confine their existence to their body alone) they think about and remember (their essential reality)... They evaluate with insight.

202. But their (devils') brothers drag them to emotionality and extremity... And they will not let them be!

203. When you do not relate a verse to them, they say, "You should have made one up!" Say, "I follow only what is revealed to me from my Rabb... This (Quran) is an insight from your Rabb (enabling you to realize and comprehend), it is a guide (to the reality) and grace for a people who believe (it elevates and matures them)."

204. When the Quran is recited, listen to it and be silent so that you may receive grace.

205. Remember and contemplate in depth your Rabb in your self, by knowing your boundary, by feeling Him, and in a modest, confidential way, without raising your voice, in the morning and evening! Do not be of the heedless!

206. Indeed, those who are with your Rabb never show arrogance and refrain from servitude... They continue their existence through Him (tasbih) **and prostrate to Him** (by feeling their nothingness in the sight of His Might). (This is a verse of prostration.)

8

AL-ANFAL

By the one who is denoted by the name Allah (who created my being with His Names in accord with the meaning of the letter 'B'), the Rahman, the Rahim.

1. **They ask you about the distribution of the spoils of war... Say, "The spoils of war are for Allah and His Rasul... Protect yourselves from Allah** (from the consequences of not living your essential reality) **and amend the relation** (brotherhood based on faith) **between you** (by observing each other's essential reality). **If you are true believers, follow Allah and His Rasul** (for your essential reality and the articulator of that reality wants you to experience your essential reality).

2. **The believers** (who are certain in their faith) **are those who, when they mention and think of Allah, their consciousness shivers** (they feel their impotence in respect of His might) **and when His signs are recited to them, it increases their faith** (to the extent they are able to contemplate)**... They trust** (submit to) **their Rabb** (they believe the Name Wakil in their essence will fulfill its function).

3. **They are the ones who establish salat** (through introspectively turning toward Allah, they realize all things are subject to His command and experientially acknowledge there is nothing in existence other than the Names of Allah, thereby manifesting the reality "Allah is pre and post eternal – the Baqi") **and they spend from what We have provided them** (material provision or spiritual provision yielded as a result of experiencing the essence of salat).

4. **They are the true believers** (whose faith is founded on enquiry and verification)**... They have degrees** (formed by the stations of the Names comprising their essence) **and forgiveness** (formed by the knowledge – the forces of Names – that covers [dissolves] the ego-self) **and generous provision** (both material and spiritual).

5. **Just as when your Rabb had taken you out of your home by making you experience the reality** (i.e. this decision was not made as a result of your emotions, but rather based on the wisdom of your Rabb) **some of the true believers were not pleased with this.**

6. Even though the Truth had become clearly apparent, they were not accepting it... As if they were deliberately going toward death.

7. Remember when Allah promised you that one of the two groups (the Quraishi army or the caravan) **will be yours... You wanted the unarmed group** (the caravan) **to be yours** (you were interested in short-term gain, the one with an easy return, whereas this was going to give you harm in the long-run)**... But Allah willed to establish the Truth with His warnings and eliminate the deniers of the reality.**

8. (He wanted) **to establish the Truth and invalidate that which is vain and baseless... even if those who commit crime against Allah dislikes it!**

9. Remember when you asked for help from your Rabb and He answered you, "Indeed I will reinforce you with a thousand angels in succession."

10. Allah did this only as good tidings and so your hearts would be assured by it... Help and victory is only from Allah... Indeed, Allah is the Aziz, the Hakim.

11. Remember when He formed a state of tranquility and security from Him, and sent down water from the sky (water symbolizes knowledge, the state of certainty and the actualization of Allah's will) **to purify you** (from ego-based emotions) **and to rid you of the filth of Satan** (fear and doubt) **and to strengthen the observation of the Truth in your consciousness and secure your feet** (with this knowledge). (This verse is an example of the symbolic/allegoric expression in the Quran. For, 'rain', when taken literally, cannot secure one's feet or cleanse one from satanic impulses. This is an example of how such verses should be construed and evaluated.)

12. Remember when your Rabb had revealed to the angels, "Indeed I am with you (since Allah cannot be literally next to the angels, this verse is referencing what is known in Sufism as 'Unity of Existence', thus, the angels are consciously aware that the power inherent within them is none other than the power of Allah)**... Secure the believers... I will cast fear into the hearts of the deniers... Strike them upon their necks** (anchor the deniers upon their delusion) **and strike all their fingers."**

13. This is because they opposed Allah and His Rasul, and separated and detached themselves from Allah and His Rasul... And whoever opposes Allah and His Rasul, indeed Allah is the Shadid al-Iqab (severe in enforcing the due consequence of an offence).

14. Here it is (the results of your deeds), **so taste it! And for the deniers of the knowledge of the reality, there is the suffering of the fire** (the flames of which burns both internally and externally).

15. O believers... When you meet those who collectively deny the knowledge of the reality, do not turn your backs on them!

16. And whoever turns his back to them, unless as a strategy or to join another troop (of believers), **will indeed return with the wrath of Allah... His abode will be fire** (suffering)! **And what a wretched destination that is!**

17. And you did not kill them, but it was Allah who killed them! And you threw not (the arrow) **when you** (illusory self; ego) **threw, but it was Allah who threw! In order to make the believers experience a good from Himself** (His grace)! **Indeed, Allah is the Sami, the Aleem.**

18. Thus it is (you have lived and seen it)! **Indeed, Allah will weaken the plot of those who refuse to experience the knowledge of the reality!**

19. If you want conquest (victory), **conquest has come to you** (at Badr)... **If you stop** (resisting the Rasul of Allah) **it is better for you... But if you return** (to duality) **We will return too!** (In this case) **even if you are a large group, it will not benefit you... Allah is certainly with the believers** (He is with those who acknowledge and experience the reality that the strength and power inherent within them belongs to Allah).

20. O believers... Obey Allah and His Rasul! Do not turn away from Him while you hear!

21. Do not be like those who hear (but do not perceive) **and say, "We have heard"!**

22. Indeed, the worst of living creatures in the sight of Allah are the deaf and dumb, who do not use their reason (who live in imitation).

23. Had Allah known any good (ability to evaluate) **in them, He would surely have made them hear... And if He had made them hear** (under the circumstances of their current creational program) **they would still have turned away!**

24. O believers, when you are invited to that which revives you (the knowledge of the reality) **attend to the invitation of Allah and the Rasul. Know well that** (if you do not attend to this invitation) **Allah will**

intervene between the person's consciousness and his heart (Allah creates a barrier between his emotions and reason, abandoning him to an emotional state of existence that comprises his hell through the system of the brain) **and prevent him. To Him you will be gathered** (you will reside in a realm in which the Absolute Reality will become apparent; you will be evaluated by the qualities of the Names that comprise your essence).

25. **Protect yourselves from a calamity, which not only strikes the wrongdoers** (but also the good among that community)**... And know well that Allah is the Shadid al-Iqab** (severe in enforcing the due consequence of an offence).

26. **O believers... Remember the days when you feared the people might harm you because you were few and weak... But He sheltered you, supported you with His aid, and provided clean blessings for you so that you would be grateful** (evaluate and be thankful).

27. **O believers... Do not betray Allah and the Rasul... Do not betray** (the knowledge and gnosis that has reached you through Nubuwwah and Risalah) **while you know!**

28. **Know well that your possessions and children are only a provocation** (objects of trial) **for you! As for Allah, the great reward is with Him.**

29. **O believers... If you protect yourselves from Allah** (not betray what has reached you with the Rasul and your natural covenant; the ability to live according to the Names comprising your essence) **He will form for you furqan** (the ability and knowledge to differentiate the right from the wrong)**, cover your misdeeds and forgive you... Allah is Dhul Fadhlil Azeem** (the possessor of great bounty).

30. **Those who deny the knowledge of the reality were plotting against you to restrain you from your cause, or to kill you or to evict you** (from your homeland). **But they plan and Allah responds to their plan by making them live the consequences of their own plan** (by turning their plot against them). **And Allah is the best of planners!**

31. **When Our signs are recited to them, they say, "Indeed we have heard... If we willed we could have said something like this... This is none other than legends from the past!"**

32. **Remember when they said, "O Allah... If this the Truth from You, then rain down upon us stones from the sky! Or afflict us with a painful suffering."**

33. But Allah would not punish them while you are among them (for you have been disclosed as grace to the worlds)**... And Allah would not afflict them while there are those who seek forgiveness.**

34. While they are prevented from (visiting the believers in) **the al-Masjid al-Haram, why should Allah not punish them?** (This verse does not contradict with the previous verse as the former verse is referring to a communal suffering while this verse is in reference to individual suffering...) **And they are not its** (al-Masjid al-Haram's) **guardians... Its guardians are only those who protect themselves... But most of them do not know** (what the al-Masjid al-Haram is).

35. Their prayer (introspection) **at the House** (Baytullah) **is none other than whistling and handclapping** (externalized methods of worship taught by their forefathers)**... So taste the suffering for denying the Truth!**

36. Those who deny the knowledge of the reality, give away their wealth in order to prevent (people) **from the way of Allah! They will spend all of it! And then this spending will cause them heartache** (painful regret)**! Then they will be overcome! And** (finally) **in hell they, the deniers of the knowledge of the reality, will all be gathered.**

37. This is so that Allah separates the filthy from the clean, and fills hell with the filthy ones stacked on top of another... Indeed, they are the very losers.

38. Tell those who deny the knowledge of the reality, if they abandon (their false beliefs) **then their past mistakes will be forgiven! But if they return to their old beliefs, then remind them of what happened to the previous people!**

39. And fight them until oppression is lifted from the believers and the Religion (the knowledge of the reality and the system and order of Allah) **becomes clearly apparent and acknowledged** (but if they forcefully prevent you from this then fight them based on the Truth 'There is no compulsion in the matters of religion.')**. If they abandon** (oppression and prevention), **certainly Allah is Basir over what they do.**

40. If they turn away, know well that Allah is your Protector... An excellent Protector (owner) **and an excellent Helper** (giver of victory He is)**!**

41. If you have believed in Allah and the day of furqan (the day of those who separate and fight in the cause of either the truth or falsity) (that is) **to that which We have revealed to Our servant** (the reinforcement of the angels) **on the day when the two groups met in opposition** (the battle of Badr) **then know that one fifth of what you obtain of spoils is for Allah** (to be spent in the way of Allah)**, the Rasul, his relatives, the orphans, the needy and the travelers who have been stranded in the way of Allah... Allah is Qadir over all things.**

42. **(Remember) when you were on the nearest side and they were on the furthest side... And the caravan was lower than you... Had you made an appointment to meet them you could not have met them in as timely a way! But Allah actualized a matter that was already decreed** (there is no coincidence)**! So that, both those who perished and those who lived would have lived its requirement, based on the clear verdict of the Truth! Certainly Allah is the Sami, the Aleem.**

43. **Allah showed them to you in your sleep as few... If He had shown them to you as many, surely you would have been discouraged and disputed over it... But Allah emancipated you... Indeed He is Aleem of what is inside you** ('your personal world created in your mind') **as its very essence** (with His Names).

44. **And remember when you met them in opposition He showed them to you as few and made you appear to them as few... Thus Allah accomplished a matter already destined! All things will eventually return to Allah.**

45. **O believers! Stand firm** (with your faith) **when you encounter a group... And engage much in the dhikr** (contemplation and remembrance of the forces of the Names comprising your essence) **of Allah so you can overcome difficulties and attain salvation.**

46. **Obey Allah and His Rasul, and do not dispute with each other or you will lose courage and your wind** (strength) **will depart... Be patient... Indeed, Allah is with those who are patient through the quality of the Name Sabur.**

47. **Do not be like those who leave their homes insolently and to be seen by others and prevent people from the way of Allah! Allah is Mu'id over what they do!**

48. **Satan made their deeds appear alluring to them and said, "No one can overcome you today! Indeed, I am with you"... But when the two armies sighted each other he turned on his heels and said, "Indeed I am not with you! Indeed, I see what you do not see... And**

indeed, I fear Allah... Allah is Shadid al-Iqab (severe in enforcing the due consequence of an offence)."

49. **Remember when the hypocrites and those who were devoid of healthy thought due to the doubt in their hearts said, "Their religion has deluded them"... But whoever places their trust in Allah** (i.e. prevents the interference of their emotions and submits to the autopilot inherent within their creational program, that is, believes that the Names comprising their essence will fulfill their functions) **indeed Allah is the Aziz, the Hakim.**

50. **And if you could but see when the angels take the deniers of the reality at death, striking their faces and their backs, saying, "Taste the scorching suffering"!**

51. **"This is the return of your deeds! And Allah does not do wrong to his servants!"**

52. **Theirs is like the dynasty of the Pharaoh and of those before them... They denied the existence of Allah in His signs** (the manifestations of His Names) **so Allah seized them upon their error... Indeed, Allah is the Qawwi, and the Shadid al-Iqab** (severe in enforcing the due consequence of an offence).

53. **Thus it is... Allah would not change His blessing upon a people** (from their essence) **until they change what is within themselves! Allah is the Sami, the Aleem.**

54. **Just like the state of the dynasty of Pharaoh and those before them! They denied the existence of their Rabb in His signs** (qualities pertaining to their Rabb) **so We destroyed them for their mistakes and drowned the people of Pharaoh! They were all wrongdoers.**

55. **The worst of living creatures in the sight of Allah are those who deny the knowledge of the reality! They will not believe!**

56. **They are those with whom you made a treaty** (the Jewish tribes in the vicinity of Medina Munawara)**... But they break their pledge every time... They do not protect themselves** (they do not beware Allah).

57. **If you catch them in war, disperse them and those behind them that perhaps they will take a lesson.**

58. **If you fear betrayal from a people, let them know in advance that you invalidate the treaty! Indeed, Allah does not like the traitors.**

59. Let not those who deny the knowledge of the reality think they can save themselves by escaping... Certainly, they cannot render Allah powerless from doing what He wills!

60. Gather your power against them as much as you are able to and prepare steeds (of war) with which you may terrify the enemy of Allah, your enemy, and others whom you do not know, but Allah knows... Whatever you spend in the way of Allah, its reward will be paid back to you in full, and never will you be wronged!

61. If they incline towards peace, then incline also (to make peace)! Rely upon Allah (hold Allah as your representative, trust that the Name Wakil in your essence will fulfill its function)! For He is the Sami, the Aleem.

62. If they want to deceive you, then sufficient for you is Allah! It is He who supported you with His help and with the believers.

63. He has joined the hearts (of the believers) as a single heart through the love of sharing! If you had spent everything on the face of the earth you could not have brought their hearts together... But Allah brought them together (through intrinsic attraction of similar frequencies). Indeed He is al-Aziz, al-Hakim.

64. O Nabi! Sufficient is Allah for you and those who follow you from among the believers.

65. O Nabi! Encourage the believers for battle! If there are among you twenty (people) who endure, they will overcome two hundred. And if there among you one hundred who endure, they will overcome one thousand of those who deny the knowledge of the reality... They are a people with no understanding!

66. Allah has now lightened your burden, for He knows you have weakness... So, if there are one hundred among you who endure, they will overcome two hundred... If there are one thousand among you, they will, with the permission of Allah (B-izni-Allah), overcome two thousand... Allah is with those who are steadfast (patient).

67. It is not for a Nabi to have captives (without war) until he is dominant in the land... You desire the goods of the world (by wishing to capture rather than to slay your opponent), but Allah desires (for you) the eternal life to come... Allah is the Aziz, the Hakim.

68. Had it not been for a previous decree of Allah regarding this matter, you would surely have suffered on account of the ransom you took.

69. So, consume the lawful and the clean among what you took of spoils... And protect yourselves from Allah. Indeed, Allah is the Ghafur, the Rahim.

70. O Nabi! Tell the captives in your hands, "If Allah knows good (faith) is in your heart, then He will give you something better than what has been taken from you, and He will forgive you! Allah is the Ghafur, the Rahim."

71. If they intend to betray you, surely they have already betrayed Allah before, and He empowered you against them! Allah is the Aleem, the Hakim.

72. Indeed, those who have believed, and migrated (for this cause), and fought in the way of Allah with their possessions and their lives, and sheltered the immigrants and helped them, they are the ones who are allies of one another... But as for those who believed but did not migrate, you are not responsible for them until they migrate! If they ask for your help in religion, then it is your debt (duty) to help them, unless it is against a people with whom you have a treaty... Allah is Basir of what you do (based on the secret of the letter B).

73. And those who deny the knowledge of the reality are the protectors of one another (they support each other)! If you do not do this also (aid and support each other) then you will be subject to provocation and degeneration on the earth.

74. Those who have believed, fought in the way of Allah and sheltered (the immigrants) and aided them, they are the believers who live their faith duly! For them, there is forgiveness and abundance of provision.

75. And those who have believed later, and migrated and fought together with you, they are also with you! Those who are related (by blood) are nearer to one another (they protect and take responsibility for eachother) in the Book of Allah Indeed, Allah is Aleem over all things (as the essence of everything with His Names)!

9

AT-TAWBAH

1. An ultimatum this is, from Allah and His Rasul, to the dualists with whom you made a treaty!

2. Travel upon the earth for four months... But know well that you can never render Allah powerless... Indeed, Allah will (eventually) disgrace those who deny the knowledge of the reality.

3. A call (adhan) from Allah and His Rasul to the people on the day of the Great Pilgrimage, that Allah and His Rasul are free from the dualists! If you repent, it is better for you... But if you turn away, know well that you cannot render Allah impotent... Give the tidings of a painful end to the deniers of the reality.

4. Except those, among the dualists with whom you made a treaty, who did not let you down (who honored the treaty) and who did not support anyone against you... Fulfill your word to them until the end of the term (of the treaty). Indeed, Allah loves those who protect themselves.

5. When the sacred months are over, kill the dualists (who break the treaty and attack you) wherever you find them. Take them captive and besiege them and watch for them, taking control of all the gateways and passages! If they repent and establish salat and give alms then clear their way... Indeed, Allah is the Ghafur, the Rahim.

6. If one of the dualists surrenders and seeks your protection, then take him into your protection so (he may be closer to you and) he may hear the word of Allah, then deliver him to a place of safety... This is (what you must do) because they are a people who do not know (the reality).

7. How can the dualists have a treaty in the sight of Allah and His Rasul, except those with whom you made a treaty at al-Masjid al-Haram? So long as they uphold their word toward you, be upright toward them... Indeed, Allah loves those who submit to His command and who protect themselves from His punishment.

8. How (can there be a treaty with them)? If they gained dominance over you they would not have observed any oath or treaty

concerning you! They satisfy you with their words, but refuse with their hearts! Most of them are corrupted in faith!

9. They exchanged the signs of Allah for a small price (worldly pleasures) and prevented people from His way. How wretched is what they do!

10. They observe neither treaty nor covenant where believers are concerned! They are the very transgressors!

11. If they repent, establish salat, and give alms, they are your brothers in Religion... Thus We clarify Our signs for a people who know.

12. But if they break their oath after pledging it and denigrate your Religion, then kill the leaders of unbelief (the coverers of the reality)... For they have no regard for their oaths... Perhaps they will desist.

13. Will you not fight with those who have broken their oaths, banished the Rasul from his homeland and who are the first to attack you? Do you fear them? Surely Allah is more deserving of your fear and awe, if you are true believers.

14. Fight them; (so that) Allah will punish them through your hands and will disgrace them, and give you victory over them and (thus) give healing to the people who believe.

15. He will remove the rage from their hearts... Allah accepts the repentance of whom He wills... Allah is the Aleem, the Hakim.

16. Or did you think that you will be left to yourselves without Allah making evident which of you have strived in the way of Allah and did not befriend (and confide in) anyone except Allah, His Rasul and the believers? Allah is Habir of all that you do (with the meaning of the Name Habir in your essence).

17. It is not possible for the dualists, who are witnesses of their own denial, to maintain the places of prostration to Allah... All of their deeds have gone in vain... In fire (Naar; radiation) they will remain forever!

18. The places of prostration to Allah can only be maintained (brought to a state of prostration to Allah) by those who believe in Allah – as comprising their essence with His Names – the eternal life to come, establish salat, give alms, and are in awe of Allah

alone... It is expected that they will be of those who attain the reality.

19. (O dualists) have you made the providing of water for the pilgrim and the maintenance of the al-Masjid al-Haram equal to the deeds of the one who believes in Allah, the essence of one's being with His Names, and the life to come and who strive in this cause? They cannot be equal in the sight of Allah! Allah does not guide a wrongdoing people.

20. Those who believe, migrate and fight in the way of Allah with their possessions and their lives, are greater in the sight of Allah by degrees... They are the ones who attain liberation!

21. Their Rabb gives them glad tidings from HU (their essence) of grace, pleasure, and Paradises that are permanent blessings (ranks) for them.

22. They will reside therein eternally... The great reward is in the sight of Allah!

23. O believers! Do not befriend your fathers and brothers if they prefer denial of the reality over belief... And whoever among you befriends them, they are the very wrongdoers.

24. Say, "If your fathers, sons, brothers, partners, tribes, possessions that you have earned, businesses that concern you, and dwellings you favor are more pleasing to you than Allah, His Rasul and striving in His cause, then wait for the command of Allah to reveal itself... Allah does not guide corrupted people (those whose consciousness have been blinded to Truth and Religion)."

25. Indeed, Allah has helped you on many battlegrounds and on the day of Hunayn... Remember how you were boasting about your great number, but it did not avail you in any way! And you felt confined (on the day of Hunayn) despite the vastness of the earth! And you turned your backs and left!

26. Then Allah disclosed a sense of tranquility and security over the believers, and revealed armies (of angels) that you could not see... (Thus) He made the deniers of the reality suffer... This is the consequence for those who deny the reality!

27. Then Allah will accept the repentance of whom He wills... Allah is the Ghafur, the Rahim.

28. O believers! Verily the dualists (who claim the existence of their ego-identities alongside the Absolute Oneness) **are contaminated** (filth)! **Let them not go near the al-Masjid al-Haram after this year! If you fear poverty** (know that) **if Allah wills He will enrich you from His bounty... Indeed, Allah is the Aleem, the Hakim.**

29. From those to whom the Knowledge (Book) **has been given, fight those who do not believe in Allah and the life to come** (beyond death), **who do not consider unlawful what Allah and His Rasul have made forbidden, and who do not embrace the understanding of the Religion of Truth** (the knowledge of the reality and sunnatullah) **until they are humbled and give the jizyah** (the cost of persisting on a false belief) **willingly.**

30. The Jews said, "Ezra is the son of Allah"... And the Christians said, "The Messiah is the son of Allah"... They say this with their mouths! They imitate those who previously denied the knowledge of the reality... May Allah kill them! How they are deluded (from the Truth)!

31. They took their rabbis and priests as Rabbs besides Allah... And the Messiah, the son of Mary! But they were ordered only to experience the awareness of their servitude to the One Uluhiyyah... La ilaha illa HU — there is no god, only HU! Subhan He is from what they associate with Him!

32. They want to extinguish the light (Nur) **of Allah with their mouths... But Allah is pleased with none other than the completion of His Nur! Even if this does not please the deniers of the reality!**

33. HU has revealed His Rasul as the reality itself and with the Religion of Truth (the valid knowledge of the system; sunnatullah) **to establish above all conceptions of religion... Even if the dualists dislike it!**

34. O believers! Indeed, many of the rabbis and clergy devour the wealth of people unjustly and prevent people from the way of Allah... As for those who hoard and hide gold and silver and not spend them in the way of Allah unrequitedly, give them the tidings of a painful suffering!

35. The day when gold and silver are heated in the fire of hell and their foreheads, sides and back are seared with it (a complete state of suffering) **it will be said to them, "This is what you hoarded for yourself, so taste** (the consequences of) **what you have hoarded!"**

36. Indeed, in the knowledge of Allah, the number of months in the period He created the heavens and the earth is twelve... Four of them are sacred (months): (Muharram, Rajab, Dhu al-Qaida and Dhu al-Hijja)**... This is the** (valid and constant) **Religion... So, do not wrong yourselves during** (these months)**... Fight with the dualists just like they fight with you collectively... Know well that Allah is with those who are protected** (a reference to the unity of existence).

37. Postponing the sacred months is only an increase in disbelief! Those who deny the knowledge of the reality are led astray by it... They make it lawful one year and unlawful another year in order to comply with (only) **the figures of what Allah has made unlawful** (and conceal the essence of the matter) **and thus make lawful what Allah has made unlawful!** (But its prohibition is in regards to Allah's command, not the qualities of the months)**... Their misdeeds were made to seem alluring to them... Allah does not guide people who deny the knowledge of the reality.**

38. O believers... What is wrong with you that when you are told, "Go forth to battle in the way of Allah" you cling heavily to the earth! Do you prefer the worldly life over the eternal life to come? While the bounties of the worldly life are nothing compared to those of the life to come!

39. If you do not go forth (to battle)**, He will punish you with a painful suffering and bring in your stead another people; you cannot harm Him at all... Allah is Qadir over all things.**

40. Indeed, Allah has aided him, even if you haven't! Remember when the deniers of the knowledge of the reality drove him out of his homeland, he was the second of the two (one of two people)**! Remember they were in the cave** (Rasulullah [saw] and Abu Bakr [ra])**... Remember he said to his friend, "Do not grieve, certainly Allah is with us"** (he was making a reference to the unity of existence)**... Allah endowed tranquility upon him and supported him with armies you did not see... He made the word of those who deny the knowledge of the reality the lowest... It is the word of Allah that is highest! Allah is the Aziz, the Hakim.**

41. Go forth to fight, whether armed heavily or lightly... Strive in the way of Allah with your possessions and your lives... This is better for you, if only you knew.

42. Had there been spoils or it been a moderate trip, they would have followed you. But it seemed difficult for them. (Despite this)

213

they will swear by Allah, "If we were able, we would have gone with you"... They are destroying themselves... Allah knows that indeed they are liars.

43. **Allah has pardoned you** (from living any discomfort due to this)! **Why did you give them permission to remain** (behind from the Battle of Tabuk) **when you had not yet distinguished with certainty the truthful ones from the liars?**

44. **Those who believe in Allah as comprising their essence with His Names and the eternal life to come, will not ask you permission** (to remain behind) **from striving with their possessions and lives... Allah knows** (as their essence with His Names) **the ones who protect themselves.**

45. **It is those who do not believe in Allah as comprising their essence with His Names and the eternal life to come, and whose consciousness is filled with doubt, who ask you for permission** (to be excused from joining the battle with you)**... In their doubts, they keep hesitating.**

46. **If they had intended to go forth** (to battle), **surely they would have made some preparation for it. But Allah knew their participation was not required so He kept them back, and they were told, "Remain with those who remain."**

47. **Had they gone to battle with you, they would not have been anything but a burden upon you. Surely they would have sought to cause provocation among you... There are among you some who listen to them. And Allah knows who the wrongdoers are** (as their essential reality with His Names).

48. **Indeed, they had already sought provocation before, and had turned things upside down for you... Until the Truth came and Allah's command became manifest, though they did not like it.**

49. **Some of them say, "Permit me, do not allow me to fall into provocation"... Be careful, they are already in the provocation! Indeed, Hell** (the state of burning) **encompasses the deniers of the knowledge of the reality** (as their very essence with the Names)!

50. **If a good reaches you it distresses them... But if a disaster strikes you, they say, "Luckily we took our precaution beforehand" and turn away in joy.**

51. Say, "Nothing will befall us except what Allah has prescribed for us! HU is our protector! Let the believers place their trust in Allah alone (believe the Name Wakil in their essence will fulfill its function)."

52. Say, "Are you watching us to see which of the two beautiful things (spoils – a quality attained at the end of a challenge – or martyrdom – one who abandons his body or both his body and his sense of identity and tastes death in this way) will befall us? We await that Allah will afflict you with suffering from Himself (from within you, illness etc.) or through our hands... So wait in hope (of whatever you wish to befall us) we are also of the waiters with you."

53. Say, "Spend willingly or unwillingly in the way of Allah, it will never be accepted of you... For you have become a people corrupted in faith!"

54. What prevents their charities (expenditures in the way of Allah) from being accepted is this: They became of the deniers of Allah, their essential reality with his Names, and His Rasul; they come to salat lazily and give charity unwillingly.

55. So, let neither their wealth nor their offspring impress you... With it, Allah only intends to punish them in the worldly life (i.e. suffering that results from becoming captivated by worldly things and hence falling far from the reality of Allah) and for their lives to depart while they are in a state of denying the knowledge of the reality (by way of a scheme).

56. They swear by Allah that they are certainly from among you! While they are not from among you! But they are people who are very afraid.

57. If they could find a place of refuge, a cave, or any place to enter (to hide), in fear they would seek refuge in it; they are a confused people!

58. And among them are some who criticize you concerning the help you give... If it were given to them, they would be pleased... But if the help is given to others they become furious.

59. If only they had been satisfied with what Allah and His Rasul gave them and said, "Sufficient for us is Allah... Soon He will give to us from His bounty, His Rasul too... Indeed, we are of those who have turned to Allah."

60. Charity is an obligation by Allah, only for the poor and the needy, and those employed to collect charity, and for the purpose of guiding toward Islam, and for the servants, the indebted, for spending in the way of Allah and for the travelers... Allah is the Aleem, the Hakim.

61. Some of them distress the Nabi (the Rasul of Allah) and say, "He believes in everything he hears (every revelation he receives)"... Say, "He lends his ears (to revelation) so that good can reach you! He believes in Allah, as comprising his essential reality with His Names, and the believers, and he is a grace to the believers among you"... As for those who harm the Rasul of Allah, there is a painful suffering for them.

62. They swear by Allah, the One who comprises their essential reality, just to please you... If they were true believers (they would have known that) it is Allah and His Rasul, their essential reality, whose pleasure they should seek!

63. Do they still not know that whoever opposes Allah and His Rasul, for him there is hellfire, in which he will reside eternally? That is the great disgrace.

64. The hypocrites fear the revelation of verses informing them of what is in their hearts! Say, "Mock as you wish! Indeed, Allah will expose that which you fear."

65. If you ask them, they will certainly say, "We were merely conversing and enjoying ourselves!" Say, "Is it Allah, your essential reality, His signs, and His Rasul that you were mocking?"

66. Make no excuse! You have denied the knowledge of the reality after believing! Even if We forgive some of you, We will subject those who are persistent in their error to suffering.

67. The hypocrite men and hypocrite women are of one another... They order what is against the command of Allah and prevent what is right; they are stingy... They have forgotten Allah, so He has forgotten them! Indeed, the hypocrites are the very corrupted ones (in faith)!

68. Allah has promised the fire of hell to the hypocrite men and women, and the deniers of the knowledge of the reality, to abide therein eternally... This is sufficient for them... Allah has cursed them (they are deprived of the Rahim quality in their Name composition). There is unceasing suffering for them.

69. (Just) like those before you... They were stronger than you in power... They were more abundant than you in wealth and offspring... They benefited from their share of worldly bounties... Like those before you benefited from their share, you also benefited from your share, and you indulged as they had indulged! Their deeds have become vain both in this world and the one to come... They are the very losers.

70. Has there not reached them the news of those before them, the people of Noah, Aad, Thamud, the people of Abraham, and the companions of Madyan and the people of Lot? Their Rasuls had come to them as clear signs! And it was not Allah who was doing wrong to them, but they were doing wrong to themselves.

71. The believing men and women are guardians of one another... They enjoin what is right, as the requisite of the reality, and prevent each other from the wrong; they establish salat and give alms (zakah), and they obey Allah and His Rasul... They are the ones to whom Allah's grace will reach... Indeed, Allah is the Aziz, the Hakim.

72. Allah has promised the believing men and women Paradises underneath which rivers flow, in which they will abide eternally... And clean dwellings in Paradises of Eden, and the pleasure of Allah, which is the most magnificent (of all blessings)! This is the great bliss!

73. O Nabi! Strive with those who deny the knowledge and the hypocrites, and do not show them any compromise! Their shelter is hell! How wretched a place of return!

74. They swear by Allah, their essential reality with His Names, that they did not say it... But indeed they did say the word of disbelief; those who deny the knowledge of the reality after accepting Islam attempted a bad thing that they will never be able to attain! They tried to take revenge just because Allah and His Rasul enriched them from His bounty... If they repent it will be better for them... But if they turn away, Allah will punish them with a painful suffering, both in this world and the eternal life to come... They have neither a protector nor a helper on the earth.

75. And among them are some who promised Allah, "If You give to us from Your bounty, we will surely give offerings and be among the righteous."

76. But when He gave to them from His bounty, they were stingy with it and turned away from their promise.

77. Because they failed to keep their promise and lied, (Allah) made them experience the hypocrisy in their consciousness, until the day they will meet (Him)!

78. Did they (still) not understand that Allah knows in detail what is in their essence, and their whisperings, and what is unknown to them (as He creates and comprises their essential reality with His Names)!

79. As for those who criticize the believers who voluntarily contribute more than they have to in charity, and those who cannot find much (due to their poverty), Allah will ridicule them... There is a painful suffering for them.

80. Ask for their forgiveness, or don't (it makes no difference)! Even if you were to ask forgiveness for them seventy times, never will Allah forgive them! This is because they denied Allah, their essential reality with His Names, and His Rasul! Allah will not enable a people whose faith is corrupted to experience the reality.

81. Those who remained behind, contrary to the wish of Allah's Rasul, rejoiced in their staying at home; they disliked the idea of striving in the way of Allah with their wealth and their lives, and said, "Do not go to battle in this heat"... Say, "The heat of the hellfire is far more intense!" If only they could comprehend it!

82. So, in thought of the recompense of their deeds, let them laugh a little but weep much!

83. If after you return from this battle those hypocrites come to you and ask for your permission to go to a new battle, say, "You will never go out (to battle) with me, you will not fight the enemy with me! You were happy to sit at home the first time, so sit at home from now on with those who stay behind!"

84. Don't ever pray the funeral prayer for any of them who have died and do not pray over their grave! Indeed, they denied Allah, their essential reality with His Names, and His Rasul, and they died as corrupt people (whose consciousness is blocked to the reality; corrupt in faith).

85. And let not their wealth and offspring impress you! Allah only wills to give them suffering with them (by way of a scheme) and for their lives to depart while they are in a state of denying the knowledge of the reality.

86. And when a surah was revealed saying, "Believe in Allah who comprises your essential reality with His Names, and strive together with His Rasul" the wealthy ones among them asked for your permission (to not go to battle) and said, "Leave us; let us be with those who sit at home."

87. They were satisfied with staying behind with the women, children and the helpless ones who could not go to battle... Their hearts were sealed (their consciousness was locked)! They can no longer understand!

88. But the Rasul and the believers with him, fought with their wealth and their lives. All good is theirs! They are ones who have been liberated.

89. Allah has prepared for them Paradises underneath which rivers flow, in which they will abide eternally... This is the great attainment!

90. Those with excuses among the Bedouins came to get permission to not attend the battle... And those who lied to Allah and His Rasul sat at home (without even offering any excuse)... A painful suffering will befall those who deny the knowledge of the reality among them.

91. There is no responsibility (for not attending battle) upon those who are in genuine financial difficulty, the ill, or those who cannot find anything to spend in this way... There is no condemnation upon those who live to do good... Allah is the Ghafur, the Rahim.

92. Nor is there any blame upon those who came to you that you might give them arms/mounts and you said, "I cannot find anything for you to ride upon" and they turned back with tears in their eyes out of grief because they could not find something to give unrequitedly for this cause.

93. Responsibility is upon those who, even though they are wealthy, ask for your permission (to not attend battle)... They are satisfied with staying back with the women, children, and the helpless ones who cannot attend the battle... So Allah sealed their hearts (locked their consciousness)... They can no longer know (the reality).

94. When you return from the battle they will give you excuses... Say, "Make no excuse... We will never believe you... Allah has (already) informed us about you... Allah and His Rasul will observe the result of your deeds and then you will be returned to the Aleem of the perceivable and the unperceivable worlds! And He will inform you of the consequences of your deeds."

95. They will swear to you by Allah, their essential reality with His Names, when you return to them, so that you would leave them alone... So leave them alone! Indeed, they are a loathsome people!

96. They will swear to you so that you may be pleased with them... Even if you were to be pleased with them, Allah will never be pleased with a people of corrupt faith!

97. The Bedouins are stronger in disbelief and hypocrisy... They are more likely to not understand the subtleties of what Allah and His Rasul reveal... Allah is the Aleem, the Hakim.

98. And among the Bedouins are some who consider what they spend in charity as loss and wait in hope that misfortune befalls you... May misfortune (of the times, the changing system and the astrological effects) fall upon them! Allah is the Sami, the Aleem.

99. But among the Bedouins are some who believe in Allah, their essential reality with His Names, and the eternal life to come, and who consider what they give unrequitedly as a means to get closer to Allah and to be a part of Rasulullah's prayers... Be careful, indeed, that (which they spend in charity) is definitely a means for closeness... Allah will include them into His grace... Indeed, Allah is the Ghafur, the Rahim.

100. And the forerunners (in faith) among the Muhajireen (those who migrated from Mecca) and the Ansar (the people of Medina) and those who followed them by observing the reality (by endowment/benevolenece) Allah is pleased with them, and they are pleased with HU! There are Paradises for them, underneath which rivers flow, in which they will abide eternally... This is the great liberation!

101. There are hypocrites both from among the Bedouins around you and the people of Medina who are persistent and canny in hypocrisy... You do not know them, We know them... We will make them suffer twice... Then they will be returned to the greatest suffering!

102. And there are some (who did not go to battle) who confessed their offences... They mixed a good deed with a bad deed... Perhaps Allah will accept their repentance... Indeed, Allah is the Ghafur, the Rahim.

103. Take from their possessions in offering, by which you may cleanse and purify them. Turn to them, and pray... Indeed, your prayer (introspection) is a source of tranquility and security for them. Allah is the Sami, the Aleem.

104. Did they not understand that Allah, who accepts the repentance of His servants and receives their offering, is HU! HU is Allah, the Tawwab, the Rahim.

105. Say, "Work! Allah, His Rasul and the believers will see your deeds... You will live the consequences of returning to the perceivable (witnessed) and unperceivable (unseen) Aleem! He will notify you of the meanings of what you do."

106. And there are others (among those who did not go to battle) who are deferred until the command of Allah... Either He will punish them or allow them to repent... Allah is the Aleem, the Hakim.

107. And there are some who have opened mosques to harm the believers, to cause disbelief and division among the believers and as a station to watch those who previously warred against Allah and His Rasul... They swear, "We intended only the best"... Allah testifies that they are certainly liars.

108. Do not ever stand to prayer in that mosque! The mosque founded on taqwa (protecting yourself in the way of Allah from the inadequacies of your identity) from the first day is more worthy of you to stand in... There are men there who love purification... Allah loves those who purify.

109. Is the one who founds his building on taqwa and the pleasure of Allah (Ridvan; the capacity to transform potentials into actions through the awareness of one's reality) better or the one who founds it on the edge of a crumbling cliff that is ready to collapse with him into the fire of hell? Allah does not enable the wrongdoing people (dualists, deniers and hypocrites) to experience the reality!

110. Until their hearts are shattered, the mosques they build will continue to be a doubt in their hearts... Allah is the Aleem, the Hakim.

111. Indeed, Allah has purchased, from the believers, their souls and their properties in return for Paradise... They fight for the cause of Allah, so they kill or are killed... It is a true promise he bears from the Torah, the Gospel and the Quran! Who can be better at fulfilling a promise than Allah? So, rejoice in this transaction with Him! This is the great liberation!

112. The repentant, the worshippers, those who are in a state of hamd (evaluating things in terms of their essential reality), the travelers, those who bow (in the sight of the Divine Might), those who prostrate (in admission of their absolute servitude), those who enjoin what is right and forbid what is wrong and protect the limits set by Allah... Give good tidings to the believers!

113. It is not for the Nabi or the believers, to ask forgiveness for the dualists, even if they are relatives, after it has become clear that they are companions of fire (for Allah does not forgive duality; Allah has endowed the brain with such a system that when the state of duality, that is, deifying an external being, is dominant in the brain, it automatically becomes unable to activate the divine qualities inherent within itself).

114. Abraham asking of forgiveness for his father was only because of a promise he had made to him... But when it became apparent to Abraham that his father was an enemy to Allah, he disassociated himself from him... Indeed, Abraham was Halim (refrained from giving impulsive reactions to events and evaluated all situations in respect of their purpose of manifestation) and gentle in nature.

115. And Allah will not let a people stray after He has enabled them to realize their essential reality until He makes clear to them what they should avoid and they do not stray from it! Indeed, Allah is Aleem over all things.

116. The dominion of the heavens and the earth is for Allah... He gives life and causes death... You have no friend or helper besides Allah.

117. Allah has indeed bestowed his bounty... He enabled the Rasul of Allah, and the Muhajireen and the Ansar who supported him in the hour of difficulty to repent just as the hearts of a group of them were about to stray. Then He accepted their repentance... He is to them the Ra'uf, the Rahim.

118. And (He also accepted the repentance of) the three who were left behind... They had felt restrained on the earth despite its vastness,

and their very being had confined them and they had thought the only refuge from Allah was yet again in Him... Then He accepted their repentance so they turn... Indeed, Allah is HU, the Tawwab, the Rahim.

119. **O believers! Protect yourselves from Allah** (for He will enforce upon you the consequences of your deeds) **and be with the devout** (those who confirm the Truth)!

120. **It is not appropriate for the people of Medina and the Bedouins surrounding them that they remain behind the Rasul of Allah and that they prefer themselves over his self! That they are faced with thirst, fatigue and hunger in the way of Allah, and that they settle in places that enrage the disbelievers, and that they have victory over the enemy is already decreed for them as necessary deeds of faith! Indeed, Allah will not leave the doers of good unrewarded.**

121. **Whatever they spend as charity – small or great – or travel upon the earth, is because it is indeed decreed for them... This is so Allah may requite their deed with the best reward.**

122. **It is not appropriate for the believers to go forth to battle all at once! A group from every division should remain behind to obtain a better understanding of Religion, so they warn the people when they return to them, that they might be cautious.**

123. **O believers! Fight those who are close to you from the disbelievers** (the deniers of the reality)! **Let them find in you intensity, determination and a rich life of faith... Know that Allah is with those who are protected!**

124. **When a surah was revealed, some of them said, "Whose faith did this increase** (what benefit did it have)?"**... As for those who believed, it has increased their faith, they are rejoicing with good tidings.**

125. **But as for those with ill thought, it has only added filth to their filth, they have died as deniers of the knowledge of the reality.**

126. **Do they not see that they are tried once or twice every year? They** (still) **do not repent, nor do they take a lesson.**

127. **And whenever a surah is revealed they look at each other and say, "Does anyone see you?" and then sneak away... Allah has turned their consciousness** (upside down) **because they are a people of no understanding.**

128. There has certainly come to you a Rasul from within yourselves, he is Mighty; your suffering grieves him... He is truly concerned for you! He is Ra'uf (compassionate) to the believers (who believe in their essential reality) and the Rahim (enables them to live the perfection in their essence).

129. But if they turn away, say, "Sufficient for me is Allah! There is no god, only HU! I have placed my trust in Him... HU is the Rabb of the Great Throne!"

10

YUNUS

By the one who is denoted by the name Allah (who created my being with His Names in accord with the meaning of the letter 'B'), **the Rahman, the Rahim.**

1. Alif, Lam, Ra... These are the signs of the Book of Wisdom (Hakim; the source of the knowledge of the reality full of wisdom).

2. Have people been astonished that We revealed to a man among them, "Warn the people and give the good tidings to those who believe they will have a lofty rank of truth (a confirmation by the manifestation of the Names)**!" Those who deny the knowledge of the reality said, "Surely, this man is a magician."**

3. Indeed, your Rabb is Allah, the One who created the heavens and the earth in six stages and then established Himself on the Throne (administers the worlds, which He created from His Names, as He wills [at a deeper level, the word Throne denotes the dimension of unity and oneness of existence]). **It is administered with His command** (He manifests Himself every instant in yet another wondrous way)**! None can intercede with another, unless the essence** (the Name composition formed according to his creation purpose) **comprising the one in need of intercession allows it! Thus is Allah, your Rabb! So, become aware of your servitude to Him! Will you still not contemplate?**

4. To Him you will return all together (This act of returning is dimensional rather than locational; it denotes the observation within one's essential reality)**... This is the promise of Allah, which He will certainly fulfill! Indeed He originates creation** (all created things are created based on the quality of the Name Mubdi collectively and without individuality; the Original Self). **Then** (at the dimension of individuality)**, returns** (based on the Name Mu'id after returning to one's essential reality) **those that have faith and do the necessary deeds required by their faith** (the constructed identity) **to their individual persona** (the constructed identity [spirit] referred to by the letter "QAF") **in order to give them the consequences of what they deserve** (i.e. experience the results of what they manifest). **As for those who deny the knowledge**

of the reality, they will drink from boiling water as a result of their disbelief and suffer a painful suffering.

5. **He** (is Allah, who) **has made the Sun as light** (energy) **of life; and the Moon as Nur** (regulator of the emotional aspect of man; the effect on the hormonal make-up and the amygdala with the force of gravity) **and determined it by stations so that you might know the number of years and calculate... Allah created these in Truth** (with the qualities denoted by His Names). **Thus He explains His signs in detail for those who can think.**

6. **In the alternation of night and day, and what Allah created in the heavens and the earth, there are many signs for those who want to be protected.**

7. **Those who doubt they can attain the awareness of the Names through returning** (to one's essential reality; becoming aware of one's origin) **and are pleased and satisfied with the worldly life, and live in their cocoon** (the world formed in their brain) **and fail to evaluate Our signs...**

8. **They are the ones who will live by burning as a result of what they manifest!**

9. **As for those who believe and perform the deeds required by their faith, their Rabb will enable them to experience the reality as a result of their faith... Rivers will flow beneath them in Paradises of Bliss** (blessings and bounties).

10. **Their call to Allah there will be, "Subhanaka Allahumma – At every instance You create anew and can never be conditioned and restricted by Your creation, we establish incomparability** (tanzih) **and denote similarity** (tasbih) **to You** (i.e. "We are in constant servitude to You by continually manifesting Your Names")**... And their call to each other will be, "Salam"** (may the meaning of the Name Salam manifest upon us constantly)**... The outcome they reach as a result of their return** (to their essential reality) **is the realization of, "Al hamdu lillahi Rabb'ul alameen – Hamd** (the evaluation of the corporeal worlds created with His Names, as He wills) **belongs to Allah, the Rabb** (the absolute source of the infinite meanings of the Names) **of the worlds** (the universe created within the brain of every individual).

11. **Had Allah hastened evil unto man when they deserved it, just as they hasten in their request of the good, their lives would have ended long ago! Leave those who doubt they can attain the**

awareness of the Names by returning (to their essential reality; becoming aware of their origin) in their excessive ways, wandering blindly.

12. When man experiences an affliction, he turns to Us and seeks help as he lies down, as he sits, or while he stands! But when We take him out of that affliction into ease, he walks away as though he never prayed to Us regarding that affliction! Thus the deeds of the transgressors are adorned to them.

13. Indeed, We have destroyed the generations before you because of their wrongdoing and denial despite Rasuls coming to them as clear proofs... Thus we requite people in error!

14. Then, after them, We made you vicegerents upon the earth, that We might see how you would behave.

15. And when Our signs are recited to them as clear proofs, those who doubt they can attain the awareness of the Names comprising their essence by returning (to their essential reality; becoming aware of their origin) said, "Bring a Quran other than this, or alter it." Say, "It is not for me to alter it of my own accord... I follow only what is revealed to me... If I rebel against my Rabb I will surely fear the suffering of that severely intense period."

16. Say, "Had Allah willed, I would not have recited it to you and He would not have notified you of its existence! Indeed, I spent a lifetime among you before... Will you not use your intellect and understand?"

17. Who does more wrong than the one who slanders against Allah or denies His existence in His signs (the manifestations of His Names)? Indeed, the wrongdoers will not be liberated!

18. They deify things besides Allah, things that are neither harmful nor beneficial! And they say, "These are our intercessors in the sight of Allah"... Say, "Are you informing Allah of something He knows not in the heavens and the earth?" Subhan He is! Free and beyond what they associate with Him.

19. Mankind was not but a single nation (created upon the natural disposition of Islam), but then they differed! (This is a reference to an ongoing phenomenon rather than a one-time incident. It denotes the reality that every human, in terms of its creation, is based on the natural disposition of Islam, yet differs after identifying with the belief system of the parents.) Had it not been for a word that preceded from their

Rabb (the decree regarding living the requirements of servitude), **He would have judged between them about what they differ.**

20. **They say, "Should a miracle not have been sent to him?"... Say, "The unknown is only for Allah! Wait! I am also with you among those who wait."**

21. **When We give the people a taste of grace and beauty after adversity, immediately they begin to strategize against Our signs... Say, "Allah is swifter in strategy... Indeed, Our Rasuls are recording what you conspire."** (Unable to see that the adversity they are exposed to is the consequence of their own deeds, they think the grace that comes after it is a sign that their deeds are not wrong and that they are on the right path. So Allah does not correct their assumption and He allows them to continue in the wrong, hence increasing their suffering. Thus, their false assumption is their conspiracy, and allowing them to continue in their wrong ways is the strategy of Allah.)

22. **HU enables you to travel on land and sea... When you are sailing in ships, and rejoicing in calm winds, a storm will hit and the waves will surge and strike from all sides! And when they think they are encompassed by the waves and in danger, they will believe that all formations are in Allah's hands of power and will pray to Him, "If You save us from this, we will surely be of the thankful."**

23. **But when He saves them, they will immediately start rampaging on the land unjustly... O mankind, your wrongfulness and rampage will only cause harm to you! You will enjoy the fleeting pleasures of the worldly life, and then to Us will be your return!** (And that is when) **We will inform you of** (the reality of) **your deeds!**

24. **The life of the world is like the water, which We disclose from the sky, with which the plants of the earth, that humans and animals eat, have been formed. And when the earth reaches its finest appearance with its produce, and the people think they are powerful and in control, Our command will manifest suddenly in an instant of the night or day! And We will convert it into a field of stubble as though it had not flourished the day before! Thus do We detail Our signs for a people who contemplate!**

25. **Allah invites to the land of Salam** (a state of existence based on the forces inherent in one's essence beyond bodily limitations) **and guides whom He wills to the straight path** (as-sirat al-mustaqim).

26. For the doers of good (ihsan) **is the Beautiful** (Names) **and more** (pleasure). **No darkness** (egotism) **will cover their faces** (consciousness), **nor derogation** (which results from deviating from one's essence). **Those are the companions of Paradise; they will abide therein eternally!**

27. As for those who have earned bad deeds, the recompense (consequence) **of their bad deed will be its equivalent! Derogation will cover them...** They have no (force) to protect them from Allah enforcing the consequences of their deeds upon them... It is as if the darkness of the night has covered their faces (consciousness)... **They will be companions of hell eternally!**

28. And the time when We will gather them all together... We will say to the dualists, "Go to your places, you and those you associate"... Then We will separate them! Their partners will say, "You were not serving us (you were worshipping your delusive ideas).**"**

29. "Sufficient is Allah as a witness between us... Indeed, we were oblivious of the essence of your servitude!"

30. There, every being will experience the consequences of what it previously sent forth! They will be returned to Allah, their True Protector, and lost will be their fantasies (objects of worship)**!**

31. Say (to the dualists), **"Who provides for you from the heavens and the earth? Or to whom belongs the powers of hearing and sight? Who brings the living** (the consciousness of being alive with the Names of the Hayy) **out of the dead** (the futile state of corporeal existence) **and brings the dead** (the state of being blinded to the reality of one's self or the reality of others; confining one's existence only to the body and assuming life is going to end once the body deteriorates under the soil) **out of the living** (while in respect of his essential reality he is alive)**? Who carries out the judgment?" They will say, "Allah"... Say, "Then why don't you be of the protected ones?"**

32. That is Allah! Your True Rabb... What can you accept besides the truth, other than error (corrupt ideas)**? (So then) how are you averted?**

33. Thus the word of your Rabb, "They will not believe" has come into effect.

34. Say, "Are there any among those you associate who can manifest creation and then return it (to its essence)**?" Say, "Allah**

manifests creation and then returns them to their essence... How are you deluded?"

35. Say, "Who among your partners can guide to the Truth?" Say, "Allah guides to the Truth... Who is more worthy of being followed, One who guides to Truth, or one who is inadequate to find the Truth for himself? What is wrong with you? How do you judge?"

36. Most of them follow only their assumptions! Indeed an assumption cannot replace the Truth! Undoubtedly, Allah knows what they do (as their essence with His Names).

37. This Quran is not the invention of those besides Allah! On the contrary, it is a confirmation of what was before it, and a detailed source of the knowledge of the reality, from the Rabb of the worlds!

38. Or do they say, "Muhammad (saw) made it up!" Say, "Then bring forth a surah similar to it and call upon whomever you can besides Allah (for assistance)! If you are true to your word."

39. No! They denied that which they do not encompass in knowledge and the reality of which has not yet been revealed to them... Thus did those before them deny! Have a look and see how the wrongdoers ended up!

40. And of them are those who will believe (the Quran) and those who won't believe! Your Rabb knows better the corrupters (as their essence with His Names).

41. If they insist on denying you, say, "For me are my deeds and for you are your deeds! You are far from what I do and I am far from what you do!"

42. And among them are those who lend an ear to you as though they are listening... But can you make the deaf (those unable to perceive) hear? Especially if they are also unable to use their reason!

43. And among them are those who look at you... But can you show the blind the right path, if they are deprived of insight?

44. Indeed, Allah does not wrong the people, even by an iota! It is the people who wrong themselves!

45. And at the time He will gather them it will be as if they had not lived (in the world) more than an hour and met each other then... Those who denied the meeting (becoming aware of their essence, the Names) will surely be in loss... They were not suitable for guidance.

46. And whether We show you some of what We promised them or We take you in death and you do not see it (nothing will change on their behalf) to Us will be their return... Then Allah is a witness over what they do.

47. There is a Rasul (an informer of the Truth) for every nation... When their Rasul comes, it will be judged between them in justice (according to what they deserve)... They will not be wronged.

48. They say, "If you are truthful, when is the fulfillment of this promise (resurrection)?"

49. Say, "I possess no harm nor benefit for myself other than what Allah wills... Every nation has an appointed time... When their time has come, they cannot postpone it for an hour, nor can they advance it."

50. Say, "Did you see (consider this): If suffering should come to you from Him in an instant of the night or day, what part of it would the guilty ones seek to hasten?"

51. Will you believe when (adversity) afflicts you? Or NOW? (Yet) you wanted to experience it with urgency!

52. Then the wrongdoers were told, "Taste the eternal suffering"... "Are you not only living the direct consequences of your own actions?"

53. They ask you "Is it (the suffering) true?"... Say, "Yes, by my Rabb, indeed, it is true! You will not be able to escape it!"

54. And if each individual (consciousness) that wronged (itself) owned everything on earth it would surely offer it as ransom! When they see the suffering, they will not even have the strength to show their regret! The judgment has been made among them according to what they deserve... They will not live anything other than what they deserve!

55. Know with certainty that whatever is in the heavens and the earth it is indeed for Allah (they are the manifestations of the meanings denoted by His Names). Know with certainty that Allah informs of the Truth... But the majority of them do not know.

56. HU gives life and takes life! To Him you will return (you will experience at the level of 'Reality of Certainty [haqq al-yakeen] that your essence is comprised of and created with the Names)!

57. O mankind! There has come to you advice from your Rabb, a healing (the remedy of healthy thought) for what is within you (consciousness), guidance (to lead you to the reality) and grace for those who believe.

58. Say, "Let them rejoice (in the things listed above) as the bounty of Allah and with His grace (not with empty fleeting pleasures)! That (what is lived with grace) is better than what they accumulate (of worldly values)."

59. Say, "Did you consider what Allah has disclosed to you of provision, of which you have made some unlawful and some lawful?" Say, "Has Allah permitted you, or are you slandering against Allah?"

60. What do those, who lie and slander about Allah, think about the Doomsday period? Indeed, Allah possesses bounty for the people... But the majority of them are not thankful (they do not duly evaluate this as the blessing of Allah).

61. Whatever state you are in, whether you are reading the Quran, or doing something else, while you are involved in it, We are always a witness over you... Nothing on the earth (body) or in the heavens (consciousness) of an atom's weight is hidden from your Rabb! (In fact) even that which is smaller or greater than it, is recorded in a Clear Book (the field of waves comprising the origin of existence; raw Data)!

62. Know with certainty! There will be no fear for the guardians (waliyy) of Allah, nor will they be grieved.

63. Those who have believed and accomplished protection.

64. There are good tidings for them both in the worldly life and in the eternal life to come... Never will the words of Allah change! This is the great liberation!

65. Let not their words grieve you... Indeed honor belongs entirely to Allah... He is the Sami, the Aleem.

66. Know with certainty! Whatever is in the heavens and the earth is indeed for Allah (for Allah to observe the qualities denoted by His Names in His knowledge, thus He has created everything from His Names with the qualities they denote)... (Then) those who pray to things other than Allah, to which they associate partnership, cannot follow this truth (due to their state of duality)... **They follow only their assumptions** (based on their illusions) **and they only lie.**

67. **HU made the night for you so that you may find tranquility in it, and the day for you to see and evaluate what is necessary... Indeed, there are signs in this for people who can perceive.**

68. **They said, "Allah has taken a son". Subhan is He! HU is the Ghani** (free and beyond being limited and conditioned by His creation)... **Whatever is in the heavens is for Him** (for the manifestations of the meanings of His Names)... **You have no inherent proof for this** (claim)! **You speak of Allah without knowledge!**

69. **Say, "Surely those who invent lies about Allah will not be liberated!"**

70. **They will benefit from the world temporarily and then to Us will be their return! Then We will make them taste the severe suffering for denying the reality.**

71. **Tell them about Noah... How he said to his people, "O my people! If my position and reminding you of the signs of Allah has become burdensome on you, then I have relied on Allah** (I believe the Name Wakil in my essence will fulfill its function)! **So, do whatever you like, you and your associates, and don't feel anxious about it! And then carry out your verdict concerning me without further ado."**

72. **"If you turn away** (because of this, then do so) **I did not ask you for any reward... My reward** (the return of what I do) **belongs to Allah alone... I have been commanded to be of those who live in submission."**

73. **But they denied him** (still)... **So We saved him and those with him in the ship and made them vicegerents... And We drowned those who denied Our signs! Have a look and see the end of those who were warned!**

74. **Then** (after Noah) **We disclosed Rasuls as clear signs** (special configurations of Names) **to many nations... But again, they failed to believe in that which they denied before... Thus We seal the hearts** (lock the consciousness) **of those who transgress!**

75. **Then after them We disclosed Moses and Aaron as Our signs to the Pharaoh and the eminent ones among his people... But they were arrogant and became a guilty people.**

76. When the Truth came to them from Us, they said, "Indeed, this is clearly magic."

77. Moses said, "Is this how you evaluate the Truth? Is this magic? Magicians will never succeed."

78. They said, "Did you come to turn us away from the belief of our forefathers and establish power on the earth? We are not believers in you (Moses and Aaron)."

79. The Pharaoh said, "Bring to me every learned magician!"

80. So when the magicians gathered, Moses said to them, "Throw what you will."

81. And when they threw, Moses said, "What you put forth is only your force of magic! Indeed, Allah will render it obsolete! Allah does not allow the work of the corrupters to end with a positive outcome!"

82. Allah will establish the Truth by His Words! Even if the guilty dislike it!

83. No one believed Moses among his people, except a group of youth, for fear of Pharaoh and his leaders... Indeed, Pharaoh was an oppressive sovereign upon the earth! Indeed, he was of the squanderers!

84. Moses said, "O my people! If you are of those who have believed in and submitted to Allah, who created you with His Names, then place your trust in Him (believe the Name Wakil in your essence will fulfill its function)."

85. They said, "We have placed our trust in Allah (we believed in the meaning of the Name Wakil, the One who provides the means for self-actualization. The One who advocates and protects those who place their trust in Him, providing them with the most auspicious outcomes. He who believes in the potential of the Name Wakil in his own essence, will have confirmed his faith in all the Names [all his potentials]. The source of the mystery of vicegerency lies in this Name!)... Our Rabb, do not make us suffer for their wrongdoing!"

86. "Manifest Your grace upon us and save us from the people who deny the knowledge of the reality."

87. We revealed to Moses and his brother, "Prepare houses for your people in Egypt... Make your houses places of worship and establish salat... Give good tidings to the believers."

88. Moses said, "Our Rabb! Indeed, it is You who has given worldly splendor and wealth to the Pharaoh and his leaders... Our Rabb, was it so they lead (people) astray from your way? Our Rabb, obliterate their wealth and give distress to their hearts! For they will not believe until they see a painful suffering."

89. (Allah) said, "Your prayer has been answered... So stand straight... Do not follow the path of the ignorant!"

90. We took the Children of Israel across the sea... The Pharaoh and his army transgressed and pursued them in enmity... Until, when drowning overtook him, he said, "I have believed, there is no god, there is only the One in which the Children of Israel believe. I am of the Muslims."

91. "NOW? But you had disobeyed before and were of the corrupters!"

92. Today We will deliver your corpse to the shore so that it may be a lesson for those who come after you! But many of the people are indeed cocooned from Our signs!

93. We have indeed settled the Children of Israel in a prominent and safe land... We provided them with clean and pure things... They did not fall into separation until knowledge came to them (with knowledge differences in opinions and interpretations arose)... Indeed, your Rabb will judge between them in the period of Doomsday, concerning that over which they differ.

94. If you are in doubt about what We have revealed to you (o man) ask those who READ Our signs in the worlds before you! Indeed the Truth has come to you from your Rabb... So do not be of those who doubt!

95. Do not be of those who deny the manifest signs of Allah! (If you do) you will be of the losers.

96. Indeed, those upon whom the word (the eternal verdict) of your Rabb has come into effect will not believe!

97. Even if every miracle came to them (they will still not believe)... Until they see the painful suffering!

98. If only the people of a single city believed and reaped the benefits of this faith! Except the people of Jonah (who felt the coming of the suffering after Jonah left them and collectively repented and believed)... When they believed, We lifted from them the suffering of worldly degradation and allowed them to benefit (from Our blessings) for a set period.

99. Had your Rabb (the reality of the Names comprising your essence) willed, all those who live on earth would surely have believed, all of them entirely... So then, will you compel the people to become believers?

100. And it is not for a soul to believe unless the unique composition of Allah's Names comprising his essence permits." And He will place (intellectual) defilement upon those who fail to evaluate reasonably!

101. Say, "Observe what is in the heavens and the earth!" But of no avail those signs will be to a people who do not believe!

102. Do they wait for the like (of the suffering) of those who came before them? Say, "Then wait... I am with you among those who wait."

103. Then (when the suffering comes) We will save our Rasuls and those who have believed... It is an obligation upon Us to save the believers.

104. Say, "O people! If you are in doubt as to my religion (then know that) I will not worship the things you worship besides Allah! I only serve Allah, the One who will cause your death! I have been commanded to be of the believers."

105. (And I have been commanded): "Direct your face as a Hanif toward the Religion (direct your spirituality and consciousness, the essence of which is a configuration of Names, to the formless essential reality of what is perceived as the corporeal worlds, free from all conceptualized ideas of god) and do not in any way be of the dualists (do not assume the existence of externalized gods besides Allah and associate partnership to Him)!"

106. "Do not turn to things besides Allah, which can neither give you benefit nor harm! If you do this, you will indeed become of those who wrong themselves!"

107. And if Allah should afflict you with an adversity, none can lift it other than Him! If He wills a good for you, none can repel His bounty either! He causes His bounty to reach whom He wills of His servants... He is the Ghafur, the Rahim.

108. Say, "O people... Indeed the Truth has come to you from your Rabb! So, whoever turns to the reality he will have turned for his own self, and whoever goes astray, he would only have gone against his own self! I am not your **Wakil** (the guide of your essence and consciousness)."

109. (My Rasul) follow what has been revealed to you and be patient until the judgment of Allah becomes manifest... He is the best of judges.

11

HUD

By the one who is denoted by the name Allah (who created my being with His Names in accord with the meaning of the letter 'B'), the Rahman, the Rahim.

1. Alif, Lam, Ra... The signs of the Knowledge (Book) have been distinctly established, and then manifested in detail from the ladun (the potential of the Names comprising one's essence) of the Hakim, the Habir.

2. (This Knowledge was revealed so that you) become aware that your servitude is only to Allah. "Indeed I am a warner and a bringer of good tidings from HU."

3. "Seek forgiveness of your Rabb (for your mistakes and shortcomings)! Then repent to Him so that He may let you enjoy your life while it lasts, and give His bounty (what they deserve of knowledge and enlightenment) to every virtuous person... If you turn away, I fear for you the suffering of that mighty period."

4. "To Allah you will return, HU is Qadir over all things."

5. Know with certainty! To hide from Him, they cover what is within themselves (they hide their real thoughts with other thoughts and conceal it)! Know with certainty! When they hide themselves behind their clothes (when they conceal their inner world) He knows what they hide and what they make apparent! Indeed He is Aleem of what is inside you ('your personal world created in your mind') as its very essence (with His Names).

6. There is no animate creature on earth whose life sustenance (provision) does not belong to Allah! He knows its state of rest (its end) and its temporary life... All of it is clear Knowledge!

7. HU created the heavens and the earth in six stages (the six states of consciousness [heavens] and body [earth]) His Throne (the dimension of Names from which His sovereignty is manifest) is upon water (the essence of the universe; the knowledge – data in the ocean of waves; the data contained within waves of energy comprising the universe). (In terms

of man, the qualities denoted by the Names are sovereign over man's consciousness and body – 80% of man is comprised of water, which is programmed to store data via certain waves of energy.) **It is to determine who among you is best in conduct... Indeed, if you say "You will certainly be resurrected after death" the deniers of the knowledge of the reality will say, "This is just clear magic** (showing the inexistent as existent).**"

8. Indeed, if We postpone the suffering from them for a set time, they will certainly say, "What detains it?" Know with certainty! The day it comes to them, it will not be averted from them! They will be enveloped by the very thing they mock.

9. Indeed, if We make man taste grace from Us and then remove it from him, he will definitely fall into despair and become ungrateful.

10. But if We make him taste a blessing after a suffering, he will surely say, "I overcame the suffering (with my own intellect)**"...** **Indeed, he is exultant and boastful!**

11. Those who are patient and engage in beneficial deeds are excepted. There is forgiveness and great reward for them.

12. (My Rasul!) Is your breast constrained and will you leave out some of what is revealed to you because they say, "Should not a treasure have been sent down with him, or an angel come with him"? (i.e. they want a miracle perceived by their eyesight rather than that which is evaluated by reason.) **You are only a warner! Allah is Wakil over all things.**

13. Or do they claim, "(Muhammad) invented it himself"... Say, "(If you claim this is a human invention) **then bring a surah like it... Call upon whomever you can** (for assistance from your deities/gods) **who have nothing to do with the meaning denoted by the name Allah...** (Go and do it) **if you are true to your word."**

14. If they do not respond to you, then know (this): It has only been revealed as the knowledge of Allah! There is no god, only HU! Will you now submit?

15. Whoever wills the worldly life and its fancy values, We will give him the results of his deeds in full... Their pay in the world will never be reduced (he who lives for the world will receive his pay in the world and terminate).

16. They are such people that in the eternal life to come there is nothing but fire for them... Their deeds will yield no return for them there. Their actions are all in vain.

17. Are they (the aforementioned) like the one who lives upon a clear proof from his Rabb? From him, a witness (Quran) follows him, and before it was the Book of Moses as a leader and a grace (confirming the things within)... They believe in it as the Truth... Do not be of those who deny it and whose place (as a result of this denial) is the promised Fire (Naar)... So do not be in doubt of it... Indeed, it is the Truth from your Rabb! But the majority of the people do not believe.

18. Who can do a greater wrong than the one who slanders against Allah? They will be presented to their Rabb! And the witnesses will say, "These are the ones who lied against their Rabb"... Be careful, the curse of Allah is upon the wrongdoers (wronging one's self and falling far from one's essential reality as a result of this).

19. They prevent from the way of Allah and seek to skew (the right path)... They are the very ones who deny their eternal life to come!

20. They were not rendering Allah powerless on earth (they cannot render the sunnatullah obsolete; everyone will certainly live the consequences of their deeds)... They have no guardian besides Allah either... Their suffering will be multiplied... For they could not perceive and evaluate with insight.

21. They are the ones who have put their own selves into loss! And lost from them are the things they invent (the deities/gods they assumed existed).

22. The truth is they will be the ones in the greatest loss in the eternal life to come.

23. Indeed, those who believe and do the deeds required by their faith and who are obedient and in awe of their Rabb, they are the people of Paradise! They will abide therein eternally.

24. The example of these two groups is like the difference in perception between one who is blind and one who is deaf! Can they be equal? Do you still not remember?

25. Indeed, We disclosed Noah to his people... He said, "I am indeed a clear warner to you."

26. "Do not worship any other than Allah... Indeed, I fear for you the suffering of a painful day."

27. The eminent among those who denied the knowledge of the reality from his people said, "We see you only as a man like ourselves... And we do not see you followed by any except the commoners (those without wealth or rank) who act based on simple views (unintelligent)... And we do not see you above us in any way either... On the contrary, we think you are lying."

28. Noah said, "O my people... Did you see? What if I have a clear proof from my Rabb and if He gave me grace (nubuwwah) but you fail to evaluate this? Should we force it upon you while you despise it?"

29. O my people... I do not want anything in return for this... The return of what I do belongs only to Allah... I cannot drive the believers away (even though you look down on them)! They will indeed unite with their Rabb... But I see you people as behaving ignorantly."

30. "O my people... If I drive them away who will help me against Allah? Can you not think?"

31. "I am not telling you the treasures of Allah are with me, or that I know the unknown... Nor am I claiming to be an angel... Nor am I telling you that Allah will never grant any good to those you belittle and despise... Allah knows best what is within them... (If I were to claim the contrary) I would surely be of the wrongdoers."

32. They said, "O Noah... You truly struggled with us... And you went too far! If you are truthful then bring upon us the thing with which you threaten us."

33. (Noah) said, "Only Allah will bring it to you, if He wills! You cannot render Allah powerless from doing what He wills."

34. "If Allah wills to misguide you, even if I want to give you advice, my advice will be of no avail. He is your Rabb, to Him you will be returned."

35. Or do they say, "He made it up"... Say, "If I have made it up, I will face the consequences of my mistake... But of your mistake, I am free!"

36. It was revealed to Noah, "None among your people, other than those who have already believed, will believe. So do not be distressed by what they do!"

37. Construct a ship according to Our revelation and as Our eyes (i.e. as the conduit of Our sight; this term is a reference to the Unity of Existence)... Do not address me concerning the (wellbeing of) wrongdoers... Indeed, they are to be drowned!

38. He was constructing the ship... The eminent ones among his people ridiculed him as they passed by... (Noah) said, "If you ridicule us, then (a time will come when) we will ridicule you just as you ridicule us."

39. "You will know soon to whom the degrading suffering will come today, and upon whom the enduring suffering will descend (in the future)."

40. So when Our command came and the water overflowed from the sources, We said, "Load upon the ship of a pair of each species, all the believers and your family, except those against whom the verdict has already been given." But only a very few had believed along with him.

41. He said, "Embark therein! Its course and its anchorage are by the One whose name is Allah! Indeed, my Rabb is surely the Ghafur, the Rahim."

42. (The ship) was sailing with them through waves as high as mountains... Noah called out to his son who was near a shore "My son! Come aboard with us (join my understanding of Religion)... Do not be with those who deny the knowledge of the reality!"

43. (But his son) said, "I will take refuge on a mountain to protect me from the water"... (Noah) said, "There is no protector today from the decree of Allah, except for whom He gives His grace"... And with a wave that came between them he was among the drowned.

44. And it was said, "O earth, swallow your water! O sky, withhold (your rain)"... The water subsided... The decree was fulfilled... (The ship) came to rest on Judiyy (a high mountain)... And it was said, "Away with the wrongdoing people."

45. Noah called to his Rabb and said, "My Rabb, indeed my son is of my family... Your declaration is true and You are the most just of judges (Your judgment manifests from everyone but as the judge within

my own essence, manifest Your judgment according to my innermost essential reality)."

46. He said, "O Noah! Indeed, he is not of your family! Indeed, (your persistence about your son against my decree) is an act not required by your faith! So do not ask of me things about which you have no knowledge! Indeed, I advise you not to be among the ignorant."

47. (Noah) said, "My Rabb! I seek refuge in You from asking for things about which I have no knowledge (into its true meaning)! If You do not forgive me and bestow Your grace upon me I will be among the losers."

48. "O Noah... Disembark, you and the nations that will be formed from those with you, in Salam and abundance from Us... We will grant them (the oncoming generations) benefit, then there shall touch them from Us (from the meanings of the Names in their essence; from their core) a painful suffering.

49. These are from the news of the unknown! We reveal these to you... Before this, neither you nor your people knew about this... So be patient... Indeed, the future is for the protected ones.

50. And to (the people of) Aad, their brother Hud had said, "O my people! Serve Allah... You cannot have a deity/god besides Him! You are only slandering (due to your dualistic approach)."

51. "O my people! I do not ask for a reward for this... My reward is with the One who created me specifically (Fatir) to fulfill this function... Will you still not use your reason?"

52. "O my people, ask for forgiveness of your Rabb... Then repent to Him so that He may disclose upon you the abundance of the sky and increase you in strength... Do not turn away as the guilty."

53. They said, "O Hud! You did not come to us as a miracle! We will not abandon our deities/gods just because you say so... We will not believe in you either!"

54. "We can only say this: One of our gods has stricken you badly!" (Hud) said, "Indeed, I hold Allah as my witness! And you also bear witness that I am disassociated and free from those with whom you associate partnership."

55. "So, scheme against me with all those you equate (associate partnership) to Him and do not offer me any respite."

56. "I have placed my trust in Allah, my Rabb and your Rabb (believed the Name Wakil in my essence will fulfill its function)... There is no animate being that He does not hold (program with the Name Fatir) by its forehead (brain) (i.e. subjugate to His command)... Indeed my Rabb is upon the right course (as-sirat al-mustaqeem).

57. "If you turn away, I have surely conveyed to you that with which I have been revealed (the knowledge of the reality)... My Rabb will bring others in your stead; you cannot harm Him... Indeed, my Rabb is Hafiz over all things."

58. When Our command actualized, We saved Hud and the believers with Him with Our grace... We saved them from a burdensome suffering.

59. Such was (the incident of) Aad... They consciously denied the signs of their Rabb (within themselves)... They rebelled against His Rasuls... And they followed the command of every obstinate oppressor.

60. They were cursed both in this world and the period of Doomsday (they fell far from their essential reality)! Know with certainty, Aad denied their Rabb! Know with certainty, distance is for Aad, the people of Hud.

61. To the Thamud (We disclosed) their brother Salih... He said, "O my people... Become aware of your servitude to Allah! You cannot have a deity/god, only HU! He formed you from the earth and flourished it with you... So ask for forgiveness of Him and repent to Him... Indeed, my Rabb is the Qarib, the Mujib (the One who responds)."

62. They said, "O Salih! Indeed, you were among us a man of promise before this! Do you forbid us to worship what our forefathers worshipped? Indeed, we are in an apprehensive doubt about that to which you invite us."

63. He said, "O my people, have a look... What if I have a clear proof from my Rabb and He gave me grace from Himself? (In this case) if I disobey Him, who will help me against Him? You cannot contribute anything to me but damage."

64. "O my people! This female camel (going about her way) is a sign for you from Allah... So, let her eat feed upon the earth of Allah... Do not touch her with harm... Lest you be seized by a suffering that is close."

65. But they hamstrung and killed her! He said, "You have three days of life left in your homes! This is a notice not to be denied."

66. When Our command became manifest We saved Salih and the believers with him with Our grace... And (we saved them) from the disgrace of that day... Indeed, your Rabb is the Qawwi, the Aziz.

67. The inevitable blast (a mighty vibrant sound) overtook them and they fell dead in their homes!

68. It was as though they had never lived there! So know with absolute certainty that (the people of) Thamud had denied their Rabb... (Again) know with absolute certainty that falling far (from their essential reality) is for Thamud.

69. Indeed, Our Rasuls (from among Our angels) came to Abraham as good news and greeted him, "Salam". He too said, "Salam" and brought a roasted calf thereafter.

70. But when he saw that they (the Rasuls) did not touch it, he found it strange and became apprehensive (fearful they might be enemies)... They said, "Do not be scared! We have indeed been disclosed for the people of Lot."

71. His (Abraham's) wife was standing nearby... She laughed... We gave her the good news of Isaac, and after Isaac, Jacob...

72. (Abraham's wife) said, "Alas for me! Will I bear a child while I am an old woman (who has reached menopause) and my husband is also old? Indeed, this is an astonishing occurrence!"

73. They said, "Are you surprised by Allah's command? The grace and abundance of Allah is upon you, o people of this house! Indeed, He is the Hamid, the Majeed."

74. When Abraham's fear left him, and he received the good news, he came to his senses and he began to argue with Us regarding the people of Lot.

75. Indeed, Abraham was a tender and sensitive-hearted person, someone who often turned to his Rabb (introspection).

76. (The angels) **said, "O Abraham! Stop arguing! The command of your Rabb is definite! An unstoppable suffering is indeed going to inflict them!"**

77. **When Our Rasuls came to Lot, he felt bad** (for them) **and worried** (that he may not be able to protect them) **and said, "This is a difficult day."**

78. **The people** (of Lot) **came to him with desire... They were used to committing bad deeds...** (Lot) **said, "O my people... Here are my daughters... They are purer for you... Be wary of your Rabb and do not disgrace me before my guests... Is there not a single right-minded man among you?"**

79. **They said, "You know we have no claim over your daughters! And you know well what exactly we are after."**

80. (Lot) **said, "If only I had enough power over you or a powerful support."**

81. (The angels) **said, "O Lot! Indeed, we are the Rasuls of your Rabb... They can never reach you! So, depart with your family in the night... Let not any among you stay behind, except your wife! For whatever strikes them is also going to strike her... Their appointed time is the morning. Is the morning not near?"**

82. **So, when Our command came We turned the city upside down and rained upon them stones of layered clay** (possibly lava from a volcanic eruption).

83. (Stones that are) **marked from your Rabb... They are not far from the wrongdoers.**

84. **And to Madyan** (We disclosed) **their brother Shuayb... He said, "O my people... Become aware of your servitude to Allah! You cannot have a deity/god, only HU! Do not reduce the measurement and the scale... I see where the good is for you... And I fear for you a time of suffering that will engulf you."**

85. **"O my people... Fulfill the measurement and the scale justly and in full, do not defraud people and do not go to extremes causing corruption on the earth."**

86. **"If you are believers, what Allah makes lawful for you is better for you. I am not your keeper."**

87. They said, "O Shuayb... Is it your introspection that tells you we should abandon what our forefathers worshipped and stop disposing of our belongings as we please! Indeed, you are the Halim and the Rashid.

88. (Shuayb) said, "O my people... Do you not see? What if I am upon a clear proof from my Rabb and He has given me provision from Himself? I do not wish to be in opposition to you by that which I have forbidden you... I only want to reform you as much as I am able to... My success is only with Allah... I have placed my trust in Him (believed the Name Wakil in my essence will fulfill its function) and to Him I turn."

89. "O my people... Let not your opposition to me drag you to crime, (whereby) you be struck by a similar thing that struck the people of Noah, or Hud, or Salih... The people of Lot are not far from you."

90. "Ask for forgiveness of your Rabb, and repent (return) to Him... Indeed, my Rabb is the Rahim, the Wadud."

91. They said, "O Shuayb... We do not understand much of what you say! The truth is, we consider you weak among us... If it were not for your respected family we would definitely have killed you! You are not in a state to prevail over us."

92. (Shuayb) said, "O my people... Is my family more powerful and unchallengeable than Allah for you? But you put Him behind your backs as forgotten... Indeed, my Rabb is Mu'id (encompassing) over what you do."

93. "O my people... Continue doing what you do according to your station. Indeed, I too am doing what I do. You will see soon to whom the degrading suffering will come and who the liar is... Observe, for I am also the Raqib with you."

94. When Our command became manifest, We saved Shuayb and the believers with Him with Our grace... while the mighty vibrant dreadful blast overtook the wrongdoers and they fell dead in their homes.

95. It was as though they had never lived there... Know with certainty, a life far from their reality is for the people of Madyan, just like the (people of) Thamud.

96. Indeed, We disclosed Moses as Our sign and with clear proof...

97. To Pharaoh and his leading men... They followed the command of Pharaoh... But the command of Pharaoh was not reflective of maturity.

98. (The Pharaoh) will stand in front of his people during Doomsday and lead them to the fire! And wretched is the place to which they are led.

99. They were cursed here (in this world) and the period of Doomsday! Wretched is the share they receive!

100. So, that is the news of those regions! We relate it to you... Of them, some are standing (and some) are like a mown harvest.

101. And We wronged them not but they wronged themselves! When the command of their Rabb became manifest, the gods they worshipped besides Allah were of no avail to them! (Their conception of god) brought them nothing but destruction.

102. Thus is the seizure of your Rabb of the cities of wrongdoers! Indeed, His seizure is painful and severe!

103. Indeed, there is a sign in this for those who fear the suffering of the life to come... That is a time when all of mankind will be gathered together! That is a time when nothing will be left hidden!

104. We only postpone it for a determined term.

105. When that period begins, no one will be able to speak except by His permission! Of them, some are wretched (faithless; befitting eternal hell) and some happy (believer; befitting eternal Paradise).

106. The wretched ones will be in the fire (Naar). They will breathe therein by moaning and sighing (from the suffering)!

107. As long as the heavens and the earth (their consciousness and body) exists they will abide therein eternally; except what your Rabb wills... Indeed, what your Rabb (the configuration of the Names comprising your essence) wills, He actualizes!

108. As for the happy ones, they are in Paradise... As long as the heavens and the earth (their consciousness and bodies) exist they will abide therein eternally, except what your Rabb wills... They will live with a continual blessing of bounties.

109. Do not fall into doubt by looking at their (apparent act of) worshipping! They are merely worshipping like their forefathers (they are not in servitude to Allah)! **Indeed, We will give them what they deserve in full and complete.**

110. Indeed, We gave Moses the knowledge of the reality, but they differed about it! Had it not been for a past word (already decreed) **by your Rabb, the matter between them would have surely been settled... Indeed, they are in doubt about it** (because of their delusion).

111. Indeed, your Rabb compensates each person in full for their deeds... For He (as their essential reality with His Names and their former) **is the Habir.**

112. So, live the reality as you have been commanded (being on the right course means the experience of the reality via the realization of one's essential reality)! **And those with you who have repented** (for the things preventing them from experiencing their reality)**... And do not transgress! For He is Basir of what you do** (based on the secret of the letter B).

113. Do not incline towards those who wrong (themselves) **for** (if you do) **the fire will touch you... You cannot have a guardian** (waliyy) **besides Allah!** (And if you do take others as guardian) **you will see no help!**

114. Establish salat at the two ends of the day and at the approach of the night... Indeed, good deeds (experiencing the reality; a pleasant lifestyle) **will remove the bad deeds** (the act of covering the reality, and the consequences of offences resulting from an ego-based existence)**... This is an advice for those with comprehension.**

115. Be patient... Indeed, Allah will not allow the rewards of those who do good to be lost.

116. Should not those who remain from the generations before you stop corruption on earth? Except for a few of those who We saved among them (none of them did this)**... The wrongdoers pursued the luxury with which they were spoilt... They became guilty!**

117. And your Rabb would not unjustly destroy the regions in which honest people reside!

118. Had your Rabb willed, He could surely have made mankind a single community (of a single faith)**! But beliefs based on differing opinions are to continue...**

119. Except for the person to whom your Rabb bestows His grace (who does not refute what the Rasul brings); for that He created them. The word of your Rabb: "I will surely fill Hell completely with the jinn and men" is fulfilled.

120. The reason why We relate the news of every Rasul is to establish your understanding... With this surah you have been notified of the Truth, and a reminder and an advice (lesson) has been given to the believers.

121. Tell the unbelievers, "Do whatever you can; for we will too."

122. "And wait (to see the result)! For we are also waiting!"

123. The unperceivable pertaining to the heavens and the earth is for Allah... The command manifests from Him in full! So, become aware of your servitude to Him, feel the presence of meaning of the Name Wakil in your essence! Your Rabb is not curtained from the things you manifest!

12

YUSUF

By the one who is denoted by the name Allah (who created my being with His Names in accord with the meaning of the letter 'B'), the Rahman, the Rahim.

1. Alif, Lam, Ra... These are the signs of the Knowledge that clearly manifests the reality.

2. Indeed, We revealed the (READable, comprehendible) Quran in Arabic (from the essential reality of man denoted by the Beautiful Names, from the dimension of Knowledge to the consciousness of man) so that you may evaluate it with your reason.

3. We (as the qualities of the Names) reveal to you (from the knowledge in your essential reality to your consciousness) this (READable, comprehendible) Quran and disclose to you an exemplary account with the best narration... Indeed, this knowledge was not apparent to you before!

4. And when Joseph said to his father, "O my father! Indeed, I saw the eleven planets, the Sun, the Moon... I saw them prostrating to me."

5. (His father) said, "My son... Do not recount your dream to your brothers, lest they set a trap for you (out of jealousy)... Indeed, Satan is a clear enemy to man."

6. "Thus your Rabb chooses you, and teaches you to see the essence of affairs, and completes His blessing upon you and the family of Jacob, like he completed upon your fathers Abraham and Isaac before you. Indeed, your Rabb is the Aleem, the Hakim."

7. Indeed, there are lessons in the incident of Joseph and his brothers for those who ask!

8. When they (his brothers) said, "Our father loves Joseph and his brother (Benjamin) more, while we are greater in number and more powerful! Indeed, our father is in clear error!"

9. "Kill Joseph or cast him out to (another) place so that his father's love will turn to you! After that you will be at ease."

10. Another one of them said, "If you want to do something, do not kill Joseph! Throw him into a well (not too deep), a caravan will (find him and) pick him up!"

11. They said, "O our father, why do you not trust us with Joseph while we only have well wishes for him?"

12. "Send him with us tomorrow so that he can freely go about and play... Indeed, we are protectors over him."

13. (Jacob) said, "Indeed, it will sadden me if you take him... I fear a wolf will eat him while you are not paying attention to him."

14. They said, "If a wolf should eat him while we are a strong group, then we will surely be losers."

15. So, when they took him and agreed to put him into the bottom of the well, We revealed to him, "Indeed, you will confront them with this affair (one day) in a place where they will not recognize you!"

16. And they came to their father in the first hours of the night, weeping.

17. They said, "O our father! Indeed we went, we were racing... we left Joseph with our possessions... and then a wolf ate him... No matter how truthfully we speak to you, you will not believe us."

18. And they came with his shirt, on which they put fresh blood... (Their father) said, "No (I do not believe you)! Your souls have enticed you to do something (bad)! So, from now on patience is most fitting for me... And Allah is my refuge against that which you assert!"

19. Then a caravan came by the well and their water-carrier let down his bucket, and when he saw, he said, "Ah, good news! There is a little boy here"... They took him out to sell him. Allah is Aleem over what they do (as their essence and the creator of their actions).

20. (Then in Egypt) they sold him for a small price, a few dirhams, to get rid of him.

21. The Egyptian who bought him told his wife, "Look after him well... I hope he will benefit us, or maybe we will adopt him as a son"... And thus We established Joseph there, and taught him to

READ the essence of life's events... The command of Allah will prevail! But most of the people are not aware!

22. When (Joseph) reached maturity, We gave him judgment and knowledge. Thus We reward the doers of good.

23. The woman in whose house Joseph lived sought to seduce him. She firmly closed the doors and said, "I am yours, come"... (Joseph) refused and said, "I seek refuge in Allah! Indeed, he (your husband) is my master, he gave me my possessions. Indeed, the wrongdoers will not succeed."

24. Indeed, she desired him... Had it not been for the proof of his Rabb (if Joseph's reason did not prevail against his feelings/emotions) he would have inclined towards her! Thus We kept bad deeds (ego-based feelings/emotions) and desires away from him! For he is of Our sincere servants.

25. And they both raced to the door... She tore his shirt from the back... And they ran into her husband next to the door... She said, "What is the punishment for the one who intends to do bad things to one's wife, other than imprisonment or a painful suffering?"

26. (Joseph) said, "It was she who sought to take advantage of me"... And a person from her household testified, "If his shirt is torn from the front she has told the truth, and he is of the liars."

27. "But if his shirt is torn from the back, then she has lied and he is of the truthful."

28. When (al-Azeez; her husband) saw (Joseph's) shirt torn from the back, he said, "This is surely the guile of you women... the guile of women is great indeed!"

29. "Joseph... Overlook this (forget it happened)... (Woman!) Ask forgiveness for your mistake... Indeed, you have made a big mistake."

30. And the news reached the women in the city, "The wife of al-Azeez tried to seduce her slave! His love has captured her heart! Indeed, we see her in clear perversion!"

31. When (the wife of al-Azeez) heard them talking behind her back she sent them an invitation and prepared for them a banquet and gave each of them a knife then called out (to Joseph), "Come out before them (and show yourself)!"... When (the women of the city) saw

him they extolled him (his handsomeness) and cut their hands (instead of what they were holding) in astonishment... They claimed, "Never! By Allah, this is no mortal; this could only be a fine angel."

32. (The wife of al-Azeez) said, "That is the one about whom you blamed me! And yes, I certainly tried to seduce him, but he sought to remain pure (and refused)! I swear, if he does not do as I order him, he will surely be imprisoned and be among the debased."

33. (Joseph) said, "My Rabb... Prison is more pleasant to me than that to which they invite me... If You do not protect me from their guile, I will incline toward them and be among the ignorant."

34. (Joseph's) Rabb responded to his prayer and warded off their guile from him! Indeed, He is the Sami, the Aleem.

35. Then (even) after seeing (so much) evidence, they decided to imprison him for some time.

36. And two young men were also imprisoned with him... One of them said, "I saw (in my dream) that I was pressing grapes for wine"... The other said, "And I saw in my dream that I was carrying bread on top of my head and the birds were eating from it"... "Inform us of the realities to which these (visions) point... Indeed, we see you of the doers of good."

37. (Joseph) said, "I will inform you of the interpretation before it is time to eat and your provision is brought to you... This is from the knowledge my Rabb has taught me... This is why I have abandoned the religion of the people, for they do not believe in Allah, the essence of the worlds (with His Names) and they deny the eternal life to come."

38. "I follow (the religion of unity) of my fathers, Abraham, Isaac and Jacob... It is not for us to associate anything/anyone (including ourselves) to Allah! This is Allah's bounty upon us and upon mankind. But the majority of the people are not grateful (do not evaluate this reality)."

39. (Joseph said), "O my companions of prison... Are diverse Rabbs of differing qualities better, or Allah, the Wahid'ul Qahhar (the only ONE under whose command lays all things)?"

40. "The things you worship besides Him exist only in name (i.e. they have no real existence), which you and your fathers have made up; there is no evidence in regards to their existence from Allah.

The judgment is Allah's alone! And he commands that you serve only Him! This is the valid (understanding of) Religion... But the majority of the people are not aware of this!"

41. "O my companions of prison... Of the two of you, one (will be let out of prison and) serve wine to his rabb (master)! As for the other, he will be crucified and the birds will eat from his head! The matter about which you inquire has been decreed as such."

42. And (Joseph) said to the one whom he assumed will be let free, "Remember me (and mention me) before your master!" But Satan made him forget to mention Joseph when he was next to his master, and Joseph remained in prison for many years.

43. The king said, "Indeed, I have seen (in a dream) seven fat cows being eaten by seven lean cows. And seven green ears (of corn) and seven dry ones... O eminent ones! Explain to me your ruling of my vision, if you can interpret dreams."

44. They said, "It is but a bunch of imaginary fables... And we are not learned in the interpretation of dreams!"

45. The one of the two (of Joseph's prison friends) who was freed, remembered and said, "I will inform you of its interpretation... Take me immediately (to the prison)!"

46. "O Joseph! O man of truth! Give us the interpretation (explain the meaning of the symbols) of seven fat cows being eaten by seven lean cows and seven ears (of grain) and seven dry ones that I may return to the people and they may know (its values)."

47. (Joseph) said, "Cultivate for seven years as you are accustomed to... And leave what you harvest in the ear, except for a little, of which you will eat."

48. "Then will come seven intense years of drought during which you will consume what you saved... Except a little, from which you will store."

49. "Then will come after that a year in which the people will be given an abundance of rain and in which they will press (an abundance of grapes, fruit, milk)."

50. The king said, "Bring him (Joseph) to me!"... But when the rasul (the king's delegate) came to him, (Joseph) said, "Return to your rabb

(your master)... **Ask him 'what happened to the women who cut their hands?'... Indeed, I am Aleem of their trap."**

51. (The King) **said** (to the women), **"What did Joseph do when you tried to seduce him?"... "Never! By Allah, we did not witness any wrong conduct from him."** The wife of al-Azeez said, **"Now the truth has become evident! I tried to seduce him... Indeed, he** (Joseph) **is of the truthful!"**

52. "This is so my master knows I did not betray him and Allah does not allow the deceit of the betrayers to be successful."

53. "I do not exonerate myself... Indeed, the soul commands malice with all its might... Except for those upon whom my Rabb bestows grace... Indeed, my Rabb is the Ghafur, the Rahim."

54. The king said, **"Bring him** (Joseph) **to me! I shall make him my special friend"...** When he spoke to him, he said, **"Indeed today you have a reliable position with us."**

55. (Joseph) **said, "Appoint me treasurer of your land. Indeed, I am a trustworthy and knowledgeable person."**

56. And thus We established Joseph in that land (Egypt)**... He could go about and lodge wherever he willed therein... We manifest Our mercy/grace when We will... We will not leave unrequited the deeds of the doers of good.**

57. The return pertaining to their eternal life to come is surely better for those who believe and protect themselves.

58. And (finally) **the brothers of Joseph came... They entered his presence... Though they did not recognize Joseph, he recognized them.**

59. After having their supplies loaded, he said, "(Next time you come for supplies) **bring to me your step-brother** (i.e. Joseph's brother Benjamin)**... As you see, I give a full measure of supplies and I am the most auspicious of accommodators."**

60. "If you do not bring him to me, neither expect a measure of supplies from me, nor approach me."

61. They said, "We will try to convince our father (to allow us) **to bring him... And we will surely succeed."**

62. (Joseph) **told his servants, "Put their capital into their saddlebags – that when they return to their family, they will recognize it and return to us."**

63. **When they returned to their father, they said, "O our father... If we do not take** (Benjamin) **with us the next time we go we will be given no supplies... We will surely protect him."**

64. (Their father) **said, "Shall I entrust you with him as I entrusted you with your brother** (Joseph) **before? Allah is the protector! He is the most Rahim of the Rahim.**

65. **When they opened their baggage they found the fee they had paid returned to them... They said, "O our father... What else can we want? The fee we paid has been returned to us! We shall get supplies for our family, watch over our brother and obtain an extra camel's load** (as Benjamin's due)**... This** (what we obtain now) **is a small quantity."**

66. (Their father) **said, "Never shall I send him with you unless you promise in the name of Allah that you will bring him back to me, except if you are completely surrounded by enemies and threatened with death"... And when they gave their solemn promise** (their father) **said, "Allah is Wakil over what we say."**

67. **And he said, "O my sons... Do not all enter from one gate... but enter from different gates...** (Though) **I cannot protect you from** (what is to come from) **Allah... The judgment is Allah's alone... I have placed my trust in Him and I turn to Him** (believe the Name Wakil in my essence will fulfill its function without failure!)**... Those who place their trust should place their trust in Him."**

68. **Their father's order to enter through different gates was not to change the decree of Allah... It was only a desire in Jacob's heart that he fulfilled... Indeed, he possessed knowledge because of what We taught Him... But the majority of the people do not know** (these realities).

69. **And when** (the brothers) **arrived next to Joseph, he took his brother** (Benjamin) **and said, "I am your brother... So do not despair over what has happened!"**

70. **So when** (Joseph) **loaded them with supplies he had a water cup put into his brother's bag... Then a messenger and his men ran after them and called out, "O people of this caravan... You are thieves!"**

71. They turned them and asked, "What is missing?"

72. They said, "The water cup of the king is missing... He who finds it will be rewarded a camel's load... I am the guarantor of this award."

73. (The brothers) said, "By Allah (i.e. a type of vow connoting astonishment)! You certainly know we have not come here to cause corruption... And we are not thieves."

74. (The Egyptians) said, "What will be the recompense if you are lying?"

75. (The brothers) said, "Its recompense will be that in whose bag the water cup is found (the owner of the bag) shall be arrested... Thus do we recompense the wrongdoers!"

76. Upon this (Joseph) started searching, he began with the other bags before his brother's bag... Then he found (the water cup) in his brother's bag and took it out... Thus We progressed (the events) in favor of Joseph. For he could not have taken his brother within the religion of the king (based on the regulations of the King) except if Allah willed... We increase in knowledge whom We will. But over every possessor of knowledge there is One who knows all.

77. (The brothers) said, "If he has stolen it, his brother has also stolen before!" Joseph kept this (slander) within himself and did not reveal it to them, "Now you are in a really bad position... Allah knows the truth of what you ascribe to whom."

78. (The brothers) said, "O Azeez... Indeed, he has a father who is very old... Take one of us in his stead... Indeed, we see you as a doer of good."

79. (Joseph) said, "We take refuge in Allah from taking one other than he in whose bag we found our possession... For then, we will indeed be wrongdoers."

80. So when they lost hope (in Joseph) they secluded themselves and spoke privately among each other... Their eldest said, "Do you not remember how your father has taken an oath from you in the name of Allah, and your guilt regarding Joseph? Indeed, I will not leave this land until my father permits me or until Allah decides for me... He is the best of judges."

81. "Return to your father and say, 'O our father... Indeed, your son has stolen... We only bear witness to what we have seen... We could not have guarded that which we couldn't see.'"

82. "Ask the people of the city and the caravan with which we have traveled... We are indeed telling you the truth."

83. (Their father) said, "No (I do not think so)! Your souls have enticed you to something (bad). So, from now on patience is most fitting for me... Perhaps Allah will bring them all back to me... Indeed, He is the Aleem, the Hakim."

84. He turned away from them and with his eyes that became white from grief he said, "Ah.. How you have done wrong by Joseph!"... He was now one trying to digest his sorrow.

85. They said, "By Allah! You are still reminiscing Joseph... You are either going to become fatally ill or die from this sorrow."

86. (Jacob) said, "I direct my sorrow and grief to Allah alone... I know about Allah things that you do not know."

87. "O my sons... Go and find out about Joseph and his brother! Do not lose hope of Allah's reviving grace... For none loses hope of the reviving mercy of Allah except those who deny the knowledge of the reality."

88. So when they (the brothers who went back to Egypt for more supplies) entered the presence of Joseph, they said, "O Azeez... Our family has fallen into a great shortness and adversity... and we have come with capital of scant worth... Give us full measure and be charitable to us from your bounty... Indeed, Allah recompenses those who are charitable."

89. (Joseph) said, "Do you remember what you did to Joseph when you were young and ignorant?"

90. (The brothers) said, "Ah! You... yes, you are Joseph, indeed?"... (Joseph) said, "I am Joseph and this is my brother... Allah has certainly bestowed his favor upon us... For whoever protects himself and is patient, indeed Allah will not allow the deeds of the doers of good to be lost."

91. (The brothers) said, "By Allah! Indeed, Allah has raised you above us... We were certainly in error."

92. (Joseph) said, "No reproach shall be uttered against you today, you shall not be condemned! Allah will forgive you... for He is the most Rahim of the Rahim."

93. "Go (to our father) with my shirt... And put it in front of him, he will see the truth... And gather the whole family and bring them to me!"

94. And when the caravan left (the land of Joseph), their father (in their own land) said, "If you do not think I am old and weakened in mind, indeed I perceive the scent (frequency) of Joseph."

95. They said, "By Allah! Indeed, you are repeating your same old error."

96. And when the bearer of good news came, he put the shirt in front of Jacob and immediately he saw the truth! (Jacob) said, "Didn't I tell you, indeed I know about Allah things that you do not know."

97. (Joseph's brothers) said, "O our father... Ask for us forgiveness of our sins... Indeed, we were mistaken."

98. (Jacob) said, "I will ask forgiveness for you from my Rabb... Indeed, he is the Ghafur, the Rahim."

99. And when they came next to Joseph, he embraced his parents and said, "Allah willing, welcome to Egypt, safe and secure!"

100. And he raised his parents to the throne... His brothers prostrated to him in respect... And (Joseph) said, "My father... This is the interpretation (actualization) of my dream before (i.e. father = sun, mother = moon, eleven brothers = eleven planets)... My Rabb has made it true (actualized it)... (My Rabb) has indeed been good to me... After Satan induced provocation between my brothers and I, He took me out of the prison and brought you from the desert... Indeed, my Rabb is Latif upon whom He wills... For He is the Aleem, the Hakim."

101. "My Rabb... Indeed, You have given to me from Your sovereignty and taught me to see the true meanings of life events... You are the Fatir of the heavens and the earth (1. Universal meaning: The dimension of knowledge comprising the essence of the universe, and the material dimension that exists based on the perception of creation, 2. Worldly meaning: The skies, with all of its dimensions, and the earth, 3. The meaning pertaining to humans: The levels of consciousness of man –

the seven stations of self/consciousness – and the body). **You are my Waliyy** (guardian/protector) **in the world and the eternal life to come** (I am experiencing the awareness of the Name Waliyy among Your names that comprise my essence at every given instance)**... Cause me to die** (take me out of the life of this material dimension) **in this submissive state and join me with the righteous** (those who fulfill the requirements of their faith)**!"**

102. **This that We reveal to you is news from the unperceivable realms... And you were not with them** (Joseph's brothers) **when they were conspiring to put together their plan.**

103. **And most of the people, although you ardently strive** (to help them) **are not experiencing true faith.**

104. (Whereas) **you do not even ask them for any payment** (to warn them of the reality). **It is simply a reminder to the worlds** (man and jinn).

105. **And there are many signs within the heavens and earth, from which they turn away and leave behind.**

106. **And most of them believe in Allah only as dualists** (by associating their assumed gods or selves)!

107. (Or) **do they give a guarantee against the punishment of Allah that will envelope them all, or the Hour** (death) **that will come upon them suddenly while they are unaware?**

108. **Say, "This is my way, I invite to Allah based on insight** (not by imitation but by experiencing the essence)**... I and those who follow me** (live with insight). **Subhan is Allah! I am not of those who associate things to Allah!"**

109. **And We have not disclosed before you any men except those in the city to whom We revealed... Have they not traveled upon the earth and seen how the end of those before them has been... The eternal life to come is surely better for those who protect themselves... Will you not use your reason?**

110. **Until the Rasuls lost hope and** (before the punishment became manifest) **they assumed they had been denied** (that is when) **Our help came to them. And whoever We willed was saved... Our punishment will not be repelled from the guilty people.**

111. Indeed, there is a lesson in their life stories for those who contemplate in depth! It (the Quran) is not a narration invented (by man)... It is a confirmation of the essential knowledge, which came before it, and a detailed narration of huda (knowledge of the reality) and grace (knowing one's self and living accordingly) for a believing people.

13

RA'D

By the one who is denoted by the name Allah (who created my being with His Names in accord with the meaning of the letter 'B'), the Rahman, the Rahim.

1. Alif, Lam, Meem, Ra... These are the signs of the Book (revealed knowledge of the reality and sunnatullah), which is revealed to you from your Rabb as the Truth... But, the majority of the people do not believe.

2. (The One whose name is) Allah is HU, who has raised the heavens (the unperceivable dimensions beyond matter – consciousness [the seven stations of the self]) upon nothing that you can see (by forming different dimensions based on different perception systems)! Then He established Himself above the Throne (made the qualities of the Names sovereign over the dimension of acts)! And He delegated the Sun and the Moon to manifest His command; each continuing their function for a specified term... He forms and directs (all) things with His command, He brings them into existence with all their details, so that you may attain certainty (i.e. the awareness of the manifestations of your Rabb's Names within your essence).

3. And it is Hu who spread the earth (made matter/the body with the capacity to form their constituents; this isn't about the roundness of the earth, but rather the capacity pertaining to the earth and the body, or the dimension of matter in general) and placed therein firmly set mountains (the organs of the body) and rivers (the continuous flow of knowledge nourishing the consciousness; the nervous system)... And from each fruit (product) its twin (the individual's formless parallel beyond matter)... He transforms the night into the day (transforms the darkness of ignorance into enlightenment; the observation of the reality, with His knowledge)... In truth, there are many signs in these for people who contemplate.

4. And on the earth (or the body) there are neighboring continents (or organs), and gardens of grapevines and crops, and groves of palms, single and clustered... All are watered and nourished (continue their existence) with one water (through the manifestation of

ONE SINGLE KNOWLEDGE throughout creation)... **Yet We favor some of their fruit over others** (based on what they provide). **Indeed, there are signs in this for a people who use their reason.**

5. And if you are astonished (at our signs because you are unable to comprehend them) **what is astonishing is their saying, "Will we be brought into a new creation and continue to live after we have become dust?"...** They are the ones who deny the knowledge that their Rabb comprises their essence (unable to comprehend their immortality due to being composed of the immortal Names of Allah)! **And they are the ones with shackles/fetters around their necks** (captives to the idea that they are merely the physical body produced by the second brain in their guts)! **They are the people of Fire** (burning/suffering)... **They will abide therein eternally!**

6. They look for trouble rather than expecting good things from You... (Whereas) **many people** (nations), **who ought to have received a lesson, were punished before them. And, indeed, your Rabb is forgiving toward people despite their wrongdoing... Indeed, your Rabb is severe in recompense** (in enforcing the due consequence of an offense).

7. Those who deny the knowledge of the reality say, "A miracle should have been revealed to him from his Rabb!"... But you are only a warner... But for every people there is a Hadi (a guide to the reality).

8. Allah knows what every female bears and what the wombs lose or exceed. In His sight everything is capacitated according to its purpose of creation.

9. He is Aleem over the unperceived and the perceived. He is the Kabir (possessor of infinite meanings)**, the Muta'ali** (His might encompasses all things).

10. Whether one conceals his thoughts or reveals it, that which is in the darkness of the night or the brightness of the day, is all the same (for Him)!

11. He has (over all His manifestations) **a system of continual/uninterrupted observation** (forces – angels) **who protect them, from front and back, by the decree of Allah... Indeed, Allah will not change the lifestyle of a people until they change themselves** (their understanding and value judgments)! **And if Allah**

wills a disaster for a people, there is no repelling it! Besides Allah, there is no helping friend for them.

12. It is HU who shows you lightning (a sudden epiphany in your brain) **as fear and hope for you, and who generates heavy clouds** (with knowledge and gnosis)... (This verse and the following verses depict the various states of humans via metaphors and symbols; however, many take these verses literally and assume they are referencing actual heavenly incidents.)

13. And the Rad (thunder – the discoveries of the Perfect Man via introspective thoughts/contemplations [The Perfect Man, Abdulkareem Al Jili]) **exalts** (tasbih) **Him with hamd** (evaluation of the corporeal worlds created with His Names, as He wills)**; and the angels** (forces within man and the universe, also exalt Him [tasbih] and fulfill their servitude to Him) **under His sovereignty... While they argue about Allah** (out of their ego-based ideas)**, He discloses thunderbolts** (the striking of the knowledge of the reality) **and enables this experience to whom He wills! He is shadid'ul mihal** (the possessor of the system called sunnatullah, which is enforced with intensity and not subject to any form of alteration or intervention).

14. To HU is the invitation of Truth! Those to whom they turn and from whom they seek help besides Allah will never respond to them (because they do not exist)! (They are) **like one who stretches out his hand for water, but it will not reach him** (for there is no tap)! **The prayer of those who deny the knowledge of the reality is only a perversion and futile!**

15. And whoever is in the heavens and the earth (matter and beyond) **and their shadows** (their conceptual existence – for the real and absolute existence is the Names of Allah) **whether willingly or by compulsion, prostrate to Allah** (they are in a state of absolute submission to the command of Allah comprising their essential reality)! (This is a verse of prostration.)

16. Say, "Who is the Rabb of the heavens and the earth?" Say, "Allah"! Say, "Have you taken allies besides Him who cannot give any benefit nor harm even to their own selves?" Say, "Can the blind be equivalent to the seeing? Or the darkness be equivalent to Nur (light of knowledge)**?" Or do they attribute partners to Allah who create like He creates and whose system resembles the system of Allah? Say, "It is Allah, who is the creator of all things... HU is the Wahid, the Qahhar."**

17. He sent down water (the qualities of the Names) **from the sky and valleys** (compositions of Names as individual forms) **flow** (as intellectual activity) **according to their capacity** (the amount of the forces in their unique composition)**... That torrent carries rising foam** (the material life)**... And from what they heat and melt in the fire in desire of ornaments and adornments, is foam like it... But foam is thrown out as unnecessary excess... Thus Allah exemplifies the truth and the falsity... But as for that which benefits people, that remains on earth... Thus Allah gives examples.**

18. For those who respond to their Rabb (who turn introspectively to their essential reality) **is the best/beautiful** (Paradise – living the beautiful manifestations of the Names comprising their essence)**... But as for those who do not respond to Him, even if they had all that is in the earth and the like of it, they would give it to ransom themselves** (from the suffering of deprivation)**... The worst result of life account will be theirs... Their refuge will be Hell... What a wretched place of rest that is!**

19. That which is revealed to you from your Rabb is the Truth. Is the one who can see the truth equivalent to the one who is blind to it? Only those with reason, who can contemplate in depth, can understand this!

20. Those (who reach the reality) **fulfill the covenant of Allah** (live according to the requirements of the knowledge of the reality manifested in their being by Allah) **and they do not break their contracts** (their natural disposition).

21. They UNIFY what Allah orders to be UNIFIED (the state of existence in which the 'constructed self' and the 'original self' are united), **and they are in awe of their Rabb** (the magnificent infiniteness of the qualities of the Names) **and fear bad accounts** (the consequence of not giving the due right).

22. They were patient (in their current state)**, and sought the face** (the paradisiacal state of existence in which the manifestations of the divine forces in one's essential reality is experienced) **of their Rabb, they performed salat and gave unrequitedly, secretly and openly from the life sustenance we disclosed to them... They nullify their wrongdoings with** (following) **good deeds... Theirs shall be the homeland of the future!**

23. (The homeland of the future is) **the Paradises of Eden** (a level of existence where one consciously experiences the forces of the Names in one's essence)... **They will enter there in unity** (experiencing the same reality) **with those who attain righteousness** (amend themselves and live coherently) **from among their parents, partners and offspring... And the angels will come to them from every gate** (the forces required to live in that state of existence will become activated within them at every level)**!**

24. (They will say) **"Assalamu alaikum** (may the force pertaining to the Name Salam become activated within you) **as a result of your patience... How beautiful is the final homeland!"** (The word 'homeland' in the Hadith "One's love for their homeland is from their faith" is a reference to this.)

25. But those who break (because of their conditionings or misevaluation of information) **their covenants** (despite the absolute submission in their natural disposition by creation) **and those who cut asunder what Allah orders to be unified/joined** (i.e. those who assume the constructed self is separate from the original self) **and those who cause corruption on the earth** (by misusing their body and becoming captives to the second brain in their guts)**, they are the ones who will be distanced from Allah** (fall far from the forces of the Names endowed within their essence)**! For them is a wretched abode!**

26. Allah increases the sustenance of life for whom He wills and decreases it for whom He wills! They rejoice and become spoiled with the worldly things, but the life of the world is merely a fleeting comfort compared to the life to come!

27. Those who deny the knowledge of the reality say, "Shouldn't he have been given a miracle from his Rabb?"... Say, "Indeed Allah misguides whom He wills and guides to the reality those who turn to Him."

28. They are the ones who have believed and consciously experience the satisfaction of remembering and feeling Allah within their essence! Let it be known with certainty that consciousness finds contentment in the remembrance of Allah (dhikrullah; to remember one's essential reality, or original self, i.e. Allah, as comprising the essence of all things with His Names)**!**

29. Those who believe and fulfill the requirements of their faith will have Tuba (the tree of Paradise) **and the bliss of experiencing what is within their essence.**

30. Thus We disclosed you to a people, before whom many nations have come to pass, so that you may recite to those who deny the Rahman and inform them of what We have revealed to you... Say, "My Rabb is HU! There is no god, only HU! To Him is my trust and to Him is my repentance and return."

31. Even if there were a Quran by (the recital of) which mountains could be set in motion, or the earth could be crumbled to pieces, or the dead could be made to speak (they would still not believe it)! No, the command is Allah's in full! Did not the believers know that had Allah willed, He would surely have enabled the realization of the absolute reality to all of mankind! As for those who deny the knowledge of the reality, adversity will not cease to strike them or near their homes because of their own misdeeds... Until the promise of Allah is fulfilled... Indeed, Allah will not fail to keep His promise!

32. Indeed the Rasuls before you were also mocked... I granted respite to those who deny the knowledge of the reality and then I seized them... How awful was the suffering that resulted from their misdeeds!

33. They ascribed partners to Allah while it is He who forms the return of what every soul outputs... Say, "Name them! Or are you informing Him of something on the earth that He does not know? Or are you talking nonsense?"... But no, the scheme of the deniers of the reality has been made pleasing to them and they have been kept back from the way (of Allah)... And whomever Allah misleads, there is no longer a guide to the reality for him!

34. There is suffering for them in the worldly life... and, surely, the suffering in the life to come will be worse! And there will be no protectors from Allah for them.

35. The example (metaphor) of Paradise for those who protect themselves is that beneath it rivers flow... Its fruit is lasting and so is its shade... This is the future for those who protect themselves... As for those who deny the knowledge of the reality, it is the fire.

36. Those to whom We (previously) gave the Book (the knowledge of the reality) rejoiced at what has been disclosed to you... but among them are some who deny part of it... Say, "I have only been commanded to serve Allah and to not ascribe any partners to Him... To Him is my invitation and to Him is my return!"

37. And thus We have revealed it as a command in Arabic... Indeed, if you follow their fantasies after the knowledge that has come to you, you shall have neither a friend nor a protector from Allah.

38. Indeed, We disclosed Rasuls before you and gave partners and offspring to them... It is not possible for a Rasul to come as a proof without the permission of Allah (B-iznillah)... There is a decreed time for the formation of every command!

39. Allah abolishes what He wills or forms (into a perceivable reality, what He wills)**, and with Him is the Mother of the Book** (primary knowledge; the knowledge of the ways in which the Names will manifest at every instant).

40. If We show you some of what We promised them (while they are alive) **or cause you to die** (without showing it to you, your function will still not change) **you are only responsible to inform... Enforcing the consequences of their deeds belongs to Us!**

41. Did they not see how we wear out the earth (the physical body) **from every way** (until it ages and dies, or the global exhaustion of the earth by cosmic or climate conditions, or the wearing out of the dualists in that time)**... Allah decrees** (this) **and there is none to chase** (adjust and change) **His decree. He is the One that instantaneously forms the subsequent stage based on what has already been formed.**

42. Those before them had also planned a trap... But the plan belongs to Allah entirely (their plan worked against them, they fell into their own trap set by sunnatullah)**... He knows the outcome of every consciousness! Those who deny the reality will also see to whom belongs the future abode.**

43. Those who deny the knowledge of the reality say, "You are not a Rasul (disclosed by Allah)**"... Say, "Sufficient is Allah and those who possess the knowledge of the reality as Witness between me and you..."**

14

IBRAHIM

By the one who is denoted by the name Allah (who created my being with His Names in accord with the meaning of the letter 'B'), the Rahman, the Rahim.

1. **Alif, Lam, Ra... This** (Book) **Knowledge** (of reality and the sunnatullah) **that We reveal to you is so you may take mankind out of the darkness** (of ignorance) **into the Nur** (light of knowledge) **based on the suitability of the Name composition comprising their being** (B-izni Rabbihim)**, to the path of the Aziz** (the One whose will to do as He likes, nothing can oppose) **and the Hamid** (the One who evaluates only Himself)**.**

2. **To Allah** (who is the Aziz and the Hamid) **belongs whatever is in the heavens and the earth** (for the observation of the qualities referenced by His Beautiful Names)**... Woe to those who deny the knowledge of the reality for the severe suffering awaiting them!**

3. **They** (who deny the knowledge of the reality) **prefer the** (limited) **worldly life to the eternal life to come and they obstruct from the way of Allah, wanting to deviate it... They are in an extreme error that is difficult to correct.**

4. **And We disclosed every Rasul with the language of his people so they may explain clearly to them... Allah sends astray whom He wills and guides whom He wills... And He is the Aziz, the Hakim.**

5. **Indeed, We disclosed Moses with miracles, saying, "Take your people out of the darkness into the light of knowledge** (Nur) **and remind them of the eternal life to come, during which the command of Allah will be realized"... Indeed, there are signs in this for everyone who is very patient and very grateful.**

6. **And when Moses said to his people, "Remember the blessing of Allah upon you...** (Remember) **how He saved you from the people of the Pharaoh... They used to afflict you with the worst torment, slaughtering your sons and keeping your females alive... In that there was a great adversity from your Rabb!"**

7. And (remember) **how your Rabb had declared, "Indeed, if you are thankful I shall increase it, but if you are ungrateful, then certainly My punishment is most severe."**

8. **Moses said, "If you and everyone on earth denied** (the reality and was ungrateful) **then** (know well that) **Allah is surely the Ghani, the Hamid."**

9. **Did not the news of those before you, the people of Noah, Aad, Thamud and those after them reach you? None knows them but Allah! Their Rasuls had come to them with proofs yet they had covered their mouths with their hands** (a gesture used by the Arabs to denote refusal of an idea) **and said, "Indeed, we deny that with which you have been disclosed, and regarding that to which you invite us, we are in a disturbing doubt."**

10. **Their Rasuls said, "Can there be doubt about Allah, the creator** (the Fatir) **of the heavens and the earth? He forgives the mistakes resulting from your humanity and gives you a chance until the end of your lifespan." They said** (to the Rasuls), **"You are but humans like us** (there is no miraculous aspect to you)**... You want to obstruct us from what our fathers used to worship... So, bring us a clear sultan** (miraculous authority, proof)**."**

11. **Their Rasuls said to them, "We are humans like you, but Allah bestows His blessing** (of risalah) **upon whom He wills of His servants... It is not possible for us to bring you a sultan** (miraculous authority, evidence) **except if it becomes manifest by the permission of Allah** (B-iznillah)**... So, let the believers place their trust in Allah** (believe the Name Wakil in their essence will fulfill its function)**."**

12. **"And why should we not place our trust in Allah when He has guided us in the way of the reality? We will surely be patient against the harm you cause us... Those who trust should place their trust in Allah** (believe the Name Wakil in their essence will fulfill its function).

13. **Those who deny the knowledge of the reality** (who live an egocentric life) **said to their Rasul, "Either we will drive you out of our land or you will turn to our belief"... Their Rabb revealed to them, "Indeed, We will destroy the wrongdoers."**

14. **"And after them We will make you dwell in that land... This is specific for those who fear My position and threat."**

15. (The Rasuls) **wanted conquest... And** (thereby) **every obstinate tyrant lost.**

16. And beyond him is Hell... He shall be given putrid water (the water of hell).

17. He will try to sip it but will not be able to swallow it... Death will come to him from all sides, but he will not die! And after that, a worse suffering!

18. The example of those who deny their Rabb (the qualities of the Names in their essence) **is like the ashes that are forcefully blown by the winds on a stormy day... They shall gain nothing from what they do... That is the biggest deviation** (from the reality).

19. Did you not see that Allah has created the heavens and the earth in Truth (with the qualities of His Names as compositions of His Names)**... If He wills, He can do away with you and bring a new creation, unique and new.**

20. This is not difficult for Allah, the Aziz (whose command nothing can oppose)**!**

21. And they are all gathered and fully exposed for Allah! The weak will say to those who were arrogant, "Indeed, we were your followers, so can you now ward off from us anything of the wrath of Allah?" (The arrogant) **will say, "Had Allah guided us, we would surely have guided you...** (But now) **whether we scream out in agony or are patient, it is all the same for us...** (For) **there is no place of escape for us."**

22. And when the matter is concluded (when the reality becomes evident), **Satan will say, "Indeed, Allah informed you of His true promise... I also promised you, but then I betrayed you... I had no authority** (power) **over you** (anyway)**... I only whispered some ideas to you and you followed my ideas** (because they resonated with your ego)**! So do not blame me, but blame yourselves! Neither can I be called to your aid, nor can you run to my aid. I had also denied your association of me with Allah before! Indeed, there is a painful suffering for the wrongdoers."**

23. As for those who believe and fulfill the requirements of their faith, they will be admitted to Paradises, beneath which rivers flow, and in which they will abide eternally, according to the Name composition comprising their Rabb (B-izni Rabbihim).

24. Did you not see how Allah explains with symbols, a pure expression (knowledge of the reality) **is like a pure tree** (the perfect man) **whose root is firmly fixed** (the core data in the brain pertaining to the original self) **and whose branches reach out to the sky** (the outcome of which is formed in the consciousness)!

25. (That tree) **produces its fruit** (knowledge and gnosis) **at all times, based on the suitability of its Name composition** (B-izni Rabbiha)... **Allah gives examples to people that perhaps they will contemplate on them and remember.**

26. **And the example of a filthy word** (a baseless idea) **is like a filthy tree** (fruitless/futile)**, devoid of a root, superficial and without a basis.**

27. **Both in the worldly life and in the eternal life to come, Allah fastens those who believe upon the word of the permanent Truth** (the Word of Unity)**! And Allah does as He wills** (Allah manifests the qualities of His Names that He wishes)!

28. **Do you not see the one who exchanges the blessing of Allah** (the knowledge of the reality) **to disbelief** (denial) **and reduces his people to a life that is not the outcome of the reality?**

29. **It is Hell on which they lean! How wretched a state of life that is!**

30. **They attributed equivalents** (gods) **to Allah, to mislead from His path! Say, "Enjoy yourselves; your destination is the fire!"**

31. **Tell My servants who have believed, to establish salat and to give from the life sustenance We have provided them, secretly or publicly, before a time comes in which there will be no exchange, nor any friendship."**

32. **It is Allah who has created the heavens and the earth, and revealed water from the sky and produced thereby fruits as provision for you and subjected ships for you to sail through the sea by His command and subjected for you the rivers!**

33. **The Sun and the Moon, which continually fulfill their functions, are in service to you** (you are constantly using the energy and various qualities of the Sun and the Moon without even realizing)... **And you benefit from the night and the day.**

34. **He has given you everything you have asked of Him** (based on your natural dispositions during the period of creation)... **If you were to count the blessings of Allah, you could not enumerate them by evaluating them... Indeed, man is most unjust and a coverer of the apparent Truth!**

35. And Abraham had said, "My Rabb, make this city secure... Protect me and my sons from worshipping idols/deities."

36. "My Rabb... Indeed, they (the deities) have led many astray... So, whoever follows me, then indeed he is of me... And whoever disobeys me, then indeed You are the Ghafur, the Rahim."

37. "Our Rabb... Indeed, I have settled some of my descendants in an uncultivated valley near your sacred house, our Rabb, so they may establish salat (experience the return of their introspection to You)! So, make those whose consciousness is open to comprehending the reality, incline toward them, and provide for them knowledge and gnosis... So they evaluate and are grateful."

38. "Our Rabb! Indeed, you know what we conceal and what we reveal... (For) nothing in the heavens and the earth can be hidden from Allah."

39. "Hamd (the evaluation of the corporeal worlds) belongs to Allah, who has bestowed Ishmael and Isaac to me in my old age... Indeed, my Rabb is Sami of the prayer in my essence."

40. "My Rabb, make me an establisher of salat (of those who experience the return of introspectively turning to the reality of the Names) and also from my descendants (create establishers of salat)! Our Rabb, fulfill my prayer." (Note: An individual such as Abraham is requesting the establishment and experience of salat; it is worth contemplating what this may mean.)

41. "Our Rabb, in that time when life accounts are openly displayed, forgive me, my parents and the faithful!"

42. And never think Allah is unaware of what the wrongdoers do! He only delays them for that time when their eyes will stare in horror.

43. (On that day) they will run ahead, their heads outstretched (looking for help), their glance in darkness... A state in which they will not be able to see themselves! They will not know what to think!

44. Warn the people of the period when the wrath (death – the beginning of an eternal suffering for those who are unprepared) will reach them! In that time, the wrongdoers will say, "Our Rabb, respite us for a short term so we may respond to Your invitation and

follow Your Rasuls"... Had you not sworn, before, that for you there would be no such end?

45. And you lived among the dwellings of those who wronged themselves! It was explained to you how We dealt with them... And We presented examples to you.

46. Indeed, they planned a trap, but their trap is with Allah (they cannot escape its consequence)! (What good is it) **even if their trap** (scheme/plot) **could move mountains!**

47. Never think Allah will fail in His promise to His Rasuls... Indeed, Allah is the Aziz'un-Zuntiqam (the enabler of a system in which the due of the deserving is irresistibly enforced)!

48. During that period the earth (the body) will be replaced by another earth (another body), and the heavens as well (individual consciousness will also be turned into another system of perception)! All will be apparent (openly evident with all their inner faces) to Allah, the Wahid, the Qahhar.

49. During that period, you will see the guilty ones tied in chains (with the ties that separated them from Allah)!

50. Their garments of liquid tar (the blackness of their ego has embodied them) and their faces covered with fire (of being curtained from the reality).

51. Allah has willed for every ego/self to live the consequences of its earnings! Indeed Allah is Sari'ul Hisab (instantly forms the results of deeds)!

52. This is a notice for mankind; let them be warned with it and know that HU is the ONE, the possessor of Uluhiyyah! Let those with reason, who can contemplate in depth, remember and evaluate (this truth)!

15

AL-HIJR

By the one who is denoted by the name Allah (who created my being with His Names in accord with the meaning of the letter 'B'), the Rahman, the Rahim.

1. Alif, Lam, Ra... These (the reality and sunnatullah) are the clear signs of THIS Knowledge, the Quran.

2. (It will be that) those who deny the knowledge of the reality (curtained from their reality) will wish with intense desire that they had been aware of their submission.

3. Leave them, let them eat and enjoy themselves, let them amuse themselves with their unending desires! Soon, they will know.

4. And We did not destroy any region that was not already decreed.

5. No population can advance nor delay their term.

6. They said, "O the one to whom remembrance (dhikr) has been revealed! Indeed, you are crazy (possessed by the jinni)."

7. "Should you not have come to us with angels if you are of the truthful?"

8. We do not reveal angels except as Truth... At that time, they will not be reprieved!

9. Indeed, it is We alone who sent down that dhikr! And, indeed, it is We who will be its guardian!

10. Indeed, We also disclosed (Rasuls) before you, among the first people who shared the same belief.

11. As soon as a Rasul came to them, they would surely ridicule him.

12. Thus We advance it in the hearts of the guilty ones.

13. They do not believe (in the reminder; knowledge)... And they do not take heed from the consequences lived by previous disbelievers.

14. Even if we had opened to them a gate from the sky and they ascended through it...

15. They would surely have said, "Our eyes have been dazzled, in fact, we are a people bewitched!"

16. Indeed, We formed constellations in the sky (the brain; specific regions [pineal gland] within the brain that enable the observation of the reality) **and adorned it for those who observe it and heed.**

17. We protected it from every accursed and rejected Satan (the sense of individualism and fear of loss formed by the amygdala).

18. Except one who steals a hearing (associates the reality that becomes manifest therein to bodily life)**, is pursued by a clear blazing ball of fire** (the Nur of the knowledge of the reality).

19. We have expanded the earth (the body is expanded such that it can contain the organs enabling the manifestations of the Names)! **And We have set firm mountains** (organs) **therein... We produced everything there in balance.**

20. And We made therein means of living both for you and for those whose livelihood does not belong to you.

21. And there is not a thing whose treasuries (the forces comprising it) **are not with us! And We disclose** (the forces/qualities) **according to its program. We manifest it** (those forces, qualities) **in the required amount.**

22. We disclosed the winds (ideas) **as fertilizers** (of new thoughts and discoveries)**... We revealed water** (knowledge) **from the sky and made you drink from it... And you are not the one that retains it.**

23. Indeed, it is We, yes We, who give life and cause death! We are the Inheritors (you are mortal, We [Al-Asma Ul-Husna – the Beautiful Names] are immortal)**!**

24. Indeed, We know who among you wants to advance and who remains behind!

25. Indeed, your Rabb, HU, will gather them! Indeed, He is the Hakim, the Aleem.

26. Indeed, We created man from an evolving cellular structure (earth + water + air).

27. **"And the jann** (a type of jinn) **We created before from 'samum' fire** (an infusing microwave radiation that is harmful to the astral body)."

28. **And remember when your Rabb said to the angels, "Indeed, I will create a human being out of dry clay, an evolving cellular structure** (the cell)."

29. **"And when I have proportioned him** (perfected his body and brain) **and breathed into Him from my Spirit** (the qualities denoted by my Names) **prostrate to him** (commence your servitude to him as his forces)!"

30. **So all of the angels** (forces) **prostrated collectively** (certain qualities of the Names began to manifest and materialize as the brain).

31. **Except Iblis! He was not of those** (forces) **who prostrated.**

32. **He said, "O Iblis! What is the matter with you that you are not with those who prostrate?"**

33. (Iblis) **said, "I have not come into existence to prostrate to a human you created from dry clay and an evolving transforming cellular structure."**

34. **He said, "Then get out from there! Indeed, you are accursed and rejected."**

35. **"Indeed, upon you is the curse** (of falling far from experiencing your essential reality) **until the time in which the truth of sunnatullah will become apparent."**

36. (Iblis) **said, "My Rabb! Reprieve me until the time they are resurrected** (with a new body after tasting death)!"

37. **He said, "Certainly, you are of those who are reprieved!"**

38. **"Until the time well known!"**

39. (Iblis) **said: "My Rabb! Because You have led me astray as the outcome of the Names expressed through me, I will surely make** (disobedience; deeds that veil from the sunnatullah) **attractive to them on earth** (their bodily lives) **and mislead them all."**

40. **"Except Your servants among them who have been given purity of essence!"**

41. He said, "This is the straight path that I have taken upon myself!"

42. "Surely you will have no power (of enforcement) over My servants... Except the corrupt ones who choose to follow you."

43. "Indeed, Hell is the place to which they are destined."

44. "It has seven gates (the seven organs – eyes, ears, tongue, hands, feet, stomach and sexual organs – which are misused to defeat their purpose)... And each gate has a section allotted to them."

45. The ones who have protected themselves will be in Paradises and springs.

46. "Enter therein as the safeguarded (with the security derived from one's faith) and in a state of certainty (salam)."

47. We have cleansed and removed from their hearts all emotions of hatred and animosity (which are derived from a view based on separation and duality rather than unity)! They will be as brothers seated on thrones facing one another.

48. They will not be affected by any weariness (energy depletion) and they will never be made to leave.

49. Tell my servants that I truly am the Ghafur and the Rahim.

50. Indeed, My punishment (the suffering resulting from falling far from My reality) is the worst punishment!

51. Inform them about the guests of Abraham.

52. How they had come to him and greeted him, "Salam"... (And Abraham had said) "We feel anxious by you."

53. (They said), "Do not be anxious! We have come to give you the good news that you shall have a son who will be Aleem (possess great knowledge)."

54. (Abraham) said, "Are you giving me this good news although old age has come upon me? What kind of good news are you giving me?"

55. They said, "We give you good news in Truth! Do not despair!"

56. (Abraham) said, "Who can despair the grace of my Rabb, except those who have gone astray (from the reality)?"

57. (Abraham) said, "O disclosed ones! What (else) is your function?"

58. They said, "The truth is, we have been disclosed for the guilty people."

59. "Except the family of Lot! We shall rescue all of them."

60. "Except for (Lot's) wife... We have decreed that she will be of those who remain behind."

61. Then the disclosed angels came to Lot.

62. (Lot) said, "Indeed, you are strangers!"

63. They said, "On the contrary, we bring (suffering as a result of their deeds) for those who are in doubt."

64. "We come to you in Truth and we are true to our word."

65. "So, take your family and leave during a portion of the night, take them away... And follow them from behind... Let none of you look back... Go to the place to which you have been commanded and leave!"

66. We conveyed to him the decree, "Indeed, their last remnants will be cut off by the morning."

67. And the people of the city came rejoicing.

68. (Lot) said, "These people are my guests... So do not shame me."

69. "Fear Allah and do not embarrass me!"

70. They said, "Didn't we tell you not to meddle in the affairs of others?"

71. (Lot) said, "Here are my daughters, if this is what you want to do!"

72. By your life, they are wandering blindly in their intoxication (of pleasure)!

73. At sunrise the terrifying vibrational blast seized them.

74. We turned them upside down and rained upon them stones of (baked) clay (volcanic lava).

75. Certainly, there are signs in this for those with discernment (who discern the true meaning of the signs).

Note: There is a hadith which states, "Rasulullah (saw) said, 'Beware (note) the discernment of a believer, for he looks with Allah's Nur – light of Knowledge – based on the secret of the letter B...'" Then he read this verse.

76. **Indeed, that city is still on people's way.**

77. **Surely there are lessons to be taken from this for those who believe.**

78. **The people of the wood** (the people of Shuayb [a.s.]) **were also wrongdoers.**

79. **Because of this We made them live the painful consequence of their deeds! Both are situated in places clearly observable.**

80. **Indeed, the people of Hijr** (the people of Thamud) **also denied their Rasuls.**

81. **We gave Our signs to them, yet they turned away.**

82. **They used to carve secure houses from mountains.**

83. **But that terrifying vibrational blast** (volcanic eruption) **seized them too in the early morning.**

84. **Their earnings did not save them.**

85. **And We have created the heavens** (the stages of manifestation pertaining to the qualities denoted by the Names) **and earth** (man's illusory world) **and everything in between them in Absolute Truth.**

86. **Certainly your Rabb is HU, Hallaq'ul Aleem.**

87. **And we have certainly given you seven of the often-repeated verses** (the quality to evaluate with your seven essential attributes) **and the great Quran** (the knowledge of the reality and sunnatullah).

88. **Do not extend your eye toward the transitory worldly bounties and pleasures that We have given to some of the deniers of reality! And do not grieve because they do not give you your due worth... Take under your wings the believers!**

89. **And say, "Indeed, I, yes I, am a clear warner."**

90. **Just as We had revealed** (the knowledge of the reality) **to those who divide and separate** (the Old and New Testaments to suit their own interests), **We have also revealed it to you!**

91. **They divided the Quran into portions** (evaluated the Quran according to their benefits)!

92. By your Rabb, all of them are going to be questioned...

93. About what they do!

94. **Then declare what you are commanded** (the knowledge of the reality and sunnatullah) **then turn away from the dualists!**

95. Indeed, We are sufficient for you against the mockers!

96. **Those who take deities/gods besides Allah** (who created the worlds and their essence with His Names)**... Soon they will know!**

97. Indeed, We know how your breast is constrained because of what they say.

98. So, engage in the tasbih of your Rabb (continue your existence through your servitude to your essential reality) **as His Hamd** (evaluation of the corporeal worlds) **and be of those who prostate** (eradicate their constructed identities/egos)!

99. And serve your Rabb (engage in the practices of prayer and servitude to your Rabb – the Names comprising your essential reality – while your ego self still exists) **until there comes to you the certainty** (until you realize the inexistence of your ego self, which is the realization of the reality of death; the experience of the Wahid'ul Qahhar. After this certainty, servitude to one's Rabb will continue as the natural outcome of this process).

16

AN-NAHL

By the one who is denoted by the name Allah (who created my being with His Names in accord with the meaning of the letter 'B'), the Rahman, the Rahim.

1. The command of Allah has come (for you to see); there is no need to rush! He is Subhan and Aliy, high and above what they associate with Him.

2. He reveals the knowledge of the reality to whom He wills among His servants with His forces (and says), "Warn with the truth that there is no deity/god, only Me! So beware of Me!"

3. He created the heavens and the earth in Truth (with His Names)... He is Aliy over what they associate with Him!

4. He created man from a single sperm... And behold, he has become defiant!

5. He also created livestock... In them are warmth (energy and clothing) and other benefits for you... And from them you eat.

6. And there is beauty for you in them when you bring them in (from pasture) in the evening and in the mornings when you let them out (to pasture).

7. They carry your loads and take you to many places that you cannot reach yourselves without difficulty! Indeed, your Rabb is the Ra'uf, the Rahim.

8. And He (created) horses, mules and donkeys for you to ride on and enjoy... And He creates so much more that you do not know.

9. The path to the target leads to Allah! But there are some who deviate from it... Had Allah willed He could have guided all of you collectively to the reality!

10. HU sent down water for you from the sky... From it comes drink and from it comes foliage in which you pasture (animals).

11. With it He causes to grow for you the crops, olives, dates and grapes of all types. Indeed, there is a sign in these for a people who think!

12. And He subjects for you the night, the day, the Sun (source of energy) and the Moon (which stimulates your hormones and senses with its gravitational force)... And the stars are subjected by and in service to His command (the stars are also a manifestation of the meanings of the Names comprising their essence)... Indeed, there is a sign in this for a people who can use their intellect!

13. And on the earth, (he subjects for you) his creation of various colors... Indeed, from this sign there are lessons to be taken for those who contemplate!

14. And it is HU who subjects the sea to your service, so that you may eat from it and extract ornaments from it to wear... You will see ships plowing through it... so that you may seek of His bounty and be of the thankful ones who evaluate.

15. He formed firmly set mountains upon the earth so that you are not shaken (organs of set functions) and rivers (people who act as a source of knowledge) by which you may find your way and reach the reality and roads (comprehensions suitable to your demeanor).

16. And much more signs! And He leads to the reality by the (Names comprising the essence of the) stars (the people of the reality, the Hadith: 'My Companions are like the stars; whoever among them you follow, you will reach the truth')...!

17. Is One who creates like One who does not create? Do you think and evaluate?

18. If you were to count the blessings of Allah, you will not be able to enumerate them! Indeed, Allah is the Ghafur, the Rahim.

19. Allah knows what you conceal and what you reveal.

20. Those to whom they turn besides Allah cannot create anything, for they themselves are created.

21. They are (living) dead, devoid of (the quality of) Hayy (the knowledge of the reality)... They are not conscious of when they will be resurrected (recreated with a new form).

22. That which you consider to be a God is the ONE possessor of Uluhiyyah! Those who do not believe in their eternal life to come,

denial has covered their consciousness; they (those who dualistically associate their own presumed existence to the existence of Allah) **are living with a strong sense of self** (ego)!

23. **Surely, Allah knows what you conceal and what you reveal... Indeed, he does not favor those who live with their egos.**

24. **When they are asked, "What has your Rabb revealed?" they said, "The myths of the past."**

25. (They say this) **that they may bear their own burdens in full on the day of Doomsday and** (some of) **the burdens of those whom they misguide without knowledge... Know with certainty, wretched is what they bear!**

26. **Those before them schemed... Allah came to their buildings from their foundations! The roof fell upon them from above them and suffering came to them from where they did not perceive** (it came and emerged from an unexpected place)!

27. **Then during the Doomsday He will disgrace them and say, "Where are my 'partners' for whom you opposed Me?" Those to whom knowledge is given will say, "Disgrace and dishonor, this day, is for those who deny the knowledge of the reality."**

28. **Those who the angels take in death while they are wronging themselves** (in a state of duality) **will say in submission, "We were not doing anything wrong"... "No! Indeed, Allah is Aleem over what you do."**

29. **"So, enter the gates of Hell as eternal dwellers therein! How wretched is the residence of the egoistic – arrogant!"**

30. **And it will be said to those who protected themselves from Allah, "What has your Rabb revealed?"... They said, "Good"... There are good things for those who engage in good deeds in this world... But the home of the life to come is surely better... How excellent is the home of those who protect themselves!**

31. (The home of those who protect themselves is) **Paradises of Eden... They will enter Paradises underneath which rivers flow... There they shall have everything they desire... Thus Allah recompenses the people of protection!**

32. The angels will say, "Assalamu alaikum" to those with pure faith who they took in death (separated from their body)! Enter Paradise as the outcome of what you did!"

33. (In order to believe) do they wait for the angels (physical death) or for the command (a suffering) of their Rabb to come? Thus did those before them! And Allah did not do wrong to them, but they had been wronging themselves.

34. So they were struck by the outcome of what they did and they were enveloped by the thing they ridiculed.

35. The dualists said, "Had Allah willed neither we nor our fathers would have worshipped things other than Him and we would not have forbidden anything other than what He says"... Thus did those before them... What can the duty of Rasuls be other than clear notification?

36. Indeed, we have disclosed a Rasul within every community saying, "Serve Allah and beware Taghut!"... Some of them, Allah guided... And upon some of them, error (misguidance) was decreed... So travel the earth and see the end of those who denied.

37. Even if you strive with ambition for their guidance, Allah does not guide those who He leads astray! They will have no helpers.

38. They swore by Allah their strongest oath saying, "Allah will not resurrect one who dies"... No, it is a true promise upon Him (the one who dies will be resurrected immediately after his death as one who has tasted death)! But the majority of the people do not know.

39. (He will resurrect all who taste death) so that He clarifies to them the thing over which they differ and so those who deny the knowledge of the reality will know that they are liars.

40. "Indeed, Our word to a thing when We intend it to be, is to say 'Be,' and it is."

41. As for those who migrate to Allah after being wronged, surely We will settle them in a good place in this world... But the reward of the life to come is definitely greater. If only they knew!

42. They are those who endured patiently and placed their trust in their Rabb.

43. And We did not disclose others before you with our revelation except for men... If you do not know, then ask those who have knowledge about the past.

44. We disclosed them with clear proofs, miracles and Zaburs (wisdom)... And We revealed to you dhikr (remembrance) so that you explain to people that which is sent down to them and so they contemplate.

45. Do those who plan a trap by which they may do bad deeds feel secure that Allah will not cause the earth to swallow them or that suffering will not come upon them from where they do not perceive?

46. Or that We will not seize them during their usual activity? They cannot render Allah powerless!

47. Or (did they feel secure) that He won't destroy them gradually? Indeed, your Rabb is the Ra'uf, the Rahim.

48. Did they not see the things Allah created, how their shadows (existence) **turn to the right** (guidance) **and to the left** (misguidance) **in prostration to Allah** (the Names comprising their essence).

49. "(All) the creatures in the heavens and the earth, and the angels (all beings and forces pertaining to the spiritual and material worlds) **prostrate to Allah** (in absolute submission to Allah) **without arrogance** (without their constructed illusory identity, ego). (This verse is a verse of prostration.)

50. They fear their Rabb who commands from within their depths and they do as they are commanded.

51. Allah has said, "Do not take two gods! HU is the ONE and only who possesses Uluhiyyah (Absolute non-dual ONEness, beyond being broken into parts or being defined as the totality of parts)... **So, fear only ME."**

52. Whatever is in the heavens and the earth is for Him! Religion is continually and eternally His! Then do you fear other than Allah?

53. Whatever blessing you have is from Allah! And when you are touched by distress you cry to Him.

54. Then when (Allah) **lifts the distress from you, behold, some of you start associating partners to their Rabb** (they ascribe the lifting of the distress to causes other than their Rabb).

55. (They do this) **to show ingratitude for what We have given them...
So, enjoy yourselves... Soon you will know.**

56. **They even put aside a portion of the things We provide them for
their illusory gods... By Allah, you shall most certainly be called to
account for the things you invent!**

57. **And they assign their daughters for Allah... HU is Subhan**
(beyond such assumptions)**! And what they like** (their sons) **for
themselves...**

58. **When the good news of a female** (child) **is given to one of them,
his face darkens in rage!**

59. **He hides himself from his people because of** (what he interprets
as) **the bad news he has been given... Will he keep her at the
expense of being despised, or hide her in the dust** (bury her alive)**?
Let it be known with certainty that evil is what they decide.**

60. **Bad attributes are for those who do not believe in the eternal life
to come... The most perfect attributes are for Allah! He is the Aziz,
the Hakim.**

61. **And if Allah were to hold responsible the people for their
wrongdoings and enforce the consequences upon them at once, He
would not have left upon the earth any creature** (DABBAH, i.e.
earthling, in human 'form' – not human)**, but He defers them until a
specified time. And when their time comes, they can neither fall
behind it nor precede it by even an hour.**

62. (The dualists) **attribute to Allah what they dislike** (claiming the
angels are His daughters)**... And they lie and claim the best future will
be theirs. Undoubtedly for them there is fire and for this they will be
at the forefront.**

63. **By Allah... We also disclosed to people before you but Satan
made their deeds attractive to them** (and they denied the messages of
the Rasuls)**! He** (Satan – illusion) **is their friend today** (too)**... There is a
painful suffering for them.**

64. **We revealed this Knowledge** (Book) **to you so that you make
clear to them that** (the reality) **which they deny and as guidance**
(knowledge of the reality) **and grace for a people who believe.**

65. **Allah disclosed from the sky** (from man's essence) **water**
(knowledge) **with which He brought earth** (the body) **to life** (made it

aware of the eternal life it possesses due to the Names of Allah) **after its death** (unconscious state – confining one's existence to the body alone)... **Indeed, this is an important sign for those who evaluate what they hear!**

66. There are lessons for you in grazing livestock (that are suitable to be sacrificed)**... We give you pure milk to drink from its** (the animals) **bellies, between its excretion and blood, which is palatable to drinkers.**

67. You obtain intoxicants and provision from the fruits of date palms and grapes... There is a lesson in this for those who use their reason.

68. And your Rabb revealed to the bee, "Make homes for yourselves from the mountains, the trees and that which they construct!" (The way bees and other creatures receive revelation, how this occurs and its meaning can be highly revealing for the thinking minds.)

69. "Then, evaluate every flower according to its program, based on the Name comprising your essence"... From its belly comes a colorful drink in which there is healing for mankind... There is a lesson in this too for those who use their reason!

70. Allah created you... Then He will cause you to die (not 'kill' you – 'cause you to die')**! And some shall be left to live until old age until they can no longer comprehend the things they once knew... Indeed, Allah is the Aleem, the Qadir.**

71. Allah has excelled some of you over others in provision. Those who have been given more are unwilling to share their provision with those of whom they are responsible... (Whereas) **they are equal with them. Do they consciously deny the blessing of Allah** (their provision of life, by claiming they earned it and taking ownership and hence associating their egos to Allah)**?**

72. Allah has made partners for you from yourselves... And made from your partners sons and grandchildren... He nourished you with clean provision... (When this is the case) **do they believe the ungrounded, baseless one? Do they cover and deny the blessing of Allah?**

73. They deify and worship things besides Allah that do not possess any sovereignty or power over anything from the heavens and the earth!

74. Do not associate similarities to Allah! (Allah is HU!) **Allah knows, and you do not know.**

75. Allah gives the example: A slave who has no power over anything and someone to whom We have provided life sustenance and who gives to others from it both secretly and publicly... Can they be equal? Hamd (the evaluation of the corporeal worlds created with His Names, as He wills) belongs to Allah! But no, the majority of them do not know.

76. And Allah gives example of two people: One of them is dumb and has no power over anything; he is a burden to his master... To whatever task he is directed he brings no good... Can he be equal to the one who duly evaluates what he possesses and who walks upon the right path?

77. To Allah belongs what is unperceivable in the heavens and the earth... The actualization of that Hour (Doomsday) is like the blink of an eye or even closer (in the sight of Allah)! Indeed, Allah is Qadir over all things.

78. Allah extracted you from the wombs of your mothers not knowing a thing... And He gave you perception, sight (evaluation) and hearts (the reflectors of the qualities of the Names to the brain; heart neurons) so that you may evaluate and be of the thankful ones.

79. Do they not see the birds in the sky that are subject to the command of Allah? None other than Allah (with the forces of His Names) holds them... In these signs are lessons for those who use their reason!

80. And Allah has made your homes a tranquil and safe place of living... And made from the hides of animals tents that you carry and use with ease during travel or during encampment, and from their wool, fur and hair for furnishing and clothing for a set time.

81. And Allah has made shadows for you, from that which He has created, and from the mountains, shelters and places of refuge, and made clothes to protect you from the heat and shields to protect you in war... Thus He completes His favor upon you so that you may be Muslims!

82. But if they turn away from you (My Rasul) then the only responsibility upon you is to inform!

83. They recognize the blessing of Allah (the Rasul) then they deny him... The majority of them are deniers of the knowledge of the reality.

84. In that period, We will bring forth a witness from every people... No permission will be given to the deniers of the reality, nor will they be asked for any excuses.

85. When the wrongdoers encounter the suffering, it will not be lightened for them and they will not be reprieved.

86. When the dualists see the partners they associated they will say, "Our Rabb! These are our partners, who are not your equal, who we gave names to and associated as partners to You"... (Their partners) will scold them and say, "Indeed, you are liars."

87. That day, the things they invented (their delusions and fabrications) will be lost from them and they will be in submission to Allah (the system, the laws of sunnatullah)!

88. We will subject to increasing suffering those who deny the knowledge of the reality and who prevent (the people) from the way of Allah, because of their corruption.

89. In that period, from every people We will resurrect a witness against themselves from within themselves... And We brought you as a witness over them! We sent down this Knowledge (Book), which explains everything in sections, as a (life) guidance and as grace and good news for those who have become aware of their submission.

90. Indeed, Allah orders justice, good conduct and generosity to relatives... And forbids immorality (ego-based behavior), bad conduct (activities that go against the requirements of faith) and oppression (wrongdoing and injustice)... He admonishes you so that you think and evaluate.

91. When you give your word to one another fulfill the covenant of Allah deservedly... Do not break your oaths after they are confirmed... For, you have held Allah witness (over your oaths)! Indeed, Allah knows what you do.

92. Do not be like the woman who untwisted her thread after it was strongly spun... Because one community is more plentiful than another, you use your oaths as means of deceit... Allah only tries you with your oaths (so that your true face is revealed and you are

unable to deny it later)... **He will make clear to you the things over which you differ in the period of Doomsday.**

93. **Had Allah willed surely He could have made you all of one faith... But He causes to stray whom He wills and guides whom He wills... You will live the consequences of your deeds!**

94. **Do not use your oaths among each other as means of deceit! Lest your feet slip after being firm** (in Islam) **and you experience wretchedness for straying away from the path of Allah... And incur a great suffering.**

95. **Do not sell the covenant of Allah for a small price... If only you knew, what is with Allah is better for you.**

96. **What is with you will surely come to an end... But what is with Allah is lasting... As for those who are patient, surely We will give them the results of their deeds, with that which is better than their deeds.**

97. **Whether man or woman, whoever believes and fulfills the requirements of their faith, We will make them live a pure-clean life... Surely We will respond to them with better than their deeds.**

98. **When you are going to recite the Quran, seek refuge in Allah from the accursed and rejected Satan** (the idea of thinking you are only the body, lest you misevaluate with delusion).

99. **"Indeed, he** (Iblis and his lineage of jinn) **has no power over those who believe** (that their Rabb is sufficient) **and place their trust in their Rabb."**

100. **"His power is only over those who take him as a guardian** (who follow the ideas he imposes upon them) **and those who associate partners with their Rabb."**

101. **And when We substitute a verse in place of a verse they say, "You are but a slanderer!" Allah knows better what He reveals! On the contrary, most of them do not know.**

102. **Say, "The Pure Spirit** (the force called Gabriel; the force of knowledge pertaining to the Names) **has brought it down from your Rabb** (the Name composition comprising your essence) **in Truth... To give endurance to the believers and as good news for the Muslims."**

103. And We certainly know that they say, "It is only a human being who teaches it"... The tongue of the one they refer to is foreign, yet this Quran is in a clear Arabic language.

104. Indeed, Allah will not guide to the reality those who do not believe in the signs that describe Him... For them there is a painful suffering.

105. Those who invent lies are only those who do not believe in the signs of Allah that describe Him... They are the very liars!

106. Except for the one who is forced (to renounce his faith) while his heart is secure in faith, whoever disbelieves (covers the reality of) Allah and opens his breast to disbelief, upon them is the wrath of Allah! And for them is a great punishment.

107. That is because they prefer the (limited – base) worldly life over the eternal life to come, and that Allah does not guide people who deny the knowledge of the reality.

108. Those are the ones whose heart and hearing (perception) and vision (evaluation) Allah has sealed! And it is they who live in their cocoons!

109. The truth is, in the life to come, it is they who will be the losers!

110. Then, indeed, your Rabb is with those who migrated after being exposed to adversity and thereafter fought and were patient... Indeed, after that, your Rabb is the Ghafur, the Rahim.

111. In that period, every soul will fight to save itself... And every soul will be compensated for what it did... They will not be wronged.

112. Allah gives the example of a city: It was safe and secure... Its life sustenance was coming to it in abundance... But (the people) were ungrateful for the blessings of Allah (they engaged in activities which, by sunnatullah, led them to be curtained)... So, Allah made them taste the envelopment of hunger and fear because of what they had been doing.

113. Indeed, a Rasul came to them from within themselves, but they denied him! So suffering overtook them while they were wrongdoers.

114. Eat from the lawful and clean things from the life sustenance Allah provides for you and be thankful for the blessing of Allah, if you are aware of your servitude to Him!

115. Allah only forbids to you the flesh of dead animals, blood, the flesh of swine, and that which has been slaughtered in the name of an 'other' than Allah... But whoever is forced by necessity can eat from them without assuming it to be lawful and transgressing the limit of necessity... Indeed, Allah is the Ghafur, the Rahim.

116. Do not make things up and say, "This is lawful, this is unlawful"... For you will have slandered against Allah! Indeed, those who invent lies about Allah will not succeed!

117. (They do this) for a brief benefit! And they will have a painful suffering.

118. And that which We have related to you before, We had also prohibited to the Jews... And We did not wrong them, but they were wronging themselves.

119. Then, indeed, your Rabb will fulfill the repentance of those who do a misdeed out of ignorance and then repent after it and correct themselves... Your Rabb, thereafter, is the Ghafur, the Rahim.

120. Indeed, Abraham was a community in himself, obedient to Allah... He was a Hanif (non-dualist who refused to accept the concept of gods/deities besides Allah)... He was not of the dualists (who ascribed partners to Allah).

121. He was thankful for His blessings... (He) had chosen and directed him to the straight path.

122. We gave him blessings in the world... He is of the righteous in the eternal life to come as well.

123. Then We revealed to you, "Follow the people (the religious understanding) of Abraham as a Hanif... He was not of the dualists."

124. The Sabbath was only enjoined upon those who differed about it (the Children of Israel)... Indeed, your Rabb will judge between them on the Day of Resurrection regarding the things about which they differed.

125. Invite to the way of your Rabb with wisdom and good advice... And struggle with them in the best way... Indeed, HU, your Rabb,

knows better who goes astray... And HU knows better who is guided!

126. And if you are to repay them for their misdeeds, then compensate them with the equivalent of the suffering with which they afflicted you... If you are patient, then indeed this is better for those who are patient.

127. Trust and rely! Your patience is through Allah! So do not grieve over them! Do not distress over the trap they conspire!

128. Allah is most certainly with those who protect themselves and who are doers of good (those who are aware that their existence is for Allah).

17

AL-ISRA

By the one who is denoted by the name Allah (who created my being with His Names in accord with the meaning of the letter 'B'), the Rahman, the Rahim.

1. Subhan is He who took His servant one night (enabled him to super sensibly and dimensionally travel by night) from al-Masjid al-Haram to al-Masjid al-Aqsa, whose surroundings We have blessed... To show him Our signs... In truth, HU is the Sami, the Basir!

2. And We gave the knowledge of the reality (Book) to Moses... And made it a guidance for the Children of Israel, so they "Do not befriend and take as guardian other than Me!"

3. O descendants of those We carried (in the ship) with Noah... Indeed, he was a grateful servant.

4. And We conveyed to the Children of Israel in the Book (the dimension of knowledge) "You will surely cause corruption on the earth twice, and you will grow your ego to the utmost!"

5. So, when the time came for the first of the two, We sent upon you Our mighty servants... They went into their homes and searched... This was a promise fulfilled.

6. Then We made you prevail over them one more time... We supported you with wealth and sons and made you numerous in warriors.

7. (We informed you that) if you do good, you do good to yourselves; and if you do bad you do it to yourselves! Then when the second time came, (We sent Our servants again) to darken their faces and make them enter the Masjid again, as they entered it the first time, and to utterly destroy all that they took with force...

8. Perhaps your Rabb will have mercy on you... But if you turn, so shall We... We made Hell a restrictive and engulfing place for those who deny the knowledge of the reality.

9. Indeed, this Quran guides to the most substantial truth and gives the good news that the people of faith who engage in beneficial practices will be given great rewards.

10. And (the news of) a painful suffering for those who do not believe in an eternal life to come.

11. Man invites his evil as eagerly as he invites his good! Man is indeed hasty!

12. We have made the night and the day as two signs... We removed the sign of the night – darkness (ignorance) – and made valid the sign of the day – brightness (knowledge)... So that you may seek bounty from your Rabb and know the number of years and its calculation... We have explained everything in detail.

13. We have wrapped the actions (fate) of every person around his neck... During the Doomsday period (one's doomsday, as in one's death or the Doomsday period in general) We will produce for him his recorded information.

14. "Read your book (knowledge) of life! Sufficient for you is your individual consciousness at this stage to discern the consequences of your actions."

15. Whoever is guided to the reality is only guided for himself and whoever goes astray (from the reality) has only gone against his own self! And no one bears the burden of another's mistakes! We will never cause suffering until We disclose a Rasul with whom We warn!

16. And when We intend to destroy a city We order its most affluent ones (to fix themselves through the Rasuls) but they continue to comply with the requirements of their corrupt beliefs... So they deserve to experience the consequence of Our warning... Thus We destroy them.

17. Many generations We have destroyed after Noah... Your Rabb is Habir and Basir of the mistakes of His servants!

18. Whoever desires the immediate world in front him, We will give to him in the world if We intend... Then We will make Hell a dwelling place for him, degraded and distanced he will dwell therein.

19. And whoever desires the eternal life to come and as believers fulfills the necessary practices of his belief, his practices will be evaluated and he will be made to live its consequence!

20. To all of them, to these and to those, We will send from the bounties of your Rabb... The bounties of your Rabb are not restricted.

21. Look how We favored some above others! Surely the eternal life to come is the greatest in terms of life stations and greatest in individual perception.

22. Do not form another god (in your head) besides Allah! Otherwise (as a result of your duality) you will be degraded and isolated!

23. Your Rabb has ordered you to serve only Him; and to treat your parents well and be giving! If one or both of them reach old age while with you, do not (so much as) sigh to them (getting fed up with looking after them), do not rebuke them, but talk to them with respect!

24. Be humble toward them with grace... Say, "My Rabb... Be merciful to them, as they tamed me when I was young."

25. Your Rabb (as the One who comprises your essential reality and consciousness; the specific configuration of the Names constituting your being) knows better what is within you (your consciousness)! If you are righteous (those who fulfill the requirements of having faith in the reality), then indeed He is Ghafur to those who repent for their inadequacies.

26. Give the relatives their rights, and also the poor and the stranded traveler... (But) do not spend wastefully!

27. Those who dissipate wastefully without knowing value are the brothers of Satan! And Satan had become ungrateful to the blessings of his Rabb!

28. And if you turn away from them (Ashab al-Suffa) due to grace you await from your Rabb, then speak to them a gentle word.

29. Do not chain your hand to your neck (an Arabic expression meaning, 'do not be stingy')! But do not extend it completely either (do not be a squanderer)... Otherwise you will be left in remorse.

30. Indeed, your Rabb will extend provision for whom He wills or restrict it! Indeed He is Habir and Basir over his servants.

31. Do not kill your children out of fear of poverty... We provide life sustenance for them and for you! Indeed, killing them is a great offence!

32. Do not approach adultery (relations outside marriage)! Indeed, that is the transgression of corporeality! It is a way with a wretched end!

33. And do not kill the one (unless it is for retribution) that Allah has forbidden! And whoever is killed unjustly, We have given his guardian an authority, but let him not exceed limits in killing (in retribution)! For he has been supported.

34. Do not approach the property of an orphan, except in the way that is best (to manage it) until he reaches adolescence. And fulfill your word! Indeed, he who gives his word is responsible for his word!

35. And give full measure when you measure, and give weights with an even balance (do not deceive with the scale)... This is both better in general and better in terms of reaching the essence of the matter.

36. Do not pursue that about which you have no knowledge (do not make decisions based on assumptions)! Indeed, hearing (perception), sight (evaluation) and the heart (the reflectors of the Names to the brain – the heart neurons copy themselves to the brain in the womb on the 120th day after conception), all of them are a responsibility upon you!

37. Do not walk upon the earth in egotism! Indeed, you can neither tear the earth nor reach the mountains in height!

38. These bad deeds, in the sight of your Rabb, are incongruent with your essential reality and yield bad results!

39. These are what your Rabb reveals to you of wisdom. So, do not form a god (in your head) besides Allah! Lest you go to Hell in remorse (of not evaluating the forces with which you have been endowed despite being warned) and cursing yourself and distanced (from your essential reality).

40. Has your Rabb chosen you for having sons and taken daughters among the angels (for Himself)? Indeed, you utter grave words!

41. And We have certainly explained (the reality) in this Quran with examples and diverse expressions so that you contemplate and remember, but it only increases them in digression.

42. Say, "If as they claim, there were other gods besides Him, then surely they would have sought a way to the owner of the Throne."

43. "He is Subhan and exalted; His sublimity is incomprehensibly above and beyond their claims (none can comprehend His sublimity)!"

44. The seven heavens (all creation pertaining to the seven states of consciousness), the earth (the body) and everything within them exalts Him (tasbih; fulfill their functions by constantly manifesting in different ways to express His Names)! There is nothing that does not exalt (tasbih) Him with hamd (evaluation of the corporeal worlds created with His Names, as He wills)! But you do not perceive their functions! Indeed, He is the Halim, the Ghafur.

45. When you recite the Quran We put between you and those who do not believe in their eternal life to come, a concealed curtain.

46. And We place over their consciousness (hearts) covers (blockages) to prevent them from understanding Him, and heaviness in their ears (they cannot perceive)! When you mention the Oneness of your Rabb in the Quran they turn back with hatred.

47. We know well how they listen to it when they lend an ear to you, yet when they whisper among each other, how the wrongdoers say, "You follow a man under a spell."

48. Look how they made comparisons to you and thus went astray! They can no longer find a way (to the reality)!

49. They said, "When we are bones and crumbled particles, will we truly be resurrected as a new creation?"

50. Say, "Be stones (biological body) and iron (spirit body) (if you like)!"

51. "Or imagine yourselves to be extraordinary (great beings in your world; consciousness) (you will still be resurrected)!" They will say, "Who will restore us (to life)?" Say, "The One who created you the first time!"... (Mockingly) they will shake their heads and say, "When is that?" Say, "Perhaps it will be soon!"

52. When He calls you (when you taste death) you will experience it as His Hamd (His evaluation) and assume you had only stayed (in the grave – the bodily life – the world) only for a little!

53. **Tell My servants to say that which is best! Indeed, Satan** (the ego-self, assuming you are only the body) **induces dissension among them... Indeed, Satan is a clear enemy to man!**

54. **Your Rabb, as your essential reality, knows you well! He gives you grace if He wills or gives you suffering if He wills! And We did not disclose you as guardian over them.**

55. **Your Rabb, as the presence in all the beings within the heavens and the earth, knows better... Indeed, We favored some Nabis over others** (in terms of their qualities)! **And to David We gave the Book of Psalms** (the knowledge of wisdom).

56. **Say, "Call upon those you assume exist besides Him! They neither possess the power to remove any distress from you nor change the state you are in."**

57. **They, whom they invoke, seek a means of closeness to their Rabb, they hope for His grace and fear His suffering! Indeed, the suffering of your Rabb is that which should be feared!**

58. **There is no country that We will not destroy before the period of Doomsday or punish it with a severe suffering! This has been recorded in detail in the Book** (the dimension of knowledge – sunnatullah – Lawh-i Mahfuz).

59. **What prevented the disclosure of Our miracles was the denial of the former people** (had you denied you would have also suffered the immediate consequences, We would have had to eliminate you)! **And We gave Thamud the female camel as an illuminating sign but** (by savagely killing her) **they wronged her! We only disclose Our miracles to frighten.**

60. **And remember when We said to you, "Indeed, your Rabb has encompassed the people** (BinNas – as their essential reality)**"... And We made the sight that We gave to you** (that which you experienced on Ascension) **and the accursed tree** (bodily life) **in the Quran only as provocation** (objects of trial) **for mankind! We frighten them... But this only increases them in transgression.**

Note: Touching the forbidden tree, the breathing of the spirit = the manifestation of the Names [the Waliyy] = Adam, who lives as a conscious being, free of all conditions, defines himself as his body [Eve] and thus, while living with the forces of the Names, reduces himself and falls away from these forces and becomes confined to living under bodily conditions on earth.

61. And remember when We told the (earthly) **angels** (the forces of the Names within the body), **"Prostrate to the Adam consciousness" and all except Iblis naturally prostrated and fulfilled the requirements** (i.e. the forces became activated)... (Iblis) **said, "Should I prostrate to the one You created from clay** (water + earth; material body)**?"** (The presence of Iblis in man is the force of suspicion/delusion and groundless fear, which does not comply with the mind [consciousness]; it assumes the existent to be inexistent and the inexistent to be existent. A. Jili)

62. (Iblis) **said, "Look at the one whom You dignified over me! Indeed, if You give me until the period of the Doomsday, I will make all his descendants, except a few, submit to me."**

63. (Allah) **said, "Go! Whoever among them follows you, indeed Hell will be the recompense of you all! The full recompense!"** (He who follows his delusion and assumes to be only the body, denying his consciousness or essence, will be subject to the hell of corporeality.)

64. "Incite (with delusion) **whoever you can among them, assault them with your horses and foot soldiers, become a partner in their wealth and children and promise them! But** (alas) **Satan does not promise anything except delusion!"**

65. "Indeed, over My servants (those who have believed in their essential reality that they are beings of Consciousness) **you have no authority** (of enforcement)**! Sufficient is your Rabb as the Wakil."**

66. It is your Rabb who drives the ship (your bodies) **for you through the sea** (knowledge) **that you may seek of His bounty! Indeed, He is the Rahim** (the One who manifests the qualities of the meanings of His Names)**!**

67. And when adversity touched you at sea, lost were all those you invoked besides Him... But when He delivered you to the land, you turned away from Him... Man is so ungrateful!

68. Did you become certain that He will not cause the land to swallow you (experience the worst of bodily corporeal life) **or that He won't send a storm** (of events to disrupt your life) **upon you? Then you would not find for yourself an advocate.**

69. Or did you become certain that He would not send you back to the sea and send upon you a hurricane of wind and drown you in that water as a result of your ungratefulness? Then you would not find for yourself an opposer against Us either!

70. Indeed, We have honored the children of Adam (the children of those created in the dimension of consciousness) **and carried them on land** (the body) **and sea** (dimension of consciousness)**... We nourished them with pure-beneficial sustenance of life... We favored them above most of Our creation!**

71. In that period, We will call every group of people with their own leader... Whoever is given their book (recorded information) **via the forces of his right side, they will confront** (read) **their deeds and no injustice will be done to them, not even as much as a thread inside a date!**

72. And whoever is blind (unable to perceive the Truth) **in this life** (outer life) **will also be blind in the eternal life to come** (inner life) **and further astray in way** (of thought)**.**

73. They were even about to tempt you into provocation against Us and make you invent things about Us, other than which We have revealed to you! (Had they been successful) **then they would have befriended you!**

74. Had We not given resistance to you and granted you stability you would have nearly inclined a little towards them!

75. In which case We would have made you taste (calamities in) **life and death in manifold! Then you would not have found a helper for yourself against Us.**

76. They were going to abuse you to drive you out of (Mecca)**... And then they would have remained only a little** (in the world) **after you** (they did this and were killed in the battle of Badr)**.**

77. This is Our established way (Sunnah) **also in regards to the Rasuls before you!** (All Rasuls are driven out of their homelands and then the people who drive them out are destroyed!) **You will not find an alteration in Our Sunnah.**

78. So establish prayer (salat) **at the time the sun sets in the west until the darkness of the night. Also, the Quran of the dawn** (the morning prayer)**... Indeed, the recitation of the Quran of the dawn is ever witnessed.**

79. And in one part of the night, pray with the Quran (experience salat in wakefulness)**! Perhaps your Rabb will disclose from within you the praised station** (manifest in you the qualities pertaining to that station... [And He already has, based on the verse "Inna fatahnalaka" i.e. "We have given you a clear conquest" 48:01.])!

80. **Say, "My Rabb, wherever I enter make me enter in Truth and from wherever I exit make me exit in Truth, and form from Yourself** (Your ladun; the potential of the Names comprising my essence) **victorious power!"**

81. **Say, "The Truth has come, and falsity has departed!** (The Truth has been informed; all false views have been invalidated.) **Indeed, falsity is bound to perish."**

82. **We reveal** (reflect from one's essence to one's consciousness) **from the Quran, healing** (information to enable healthy thought) **and grace** (reminder of the qualities pertaining to one's essential reality) **for those who believe! But this only increases the frustration of the wrongdoers** (those who deny their essential reality and hence wrong themselves).

83. **When We bestow favor upon man he turns away and distances himself! And when he is touched by an unfavorable circumstance he falls into despair.**

84. **Say, "Everyone acts according to his own creation program** (natural disposition; fitrah)**" This is why your Rabb** (who is the Fatir) **knows best who is on the right path!"**

85. **And they** (the Jews) **ask you,** (O Muhammad) **about the spirit. Say, "The spirit is under the command of my Rabb** (Amr; the manifestation of the Names). **And you have been given little of this knowledge** (this answer is for the Jews who asked this question)**."**

86. **And if We willed We could surely remove that which We revealed to you. Then you would not find for yourself an advocate against Us...**

87. **Except as grace from your Rabb! Indeed, His favor upon you is great!**

88. **Say, "Indeed, if mankind** (the species) **and the Jinni were to gather to produce the like of this Quran and were to support each other, they could still not produce the like of it!"**

89. **Indeed, We have explained all** (truths) **in this Quran with all kinds of examples, but the majority of people cover the reality** (by taking the examples literally).

90. They said, "Never will we believe you until you bring forth for us a spring from the ground."

91. "Or (until) you have a garden of palm trees and grapes, and make rivers gush forth within them with mighty force."

92. "Or you make the heaven fall upon us in fragments as you have claimed or you bring Allah and the angels before us as warrantors." (They say this because they fail to understand the One referenced by the name 'Allah' and think of Him as a god in the heavens.)

93. "Or you have a house made of gold or you soar into the sky... And even then we will not believe you soared into the sky until you bring down to us a tangible written book we may read!"... Say, "Subhan is my Rabb! What am I but a human with a Rasul function?"

94. What prevents people from believing when a reality comes to them is their word, "Allah has disclosed a human Rasul!"

95. Say, "If it were angels who walked the earth as its inhabitants then surely We would have sent upon them from the heaven an angel Rasul."

96. Say, "Sufficient is Allah, as my essential reality with His Names, as Witness between me and you! Indeed, He is Habir, Basir concerning His servants."

97. Whoever Allah guides to the reality, he is the one who finds the Truth! And whomever he leads astray, he can no longer find a friend besides Him! We will resurrect them during the Doomsday period as blind (unable to see the Truth), dumb (unable to speak the Truth) and deaf (unable to perceive the Truth)! Their abode will be Hell! As its flames subside We will increase them in fire!

98. That is the result of what they did! For they denied Our signs, which were inherent within themselves, and the knowledge of the reality and said, "Will we really be resurrected with a new creation when we are a pile of bones and crumbled particles and dust?"

99. Did they not see that Allah, who created the heavens and the earth, is Qadir to create the likes of them? They have been appointed a life span about which there is no doubt. But the wrongdoers approach only as coverers of the Truth.

100. Say, "If you possessed the depositories of the grace of my Rabb, you would stingily withhold it out of fear that it would finish"... Man is so stingy!

101. Indeed, We gave Moses nine clear miracles... Ask the Children of Israel about how when he (Moses) came to them, the Pharaoh had said, "Indeed, I think, O Moses, you are but a magician!"

102. (And Moses said to Pharaoh), "Indeed, you know well that none has disclosed these proofs to verify my authenticity other than the Rabb of the heavens and the earth... Indeed, I think, O Pharaoh, that you are but a loser!"

103. So (Pharaoh) intended to drive them out of the land, but We drowned him and those with him altogether!

104. Then We told the Children of Israel, "Dwell in the land... When the afterlife comes due, We will gather you altogether."

105. We revealed it as the Truth, and as the Truth is descended! We disclosed you only as a bringer of good news and a warner."

106. We separated the Quran into chapters, completing one another, so that you may recite it to the people over a prolonged period, giving them the chance to digest it... We sent it down part by part.

107. Say, "Believe in it or do not believe in it! Those who were given knowledge before it, when it (the Quran) is recited to them, they prostrate in respect." (This is a verse of prostration.)

108. And they say, "Subhan is our Rabb! Indeed, the promise of our Rabb will be fulfilled."

109. They fall upon their faces in prostration with tears... (The recital of the Quran) increases them in humble submission and awe!

110. Say, "Turn to Allah or turn to the Rahman; with whichever understanding you turn, to HU belongs the Most Beautiful Names (all the Names reference the ONE! The Beautiful Names are references to the various qualities of the ONE; there is no other than HU)! Do not raise your voice during prayer, but do not conceal it completely either; seek a way between them."

111. And say, "Hamd (the evaluation of the corporeal worlds as He wills) belongs to Allah, who has not taken a son, who has no partner in His dominion, and therefore has no need of a guardian" and

glorify Him through takbir (experience His magnificent might; Allahu Akbar)!

18

AL-KAHF

By the one who is denoted by the name Allah (who created my being with His Names in accord with the meaning of the letter 'B'), the Rahman, the Rahim.

1. **Hamd** (the evaluation of the corporeal worlds as He wills) **belongs to Allah, who has disclosed to His servant the knowledge of the reality and sunnatullah (Book) in which there is no discrepancy.**

2. **It is (a) straight (Book)... from His ladun to warn against a severe suffering and to give the good news to the believers, who fulfill the requirements of their faith, that they will have a good reward.**

3. **Those** (believers) **will reside therein forever.**

4. **And to warn those who say, "Allah has taken a son."**

5. **Neither they, nor their forefathers, have any knowledge of it! Grave is the word their mouths utter! They speak nothing but lies!**

6. **So, if they don't believe in this warning, will you ruin yourself in grief over them?**

7. **We adorned everything on earth** (or the bodily life) **for it, so that it may become apparent who will display the best conduct!**

8. **We will certainly turn everything on earth** (the body) **into barren soil!**

9. **Or did you think that** (only) **the Asab-i Kehf** (companions of the cave) **and the inscription** (on stone) **were among Our wondrous signs?**

10. **And when the youths retreated to the cave and said "Our Rabb** (the Name composition comprising our essential reality)**, grant us a grace** (a blessing with your favor) **from Yourself** (Your ladun) **and form within us a state of perfection in this matter."**

11. **So We cast** (a veil) **over their ears** (closed their perception to the world; put them to sleep) **in the cave for many years.**

12. **Then We revived them** (with a new understanding of life) **that We might know** ('Know' here denotes 'reveal' so that they may know – Elmalili Tafsir, Vol 5, Pg 3226) **which of the two factions were most precise in calculating the time they had remained there.**

13. (My Rasul) **We narrate their story to you in truth... Indeed, they were youths who believed in their Rabb** (B-Rabbihim; as their essential reality in their consciousness)**... Hence, We increased them in experiencing their essential reality.**

14. **We put a nexus in their hearts** (fixed their consciousness upon a state of constant observation)**! They** (those youths) **stood up and said, "Our Rabb** (the dimension of Names comprising our essence) **is the Rabb of the heavens and the earth** (the One who forms everything in existence with His Names)**! Never will we accept a god** (an administrator in existence) **besides Him** (equivalent to Him)**! For if we speak the contrary, we would have spoken an absurd thing that defies the mind and logic."**

15. **These, our people** (who have deified the results of their baseless assumptions) **have taken gods besides Him... If only they can show a clear proof of the power of these gods! So, who is more unjust than one who lies and slanders against Allah?**

16. **Since you have distanced yourselves from them and the things they worship besides Allah, retreat to the cave so your Rabb may spread His grace over you and form a benefit for you from what you do.**

17. **When the sun rises it turns from the right side of the cave... And when it sets it passes from their left side... They are within an open space thereof... This is a sign of Allah... Whoever Allah guides** (to his essential reality) **is enabled to reach the reality... And whoever He leads astray, never will you find for him a friend/guide to enlighten him.**

18. **You would have thought they were awake though they lay asleep** (as though dead)**... We turned them to the right and to the left... And their dog stretched his forelegs at the entrance** (of the cave)**! Had you seen them in that state, you would have turned away from them in flight; you would have been apprehensive and frightened!**

19. **Thus We revived them** (resurrected) **them** (a quality of the Name Baith manifested upon them). **so that they may question one another about what they experienced... One of them said, "How long have**

you remained?" Some of them said, "We have remained a day or a part of a day"... The others said, "Your Rabb knows better how long you remained... So send one of you with this silver coin (money) to the city and let him see what food is clean and bring back some sustenance for you; let him be cautious and not let others be aware of you."

20. "For if they become aware of you they will stone you to death or turn you to their belief... Then you will never have the opportunity to succeed!"

21. So We informed them about them, so that they know the word of Allah (resurrection) is Truth, and that of the hour (of death) there is no doubt! When they were arguing about the affair among themselves they said, "Construct over them a building. Their Rabb knows best about them (about what they are)" Those whose word prevailed over the matter said, "Surely, we will construct over them (the people of the cave) a masjid (a prayer house)."

22. They will say, "They were three, the fourth was a dog"... "They were five, the sixth was a dog"... This is merely guessing at the unknown (ranting and fabricating about things they do not know)! They will say, "They were seven, the eighth was a dog"... Say, "My Rabb knows better their number... None knows them except a few"... Do not argue about them other than exchanging ideas and do not ask them anything about them!

23. Do not say "I will definitely do it tomorrow" about anything (for you do not know if Allah wills that thing or not)!

24. Except when adding, "Insha Allah – If Allah wills" (you cannot know how Allah's new manifestation will be)! And remember (dhikr) your Rabb (the Names comprising your essence) when you forget! And say, "I hope my Rabb enables me to attain perfection in His closeness (the dimension of the Reflection of Attributes, in the experience of the unity of existence. [See the topic of the Reflection of Divine Attributes in The Perfect Man, by Abdulqadir al-Jili.])

25. (And some say) they remained in their cave for three hundred years and added nine to it.

26. Say, "Allah knows best how long they remained... To Him belongs the unknown (aspects) of the heavens and the earth! He is One whose sight and hearing cannot be comprehended with the

mind! They have no friend or guardian besides Him! And there is none to share His verdict!"

27. **Recite** (decipher – understand) **what has been revealed to you** (to your consciousness) **of the Book of your Rabb** (the knowledge pertaining to the dimension of the Names comprising your essence)! **There is none to change His words! And you will never find a refuge other than Him.**

28. **Keep yourself** (consciousness) **patient with those who pray to their Rabb, in the morning and the evening, seeking His countenance! Do not turn away from them desiring the adornments of the worldly life! And do not obey the one whose perception has been confined in his cocoon, deprived of remembering Us, and who follows his baseless ideas, and whose case has gone beyond all bounds!**

29. **Say, "The Truth is from your Rabb! So, whoever wills – let him believe, and whoever wills – let him deny!" Indeed, We have prepared for the wrongdoers a fire whose enormous waves have surrounded them from all sides! If they call for relief, they will be relieved with water like molten lead, which scalds their faces! How wretched a drink; how wretched an abode!**

30. **Indeed, those who have believed** (that the One denoted by the name Allah is manifest with His Names, and that He is the Ahad and the Samad) **and who fulfill the requirements of their faith, surely We will not allow to be lost the results of their righteous deeds!**

31. **For them there will be Paradises of Eden underneath which rivers flow, they will be adorned therein with bracelets of gold and will wear green garments of fine silk and brocade, resting on couches... How excellent a return and how favorable an abode** (a metaphoric narration of the heavenly state of life; please refer to 13:35 and 47:15).

32. (My Rasul) **present to them the example of the two men: We gave two gardens of grapevines to one of them, and encircled them with date palms and placed crop fields between them.**

33. **Both the gardens produced their fruits and did not fall short in anything... And We caused a river to gush forth between the two gardens.**

34. (This man) **had other means of income as well... So, when he came across the other man, he said, "I am greater than you in wealth and mightier in number."**

35. And he entered his garden, wronging himself, he said, "I do not think this wealth will ever perish."

36. "I do not think the Doomsday will occur! And, if I am indeed returned to my Rabb, I am sure I will find even a better life than this."

37. His friend said to him, "Are you denying your essence? He created you from dust, then created you from a sperm drop and then made you into a conscious man!"

38. "Thus HU is Allah, my Rabb! I do not associate anything with my Rabb (the Names comprising my essence)!"

39. "If only you had said, when you entered your garden, "MashaAllah (this formation is by the will of Allah) la kuwwata illa Billah – power (which appears to manifest on me) belongs only to Allah"... Although you see me less in wealth and children."

40. "It may be that my Rabb will give me a better Paradise (garden) than yours and will send upon your garden a calamity from the sky and it will become a dry, dusty ground."

41. "Or the water (of your garden) will be sunken down (into the earth) and you will not be able to find it again."

42. And his wealth was encompassed and ruined! In the end he was rubbing his hands about (in loss) over what he had spent on his garden, which had collapsed upon its trellises, saying, "I wish I had not associated anything with my Rabb."

43. He had neither a helper besides Allah, nor the strength to fend for himself!

44. Thus, as can be seen, the manifestation of the Name Waliyy belongs only to Allah, the Truth (Allah is the One who enables the state of wilayah)! He is better in giving reward and better in enabling the experience of an outcome.

45. Present to them the example of the worldly life... (The life of this world) is like water We bring down from the sky, which mixes with the vegetation of the earth... then (the vegetation) becomes dry remnants scattered by the winds... Allah is Muqtadir over all things.

46. Wealth and children are but the adornments of the worldly life (they are transient and temporary – bound to perish)! But the enduring

deeds done as the requirements of faith are better both as reward in the sight of your Rabb, and as expectation.

47. **The day We make the mountains walk** (render dysfunctional the organs) **you will see the earth naked! We will gather all of them, such that none will be disregarded!**

48. **They will be presented to their Rabb in rows** (according to the level of their faith)**! Indeed, you have come to Us as We created you the first time** (cleansed from the identity, as pure consciousness)**... Perhaps you did not think We will form this phase for you!**

49. **"The book** (the full record of an individual's life) **will be laid open, and those who are guilty will be filled with dread at the information they see and will exclaim: 'Oh, woe unto us! What kind of a book** (recorded information) **is this! It leaves out nothing, small or great, but takes all our thoughts and deeds into account!' They will find in their presence all that they have done! Your Rabb does not wrong anyone."**

50. **"And** [mention] **when We said to the angels, 'Prostrate to Adam,' and all but Iblis prostrated. He was of the jinn...** (thus, in favor of his ego) **he disobeyed the command of his Rabb** (he did not have the knowledge of the reality [the jinni have no apprehension of the knowledge of the reality], they live purely by the ego. A.H.)**. So do take him** (Iblis) **and his offspring as friends in My stead despite their enmity towards you! How bad a choice of friends for the wrongdoers!**

51. **I did not hold them** (the jinni) **witness to the creation of the heavens and the earth, or to the creation of themselves! Never can those who lead the people astray be in servitude to Me!**

52. **During that time when it is said, "Call My partners whom you assumed existed", and they will call upon them, but they will not respond to them... We have put an unsurpassable barrier between them.**

53. **When the guilty ones saw the fire, they were certain they were going to fall in... There was no other destination for them but the fire!**

54. **Indeed, in this Quran We have presented the truths with every kind of example for the people! But man has ever been most keen on arguing against the reality.**

55. What can prevent the people from believing and asking for forgiveness of their Rabb when there has come to them a guide (Rasul) leading them to the path of the reality, other than waiting for the precedent of the former people to befall them, or for the punishment to appear directly in front of them!

56. We disclose the Rasuls only as givers of good tidings and as warners... Those who deny the knowledge of the reality strive to cover the Truth with baseless ideas! They took My signs and the things of which they are warned as amusement (they did not take it seriously enough to evaluate it)!

57. Who can do more wrong than the one who is reminded of the proofs of his Rabb (inherent divine qualities), but turns away from them and forgets what he prepared and put forth with his own hands? Indeed, We have imprisoned them into their cocoons for not realizing the truth (due to their denial) and placed a heaviness into their ears! Even if you invite them to the reality they will never attain guidance!

58. Your Rabb is the Ghafur and possessor of grace! Had He willed to enforce the consequences of their doings immediately, surely He would have hastened the suffering (death)! Rather, there is an appointed time for them, from which they will never be able to escape.

59. These are the cities We destroyed for having wronged, and We had appointed a time for their destruction.

60. And Moses said to the youngster in his service, "I will continue traveling until I reach the junction of the two seas, even if it takes me many years."

61. But when they reached the junction of the two seas, they forgot their fish (there)... So, it (the fish) took its course into the sea and was gone!

62. A little after they passed (their meeting point), Moses said to his servant, "Bring us our lunch; this journey has certainly exhausted us..."

63. (Moses' servant) said, "Did you see? I forgot the fish near the rock... Satan made me forget to remind you! And it (the fish) wondrously (came to life) and delved into the sea!"

64. (Moses) said, "That is what we have been seeking!"... So they returned, following their footprints.

65. And they found a servant from among Our servants to whom We had given (gifted) grace (enabling him to experience his reality) and had disclosed through him Our Knowledge (the manifestation of divine attributes as the pleasing self [nafs-i mardiyya])from Our ladun.

66. Moses said to him, "I would like to follow you so that you teach me from the knowledge that has been disclosed through you!"

67. (Khidr) said, "You will not be able to bear being with me (your creational program and function are tuned for the exterior; the perception of the eye, you cannot comprehend the interior dimensions of the unknown due to the requirements of your specific function)!"

68. "How can you bear to witness an event when you are unaware of its essential reality?"

69. (Moses) said, "With the will of Allah you will find me to be of those who are patient; I will not object to you in any of your affairs."

70. (Khidr) said, "If you are to follow me, you shall not ask me any questions (regarding how and what I do) until I explain to you the reality of it!"

71. So they set out, until when they embarked on a boat (Khidr) made a hole in the boat. (Moses) said, "Have you made this hole so its people may drown? Indeed, you have done a grave thing!"

72. (Khidr) said, "Did I not tell you that you cannot bear being with me?"

73. (Moses) said, "Do not rebuke me for forgetting (my word); do not make my job difficult for me."

74. So they continued on their way, until when they met a little boy, Khidr killed him! (Moses) said, "You have killed an innocent person other than for retribution? You have certainly done a horrendous thing!"

75. (Khidr) said, "Did I not tell you that you cannot bear being with me?"

76. (Moses) said, "If I should ask you about (anything) after this then do not keep me as a companion! Let this be my final excuse!"

77. So they continued on their way... Finally they reached a town and asked for some food from its people... But they refused to offer their hospitality... Then they (Moses and Khidr) saw a wall about to collapse. (Khidr) restored the wall. (Moses) said, "If you wished you could have obtained a payment for this job."

78. (Khidr) said, "This (your third objection) has marked the end of our companionship! I shall give you the interpretation (the inner meanings) of the things you could not bear witnessing."

79. "Let us start with the boat: That boat belonged to the poor people working at sea. I willed to make it faulty because they were to meet a king who would seize every boat by force (since the king was not to take a damaged boat, I actually salvaged the boat for the people in order to help them).

80. "As for that little boy, his parents were both believers but we feared he would make them fall into transgression and disbelief (through the person he was to become when he grew older)!"

81. "So we wanted their Rabb to substitute for them one who is better, purer and closer to His grace."

82. "As for the wall: It belonged to two orphan boys in that city... Underneath it there was a treasure that belonged to them (the two orphan boys)... And their father was a righteous man... So your Rabb willed for those two boys to grow older and reach maturity and extract their treasure as grace from your Rabb... I did not do these things out of my own accord! So, this is the interpretation (inner meanings) of the things that you could not bear to witness."

83. They ask you about Dhul-Qarnayn... Say, "I will recite to you a dhikr (remembrance) about him."

84. We established him upon the earth and made easy for him every path (to attain his wishes).

85. So he followed a way.

86. When he finally reached the place where the sun set, he found it setting in dense, dark water... And he found people there! We said, "O Dhul-Qarnayn! You can either punish them or do good for them."

87. (Dhul-Qarnayn) said, "We will punish the one who does wrong... And he will be returned to his Rabb and He will punish him with an indescribable torment."

88. But whoever believes (in the reality) and fulfills the requirements of his faith the return of this is best for him... We will apply Our command of ease on him.

89. Then he (Dhul-Qarnayn) followed (another) way.

90. Until he came to the place of the rising sun (the place where the sun rises from the lowest point in the north without actually setting). He found it rising upon a people for whom We had not made a cover (against the sun) (i.e. the sun never disappeared).

91. Thus it is... We had encompassed him with what he had.

92. Then he (Dhul-Qarnayn) followed one other way.

93. Finally he reached a place between two mountains... He found people there who were almost unable to evaluate any warning.

94. They said, "O Dhul-Qarnayn! Indeed, Gog and Magog are causing corruption on earth! So, shall we pay you a price so that you make a barrier between us and them?"

95. (Dhul-Qarnayn) said, "That which my Rabb manifests through me is better... But assist me with your strength and I will make between you and them a barrier."

96. "Bring me the blocks of iron..." Until when We leveled both sides, he said, "Blow (with bellows)"... Until it (the iron) became red hot, he said, "Bring it to me, that I may pour molten copper over it."

97. So they were neither able to pass over it nor penetrate through it!

98. (Dhul-Qarnayn) said, "This is a grace from my Rabb... So, when the promise of my Rabb comes, He will make it level... The promise of my Rabb is true."

99. That day We will leave them alone, they will surge over each other like (two different kinds of) waves! And the Horn will be blown, and We will have gathered all of them together.

100. And We will display Hell clearly before the eyes of those who deny the knowledge of the reality!

101. **Their insight** (perception) **was blocked from my dhikr** (remembrance)! **And their capacity was inadequate to perceive and comprehend!**

102. **Did those who deny the knowledge of the reality think they can leave Me** (deny the quality of the Name Waliyy in their essence) **and take my** (external) **servants as guardians! We made hell an abode for the deniers of the knowledge of the reality.**

103. **Say, "Shall I inform you of the greatest losers as a result of their deeds?"**

104. **They are the ones whose efforts in the worldly life have gone to waste while they thought they were doing good!**

105. **They are the ones who deny the signs** (Names) **of their Rabb within themselves and the meeting with Him** (that they will experience the manifestation of the Names in their consciousness) **and thus whose deeds are in vain! And We shall give them no weight** (importance) **in the Doomsday period.**

106. **That is the hell in which the deniers of the knowledge of the reality will reside; that is the recompense for mocking My signs and Rasuls!**

107. **Indeed, those who believe** (in the reality) **and fulfill its requirements, their place of residence will be Gardens of Paradise.**

108. **They will abide therein eternally... They will never want to leave.**

109. **Say, "If the ocean were ink for the words** (the manifest meanings) **of my Rabb, surely the ocean will be exhausted before the words of my Rabb came to an end! Even if we added another ocean like it!"**

110. **Say** (my Rasul), **"I am merely a man like you** (therefore you are also like me) **except that the Unity of Uluhiyyah is revealed to my consciousness** (the knowledge of Allah is disclosed through me; Risalat)! **So, whoever expects to meet their Rabb** (experience the requirements of the reality of the Names) **let him fulfill the requirements of his faith and** (continue) **serving His Rabb and not assign any partners to Him!"**

19

MARYAM

By the one who is denoted by the name Allah (who created my being with His Names in accord with the meaning of the letter 'B'), the Rahman, the Rahim.

1. Kaf, Ha, Ya, 'Ain, Sad.

2. Remember (dhikr) the grace of your Rabb to His servant Zechariah.

3. When he had introspectively turned to his Rabb.

4. "My Rabb... Indeed, my bones have weakened, and my hair has become white! My Rabb, never have I been disappointed in my prayers to You..."

5. "Indeed, I fear what the successors after me may do. And my wife is barren! So, grant from ladun (the potential of the Names comprising my essence) a successor for me."

6. "Who will be my heir and the heir of the family of Jacob... And, my Rabb, make him of those who live according to Your pleasure."

7. "O Zechariah... We give you the good tidings of a boy whose name will be John... We have not assigned this name to anyone before him."

8. (Zechariah) said, "My Rabb, how can I have a son when my wife is barren and I have reached the extreme in old age?"

9. "Thus it is," your Rabb says, "It is easy for Me... For when you were nothing (worthy of mention), I created you."

10. (Zechariah) said, "My Rabb! Give me a sign..." He said, "Your sign is that you will not be able to speak to the people for three nights, although being sound/healthy in body."

11. So (Zechariah) came out of the shrine and signaled to them to exalt (tasbih) in the morning and evening.

12. "O Zechariah! Hold firmly onto the knowledge of the reality!" When We taught (John) the reasons underlying matters and the ability to read the system, he was only a child!

13. And We bestowed him with a spiritual life and purity (alms) from Our ladun... He was ever so sensitive in protection!

14. He was kind to his parents; he was neither a tyrant nor a rebel.

15. Salam was upon him on the day he came to the world, the day he tasted death, and the day he was resurrected as an immortal (this denotes resurrection takes place immediately after death).

16. And remind them of Mary in the knowledge that came to you... How she withdrew from her family and retreated to a (far) place in the east (of the shrine).

17. She secluded herself from them... We disclosed Our Spirit (the form of knowledge, wave, materialized data) to her, and he appeared to her as a full human.

18. (Mary) said, "I seek refuge in the Rahman from you, (so do not approach me) if you are of the protected!"

19. (The Spirit) said, "I am the Rasul of your Rabb! I have been disclosed to grant you a pure son."

20. (Mary) said, "How can I have a son when no man has touched me and I have not been unchaste?"

21. "Thus it is!" your Rabb says, "It is easy for me! We will disclose him as a miracle for the people and as a grace from Us. This is a matter decreed (already done)!"

22. So (Mary) conceived him (Jesus) and withdrew with him to a remote place.

23. When the pain of childbirth drove her to grasp the branch of a palm tree, she exclaimed, "Oh, I wish I had died before this and was completely forgotten."

24. Then a voice below her said, "Do not grieve, your Rabb has formed a stream beneath you."

25. "Shake the branch of that palm tree toward yourself and it will drop upon you ripe fresh dates."

26. "So eat, drink and be happy! And if you see anyone, say, 'I have vowed a fast (of silence) for Rahman, I will not speak today to anyone.'"

27. When (Mary) came to her family with him in her arms, they said, "O Mary... Indeed, you have done a terrible thing!"

28. "O sister of Aaron! Your father was not an indecent man... And your mother was not an unchaste woman."

29. As Mary had vowed fast she only pointed to the child (suggesting they should ask him)... They said, "How can we talk to a baby in a cradle!"

30. (Baby Jesus) spoke, "Indeed, I am a servant of Allah; He gave me Knowledge (Book) and made me a Nabi."

31. "He made me prosperous wherever I may be... He enjoined upon me salat (living in a constant state of introspective turning to my Rabb) and purity, for as long as I live!"

32. "He made me kind to my mother, not a tyrant destitute!"

33. So Salam is upon me on the day I came to the world, the day I taste death, and the day I am resurrected as an immortal."

34. Thus was Jesus, the son of Mary... The truth about which they fall into doubt!

35. It is not for Allah (the Ahad the Samad other than whom nothing exists) to take a son, Exalted (Subhan) is He! If He decrees an affair He only says to it "Be", and it is.

36. Indeed, Allah is my Rabb and your Rabb! Realize your servitude to Him... This is the straight path.

37. Then those of differing opinions (blinded from the Unity of Uluhiyyah) fell into dispute (slandered Allah)... Woe to those who deny the knowledge of the reality during that dreadful time!

38. They will hear and see (the reality) the Day they come to Us! But the wrongdoers today, are in clear error.

39. So, warn them about the period of longing when the consequences of matters will be faced! Their matter will be concluded while they are cocooned and in a state of disbelief.

40. **Neither the earth nor anything on it will remain! All of them will be returned to Us** (their essential reality).

41. **Remember** (dhikr) **Abraham in the knowledge that came to you! Indeed, he was a man of Truth, a Nabi.**

42. **(Abraham) said to his father, "O my father... Why do you worship things that cannot hear you, see you or benefit you in any way?"**

43. **"O my father... Indeed, the knowledge that has not been disclosed to you has been disclosed to me! So follow me and I will guide you to a straight path."**

44. **"O my father... Do not serve the Satan! Indeed, Satan disobeyed the Rahman."**

45. **"O my father... I fear that a punishment will touch you from the Rahman and you will become a companion of Satan** (become confined within the bounds of the physical body in the life to come)."

46. (His father) **said, "Are you turning away from my gods, O Abraham? I swear if you do not desist, I will have you stoned to death... Stay away from me for a prolonged time!"**

47. **(Abraham) said, "Salam be upon you. I will ask forgiveness for you of my Rabb. Indeed, He is ever generous to me."**

48. **"I will distance myself from you and those you invoke besides and pray to my Rabb. I expect not to be disappointed as a result of introspectively turning to the divine qualities within my essence."**

49. **When** (Abraham) **left them and those they invoked besides Allah, We bestowed him with Isaac and Jacob... We made each of them a Nabi!**

50. **We bestowed them from Our grace and granted them the supreme force of articulation of the knowledge pertaining to Truthfulness** (the experiential confirmation of the reality).

51. **And remind of Moses too from the knowledge that came to you... Indeed, he was chosen** (aware of his servitude to Allah)**, and he was a Rasul and a Nabi.**

52. **We called to him from the right side of the mount** (the right side of his ego, from his essential reality) **and brought him to a state of nearness** (a state in which he was able to hear the calling of the reality).

53. And We gave to him from Our grace, his brother Aaron as a Nabi.

54. And remember Ishmael from the knowledge that came to you... Indeed, he was true to his promise (that he will not be negligent of his servitude to Allah), **and he was a Rasul and a Nabi.**

55. He used to command his family to experience salat and purity. In the sight of his Rabb he was in the state of the pleasing self (state of selflessness).

56. And remind of Idrees from the knowledge that came to you... Indeed, he was a man of Truth and a Nabi.

57. We raised him to an exalted station!

58. They are those upon whom Allah bestowed favor from among the Nabis, the descendants of Adam, and of those We carried with Noah (on the boat), **and of those We lead to the reality from the descendants of Abraham and Israel** (Jacob) **and whom We chose** (from pre-eternity). **When the proofs of the Rahman's existence are recited to them they prostrate** (in state of pure observation and certainty) **and cry.** (This is a verse of prostration.)

59. But there came after them descendants who neglected prayer (introspective turning to one's essence) **and followed their desires** (the impulses driven by the idea of being the body and baseless ambitions)... **They will soon find themselves in the pit of Gayya** (the pit of hell from which they will not be able to escape).

60. Except those who repent, believe and fulfill the requirements of their faith... They will enter Paradise and will not be subject to injustice in any way.

61. Rahman has promised His servants from the unknown Paradises of Eden (reflection of attributes)**... Indeed, His promise has been fulfilled.**

62. They will not hear any gossip there, only "Salam" (the meaning of the Name Salam will manifest and hence their speech will be about the reality disclosing from their own essence)**... And they will have their sustenance therein, morning and evening.**

63. This is the Paradise that We will give as inheritance to Our servants who protect themselves (not only in action, but also in thought)**!**

64. We only become revealed (dimensionally) with the command of your Rabb! Everything within and outside and beyond our knowledge belongs to Him! The concept of forgetfulness does not apply to Him!

65. Everything between the heavens and the earth belongs to your Rabb... So become aware of your servitude to Him and persevere in your worship to Him... Have you ever heard of or come to know anyone like Him?

66. Man says, "Will I be brought forth as an immortal after I have died?"

67. Does man not remember that We created him before while he was nothing?

68. By your Rabb, We will resurrect them together with the devils... And We will surely gather them around Hell on their knees.

69. Then from every group We will extract (for the fire) those who were most fierce in denying the Rahman.

70. For We know well who has deserved to burn in fire.

71. <u>And there is none among you who He will not pass through (experience) Hell</u>! This is, by your Rabb, a definite decree.

72. Then We will save those who protected themselves (who exhibit the forces that become manifest as a result of living ones' reality) and leave the transgressors on their knees!

73. When Our proofs are clearly recited and informed to them, those who deny the knowledge of the reality said to the believers, "Which of the two factions are better in position and association?"

74. We have destroyed many generations before them who were better in wealth and appearance.

75. Say, "Whoever is in error, let the Rahman extend his time! Until they see that which has been promised to them, the punishment, or that hour (of death or Doomsday) they will know who is more evil and weaker in army!"

76. Allah increases in knowledge (of the reality) those who are on the right path! In the sight of your Rabb the deeds of faith are better in return and better as merit.

77. Did you see the one who denied Our signs and said, "I will most definitely be given wealth and children"?

78. Has he attained knowledge from the unknown or taken word from the Rahman?

79. No! We will record what he says and extend his suffering extensively.

80. He will lose what he says and We will be his inheritor... And he will come to Us alone.

81. They took deities besides Allah as a source of supremacy for themselves.

82. No! (Those deities) are going to deny their worship and oppose them!

83. Did you not see how We sent the devils upon those who deny the knowledge of the reality so they play with them (by inciting suspicion and groundless fear and illusion in them).

84. So do not be impatient concerning them... We only count the days for them.

85. In the period when We gather the protected ones to the Rahman to receive His offerings!

86. And dispatch the guilty ones to Hell, yearning for water!

87. None in the sight of Allah will be able to intercede except those who have been given a covenant from the Rahman (those through whom the Names have become manifest from their essential reality)!

88. They said, "Rahman has taken a son!"

89. Indeed, you have done an atrocious thing.

90. Because of this the heavens almost shatter, the earth splits open and the mountains collapse in devastation!

91. Because they attribute a son to the Rahman!

92. Such concepts like taking a son are not befitting for the Rahman.

93. Whoever is in the heavens and the earth is in servitude to the Rahman!

94. Indeed, (Rahman) knows them in detail and in many ways!

95. In the period of the Doomsday, all of them will come to Him as ONE.

96. Those who believe and fulfill the requirements of their faith, Rahman will form love for them.

97. We have made it easy through your narration so that you give good tidings with it to the believers and warn the stubborn ones with it.

98. And We have destroyed many people before them... Do you feel any of them or hear any of their whisperings now?

20

TA-HA

By the one who is denoted by the name Allah (who created my being with His Names in accord with the meaning of the letter 'B'), **the Rahman, the Rahim.**

1. O man (pure Muhammadan consciousness, the original Self metaphorically described as the totality of the Names taught to Adam and the Spirit that was blown into Adam)!

2. We did not reveal the Quran for you to be miserable.

3. It (the revealed knowledge) **is only a reminder** (of its reality) **to a consciousness that is open to awe** (perceptive to the might of Allah)!

4. It is sent down in parts from the creator of the earth (body) **and the great heavens** (the forms and levels of consciousness manifesting from the dimension of Names).

5. Rahman is established on the Throne (Rahman established His sovereignty by creating the worlds [the existential world created by the potential of the Names inherent in one's brain] with His Names, i.e., in the quantum potential, Rahman observes His knowledge through His knowledge).

6. Whatever is in the heavens (consciousness) **and the earth** (manifest action) **and everything in between** (in one's imagination) **and beneath the earth** (the depths of his body) **is for Him** (for the manifestation of His Names).

7. And if you speak your thoughts (or conceal them) **know that indeed He knows the secret** (in your consciousness) **and what is even deeper** (the actual Names that compose it).

8. It is Allah! There is no deity-god, only HU! The Beautiful Names belong to Him (He creates what He wills with those qualities)!

9. Has the story of Moses reached you?

10. How he (Moses) saw a fire and said to his people, "Stay here, indeed I have sensed fire... Perhaps I will bring you an ember from it or find a guide near that fire."

11. When he came close (to the fire) he perceived a calling, "O Moses."

12. "Indeed, I am your Rabb! Take off both your sandals (let go of your physical and mental conditionings and remain as pure consciousness) for you are indeed in your sacred valley of Tuwa!"

13. "I have chosen you! So, perceive the knowledge that is being revealed!"

14. "Indeed, I am Allah! There is no deity-god, only Me! So serve Me (by manifesting the qualities of My Names)! And experience salat to remember Me!"

15. "Indeed, the hour (of death) will come... But I will keep its time hidden so that everyone will see and experience the consequences of their own deeds."

16. "Do not let those who don't believe (in the eternal life to come upon death) and who follow their baseless illusions distract you from it (the truth that all shall return to Allah) lest you be destroyed!"

17. "What is that in your right hand, O Moses?"

18. (Moses) said, "It is my staff... I lean on it, I beat down leaves for my sheep with it and it also serves my other needs."

19. "Let go of it, O Moses!"

20. So he threw it... And behold, it became a moving serpent!

21. "Take hold of it and have no fear! We will return it to you with its initial appearance!"

22. "And now put your hand in your chest, as another miracle, it will come out white without blemish or illness!"

23. "Thus We show Our biggest miracles to you!"

24. "Go to Pharaoh! Indeed, he has transgressed all bounds!"

25. (Moses) said, "My Rabb, expand my consciousness (so that I may digest these and apply their requisites)."

26. "Ease my task for me."

27. "Untie the knot in my tongue."

28. "So that they understand (the intricacy of) my words."

29. "And appoint for me a helper from my people."

30. "My brother Aaron."

31. "Strengthen me through him."

32. "Let him share my task."

33. "So that We may glorify (tasbih) You much."

34. "And remember (dhikr) You much!"

35. "Indeed, You are Basir over us!"

36. He said "You have been granted your request, O Moses!"

37. "Indeed, We had also bestowed Our favor to you once more (before this)."

38. "We had revealed to your mother that which was revealed."

39. "Place him (Moses) in a chest and cast the chest into the river... The river shall take him to the shore where he shall be taken by an enemy of Mine and his! I have placed My love upon you... So that you may be raised directly under My sight."

40. Recall when your sister walked along and said (to the family of Pharaoh), "Shall I show you one who will embrace him and take care of him?" Thus We returned you to your mother so that she may be happy and not grieve... And you killed someone and We delivered you from that trouble... We subjected you to trial after trial... And recall how you stayed among the people of Madyan (with Shuayb a.s.) for many years... And then, as decreed by your fate, you came here!"

41. "I have chosen you for Myself."

42. Go, you and your brother, with My miracles... And do not show any weakness when remembering Me!"

43. "Go both of you to Pharaoh! Indeed, he has transgressed all bounds."

44. "But speak gently with him! Perhaps he will contemplate and evaluate or feel awed!"

45. "Our Rabb! Indeed, we are afraid that he will put too much pressure on us or go overboard."

46. "Do not be afraid! Indeed, I hear and see with and through you (the secret of the unity of existence; non-duality)" (Hadith Qudsi: "...I will be the ear by which My servant hears and the eyes with which My servant sees...")

47. "So go to him and say, 'We are indeed the Rasuls of your Rabb! Send the Children of Israel with us and do not torment them! Indeed, We have come to you as miracles from your Rabb... May salam be upon those who follow the guide'."

48. "It has been revealed to us that suffering will be upon those who deny and turn away."

49. (Pharaoh) asked, "Who is your Rabb, O Moses?"

50. (Moses) said, "Our Rabb is He who gives everything its existence and qualities and then eases for it its way."

51. (Pharaoh) asked, "What about the previous generations? What will happen to them (for they have not seen this reality)?"

52. (Moses) said, "Their knowledge is the knowledge with my Rabb... My Rabb neither does wrong nor forgets."

53. It is He who made the earth like a cradle for you and opened pathways therein and disclosed water from the sky and produced pairs of various plants with it.

54. So eat and graze your animals... Indeed, there are signs in this for those with healthy thought.

55. We created you from it! And We will return you to it! And from it We will bring you forth (resurrect you) one more time.

56. Indeed, We have shown him (Pharaoh) all of Our signs... But he denied them and refrained from accepting.

57. He said, "Have you come to drive us out of our land by means of your magic, O Moses?"

58. "We will bring you magic to match yours... So, appoint a time for both of us and let us meet in an appropriate place."

59. (Moses) said, "The meeting day will be the day of the festival... Let the people assemble at late morning."

60. So Pharaoh turned (went) away and gathered his tricks (magicians) and came.

61. Moses said to them, "Woe to you... Do not make up lies against Allah lest He destroys you with a punishment... He who slanders has most definitely lost."

62. (The magicians) argued among themselves over their affair, whispering secretively to one another.

63. (Pharaoh's magicians) said, "These two are nothing but magicians... They want to drive you out of your land with their magic and destroy your exemplary lifestyle."

64. "So put together your tricks and come forward in a line... Whoever prevails today has surely attained salvation"

65. They said, "O Moses! Either you throw first or we shall be the first to throw."

66. (Moses) said, "No, you throw"... And behold! By their magic, their ropes and staffs appeared (in his imagination) as though they were moving rapidly towards him.

67. Moses felt apprehensive inside!

68. We told him, "Do not be afraid! Indeed, you, yes you, shall prevail"

69. "Leave that which is in your right hand and let it swallow what they have wrought... For they have only wrought a magician's trick... A magician shall never succeed wherever he may go."

70. The magicians then prostrated and said, "We believe (in scope of the letter B) in the Rabb of Aaron and Moses."

71. (Pharaoh) said, "Have you believed him without my permission! Indeed, he is your master in teaching you magic... I will certainly cut your hands and feet off on opposite sides and crucify you on the trunks of the palm-trees... You will surely know whose punishment is more severe and lasting!"

72. They said, "After the clear sign that has come to us we will never prefer you over our creator... So, decide whatever you will! Your jurisdiction applies only in the life of this world."

73. "We have indeed believed in our Rabb so that He may forgive us our mistakes and our sorcery... Allah is better and lasting."

74. The truth is, he who comes to his Rabb as guilty, hell shall be for him... Therein he will neither die (and be freed) nor will he experience living!

75. But he who comes to Him as a believer and as one who has fulfilled the requirements of his faith, the highest ranks shall be for them.

76. Paradises of Eden underneath which rivers flow... They will abide therein eternally... This is the recompense for those who purify themselves.

77. Indeed We revealed to Moses, "Take my servants and travel by night... Strike for them with your staff a dry path through the sea! Let them (walk) without fear of being caught or fright (that they will drown)!"

78. Pharaoh pursued them with his army and the sea engulfed and drowned them.

79. Pharaoh led his people astray; he did not guide them to the right path.

80. O Children of Israel! Indeed, We delivered you from your enemy and made a covenant with you on the right side of Mount Sinai... We sent manna and quail upon you.

81. So, eat what is clean from the sustenance with which We nourish you and do not go to excess... Lest you incur My wrath (as a result of your deeds)... For whoever incurs My wrath, surely he is in a serious downfall.

82. Indeed, I am Gaffar over those who repent (who become aware of their actions that do not befit their essential reality and turn back with regret), who believe and fulfill the requirements of their faith, and who then find the right way.

83. "What is it that makes you distance yourself from you people with such haste, O Moses?"

84. (Moses) said, "My Rabb, I hasten to attain your pleasure. They are following in my footsteps..."

85. (His Rabb) said, "Indeed, We have tried your people after you left them, to make them see their own level of understanding... Samiri (a man of sorcery and magic who fled from Pharaoh's palace and joined them) has led them astray!"

86. Moses returned to his people in anger and sorrow... He said, "O my people... Had not your Rabb made you a good promise? Was the time of the promise too long for you? Or did you will to incur the wrath of your Rabb and that is why you did not keep your promise?"

87. They said, "We did not defy you consciously... But we were carrying heavy loads of the people's ornaments and so we threw them (into Samiri's fire)... for that is how Samiri had thrown them (so we imitated him)."

88. (Samiri) made a statue of a calf for them that produced a roaring sound... Whereupon they said, "This is your deity-god and the deity-god of Moses, but Moses has forgotten it!"

89. Do they not see that it (the calf) cannot give them any response and has no power to harm or benefit them!

90. Indeed, Aaron had told them, "O my people... You have only been tested with it... Most certainly your Rabb is Rahman... So follow me and obey my command!"

91. They said, "We will continue to worship this (calf) until Moses returns to us."

92. (Moses) said, "O Aaron! Why did you not prevent them when you saw they had gone astray?"

93. "Why did you not follow me (and show them the right way)? Have you rebelled against my command?"

94. (Aaron) said, "O the son of my mother! Stop seizing me by hair and beard! Indeed, I was afraid that you would say, 'You have caused dissension among the Children of Israel and did not follow my word.'"

95. (Moses) said, "What is your purpose, O Samiri?"

96. (Samiri) said, "I perceived what they perceived not! So, I took a little of the Rasul's product (by using the force of the letter B he informed us about) and threw it (into the blend of molten gold)... This is what my (inner) self (the force within my essence) prompted me to do."

97. (Moses) said, "Begone! Indeed, throughout your whole life you will say, 'do not touch me' to people... And you will be faced with an end from which you will never be able to escape... Look at the deity-god you keep worshipping! We will most definitely burn it until it becomes dust and then scatter it into the sea."

98. The possessor of Uluhiyyah is Allah alone... There is no deity-god, only HU! He encompasses everything (in every aspect) with His knowledge!

99. Thus We relate to you some of the news of past events... In truth, We have given you a reminder (dhikr) from Our ladun (the potential of the Names comprising your essence).

100. So, whoever turns away from it (the reality that is being reminded), indeed, he will bear a heavy burden in the period of the Doomsday.

101. They will live the consequences of their mistakes forever! A grievous burden it (their mistake) will be for them during the Doomsday period!

102. The day the Horn will be blown! We will resurrect the wrongdoers that day; their eyes will be filled with terror.

103. They will murmur among themselves, "You remained (in the world) only for ten (hours)."

104. We (as their essential reality) know better what they will say; the most learned of them will say, "You stayed only one day."

105. They ask you of the mountains... Say, "My Rabb will turn them into dust and scatter them."

106. "He will leave their places bare and flat."

107. "You will see neither pits there nor any humps."

108. At that time, they will follow the inviter from whom none can escape... All voices will be silenced with the fear of the Rahman... You will hear nothing but a moaning coming from the depths.

109. Intercession will be of no avail that day... Except for the one to whom the Rahman gives permission and who is pleased with His word (who says "only Allah")!

110. He knows what is before them and behind them (their past and future)**... They cannot encompass His knowledge.**

111. All faces will bow down humbly before the Hayy and Qayyum One... He who bears a burden (who has died without becoming aware of his vicegerency) **will indeed be in loss.**

112. He who does good work as a believer will not fear injustice or being wronged.

113. Thus We revealed the Quran in Arabic, and explained within in it all kinds of warnings and consequences. It is hoped that they will protect (purify) **themselves or heed the advice** (of the Quran).

114. Supreme is Allah, the Maleek (the Sovereign One who has providence over all things)**, the Truth. Do not hasten to** (recite) **the Quran before its revelation is completed to you and say, "My Rabb, increase my knowledge."**

115. We had informed Adam before this... But he forgot... We did not find him determined (in complying with the warning).

116. When We said to the angels (the forces pertaining to earth)**, "Prostrate to Adam", they all prostrated immediately, except for Iblis... Who refrained!**

117. We said, "O Adam, indeed this (Iblis; the illusive idea that you are the body) **is an enemy to you and your partner** (your body)**! Do not let it drive you out of Paradise** (reduce you from being in the state of universal consciousness to corporeality; individual consciousness) **lest you become one who suffers** (in misery of being confined to the body and thus burns with the consequences of this limitation)**!"**

Note: The reality denoted here, according to my observation, is as follows: While the being referenced as 'Adam' is inexistent, it becomes manifest as a 'conscious being' through the 'blowing of the Spirit,' which is a metaphoric expression signifying the Names of Allah. This manifestation takes place in the brain, that is, the physical body. The 'Spirit of the Names,' or in other words, this conscious, angelic being comprised of pure data, is essentially free of gender. However, once the brain is programmed to accommodate for this manifestation and goes through the various stages of development, the organs and a group of neurons referred to as the 'second brain' in the gut, send signals to the brain, embedding within it the notion, "I am this body." This thought is then exploited by Iblis and hence Adam is reduced to a state of accepting itself as the physical body. In other words, a species of the jinni (invisible energy beings), called Iblis, sends impulses to one's brain provoking the idea that they are comprised merely of their physical body (symbolized as their 'partner') hence covering the reality of the Universal Consciousness. The brain lives completely within its own illusory world! For the individual consciousness arising in the brain is based totally on the accumulation of the genetic information, the conditionings, the value judgments, and the emotions and ideas produced as a result of them; all received by the brain to form its database. And the 'intellect' is used in light of this database. So, the individual, or the 'identity' that is formed as the person, is asked to 'believe' in the Universal Consciousness (comprised of the Names of Allah) and live by the qualities within his 'original self' in order to become aware of the (angelic) forces inherent within his essence. Hence, to remind him of this, Knowledge (in the form of a Book) is sent! The purpose is to remind man of his original self; pure universal consciousness, which is free from all forms and concepts; an angelic force (Nur) based on the knowledge of Allah. Universal consciousness is also referred to as 'fuad' (the reflectors of the qualities of the Names to the brain – the heart neurons) as it reflects the heart, or more precisely, the reality. One's capacity to comprehend the reality referred to as 'fuad' is determined in the mother's womb on the 120th day after conception. On this day, the brain is either embedded with this capacity, in which case the person is characterized as 'fortunate' (sa'id) or not, in which case the person is not endowed with this capacity, and hence characterized as 'unfortunate' (sha'ki.) After this, these neurons continue carrying out their function from the brain to which they are copied. I believe one aspect of 'mirror neurons' pertains to this event. As for the body, which, as the partner, or form of consciousness, is endowed with a specified life span, has been expressed in various ways: In terms of its material make-up it is called the 'dabbat'ul ardh', in terms of its common qualities with other animals it is referenced as 'an'am' and in respect of stimulating limiting or obstructive ideas within the brain in regards to the angelic qualities of consciousness, it has been called 'satan.' A human is essentially universal consciousness; however, when consciousness opens its eyes within the human body, it forgets its origin. Due to this, 'dhikr' or 'reminders' are sent. The knowledge contained within the Quran is such a reminder. It is here to remind man of his essential self. The limitation arising from the brain thinking 'I am this body' is symbolic of a conditioned hell-like bodily lifestyle. On the other hand, observation pertaining to the angelic realm of consciousness signifies a paradise-like state of life. All such concepts and depictions employed in the Quran are metaphoric and allegoric expressions. Since Paradise denotes a life related to consciousness in which the qualities of the Names are manifest, the biological body and anything connected to it, is invalid and unnecessary in this dimension. Hence it is said Paradise is a state of life that is beyond perception. The details of this topic can be a book on its own, but I felt it necessary to share this much here to stress the importance of proper construal of metaphors in the Quran. I ask forgiveness for any inadequate or improper observation I may have, only Allah knows its reality.

118. **"You will not** (feel) **hungry therein** (for there is no biological – material body) **nor naked!"**

119. **"Indeed, you will neither be thirsty therein** (due to not having a biological – material body) **nor hot from the sun!"**

120. Then Satan incited him, "O Adam, shall I inform you of the tree of immortality and of a possession that never deteriorates?"

121. They both (consciousness and body) **ate from it** (the tree of corporeality)**! So they perceived their body and tried to cover it with the leaves of Paradise** (they tried to cover their sense of corporeality with the awareness of their non-corporeal eternal nature). **And Adam disobeyed his Rabb** (succumbed to his ego) **and his way of life erred** (as a result of being veiled to the reality of the Names comprising his essence).

122. Then his Rabb chose him and purified him, He accepted his repentance and enabled him to reach his essential reality!

123. (His Rabb) **said, "Go down both of you** (consciousness and its bodily partner that will eventually be left behind) **as enemies to one another! When guidance** (reminder of your reality) **comes to you from Me, whoever follows My guidance** (the reality of which I inform you) **he will not deviate and will not become unfortunate!"**

124. And he who turns away from My dhikr (the absolute reality of which I have reminded him)**, indeed, he will have a restricted life** (limited by the conditions of his body and mind)**, and We will resurrect him as blind in the period of Doomsday."**

125. (Then) **he will ask, "My Rabb, why have you raised me up as blind, while my eyes were able to see** (in the world)**?"**

126. (His Rabb) will say, "Thus it is... Just as Our signs came to you and you forgot (to evaluate) them, so will you be forgotten (deprived of the things you did not remember) in this period!"

127. Thus, the one who squanders his life (his potential of vicegerency) and denies the signs of his Rabb within his own essence, lives its consequences! And the suffering to come is even more intense and lasting.

128. Even though they walk upon the remnants of the generations who were destroyed before them, do they not see the Truth? Indeed, there are many proofs for those who are intelligible enough to take a lesson.

129. If it were not for a decree and a set life span already determined by your Rabb, the suffering (immediate death) would have been inescapable!

130. So be patient about what they say... Glorify (tasbih) your Rabb as His Hamd (by feeling the One who manifests Hamd within you) before the sun rises and before it sets! And glorify (tasbih; experience your essential reality) in a part of the night (I'sha) and in the middle of the day (zuhr) so that you may attain the state of pleasure (observing).

131. And do not shift your eyes to the transitory wealth (given to) some of them as the ornaments of the life of this worldly life to test them! The provision of your Rabb is better and more lasting.

132. Command your relatives to experience salat (introspective turning to one's Rabb) and be constant in its observance! We ask for no sustenance from you, (on the contrary) it is We who provides your sustenance! The future is for those who protect themselves.

133. They said, "Why hasn't he brought a sign from his Rabb!"... Did not the clear signs of the previous knowledge reach them?

134. If We had destroyed them with a suffering before this they would have said, "Our Rabb, why didn't you disclose a Rasul so that we may have followed Your signs before being humiliated and disgraced?"

135. Say, "Everyone is waiting and observing, so you wait too! You shall know soon who the people of the straight path who attain the reality are!"

AL-ANBIYA

By the one who is denoted by the name Allah (who created my being with His Names in accord with the meaning of the letter 'B'), **the Rahman, the Rahim.**

1. **The time for the people to see the consequences of their deeds has drawn near! Yet they are in a heedless state within their cocoons!**

2. **They listen to every new admonition from their Rabb in mockery!**

3. **They are consumed by entertainment! Those who wrong themselves whisper among one another, "Is he not a mortal like you? Will you succumb to his magical words when you can see the truth of it?"**

4. (Rasulullah saw) **says, "My Rabb knows what is spoken in the heavens and the earth... He is the Sami and the Aleem."**

5. **And they say, "He only talks of delusive dreams! He is probably making them up... No, he is a poet!** (If this isn't the case, then) **let him show his miracle as did the Rasuls before him!"**

6. **None of the people of the cities We destroyed before them had believed... So, how will these believe?**

7. **And We did not disclose anyone to them with a revelation before you, other than men... If you do not know, then ask those who possess knowledge of the past.**

8. **And We did not form them** (the Nabis and Rasuls) **with bodies that did not need any food! Nor were they to live forever!**

9. **Then We fulfilled Our promise to them and We saved them and those We willed to save, and destroyed those who exceeded their bounds.**

10. **Indeed, We have revealed Knowledge to you in which there is remembrance** (of your essential reality) **for you! Do you not understand?**

11. We have destroyed many wrongdoing communities and formed new communities after them.

12. When they feel Our intensity, behold, they begin to flee!

13. "Do not flee, but turn back to the places in which you became spoilt so that you may be questioned."

14. They said, "Woe to us! We have indeed become wrongdoers!"

15. And they continued to argue... Until We turned them into mowed crop and extinguished fire.

16. And We did not create the heavens and the earth as a game for them (they have great functions)!

17. If Our wish was to create games and entertainment, surely We would have done so from within Our Own ladun. But this isn't what We do!

18. On the contrary, We bring the Truth (the reality) down upon falsity (delusive ideas) and crush to pieces its system of thought... And behold, it will be destroyed and gone... Woe to you for the things you describe!

19. And whoever is in the heavens and the earth is for Him (to manifest His Names)! And those who are with Him are neither egotistic nor full of self-importance, nor do they grow weary!

20. The night and the day glorify (tasbih) Him (by fulfilling their creational purpose) continually!

21. Or have they taken deities on earth who can bring to life (enable the experience of one's essential reality) those who are dead in their grave (unaware of the consciousness in their body)?

22. Had there been within both (the heavens and the earth) gods besides Allah, surely this system would have lost its order. Allah, the Rabb of the Throne, is beyond the definitions they attribute to Him.

23. He is not questioned (called to account) for what He does! But they will be questioned (they will live the consequences of their actions)!

24. Or have they taken deities besides Him? Say, "Bring your proofs! This ("La ilaha illa Allah") is the reminder (of the reality) of those who are with me and the reminder (of the reality) of those

before me... No, most of them do not know the Truth... and thus they turn away.

25. And We have not disclosed any Rasul before you to whom We have not revealed, "There is no deity-god, only Me! So, become aware of your servitude to Me."

26. They said, "Rahman has taken a son"! Subhan He is! On the contrary, they (Jesus and the angels who they claim to be Allah's daughters) are His honored servants.

27. Their word does not get ahead of His command! They fulfill His command.

28. He knows what is before them and behind them... They only intercede for those who have attained His pleasure... They shiver in awe of Him.

29. Whoever among them says, "I am a god besides Him," We will make him live the consequence of this as Hell. Thus will be the result to which we will subject the wrongdoers.

30. Do those who deny the knowledge of the reality not see that the heavens and the earth were joined together (at the sub-atomic level) and We separated them (through densified levels of perception). We have created every living thing from water (H_2O)... Do they still not believe?

31. And We set firm mountains upon the earth (the organs in the body)... And placed wide pathways between the mountains so that they find the right way.

32. And We made the sky a protected ceiling... But they disregard His signs.

33. It is HU who has created the night, the day, the Sun and the Moon. Each traverses its own orbit (in the ocean of waves – energy)!

34. And We have not granted eternal life to any human before you! Can it be possible that you die and they live forever?

35. Every soul (consciousness) will TASTE death! We test you with the good and the bad so that you discover the forces within yourself... And to Us you will be returned.

36. When those who deny the knowledge of the reality see you, all they can do is belittle you by saying, "Is this the one who talks of

your gods!" Yet, when they are reminded of the Rahmaniyyah of their essence, they deny it!

37. Man has been created as one who wants immediate results (hasty)! I will show you My Signs (and what they mean) soon... But do not be hasty (for their formation)!

38. They say, "If what you say is true, when will this promise be fulfilled?"

39. If only those who deny the knowledge of the reality knew the time when they would not be able to ward off the fire neither from their faces (their internal world) nor from their backs (their external world); if only they knew the time when they will not be helped!

40. Rather, it (the fulfillment of the promise through death, the disconnection caused by the loss of life in the body) will come to them suddenly and confound them! And they will neither have the power to ward it off nor will they be reprieved.

41. Indeed, Rasuls that came before you were also mocked, but those who mocked were engulfed by all sides by the very thing they belittled.

42. Say, "Who, in your night and day, will protect you from the Rahman (the suffering that results from not fulfilling the requirements of the qualities pertaining to the Rahman quality in your essence)?" No, they turn away from the remembrance (dhikr) of their Rabb!

43. Or do they have deity-gods besides Us who will protect them? Whereas they (their assumed gods) neither have the power to help themselves, nor will they be supported by Us.

44. No, We allowed them and their forefathers to benefit (from the blessings of this world). To such extent that their life span seemed too lengthy to them (as though it was never going to end)! Do they not see that We come to the earth (the body) and reduce it from its borders (so that it becomes old and tastes death)... Are they the prevalent ones?

45. Say, "I am only warning you through the revelation." But the deaf cannot hear the calling when they are warned!

46. Indeed, if only a waft of the suffering touched them from their Rabb, they would say, "Woe to us! We were indeed wrongdoers."

47. We shall set up scales according to the measures of Uluhiyyah during the Doomsday period! No being (individual consciousness;

sense of self) **shall be wronged in the least. We will weigh even an action as little as a grain of mustard. We** (the quality of Hasib in one's essence) **are sufficient as reckoners.**

48. Indeed, to Moses and Aaron We gave the Furqan (the ability and knowledge to differentiate the right from the wrong) **as light and as a reminder for those who want to be protected.**

49. Those who are in awe of their Rabb... And who tremble from that Hour.

50. And this, what We reveal, is a blessed reminder! Are you deniers of it?

51. Indeed, We gave maturity (mature thought – the quality of being a Hanif) **to Abraham before this... And We knew him well.**

52. When he asked his father and people, "What are these statues that you worship?"

53. They said, "We saw our fathers worship them (so we are imitating them).**"**

54. (Abraham) **said, "Indeed, you and your fathers have been clearly misguided!"**

55. They said, "Have you come to us as the Truth or are you playing us?"

56. (Abraham) **said, "No** (this is not a game)**! Your Rabb is the Rabb of the heavens and the earth, who created them with a specific function and system! And I bear witness to that."**

57. "By Allah, when you turn your backs and go, I will definitely devise a trap for your idols."

58. So (Abraham) **broke all of them into pieces except the biggest one of them, in case they wanted to resort to him for enquiry.**

59. They said, "Whoever has done this to our deities is surely a wrongdoer."

60. They said, "We had heard about a young man called Abraham talking about (the invalidity of) **them."**

61. They said, "Seize him and bring him here in front of all the people so that everyone may bear witness to this."

62. They said, "Was it you, O Abraham, who did this to our gods (statues – idols)?"

63. (Abraham) said, "No! Rather, it was the biggest one of them who did it. Ask them, if they can actually speak!"

64. After some thought, they said to (one another), "Indeed, it is you, yes you, who is in the wrong."

65. Then, feeling confused, they went back to their previous thought and insisted, "But you know they cannot speak!"

66. (Abraham) said, "So do you worship things besides Allah who can neither give you any benefit nor any harm?"

67. "Woe to you! And woe to the things you worship besides Allah! Do you not use your intellect?"

68. They said, "Burn him (Abraham) and support your deities... if you are able to do something (then at least do this much)."

69. We said, "O Fire... Be cool and safe (enable the state of salam) on Abraham!"

70. They wanted to trap him, but We rendered their plan useless!

71. We saved him (Abraham) and Lot, and brought them to the land that We made prosperous for the people.

72. We bestowed him with Isaac and also gave him Jacob, and made all of them righteous.

73. We made them leaders who guided people to the reality by Our command. We revealed to them the doing of good, observance of prayer and the giving of alms... They were aware of their servitude.

74. As for Lot, We gave him judgment and knowledge... And We saved him from that city in which bad deeds were practiced... Indeed, they were bad people with corrupted beliefs.

75. We admitted him into Our grace... Indeed, he was of the righteous.

76. And Noah... He had turned to us before and We responded to him, and saved him and his people from that great distress.

77. We had helped him against the people who denied Our signs... Indeed, they were a bad people... So, We drowned them all.

78. And remember David and Solomon too... How the two of them both made a judgment concerning the field and how the sheep of the people strayed into the field (and grazed at night)... We were witnesses to their judgment.

79. We gave Solomon the right understanding of the matter! To each of them We gave judgment and knowledge. While David engaged in Our glorification (tasbih), We gave the mountains and the birds to his service. We were the doers.

80. We taught (David) the art of making shields to protect you in battle... Do you give thanks now?

81. And We subjected Solomon to the storm... Which blew with his command towards the land that bestowed prosperity! For it is We who have knowledge of all things.

82. And there were also devils in his (Solomon's) service (entities that served him), who dived to the depths of the sea for him and performed other tasks... We kept a watch over them.

83. And remember when Job said to his Rabb, "Indeed, this ailment has thoroughly exhausted me and You are the most Rahim of the Rahim (the One who manifests the infinite qualities of your Names with Your grace [arhamurrahimeen])."

84. So We responded to him and saved him from his ailment... And, as an act of Our grace and a reminder for the worshippers (who fulfill the required practices until they attain the state of certainty), We gave his people and the like of them to him.

85. Ishmael, Idris, Dhul Kifl... They were all patient.

86. We admitted them into Our grace... Indeed, they were among the righteous.

87. And Jonah... Remember how he went away in anger thinking We would not try him! Then he cried out in darkness, "There is no deity-god (there is no 'me') only You (the Names comprising my essential reality)! I glorify You (through my function that manifests your Names)! Indeed, I have been of the wrongdoers."

88. So We responded to him and saved him from the distress in which he had fallen! Thus We save the believers.

89. And mention Zechariah when he called out to his Rabb, "My Rabb... Do not leave me on my own in life (grant me an heir)! You are the best of heirs."

90. So We responded to him and bestowed him with John and made his wife fit to bear a child... They used to hasten to do good and pray to Us in hope and fear; they were in awe.

91. And the one who guarded her chastity (Mary)... We breathed Our Spirit into her (the embryo in her womb – like the creation of Adam) (We created Jesus [a form of consciousness] by manifesting the special meanings of some of Our Names)... We made her and her son a sign for all the worlds.

92. Indeed, this community of yours in one community! And I am your Rabb! So become aware of your servitude to Me!

93. But they divided their affairs (the understanding of religion and the system) into factions... To Us they shall all return.

94. Whoever put forth a beneficial deed, as a believer, will receive the return of his deed! We record all of them!

95. There is a prohibition on any city that We have destroyed; they shall not return!

96. But when the doors of Gog and Magog are opened, they will rapidly descend from every elevated place (perhaps spaceships)!

97. When death draws near, behold, those who denied the knowledge of the reality will stare in horror! Woe to us! We were indeed living in our cocoon world (unaware of this reality)! No, we were indeed wrongdoers."

98. You and the things you worshipped besides Allah will be fuel for the fire of hell! You will arrive there!

99. If they had really been gods they would not have entered therein! But they will all remain there forever.

100. There will be intense stertorous moaning there for them and they will not hear anything else (as a result of their deafness to the reality in the world)!

101. As for those to whom beauty and happiness has been bestowed from Us, they will be kept far away from Hell.

102. They will not hear the rumbling sound of it (Hell)... They will live forever among whatever their souls desire.

103. The great horror will not scare them (as the concept of death will be removed) and the angels will greet them, saying, "This is the day that you have been promised."

104. That day We will roll up the heavens like a scroll of paper! And We will return it to a state like We first created (the heavens and earth were joined together)! This is Our promise! It is Us who will fulfill it!

105. Indeed, We have already written in the Psalms (Book of Wisdom) following the Reminder (the previous knowledge that came as reminders), "My righteous servants (the vicegerancy principle) shall inherit the earth (the administration of the body with the forces of the Names)!"

106. Indeed, there is explanatory information in this for the worshippers (who engage in practices of purification).

107. And We have revealed you only as grace to the worlds (people)!

108. Say, "It has been revealed to me that what you think of as god is the ONE, possessor of Uluhiyyah! So, are you Muslims (aware of your submission)?"

109. If they turn away say, "I have informed you all in fairness... I do not know if what you have been promised (death) is near or far."

110. "Indeed, He knows the thoughts you reveal and that which you conceal."

111. "I do not know, perhaps a reprieve is a trial for you (so that you experience and see the Truth about yourselves) and a limited benefit."

112. He said, "My Rabb, judge with Truth! Against your baseless definitions Our Rabb, the Rahman is the Mustaan (the Helper we seek)!"

22

AL-HAJJ

By the one who is denoted by the name Allah (who created my being with His Names in accord with the meaning of the letter 'B'), the Rahman, the Rahim.

1. O people! Protect yourselves from your Rabb (from what He will enforce upon you as the consequences of your deeds)! The earthquake of that Hour is tremendous indeed.

2. When that time comes, every suckling (nourisher) will forget the child she has suckled and every pregnant woman shall drop her burden! The people will appear to be drunk, yet they will not be drunk. Intense is the wrath of Allah.

3. And among the people are some who argue about (the One referred to as) Allah without any knowledge, and they follow every rebellious Satan (those with corrupted thoughts).

4. About him (Satan – the idea of being only the body) it has been written, "Whoever follows him, indeed he will lead him astray and guide him to the fire."

5. O people... If you are in doubt of being resurrected (to continue your life with a new form after death, then consider that) We first created you from dust, then from a drop of sperm, and then a genetic structure, an embryo, and then a lump of flesh, half formed half not – this We let you know openly and clearly! And We hold in the womb whom We will for a specified time, and then We bring you out as a child, and then (provide you with whatever is necessary) for you to reach maturity... Some of you are taken (early) in death and some are left until he reaches the most decrepit age, forgetful of what he once knew... You will see the earth dead, but when We send water upon it, it will quiver and swell and grow plants of every beautiful pair (He who enlivens the dead earth will also enliven you after your death)!

6. This is how it is. For Allah is the Truth (the clearly observable One)! Indeed He will enliven the dead (with the knowledge of the reality)... For He is Qadir over all things.

7. That Hour (death) **will definitely come – there is no doubt about it. And Allah will definitely resurrect the beings** (individual forms of consciousness) **in their graves** (bodies) (to continue their lives through new bodies)**!**

8. And among the people are some who argue about (the One referenced as) **Allah without any knowledge about Him and without any true guidance, and without revelation** (knowledge that projects from the reality of the Names to one's consciousness).

9. He turns his back to the reality to mislead the people from the way of Allah! There is disgrace for him in the world! And We will make him taste the suffering of the dreadful fire during Doomsday!

10. This is the result of what your hands have put forth. Indeed, Allah is never unjust to His servants (Allah is not the cause of your dual perception; it is the ego or your constructed identity that attributes a separate existence to itself, hence causing duality [shirq], which leads to suffering).

11. And there are some among the people who accept his servitude to Allah in one aspect (in respect of what suits him). **When he is touched by good he is made joyful by it... But if he is touched by an affliction he turns his back** (and denies his servitude)**... Such are the ones whose lives in this world and the next are lost. This is a clear loss indeed!**

12. He turns to things besides Allah, which neither benefit him nor harm him... This is a real deviation (from the Truth)**!**

13. He turns to things that have more harm than benefit... How wretched the protector and how wretched the friend (he deifies)**!**

14. Indeed, Allah will admit those who believe and fulfill the requirements of their faith to Paradises underneath which rivers flow... Indeed, Allah does as He wills (He forms what He wills to manifest from His knowledge with Power; Knowledge – Will – Power).

15. Whoever thinks Allah (the forces of the Names within his essence) **will not aid him in this world and the life to come, should turn** (in contemplation) **to the sky** (to his consciousness) **and cut off** (his bodily tie from his consciousness) **and see if the trap he has fallen into** (by assuming he exists only of the body) **can remove that which enrages him** (the truth that he is the servant of his Rabb).

16. Thus We revealed him with clear signs... Allah enables the observation of his innermost essential reality to whom He wills.

17. Indeed, Allah will segregate the believers (according to what they deserve), the Jews, the Sabaeans (who don't believe in Allah but deify and worship the stars), the Christians, the Magians (who worship fire) and the dualists during Doomsday. Surely Allah is witness to all things.

18. Do you not see that to Allah prostrates whoever is in the heavens and whoever is on the earth, the Sun, the Moon, the stars, the mountains, the trees, the moving creatures and many of the people? But upon many the suffering has been justified. And he whom Allah humiliates – for him there is no bestower of honor. Indeed, Allah does what He wills.

19. These two opposing groups disputed about their Rabb... And for those who deny the knowledge of the reality, garments of fire have been cut and prepared for them and boiling water will be poured over their heads.

20. With that boiling water their interior and their exterior will be melted.

21. And there will be maces of iron for them.

22. Every time they try to escape (the irredeemable condition in which they found themselves as a result of their failure to recognize the reality) they will be returned to it and told, "Taste the pain of burning!"

23. Indeed, Allah will admit those who believe and fulfill the requirements of their faith to Paradises underneath which rivers flow... There they will be adorned with golden bracelets and pearls... There their garments will be of silk.

24. They will be guided to healthy thought and to the way of Hamid (the evaluation of what has been endowed).

25. Indeed, those who deny the knowledge of the reality prevent others from the way of Allah and from al-Masjid al-Haram, which has been made equal for its residents and for those coming from other places... Whoever does wrong by going against the requirements of the reality, We will make him taste the painful suffering.

26. We had prepared for Abraham the site of the House, saying, "Do not associate anything with Me! And purify My House for those who circumambulate it, turn to it standing upright (with their ego-identities), who prostrate (without their ego-identities) and who bow (in submission)!"

27. "Proclaim to people that they experience the pilgrimage (invite them to the Baytullah) so that they come to you from near and far and on every kind of vehicle."

28. "So that they witness its benefit for them... And let them sacrifice the animals – remember We provided for them and remember the name of Allah thereby... Eat from them and feed the poor and the needy."

29. Then let them end the filth (of their egos) and fulfill their vows and circumambulate the Ancient Houses (honorable – free house)."

30. Thus it is... Whoever respects that which is respectable by Allah and fulfills its requirements, this will be better for Him in the sight of his Rabb... Except that with which you have been informed, livestock (camel, cattle, sheep) has been made lawful to you... So abstain from the filth of idols and fabrications.

31. Do not associate anything to Allah (do not assume other gods besides Him)! Whoever associates partners to Allah, one's essential reality with His Names, he is like one who has fallen from the sky and is snatched by a bird or carried away to a distant place by the winds.

32. Thus it is... Whoever respects and obeys the rules of Allah, indeed that is the result of consciousness seeking protection.

33. There are benefits in them for you for an appointed time... Then they will reach the Ancient House (honorable free house, the House of Allah, the heart).

34. And for every people We have appointed a place (of worship – as the requisite of the Rahman reality)... That which you think of as God is the One possessor of Uluhiyyah! So become aware of your submission to Him! And give good news to those who are susceptive to the awareness of submission and obedience!

35. They are the ones, when the name 'Allah' is mentioned, to whom its meaning generates awe in their consciousness... They are the ones who are patient against what afflicts them, and who

establish salat (prayer)... They give to others from the life sustenance with which We nourish them.

36. And We have also made the camels from the laws of Allah for you; there is good in them for you... When they are standing with one of their front legs tied, remember Allah... And when they fall down, eat from them and feed those who are present there and whoever asks for it... Thus We have subjected them to you so that you may be thankful.

37. Neither their flesh nor their blood will ever reach Allah, it is your taqwa (benefits acquired through obedience) that reach Him... Thus Allah has subjected them to you, that you may glorify Allah (say takbir) to the extent He endows you with the realization of the reality... Give glad tidings to those who do good!

38. Indeed, Allah will defend the believers! Indeed, Allah does not like the betrayers (who betray a given trust) and the ungrateful (who do not appreciate what they have been given)!

39. Permission (to fight) has been given to those who are attacked... This is because they have been wronged! Indeed, Allah has the power (Qadir) to grant them victory.

40. They are those who have been unjustly driven out of their homeland, only because they said, "Our Rabb is Allah"... If Allah did not repel some people by means of others, surely the monasteries, churches, synagogues and mosques in which the name of Allah is much remembered would have been demolished... Allah will surely help those who help (contemplate, exercise abstinence and struggle for) Him... Indeed, Allah is the Qawwi, the Aziz.

41. If We give them a place on the land they will establish salat, give alms, judge with integrity and prevent from bad conduct... The outcome of all affairs belongs to Allah.

42. If they deny you, (know that) the people of Noah, Aad and Thamud had also denied.

43. And the people of Abraham and Lot.

44. And the people of Madyan... And Moses was also denied... So I gave respite to those who deny the knowledge of the reality, and then I seized them... How terrible was my recompense for denying Me!

45. There were many nations given to wrongdoing that **We destroyed**... **Its roofs and walls collapsed upon itself**... **Only deserted wells and ruins of castles remain there now**...

46. Did they lack consciousness with which to evaluate and ears with which to perceive that they did not travel the earth and take a lesson? The truth is, it is not their eyes that are blind, but the (inner) eyes of their hearts (within their brain) that are blinded!

47. They ask you to hasten the suffering... In the sight of your Rabb (the perception at the level of your essential reality manifested by the forces comprising your being) **one day is like one thousand** (earthly) **years!** (Allah knows best but I believe this verse is in reference to the perception pertaining to the dimension of life after death, for 'your Rabb' connotes the state of consciousness [the perception of time in one's brain or cocoon reality] as a result of one's individual Rabb or composition of Names. This is not in reference to the 'Rabb of the worlds'.)

48. There were many nations given to wrongdoing to which I gave respite... I seized them all... All things shall return only to Me!

49. Say, "O people... I am indeed a clear warner for you."

50. For those who believe and fulfill the requisites of their faith, there is forgiveness and a generous sustenance of life.

51. As for those who strive to invalidate Our signs, they are the people of Hell!

52. And We have not disclosed any Rasul (the informer of the reality) or Nabi (one who conveys the divine laws) before you (to inform of the reality and gnosis) whose Satan (ego-identity forming his persona) has not induced an idea (as necessitated by his duty) when he conveyed! Allah renders the suggestions of Satan invalid, then firmly establishes His own signs! Allah is the Aleem, the Hakim.

53. An idea that is induced by Satan (from the ego-consciousness produced by the effect of the amygdala) is an object of trial for those who are devoid of healthy thought and whose consciousness is covered (one whose essential angelic forces are blocked and who is indulgent of bodily and egoistic pleasures)... Indeed, the wrongdoers are on a path without return!

54. As for those to whom knowledge has been given, let them know that (what reflects to their consciousness) is the Truth from their Rabb and let them believe in it and let their consciousness be in awe of Him... Indeed, Allah will guide those who believe to the reality.

55. As for those who deny the knowledge of the reality, they will remain in doubt (of the truth of Oneness) until death comes to them suddenly or the suffering of the period in which all hope will be lost...

56. At that time, the sovereignty (the entire existence) will be for Allah; He will judge between them! Those who believe and engage in the necessary deeds will be in Paradises of Bliss.

57. But those who deny the knowledge of the reality and Our signs, there is a humiliating and disgracing suffering for them.

58. As for those who migrate for the cause of Allah and are then killed or die, Allah will nourish them with a beauteous sustenance of life! Yes, indeed, Allah is HU! He is the One who nourishes with the best sustenance!

59. He will admit them to a life with which they will be well-pleased. Indeed, Allah is the Aleem, the Halim.

60. Thus it is... Whoever retaliates to the same extent as he has suffered and then is subject to suffering again, Allah will surely help him... Indeed Allah is the Afuw, the Ghafur.

61. Thus it is... For Allah transforms the night into the day and the day into the night (things continuously alternate between opposites)! Indeed, Allah is the Sami, the Basir.

62. Thus it is... For Allah is HU! He is the Truth (the real existence)! The things to which they turn besides Him are delusive inexistent things (assumed to exist by the individual consciousness due to its false data)! Indeed, Allah is the Aliy, the Kabir.

63. Did you not see how Allah disclosed water from the sky and the earth became green... Indeed, Allah is the Latif, the Habir.

64. Everything in the heavens and the earth is for Him (for the observation of the qualities of the Names)! Indeed, Allah is the Ghani, the Hamid.

65. Did you not see how Allah subjected everything on the earth and the ships that sail on the sea to your service... He protects the sky from the collision (of meteors)... Except what forms with His permission... Indeed Allah is Ra'uf and Rahim to mankind.

66. It is HU who gave you life (with consciousness)... Then He will cause you (your ego-self identity) to die and then give you life again (real and immortal life)... Indeed, man has limited ability of evaluation.

67. We have appointed for every community a way (an understanding and style) of worship... So, let them not dispute with you on this matter (do not argue) just invite them to your Rabb... Indeed, you are on a path that leads to the reality!

68. If they argue with you say, "Allah (as the creator) knows best what you do."

69. Allah will judge between you on that which you argue during Doomsday.

70. Do you not comprehend that Allah knows everything in the heavens and the earth (as He comprises the essence of all things with His Names)... Indeed, they are all within the scope of His knowledge... Indeed, this is easy for Allah.

71. Yet they worship something besides Allah that has no power and about which they have no knowledge! There is no helper for the wrongdoers.

72. When Our verses are clearly recited to them, you will see the denial and refusal on the face of those who deny the knowledge of the reality! It is almost as if they are going to attack those who inform them of Our proofs... Say, "Shall I inform you of something worse than this? The fire (that will burn you)! Allah has promised it to those who deny the knowledge of the reality... How wretched a place of return it is!"

73. O people! Here is an exemplary lesson for you; so listen to it! Even if the things to which you turn besides Allah were to gather, they could not create even a fly! And if a fly was to snatch something away from them, they could not recover it from the fly... Helpless is the seeker and the sought!

74. They did not justly appraise (the manifestations of the qualities denoted by the Name) Allah... Indeed, Allah is the Qawwi and the Aziz (One who is powerful and whose use of His power is unchallengeable).

75. Allah selects Rasuls from both angels and mankind... Indeed, Allah is the Sami, the Basir.

76. He knows their future and their past... All affairs return to Allah.

77. O believers! Bow (with the awareness of His sovereignty everywhere over every iota of existence) **and prostrate** (feel the 'inexistence' of your ego-based 'identity') **and comprehend your servitude to your Rabb; no, engage** (in truthful/righteous deeds) **so that you may attain liberation!**

78. Strive for Allah, as you should strive for His Truth (not driven by the ego)**! He has chosen you and imposed upon you no hardship in the matter of religion, the** (religious understanding) **of the people of your father Abraham... Previously and today, He has given you the name 'Muslims – those who have submitted** (those who decipher the mechanics of the system, and disclose Unity) **– so that the Rasul** (Muhammad saw) **can be a witness over you, and you can be a witness over mankind! So establish prayer** (salat) **and give alms and connect wholly to Allah, your essential reality with His Names! He is your Protector** (your owner and former of all your actions)**... An excellent Protector and an excellent helper.**

23

AL-MU'MINUN

By the one who is denoted by the name Allah (who created my being with His Names in accord with the meaning of the letter 'B'), **the Rahman, the Rahim.**

1. Indeed, the believers are liberated!

2. They (the believers) **are in the experience of duly observing Allah in their prayer** (salat);

3. They turn away from empty discourse and engagements;

4. They do whatever is necessary to cleanse and purify (zakat);

5. They protect their sexual organs from relationships out of wedlock,

6. Except from their spouses or what their right hands possess... For they are not condemned.

7. So, whoever wants more than this (with alternative sexual desires) **they are the very transgressors.**

8. Those (believers) **are faithful to what they have been entrusted with and true to their word.**

9. They observe their prayers (salat; their introspection toward – observation of Allah is constant).

10. They are the inheritors!

11. And they, who have inherited Paradise, will live therein forever.

12. Indeed, We have created man from a line (sperm; a genetic formation) **of wet clay** (a mixture of clay, water and minerals).

13. Then We placed him as a drop in a safe place.

14. Then We developed that drop into an embryo (a genetic form) **and then into a lump of flesh, and then We developed them into bones, and then finally clothed the bones with flesh... Then We**

composed him with a new creation (by forming the spirit)... **Exalted is Allah, the most beautiful of Creators!**

15. After this, surely you will die (and move on to a life without a biological body).

16. Indeed, during Doomsday (after your death) **you will be resurrected** (with a new body in a new dimension of life).

17. Indeed, We have created seven paths above you (the life paths of the seven states of consciousness – all creatures in the universe are subject to living one of these states)... **We are not unaware of their creation.**

18. We disclosed water from the sky in due measure and lodged it in the earth (gave life to earth – the body - with it)... **Indeed, We have the power to take it away.**

19. With it We formed for you palm groves and vineyards (Paradises – the beauteous experiences of the dimension of consciousness) **in which there are many fruits** (gnosis, realizations) **and you eat these.**

20. Also (with that water) **a tree growing on Mount Sinai** (the place where Moses met with his Rabb) **that produces oil and a condiment** (olives) **for those who eat it.** (While a fig is symbolic of unity within multiplicity, an olive is a direct symbol of unity in Sufism.)

21. And surely there are lessons in livestock (sacrificial animals; the animalistic forces within the body) **for you... We feed you from that which is in their bellies... There are many benefits in them for you and you eat them too.**

22. And you ride on them (animals) **and ships.**

23. Indeed, We disclosed Noah to his people and he said to them, "O my people! Serve Allah (become aware of your servitude to Allah)! **You cannot have a god besides HU! Do you still not fear and protect yourselves?"**

24. The leaders among his people who denied the knowledge of the reality said, "He is only a mortal being like yourselves... He wants to make himself superior to you... Had Allah willed (instead of sending a mortal) **He would have sent angels... We have not heard a thing like this from our forefathers."**

25. "He is a man possessed (by the jinni)... **So, observe him for a while."**

26. (Noah) said, "My Rabb! Help me against their denial."

27. Whereupon We revealed to (Noah), **"Build the ship as Our eyes** (under our supervision; a reference to the unity of existence – non-duality) **and Our revelation... When** (the water) **starts** (to rise) **and the oven boils** (obviously this doesn't refer to a steam boiler!) **take on board a pair of every couple and your family, except those for whom the decree has been already made. Do not address me in favor of the wrongdoers! They shall most certainly drown!**

28. "When you and those with you board the ship say, 'Hamd (the evaluation of the corporeal worlds as He wills) **belongs to Allah, who saved us from the wrongdoers.'"**

29. "And say, 'My Rabb, settle me in a sacred location... You are the best of settlers."

30. Indeed, there are signs in this... Surely We will try you (so that the person may see his own capacity).

31. Then, We created a new generation after them.

32. We disclosed a Rasul from among them, who said, "Serve Allah... You have no god besides Him... Do you still not fear (the results of your deeds) **and protect yourselves?"**

33. The conservative leaders among his people who denied the knowledge of the reality and the eternal life to come, and on whom We had bestowed the comforts and opportunities of the worldly life, said, "He is no more than a mortal like yourselves... He eats what you eat and drinks what you drink."

34. "Indeed, if you follow a mortal like yourselves, you will definitely become of the losers."

35. "Does he (the Rasul) **promise you that when you die, and become dust and bones, that you will definitely be brought forth** (to a new dimension)**?"**

36. "Alas, alas... Far-fetched is such a thing!"

37. "It (life) **comprises only of the worldly life! Your death and your life are here! Living with a new form after death cannot be!"**

38. "He (the Rasul) **is a liar, slandering against Allah! We do not believe him!"**

39. (The Rasul) said, "My Rabb! Help me against their denial of me!"

40. He was answered, "In but a short while they are to be sorry."

41. A frightening wave of blasting sound overtook them in Truth, and We turned them into dregs! The crowd of wrongdoers will be forced to face the consequence of their farness!

42. Then, after them, We formed new generations.

43. No community can hasten nor delay their term!

44. Then We disclosed Our Rasuls in succession... Every time their Rasul came to a people, they denied him... So We destroyed them in succession (made them live the consequence of their deeds) and turned them into exemplary stories... Let the unbelieving crowd live the consequences of their remoteness!

45. Then We sent Moses and his brother Aaron to them as Our proofs and unchallengeable force.

46. To Pharaoh and his chiefs... But they showed only arrogance and they were an obstinate people.

47. In fact they said, "Shall we believe in two men like ourselves while their people are our servants?"

48. They denied the two, and thus became of the perished ones.

49. Indeed, We gave the knowledge of the reality to Moses so that they (the Children of Israel) can attain the reality.

50. We made the son of Mary a miracle... And We placed the two of them on a high ground with a fresh spring.

51. O Rasuls... Eat from the clean foods and engage in beneficial deeds... Indeed, I am Aleem over what you do (all of your deeds have a consequence).

52. And this is your people as a single community... And I am your Rabb, so protect yourselves (from what I can subject you to)!

53. (While religion – the system is one) they fragmented their affairs among each other with various interpretations... Each group is pleased with their own acceptance.

54. Leave them in their cocoon for a while!

55. Do they think that by giving them wealth and sons (the ornaments of the worldly life).

56. We are hustling about for their good! No, they are not aware!

57. They are those who (as a result of observing the reality) shiver in awe of their Rabb.

58. They believe in the signs of their Rabb within their being.

59. They are those who do not associate partners to their Rabb (they are conscious of the fact that what manifests through them are the Names of their Rabb – they have annihilated their ego-identities in the reality – Allah).

60. They are those who give what they give with the thought that they will return to their Rabb.

61. They hasten to do good... They excel in the race of doing good.

62. Never will We offer an individual form of consciousness that which is beyond their capacity... There is Knowledge of the Truth (showing what each individual deserves according to its creational purpose)... They will not be subject to injustice!

63. But their consciousness is cocooned from this... And besides this, there are the deeds they continue to do (driven by ego-based temptations and bodily vulnerabilities).

64. When finally We seize them with suffering in the confession out of their remorse, they will groan and beseech.

65. "Do not cry for help today! Indeed, you cannot receive any help from Us!"

66. "My signs used to be shown to you yet you used to turn back on your heels."

67. "In arrogance towards it, you used to live deliriously in the night!"

68. Did they not duly ponder over that word? Or has something that has not previously come to their forefather come to them for the first time?

69. Or do they not recognize the Rasul and (hence) they deny him?

70. Or do they claim, "He is possessed"? On the contrary, he has come to them as the Truth! But the majority of them do not like the Truth!

71. If the Truth had been in accord with their desires, the heavens, the earth and everything in between them would have perished... No, We gave them their dhikr (knowledge to remind them of their essential reality)... But they turned away from their own dhikr (the knowledge pertaining to their own essence).

72. Or is it that you ask of them a fee? The endowment of your Rabb is better... He is the One who best nourishes with the sustenance of life.

73. Indeed, you call them to the straight way.

74. Those who do not believe in their eternal life to come deviate from that straight way.

75. If We show mercy to them and relieve them of their afflictions they will surely persist in their transgression (rebellion against their reality) wandering blindly.

76. We have indeed seized them with suffering... They did not surrender to their Rabb and supplicate!

77. Until We open upon them a gate of intense suffering, suddenly they will be left hopeless in that suffering.

78. It is HU who has formed for you hearing (perceptive force) sight (eyes) and hearts (the reflectors of the meanings of the Names to the consciousness – the heart neurons)... How little you thank!

79. It is HU who has created you on the earth (the body) and multiplied you... You will be gathered unto Him!

80. It is HU who gives life and causes death... The transformation of the night and day is for Him... Do you still not comprehend?

81. But they said what those before them said.

82. They said, "When we have died, and become dust and bones, will we really continue to live with a new form?"

83. "Indeed, we and our forefathers have been warned with this before. This is nothing but fables of the past."

84. Say, "For who is the earth and everything within it? If you know it (then tell me)."

85. They will say, "For Allah!" Say, "Will you still not contemplate and evaluate?"

86. Say, "Who is the Rabb of the seven heavens and Mighty Throne?"

87. They will say, "For Allah!" Say, "So, will you not fear and protect yourselves?"

88. Say, "Who is the one in whose hand (knowledge and power) lies the sovereignty (the depths, the essence) and who protects (everything with His very existence) yet who is not in need of protection? Speak, if you have knowledge!"

89. They will say, "Allah!" Say, "So, how is it that you are deluded (by your world)?"

90. No, We came to them as the Truth... They are liars indeed.

91. Allah does not take sons! There is no god besides Him either! Otherwise, each god would have walked away with what He created and some would have been superior to others! Exalted (Subhan – beyond) is Allah what they attribute to Him."

92. He knows the unknown and the manifest... He is exalted above their association (duality)!

93. Say, "My Rabb, if you are to show me that with which they have been threatened..."

94. "Then do not hold me among the wrongdoers, my Rabb!"

95. We certainly have the power to show you that with which we threaten them!

96. Repel evil (falsity) with what is best (the Truth, system consciousness)! We are well aware of what they say (about you).

97. And say, "My Rabb (the protective Names within my essence), I seek refuge in You from the incitements of the satans (that call to corporeality)."

98. "And I seek refuge in You (your protective Names within my essence), my Rabb, lest they be around me."

99. When death comes to one of them, he says, "My Rabb, send me back (to the worldly life)."

100. "So that I might do righteousness in that which I left behind (i.e. a faithful life that I did not heed or give importance to; the potential that I did not utilize and activate)." **No!** (It is impossible to go back!) **His words are invalid!** (His request is unrecognized in the system) **and behind them is a barrier** (an isthmus; a difference of dimension) **until the Day they are resurrected** (they cannot go back; reincarnation, being re-born for another worldly life, is not possible!).

101. **So when the Horn is blown** (when the process of resurrection, i.e. a new beginning commences)**, no relationship** (worldly interactions, family relations, titles or familiar faces) **will there be among them that Day, nor will they ask about one another** (in terms of earthly relations).

102. Those whose scales weigh heavy are the ones who will be saved.

103. And those whose scales weigh light, they are the ones who will be losers. They will abide in the place of burning eternally!

104. That fire will scorch their faces... Their faces will be strained with the suffering therein and their teeth will protrude out!

105. "Were My signs not shown to you? Did you not deny them?"

106. They said, "Our Rabb! Our desires overcame us and lead us to misery, we became a people misguided and lost."

107. "Our Rabb... Take us out from here... If we go back (and repeat our mistakes) then surely we would be wrongdoers."

108. He said, "Remain therein... And do not turn to Me!"

109. Indeed, among my servants there were some who used to say, "Our Rabb, we have believed... Forgive us and grant Your grace upon us... You are the best of those who are Rahim."

110. But you made fun of them! In fact, this state of yours made you forget my dhikr (remembering my existence within your essence)! You used to laugh at them."

111. I have rewarded them this day for their patience... They are the ones who have attained true liberation."

112. He said, "How long have you remained on earth (the bodily life)?"

113. They will say, "We remained a day or part of a day; ask those who count."

114. He said, "You remained there only a short while, if only you knew!"

115. "Did you think We created you without purpose and that you would not be brought back to Us?"

116. Exalted is Allah, the Maleek and the Truth! There is no god, only HU! He is the owner of the Bounteous Throne.

117. Whoever turns to another god besides Allah, of whose divinity he can never have any proof, he will face its consequence in the sight of his Rabb! Certainly those who deny the knowledge of the reality can never be liberated.

118. Say, "My Rabb, forgive and bestow Your grace! You are the best of those who are Rahim!"

24

AN-NUR

By the one who is denoted by the name Allah (who created my being with His Names in accord with the meaning of the letter 'B'), the Rahman, the Rahim.

1. This is a chapter that We have revealed and (the rules that We) made obligatory... We have revealed clear signs in it so that you may remember and contemplate.

2. As for the adulterer and the adulteress (who engage out of wedlock), flog each one with a hundred strikes! Let not pity for them prevent you in the religion (system) of Allah if you have believed in Allah, your essential reality with His Names, and the eternal life to come (for this punishment is out of mercy and love)... And let some of the believers witness their punishment.

3. For an adulterer (who engages in sexual relations out of wedlock) can only marry an adulteress or a polytheist (dualist) woman. And an adulteress can only marry an adulterer or a polytheist (dualist) man. This has been forbidden to the believers.

4. Those who slander against chaste women (accuse them of adultery) without bringing four witnesses, flog them with eighty strikes and never accept their testimony again... They are the ones whose faith has become corrupt.

5. Except those who repent and correct themselves... Indeed, Allah is the Ghafur, the Rahim.

6. Those who accuse their own wives of adultery and have no witness other than themselves, shall swear four times 'by Allah' that they are among the truthful ones.

7. And the fifth time that Allah's curse may be upon him if he is of the liars.

8. (And the woman in defense) shall ward off the punishment from herself by swearing four times 'by Allah' that he is a liar.

9. And the fifth time that Allah's curse may be upon her if he is of the truthful.

10. What if Allah's bounty and grace had not been upon you and Allah had not been the Tawwab and the Hakim!

11. Indeed, those (hypocrites) who came to you with that slander (in regards to Aisha r.a.) is a group among you who have come together only to accuse. Do not think it (that slander against you) is harmful to you! On the contrary, it is beneficial for you... Each one of them shall be held to account of their own crime. And their ringleader, who took the greater part of the crime, shall be subject to great suffering.

12. Should not the believing men and believing women have thought well of each other and said, "This is a clear slander"?

13. Should they (the slanderers) not have brought forth four witnesses? Since they could not bring the witnesses, they are definitely liars in the sight of Allah.

14. If Allah's bounty and grace had not been upon you in the world and the eternal life to come, a terrible suffering would have afflicted you for your slandering.

15. You accuse based on rumors and speak of things of which you have no definite knowledge as if this is a trivial matter... Yet in the sight of Allah this is a great (crucial) thing!

16. And when you heard (that lie) should you not have said, "It is not our business to speak of such things! We exalt you! This is a great slander!"?

17. Allah warns you so that you never repeat the like of it again, if you are believers!

18. Allah explains His signs to you... Allah is the Aleem, the Hakim.

19. Those who enjoy spreading indecent rumors among the believers shall be subject to a terrible suffering in the world and the eternal life to come... And Allah knows; you do not know.

20. What if Allah's bounty and grace had not been upon you! Indeed, Allah is the Ra'uf, the Rahim!

21. O believers... Do not follow Satan's steps (bodily impulses)! Whoever follows the steps of Satan, let him know with certainty that

Satan only commands indecency (extreme indulgence in corporeality) and transgression... Had it not been for Allah's bounty and grace upon you none of you could have been purified and shown any progress... But Allah purifies (from the illusory self; ego) whom He wills... Allah is the Sami, the Aleem.

22. Let not those among you who are graceful and wealthy swear not to give to their kindred, the needy and those who have migrated for the cause of Allah... Would you not like Allah to forgive you? Allah is the Ghafur, the Rahim.

23. Those who live in their cocoons devoid of the knowledge of the reality and accuse the believing chaste women are most definitely cursed both in this world and the eternal life to come... There is a great suffering for them.

24. In that time, their tongues, hands and feet will testify against them about what they did.

25. In that time, Allah (as the requisite of sunnatullah) will make them live the consequences of their deeds in full and they will know that Allah is clearly the Truth itself.

26. Women with corrupt thoughts and ways are for men with corrupt thoughts and ways; and men with corrupt thoughts and ways are for women with corrupt thoughts and ways... Women with pure and good thoughts are for pure men, and men with pure thoughts are for pure women with good thoughts... They are far from their (the slanderers) claims... There is forgiveness and a generous sustenance of life.

27. O believers! Do not enter into houses other than your own without permission and without greeting (salam) its residents! This is better for you; perhaps you will contemplate upon this.

28. If there is no one home do not enter until permission has been given to you... If you are told to go away, then go away... This is more pure for you... Allah (based on the reality denoted by the letter B) is Aleem of what you do.

29. There is nothing wrong in you entering uninhabited houses in which there are things that belong to you... Allah knows what you reveal and what you hide.

30. **Tell the believers to lower their gaze** (refrain from looking with sexual desire) **and guard their sexual organs... This is purer for them... Indeed, Allah knows what you do** (as their creator).

31. **Tell the believing women to lower their gaze** (refrain from looking with sexual desire) **and guard their sexual organs and not to reveal their adornments, except what is normally apparent... And let them hang their shawls over their chests** (to cover their breasts)**... Let them not reveal their adornments** (that Allah has bestowed on them)**, except to their husbands, their fathers, or their husbands' fathers, or their sons, or their husbands' sons, or their brothers or their brothers' sons or their sisters' sons or maidservants or those whom their right hands possess** (bondmaids) **or their male attendants who have no sexual desire or male children who are not yet aware of the private parts of women. Nor should they stamp their legs while walking to draw attention to their breasts... O believers, repent to Allah all together, so that you may attain liberation.**

32. **Marry those among you who are single and the righteous ones among your male slaves and female slaves! If they are poor, Allah will bestow wealth upon them from His grace... Allah is the Wasi, the Aleem.**

33. **Those who do not have the means to marry should keep themselves chaste until Allah bestows wealth on them from His grace... Sign a contract with your slaves who request a deed of freedom, if you find them promising, and give to them from the wealth Allah has given you. If your bondmaids wish to remain chaste, do not force them into prostitution for the sake of temporary worldly benefits... But if anyone forces them, after they have been forced, Allah will be Ghafur and Rahim to them.**

34. **Indeed, We have revealed clear signs of the Truth to you and examples of those who came before you and exemplary admonition for those who want to protect themselves.**

35. **Allah is the Nur** (NUR is knowledge – life; the essence comprising of knowledge [data]) **of the heavens and the earth... The example of His light** (the manifestation of His knowledge) **is like a lantern** (the brain) **in which there is a lamp** (individual consciousness) **and that lamp is within a glass** (universal consciousness)**! That glass** (universal consciousness) **is like a star made of pearl** (Name compositions given functions according to their creational purposes) **lit from an olive tree** (the consciousness of Unity within the essence of man)**, neither of the east or the west** (free from time and location)**. The** (tree's) **oil** (the observation of the reality in consciousness) **would almost glow even if untouched by fire** (active cleansing)**... It is light upon light!** (The individualized manifestation of the knowledge of the Names)**... Allah** (the Names [the various compositions of the structural qualities constituting existence] within the essence of man) **enables the realization of His Nur** (the knowledge of His reality) **to whom He wills. Allah provides mankind with examples... Allah knows all** (as He is 'all', through the qualities of His Names).

36. (That Nur; knowledge of the reality) **is in the houses** (brain, individual consciousness) **that Allah has allowed to be raised and in which He has allowed His name to be remembered** (observed, based on their capacity)**! Morning and evening** (both extrinsic and intrinsic observation) **they are in remembrance therein!**

37. **They are men who, neither trade nor worldly dealings distracts from the dhikr of Allah** (remembering their essential reality) **and performance of salat** (experiencing their essence) **and giving of zakah** (unrequited sharing)**! They fear a time of transformation due to what their eyes will see** (the extrinsic observation of the reality) **in their hearts** (the reality in their essence that will become manifest in universal consciousness).

38. **Hence, Allah will make them live the consequences of their deeds in the best of ways and will bestow more upon them from His bounty... Allah nourishes with sustenance whom He wills without measure!**

39. **As for those who deny the knowledge of the reality, their works are like a mirage in the desert! When finally he reaches it** (the mirage; his works, through death) **he finds nothing! He will find Allah with him** (in his own essence and realize He comprises his essential reality with His Names, but alas, he will be at a point of no return to evaluate this)**! So Allah will make him live the consequences of his past life in full! Allah is swift at reckoning!**

40. **Or** (the consequence of his life) **will be like darkness within a deep ocean, covered by a wave upon a wave and overcast with clouds! Darkness upon darkness! If he** (the one engulfed by it) **reaches out his hand he will hardly be able to see it... Whoever Allah withholds His Nur** (knowledge) **from shall forever be deprived of Nur** (knowledge)**!**

41. **Did you not see how everything in the heavens and the earth and the rows of birds glorify** (tasbih) **Allah** (by actualizing their function of servitude)**... Each knows his own salat** (the actualization of the Names

composing his own essence) **and tasbih** (the function resulting from his salat)**... Allah is Aleem over what they do.**

42. The existence of the heavens and the earth is for Allah (He creates them in His knowledge to observe the meanings He wills) **and to Allah the return shall be!**

43. Did you not see how Allah drives the clouds (ideas) **then joins them** (unifies them with wisdom) **then piles them into layers** (the system and order)**! Thus you will see rain** (grace) **pouring from among them...** (A cloudburst of the knowledge of the reality) **will pour out from the mountainous masses of clouds** (source of grace)**... He will make it fall upon whom He wills and turn it away from whom He wills! The intense flash of His lightning** (a sudden epiphany pertaining to the Absolute Essence in one's consciousness) **will nearly make the observable unobservable!**

44. Allah transforms the night and day into one another (the alternation between intrinsic and extrinsic observation)**! Indeed, there is wisdom in this for those with insight.**

45. Allah has created every creature (animate being) **from water...** **Some of them crawl upon their bellies; others walk on two legs and others on four... Allah creates what He wills... Indeed, Allah is Qadir over all things.**

46. Indeed, We have revealed explanatory signs. Allah leads whom He wills to the straight path.

47. They say, "We have believed in Allah, who comprises our essential reality with His Names, and the Rasul (His command manifesting as His Rasul)**" yet after having said this, a group of them will turn away! They are not believers!**

48. And when they are called to Allah and His Rasul so that they may judge between them, you will see a group of them turn away.

49. Yet, if the truth is in their favor, they are quick to accept and obey it!

50. Are they devoid of healthy thoughts or have they fallen into doubt? Or do they fear Allah and His Rasul will be unjust to them? No, they are the very wrongdoers.

51. When they are invited to Allah and His Rasul so that they may judge between them, the believers will only say, "We hear and we obey"... They are the ones who are liberated.

52. Whoever obeys Allah and His Rasul and experiences the awe of Allah and protects himself from Him, they shall attain their desires.

53. They (the hypocrites) swear by Allah that they will definitely go forth if you order them to... Say "Do not swear... (What is expected of you) is obedience... Indeed, Allah is Habir of what you do."

54. Say, "Obey Allah and obey His Rasul!" If you turn away, then upon him is only that with which he has been charged (the duty to inform) and upon you is that with which you have been charged (the duty to obey)! If you obey him you will find guidance! There is no responsibility upon the Rasul other than clear notification!

55. Allah has promised those among you who believe and fulfill the requisites of their faith that He will grant them vicegerency on earth just as He had granted it to those before them... And that He will establish for them their religion (lifestyle based on faith) that He has chosen for them and with which He is pleased, and replace their fears with security... So, let them be in servitude to Me and not associate any partners to Me! And whoever denies the knowledge of the reality after this, they are the ones who are corrupt in faith.

56. Establish salat, give zakah (alms) and obey the Rasul so that you may attain grace.

57. Do not think that those who deny the knowledge of the reality will render (the religion and the system) helpless (and invalid)! Their abode shall be fire! What a wretched place of return!

58. O believers! Let those who your right hands possess and who have not yet reached adolescence ask for your permission on three occasions: Before the morning prayer, when you have taken off your garments at noon, and after the evening prayer... These are the three occasions of nakedness... There is no blame upon you or them (other than these three times) to be around you. Thus Allah explains His signs to you... Allah is the Aleem, the Hakim.

59. When your children reach adolescence, let them ask for permission as their elders do... Thus Allah explains His signs... Allah is the Aleem, the Hakim.

60. There is no blame on women who have passed the age of marriage if they do not wear their outer clothing, provided they do not do so with the intention to provoke others with their adornments... It is better for them to be chaste... Allah is the Sami, the Aleem.

61. There is no harm if the blind, the lame, the sick or you yourselves eat in your own houses, or in the houses of your fathers, or mothers, or brothers, or sisters, or paternal uncles, or paternal aunts, or maternal uncles, or maternal aunts, or in houses whose keys you are in charge of, or in the house of a friend... There is no blame upon you whether you eat together or separately. But when you enter houses, salute one another with a greeting from Allah that is blessed and good... Thus does Allah expound to you His signs, so that you may use your intellect.

62. The believers are only those who believe in Allah, their essential reality with His Names, and His Rasul... When they are with him on a matter of common concern, they do not leave until they have asked for his permission... Indeed, those who ask you for your permission, they are the ones who believe in Allah, as their essential reality with His Names, and His Rasul... When they ask you for your permission regarding some of their affairs, grant it to whomever you please and ask for forgiveness for them from Allah... Indeed, Allah is the Ghafur, the Rahim.

63. Do not treat the invitation of the Rasul like the calling of one of you to another. Allah knows those who hide behind others and secretly slip away... So, let those who oppose His command beware being stricken by an affliction or a painful suffering!

64. Be careful! Whatever is in the heavens and the earth is for Allah (to manifest His Names)! He knows well what state you are in... At the time they are returned to Him, He will inform them of what they have done... Allah (as the essential reality of all things with His Names) is the one who knows.

25

AL-FURQAN

By the one who is denoted by the name Allah (who created my being with His Names in accord with the meaning of the letter 'B'), **the Rahman, the Rahim.**

1. **Sublime is He who revealed the furqan** (the criterion by which the reality may be differentiated from falsity) **to his servant as a warner to the worlds** (all humanity).

2. **The existence of the heavens and the earth is for Him! He is free from the concept of begetting a child! He has no partner in all of existence! It is He who has created all things and formed them according to His determination!**

3. **Yet they have taken deities besides Him, who create nothing and are created themselves, who have no power to cause benefit or harm to themselves, and who have no attribute to form life, or death, or life after death.**

4. **Those who deny the knowledge of the reality say, "This** (Quran) **is only a lie that he has forged. And others** (the Jews) **have helped him at it"... In truth, they have committed a great injustice and perjury.**

5. **They said, "These are the fables of the past that he has had written down, to read in the morning and evenings."**

6. **Say, "It has been revealed by the One who knows the secrets of the heavens and the earth! Indeed, He is the Ghafur, the Rahim."**

7. **They said, "What kind of a Rasul is he? He eats food and walks about in the markets... Shouldn't an angel have been sent to him, accompanying him as a warner?"**

8. **"Or shouldn't he have been given a treasure or a garden with exclusive produce..." The wrongdoers spoke among each other saying, "You are following a man who is bewitched."**

9. **Look how they went astray because of the comparisons** (incorrect evaluations) **they made to you! They can no longer find a way out!**

10. **Exalted is He who, if He wills, can give you better things than this; who can form Paradises underneath which rivers flow and make palaces for you.**

11. **But they denied the Hour** (their eternal life to commence ensuing death)**... And We have prepared a blazing fire for those who deny the consequences of that Hour.**

12. **They will hear its outburst of rage and intense roar even before they enter it** (while they are in the dimension of the grave).

13. **When they are bound** (helpless) **and thrown into a narrow space, they will plead for death** (they will realize death is the only way out from the suffering that has befallen them).

14. **"Wish for not one death but many deaths today! (Alas, you shall not die!)"**

15. **Say, "Is this better or the Paradise that has been promised to those who protect themselves? That Paradise is the consequence** (of their life) **and a place of return** (to their essence)**."**

16. **They shall forever find whatever they desire therein. This is a binding promise upon your Rabb!**

17. **At the time when He gathers them and those who they deified/worshipped besides Allah, and says, "Did you mislead my servants or did they go astray from the path** (leading to their essential reality) **themselves?"**

18. **They** (the objects/idols of their worship) **will say, "Subhan, You are! It is not possible for us to take besides You any guardians. But when You provided comforts for them and their fathers, they forgot the knowledge of the reality and indulged in bodily pleasures eventually leading to their ruin."**

19. (He will say to those they worshipped besides Allah): **"They have truly denied the things you've said... You can neither have the strength to ward off** (the suffering) **from yourselves nor find any help! Whoever does wrong from among you We will subject him to a great suffering."**

20. **The Rasuls We disclosed before you also ate food and walked about in the markets! We have made you objects of trial for one another... Will you be patient? Your Rabb is the Basir.**

21. **Those who did not expect to meet Us** (to experience the manifestation of Our Names in their essence) **said, "Should not an angel been sent down to us or should we not be able to see our Rabb** (with our eyes)**?"** (Unable to comprehend the intrinsic reality within their essence and incessantly seeking an external god!) **Indeed, they were full of arrogance and self-importance, and they transgressed and disobeyed.**

22. There is no good news for those who are guilty of denying the reality at the time when they see the angels! They will say, "It (good news and the ability to administer with the forces of the Names) **has been forbidden to you, forbidden!"**

23. When the actual doer becomes evident, they will realize the good work they did does not belong to them! (All of their works have been in vain. For, while you assume you are the doer, it is Allah who does a good deed through you!)

24. The people of Paradise will have the best residence and the finest lodging as their eternal abode.

25. The time when the sky (consciousness) **is split open with its clouds** (the grace that enables the realization of the reality) **and the angelic forces** (the reality of the Names) **become manifest one after another!**

26. The time when the reality that sovereignty belongs to ar-Rahman (will be experienced)**! A time of great difficulty for those who deny the knowledge of the reality** (the reality of the Names within their essence)**!**

27. At that time, the one who wronged himself (by failing to experience the reality of his original self) **will bite his hands and say, "I wish I had walked on the path of the Rasul."**

28. "Woe to me, I wish I had not befriended him (the body demon, the idea "I am the body" produced by the second brain in one's gut)**!"**

29. "Indeed, it led me astray from the remembrance (of the knowledge of the reality reminding me of my essence)**... Satan** (delusion – thinking you are the body) **is man's great deserter** (deserting him and leaving him helpless)**."**

30. The Rasul (one who READs his essential reality) **said, "O Rabb! Indeed, my people have abandoned the Quran** (experiencing the requisites of their essential reality and turned to bodily pleasures instead)**!"**

31. And thus, for every Rasul, enemies were formed from among the deniers of the reality... Sufficient is your Rabb, which comprises your essence, as the Hadi (One who enables the realization of one's essential reality) and the Nasir (the One who aids in the process of attaining this liberation).

32. Those who deny the knowledge of the reality say, "The Quran should have been revealed to him all at once (like those revealed to the Children of Israel)." (Whereas) We (revealed it as thus) to anchor it in your heart (the reflectors of the Names to your brain) and made you recite it in sections (so that you may find each denoted quality within your own essence).

33. Every time they came to you with a problem, We came to you with the best explanation and as the Truth.

34. Those who will be gathered in hell, whose essences have darkened and whose faces look down, those are worse in position and most astray in way.

35. Indeed, We gave Moses the knowledge of the reality and the instructions of application, and appointed his brother Aaron as an assistant.

36. Then We said, "Go, both of you, to the people who have denied Our signs in their essence!" And We made them miserable!

37. And when the people of Noah denied their Rasul We drowned them and made them an exemplary lesson for the people... We have prepared a tragic suffering for the wrongdoers.

38. And Aad (the people of Hud) and Thamud (the people of Salih) and the companions of the Rass (the unstable well) and many generation between them...

39. We had given each of them lessons... (In the end) We destroyed them all.

40. Surely they came upon the city upon which We showered wrath (the destroyed city of the people of Lot)... Did they not see it? No! They did not expect to be resurrected and returned to their essence after death!

41. When they see you they only make a mockery of you, "Is this the one Allah has disclosed as His Rasul!"

42. "Had we not been steadfast (upon our deities) he (the Rasul) would have lead us astray from our gods"... When they see the suffering they will know whose path is astray.

43. Did you not see the one who has deified his 'hawa' (instinctual desires, corporeality, illusory self)..! Are you going to be his representative?

44. Do you actually think most of them can hear or use their intellects? They are like cattle, no, perhaps they are even more astray (from being a human) in their way!

45. Did you not see how your Rabb lengthens the shadow (the ego-self, when the sun of the reality has not yet fully risen)? Had He willed surely He could have made it constant (immobile)... Then We made the Sun (the awareness of the reality) a proof for them.

46. Then We withdrew (seized) it (the lengthened shadow) to Us with an easy withdrawal (made it feel its inexistence with the awareness of the reality).

47. It is He who made the night a cover for you and sleep a form of death... And made the day a time for rising (awakening).

48. It is HU... Who sends the winds as heralds of His grace (rain)... We have disclosed pure water from the sky.

49. So that We may bring life to a dead land and nourish with it many animals and humans of Our creation.

50. Indeed, We have explained it (the Quran) to them in many ways (so that they may remember and contemplate)... But the majority of the people deny the reality.

51. Had We so willed, We would have disclosed a warner in every city.

52. Do not follow those who deny the knowledge of the reality, struggle vigorously with them by means of this (the Quran) with all your strength!

53. It is HU... Who releases the two bodies of water (universal and individual consciousness – the body): one sweet (the original self) and the other salty and bitter (the ego identity assuming it is the body)! And formed a barrier of enmity (opposition) between them (remember the verse 'descend as enemies to one another')!

54. It is HU who has created a human (the biological body of man) from water and formed the relations of blood (genetic-based) and matrimony! Your Rabb is the Qadir.

55. They worship things (they take as deities) besides Allah who neither benefit them not harm them! One who denies the knowledge of the reality supports that which is against his Rabb.

56. We disclosed you only as a giver of good news and as a warner.

57. Say, "The only thing I ask for in return is for you to find the path to your Rabb!"

58. Place your trust in the Ever-living One who does not die (comprising your essence with His qualities) and glorify (tasbih) Him (as His hamd)! It is enough that He is Habir (aware) of the mistakes of His servants!

59. It is He who has created the heavens, the earth, and everything in between in them in six stages, and then established His sovereignty upon the Throne (the various waves of data created with the qualities of the Names of Allah)... He is the Rahman! Ask one who is Habir (informed of the reality) about Him!

60. When they are told, "Prostrate to Rahman" (i.e. feel your inexistence in the sight of your essential Names-based reality) they say, "What is Rahman? Why should we prostrate to something you tell us to?"... This (offer) increases their hatred even more. (This verse is a verse of prostration.)

61. So magnificent is He Who forms constellations in the skies (the materialization of the various compositional groups of His Names at the macro level) and forms an object (the Sun) of radiance (Nur) and an illuminating reflection (the Moon – the reflector of light) (each of them have different functions)!

62. It is HU who makes the night and the day as successors to each other for those who want to realize and evaluate the Truth.

63. The servants of Rahman (who are aware of their Names-based essence) live on earth (in the body) consciously and without an ego... When the ignorant ones (who are veiled from the reality) try to provoke them they say, "Salam!"

64. **They spend their nights in prostration** (with the awareness of their inexistence) **and standing** (in the observation of the Qayyum within their essence) **before their Rabb.**

65. **They say, "Our Rabb... Ward off the suffering of hell from us! For indeed its suffering is tormenting to man!"**

66. **"Indeed, that state and place of burning is atrocious!"**

67. **They are those who neither squander when unrequitedly giving nor withhold stingily... But keep a just balance between the two.**

68. **They do not turn to a god besides Allah, or take a life that Allah has forbidden except by right** (retribution) **and do not commit adultery... And whoever does that shall face its consequence!**

69. **Burning will be multiplied for him during Doomsday and he will abide forever in disgrace** (abandoned, alone).

70. **Except he who repents, believes and fulfills the requisites of his faith! Allah will change their bad deeds into good deeds... Allah is the Ghafur, the Rahim.**

71. **And whoever repents and does righteous deeds, he will indeed return to Allah as one whose repentance is accepted.**

72. **They are those who never bear false witness... When they encounter rumors and empty discourse, they pass by with dignity.**

73. **When they are reminded of the signs of the existence of their Rabb within their beings** (essence) **they do not remain deaf and blind** (to that Truth)**!**

74. **They say, "Our Rabb... Grant us partners** (or bodies) **and children** (the fruits of our bodily endeavors) **who will cause us joy** (Paradise life) **and make us leaders worthy of being followed for those who want to be protected."**

75. **They will be rewarded with mansions** (higher states of life) **for being patient** (against the conditions of the worldly and bodily life)**! There they will be greeted with life and salam** (the actualization of the forces of the Names).

76. **They will abide therein forever... What a blessed station and abode!**

77. Say, "If it wasn't for your introspection my Rabb would not hold you in esteem! Truly you have denied... Soon you will live the inevitable consequence!"

ASH-SHU'ARA

By the one who is denoted by the name Allah (who created my being with His Names in accord with the meaning of the letter 'B'), the Rahman, the Rahim.

1. Ta, Sin, Meem.

2. These are the signs of the clear Knowledge (sunnatullah).

3. Are you going to destroy yourself because they don't believe?

4. If We so will, We could reveal a miracle upon them from the heavens and they will be forced to bend their necks and accept the command!

5. But whenever a new reminder comes to them from ar-Rahman they turn away from it.

6. Indeed, they have denied! But the news of the thing they mock will come to them soon.

7. Did they not see the earth, how much We have produced therein from every generous couple (double stranded DNA)?

8. Indeed, there is a sign in this... But most of them have not believed (in the Truth, in their Truth).

9. Indeed, your Rabb is HU, the Aziz, the Rahim.

10. And remember when your Rabb called to Moses, "Go to the wrongdoing people!"

11. "To the people of Pharaoh... Will they not fear and protect themselves?"

12. (Moses) said, "My Rabb, I fear that they will deny me!"

13. "I feel constricted and tongue-tied, so appoint Aaron (for this task instead)!"

14. "I fear they will kill me, for I am guilty of a crime about which they are right!"

15. He said, "No! Never!... Go, both of you, as Our miracles – proofs... Indeed, We are ONE with you, listening."

16. "Go, both of you, to Pharaoh and say, 'Indeed, We are the Rasuls of the Rabb of the worlds (the creator of everything in existence with the qualities of His Names).'"

17. "Send the Children of Israel with us."

18. (Pharaoh) said, "Did we not raise you and tame you while you were a child among us? Did you not spend many years of your life with us?"

19. "And you did that deed! (Killed one of Pharaoh's people)... You are of the ungrateful!"

20. (Moses) said, "When I did that deed I was not aware of myself."

21. "So I fled from you out of fear... Then my Rabb granted me a command and made me of the Rasuls."

22. "And this favor of which you remind me is no more than the result of your enslavement of the Children of Israel!"

23. Pharaoh said, "And what is the Rabb of the worlds?"

24. (Moses) said, "The Rabb (creator with His Names) of the heavens, the earth, and everything in between, if you are of the people of certainty (you will know)!"

25. (Pharaoh) said to those around him, "Do you hear him?"

26. (Moses) said, "Your Rabb and the Rabb of your forefathers."

27. (Pharaoh) said, "This Rasul who has been disclosed to you is most definitely possessed." (Most of the Rasuls have been accused of being possessed after they have conveyed the reality.)

28. (Moses) said, "The Rabb of the east, the west and everything in between... If you use your intellect!"

29. (Pharaoh) said, "Indeed, if you take anything besides me as god I will surely imprison you!"

30. (Moses) said, "Even if I have come to you with something clear (proof)?"

31. (Pharaoh) said, "Then show it, if you are of the truthful?"

32. (Moses) released his staff, suddenly it appeared as a serpent!

33. (Moses) drew out his hand (from his shirt) the observers saw it to be bright white!

34. (Pharaoh) said to his leaders, "Indeed, he is a learned magician..."

35. "He wishes to drive you out of your land with his magic... What do you advise?"

36. They said, "Seize him and his brother... And send heralds to the cities..."

37. "Let them gather all the skilled magicians and bring them to you!"

38. So the magicians assembled at a specified time and place.

39. And it was said to the people, "Have you all gathered?"

40. "If they prevail we will probably follow the magicians" said the people.

41. When the magicians came they said to Pharaoh, "And what if we prevail, will we be rewarded?"

42. "Yes" (said Pharaoh)... "In that case you will be of those most near to me."

43. Moses said to them, "Throw what you have in your hands!"

44. So they threw their ropes and staffs and said, "By the might of Pharaoh, indeed, it is we who will prevail."

45. Then Moses threw his staff, and alas, at once it devoured their apparitions!

46. Upon seeing this, the magicians prostrated in front of Moses!

47. They said, "We believe in the Rabb of the worlds..."

48. "The Rabb of Moses and Aaron!"

49. (Pharaoh) **said, "Have you believed in Him without my permission? Surely he is your leader in teaching you sorcery... Soon you will know... I will cut off your hands and feet on opposite sides and have you all crucified."**

50. (The magicians who now believed) **said, "No harm! Indeed, to our Rabb we will return."**

51. "As the first believers, we hope that our Rabb will forgive us for our mistakes."

52. We revealed to Moses, "Travel with My servants by night... You will be pursued."

53. Pharaoh sent heralds to the cities...

54. "They (the Children of Israel) **are an insignificant minority!"**

55. "But they are enraging us!"

56. "Indeed, we are a well-prepared people," said Pharaoh.

57. Thus We made them leave their gardens and springs.

58. Their treasures and wealth!

59. Thus it is... And then We made the Children of Israel inheritors of them (the dynasty of Pharaoh).

60. (Pharaoh and his army) **pursued them as the sun rose.**

61. When the two groups saw each other Moses' companions said, "They have caught up to us."

62. "No!" said Moses, "My Rabb is with me; He will show us the way (to liberation)**!"**

63. We revealed to Moses, "Strike the sea with your staff"... (When he did) **the sea parted into two; each part was like a big mountain.**

64. We made the others (who were following) **approach that place too.**

65. Then We saved Moses and all those with him.

66. Then We drowned the others.

67. Indeed, there is a miracle – a lesson – in this! Yet most of them have not believed.

68. Indeed, your Rabb is HU, the Aziz, the Rahim.

69. Tell them about Abraham too.

70. How he had asked his father and his people, "What is that which you serve?"

71. They said, "We serve our idols; we are constantly engaged in them."

72. (Abraham) said, "Do they hear you when you pray to them?"

73. "Or do they help or harm you?"

74. They said, "No! But we found our forefathers doing the same (so we are imitating them)!"

75. (Abraham) said, "Think! What are you serving...?"

76. "You and your forefathers!"

77. "They are definitely my enemies... Only the Rabb of the worlds..."

78. "Who created me... It is He who guides me (to my essential reality)."

79. "Who gives me food and drink."

80. "It is He who heals me when I am sick."

81. "And He who takes life and gives life."

82. "And it is He who I hope will forgive me for my mistakes during the period when the laws of Religion are in effect."

83. "My Rabb, grant me a judgment and include me among the righteous ones!"

84. "And allow me to convey the Truth to the generations to come after me!"

85. "Make me one of the inheritors of your Paradise of Bliss!"

86. "Forgive my father! Indeed, he is of those who have gone astray from the right faith!"

87. "Do not disgrace me during the resurrection period!"

88. "The time when neither wealth nor sons will be of any avail."

89. "Only he who has come to Allah with a sound heart (in whose consciousness the reality has become manifest)!"

90. (The life of) **Paradise has been brought near to the protected ones.**

91. **And for those who have deviated from the reality, Hell has been brought in front of them!**

92. **They are asked, "Where are the things you worshipped?"**

93. **"The things you worshipped besides Allah... Can they help you or can they even help themselves?"**

94. **They** (the things you worshipped) **and those of you who have deviated from their essential reality and worshipped those idols will be thrown face down into Hell!**

95. **And** (so will) **the armies of Iblis.**

96. **They argue therein, saying:**

97. **"By Allah, we were definitely in clear corruption!"**

98. **"When we held you equal to the Rabb of the worlds."**

99. **"It was the guilty** (who denied the reality) **who led us astray."**

100. **"And we have no intercessor."**

101. **"And we have no trustworthy friend."**

102. **"If only we can go back** (to the reality) **and attain the results of faith."**

103. **There is indeed a lesson in this... Most of them have not believed** (in their essential reality).

104. **Indeed, your Rabb is HU, the Aziz, the Rahim.**

105. **The people of Noah also denied the Rasuls.**

106. **When their brother Noah said to them, "Do you not fear and beware?"**

107. **"I am indeed a trustworthy Rasul for you."**

108. "So, protect yourselves from Allah (for He will most definitely subject you to the consequences of your deeds) and obey me!"

109. "I do not ask you for anything in return... It is the Rabb of the worlds who will make me live the consequences of my working!"

110. "So, protect yourselves from Allah (for He will most definitely subject you to the consequences of your deeds) and obey me!"

111. They said, "Why should we believe in you when your followers are but the lowest of classes?"

112. (Noah) said, "I have no knowledge of their doings..."

113. "My Rabb knows the consequences of their deeds... If only you had become conscious of it!"

114. "I am not one to drive believers away!"

115. "I am only a clear warner!"

116. They said, "Indeed, O Noah, if you do not desist, you are going to be stoned to death!"

117. (Noah) said, "My Rabb... My people have most certainly denied me!"

118. "So part me from them (so that they get what they deserve, for, while a Rasul is among them, they shall not be subject to suffering) and save me, and those who are with me from among the believers."

119. So We saved him and the ark full of those who were with him.

120. Then We drowned the rest!

121. Indeed, there is a miracle – lesson – in this... But the majority of them are not believers!

122. Indeed, your Rabb is HU, the Aziz, the Rahim.

123. Aad (the people of Hud) also denied the Rasuls.

124. When their brother Hud said, "Do you not fear (and protect yourselves)?"

125. "Certainly, I am a trustworthy Rasul for you."

126. "So, protect yourselves from Allah (for He will most certainly make you live the consequences of your deeds) and obey me."

127. "I do not ask you for anything in return... The return of my works belongs to the Rabb of the worlds."

128. "Do you build mansions on every hilltop and amuse yourselves?"

129. "And make castle-like houses as though you will forever?"

130. "You rely on your strength and abolish all rights and seize all that you can!"

131. "So, protect yourselves from Allah (for He will most definitely subject you to the consequences of your deeds) and obey me."

132. "Protect yourselves from the One who assists you with all the blessings that you know."

133. "And gave you cattle (sacrificial animals) and sons."

134. "And gardens and springs..."

135. "Truly, I fear for you as the suffering of a tremendous time is upon you."

136. They said, "Whether you admonish us or not, it is all the same for us!"

137. "These are only the fables of the past!"

138. "And we will not be subject to any suffering!"

139. And thus they denied him, and We destroyed them! Indeed, there is a miracle – a lesson – in this! But most of them are not believers.

140. Indeed, your Rabb is HU, the Aziz, the Rahim.

141. Thamud also denied the Rasuls.

142. Their brother Salih said to them, "Do you not fear and beware?"

143. "I am most certainly a trustworthy Rasul."

144. "So protect yourselves from Allah (for He will most definitely subject you to the consequences of your deeds) and obey me."

145. "I do not ask you for anything in return... The return of my service belongs only to the Rabb of the worlds!"

146. **"Do you think you will always be safe** (regardless of whatever you do)?**"**

147. **"In Paradises** (gardens) **and springs..."**

148. **"With crops and date-palms with fruit buds!"**

149. **"Skillfully and cheerfully hewing out houses in the mountains!"**

150. **"So, protect yourselves from Allah** (for He will most definitely subject you to the consequences of your deeds) **and obey me."**

151. **"Do not follow the orders of those who exploit their authority!"**

152. **"They** (who exploit their authorities) **guide people in the world to the wrong, rather than being corrective."**

153. **They said, "You have been bewitched** (influenced).**"**

154. **"You are only a man like us** (but you think you are different)! **Then show us a miracle if you are truthful!"**

155. **(Salih) said, "Here is an** (unattended) **she-camel... She has a turn of drinking water, as do your camels..."**

156. **"Give her no harm** (otherwise) **an intense period of suffering will overtake you."**

157. (Taking no heed of this warning) **they viciously slaughtered her; and became very regretful.**

158. **So the suffering struck them! Indeed, there is a sign – a lesson – in this... Most of them have not believed!**

159. **Indeed, your Rabb is HU, the Aziz, the Rahim.**

160. **The people of Lot also denied the Rasuls.**

161. **When Lot asked them, "Do you not fear and beware?"**

162. **"Indeed, I am a Rasul you can trust."**

163. **"So, protect yourselves from Allah** (for He will most definitely subject you to the consequences of your deeds) **and obey me!"**

164. **"I do not ask you for anything in return... The return of my service belongs only to the Rabb of the worlds."**

165. "Do you wish to (leave the females and) sleep with men (instead)?"

166. "You leave your women whom your Rabb has created for you! No, you are indeed a people who transgress all bounds!"

167. They said, "O Lot, if you do not desist (your lecturing) you will surely be driven out (of here)!"

168. (Lot) said, "In truth, I abhor this act of yours!" (Note the hatred is expressed in reference to the action not the doer.)

169. "My Rabb, save me and my people from what they do."

170. So We saved him and his people.

171. Except the old woman (Lot's wife who did not believe) who did not wish to join them!

172. Then We totally destroyed the rest!

173. And We poured such a rain upon them! Dreadful is the rain that befalls the forewarned!

174. Indeed, there is a sign – a lesson – in this... But most of them have not believed.

175. Indeed, your Rabb is HU, the Aziz, the Rahim.

176. The dwellers of the forest (the people of Shuayb) also denied the Rasuls!

177. When Shuayb said to them, "Do you not fear and beware?"

178. "Indeed, I am a Rasul you can trust."

179. "So, protect yourselves from Allah (for He will most definitely subject you to the consequences of your deeds) and obey me!"

180. "I do not ask you for anything in return... The return of my service belongs only to the Rabb of the worlds."

181. "Give full measure... Do not defraud people with the scale and cause loss to them!"

182. "Weigh with correct scales!"

183. Do not deprive people of their rights and corrupt the order; do not go to excess in the land."

184. "**Protect yourselves from the One who created you and those before you** (as He will subject you to the consequences of your deeds just as He subjected those before you)!"

185. "They said, "You are bewitched (influenced)!"

186. "You are a man like us! We think you are a liar!"

187. "If you are truthful, then cause fragments from the sky to fall on us."

188. (Shuayb) said, "My Rabb knows better what you do (as the creator)."

189. Thus they denied Him and the intense suffering of that dark day caught them... Indeed, it was a tremendous time of a suffering.

190. Indeed, there is a sign – a lesson – in this too... But most of them have not believed!

191. Indeed, your Rabb is HU, the Aziz, the Rahim.

192. Indeed, (the Quran) is the revelation of the Rabb of the worlds (a dimensional descent from your Names-based essence to your consciousness)!

193. The Trustworthy Spirit (the knowledge of the Names reflecting to your heart) came down with (Gabriel)!

194. To your heart (consciousness) so that you may be of the warners (based on this knowledge)!

195. In a clear Arabic language!

196. And, indeed, it (this knowledge of the reality) also formed part of the wisdom of those before you.

197. Was it not a proof for them that it was known by the scholars of the Children of Israel?

198. Had We revealed it to someone who did not know Arabic,

199. And he recited it to them, they would still not have believed.

200. Thus We insert it in the minds of those who are guilty (of denying the reality)!

201. They do not believe until they see a tragic suffering.

202. It (suffering of death) **comes to them suddenly, at a time when they least expect it!** (Death is the biggest suffering, as through the experience of death, one observes his essential reality and realizes how much he failed to give its due right, and that he no longer has the opportunity to compensate, falling into the suffering of deep regret.)

203. And they say, "Will we be given additional time?"

204. Do they want Us to hasten the manifestation of Our suffering upon them?

205. Thus you see... If We give them enjoyment for many years with various blessings,

206. Then the thing of which they are warned comes to them...

207. Neither their possessions nor the pleasures they enjoyed will give them any benefit!

208. And We have never destroyed a city to which a warner has not come.

209. (First) **a reminder is given! We are not unjust!**

210. It was not the devils that formed (the Quran)!

211. It does not suit them to do so! Nor do they have the power to do so!

212. They are indeed devoid of the capacity to perceive!

213. So do not turn to any concept of god/godhood when (the reality of) **Allah** (is clearly evident)! **Otherwise you will be among those subject to the suffering!**

214. Start your warning from those who are closest to you!

215. Take those who follow you from among the believers under your wing!

216. If they disobey you say, "I am free (disassociated) **from what you do!"**

217. Place your trust in the Aziz the Rahim (the Names comprising your essential reality)!

218. Who sees you when you arise (to fulfill your function)...

219. And that you are among those who prostrate!

220. Indeed, He is HU, the Sami, the Aleem.

221. Shall I inform you on whom the devils descend?

222. They take under their influence those who are responsible of betraying themselves!

223. Those who betray themselves give ear to (the devils – delusive ideas in their subconscious) and most of them are liars.

224. And the poets (who incite the emotions and guide people to worship things they take as deities) – only those who have truly deviated follow them.

225. Do you not see how they live in the world of fantasy and doubt!

226. They say things that they cannot do!

227. Except those who believe (in the reality) and fulfill the requisites of their faith, who remember Allah much and who attain victory after being wronged... Those who wrong (themselves) will soon comprehend the kind of transformation they will undergo (but alas, it will be too late)!

By the one who is denoted by the name Allah (who created my being with His Names in accord with the meaning of the letter 'B'), the Rahman, the Rahim.

1. Ta, Sin... These are the verses of the Quran (the knowledge of the reality and sunnatullah) and the signs of a Clear Book (the clearly evident system and order).

2. As guidance to the reality and good news for the believers!

3. Who perform salat (experience ascension [miraj] by turning to Allah) and give from their possessions in order to become purified and refined; it is they who have attained certainty of their immortal life to come.

4. As for those who do not believe in their immortal life to come, We have adorned their deeds to them and made it appear (as pleasurable), they falter and wander, blinded (to the reality).

5. They are the ones who will have the worst suffering! And in the life to come, they will be the greatest losers!

6. You (through your consciousness) have certainly received this Quran from the ladun (the potential of Names in your essence) of One who is Hakim and Aleem.

7. When Moses said to his people, "I have perceived a fire... I will either bring news from it or a burning ember with which you can warm yourselves."

8. When (Moses) came to (the fire), he perceived a voice, "Blessed is the one in that fire and the one near it! Allah the Subhan is the Rabb of the worlds!"

9. "O Moses! Indeed, I am Allah, the One who is Aziz and Hakim!"

10. "Throw your staff!"... When Moses saw his staff moving like a snake he turned and fled without looking back... "O Moses, do not be afraid! Indeed, the Rasuls have no fear in my presence!"

11. "Except the one who does wrong (to himself)! As for one who does wrong and then corrects himself, I am the Ghafur, the Rahim."

12. "Put your hand inside your cloak... It will come out white without blemish... These are among the nine signs for Pharaoh and his people (to whom you have been disclosed as a Rasul)! Indeed, they have become corrupt in faith."

13. When Our miracles came to them in all their clarity, they said, "This is clearly magic."

14. Even though they felt close to and certain (about the realities Moses expounded to them) they deliberately denied it, wrongfully and out of arrogance... Look and see how the corrupters ended up!

15. Indeed, We gave knowledge to David and Soloman... They both said, "Hamd be to Allah who has exalted us above many of His believing servants."

16. Solomon succeeded David and said, "O people... We have been taught the language of birds (the ability to communicate with other creatures) and endowed with (the blessing of having knowledge about) all things... This is indeed a clear favor!"

17. An army was formed for Solomon, from the jinni, men and birds. They were arranged together, recruited and administered (by Solomon).

18. When they came to the Valley of the Ants, one female ant said, "Ants! Go into your dwellings lest Solomon and his army inadvertently crush you."

19. (Solomon) smiled at her words and said, "My Rabb... Enable me (with the Name Rahim in my essence) to be thankful for the blessings You have granted me and my parents, and to do righteous deeds that please You, and include me among Your righteous servants with Your grace.

20. Then (one day, Solomon) inspected the birds and said, "Why can't I see Hoopoe... Is he lost?"

21. "Unless he gives me a valid excuse for his absence I will punish him or execute him."

22. Then (Hoopoe) **came shortly after and said, "I saw something you do not know and I have come to you with reliable news from Sheba."**

23. "I found a woman ruling over them (Shebeans) **and she has been given of all things and she has a throne of sovereignty."**

24. "I found her and her people worshipping the Sun instead of Allah... Satan has made their deeds appear pleasing and right to them and diverted them from the (right) way! Thus they cannot find the path of the reality."

25. "(They have been deceived by their illusions) **to not prostrate to Allah, who brings forth what is hidden in the heavens and the earth and who knows what you conceal and what you reveal."** (This is a verse of prostration.)

26. "Allah, there is no god, only HU, the Rabb of the Great Throne!"

27. (Solomon) **said, "Let us see if what you say is the truth or if you are of the liars."**

28. "Take this letter of mine and deliver it to them! Then leave them and see the state of their understanding."

29. (Queen Sheba) **said, "O eminent ones! An important and valuable letter has been delivered to me."**

30. "The letter is from Solomon; indeed (the beginning of it) **reads: 'By the one who is denoted by the name Allah** (who created my being with His Names in accord with the meaning of the letter 'B'), **the Rahman, the Rahim.'"**

31. (And says) **"Do not be haughty with me but come to me in submission!"**

32. "O eminent ones... What would you advise me... I did not want to decide without consulting you."

33. They said, "We are both strong and mighty warriors... The decision is yours to make! You decide on your command."

34. (Sheba) **said, "When kings enter a country they thrash it and render the powerful ones powerless... This is what they do!"**

35. "So I shall send them a gift and see with what (news) my envoys (bearing the gifts) will return."

36. When (the envoys) came to Solomon (with the gift) he said, "You think you can stop me with your gifts? But that which Allah gave me is better than that which He has given you! Only those like you will rejoice with such gifts!"

37. "Go back (and tell) them... I swear I will come with forces that they will never be able to withstand and drive them out of there, helpless and disgraced!"

38. (Solomon told his eminent ones), "O counselors... Who can bring me her throne before they come to me in submission?"

39. A demon from among the jinni said, "I will bring it before you get up from your seat... You can me trust me that I have enough power to do this."

40. But one who had an understanding of the knowledge of the reality (who had the ability to act with the forces of the Names; Reflection of Divine Attribute) said, "I will bring it to you before you blink your eye"... When Solomon saw the throne placed before him, he said, "This is from the bounty of my Rabb... To see whether I will be grateful or ungrateful... And whoever is grateful, his gratitude is for his self (the realization and evaluation of the perfection of his essence)... And whoever is ungrateful, surely my Rabb is the Ghani, the Karim."

41. (Solomon) said, "Disguise her throne, and let us see if she can find the Truth or if she is of those who are not guided."

42. When (Sheba) arrived she was asked, "Is your throne like this?"... She said, "It looks like it... We had been given knowledge before this and we had become Muslims (submitted)."

43. And that which she worshipped besides Allah had stopped her... Indeed, she was from a people who denied the knowledge of the reality.

44. Then she was told, "Enter the palace"... When (Queen Sheba) saw it she thought it was deep water and pulled her skirt up... (Solomon) said, "It's just a palace made of crystal glass"... (Sheba) said, "My Rabb... I have wronged myself (by worshipping an external force, the Sun) but now I have submitted myself, along with Solomon, to Allah, the Rabb of the worlds!"

45. Indeed, We disclosed to Thamud, their brother Salih, who said, "Serve Allah!"... But they divided themselves into two groups opposing one another.

46. (Salih) said, "O my people! Why do you hasten on the bad rather than the good? Will it not be better for you to repent to Allah so you may be shown mercy?"

47. They said, "Because of you and your followers we have been subject to an evil omen." (Salih) said, "Your evil omen is with Allah... No, you are a people being tried."

48. There was in that city a gang of nine men who caused corruption and rebelled.

49. Swearing with the oath, "By Allah" they said, "Let us attack (and kill) him and his family in the night, and to his guardian, we shall say, 'We are unaware of his and his family's death; indeed, we are telling the truth.'"

50. Thus they devised a trap but We also devised a trap, of which they were unaware.

51. Look at the result of their traps! We completely destroyed them and their people!

52. Here are their houses, demolished and ruined, because of their wrongdoing... Indeed, there is a sign – a lesson – in this for a people with understanding.

53. We saved the believers and those who protected themselves.

54. And Lot... How he said to his people, "You are deliberately engaging in that shameless act!"

55. "Do you leave the women and lustfully sleep with men? No, you are a people in ignorance."

56. His people answered, "Drive Lot's family out of the city! They are people who live purely."

57. So We saved him and his people, except his wife... We ordained her to be one of those who stayed behind and perished.

58. And We showered such a rain upon them! Atrocious is the rain that befalls the forewarned!

59. Say, "Hamd belongs to Allah... Salam to His chosen servants upon whom He bestows purity... Is Allah better or those they ascribe as partners to Him?"

60. Or the One who created the heavens and the earth, and who disclosed water for you from the sky? With it We made blissful gardens... It is not possible for you to have made even a single tree to grow in them... A god besides Allah? No, they are a people who have deviated from the Truth.

61. Or is the One better, who made the earth (the body) a stable station, and formed rivers (veins) between them, and fixed mountains (organs) therein and made a barrier between the two seas (consciousness – body)? A god besides Allah? No, the majority of them do not understand.

62. Or is the one better, to whom you pray when you are feeling down and who saves you from your suffering and appoints you vicegerents on earth? A god besides Allah? How little you recall these facts and how little you think...

63. Or the One who guides you (shows you the way to reality) on the land (material world) and in the sea (the world of knowledge – ideas) and who discloses the winds (the Rasuls) as heralds of His grace? A god besides Allah? Exalted is Allah above what they associate with Him.

64. Or the One who manifests the creatures and then returns them (to their initial state) and nourishes you with sustenance from the sky and earth? A god besides Allah? Say, "Bring your definite proof then, if you are of the truthful."

65. Say, "No one in the heavens and the earth knows the unknown besides Allah... And they are not aware of when they will be gathered!"

66. Whereas they have an accumulation of knowledge about the eternal life to come. No, they are in doubt thereof... No, they are blind to it!

67. Those who deny the knowledge of the reality say, "When we and our forefathers have become dust, will we really be brought back?"

68. "Indeed, we and our forefathers have been warned with this before! This is nothing but fables from the past."

69. Say, "Observe the earth and see the how the guilty ones ended up."

70. Do not grieve over them... And do not feel distressed by their schemes!

71. They say, "If you are telling the truth, when will it be fulfilled?"

72. Say, "Perhaps a part of what you want to hasten is close behind you!"

73. Indeed, your Rabb is bountiful to mankind... But the majority of them are not grateful.

74. Indeed, your Rabb knows what they conceal within and what they reveal.

75. There is no unknown in the heavens and the earth that is not already recorded in the Clear Book (of the universe, and clearly apparent in existence)! (That it is 'unknown' is according to the perceiver! If Allah wills He can change what appears to be unknown and make it known.)

76. Indeed, this Quran narrates and explains most of the things over which the Children of Israel differed.

77. Indeed, (the Quran) is a guide to the reality and grace for the believers.

78. Indeed, your Rabb will judge between them from within their essence... HU is the Aziz, the Aleem.

79. So place your trust in Allah! Indeed, you are upon the manifest Truth.

80. Indeed, you cannot make the dead (those who live unconsciously) hear; when they turn their backs (to the Truth) and go, you cannot make the deaf hear!

81. You cannot show the right way to the blind to guide them out of their wrong way! You can only make those hear, who have believed in Our signs within their essence as a result of their submission.

82. When the command (their own Doomsday [death] or the time prior to the general Doomsday) reaches them, We will produce a dabbah from the earth (a talking form from the earth [the body] during the experience of parting from the body, i.e. death) which will tell them that man had no certainty in Our signs (they were unable to observe the qualities of the Names that comprise their being)!"

83. During that time We will assemble as groups those who denied Our signs from every community... They will all be dispatched together.

84. When they come, Allah will say, "Did you attempt to deny My signs even though they were beyond the scope of your knowledge? What was it that you did?"

85. The verdict has reached them because they did wrong (to themselves)! They can no longer talk!

86. Did they not see how we made the night for them to find tranquility in and the day as observable... Indeed, there are signs in this for a people who believe.

87. During that time, when the Horn is blown (when the spirit is blown out of the body, i.e. when death is experienced or when the dead are blown out of their graves during the time of gathering) everyone in the heavens (those who have found themselves at the level of consciousness) and everyone on earth (living at the bodily state), except whom Allah wills, will be struck with terror! All shall come to Him with their necks bent down (in utter humility).

88. You see the mountains (the organs in your body) and think they are firmly fixed, but they move and pass away as the clouds (ideas – thoughts) move and pass away (by transforming into various understandings)... (The blowing of the Horn and all that pertains to it) is the art of Allah such that He has made all things an unalterable reality to experience. Indeed, He is Habir of what you do (as their Creator).

89. Whoever comes with good traits shall be given what is better... During that time they will be secure from what they fear.

90. And whoever comes with badness, their faces will be overturned in the fire... "You shall only live the consequences of your own deeds!"

91. "I have only been ordered to serve the Rabb of this city... Which He has made respectable, and everything belongs to Him! I have been ordered to be of those who are (aware of their) submission!"

92. "And to inform of the Quran!" So whoever accepts the reality will walk on this path to experience this Truth within his being... And whoever goes astray, say, "I am only of those who warn!"

93. Say, "Hamd belongs to Allah! He is going to show you His signs, and you are going to recognize them!" Your Rabb in not unaware of what you do."

AL-QASAS

By the one who is denoted by the name Allah (who created my being with His Names in accord with the meaning of the letter 'B'), **the Rahman, the Rahim.**

1. Ta, Sin, Meem.

2. **These are the signs of the Clear Book** (clearly manifest system and order).

3. **We shall narrate some of the news of Moses and Pharaoh, as Truth, for people who believe.**

4. **Indeed, the Pharaoh had established supremacy in that land and had divided the people into various classes. Seeking to weaken and debase one class, he was slaying their sons and sparing their women...** Indeed, he was of those who caused corruption.

5. **So We wished to favor those who were left helpless and abased, and make them leaders and inheritors.**

6. **And to secure them in that land, and to subject the Pharaoh and Haman** (his high priest) **and their forces to the very thing they feared!**

7. **We revealed to Moses' mother, "Suckle him, and then when you fear for him, leave him in the river** (Nile)**... Have no fear or grief! Indeed, We will return him to you and make him of the Rasuls!"**

8. **Then Pharaoh's family found him as a lost child and picked him up... Later to become an enemy and a source of grief for them... Indeed, the Pharaoh and Haman and their forces were doing wrong things!**

9. **The Pharaoh's wife said, "He will be a source of joy, for both me and you. Do not slay him! Perhaps he will be beneficial for us or we can adopt him as our son"... They were not aware.**

10. **And the heart of Moses' mother became full with the thoughts of her son... Had We not given her a sense of security to be of the believers, she would nearly have disclosed his identity.**

11. (Moses' mother told Moses' sister) **"Watch him"**... **So she watched him from afar without them noticing.**

12. First we forbade wet nurses to him, (Moses didn't suckle any wet nurse) **then** (his sister) **said, "Shall I tell you of a family who will raise him on your behalf and take good care of him?"**

13. Thus We returned him to his mother so that she may be comforted and not grieve and so that she may know the promise of Allah is True... But most of them do not know.

14. When (Moses) **reached maturity** (when he was 33 years old) **and when he reached the age of** (40, when one is able to duly evaluate affairs through maturity) **We bestowed him with the law and knowledge... Thus We reward the doers of good.**

15. (Moses) **entered the city at an hour when all had withdrawn to their homes... He saw two men trying to kill one another... One from his own people and the other from his enemies. The one who belonged to his people asked for his help against the enemy... So Moses struck him with his fist and killed him... Then he said, "This is Satan's doing** (bodily pursuits and ties). **Indeed, he** (Satan, the thought you are the body) **is an open enemy."**

16. He prayed, "My Rabb! I have indeed wronged myself (my essential reality, by thinking I belong to the world of the body), **forgive me!"... He** (his Rabb) **forgave him. Indeed, HU is the Ghafur, the Rahim.**

17. (Moses) **said, "My Rabb, I swear by the favors You have bestowed within my being, I will not** (get caught up by a sense of belonging and) **help the guilty ones."**

18. (Moses) **apprehensively waited for the morning in the city, watchful** (of his surroundings)... **And then, alas, the man who had asked for his help the day before was** (again) **crying out for his help... Moses said to him, "Indeed, you are clearly a misguided man!"**

19. When (Moses) **wanted to catch the one that was an enemy to them both, the man said, "O Moses, do you want to kill me just as you killed a man yesterday? You just want to become a tyrant in this city, you do not want to set things right!"**

20. Then a man came running from the far end of the city saying, "O Moses! The authorities of the city are talking about executing you... Flee from here... Indeed, I am one of your well-wishers."

21. Upon this (Moses) departed from there, fearful and watchful (of his surroundings) and said, "My Rabb, save me from the wrongdoing people!"

22. When he made his way towards Madyan (the city of Shuayb) he said, "I hope my Rabb guides me to the even (most correct) path!"

23. When he reached the wells of Madyan he saw a group watering their flocks. And he saw two ladies waiting to water their flocks, so he asked them, "What are you waiting for?" They said, "We cannot water (our flocks) until the shepherds water (their flocks) and go... And our father is an old man, he cannot do this!"

24. Then Moses watered (their flocks) for them... Then he went back to the shade and said, "My Rabb, indeed, after (I fled from) the good that You had bestowed upon me, I have become very needy!"

25. One of those young ladies shyly came to Moses and said, "My father invites you that he may reward you for watering our flocks"... When (Moses) came to Shuayb and told his story, (Shuayb) said, "Do not be afraid! You have escaped from the wrongdoing people!"

26. One of them (the girls) said, "O father, hire him... Indeed, he is the best one you can hire; he is strong and trustworthy."

27. (Shuayb said to Moses) "I wish to marry you to one of my girls on the condition that you work for me for eight years, but if you complete it to ten years, that will be the reward of your essence! I do not wish to cause you difficulty... InshaAllah, you will find to be of the righteous ones."

28. (Moses) said, "That (condition) is between me and you! Whichever of the terms I complete there shall be no blame on me... Allah is Wakil to what we say."

29. When Moses completed that term he set out with his family, then perceived a fire in the direction of Mount Sinai... He said to his family, "Stay here, indeed I have perceived a fire... Maybe I will bring news from it to you or a burning ember with which you can warm yourselves."

30. When he came to it, he was called from a tree from the side of the blessed spot, the Valley of Aymen, "O Moses! Indeed, I am Allah, the Rabb of the worlds!"

31. "Throw your staff!" When Moses saw it move like a small thin snake he turned in flight and didn't look back... (Allah said), "O Moses, come back and do not be afraid! Indeed, you are of the secure!"

32. "Put your hand inside your shirt, it will come out shining white and unblemished! And put your arms down and relax! These are signs for Pharaoh and his leaders, two signs from your Rabb... Indeed, they are a people who are corrupt in faith."

33. (Moses) said, "My Rabb, indeed I have killed someone from them, and I fear they may kill me because of this."

34. "My brother Aaron is more eloquent than I am in speech! Send him with me as my supporter. Indeed, I fear they will deny me."

35. (Allah) said, "We will strengthen your arm through your brother and We shall give you both such a power that they shall not be able to reach you (Our signs)! You two and those who follow you shall prevail."

36. When Moses came to them as Our clear proofs, they said, "This is contrived magic! We did not hear such things from our forefathers."

37. Moses said, "My Rabb knows better who has come from Him as True guidance and whose the abode shall be in the end... Indeed, the wrongdoers will not be liberated."

38. The Pharaoh said, "O nobles... I know of no god for you besides myself! O Haman, burn a fire of bricks and build (with bricks) a high tower for me, perhaps I will climb it and see Moses' Supreme God! But in truth, I think he is of the liars!" (The Pharaoh, who had attained the ancient knowledge of the reality, chose to use this in favor of his bodily existence and bodily pursuits rather than using it to observe the comprehensiveness of consciousness upon existence, and thus fell to the state of the inciting self. This is why rather than conveying the knowledge of the reality to him and calling him to believe in Allah, Moses warns him by calling him to believe in the 'Rabb of the worlds.' In other words, he invites him to believe in the Names, which are manifest throughout, and administer the entire existence, rather than experiencing his understanding of this unity through his corporeality.)

39. Him and his forces were unjustly arrogant on earth thinking they would not be returned to Us!

40. So We seized him and his army and threw them into the sea... Look at the end of the wrongdoers!

41. We made them leaders who called to the fire... And they will not be helped during Doomsday.

42. We have caused a curse to follow them in this world... And on the Day of Judgment they will be looked upon with hatred.

43. Indeed, after destroying the first generations, We gave the knowledge of the reality (Book) to Moses, to guide the people to the reality and as grace (discovering and experiencing the forces of the Names inherent within themselves); **perhaps they will remember and evaluate.**

44. You were not on the western side when We gave that command to Moses... Nor were you among the witnesses.

45. We formed many generations in the meantime, who lived and passed away... You were not among the people of Madyan either to recite Our signs to them... It is Us who discloses the Rasuls!

46. You were not on the side of Mount Sinai when We addressed (Moses)... But We have sent you as grace from your Rabb, so that you may warn people to whom no warner has come (this is why this knowledge was revealed to you). **Perhaps they will contemplate on it.**

47. And if it wasn't for when an affliction befalls them as a result of their own doings (due to sunnatullah), they say, "Our Rabb... If only You had disclosed a Rasul to us so we could have followed Your signs and become of the believers." (We would not have disclosed a Rasul.)

48. But when the Truth (Rasul) comes to them from Us, they say, "Why hasn't he been given the like of what was given (as miracles) to Moses?" Had they not previously denied what was given to Moses? And they had said, "It is two works of magic supporting each other and we deny them all."

49. Say, "If you are true to your word then bring a knowledge (Book) from Allah that shows a better way than these two (the Quran and the Old Testament) so that we may follow it!"

50. If they do not accept your offer, know that they merely follow their baseless fantasies! And who is more corrupt than he who follows fantasies and imaginations without (the knowledge of the reality manifesting from within themselves) **from Allah** (the Names comprising their essence)**? Indeed, Allah does not guide** (to the realization of their essential reality) **the wrongdoing people.**

51. Indeed, We made Our Word reach them repeatedly... Perhaps they will remember and contemplate!

52. Those to whom We gave the knowledge of the reality (Book) **before this are ones who believe in it** (their essence).

53. When they are informed of it, they say, "We have believed in it... Indeed, it is the Truth from our Rabb... We were aware of our submission to Him before it as well!"

54. They will be rewarded twice because of their patience... They repel the bad with good, and give unrequitedly from the sustenance with which We nourish them.

55. When they hear empty discourse and gossip they turn away from it and say, "For us is the result of our deeds and for you is the result of your deeds! Salam be upon you! We will have nothing to do with the ignorant! (We have nothing to talk about with those who fail to comprehend the reality.)

56. You cannot lead the one you love to the reality! But Allah can lead whom He wills to the reality! HU knows who are to experience the reality! (For He has created them with a specific capacity and aptitude with His Names.)

57. They said, "If we were to follow the reality with you we would be uprooted and driven out of our land"... Did We not establish them in a safe place, to which fruits of all things are brought forth as life sustenance from Us (as Our bounty)**? But most of them do not know** (its value).

58. We destroyed many cities in which the people had become spoilt with the comforts of the worldly goods! Here are their dwellings! None have inhabited them after them, except a few! We were the inheritors.

59. Your Rabb will never destroy a city until He discloses therein a Rasul among its leaders! We have only destroyed cities whose people were wrongdoers.

60. The things that you have been given are only the goods of the worldly life and its adornment (its agent of pleasure)! That which is with Allah is better and more lasting... Do you not comprehend?

61. Can someone to whom We have made a gracious promise and who sees it fulfilled be compared to someone We have allowed to enjoy the transitory goods of the worldly life and who will be of those brought forth with force during Doomsday?

62. During that time they (those who claimed to believe in Allah but then deified other things besides Him) will be addressed, "Where are my alleged 'partners'?"

63. Those who deserved the charge will say, "Our Rabb... These are the ones whom we misguided and led astray... Just as we corrupted ourselves we corrupted them too... To You we have turned, the judgment is Yours... They didn't worship us anyway."

64. It will be said, "Call your partners!" And they will call them... But they (their partners) will not respond to them, and they will see the suffering! If only they had found the right way!

65. During that time He will call out to them, "What response did you give to the Rasuls?"

66. But at that time all news pertaining to the past will be shut off to them! They will not be able to ask one another either!

67. But whoever turns from the wrong with regret and believes and fulfills the requisites of their faith, it is hoped they will be among those who will attain liberation.

68. Your Rabb (the reality of the Names comprising your essence) creates and chooses as He pleases, they have no free will (or choice)! Allah is Subhan! He is Aliy over what they associate with Him!

69. Your Rabb knows what they conceal within and what they reveal.

70. HU is Allah, there is no god, only HU! Hamd belongs completely to Him and the judgment belongs to Him; to Him you will be returned.

71. Say, "Think... If Allah makes the night continuous upon you until the time of Doomsday, is there a god besides Allah who can be your light? Do you not hear?"

72. Say, "Think... If Allah makes the day continuous upon you until the time of Doomsday, is there a god besides Allah who can make a night for you in which you can find tranquility? Do you not see this?"

73. He formed the night and the day for you out of His grace so that you may rest (in the night) and ask for His favor (in the day) and be thankful (evaluate).

74. And He will call out to them at that time, "Where are those you assumed were My partners?"

75. And We will extract a witness (a Rasul) from every community and say, "Bring your definite proof!" And they will know that the Truth belongs to Allah! And all the things they invented will be lost from them!

76. Indeed, Qarun was from the people of Moses but he transgressed and did wrong to them... We had given them such treasures that even their keys would have burdened a group of strong men... And when his fellow citizens said to them, "Do not exult, indeed Allah does not like those who exult and go to extremes."

77. "Seek the (things that will enable you to attain the) abode of the future from what Allah has bestowed to you, and do not forget to take your portion of the world! And do good unto others just as Allah does good unto you! Do not cause corruption in the land! Indeed, Allah does not like those who cause corruption!"

78. (Qarun) said, "I have been given (these treasures) because of the knowledge I possess!" Did he not know that Allah has destroyed people in the past who were stronger than he, and much greater in wealth! The guilty will not be asked to explain their mistakes (they will only be subjected to their consequences)!

79. When (Qarun) went forth to his people demonstrating his wealth, those who desired the life of the world (carnal state of existence) said, "If only we were given the like of what Qarun has been given... He really is a fortunate man!"

80. But those who had been given knowledge said, "Woe to you! Allah's reward is better for those who believe and fulfill the requisites of their faith... but only those who are patient will attain it!"

81. Then We made the earth swallow (Qarun and) **his dwelling! And there was nobody besides Allah that could have helped him...** He **was not of those who saved themselves!**

82. Those who wanted to be in his (Qarun's) **place the day before was now saying in the morning, "Ah! So it is Allah who increases the life sustenance for whom He wills and restricts it** (for whom He wills)! **If Allah had not protected us out of His favor, we would surely have been swallowed up also... Ah! So** (it is true that) **those who deny the knowledge of the reality cannot succeed!"**

83. The land of the future (the dimension of immortality)! **We form it in the world** (the life of the body) **for those who do not act superior to others and who comply with the order... The blessed future is for those who are protected** (for the sake of Allah)!

84. Whoever comes with beauty (the qualities of the Names that they have manifested) **will be rewarded with something better... And whoever comes with the bad** (deeds driven by the assumption that they are the body, which is bound to deteriorate) **will find nothing else but the consequences of their own deeds!**

85. The One who has made the Quran (complying with the knowledge of the reality and sunnatullah) **obligatory upon you will surely make you reach the final goal! Say, "My Rabb knows better who has come as a guide to the reality and who is clearly in corrupt faith."**

86. You never expected the Book (the knowledge of the reality and sunnatullah) **would be disclosed through you; it was the grace of your Rabb! Never support those who deny the knowledge of the reality!**

87. And let them not prevent you from fulfilling the requisites of the signs of Allah that have been revealed to you! Call to your Rabb and do not be among the dualists (polytheists).

88. Do not turn to (assume the existence of) **a god** (exterior manifestations of power or your illusory self) **besides Allah. For there is no god, only HU! Everything** (in respect of its 'thing'ness) **is inexistent, only the face of HU** (only that which pertains to the Absolute Reality) **exists!.. The judgment is His... To Him** (the awareness of the Names comprising your essence) **you will be returned!**

29

AL-ANKABUT

By the one who is denoted by the name Allah (who created my being with His Names in accord with the meaning of the letter 'B'), the Rahman, the Rahim.

1. **Alif, Lam, Meem!** (His knowledge in His knowledge with His knowledge!)

2. **Do people think they can get away with just saying, "We believe" and not be confronted with who they really are through trial!**

3. **Indeed, those before them were also tested with objects of trial...** **Allah** (not an external god-deity but their very essential reality) **certainly knows and will expose those who are truthful** (to their word) **and those who are liars.**

4. **Or do those who do bad deeds think they can outrun Us... What bad judgment they have!**

5. **Whoever hopes to meet with Allah** (to experience the manifestations of the One referenced as 'Allah' in one's consciousness, according to one's natural disposition), **indeed** (let them know that) **the term of the bodily life, which is also Allah's discretion, will come to an end! HU is the Sami, the Aleem.** (This definition at the end of the verse points to the 'incomparability' [tanzih] of Allah through HU, and the 'similarity' [tashbih] quality of Allah by giving references to His Names, in order to form a non-dual unified view for the reader, according to my understanding.)

6. **So, whoever strives with determination** (to live this faith; this reality) **strives only for his own being.** (The greatest Jihad [strife] is the one done against one's self!) **Indeed, Allah is Ghani from the worlds** (in terms of His Absolute Essence, Allah is free from being conditioned and limited by the manifested compositions of His Names)!

7. **As for those who believe and fulfill the requisites of their faith, surely We will erase their bad deeds** (the traits of their ego) **from them and reward them with the best of their deeds!**

8. And We have enjoined upon man to be kind to his mother and father... But if they bid you to associate with Me that which goes against your knowledge, then do not obey them! To Me is your return... I will inform you of (the meanings of) your deeds.

9. As for those who believe and fulfill the requisites of their faith, surely We will include them among the righteous.

10. And there are some among the people who say, "We believe in Allah, our essence with His Names," but when they encounter hardship in the way of Allah they mistake the provocation of man for the punishment of Allah. And if victory comes to them from their Rabb, they say, "We were really with You." Does Allah (as the creator with His Names) not know better what is in the breasts (the brains of people)?

11. Surely Allah knows those who believe, and those who are hypocrites (the two-faced who use their intellect in favor of their vested interests rather than for the sake of the Truth).

12. Those who deny the knowledge of the reality say to the believers, "Follow our understanding and we will bear your mistakes (sins)!" The deniers cannot bear the responsibility of their mistakes... Indeed, they are liars.

13. They will indeed bear their own burdens and (other) burdens along with their own... And they will definitely be held responsible for their fabricated ideas during the Doomsday period.

14. And We have disclosed Noah to his people and he stayed for a thousand years less fifty among them! But the deluge overtook them upon their wrongdoing.

15. We saved him and the people of the ark, and made it an exemplary lesson for the people.

16. And Abraham... How he said to his people, "Serve Allah and protect yourselves from Him! This is better for you if you understand."

17. "You worship idols besides Allah and you invent things! The things you worship besides Allah cannot give you any life sustenance! Ask for your sustenance from Allah (your essence)... Pray to him and be thankful to Him... Unto Him you are returned."

18. "And if you deny, (know well) that the people before you also denied... Upon the Rasul is only (the responsibility) of clear notification."

19. Did they not see how Allah originates the creation and then returns them (to their origin or to a new creation for the second time)... Indeed, this is easy for Allah.

20. Say, "Examine the earth (the body) and look at how He originated creation... After this Allah will form your second life (the body of your future life)... Indeed, Allah is Qadir over all things."

21. "He gives suffering to whom He wills and grants mercy to whom He wills... To Him you shall be transformed (you will realize that the Names comprise your essence)!"

22. "You cannot render Him powerless neither on the earth nor in the heavens! You have no guardian or helper besides Allah."

23. Those who deny the signs of Allah in their being and the meeting with Him, it is they who have lost hope in My grace; there shall be intense suffering for them!

24. But the answer of the people (of Abraham) was, "Kill him or burn him!" But Allah saved him from the fire... Indeed, there are signs in this for people who believe.

25. And (Abraham) said, "You have deified idols besides Allah because of your emotional ties to each other (to your ancestors) in the worldly life. Because of this you will disown and curse one another during Doomsday! Your abode is fire and you have no helper."

26. After this Lot (his nephew) believed him and said, "I shall migrate to my Rabb!"... Indeed, He is HU, the Aziz, the Hakim.

27. And We gave Isaac and Jacob to (Abraham)... and We formed Nubuwwah and knowledge in his descendants... We gave his reward in the world... And in the eternal life to come he is indeed among the righteous.

28. And Lot... How he said to his people, "Indeed, you commit an indecency that no one has committed before you!"

29. "Indeed, you sleep with men and sever (the natural process of reproduction), and you do this in public." But their answer was, "So, bring the punishment of Allah then, if you are true to your word!"

30. (Lot) said, "My Rabb, help me against these corrupting people!"

31. When our Rasuls came to Abraham as good news, they said, "Indeed, we will destroy the people of this region... For they have become people who do wrong to themselves."

32. (Abraham) said, "But Lot is also there?" They said, "We know who is there... Surely we will save him and his family... Except his wife, she has become of those who remain behind."

33. When Our Rasuls came to Lot he felt distressed for them and great discomfort (about what may transpire)... (Our Rasuls) said, "Do not fear or grieve! Indeed, we are here to save you and your family... Except your wife, she has become of those who remain behind."

34. "Indeed, we will disclose a suffering from the sky upon the people of this region because of their corrupt beliefs."

35. And indeed, We have left a clear exemplary sign (from that region) for those who use their intellect.

36. And to Madyan (We disclosed) their brother Shuayb... He said, "O my fellow citizens... Worship Allah, believe in the eternal life to come, and do not cause corruption on the earth."

37. But they denied him (Shuayb)... And thus the intense quake seized them and they were left fallen on their knees in their homes.

38. And (We did the same thing to) Aad and Thamud... You should have understood this from the state of their dwellings... Satan (their ego) had made pleasing to them their deeds and averted them from the (True) path... Even though they were endowed with the ability to perceive the reality!

39. And (We did the same thing to) Qarun, Pharaoh and Haman... Indeed, Moses came to them as clear proofs but they were arrogant (full of ego) on the earth... But they could not escape (Our power)!

40. We seized each one with the result of his own wrongdoing... Upon some We disclosed a cyclone! Some were seized by the terrible billowing sound! And some We caused the earth to swallow up... And some We drowned... And Allah did not cause them to suffer, but it was they (their constructed self, ego- identity) who caused their own suffering.

41. The example of those who take friends besides Allah (by deifying each other) is like that of a female spider who takes a home...

Indeed, the weakest of homes is the home of a female spider! If only they knew.

42. Indeed, Allah knows the things to which you turn besides Him... HU, the Aziz, the Hakim.

43. Thus We emphasize these examples to people! But none can duly evaluate them with their intellect other than those of knowledge!

44. Allah created the heavens and the earth in Truth (with the qualities pertaining to His Names)! Indeed, there is a sign in this for those who believe.

45. Read and inform the knowledge (Book) that has been revealed to you, and establish salat... Indeed, salat keeps immorality (going to excess as a result of corporeality) and bad deeds (things that go against sunnatullah) away... Indeed, the dhikr (remembrance) of Allah is Akbar (enables one to experience Akbariyyah – Absolute Magnificence)! Allah knows the state you are in.

46. Except those among them who do wrong! Strive in the best of ways with those to whom the knowledge has been given in the past and say, "We believe in what has been revealed to us and what has been revealed to you... Our God and your God is ONE! To Him we have submitted."

47. Thus We have revealed the Book (knowledge of the reality and sunnatullah) to you... Those to whom We have given a Book believe in Him (as their essential reality)... And among these are also some who believe in Him (their essence)... Only those who deny the knowledge of the reality (those whose hearts have been sealed) deliberately deny Our signs.

48. And you did not recite any book (like the Torah and the Bible) before (the knowledge we disclosed), nor did you inscribe it with your right hand... (Hence, he may be literate in the general sense). Otherwise, (had you been literate) the ones who wish to falsify your words would surely have had doubt.

49. On the contrary, it (the Quran) comprises clear signs within the depths of those to whom the knowledge has been given... Only those who do wrong to themselves deny Our signs (that are inherent in their essence).

50. They said, "He should have been given miracles from his Rabb!"... Say, "Miracles are only from Allah... I am only a clear warner."

51. Is it not sufficient for them that We revealed to you the knowledge that they are informed of? Indeed, there is grace and an admonition in this for people who believe.

52. Say, "Sufficient for me is Allah, who comprises my essence with His Names, as a witness between you and I! He knows what is in the heavens and the earth! Those who believe in falsehood (that they are the body that is bound to deteriorate) and deny Allah, the essence of their being with His Names, they are the very losers!"

53. They want you to hasten the suffering (death) for them. Had their life span not been determined, surely the suffering would have come to them! But it will definitely come to them, suddenly, when they are unaware.

54. They want you to hasten the suffering (death) for them... Indeed, Hell has encompassed those who deny the knowledge of the reality (this very moment)!

55. At that time suffering will cover them from above (their consciousness) and below (their bodies) and it will be said, "Taste the consequences of your deeds!"

56. O my servants who believe! Indeed, my earth is spacious! (The capacity of your brain is expansive! Note that while the body and the brain, in terms of their material make-up, are denoted by the word 'earth', the functions of the brain, its neuronal activities and its manifestation of data, are referred to as 'heavens.' The reason why 'heavens' is used in the plural form, according to my understanding, is due to the various levels of manifested data and knowledge. Hence, by saying 'My earth is spacious,' there is an indication as to the vastness of the capacity of the brain and a proposal to use it as its highest level of performance in order to attain knowledge. For, the main concern is not in regards to objects that are to deteriorate under the earth but to the necessary acquisitions pertaining to an eternal life.) Serve only Me!

57. Every being (individual consciousness) will taste death... And then to Us you shall be returned!

58. As for those who believe (in their essential reality) and fulfill the requisites of their faith, We will definitely prepare elevated

chambers for them underneath which rivers flow... They will abide therein eternally... Beautiful is the reward of those who labor!

59. They are those who are patient and place their trust in their Rabb (they believe in the quality of the Name Wakil in their essence and trust in its function)!

60. And there are many creatures that do not carry their own sustenance... Allah gives both their sustenance and yours... HU is the Sami, the Aleem.

61. Indeed, if you were to ask them, "Who created the heavens and the earth, and who gave their function to the Sun and the Moon?" Surely they will say, "Allah"... How then do they turn (to duality despite the Truth)?

62. Allah increases the life sustenance for whom He wills among His servants and decreases it (for whom He wills)! Indeed, Allah is Aleem of all things.

63. And indeed, if you were to ask them, "Who discloses water from the heavens (knowledge in the consciousness) and brings the earth (the body) back to life after its death (while you were living lifelessly deprived of the consciousness of the reality)?" Surely they will say, "Allah"... Say, "Hamd belongs to Allah!" No, most of them do not use their reason and evaluate!

64. And this apparent and perceived worldly life (the lowest state of consciousness) is no other than an amusement (a delusive diversion in relation to the real) and a game (in which we merely play our roles in the script)! As for the eternal abode, that is the true state of conscious life. If only they could comprehend!

65. When they board the ship they divert all their faith to Him and pray to Allah... But when He delivers them to the land, alas, they fall into duality!

66. So they (turn to duality and) show ungratefulness to the things We have given them (the forces and qualities within their essence) and benefit (from temporary things)! Soon they will understand!

67. Did they not see how We made it a safe Sanctuary (Harem) while people were being taken away from around them... Do they still believe in falsehood (that they are nothing but the body, and bound to deteriorate upon death) and ungratefully deny the favor of Allah (the forces of the Names in their essence)?

68. Who does greater wrong than he who invents a lie about Allah or denies that which comes as the Truth (Rasul)? Is Hell not the dwelling place of those who deny the knowledge of the reality?

69. And those who strive (against their egos) **to reach Us, We will surely enable them to reach Our ways** (by enabling them to realize their innermost essential reality... The ability to observe the manifestations of Allah's names ubiquitously). **Indeed, Allah is with those who have certainty** (those who turn to Allah as though they see Him, i.e. the manifestations of the qualities of His Names).

30

AR-RUM

By the one who is denoted by the name Allah (who created my being with His Names in accord with the meaning of the letter 'B'), the Rahman, the Rahim.

1. Alif, Lam, Meem.

2. The Romans (Byzantines) have been defeated!

3. In a nearby land... They (the Byzantines) will be victorious after this defeat.

4. Within a few years... The judgment is Allah's from beginning to end! Then those who have believed will rejoice (for the word of Allah will have been fulfilled).

5. With the help of Allah... He gives victory to whom He wills! HU is the Aziz, the Rahim.

6. (This is) the promise of Allah; He does not fail in His promise! But the majority of the people do not know.

7. Living in their cocoons, they are unaware of the eternal life to come; they only know and recognize the material aspect of the worldly life!

8. Do they not contemplate on their own selves (their own essential reality)? Allah created the heavens, the earth and everything between the two only as the Truth, and with a defined lifespan! Indeed, most of the people deny they will meet with their Rabb.

9. Do they not travel the earth and see the end their predecessors met? They (the predecessors) were mightier than them (the present people)... They cultivated the earth more and built upon it more than these have built... Their Rasul also came to them as clear proofs. So, it was not Allah who did wrong to them, but it was they who wronged themselves.

10. Then the end of those who did wrong (to themselves) was the worst! For they had denied the signs of Allah, and they mocked them.

11. Allah originates creation, then He will restore it, and then to Him you shall be returned.

12. During that time the guilty (the dualists) will be silent in hopelessness.

13. There was no intercession from the partners they ascribed, for they saw the invalidity of those partners!

14. At the time of that hour (death), (the believers and the people of duality) will be sorted.

15. Those who believe and fulfill the requisites of their faith will rejoice in a blissful environment.

16. And those who deny the knowledge of the reality and Our signs in their essence and who deny the eternal life to come, they will forcefully remain in that suffering.

17. Subhan is Allah, in your evening and in your morning!

18. Hamd belongs to Him in the heavens and the earth... At midday when the sun is at its peak and late afternoon when it begins to set!

19. He brings the living out of the dead and the dead out of the living, and gives life to earth after its death... Thus you will also be brought forth.

20. It is from His miracles – signs – that He created you from dust... Then you dispersed as humans (thinking you are merely the body, whereas you have been created as vicegerents)!

21. It is from His signs that He creates partners (body) from your selves (your consciousness formed by a composition of Names) so that you may settle and find repose therein, and so that He forms between you love and grace... Indeed, there are many signs in this for people who contemplate.

22. It is from His signs... The creation of the heavens (levels of consciousness) and the earth (brain – body) and the differences of your language and color... Surely, there are signs in this for those of knowledge (humanity).

23. It is from His signs that you sleep in the night and ask from His bounty in the day... Indeed, there are signs in this for people who perceive.

24. It is from His signs that He shows you a lightening (a sudden strike of the reality) giving rise to both fear and hope... He discloses water (knowledge) from the sky (the dimension of Names [data] comprising the essence of your brain) and brings the earth (the idea of being the body) to life after its death (after being unconscious of the reality)... Indeed, there are signs – lessons – in this for people who can use their intellect.

25. It is from His signs that the heavens (consciousness) and the earth (the body) continue to subsist by His command... And then when He calls you from the earth (your body) you will come out (with the angelic force of Azrael)!

26. And to Him belongs whoever is in the heavens (conscious beings) and the earth (bodily beings). Thus, all are in a state of devout obedience to Him (in manifesting the qualities of His Names)...

27. It is HU who manifests creation and then returns it! And that is easy for Him (to do)! And to Him belongs the greatest examples in the heavens and the earth. HU is the Aziz, the Hakim.

28. He gives you an example from yourselves: Will you accept to be partners in your provisions (wealth) with your servants? Yet do you not accept to be partners with them in wealth and fear them as you fear yourselves? Thus, We diversify the lessons for people who use their intellects.

29. No, the wrongdoers ignorantly follow their empty desires and fantasies... Who can guide the one who Allah leads astray? And they have no helpers.

30. Set your face (consciousness) as a Hanif (without the concept of a deity-god, without making shirq to Allah, i.e. with the consciousness of non-duality) towards the One Religion (the only system and order), the natural disposition (fitrah) of Allah (i.e. the primary system and mechanism of the brain) upon which Allah has created man. There is no change in the creation of Allah. This is the infinitely valid system (deen al-qayyim), but most people do not know.

31. As those who have turned to Him, protect yourselves from Him (as His system and order will automatically enforce upon you the

consequences of your deeds) **and establish salat, and do not be of the dualists!**

32. Do not be of those whose religious understanding is fragmented and who are divided into sects... Where every sect rejoices with their own (religious approach)**!**

33. When an affliction touches the people they turn to Him in prayer... Then, if He lets them taste grace from Him, at once some of them begin to ascribe partners to Him.

34. So that their ungratefulness towards what He has given them may become apparent... Enjoy (the temporary pleasures)**, soon you will know.**

35. Or did We reveal a powerful proof to them, and that is why they are in duality?

36. When we make people taste grace they rejoice with it... But when they live something bad as a result of their own doing, at once they fall into despair!

37. Did they not see how Allah increases or constricts the life sustenance of whom He wills... Indeed, there are signs in this for people who believe.

38. Give your relatives their due rights, and the needy and the traveler... This is better for those who desire the countenance of Allah! They are the ones who, going against all odds, achieve and attain liberation!

39. What you give in usury to gain in value through other people's wealth will not increase in the sight of Allah! But what you give as alms (purification) **seeking the countenance of Allah will be multiplied manifold!**

40. It is Allah who created you, and then nourished you with sustenance of life, then He will cause you to die (make you taste death) **and then bring you to life** (in a new dimension of existence)**! Can any of your 'alleged partners' do these things? Exalted is HU from the partners they ascribe to Him, the Aliy.**

41. Corruption has appeared on land and sea so (Allah) **can make people taste the consequences of what they do! Perhaps they will turn back.**

42. Say, "Travel throughout the earth and see the end met by those before you! Most of them were dualists!"

43. Direct your face towards the Right Religion (Islam; the reality that everything is in a state of absolute submission to Allah), before there comes from Allah the time (of death) that cannot be repelled, a time when people will be divided into groups.

44. Whoever denies, his denial is at his own expense... And who ever believes and fulfills the requisites of his faith, he would have prepared (the results of his good deeds) for his own self.

45. So that (Allah) rewards from His bounty those who believe and fulfills the requisites of their faith... Indeed, He does not like those who deny the knowledge of the reality!

46. It is from His signs that He discloses the winds as heralds of good news, that He makes you taste His grace, and the ships sail at His command... So that you ask from His bounty, evaluate and be thankful.

47. Indeed, We disclosed Rasuls to their people before you who came to them as clear proofs... And We took revenge from the guilty... It is incumbent upon Us to help the believers.

48. It is Allah who discloses the winds (inspirations) and drives the clouds (the thoughts in the individual's database) with it, and spreads them in the sky (consciousness) and fragments them (allows them to be analyzed) so that rain (the ascertained knowledge) emerges from among them... When He causes it to fall upon whom He wills from His servants, immediately they rejoice with the good news.

49. Whereas before this (the rain – knowledge) came to them, they were confounded (unable to tell the difference between the reality and falsity).

50. So observe the works of Allah's grace, how He gives life to the earth (with knowledge) after its death (thinking you are the body, or 'matter', when you have been created as an immortal and a vicegerent, at the highest state of existence). Indeed, He is the One who gives life (immortality) to the dead! HU is Qadir over all things.

51. But if We disclose a wind and they see it (their crops) turn yellow, immediately they become ungrateful.

52. **Indeed, you cannot make the dead** (those who ignorantly think they will deteriorate and become non-existent) **hear; nor can you make the deaf hear when they turn their backs** (to the Truth) **and go!**

53. **And you cannot take the blind out of their corrupt beliefs and show them the reality! You can only make the Muslims** (those who have submitted) **hear, those who have believed in Our signs within their essence!**

54. **It is Allah who created you with weakness** (unaware of the reality)! **Then after your weakness He formed strength** (made you aware of your essential reality – your Rabb)! **Then, after this strength, He made you weak** (aware of your helplessness in the sight of Allah) **and gave you white hair** (wisdom)... **He creates what He wills... HU is the Aleem, the Qadir.**

55. **At that hour** (death) **the guilty will swear they did not remain** (in the bodily life) **for more than an hour... Thus they were deluded** (a day in the sight of your Rabb is a thousand years of bodily life).

56. **And those to whom knowledge and faith has been given said,** "**Indeed, you remained in Allah's Book** (the 'Read'able Book or the state of existence defined as the Clear Book) **until the time of resurrection** (when you are given a new form to continue your life with)... **And so this is the time of Resurrection... But you did not understand the reality!**"

57. **During that time the excuses of those who wronged** (themselves) **will be of no avail to them, and they will not be asked to correct** (with a positive action) **their condition either.**

58. **We have attenuated all kinds of examples in this Quran! Indeed, if you bring them a proof, those who deny the knowledge of the reality will say, "You are fabricators!"**

59. **Thus Allah seals the consciousness of the ignorant!**

60. **So be patient! Indeed, the promise of Allah is true! Those who have not reached the state of certainty are not going to be able to take you lightly** (when Our promise is fulfilled)!

31

LUQMAN

By the one who is denoted by the name Allah (who created my being with His Names in accord with the meaning of the letter 'B'), the Rahman, the Rahim.

1. Alif, Lam, Meem.

2. These are the signs of the Book of Wisdom (knowledge).

3. As grace and guidance to the reality for those who turn to Allah as though they see Him (the doers of good).

4. They are those who establish salat and give alms, and they are certain about their eternal life to come.

5. They are upon the knowledge of the reality from their Rabb and it is they who are liberated.

6. And there are some among the people who engage in idle talk, without any basis, to lead (people) astray from the way of Allah. There is a humiliating suffering for them.

7. And when he is informed of Our signs he turns away with arrogance as if he has not heard it, as if there is deafness in his ears... Give him the news of an intense suffering!

8. As for those who believe and fulfill its requisites, for them there are Paradises of Bliss (a life adorned with the Rahim qualities of the Names).

9. They will abide therein eternally... It is the true promise of Allah! HU is the Aziz, the Hakim.

10. He created the heavens without pillars (the dimensions of knowledge and consciousness subsist directly as the meanings of the Names) so that (your self-consciousness can develop) and set firm mountains (organs) upon the earth (the body) so that you are not shaken, and formed every creature (animalistic properties)... We disclosed water (knowledge – the consciousness with which one can become aware of his essential self) from the heavens (universal

consciousness) **and formed in it of every generous pair** (your spirit – character for your eternal life to come).

11. **This is the creation of Allah... So, show me what those other than Him have created? No, the wrongdoers are plunged in clear error.**

12. **Indeed, We gave wisdom** (an intellect based on systematic thinking) **to Luqman, so that he may be grateful to Allah... And whoever is grateful, his gratitude is for his own self... And whoever denies** (the blessings within his essence), **Allah is indeed the Ghani, the Hamid.**

13. **And when Luqman admonished his son, "O my son! Do not associate partners with Allah, who comprises your essence with His Names! Assuredly, duality is a great wrongdoing!**

14. **We enjoined upon man his parents... His mother carried him in weakness upon weakness... And his weaning from breastfeeding is within two years... "Be grateful to Me and to your parents; to Me is the return!"**

15. **But if they force you to associate with Me that which goes against your knowledge, then do not obey them! Be kind to them in terms of worldly relations, but follow the one who turns to Me! Your return is to Me. I will notify you about the things you do.**

16. **"O my son... Indeed, if the thing you do is the weight of a mustard seed and it is inside a rock or in the heavens or beneath the earth, Allah will bring it forth** (as the result of your essence)**... Indeed, Allah is the Latif, the Habir."**

17. **"O my son... Establish salat... Make your judgments based on your faith; enjoin the good and forbid the bad. And be patient with what afflicts you! Indeed, these are things that require determination."**

18. **"Do not turn away from people in arrogance and do not walk upon the earth boastfully! Indeed, Allah does not like those who are arrogant and proud with their possessions!"**

19. **"Know your boundaries in life, with balance, and lower your voice! Indeed, the ugliest of sounds is the voice of donkeys."**

20. **Do you not see how Allah has subjected all that is in the heavens and the earth to your service and spread His apparent and concealed blessings upon you... And among the people are some**

who dispute about Allah without any basis in reality, and no enlightening knowledge.

21. When they are told, "Follow what Allah has revealed" they say, "No, we follow the ways of our ancestors"... Even if Satan (bodily desires) calls them to the suffering of a blazing fire?

22. And whoever submits his face (consciousness) to Allah as a doer of good, has surely grasped a strong handle... All affairs return to Allah!

23. And whoever denies, do not let his denial upset you! Their return is to Us; We will inform them of the things they do... Indeed, Allah, as the Absolute Essence of the Names comprising your being, is the Aleem.

24. They will enjoy the pleasures of the world for a short while... Then We will subject them to an intense suffering.

25. Indeed, if you were to ask them, "Who created the heavens and the earth?" they will surely say, "Allah"... Say, "Al-hamdu-lillah – Hamd belongs to Allah!"... But no, most of them cannot understand!

26. Whatever is in the heavens and the earth is for Allah (to observe the manifestation of the qualities of His Names). Indeed, Allah is HU, the Ghani, the Hamid.

27. If all the trees on earth were pens and the sea (were ink) and seven more seas were added to it, the words of Allah would not cease... Indeed, Allah is the Aziz, the Hakim.

28. The creation and resurrection of all of you with a new form in a new dimension of life is just like that of a single being... Indeed, Allah is the Sami, the Basir.

29. Did you not see how Allah transforms the night into the day, and the day into the night! He has appointed functions to the Sun and the Moon! Each one fulfills its own function for a specified time... Allah is Habir of what you do (as its creator).

30. That is because Allah is HU, the Truth (the Absolute Reality)... Indeed, the things to which they give names other than Allah are baseless empty things! Indeed, Allah is HU, the Aliy, the Kabir.

31. Did you not see how the ships sail through the sea as a blessing from Allah so that He may show you of His signs? Indeed, there lessons in this for those who are patient and grateful.

32. And when waves cover them like dark clouds they devote their faith purely to Allah and pray... But when We deliver them to the land, some of them take the middle path. And none deliberately denies Our signs, except those who are brutal and ungrateful.

33. O people! Protect yourselves from your Rabb (for He will definitely enforce the consequences of your deeds upon you) and fear the time at which no father will avail his son and no son will avail his father! Indeed, the promise of Allah is true! Do not let the worldly life deceive you... And do not let the deceiver (your deluded ego) deceive you about Allah (by making you think he is your essential reality so nothing will happen to you, veiling you from sunnatullah)!

34. Indeed, the knowledge of that hour (death) is with Allah, He sends down the rain, He knows what is in the wombs; no one knows what the future will bring, and no one knows where they will die! Indeed, Allah is the Aleem, the Habir.

AS-SAJDA

By the one who is denoted by the name Allah (who created my being with His Names in accord with the meaning of the letter 'B'), **the Rahman, the Rahim.**

1. Alif, Lam, Meem.

2. This is the knowledge (Book) **of the reality and sunnatullah revealed from the Rabb of the worlds** (the Rabb of 'humans')! (In many places throughout the Quran the word 'worlds' has been used to denote 'humans'. This is worth examining and contemplating.)

3. Or do they say, "He made it up"! Never! It is the Truth from your Rabb so that with it you may warn the people to whom no warner has come before you... Perhaps they will (evaluate and) **attain the reality.**

4. It is Allah who created the heavens (the levels of the self and consciousness) **and the earth** (the body – brain) **and everything in between them in six stages** (the six stages in terms of the creation of humans are: 1. Sperm/egg; 2. Conception [zygote]; 3. Cell division; 4. Cellular differentiation; 5. The formation of the organs; and 6. Specialization of organs with various functions and the formation of consciousness and the senses) **and then He established Himself on the Throne** (commenced administration in the world of acts with His Names)**... You have no guardian or intercessor besides Him... Do you still not contemplate and evaluate this?** (There are two ways of looking at this verse according to my understanding: In respect of man's external world and in terms of man's existence.)

5. He governs the earth (the brain) **from the heaven** (through the cosmic electromagnetic energy emanating from the qualities of the Names in the form of celestial constellations [star signs] that affect the second brain in the gut and thus one's consciousness, or from an internal perspective, through the Names that become manifest in one's brain based on the holographic reality)**... Then it will ascend to Him in a time, the extent of which is a thousand years** (the ascension to the life of the spirit-body or a dimensional return to one's essence).

6. Thus (Allah) **is the Knower of the unknown** (unperceivable) **and the manifest** (perceivable), **the Aziz, the Rahim.**

7. It is He who has created everything perfectly! He began the creation of man from clay (the eggs).

8. Then He made his lineage from a basic fluid (sperm).

9. Then He proportioned him (formed his brain such that the neurons evaluate the various wavelengths to manifest the meanings of the Names) **and breathed into him from His own Spirit** (the act of breathing into something goes outward from within, that is, the manifestation of the Names within the data level of the brain is referred to as 'Allah's spirit' in existence)**... And He made for you hearing** (perception), **sight** (vision) **and hearts** (the reflectors of the meanings of the Names to the brain – heart neurons)**... How little you thank** (evaluate)!

10. They said, "When we have become nothing beneath the earth, will we continue life with a new form?" No, they refuse to be enlightened about the manifestation (meeting) **of their Rabb** (with His Names) **through their existence.**

11. Say, "The angel of death (the force of death – the force that pulls one from the biological-body to a life in the domain of the spirit-body) **who has been entrusted with you** (a function that is already present in your system) **that will cause you to die** (separate you from your body)! **Then to your Rabb you will be returned** (You will realize your essential reality)."

12. You should see the guilty ones (who deny the knowledge of the reality) **when they bow their heads in the sight of their Rabb and say, "Our Rabb... We have seen and perceived the Truth! So return us** (to the world – the life of the body) **so we may fulfill the requisites! Indeed, we have attained certainty** (now)."

13. If We had so willed, We could have enabled every being (illusory self; ego) **to realize its essential reality, but My word: "I will surely fill Hell** (the conditions to manifest the specific configuration of the qualities of the Names that result in an infernal state of life) **with jinn and man all together" is in effect.**

14. So taste (the suffering) **for having forgotten the meeting of this day! In truth, We have also forgotten you! Taste the eternal suffering because of your deeds!**

15. Only those believe in Our signs who, when they are reminded, they prostrate and selflessly glorify their Rabb (fulfill their functions) as His Hamd. (This is a verse of prostration.)

16. They arise from their beds (at night) and pray to their Rabb with fear and with hope... They unrequitedly give from the life sustenance with which We have provided them!

17. And no one knows the blessings of joy kept hidden in store for them as a result of their deeds!

18. Is one who believes equal to one with corrupt beliefs? They are not equal!

19. Those who believe and fulfill the requisites of their faith, there are Paradises of Refuge for them, as a result of what they have done (an experience that will emerge from within their essence).

20. As for those with corrupt beliefs, their abode is fire! Every time they want to leave they will be returned to it and told, "Taste the suffering of the fire that you denied!"

21. And We will surely make them taste the nearer suffering (in their world) before the greatest (eternal) suffering, that perhaps they will turn back.

22. And who does more wrong than the one who, when he is reminded of the signs of his Rabb within his own essence, turns away from them? Indeed, We will make the guilty taste the results of their doings!

23. Indeed, We gave the knowledge (the Book) to Moses... So do not be in doubt (now) of having reached it (the knowledge)! We have made it a guide for the Children of Israel.

24. And when they are patient, We made leaders among them, under Our command, to guide them to the reality! They were certain of Our signs!

25. Indeed, your Rabb is HU and He will judge between them during Doomsday regarding the things over which they dispute.

26. Did it not show them the Truth, how We destroyed so many generations before them, as they walk upon their dwellings? Indeed, there are lessons in this... Do they still not perceive?

27. Did they not see how We channel the water to a barren land and with it We bring forth the crops from which they and their animals eat? Do they still not see?

28. They say, "When will be the conquest (the absolute conquest [fath] – the complete unveiling of the reality through the experience of death) if you are of the truthful?"

29. Say, "During that time when the conquest is experienced, the belief of those who were in denial of the knowledge of the reality (before tasting death) will be of no avail to them, and they will not be reprieved."

30. So turn away from them and wait. Indeed, they are also waiting!

33

AL-AHZAB

By the one who is denoted by the name Allah (who created my being with His Names in accord with the meaning of the letter 'B'), **the Rahman, the Rahim.**

1. O Nabi! Be of those who protect themselves from Allah (as He will most definitely enforce the consequences of your deeds upon you)! **And do not obey those who deny the knowledge of the reality and the hypocrites** (the two-faced)! **Indeed, Allah is the Aleem, the Hakim.**

2. Follow what has been revealed (inspired) **to you from your Rabb...** **Indeed, Allah is Habir of what you do** (as their creator).

3. Place your trust in Allah! Sufficient for you is Allah, your essential reality with His Names as the Wakil.

4. Allah has not formed two hearts in any man's chest cavity! And He has not made your partners, (whom you call your mothers and forbid to yourselves) **your mothers. And He has not made your adopted sons your real sons. This is merely your baseless talk! Allah informs of the Truth and leads to the right path!**

5. Address them (your adopted sons) **by** (the names of) **their fathers...** **This is more just in the sight of Allah. If you do not know their fathers, then they are your brothers and friends in religion... And there is no blame upon you for that in which you erred... Except for the things you did with deliberate intention... Allah is the Ghafur, the Rahim.**

6. The Nabi is of higher priority to the believers than their own selves! His spouses are their (the believers') **mothers! And relatives are of higher priority in Allah's Book** (in terms of inheritance) **than** (other) **believers and emigrants... Except the good you do for your friends in the way of religion... This is a law from the revealed knowledge.**

7. And We took a pledge from the Nabis: from you, Noah, Abraham, Moses and Jesus, the son of Mary... We took a solemn covenant from them.

8. So that the truthful may be questioned of their Truth (so that they may be tried)... And He has prepared a severe suffering for those who deny the knowledge of the reality.

9. O believers... Remember the blessing of Allah upon you... When armed forces (in the Battle of the Trench) came to you and We disclosed a storm and invisible forces upon them... Allah is Basir of what you do (as their creator).

10. And when they came to you from above and from below... And your eyes shifted and your hearts reached your throats! You were in various assumptions about Allah.

11. There the believers were tried and severely shaken.

12. And the hypocrites and those in whose hearts is disease (devoid of healthy thought) said, "Allah and His Rasul have not promised us anything except delusion."

13. And a group of them said, "O people of Yasrib (the previous name of Medina)! There is no place here for you to stay, go back!" And another group asked permission of the Nabi saying, "Indeed, our houses are unprotected"... While they (their houses) were not unprotected... They wanted nothing other than to flee.

14. If their houses were forcefully entered upon from all its (the city's) surrounding and they were required to turn back from their religion, they (the hypocrites) would surely have done so...

15. Indeed, they had promised Allah before that they would not turn their backs and flee... And a promise made to Allah will be questioned (its consequence will be inescapably experienced)!

16. Say, "If you are trying to flee from death or from being killed, your fleeing will be of no benefit to you... Even if you were to escape, your gain will be near to nothing (as the life of the earthly life is so very short)!"

17. Say, "Who can protect you against (the will of) Allah if He wills (to manifest) a bad thing on you or (wills to manifest) grace?" They cannot find a friend or a helper besides Allah.

18. Allah already knows those among you who cause obstruction and say to the people, "(Leave the Rasul and) come to us!" Only a few of them come to battle anyway.

19. They are stingy (two-faced) **towards you! When the fear of battle – death – comes, you will see them looking at you, their eyes turned like someone overcome by the fear of death... And when their fear passes, greedy for acquisitions, they will hurt you with their sharp tongues... They are not believers! And so Allah has rendered their deeds worthless... This is easy for Allah.**

20. They think the confederates (Ahzab – supporting forces in combat) **have not gone... If the confederates should come, they would prefer to stay in the desert with the Bedouins, contending themselves with your news! Even if they were among you, they would take very little part in fighting.**

21. Indeed, there is a perfect example in the Rasul of Allah for those who hope for Allah and the eternal life to come, and remember Allah much!

22. When the believers see the confederates (Ahzab – groups that come as reinforcement) **they say, "This is the promise of Allah and His Rasul... Allah and His Rasul have told the truth"... This only increases them in faith and submission.**

23. Among the believers are men who have kept their word to Allah... They had pledged their life and they fulfilled it (they tasted death for the cause of Allah)**... and some who are still waiting** (to fulfill it)**... They did not change** (their stance)**!**

24. Thus, Allah will reward the devout (the truthful; those who confirm the reality) **due to their truthfulness** (their pure and sincere belief) **and subject the hypocrites to suffering if He wills, or accept their repentance. Indeed, Allah is the Ghafur, the Rahim.**

25. Allah repelled those who deny the knowledge of the reality with their own rage, having not attained any good! And sufficient was Allah for the believers in battle... Allah is the Qawwi, the Aziz.

26. He brought down from their fortresses those who supported them among the People of the Book, and cast worry into their hearts... You killed a group of them, and took captive another.

27. He made you inheritors of their land, homes, properties and a land that you have never trodden... Allah is Qadir over all things.

28. O Nabi... Tell your partners, "If you want the adornments of the worldly life, then come, let me give you your compensation for separation, and set you free graciously."

29. "But if you desire Allah and His Rasul and the eternal life to come, then indeed, Allah has prepared for the doers of good among you women (who have turned to Allah as though they can see Him) a great reward."

30. O wives of the Nabi... Whoever among you should commit a clear immorality – an act of transgression – the punishment will be two-fold! This is easy for Allah.

31. And whoever among you obeys Allah and His Rasul and fulfilles the requisites of their faith, We will give their reward twice... We have prepared a generous – abundant – life sustenance for them.

32. O wives of the Nabi... You are not like any other women! If you want to be protected, do not talk flirtatiously (with men)! Lest the inconsiderate one in whose heart there is sickness should become hopeful! Speak with appropriate speech to avoid misunderstandings!

33. Stay in your homes... Do not walk (flirtatiously) like the women in the former times of ignorance, revealing yourselves (to provoke and entice)... Establish salat, give alms and obey Allah and His Rasul! O people of the (Rasul's) household, Allah only wants to remove impurity (all restrictions pertaining to worldly and bodily addictions) from you and purify you!

34. Remember (recite) the verses of Allah in your homes and what has been informed of wisdom... Indeed, Allah is the Latif, the Habir.

35. Indeed, for men who have accepted Islam and women who have accepted Islam, obedient men and obedient women, truthful men and truthful women, patient men and patient women, men in awe (of the reality) and women in awe, charitable men and charitable women, men that experience fasting and women that experience fasting, men who guard their chastity and women who guard their chastity, men who remember Allah much and women who remember Allah much – Allah has prepared forgiveness and a great reward.

36. <u>When Allah and His Rasul make a judgment regarding an affair, believing men and women have no choice in their own affair! Whoever disobeys Allah and His Rasul, they have clearly plunged into a corrupt faith!</u>

37. And recall when you told the one to whom Allah and you bestowed favor (the Rasul's adopted son, Zayd), **"Keep your wife and protect yourselves from Allah,"** but you were concealing within your thoughts that which Allah was to disclose, and you feared the people (would misunderstand and turn away from the way of Allah)! (Whereas) **Allah has more right to be feared! When Zayd divorced her, We married her** (Zaynab) **to you, so that there may be no discomfort or obstacle upon the believers concerning marrying the ex-wives of their adopted sons once their relationship ends... The command of Allah is fulfilled!**

38. There is no responsibility upon the Nabi about that which Allah has imposed upon him! Such was also the sunnatullah for those who came before him... The command of Allah is a decreed (planned) **destiny** (its fulfillment is definite)!

39. They (the Rasuls) **convey the risalah** (the knowledge of the reality) **of Allah, they are in awe of Him and they are not in awe of anyone but Him... Sufficient is Allah as the Hasib!**

40. Muhammad is not the father of any one of your men... But he is the Rasul of Allah, the final of Nabis (the summit of perfection – the final one)**... Allah is Aleem over all things** (in respect of the mystery of the letter B).

41. O believers! Remember Allah much!

42. Glorify (tasbih) **Him morning and evening** (constantly)!

43. It is HU who reflects upon you and His angels (the forces of His Names)**, to bring you out of the darkness** (of your formed illusory identities) **into the Nur** (life based on the knowledge of the reality)! **And is ever, Rahim to those who believe in their essential reality.**

44. Their greeting when they unite with Him (through death) **is "Salam"... And He has prepared a generous – noble – reward for them.**

45. O Nabi... Indeed, We disclosed you as a witness, a giver of good news and a warner;

46. As a source of light who calls to (the reality of) **Allah with His permission!**

47. So give the good news to the believers that there is a great bounty for them from Allah!

48. And do not follow those who deny the knowledge of the reality and the hypocrites! Do not heed their persecutions! Place your trust in Allah! Sufficient for you is Allah, your essential reality with His Names, as the Wakil.

49. O believers! When you marry believing women and then divorce them without having touched them, you have no right to determine a waiting period concerning them... Immediately pay their separation compensation and release them with ease.

50. O Nabi! We have made exclusively lawful for you, your wives to whom you have given their dowries, as well as what your right hand possesses (bondmaids) from among the captives of war whom Allah has bestowed upon you; and the daughters of your paternal uncles and aunts, the daughters of your maternal uncles and aunts, who have migrated with you; and any believing woman who has granted herself to the Nabi, provided the Nabi also wants to marry her... This does not apply to the other believers... We know exactly what We have made obligatory upon them concerning their wives and their bondmaids... (We explain this) in order that there may be no blame upon you... Allah is the Ghafur, the Rahim.

51. You may put aside whom you will of them and take for yourself whom you will... And there is no blame on you if you take (again) one (whose turn) you put aside... This is most appropriate so that they may be comforted and not grieve and that they may be well pleased with what you give them... Allah knows what is in your hearts... Allah is the Aleem, the Halim.

52. No (other) women after this is lawful to you... You cannot exchange them for other wives even if their beauty is pleasing to you! Except for your bondmaids... Allah is Raqib over all things.

53. O believers... Do not enter the house of the Nabi unless you are permitted for a meal... (And not) without waiting (for the meal) to be ready... But go when you are invited, and after you have your meal, leave without lingering in idle talk... For this (reckless behavior of yours) distresses the Nabi, yet he is hesitant to tell you (for he does not want to hurt you), but Allah does not hesitate to disclose the truth! And when you ask (his wives) for something ask them from behind a curtain... This is purer for your hearts and their hearts... It is not conceivable for you to distress the Nabi, or marry his wives after him, ever... Indeed, this is grave in the sight of Allah.

54. Whether you reveal something or conceal it, Allah is most definitely Aleem over all things (as their creator).

55. There is no blame upon them for appearing before their fathers, sons, brothers, nephews, other believing women and their maids... Protect yourselves from Allah... Indeed, Allah is a witness over all things!

56. Indeed, Allah and His angels bestow blessings upon the Nabi... O believers, send blessings (turn to) him and greet him in submission!

57. As for those who cause distress to Allah and His Rasul, Allah has cursed them in the world and the eternal life to come, and prepared a degrading suffering for them.

58. As for those who cause distress to believing men and believing women by accusing them of things they have not done, they have indeed taken upon themselves (the responsibility of) slander and an obvious error.

59. O Nabi! Tell your wives, daughters and the wives of the believers to wear their outer garments... This will enable them to be recognized and thus not abused... Allah is the Ghafur, the Rahim.

60. If the two-faced, those with sickly thoughts and those who are spreading rumors in Medina do not desist, We will indeed send you upon them and then they will be only remain as your neighbors for a short while.

61. Accursed, wherever they are found, they will be seized and killed.

62. Such was also the way of the sunnatullah for those who passed on before them... And there is no change in the sunnatullah!

63. People ask you about the Hour (of death)... Say, "Its knowledge is with Allah alone"... Who knows? Perhaps the hour is close!

64. Indeed, Allah has cursed those who have denied the knowledge of the reality and prepared for them a blazing fire.

65. They will abide therein eternally... And they will not find any friend or helper.

66. At the time when their faces (consciousness) are turned into fire (burning in remorse) they will say, "Woe to us! If only we had obeyed Allah; if only we had obeyed the Rasul."

67. And they shall say, "Our Rabb... Indeed we followed our leaders and elders, but they lead us astray from the path (of the Truth)."

68. "Our Rabb, give them double suffering and curse them with a mighty curse."

69. O believers! Do not be like those who caused distress to Moses! Allah cleared Moses of their allegations... He submitted himself in the sight of Allah.

70. O believers! Protect yourselves from Allah (His system by which He will enforce upon you the consequences of your deeds) and speak the solid truth!

71. (So that Allah) may correct your actions and cover your mistakes... Whoever obeys Allah and His Rasul has indeed attained a great success.

72. Indeed, we offered the Trust (living consciously of the Names) to the heavens (consciousness of the self, ego) and the earth (the body) and the mountains (the organs), and they declined to bear it (their Name compositions did not have the capacity to manifest it) and feared it; but Man (the consciousness to manifest the Names that compose vicegerency) undertook to bear it. Indeed, he is unjust (insufficient in duly living his reality) and ignorant (of the knowledge of His infinite Names).

73. Allah will cause suffering to hypocrite men and women, and dualist men and women, and accept the repentance of the believing men and women... Allah is the Ghafur, the Rahim.

34

AS-SABA

By the one who is denoted by the name Allah (who created my being with His Names in accord with the meaning of the letter 'B'), the Rahman, the Rahim.

1. Hamd be to Allah, to whom everything in the heavens (levels of consciousness) and earth (the body) belongs! And Hamd belongs to Him in the eternal life to come as well! HU is the Hakim, the Habir.

2. He knows whatever goes into the earth (the body) and whatever comes forth from it; and whatever is disclosed from heaven (consciousness) and whatever (dimensionally) ascends to it... HU is the Rahim, the Ghafur.

3. Those who deny the knowledge of the reality say, "The hour (of death by which the reality will become apparent) will not come to us"... Say, "No, I swear by my Rabb, the knower of the unknown, that it will indeed come to you! Not even an iota's weight in the heavens and the earth is hidden from Him! (In fact) what is even smaller than that or greater, are all in the Clear Book (the 'world of acts,' which is the manifest world).

4. (This is so) that He may reward those who believe and fulfill the requisites of their faith! There is forgiveness for them and a generous sustenance of life.

5. As for those who rush about to invalidate Our signs, for them there is an intense suffering (filth, illusion).

6. Those to whom the knowledge has been given, know that what has been revealed to you is the Truth itself guiding to the reality of the One who is the Aziz, the Hamid.

7. Those who deny the knowledge of the reality say, "Shall we show you the man who claims to be a Nabi and that you will be (recreated) in a new creation after completely disintegrating into dust and particles?"

8. "Has he invented a lie about Allah or is he afflicted with madness?" On the contrary, those who do not believe in their eternal life to come are in suffering and a deviation that is extremely far (from the reality).

9. Did they not see what is before them and after them (past and future) of the heaven (consciousness) and earth (the body)? If We should will, We could cause the earth to swallow them (drown them in corporeality by means of our Names) or make fragments from the sky fall upon them (turn all their thoughts upside down)! Indeed, there is a sign in this for every servant who turns (to his reality).

10. Indeed, We bestowed a favor upon David from Us. We said, "O mountains (beings with an ego) repeat My tasbih with him and the birds (those who observe with the knowledge)!" And We softened (belief in the reality) for him that which is sharp (iron-bullet like truth).

11. "Form an exquisite thought system to shield you, and fulfill the requisites of your faith! Indeed, I am Basir of what you do."

12. And to Solomon we subjected (that which moves like the) wind, whose morning course was a month and evening course a month! We caused a fount of copper to flow for him! And by the permissibility of his Rabb, some (the Ifrit type) of the jinni (invisible beings) worked before him. And whoever abandons Our command We will make him taste the suffering of a scorching fire. (If we consider this 'fount of copper' in light of the 'molten copper' Dhulqarnain uses to build the set against the Agog and Magog, it becomes obvious that this is not in reference to a physical-material situation in the general sense, but to something else altogether. Also taking into account the fact that both Dhulqarnain [one with double horns – or antennas perhaps?] and Solomon had providence over invisible beings, approaching this not as the iron element per se, but the use of the force in its elemental composition may allow us to gain different perspectives. I do not wish to delve into this any further.)

13. They made for him (Solomon) whatever he desired: temples, statues, pools like reservoirs and stationary vessels... "Work for gratitude (true gratitude is the result of evaluation), O generation of David! So few of My servants are grateful (able to evaluate)."

14. When We commanded (the tasting of) death for him (Solomon), none made evident this truth to them (the jinni) other than the worm that ate away at his staff! When finally his staff (decomposed) and he fell down, the (Ifrit type) jinni realized (he had died)... But if they

34. To whichever city We sent a warner, the spoilt affluent ones therein said, "Indeed, we will not accept this knowledge of the reality sent through your Risalah."

35. And, "We are more powerful than you, both with our wealth and our offspring... We will not be subject to suffering!"

36. Say, "Indeed, my Rabb expands the life sustenance (provision) for whom he wills and constricts it for whom He wills (wealth is not acquired; it is a bestowal by Allah)... But the majority of the people do not know (this truth)."

37. It is neither your wealth nor your offspring that can bring you nearer to Us ('the Station of Nearness' – conscious application of the qualities of the Names of Allah), but being a believer and fulfilling the requisites of your faith... For them the rewards of their deeds will be multiplied manifold. They are safe within elevated stations.

38. As for those who rush about to invalidate Our signs (warnings), they will be held in constant suffering.

39. Say, "Indeed, my Rabb expands the life sustenance (physical and spiritual nourishment) for whom He wills among His servants and constricts it (for whom He wills)! If you give something (unrequitedly for the sake of Allah), He will replace it with something else... HU is the absolute Razzaq, the sustainer with His sustenance.

40. At that time He will gather them all and say to His angels, "Was it only these who served you?"

41. (The angels) will say, "Subhan, You are. It is You who is our guardian not them... On the contrary they used to worship the jinni, most of them had believed in them (as their gods)."

42. And that is the time during which no one can be of any benefit or harm to another... And to those who wronged themselves, We will say, "Taste the suffering of the very burning that you denied!"

43. And when Our verses were openly recited to them, the (wrongdoers) said, "This man intends to avert you from what your forefathers have been worshipping"... And, "These are nothing but fabrication"... When the Truth came to those who denied the knowledge of the reality, they said, "This is clearly magic."

44. **Whereas We had not given them any information** (that they can use against you) **for them to take a lesson. And We had not disclosed any warner to them before you either.**

45. **But those before them had also denied** (a genetic attribute)! (While) **these have not even attained a tenth of what We had given them...** (Despite this) **they denied Our Rasuls... So, look at the result of My denial of them!**

46. **Say, "I give you only one advice: Contemplate upon Allah, either in pairs or individually! There is no madness in the one who is protecting you... He is only a warner to you before a severe suffering!"**

47. **Say, "If I have asked for something in return, keep it... My payment is only from Allah... HU is Shahid over all things."**

48. **Say, "Indeed, my Rabb projects the Truth in all its might! He is the Knower of the Unknown!"**

49. **Say, "The Truth has become evident! Falsity can neither create something new nor restore the old!"**

50. **Say, "If I deviate** (from the right belief) **this deviance will be from my consciousness** (the misleading of my mind)! **But if I attain the reality this will be with what my Rabb reveals to me... Indeed, He is the Sami, the Qarib."**

51. **You should see them when they are in fear and terror! They have nowhere to run; they are seized from close by!**

52. **They said, "We have believed in Him** (as the One in our essence)"... (But if that were really the case), **how could they have fallen so far!**

53. **They had denied the reality before, indulging in conjectures about their unknown, far from the reality.**

54. **A barrier is put between them and their desires, as done in the past to their like! Indeed, they are in a discomforting doubt.**

35

FATIR

By the one who is denoted by the name Allah (who created my being with His Names in accord with the meaning of the letter 'B'), the Rahman, the Rahim.

1. **Hamd belongs to Allah, the Fatir** (who creates everything programmed according to its purpose) **of the heavens and the earth, who discloses the angels** (conscious forces driving specific functions) **as Rasuls with two, three, four functions! He adds to His creation whatever He wills... Indeed, Allah is Qadir over all things.**

2. **If Allah wills to bestow grace upon people, no one can withhold it! And if He withholds it, none can disclose it thereafter! HU is the Aziz, the Hakim.**

3. **O people... Consider the blessing of Allah upon you! Is there, besides Allah, a creator who creates for you sustenance from the heaven** (the data in your brain) **and the body** (the brain – body)? **There is no deity-god, only HU! How you deviate** (from the Truth)!

4. **If they deny you,** (know that) **they denied all the Rasuls before you too! The judgment regarding what transpires belongs to Allah.**

5. **O people! Indeed, the promise of Allah is true! Let not the life of the world** (the bodily life) **deceive you... And let not the great deceiver** (your mind) **make you arrogant towards Allah!**

6. **Indeed, the devil** (the conception formed in the brain via the impulses sent by the organs in the body that your existence in confined to the body) **is an enemy to you** (taking you away from Allah, your essential reality)! **So, take him as your enemy! It** (the belief that you are only the body) **invites its followers to become companions of a blazing fire!**

7. **There is severe suffering for those who deny the knowledge of the reality. As for those who believe and fulfill the requisites of their faith, there is forgiveness and a great reward for them.**

8. (How can) **the one whose bad deeds are made to seem attractive, so he thinks he is good** (be equal to those who are truly good?)!

449

Indeed, Allah leads astray whom He wills and guides whom He wills... So, do not despair over those who are in loss! Indeed, Allah is Aleem of what they do (as their Creator).

9. It is Allah who disclosed the winds (rahmani knowledge) and thus drives the clouds (the black clouds formed in one's mind as a result of emotions and conditionings)... Then We drove them (the rahmani knowledge) to a dead land (consciousness) and gave life to the earth (the body) while it was dead! Thus is the resurrection (the return to the essence)!

10. Whoever desires honor (let him know first that) honor belongs entirely to Allah (one who thinks of himself as a separate being cannot have honor due to the duality he is in)! Creations, good and pure, reach Him, and are raised by fulfilling the requisites of faith (the word 'raise' here refers to the fulfilling of the deeds that are the requisites of one's faith in his essential reality as they save one from the ego and enable one to reach Allah). But those who scheme bad things, for them there is a severe suffering... And their schemes will amount to nothing!

11. Allah created you from dust, then from a fertilized cell, then formed you as pairs (double helix DNA). No female (producer) can either become pregnant (produce) or give birth (form a new creation) outside His knowledge (what is recorded in the genetic helix)... The life span of each living being is indeed recorded in a book (the creational genetic codes)! This is certainly easy for Allah.

12. Not equal are the two seas! One is sweet and quenches thirst, pleasing and easy to drink... The other is salty and bitter... From each one you eat fresh meat and extract ornaments to wear... And you see ships sailing through them, so that you seek of His bounty and are grateful.

13. He transforms the night into the day, and the day into the night... He has given functions to the Sun and the Moon... Each one runs its course for a specified time... Thus is Allah, your Rabb! Sovereignty is for Him (for the manifestation and observation of His Names)! Those to whom you turn besides Him (assuming they exist) do not have sovereignty over the membrane of a date seed.

14. If you call out to them, they will not hear your call! And if they do, they cannot respond to you! (Furthermore) they will deny your deification of them during Doomsday... None can inform you like the One who is Habir.

15. O people! You are in (absolute) **need of Allah** (for you exist with His Names)! **But Allah is the Ghani, the Hamid.**

16. If He wills he can do away with you and manifest a completely new creation (of His Names)!

17. This is not (a problem) **for Allah, who is the Aziz** (the possessor of irresistible force)!

18. No bearer of guilt can bear the burden of another... And if one whose burden is heavy, calls out for his burden to be carried, nothing of it will be carried... Even if it is a relative! You can only warn those who are in awe of their Rabb, their unknown, and who establish salat... Whoever purifies and cleanses himself only purifies for the benefit of his own self. The return is to Allah.

19. Not equal are the blind and the seeing.

20. Nor are the darknesses (ignorance) **and Nur** (knowledge)!

21. Nor are the shade (consciousness; the forces of the Names) **and the heat** (the bodies)!

22. And not equal are the living (through the knowledge of the reality) **and the dead** (those who think they will become inexistent with death)! **Indeed, Allah will enable whom He wills to hear... But you do not have the function to make hear those who are in their graves** (cocoons – those who are living in the world projected by their brain)!

23. You are certainly only a warner!

24. Indeed, We have disclosed you as the Truth, as a giver of good news and as a warner! There is no community to whom a warner has not come.

25. If they deny you, (then know that) **those before them also denied. Their Rasuls came to them as clear proofs and wisdom and enlightening information.**

26. Then I seized those who denied the knowledge of the reality... And how was My reproach (for denying Me)!

27. Did you not see how Allah disclosed water (knowledge) **from the sky... With it We produced fruits of various colors** (various thoughts)**... And in the mountains** (beings with egos) **tracts of white, red of various shades and black** (various lifestyles and life paths).

28. And there are also those with various colors among the creatures (different bodies – races) **and cattle** (animalistic properties)! **Among His servants, only those who have knowledge** (of what is denoted by the name Allah and who are aware of its Might) **are truly in awe of Allah** (realize their nothingness in respect of His magnificence)! **Indeed, Allah is the Aziz, the Ghafur.**

29. Indeed, those who 'read' Allah's Book, establish salat and who give unrequitedly, both secretly and openly, in the way of Allah from the sustenance with which We nourish them, can be sure they have made an investment that will never incur a loss!

30. He gives to them what they deserve in full and increases it from His bounty... Indeed, He is the Ghafur, the Shakur.

31. That which We have revealed to you from the knowledge (Book) **of the reality and sunnatullah is the very Truth that confirms what came before it! Indeed, Allah, as the presence with His Names in His servants, is the Habir and the Basir.**

32. Then We made the servants whom We chose inherit the knowledge of the reality and sunnatullah! Some of them wrong themselves (their lifestyles do not do justice to this knowledge) **and some who are moderate** (are in tune with their essence some times and fall into corporeality at other times) **and some who, with the permission of Allah** (B-iznillah; the permissibility of the Names manifesting from his essence), **advance with the good they do – their lifestyles... This is surely a great bounty, supremacy!**

Note: A hadith in relation to this verse: Narrated by Abu Darda (ra), "I heard the Rasul of Allah (saw) recite this verse (32nd verse) after which he said, 'He who advances ahead with his good deeds will go to Paradise without giving any account... The moderate one will be called to an easy account... But the one who wrongs himself, he will be made to sit at a station until sadness and sorrow afflicts him, then he will be admitted to Paradise' then he recited the verse, 'Hamd belongs to Allah (the possessor of all forces) who has removed from us all sorrow... Indeed, our Rabb is the Ghafur, the Shakur.' (34th verse)" (Musnad-i A. Hanbal)

33. They will enter Paradises of Eden (a life established upon the forces of the Names)**... There they will be adorned with bracelets of gold and pearls... There their garments will be silk.**

34. (Those who enter the life of the Paradise of Eden) **say, "Hamd belongs to Allah** (the possessor of all forces) **who has removed from us all sorrow... Indeed, our Rabb is the Ghafur, the Shakur."**

35. He who, from His bounty, has settled us in an everlasting abode (a body/form by which we are enabled to experience the life of Paradise)**... In it neither fatigue nor weariness can touch us.**

36. As for those who deny the knowledge of the reality, there is a hellish burning for them... Death will not be decreed for them, so they cannot die nor will their suffering be lightened... This is how We recompense everyone who is ungrateful (of the knowledge of the reality).

37. They will cry therein, "Our Rabb! Take us out (from our conditionings) **so we may do what is necessary, rather than what we were doing"...** (They will be answered)**, "Did We not allow you life enough for those with the capacity to contemplate therein to contemplate? And a warner came to you! So taste** (what you have prepared for yourself)**! There are no helpers for the wrongdoers."**

38. Indeed, Allah knows the unknown of the heavens (the capacity of the brain founded on the reality of the Names) **and the earth** (what is contained within the brain)**... Indeed, He, as the Absolute Essence of what is within your breasts** (your depths)**, is Aleem** (of the reality).

39. It is HU who has made you vicegerents upon the earth (the caliphate attribute is 'established' not 'created'. This fine distinction should be pondered upon with care!)**... Whoever is ungrateful** (whoever denies his vicegerency for the sake of individual values and bodily pleasures) **denies** (the reality) **against himself! And the denial of those who deny the knowledge of the reality increases them only hatred in the sight of their Rabb!**

40. Say, "Did you see your alleged partners – friends whom you worshipped besides Allah? Show me, what did they create on earth (what did they administer in your body)**?"... Or do they have a share in the heavens** (did they form a new understanding of knowing the self in your consciousness while you thought you were your body)**? Or did We give them the knowledge of the reality** (the Book) **on which they are standing as evidence? On the contrary, the wrongdoers do not promise each other anything but delusion.**

41. Indeed, Allah is holding the heavens and the earth lest they cease their functions! For if they were to cease their functions none

can hold them (in place) other than Him... Indeed, He is the Halim, the Ghafur.

42. They swore in the name of Allah (saying Billahi) with all their strength that if a warner came to them, they would be more guided than (any) of the previous people... But when a warner came to them, (this) increased nothing in them except for hatred!

43. (They turned away) in arrogance (egotistically), scheming evil... But the scheme of evil encompasses only those who scheme it! Are they awaiting one who follows a way other than the sunnah (the system and order of Allah) that the previous people followed? You will never encounter an alternative for sunnatullah. You will never find an alteration in the sunnatullah!

44. Did they not travel the earth and see with insight the end met by those before them? They (the previous people) were mightier than they... Nothing in the heavens or the earth can render Allah ineffective! Indeed, Allah is the Aleem, the Qadir.

45. Had Allah willed to subject people to the consequences of their actions immediately, there would be no creature (human body) left (alive) on earth! But He provides respite until the end of the specified term (for their bodily life). When their death comes (their affairs in the world will end)! Indeed, Allah, with His Names, is Basir within the very existence of His servants.

36

YA-SIN

By the one who is denoted by the name Allah (who created my being with His Names in accord with the meaning of the letter 'B'), **the Rahman, the Rahim.**

1. Ya Sin (O Muhammad)!

2. And the Quran full of wisdom (which he disclosed)!

3. You are most definitely of the Rasuls.

4. Upon a straight path.

5. With the comprehensive knowledge disclosed to you by the One who is the Aziz, the Rahim.

6. So that you may warn a people whose forefathers have not been warned and thus who live cocooned (from their reality, the sunnatullah).

7. Indeed, the word ("Hell will be filled with the majority of humans and the jinni") **has come true for most of them! Because of this they do not believe.**

8. Indeed, We have formed shackles (conditionings and judgments) **around their necks up to their chins! Their heads are aloft** (they are unable to see their essential reality; they live driven by their egos)!

9. And We have formed a barrier before them and after them (they can neither see their future nor take lessons from their past) **and thus We covered them... They can no longer see.**

10. Whether you warn them or do not warn them, it is all the same; they will not believe!

11. You can only warn the one who remembers (the reality that is reminded) **and who is in awe of the Rahman, as his unknown. Give him the good news of forgiveness and an abundant reward.**

12. Indeed, it is We, yes only We, who can bring the dead to life! We write their deeds and what they put forth! We record everything (with all its detail) **in a Clear Book** (in their brains and their spirits).

13. **Give them the example of the people of that city to which the Rasuls had come.**

14. **When We sent two Rasuls to them and they denied them both...** Upon this **We sent a third one and strengthened him, and they** (the Rasuls) **said, "Indeed, We have been disclosed to you."**

15. **They responded, "You are not but mere humans like us... And the Rahman has not disclosed anything... You are but liars."**

16. (The Rasuls) **said, "Our Rabb knows, we have indeed been disclosed to you."**

17. **"We are only responsible for clear notification."**

18. **They said, "Indeed, we think you are a bad omen... So, if you do not desist we will definitely stone you to death and a severe suffering will afflict you from us."**

19. **They said, "Your bad omen is from you...** (Is it a bad omen) **because you are reminded** (of your reality)**? No, you are a wasteful people."**

20. **Then a man came running from the farthest end of the city, saying, "O my people, follow the Rasuls."**

21. **"Follow those who do not ask you for anything in return, who are upon the reality!"**

22. **"How can I not serve the One who gave me this disposition? To Him you will be returned."**

23. **"Shall I take gods besides Him! If the Rahman wills to manifest adversity, their intercession will neither benefit me nor protect me..."**

24. **"In that case, I would be in clear error!"**

25. **"I have indeed believed in the Rabb manifest in you, listen to me!"**

26. (They were told) **"Enter Paradise!"** He said, **"I wish my people knew my state!"**

27. "How my Rabb forgave me and placed me among those who are the receivers of generosity (the Name Karim)."

28. After that We did not disclose upon his people any army from the heavens, nor would We have done so.

29. There was only a single cry, and immediately they were extinguished!

30. What a loss for those servants! Whenever a Rasul came to them, they used to mock and ridicule his message.

31. Did they not see how many generations We destroyed before them, and that none of them will return!

32. And indeed, all of them will be brought present (forcefully).

33. The dead earth is also a sign for them! We brought it to life, and brought forth from it produce of which they eat...

34. And formed therein gardens with date palms and grapevines, and caused springs to gush.

35. So that they eat its fruit and what their hands produce... Are they still not grateful?

36. Subhan is He who created all pairs (DNA helix) from what the earth (body) produces and from themselves (their consciousness) and from that which they don't know!

37. The night is also a sign for them! We pull the day (light) out of it and they are left in darkness.

38. And the Sun runs on its course! This is the determination of the Aziz, the Aleem.

39. As for the Moon, We have appointed stations to it... Until it finally becomes like an old date stalk.

40. Neither will the Sun overtake the Moon nor the night outpace the day! Each floats in its own orbit.

41. And a sign for them are the ships We carried full with their progeny!

42. And that We created for them the like of it in which they can ride!

43. And if We should will, We could drown them, and there will be none to help them, nor will they be saved!

44. Except if We give them a specified life term as grace from Us so that they may benefit.

45. But when they are told, "Protect yourselves from what is before you (the things you will encounter) and what is behind you (the consequences of the things you did in the past) so that you may receive grace" they turn away.

46. And no proof comes to them of the signs of their Rabb from which they do not turn away.

47. And when they are told, "Give unrequitedly from the sustenance with which Allah nourishes you," those who deny the knowledge of the reality say to the believers, "Shall we feed those who, if Allah had willed, He would have fed? You are only in clear error."

48. They say, "If you are true to your word, (tell us) when will this promise (be fulfilled)?"

49. They do not await anything except a single cry (the blowing of the horn [body]), which will seize them while they are disputing.

50. At that time they will neither have the strength to make a bequest nor will they be able to return to their families!

51. And the horn has been blown! At once you will see them leave their graves (bodies) and hasten towards their Rabb (to the realization of their essence)!

52. They will say, "Woe to us! Who has delivered us from our sleeping place (the world) to a new state of existence? This must be the promise of the Rahman; the Rasuls have indeed told the Truth." (Hadith: Mankind is asleep; with death, they will awaken!)

53. Only a single blow (of Israfil's horn) took place... At once they are all brought present before Us.

54. At that time, no soul shall be wronged in any way... You will not be recompensed, except for what you did (you will only live the consequences of your own actions)!"

55. The people of Paradise, at that time, will be occupied with the joy and amusement of the blessings of Paradise.

56. They and their partners shall recline on couches in the shade.

57. They shall have fruits therein... And whatever pleasurable things they shall desire.

58. "Salam," a word from a Rahim Rabb shall reach them (they will experience the manifestation of the Name Salam)!

59. "O guilty ones! Stand apart!"

60. O Children of Adam... Did I not enjoin upon you (inform you), O children of Adam, that you not serve Satan (body/bodily and unconscious state of existence deprived of the knowledge of the reality; ego driven existence), **for indeed, he** (this state of unconsciousness) **is to you a clear enemy?**

61. And that you serve only Me (experience and feel the requisites of the reality), **as this is the straight path** (sirat al-mustaqim)?

62. Indeed, (your belief that you are only the body and that you will become inexistent when you die) **has caused many of you to go astray! Did you not use your intellect?**

63. So, here is the Hell that you have been promised!

64. Experience the results of denying your essential reality now!

65. We will seal their mouths at that time, their hands will speak to Us, and their feet will bear witness about what they have done.

66. And if We willed We could have blinded their eyes and they would have rushed about on the path... But how could they see (this Truth)?

67. And if We willed We could have paralyzed them in their places (fixated them upon their current understanding) **and they would not be able to move forward, nor go back to their old states.**

68. And to whom We grant a long life, We weaken in creation. Do they still not use their intellect?

69. We did not teach him poetry! Nor is it befitting for him! It is only a reminder and a clear Quran!

70. To warn the living and justify the word against the deniers of the reality.

71. Do they not see how We created sacrificial animals for them among Our creation... And they are their owners?

72. We tamed them (cattle) for them... And on some of them they ride, and some of them they eat.

73. And for them therein are benefits and drinks... Are they still not grateful?

74. They took gods besides Allah, hoping they could be helped!

75. They (the gods) cannot help them! (On the contrary) they are like soldiers (in service) to their gods!

76. So, let not their words grieve you... Indeed, We know what they conceal and what they reveal.

77. Did man not see how We created him from sperm... Despite this, he is now an open enemy!

78. He forgets his own creation and presents for Us an example saying, "Who will give life to the bones when they have rotted away?"

79. Say, "He who brought them to life in the first place will resurrect them and give them life! HU is Aleem of every creation with His Names."

80. It is He who produced fire for you from a green tree, from which you kindle fire!

81. Is He who created the heavens and the earth not able to create their like with His Names? Yes! HU is the Hallaq, the Aleem.

82. Indeed, when He wills a thing, His command is 'Kun – be' (He merely wishes it to be), and it is (formed with ease)!

83. Subhan is He in whose hand (governance) is the Malakut (the force of the Names) of all things, and to Him you will be returned (the illusory self – ego will come to an end and the Absolute Reality will be discerned).

37

AS-SAFFAT

By the one who is denoted by the name Allah (who created my being with His Names in accord with the meaning of the letter 'B'), **the Rahman, the Rahim.**

1. By those (forces that form the various dimensions) **lined up in rows.**

2. And those who drive away with intensity (the things which prevent and blind one from Allah).

3. And those who recite the dhikr (remembrance).

4. Indeed, (that which you think of as) **your god is One** (the Wahid)!

5. He is the Rabb (the One who manifests with His Names) **of the heavens and the earth and everything in between, and the Rabb of the Easts** (origin – that which will become manifest)!

6. Indeed, We have adorned earth's heaven (configured man's brain) **with planets** (astrological data).

7. And protected it (earth's atmosphere) **from every rebellious Satan** (the purified consciousness is beyond the reach of illusory impulses).

8. Thus they (those devils) **cannot listen to the exalted assembly** (Mala-i Ala) **and are pelted from every side.**

9. Rejected... For them is a constant suffering.

10. Except if one snatches a word, a blazing flame shall pursue him.

11. So, ask them (those who deny you) **what they think. Are they more powerful in terms of their creation or** (those) **that We created? Indeed, We created man from a sticky clay.**

12. No, you are surprised by their mockery.

13. Even when they are reminded, they do not remember and take heed!

14. When they see a sign, they ridicule it.

15. They say, "This is plainly an effect of sorcery."

16. "Will we really be resurrected after we die and become dust and bones?"

17. "Along with our forefathers?"

18. Say, "Yes, indeed! (You shall be resurrected) with your heads lowered and in misery."

19. A single cry and then they will be looking on!

20. "Woe to us! This is the Day of Religion!" they will say.

21. "This is the time of discernment, which you denied!"

22. Gather those wrongdoers (individual consciousness) and their partners (the bodies) and the things they deified and served...

23. Besides Allah! And send them to path of Hell!

24. Stop them! Indeed, they are responsible!

25. What is wrong with you (today) that you are not helping each other?

26. Rather, today, they have succumbed and surrendered!

27. They will question and blame each other!

28. "Indeed, you came to us from the right (as though you are informing us of the Truth)?"

29. "No, rather, you yourselves did not believe (in what you were taught)!"

30. "And we had no authority over you... But you were a transgressing people."

31. "But now our Rabb's word has come into effect! Now we are bound to taste (the suffering)."

32. "We led you astray, but indeed we were astray!"

33. Indeed, they will be partners in the suffering.

34. This is how We deal with those who are guilty of duality!

35. When they were told to accept the Truth, "There is no god, only Allah," they were egocentric!

36. Saying, "Shall we leave our gods for a poet possessed?"

37. No, rather, he has come as the Truth and confirmed the Rasuls.

38. Indeed, you will be tasters of the painful suffering!

39. And you will not be recompensed, except for what you did (your own actions)!

40. Except for (exempt from suffering are) **Allah's servants who have been guided to sincerity** (purity).

41. There is a known (pre-determined) **provision for them.**

42. Fruits (the products of the forces they attained)... **They will be receivers of generosity** (the Name Karim).

43. In the Paradises of Bliss.

44. On thrones facing one another.

45. Cups (forces) **from a flowing spring** (the reality of the Names) **are passed around.**

46. White (with the light of gnosis) **cups** (forces) **and pleasing to the drinkers** (its users).

47. There is no deviating effect in them... Nor will they be intoxicated from it (they will never lose consciousness)!

48. Besides them will be those whose glances will be directed upon them, illuminating (their lives).

49. As though they are eggs closely guarded (assisting in the manifestation of inherent forces).

50. They (those in Paradise) **will approach one another and inquire.**

51. One among them will say, "Indeed, I had a friend."

52. "Who used to say, 'Are you really of those who confirm (this knowledge)?'"

53. "Will we really be recompensed once we have died and become dust and bones?"

54. He will say, "Have you witnessed (this event you speak of)?"

55. Now they have experienced this, in fact they saw him right in the middle of Hell.

56. He said, "By Allah, you almost rolled me into this pit."

57. "Had it not been for the favor of my Rabb, I would definitely have been of those brought forcefully before the gate (of Hell)."

58. "Are we not of those who are freed from the condition (restriction) of the body?"

59. "Except for our first experience of death (we shall not die again)! And we are not to be punished either."

60. "Indeed, this is the great success."

61. So let those who work, work for this!

62. Is this better, in terms of disclosure, or the Zaqqum tree (the person's body)? (Up to here, the subject was in regards to the experience of the paradisiacal state of existence, brought into effect by the forces of the Names the person manifests through faith. After this, the subject changes, via various examples and similitudes, to the hellish state of existence produced by the belief 'I am this body' and the pursuit of bodily pleasures.)

63. Indeed, We made it (the Zaqqum tree – the body) an object of trial (to see if they will remember their essence or if they will live as though they are the body).

64. Indeed, it is a tree (biological body) sourced in Hell (producing the sense of burning).

65. Its fruits (the result of thinking you are the body) are like the heads of the devils (the instinctual impulses).

66. Indeed, they will eat from it (throughout their worldly life) and fill their bellies with it.

67. After this there will be scalding water (the ego self) for them.

68. Then indeed, their place of return will be Hell.

69. For they found their forefathers astray (from the reality).

70. So they incessantly follow in their footsteps.

71. **Indeed, most of the former people before them had also gone astray** (from the reality)!

72. **And indeed, We had disclosed warners within them.**

73. **Look at how those who were warned ended up!**

74. **Only the servants of Allah, who were guided to sincerity** (purity), **were exempt from this.**

75. **Indeed, Noah had turned to us... And We are the best of responders.**

76. **We saved him and his family from a great affliction.**

77. **And We continued his progeny.**

78. **And made sure he was remembered by later generations.**

79. **Salam be to Noah among the people.**

80. **Thus We reward the doers of good** (those who observe none other than Allah)!

81. **Indeed, he is of Our believing servants.**

82. **Then We drowned the rest** (the dualists).

83. **Indeed, Abraham was of the same understanding.**

84. **He had turned to his Rabb with a sound heart** (experiencing the reality of the Names in his consciousness)!

85. **When** (Abraham) **had asked his people, "What are you worshipping?"**

86. **"Are you taking gods besides Allah by inventing baseless things?"**

87. **"What do you think the Rabb of the worlds is?"**

88. **Then** (Abraham) **observed the stars** (through his intellect) **and contemplated...**

89. **He said, "I am sickened** (by what you do)!"

90. **And they turned away from him and departed.**

91. So (Abraham) **approached their gods and said, "Will you not eat?"**

92. "Why won't you speak?"

93. Then approaching them he struck the idols with his right hand!

94. Upon seeing this, his people came back in a rush.

95. (Abraham) **said, "How can you take as gods and worship things you carve with your own hands?"**

96. "While it is Allah who created you and all your doings!"

97. They said, "Build a furnace and throw him into the burning (fire)**!"**

98. They intended a trap for him... But We debased them to the lowest of the low.

99. (Abraham) **said, "Indeed, I will go to by Rabb... He will guide me."**

100. (Abraham) **said, "My Rabb, grant me from among the righteous!"**

101. So We gave him the good news of a Halim son.

102. When (his son Ishmael) **reached the age when he could walk with him** (Abraham) **said, "O my son! Indeed, I have seen in my dream that I was sacrificing you... What do you say about this?"** (His son) **said, "O my father... Do as you are commanded! InshaAllah, you will find me to be of the patient."**

103. And when they had both submitted and he lay him (Ishmael) **down upon his forehead...**

104. We called out to him, "O Abraham!"

105. "You have indeed fulfilled your dream... Thus We requite (enable the consequences upon) **the doers of good** (those who observe none other than the Truth)**."**

106. Indeed, this is a clear affliction (a learning experience that leads to awareness/comprehension)**!**

107. And We ransomed him with a great sacrifice.

108. And made sure he was remembered by later generations.

109. Salam be to Abraham.

110. **Thus We requite the doers of good** (those who fulfill their servitude as though they can see Allah).

111. **Indeed, he is of our believing servants.**

112. **And We gave him the good news of Isaac, a Nabi from among the righteous.**

113. **And We blessed him and Isaac with prosperity...** There are doers of good from among both of their descendants and those who clearly wrong themselves.

114. **And We also bestowed Our favor upon Moses and Aaron!**

115. **We saved those two and their people from a great affliction.**

116. **We helped them and they prevailed.**

117. **We gave to those two** (Moses and Aaron) **the explicit knowledge.**

118. **And guided them to the straight path.**

119. **And made sure they were remembered by later generations.**

120. **Salam be to Moses and Aaron!**

121. **Thus We requite the doers of good** (those who serve Allah as though they can see Him)!

122. **Indeed, both of them were of our believing servants.**

123. **Indeed, Elias was also of those disclosed.**

124. **When he said to his people, "Will you not protect yourselves?"**

125. **"Do you worship Baal** (a statue with four faces made of gold) **and abandon the most beautiful of creators?"**

126. **"Your Rabb is Allah, the Rabb of your forefathers!"**

127. **But they denied him** (Elias)! **Indeed, they were forcefully brought to presence!**

128. **Except those servants of Allah who have been guided to sincerity** (purity).

129. And we made sure he was remembered by later generations.

130. Salam be to those who follow the way of Elias!

131. Thus We requite the doers of good (those who serve Allah as though they can see Him).

132. Indeed, he is of Our believing servants.

133. Indeed, Lot was also of those who were disclosed.

134. When We saved him and those close to him all together.

135. Except the old woman (Lot's wife who was an unbeliever) **among those who remained.**

136. Then We destroyed the others!

137. Indeed, you pass by their homes in the morning...

138. And at night... Do you still not use your intellect?

139. Indeed, Jonah was also of those who were disclosed (a manifestation of the knowledge of the reality).

140. When he ran away to the ship (returned to his ordinary life despite the knowledge of the reality, thinking he was of no benefit to his people).

141. (Jonah) **drew lots** (made a choice) **and was among those whose proof was invalidated** (his choice led him astray)...

142. Then the fish (the life of the world) **swallowed him** (Jonah) **while he was blaming himself** (confused with feelings of guilt);

143. Had (Jonah) **not been of those who remember** (their essential function; had he not turned his countenance towards Allah through remembrance – taspih, feeling his essence);

144. He (Jonah) **would have remained inside the fish until the time of resurrection** (he would have remained in a state of corporeality until his time of death).

145. But We cast him onto the land (where the forces are not known), **while he was ill** (and worn out).

146. And caused a gourd tree (a trunkless tree) **to grow over him** (manifested fruits of divine gnosis through him).

147. And disclosed him (Jonah) to a hundred thousand (people) **or more.**

148. They believed, so We made them live in joy for some time.

149. So, ask them (the unbelievers), **"Are daughters for your Rabb, while sons are for them?"**

150. Or did We create the angels as females while they were watching?

151. Be careful, they slander and say:

152. "Allah has begotten children (Allah has a son)**! Indeed, they are liars!"**

153. Has (Allah) **chosen daughters over sons?**

154. What is wrong with you? How do you make such judgments?

155. Do you not remember and think?

156. Or do you have clear evidence?

157. If you are truthful then present what you know!

158. And they have assumed between Him (Allah) **and the jinn** (conscious beings outside the human capacity of perception) **a connection** (i.e. associated divinity to them), **but the jinn know well that, indeed, they** (who made such assumptions) **shall surely be summoned** (will realize such a connection does not actually exist)**!**

159. Allah is far beyond what they attribute to Him!

160. Except those servants of Allah who have been guided to sincerity (purity) (the rest are of those who shall be summoned).

161. Indeed, neither you nor what you worship,

162. Can never turn (those who are pure in essence) **against Him!**

163. Except those who are to burn in Hell.

164. (All the manifest angelic forces of the Names will say), **"There are none among us without an assigned function!"**

165. "Indeed, it is us, yes us, who are lined up in rows (forming the dimensions of existence and all that is contained within them).**"**

166. "Indeed, it is us, yes us, who engage in taspih (effectuate their servitude by fulfilling their functions)."

167. Indeed, they (the dualists) were saying:

168. "If only we had been passed down the knowledge from our forefathers..."

169. "Surely, we would also have been of the servants of Allah who have been guided to sincerity (purity)."

170. But now they denied the knowledge of the reality... Soon they will know!

171. And Our word has been fulfilled for Our disclosed servants:

172. That indeed, they will be given victory.

173. And indeed, Our soldiers are victorious!

174. So leave them for a time!

175. And observe them... Soon they will see!

176. Do they want to hasten the manifestation of Our punishment (death)? (Death is the beginning of suffering for those who deny their essential reality, while grace for the believers.)

177. How wretched is the awakening of those who were forewarned when it befalls them!

178. So leave them for a time.

179. Observe them... Soon they will see.

180. Your Rabb, the possessor of might, is far beyond what they ascribe!

181. Salam be to those who have been disclosed!

182. Hamd belongs to the Rabb of the worlds.

38

SAAD

By the one who is denoted by the name Allah (who created my being with His Names in accord with the meaning of the letter 'B'), the Rahman, the Rahim.

1. Saad... The Quran which is the reminder of your essential reality!

2. Look at those who deny the knowledge of the reality, yet think they are esteemed, how they are disconnected from the Truth!

3. How many a generation We have destroyed before them while they called out in agony! But it was not possible for them to escape!

4. Those who deny the knowledge of the reality are surprised that a warner has come to them from among themselves and say, "This is a magician and a liar."

5. "Has he reduced our gods to one god? This is a strange thing indeed!"

6. Their leaders walked on saying, "Continue and remain constant to your gods! For this is how it should be!"

7. "We have not heard this from the previous people! This (concept of non-duality and oneness) is but a fabrication!"

8. "Was the remembrance (dhikr) disclosed to him out of all of us?" No! They are in doubt of My remembrance (Me reminding them of their essence)! No, they have not yet tasted My punishment (death; the means to realizing the Truth)!

9. Or are the treasures (blessings) of your Rabb, the Aziz, the Wahhab, with them?

10. Or is the sovereignty of the heavens, the earth and everything between them theirs? If that is what they think then let them form the causes and rise (and see what they will gain)!

11. They are but defeated soldiers, remnants of those who are joined in disbelief.

12. Before them, the people of Noah, Aad (the people of Hud) and Pharaoh the owner of (mansions built upon) columns denied.

13. And Thamud (the people of Salih), the people of Lot (those who were destroyed by their bodily desires) and the people of the thicket (the people of Shuayb)... They were people who were joined in disbelief!

14. All of them denied the Rasuls... Thus, they deserved the wretched consequence of their deeds!

15. They only await a single cry (death) for which there is never delay.

16. They (mockingly) said, "Our Rabb! Hasten for us our share before the time during which the consequences of all deeds will be clearly faced!"

17. Be patient over what they say and remember David, the possessor of strength... Indeed, he was one who repeatedly turned to his essence.

18. Indeed, We subjected the mountains (those with ego) to fulfill their functions (taspih) in the evening and when the Sun rises to him.

19. And the assembled birds (those who believed in him)... All of them were those who repeatedly turned (to their essence).

20. We strengthened his sovereignty and gave him wisdom (the knowledge of causes) and discernment in speech (the ability to logically distinguish the right from the wrong).

21. Has the news of their argument come to you? How they climbed the wall and reached the prayer chamber?

22. How they entered upon David and he was alarmed by them... They said, "Do not be afraid, we are two adversaries, some of whom have wronged the other (this is a plural expression)... So, judge between us with truth; do not be unjust and guide us to middle/even (most correct) path."

23. "Indeed this, my brother, has ninety-nine ewes, and I have one ewe, so he said, 'Give her to me' and made me do so!"

24. (David) said, "He has certainly wronged you by adding your only ewe to his ewes... Indeed, many close associates oppress each other in similar ways... Only those who believe and fulfill the requisites of their faith are different... But they are so few!" David thought We had tried him and asked for forgiveness of his Rabb and turned to Him in prostration! (This is a verse of prostration.)

25. So We forgave him for him... For him there is closeness from Us and a good return.

26. O David! We have made you a vicegerent on earth! So judge between the people with Truth and do not follow your desires (thoughts and feelings not based on the Truth)! For this will lead you astray from the way of Allah... As for those who go astray from the way of Allah, they will be subject to intense suffering for forgetting the time of facing consequences.

27. And We did not create the heavens, the earth and everything in between without a function! Thinking (it has no function and purpose) is the assumption of those who deny the knowledge of the reality! So, woe to those who deny the knowledge of the reality in their burning (world)!

28. Or shall We treat those who believe (in their essential reality) and fulfill the requisites of their faith like those who live on earth (driven by their bodily lives) with corrupt beliefs? Or shall We treat those who protect themselves for Allah like the wicked ones (those who live against their natural disposition)?

29. This divine knowledge that We disclosed to you is for them to contemplate upon in depth and for the intelligent ones who have reached the essence to remember (the reality)!

30. And to David We bestowed Solomon; a beautiful servant he was! Indeed, he was one who repeatedly turned back (experienced his essential reality).

31. When there appeared before him in the afternoon (glamorously) well-bred poised racehorses.

32. (As he watched them, Solomon thought to himself): "I turned away from the remembrance (observation) of my Rabb to my love of horses"... And the horses disappeared from sight!

33. "Bring them back to me" (said Solomon)... And began to stroke their legs and necks (this time with conscious observation).

34. Indeed, We tried Solomon and placed a lifeless body on his throne (an heir with no faith)... Then he turned in repentance.

35. "My Rabb, forgive me (cover my identity) and bless me with a quality no one will ever need after me (a quality specific to me)... Indeed, you are the Wahhab"

36. So We subjected (that which moves like) the wind to his command; with it, he traveled wherever he willed, without causing harm to anything.

37. And We also subjected the devils to his service; the builders and divers!

38. And others chained together in fetters...

39. This (sovereignty over which you can rule) is Our gift to you; so grant or withhold, use it without limit!"

40. Indeed, for him there is closeness to Us and a good return.

41. And remember Our servant Job, when he called to his Rabb, "Indeed, Satan (the feeling of being this body) has given me hardship and torment."

42. So We said, "Strike the ground with your foot! This is the cool spring (the knowledge of the reality) that you can drink and bathe in."

43. And We granted him, his family and the like of them as grace from Us and a reminder for the intelligent ones who contemplate.

44. "Take in your hand a bunch and strike with it so that your promise may be fulfilled!" We found him to be patient... A beautiful servant he was! Indeed, he was one who repeatedly turned back (to Allah – one who often experienced his essential reality).

45. And remember our powerful and insightful servants Abraham, Isaac and Jacob as well!

46. Indeed, We bestowed upon them a pure life with the remembrance of their true home (their essential reality).

47. They are indeed in Our sight chosen, refined and purified.

48. And remember Ishmael, Elisha and Dhul-Kifl! All of them were among the outstanding.

49. This is a reminder! Indeed, there is a good place of return for those who are protected.

50. Paradises of Eden, whose gates are opened to them.

51. They will make themselves comfortable and ask for abundant fruits and drinks therein.

52. And with them will be peers (bodies) whose glances will be turned to them (to what they manifest). (Heavenly bodies suitable to their manifestation capacity who are ready to actualize the meanings manifesting from the forms of consciousness and have realized their essential reality with the Names [who have reached the station of certainty to their Rabb].)

53. This is it! This is the time of facing the consequences of your deeds, which you were promised!

54. Indeed, this is our life sustenance, which is never depleted!

55. This is it! Indeed, there is a wretched place of return for those who transgress.

56. Hell, on which they will lean! A wretched abode it is!

57. This is it! Let them taste it! Scalding water (burning ideas pertaining to the identity-self) and purulence (situations resulting from actions based on the idea of being the body)!

58. And others with their partners (both the identity-self and a matching body)!

59. This is a group enduring (hell) with you... They (those who led them astray) will say, "It is useless to say 'Welcome' (a re-assurance of comfort) to them... Indeed, they are subject to burning."

60. They (who followed those leaders) will say, "No, in fact it is you who is not 'welcome' (no well-being for you)... For it was you who led us to this (hell)! What a wretched settlement!"

61. They said, "Our Rabb! Whoever brought this upon us, double his suffering of burning."

62. They said, "Why can't we see the men who we used to think of as evil here?"

63. "We used to mock them... Or is our vision unable to see them here?"

64. Indeed, this will transpire... The quarreling of those who will burn!

65. Say, "Indeed, I am a warner! There is no god and the concept of godhood is invalid; there is only Allah, the Wahid, the Qahhar..."

66. "The Rabb of the heavens and the earth and everything in between, the Aziz (whose might is unchallengeable), the Gaffar."

67. Say, "(The Truth about) HU is a mighty news!" (If you can comprehend the meaning and value of this news!)

68. "But you turn away from it (from what you can gain from the reality disclosed by that mighty Truth)!"

69. "I have no knowledge of the discussions of the Mala-i Ala (the Exalted Assembly of angels)."

70. "It has not been revealed to me, except that I am a clear warner!"

71. And when your Rabb said to the angels, "Indeed, I will create a human being from clay (water plus minerals)."

72. So when I have proportioned him (formed his brain) and breathed into him (manifested through him; the word 'breath' which is 'nafh' in Arabic literally means to blow out, i.e. to project explicitly, to manifest, to materialize) of My spirit (My Names) prostrate to him (accept his sovereignty and administration).

73. So the angels prostrated, all of them entirely.

74. Except Iblis; he (relying on his mind) was arrogant and became of those who deny the knowledge of the reality (those who cannot recognize the essential reality of others due to their egos).

75. He said, "O Iblis (he who is in duality)! What prevented you from prostrating to that which I created with my two hands (knowledge and power)? Did your ego prevent you, or did you think you were among the Alun (sublime angelic forces to whom prostration to Adam does not apply)?"

76. (Iblis) **said, "I am better than him; You created me from fire** (radiation – burning waves – this word is the same word used to refer to the hellfire) **and created him from clay** (a cell-based material body)."

77. (Allah) **said, "Get out from there, for you are rajim** (fallen far from your essential reality)!"

78. "And certainly, upon you is My curse (separation from Me; inability to experience your essential reality, being trapped within your ego) **until the Day of Recompense** (the period in which the reality of the system will become clearly evident and thus experienced).

79. (Iblis) **said, "My Rabb! Reprieve me until the time of** (their death) **resurrection** (so that I may use my forces against them)."

80. (Allah) **said, "Indeed, you are of those reprieved!"**

81. "Until the specified time!"

82. (Iblis) **said, "I swear by Your might** (the unchallengeable power within my essence denoted by the secret of the letter B)**, I will surely mislead them all** (deviate them from spirituality, by making them confine their existence to their physical body and making them pursue their bodily pleasures).

83. "Except, among them, who are pure in essence (those to whom You have bestowed the experience of their essential reality)."

84. (Allah) **said, "You have spoken the truth** (in regards to my sincere-pure servants) **and let me also tell you a truth..."**

85. "I will surely fill hell with you and those who follow you, all together."

86. Say, "I do not ask you for anything in return for what I am informing you and I have not come to you with baseless claims."

87. "It is nothing other than a reminder for the worlds (humans)."

88. "You shall understand what it is before long (at the time of death)!"

39

AZ-ZUMAR

By the one who is denoted by the name Allah (who created my being with His Names in accord with the meaning of the letter 'B'), the Rahman, the Rahim.

1. This knowledge has been dimensionally disclosed to your consciousness from Allah, the Aziz, the Hakim!

2. Indeed, We have revealed the knowledge to you in Truth (disclosed it from the dimension of Names comprising your essence)! So, live the religion with the awareness of your servitude to Allah (the absolute judge and sovereign of the system and order within existence)!

3. Pay heed, genuine religion (the absolute system and order) is for (the manifestation of the Names of) Allah! Those who befriend others besides Him (assuming they have divine qualities) say, "We only worship them so they may take us closer to Allah"... Indeed, Allah will judge between them regarding that over which they argue... Indeed, Allah does not guide to the reality those who lie and deny the Truth.

4. If Allah had willed to have a child, He would surely have chosen from His creation... He is Subhan! Allah is the Wahid, the Qahhar!

5. He brought into existence the heavens and the earth as the Truth (with the qualities of His Names) while they were inexistent! He turns the night into the day and the day into your night... It is He who has appointed functions to the Sun and the Moon... Each one traverses its own orbit for a specified term... Pay heed, HU is the Aziz, the Gaffar.

6. He created you from a single soul (referenced as the cosmic consciousness – the universal self – the reality of Muhammad – the angel denoted as the Spirit)! Then (based on the holographic principle) He created his partner (the body), then manifested for you from the livestock eight mates (controllable animalistic senses)... He creates you in the wombs of your mothers within three darknesses, (transforming you from one) creation (to another) creation. That is Allah, your Rabb; to Him belongs sovereignty (the manifestations of the qualities

478

denoted by His Names)! **There is no god; only HU! How can you not see the reality!**

7. But if you cover the Truth (be ungrateful) (and do not evaluate your vicegerency [your ability to administer with the forces of the Names within your essence] on earth [the body] you will be curtained from your reality)**, indeed, Allah is Ghani from you!** (Allah) **is not pleased with his servants covering** (their essential reality and being ungrateful to their essence)**! If you are thankful** (and evaluate) **He will be accepting of you... No one can bear the burden of another! Then to your Rabb is your return! He will disclose to you the results of your deeds... Indeed, He is Aleem of what you contain inside** (your consciousness) **as its Absolute Essence** (he knows all that you reveal and conceal in full).

8. And when adversity touches man (as grace, in order to cleanse and develop him)**, he turns to Him and prays to his Rabb... Then when** (his Rabb) **bestows on him a favor from Himself, he forgets he had prayed to Him before and attributes equals to Allah to mislead from His way... Say, "Live a little in your denial... Indeed, you are of the people of the fire!"**

9. (Is this better or) **one who experiences prostration in the part of the night and stands** (with the Qayyum) **preparing for the requisites of the eternal life to come** (in a state of complete submission)**, in hope of the grace of his Rabb** (the manifestations of the various qualities pertaining to the Names comprising his essential reality)**? Say, "Can one who knows be equal to one who does not know? Only those with intellects that contemplate can discern this."**

10. Say, "O my servants who have believed, protect yourselves from your Rabb (for He will most definitely subject you to the consequences of all your deeds)**! For those who do good in this world... The earth of Allah** (the brain's capacity to manifest the Names) **is spacious... The reward of this will be given without account only to those who are patient."**

11. Say, "I have certainly been commanded to serve Allah without assuming any other agent in the system and order besides Him."

12. "I have been commanded (created) **to be the first of those who experience the awareness of their submission!"**

13. Say, "Indeed, I fear the suffering of a tremendous time, if I rebel against my Rabb (if I ignore His absolute administration within my existence)!"

14. Say, "So let me serve Allah without attributing any other agent besides Him within His system and order..."

15. "And you worship what you will besides Him!" Say, "The truth is, the losers during Doomsday are those who mislead themselves (their own consciousness) and their people (their bodies)! Be careful! That is the very loss!"

16. There are layers of fire above them (in respect of their consciousness) and levels beneath them (in respect of their bodies)... This is (the Truth); Allah manifests its fear in His servants! O my servants, protect yourselves from Me (for I will subject you, based on sunnatullah, the consequences of all your deeds)!

17. For those who refrain from deifying and worshipping their bodies (Taghut) and turn to Allah, there is good news... Give the good news to the servants (who manifest the qualities of the Names)!

18. They are (my servants) who listen to the word of Truth and follow the best (most protective) of it... Those are the ones Allah has guided to the reality and those are the ones with intellects capable of contemplation!

19. Can you save the (unfortunate) one who has been created to suffer from burning?

20. But those who protect themselves from their Rabb, there are chambers (ranks of Paradise) for them built above them (in the dimension of consciousness) underneath which rivers flow... This is the promise of Allah... There is never a change in the promise of Allah!

21. Did you not see that Allah disclosed water (knowledge) from the sky (consciousness, where the Names become manifest) and made it flow into springs (the brain) in the earth (the body)... Then He produces crops (products) of varying colors (dispositions) with its forces... Then they dry and you see them turned yellow (all things you value during its formation lose value after it is formed and lost)... Then He makes them scattered debris! Indeed, there is a lesson in this for intellects that contemplate!

22. Is he whose heart (essence) **Allah has expanded towards comprehending Islam, not upon a Nur** (knowledge) **disclosed by his Rabb** (his essential reality)? **Woe to those whose hearts are constricted** (tightened) **with the remembrance of Allah! They are experiencing clear deviation** (from the reality)!

23. Allah has sent down the best knowledge (in detail)**, allegoric and repeating** (with dual explanations and meanings)**... Causing the skins of those who are in awe of their Rabb to creep... Then their bodies and consciousness soften** (become receptive) **to the remembrance of Allah... This is the guidance of Allah by which He guides whom He wills to the reality! But one who Allah leads astray – there is none who can guide him.**

24. The one who will (helplessly) **try to shield himself with his face from the worst of punishments during Doomsday? The wrongdoers are told, "Taste what you have earned!"**

25. Those before them denied and suffering came to them from a place of which they were not aware.

26. Allah made them taste disgrace in the worldly life. But the suffering of the eternal life to come is surely greater! If only they knew!

27. And We have certainly presented for the people in this Quran from every kind of example that they might contemplate (remember their forgotten reality)!

28. (We revealed) **an Arabic Quran, flawless and without complication that perhaps they will understand and protect themselves.**

29. Allah presents an example: A man in the service of quarreling partners and a man who has submitted to only one master... Can they be equal in condition? Hamd belongs to Allah! No, the majority of them do not know!

30. You will most certainly taste death and they will most certainly taste death!

31. Then, during Doomsday you will most certainly be brought together before your Rabb.

32. Who can be worse than the one who lies about Allah and denies His intrinsic Truth when it comes to him? Is Hell not the dwelling place for those who deny the knowledge of the reality?

33. As for he who has brought the Truth (about being a servant to Allah and the reality of vicegerency being an experience in the body) and confirmed it (Hadhrat Abu Bakr) they are the protected ones!

34. For them there is everything they desire from their Rabb! This is the reward for the doers of good (those who serve Allah as though they can see Him)!

35. So that Allah may remove from them even the worst of their past deeds and reward them with the best of their deeds.

36. Is Allah not sufficient for His servant who He has created with His Names? Yet they threaten you with things besides Him! And whoever Allah leads astray – there is none who can guide him.

37. He who Allah guides (enables the observation of his innermost essential reality) can never be led astray! Is Allah not the Aziz (the One who manifests the qualities of this Name on His servants) and Zuntiqam (One who enforces the consequences of all deeds without any emotional interference)?

38. Indeed, if you were to ask them, "Who created the heavens and the earth?" They will surely say, "Allah"... Say, "Then have you seen (the place of) those you name besides Allah? If Allah wills an affliction for me, can they remove that affliction? Or if Allah wills grace for me, can they prevent His grace from me?" Say, "Sufficient is Allah for me! Those who trust, place their trust in Him as their Wakil!"

39. Say, "O my people! Do whatever you can, according to your understanding; as I too am doing... Soon you will know..."

40. "To whom is the degrading suffering (death) coming and to whom is the constant suffering (Hell) coming?"

41. Indeed, We disclosed that knowledge to you as the Truth for the people! So, whoever turns to the reality has turned for his own sake! And whoever deviates (from the reality) deviates against his own self! You are not their Wakil!

42. Allah causes people to die (renders their bodies dysfunctional) when it is time for them to taste death... And those that have not

died, (He takes to the world of consciousness) **during their sleep...
Then He keeps those for whom He has decreed death and releases
the others until a specified time... Indeed, there are signs in this for
people who contemplate.**

**43. Or did they take intercessors besides Allah? Say, "What if they
do not possess anything and are unintelligent?"**

44. Say, "Intercession belongs entirely to Allah! (For) **the
sovereignty of the heavens and the earth belongs to Him! Then to
Him you will be returned."**

**45. When they are reminded of the Oneness of Allah, those who do
not believe in their eternal life to come are not pleased! But when
those besides Him are mentioned, immediately they rejoice as
though they have been given good news!**

**46. Say, "O my Allah, the Fatir of the heavens and the earth, the
One who knows the unknown and the manifest, You judge between
Your servants over that which they dispute!"**

**47. If those wrongdoers had everything on the earth and the like of
it they would have given it to ransom themselves from the worst of
the suffering during Doomsday!** (For) **they encountered from Allah
that which they did not the least expect!**

48. The bad (consequences) **of their deeds became apparent to them;
the very thing they mocked enveloped them!**

**49. When man is afflicted with harm or an ailment he calls upon Us
for help... Then, when We bestow Our favor upon Him, he says, "It
was given to me because of my knowledge"... No, it** (the favor) **is an
object of trial! But the majority of them do not know this.**

**50. Those before them had also said it... But their earnings did not
give them any benefit.**

**51. In the end, the bad consequences they earned struck them...
And those who did wrong will be struck by the bad consequences
they earn... They cannot render** (Us) **helpless!**

**52. Did they not know that Allah extends and expands provision for
whom He wills and constricts it** (for whom He wills)**! Indeed, there
are signs in this for a people who believe.**

53. Say, "O my servants who have transgressed against themselves
(who have squandered their lives in pursuit of bodily pleasures rather than

duly experiencing their essential reality)! **Do not lose hope from the grace of Allah! Indeed Allah forgives all mistakes** (of those who repent)**... Indeed, He is the Ghafur, the Rahim."**

54. **Turn to your Rabb** (in repentance) **and surrender to Him before the suffering** (death) **comes... You will not be helped thereupon!**

55. **Before the suffering** (death) **comes to you suddenly while you are not aware, follow the best of what has been revealed to your from your Rabb!**

56. **A soul** (during that time) **will say, "Look at the longing** (the loss) **I have fallen into due to my inadequacy in knowing Allah! Indeed, I was among the mocked!** (I was unaware of the seriousness and importance of the matter!)**"**

57. **Or he shall say, "Had Allah guided me, I would surely have been among the protected ones."**

58. **Or when he sees the suffering he shall say, "If only I had another chance** (at a life with a body – brain) **so that I could be among the righteous."**

59. **"No, My signs came to you but you rejected and denied them, you were arrogant and you were of those who denied the knowledge of the reality!"**

60. **During Doomsday you will see the faces of those who lied about Allah blackened... Is Hell not the residence for those who were arrogant?**

61. **Allah leads those who protect themselves to liberation by their attainments! Bad does not touch them, nor will they grieve.**

62. **Allah is the Khaliq of all things... HU is Wakil over all things.**

63. **The keys of the heavens and the earth belong to Him! As for those who deny the existence of Allah in His signs, they are the very losers!**

64. **Say, "Do you order me to worship things besides Allah, O ignorant ones!"**

65. **I swear it was revealed to you and those before you, "Indeed, if you associate anything to Allah** (if you live in a state of duality – shirq) **all your work will become worthless and you will surely be of the losers!"**

66. **No, serve only Allah and be of those who are thankful** (evaluate the blessing of what it means to be a servant)!

67. **They could not duly appraise Allah! During Doomsday the earth will be within His grip and the heavens will be folded with His right hand... He is beyond what they associate with Him, He is the Aliy.**

68. **And the Horn is blown! And whoever is in the heavens and the earth will be struck by it and faint, except whom Allah wills... Then it is blown again, and they are all standing, looking on.**

69. **And the earth will shine with the light (Nur) of your Rabb, the Nabis and the witnesses will be brought and it will be judged between them in Truth without wronging anyone.**

70. **Every soul shall be given its due in full... He knows best what they do** (as the creator of their actions).

71. **Those who deny the knowledge of the reality will be driven to Hell in groups... When finally they reach it, its gate will open and its keepers will say, "Did there not come to you Rasuls from within you, informing you of the signs of your Rabb and warning you of the meeting of this day?" They will say, "Yes"... But alas, the promise of the suffering will have fulfilled itself upon those who deny the knowledge of the reality.**

72. **It will be said, "Enter the gates of Hell; you will abide therein eternally... Wretched is the place for the arrogant who could not let their egos go!"**

73. **But those who protect themselves from their Rabb** (who protect themselves from living a life based on their bodies) **will be driven to Paradise in groups... When they reach it and its gates are opened its keepers will say, "Salam to you! You have done well** (your formation is based on Truth)**... Enter to abide therein eternally!"**

74. (Those who are in Paradise) **will say, "Hamd be to Allah who has fulfilled His promise and made us inherit the earth** (this place)**... We live in Paradise in whichever state we desire... How beautiful is the reward of those who fulfill the requisites of their faith!"**

75. **And you will see the angels surrounding the Throne** (of sovereignty – the state of the manifestation and observation of the Names) **exalting their Rabb and expressing His Hamd... All shall be judged in Truth and it will be said, "Hamd belongs to Allah, the Rabb of the worlds."**

AL-MU'MIN

By the one who is denoted by the name Allah (who created my being with His Names in accord with the meaning of the letter 'B'), the Rahman, the Rahim.

1. Ha Meem!

2. The revelation of the knowledge (about the reality and sunnatullah) is from Allah, the Aziz, the Aleem.

3. The forgiver of mistakes, the acceptor of repentance (the return to one's essence), the One who is severe in enforcing the due consequence of an offence, the One whose favor and bounty are abundant... There is no god, only HU! The return is to Him.

4. None will dispute and argue about the signs of Allah other than those who deny the knowledge of the reality! So, do not let their (uninhibited and cheery) activity throughout the land deceive you.

5. The people of Noah denied before them, and all people who opposed the reality denied after them. Every nation intended to seize (render dysfunctional, kill) their Rasul... They fought to invalidate the Truth by spreading falsehood... So, I seized them... And how was My recompense for their mistakes?

6. Thus, the word of your Rabb, "Their place is Fire," regarding the deniers of the knowledge of the reality has been fulfilled.

7. The carriers of the Throne and the (conscious) forces around it (the loci of the manifestation of Allah's power) glorify (tasbih) their Rabb as His hamd (manifest the Name Hamid); they believe in Him (as their essential reality) and ask forgiveness for the believers (for their inadequacy to duly live the requisites of their essential reality) saying, "Our Rabb, You encompass all things with Your grace and knowledge... Forgive those who repent and follow Your way, and protect them from the suffering of burning!"

8. "Our Rabb... Admit them to gardens of Eden, which you have promised them, and whoever attained purity among their fathers,

spouses and offspring... Indeed, You, yes You, are the Aziz, the Hakim."

9. "Protect them from bad deeds resulting from arrogance – corporeality... And he whom You have protected is he upon whom You have indeed bestowed Your grace... That is the great attainment!"

10. Indeed, those who deny the knowledge of the reality will be told, "The hatred of Allah is greater than your hatred of one another... Remember, you were invited to faith, but you refused in denial!"

11. They said, "Our Rabb, you have made us die twice (the experience of separation from the body and the state of selfless existence during mahshar [see 6:94]) and brought us to life twice (with a new identity) and we have confessed our mistakes! So, is there a way out of this state?"

12. The reason why you are in this state is: When Allah invited you to His Oneness (when you were offered to cleanse yourselves from your illusory identities), you covered (denied) it! If it were duality (to which you were invited) you would surely have believed in it... The judgment belongs to Allah, the Aliy, the Kabir (the One whose judgment of His manifest forces you cannot refuse)!

13. It is HU who shows you His signs and sends down provision (knowledge pertaining to your essence) from the heavens (to your consciousness)... But none can remember and contemplate upon this, except he who turns (to his essential reality)!

14. So, even if those who deny the knowledge of the reality detest religion, turn to Allah with the knowledge that He is the essential reality of the system!

15. He is the raiser of degrees, the owner of the Throne... He sends the spirit (the comprehension of the Names to the consciousness) from His command, to warn of the time when the Truth will be discerned!

16. At that time they will be exposed in every sense! They cannot hide anything from Allah... To whom belongs all sovereignty this Day (this moment, now, in the sight of Allah time is only this present moment)? To Allah, the Wahid, the Qahhar (the One whose absolute verdict applies beyond the concepts of time and space).

17. During this period every individual consciousness will be requited for what he has done (face the consequences of his deeds)! **No injustice will be done in this time! Indeed, Allah is swift in reckoning** (He instantly puts into effect the consequences of one's actions).

18. Warn them with the nearing time of death! At that time, their hearts, full of sorrow, will come right up to their throats! The wrongdoers will have neither a friend nor a chief to follow (to save them).

19. He knows the perfidy of the eyes (dualistic perception) **and what the hearts conceal.**

20. Allah judges in Truth... Those from whom they seek help besides Him have no judgment over anything! Indeed Allah is the Sami, the Basir.

21. Did they not travel throughout the earth and see the end of those before them? Those (before them) **were mightier than them in strength and more advanced in terms of what they formed on earth... But Allah seized them with the product of their own mistakes... And there were none to protect them from Allah** (their essential reality).

22. The reason for this was: Their Rasuls came to them with clear evidence, but they denied them... So Allah seized them... Indeed, He is the Qawwi and severe in enforcing the due consequence of an offence.

23. Indeed, We disclosed Moses with Our signs and a clear and undeniable evidence.

24. To Pharaoh, Haman and Qarun... But they said, "He is a great lying sorcerer."

25. When (Moses) **brought them the Truth from Us they said, "Slay the sons of those who believe with him and keep alive their females"... But the plots of those who deny the knowledge of the reality amount to nothing!**

26. Pharaoh said, "Leave me to slay Moses... And let him call his Rabb (for help)**... Indeed, I fear that** (Moses) **will change your understanding of religion or cause trouble in the land."**

27. Moses said, "Indeed, I seek refuge in my Rabb and your Rabb from the arrogant ones who do not believe in the time in which they will face the consequences of all their doings."

28. A man from among the family of Pharaoh who had believed, but not revealed it until that time, said, "Are you killing a man simply because he says 'My Rabb is Allah' when he has come to you with clear proofs from your Rabb? If he is lying, his lies are against him... But if he is telling the truth, the suffering of which he warns you will afflict you! Indeed, Allah does not guide those who squander (their resources within their essence) and who lie."

29. (That man said), "O my people! As the masters upon earth, abundance is yours today... But if it were to afflict us, who can help and save us against the wrath of Allah?" Pharaoh said, "I am not presenting to you an opinion other than my own and I am not guiding you, except to the only way out."

30. Then said the man who believed, "O my people! Indeed, I fear for you something like what befell those who united against the reality."

31. "Like what befell the people of Noah, Ad (the people of Hud) and Thamud (the people of Salih), and those who came after them... Allah does not will injustice for His servants."

32. (The believing man said), "O my people... I truly fear for you a time when there will be mournful wailing."

33. During that time, when you will turn and try to escape, there will be none to protect you from Allah! And whoever Allah misleads, there is none to guide him.

34. Previously, Joseph had also come to you with clear proofs... And when he died, you had said, "Allah will never disclose another Rasul after him"... Thus Allah misleads those who transgress and who are full of doubt.

35. They are those who dispute the signs of Allah without having received any solid evidence... This (conduct) is intensely hateful in the sight of Allah and the believers... Thus, Allah seals every arrogant and tyrannical consciousness.

36. Pharaoh said, "O Hamam! Build for me a high tower that I may reach the ways."

37. "The ways of the heavens... So that I may understand the god of Moses! For I certainly think he is a liar!"... And thus was made attractive to Pharaoh his bad deeds and thus was he prevented from the way (to his essential reality)... Pharaoh's plan amounted to nothing but loss!

38. The believer (from among Pharaoh's family) said, "O my people... Follow me, so that I may guide you to the way of maturity."

39. "O my people... This worldly life is only a temporary enjoyment of fleeting pleasures! The eternal life to come is indeed the home of permanent settlement!"

40. "Whoever does a bad deed will only be recompensed by the like thereof, but whoever, male or female, fulfills the requisites of their faith, they will be admitted to Paradise... A life in which they will be nourished with a variety of eternal sustenance!"

41. "O my people... How odd it is that while I call you to salvation, you call me to the Fire!"

42. "You call me to deny Allah, the One comprising my essence with His Names, and to associate with Him that of which I have no knowledge! While I call you to the One who is the Aziz, the Gaffar."

43. "The Truth is: That to which you invite me has no place in this world or the eternal life to come... Indeed, our return is to Allah... And indeed those who squander (their lives) are the companions of the Fire!"

44. "You will soon remember what I tell you! I leave my affair to Allah! Indeed, Allah is Basir over His servants."

45. Thus Allah protected Him (the believing man) from the evil (Pharaoh) plotted... And the family of Pharaoh was encompassed by the worst of sufferings.

46. The (wretched) Fire! They will be brought to it in the morning and the evening... And when that time comes, it will be told, "Place the family of Pharaoh in the worst of suffering!"

47. When they argue with one another in the Fire, the weak ones will say to those who were arrogant, "We were your followers... Can you now relieve us from some of this Fire?"

48. But the arrogant ones will say, "In truth, we are all in it together... Indeed, Allah has judged between His servants!"

49. Those in the Fire (an ocean of radiation) will say to the keepers of Hell, "Plead to your Rabb, that He may relieve us from this suffering at least for one day!"

50. (The keepers) will say, "Did your Rasuls not come to you as clear proofs?"... "Yes" they will say... "Then pray yourself!" the keepers will say... The prayer of those who deny the knowledge of the reality is nothing but a baseless attempt.

51. Indeed, We will help Our Rasuls and the believers both in the worldly life and during the time when the witnesses stand.

52. During that time their excuses will not give the wrongdoers any benefit... The curse (having fallen far from the forces of the Names of Allah) is upon them and theirs is the worst abode!

53. Indeed, We gave Moses the guidance (the knowledge of the reality) and made the Children of Israel inherit the knowledge!

54. As guidance to the reality and a reminder for those with intellects that contemplate!

55. Be patient! Indeed, the promise of Allah is Truth! Ask forgiveness for your mistakes! Glorify (tasbih; experience your essential reality) your Rabb as His hamd (by feeling the One who manifests hamd within you) in the morning and evening!

56. Those who dispute the signs of Allah without having received any solid proof contain nothing inside themselves except for an unattainable arrogance (i.e. they can never reach enlightenment in regards to the reality of true Greatness)! So, seek refuge in Allah, your essential reality with His Names... Indeed, He is HU, the Sami, the Basir.

57. Surely the creation of the heavens and the earth is much greater than that of humans! But the majority of humans do not know.

58. The blind one and the one who sees, the believer who fulfills the requisites of his faith, and the one who denies and does bad deeds are not equal! How little you remember and contemplate!

59. That Hour will most definitely come; there is no doubt about it... But the majority of the people do not believe!

60. Your Rabb said, "Pray to Me, so that I may respond to you! Indeed, those who do not pray out of their arrogance will enter Hell with their necks bent low."

61. It is Allah who created the night so that you may find tranquility therein, and the day so that you may see and evaluate! Indeed, Allah is full of bounty to humans... But the majority of the people are ungrateful!

62. This is your Rabb Allah, the Creator of all! There is no god, only HU! How you are turned away (from the Truth)!

63. Those who deliberately deny the signs of Allah are thus turned away!

64. It is Allah who made earth a place of residence for you and the heavens your edifice (that which adorns the earth [or body] with what it contains)... He proportioned you (gave you specific properties) and beautified your forms (of meaning) and nourished you with good sustenance (of knowledge and gnosis)! Thus is Allah, your Rabb! Sublime is the Rabb of the worlds (humans)!

65. HU is the Hayy! There is no god, only HU! Turn to Him with the knowledge that He is the essential reality of the system. Hamd belongs to Allah, the Rabb of the worlds (humanity).

66. Say, "I have been forbidden to worship those you deify besides Allah once proofs have come to me from my Rabb, and I have been commanded to submit to the Rabb of the worlds."

67. It is HU who created you from dust, then from sperm, then a clot (embryo)... Then He brought you out as a child; then gave you life allowing you to mature and reach old age... And some of you are taken in death before that... so that you reach the specified term and use your intellect.

68. It is HU who gives life and takes life! When He decrees a matter, He only says, 'Be' (wills it to be) and it is!

69. Did you see those who dispute the signs of Allah? How they are averted (from the Truth)?

70. They are those who deny the knowledge pertaining to their essence and the Rasuls We have disclosed! But soon they will know!

71. When the shackles (the conditionings and value judgments of their identities) and chains (addictive tendencies) are around their necks, they will be dragged!

72. Into the boiling water (burning thoughts)... And then in the Fire (ocean of radiation) they will be burnt!

73. Then they will be told, "Where are those you ascribed as partners..."

74. "Besides Allah!" They will say, "They are gone from us... No, indeed, we had previously turned to things that didn't exist!"... Thus Allah averts those who deny the knowledge of the reality.

75. This is for overindulging and exulting in arrogance on the earth without right.

76. Enter the gates of Hell to abide therein eternally... Wretched is the abode of the arrogant (egocentric) ones!

77. Be patient! Indeed, the promise of Allah is Truth! Whether We show some of what We have promised them to you or We cause you to die (without showing you, it does not matter, for in any case), they will be returned to Us.

78. Indeed, We have also disclosed Rasuls before you... Among them are some whose stories We have narrated to you, and some whose stories We have not... It is not possible for a Rasul to bring a miracle outside the permission of Allah! When the command of Allah comes, it will be judged with Truth, and those who pursue falsity will be in loss!

79. It is Allah who made the grazing animals for you, some upon which you ride, and some which you eat.

80. There are (other) benefits in them for you... To reach your destination upon them... And you are carried upon them and upon ships.

81. (Allah) shows you His signs... Which of Allah's signs do you deny!

82. Did they not travel throughout the earth and see the end of those before them! They (the previous people) were greater in number, mightier in strength, and more advanced in terms of what they produced on earth. Yet what they earned did not save them!

83. When their Rasuls came to them as clear proofs, they relied on their own knowledge and exulted! The very thing they mocked has encompassed them!

84. When they saw Our rage they said, "We believe Allah, the One who comprises Our essence with His Names, is One; and disbelieve in what we ascribed to Him."

85. But the faith they developed after seeing Our rage did not benefit them! This is the sunnatullah of Allah established upon His servants for ages! Thereupon those who denied the knowledge of the reality are in loss!

By the one who is denoted by the name Allah (who created my being with His Names in accord with the meaning of the letter 'B'), **the Rahman, the Rahim.**

1. **Ha, Meem.**

2. **This is a revelation** (an explanation) **from the Rahman and Rahim One!**

3. **For people who understand, it is the knowledge, whose signs are expounded as an Arabic Quran!**

4. **As a giver of good news and a warner... But the majority of them have turned away** (from these truths)**! They do not hear!**

5. **They say, "Our consciousness is cocooned from that to which you call us, there is heaviness in our ears, and there is a curtain between you and us! So, do whatever you may, we too are doing."**

6. (My Rasul) **say, "I am a human like yourselves; however, it has been revealed to me: That which you think as god is One, possessor of Uluhiyyah! So, turn to Him and ask Him for forgiveness... Woe to those who are in duality** (who fail to understand the Oneness of existence and ascribe partners to Allah)**!"**

7. **Those** (dualists) **do not give unrequitedly for Allah and they deny their eternal lives to come.**

8. **But those who believe and fulfill the requisites of faith, there is an unending reward for them.**

9. **Say, "Do you really deny the One who has created the earth in two periods** (in reference to earth this refers to the period of materialization of earth and the formation of animate beings; in reference to the body, it refers to the time between conception until the 120th day, to the time of birth. Allah knows best)**! Do you equate** (assume the existence of) **other gods to Him! He is the Rabb of the worlds** (the One who forms with the Names of Allah every instance of the process of creation – from the point it is willed and its formation, to the end of its

existence – creating all the required and appropriate qualities necessary for its actualization)!"

10. **And he formed firmly set mountains** (egos) **on the earth** (the body) **and gave abundance therein and determined the sustenance for the continuation of its creatures in four periods, without distinction, for those who ask** (according to their capacities).

11. **Then established Himself in the heaven** (to manifest some of His Names) **while it was in smoke form** (natural formless self) **and said to it** (consciousness) **and to the earth** (the body), **"Come willingly or by compulsion** (to manifest My Names)!" **They both said, "We come willingly to obey!"** (The heaven = intellectual state; and the earth = bodily organs. Both willingly manifest the qualities of the Names.)

12. **Thus He decreed there to be seven heavens** (the seven states of consciousness – self) **and revealed to each heaven its function! And He adorned the nearest heaven** (of earth) **with lamps** (enlightening ideas) **and protected it. That is the determination of the Aziz, the Aleem!**

13. **But if they turn away say, "I warn you with the thunderbolt like the thunderbolt of Aad and Thamud!"**

14. **When their Rasuls came to them from in front** (with what they knew) **and from behind** (with what they did not know) **and said, "Do not idolize others; serve and worship only Allah!" They said, "Had our Rabb willed, He would surely have disclosed angels... We deny that** (knowledge of the reality) **with which you have been disclosed."**

15. **As for Aad** (the people of Hud), **they were arrogant on earth without right and said, "Who is mightier than us in strength?" Did they not see that Allah, who created them, is mightier than them in strength! They denied Our signs consciously** (and deliberately)! (They thought the forces pertaining to Our Names belonged to their assumed selves.)

16. **So We disclosed an icy wind upon them during days of misfortune, so that they taste the suffering of disgrace in the worldly life! But surely the suffering of the eternal life to come is more disgracing... And they will not find any help!**

17. **As for Thamud** (the people of Salih) **We guided them but they preferred blindness over guidance** (reality)... **So, the thunderbolt of the humiliating suffering seized them as the result of their conduct.**

18. We saved those who believed and protected themselves.

19. When that time comes the enemies of Allah will be gathered together and driven to the Fire.

20. When they (the enemies of Allah) come there, their ears (hearing), eyes (sight) and their skins (their whole body) will testify against them about what they used to do.

21. They will ask their bodies, "Why did you testify against us?"... They will say, "Allah, who makes all things speak, made us speak... He created you the first time... And now to Him you are returned."

22. And you did not expect your hearing, sight and bodies to testify against you (so you lived as you liked)... You thought Allah was unaware of most of your doings!

23. Your mistaken assumption about your Rabb has brought you to perdition, and you have become among the losers.

24. So even if they patiently endure it (thinking it will pass) the Fire is their abode! If they try to please (their Rabb, presenting excuses) they will not be of those whose excuses are accepted and appeased.

25. And we have appointed for them companions (those with satanic ideas from among the jinn and man) who made attractive to them their actions and desires. And the sentence concerning the jinn and man that had passed before them has now come into effect upon them. Indeed, they were all losers.

26. Those who denied the knowledge of the reality said (to those who listened to the Rasul of Allah), "Do not listen to the Quran, talk baseless things in regards to it, perhaps you will overpower it!"

27. Indeed, We will subject those who deny the knowledge of the reality to an intense suffering and We will surely make them face the consequences of their deeds!

28. Fire is the result of the deeds of Allah's enemies! For them is the home of eternity therein! As the recompense for consciously denying Our signs (refusing to accept their Rabb)!

29. Those who deny the knowledge of the reality say, "Our Rabb... Show us the two who misled us from among the jinn and man so that we may place them under our feet that they may be among the lowest!"

30. Indeed, angels will descend upon those who say, "My Rabb is Allah" and who live their lives accordingly (the Jamal forces of the divine attributes will manifest, which means), "Do not fear and do not grieve but be happy with your Paradise, which you have been promised..."

31. "We are your friends (Waliyy) in the worldly life and the eternal life to come! You will have therein whatever your consciousness desires... And whatever you request therein, you shall have!"

32. As the disclosure (manifestation) of the Rahim, the Ghafur (the Jamal attributes)."

33. Who is better in speech than one who invites to Allah and fulfills the requisites of faith and says, "Indeed, I am of those who experience their absolute submission"?

34. The good deed and the bad deed are not equal! Repel (the bad) with that which is best... Then you will see, the person who had enmity towards you will be like as though he was a devoted friend!

35. Only those who are patient are granted this (quality)... And only those who have been given a great grant are allowed (this patience).

36. If an impulse from the Satan seduces you, immediately seek refuge in Allah, the One who comprises your essence with His Names (activate your inherent forces of the Names)! Indeed, He is HU, the Sami, the Aleem.

37. The night (intrinsic qualities), the day (extrinsic qualities), the Sun (the intellect) and the Moon (emotions) are all of His signs! Do not prostrate (idolize) to the Sun or the Moon, but prostrate to (their creator) Allah (listen to your intuition, which is inspired by the Names, for there is always an inner voice guiding you to what is right before you commit a deed); if you are conscious of your servitude to Him! (This is a verse of prostration.)

38. If they continue to be arrogant (egotistic), then (let them know) that those who are near their Rabb (conscious of their essential reality) tasbih Him (live with the awareness of their servitude to their Rabb) by night and by day without becoming weary!

39. It is from His signs that you see the earth (body) in a state of awe... When We disclose water (knowledge of the reality) upon it, it quivers and awakens! Indeed, the One who has given life to it (one

devoid of knowledge) **is the One who gives life** (Muhyi) **to the dead! Indeed, He is Qadir over all things.**

40. Those who pervert Our signs from their intended purpose are not concealed from Us. So, is the one who is thrown into the Fire better or the one who is secure during Doomsday? Do as you wish! Indeed, He is Basir of what you do (as their creator).

41. Indeed, they deny the knowledge reminding them of their essential reality! Indeed, that knowledge (reminding them of their essential reality – dhikr) **is mighty!**

42. Falsehood cannot reach it, from its front (directly) **or its back** (indirectly)**! It is a** (dimensional) **disclosure from the One who is the Hakim, the Hamid.**

43. (O Rasul of Allah!) **You are not told anything different to what previous Rasuls were told! Indeed, your Rabb is both forgiving and One who subjects to severe suffering.**

44. Had We made it a Quran not in Arabic, surely they would have said, "These verses should have been understandable! A non-Arabic (Quran) **to an Arabic speaking** (Rasul? How can that be?)**"... Say, "It is guidance and healing** (enabling healthy thought) **for the believers!" As for those who do not believe, there is heaviness in their ears; it is an unperceivable object for them!** (Thus it is as though) **they are being called from a distant place.**

45. Indeed, We gave the knowledge (Book) **to Moses, but they differed in regards to it... And if it were not for the decree of your Rabb it would surely have been judged between them... Indeed, they are in dubious doubt about it.**

46. Whoever fulfills the requisites of faith, it is for their own sake! And whoever does bad, it is against their own selves. Your Rabb is not unjust to His servants.

47. The knowledge of that Hour (death) **belongs to Him! Outside His knowledge, neither fruits emerge from their buds, nor a female conceives or gives birth! The day when He** (Allah) **calls out, "Where are my partners?" They say, "No one has witnessed such partner, this we confess!"**

48. That which they previously uttered is lost from them and they realized they have no place of escape.

49. Man is not weary of asking for good things... But if bad afflicts him, at once he loses hope and falls into despair.

50. Indeed, if We make him taste Our grace after an affliction, he will surely say, "This is my right... I don't think that Hour (Doomsday) will come to pass... Indeed, if I were to be returned to my Rabb I will have the best of things from Him anyway!" Indeed, We will inform those who deny the knowledge of the reality of what they do... Indeed, We will make them taste severe suffering.

51. When We bestow a favor upon man, he turns away and distances himself! But when a bad thing afflicts him, he prays extensively.

52. Say, "Think, if (this knowledge) is from Allah and you have denied it, who can be more corrupt than one who has gone astray (from the reality) to this extent!"

53. We will show them Our signs in the horizons (externally) and within themselves until it becomes clearly evident to them that it is the Truth! Is it not sufficient that your Rabb is a witness over all things?

54. Pay heed! Indeed, they are in doubt about the meeting of their Rabb (from experiencing the manifestation of their Rabb from within their essence)! Be careful! Indeed, He is Mu'id (encompassing) over all things (forms all things with the qualities of His Names)!

42

ASH-SHURA

By the one who is denoted by the name Allah (who created my being with His Names in accord with the meaning of the letter 'B'), the Rahman, the Rahim.

1. Ha, Meem.

2. Ayn, Seen, Qaf.

3. Thus does Allah, the Aziz, the Hakim, reveal to you and those before you!

4. Whatever is in the heavens and the earth is for Him... He is the Aliy, the Azim.

5. The heavens almost break from above them (what will come out?)! The angels glorify (tasbih) their Rabb as His hamd, (they carry out their function) and ask forgiveness for those on earth... Pay heed, Allah is the Ghafur, the Rahim.

6. Those who have taken friends besides Him, Allah observes them... You are not responsible for their actions.

7. Thus We revealed it to you as an Arabic Quran so that you may warn the people of Mecca with it and inform them of the intensity of that time of gathering, about which there is no doubt! A group (of them) will be in Paradise, and a group (of them) will be in flames of Fire.

8. Had Allah willed He would surely have made them a single community (of a single faith)... But Allah includes whom He wills to His grace! As for the wrongdoers, they have neither a guardian friend nor a helper!

9. Or did they take other friends besides Him? Allah is HU, the Waliyy HU gives life and takes life! HU is the Qadir One over all things.

10. Whenever you disagree about something its judgment belongs to Allah! Thus is Allah, my Rabb! I have placed my trust in Him... And to Him I turn!

11. He is the Fatir of the heavens and the earth! He has formed for you partners from your selves (the original self + constructed identity self) and from the cattle (animalistic body) mates (biological + radial [spirit] body)... Thus He multiplies you! There is nothing that resembles Him! He is the Sami, the Basir.

12. The keys (the forces to manifest the qualities) of the heaven and the earth belong to Him! He extends and expands provision for whom He wills, or constricts it! Indeed, He is the Aleem (the Knower) of all things (as their very creator with His Names).

13. He has ordained for you of the single religion (the absolute valid system and order of Allah) what He enjoined upon Noah, what We revealed to you, and what We enjoined upon Abraham, Moses, and Jesus – to establish the religion and not to be in division therein! This to which you call them (the truth of 'La ilaha illaAllah – the reality of the system) is too great for the dualists (to comprehend)! Allah chooses for Himself whom He wills and guides those who turn to Him to (realize their inner) reality!

14. And they fell into division, after the knowledge (of the reality) came to them, out of jealousy between themselves! Had their life-span not been already decreed by your Rabb, surely the matter between them would have been concluded! As for those who were granted inheritance of the knowledge after them (the people of the Book), they are in dubious doubt concerning it (the Quran).

15. So, invite them (for this reason)! Remain on the right course of your natural disposition, as you have been commanded! Do not follow their baseless desires and ideas! Say, "I believe in the knowledge disclosed by Allah! I have been commanded to be just! Allah is both our Rabb and your Rabb. Our deeds are for us and your deeds are for you. There is no need for a battle of proofs between us! Allah will bring us together! To Him is the return."

16. The proofs of those who still argue about Allah after He has been responded to are invalid in the sight of their Rabb... Upon them is wrath and intense suffering.

17. It is Allah who has revealed the knowledge of the reality and sunnatullah and the judgment (reasoning)... Who knows, perhaps the Hour (of death) is close!

18. Those who do not believe they will live it are impatient for it! But those who believe, tremble with fear of it, for they know it is most definitely the Truth! Pay heed, those who argue about the Hour (doubtful about a life in a new dimension after death) are indeed very astray from the truth of the matter!

19. Allah is the Latif One over His servants, He provisions whom He wills... He is the Qawwi, the Aziz.

20. And whoever wants the blessings of the eternal life to come, We will increase it for him! And whoever wants the blessings of the world, we will give it to him – but he will have no share in the eternal life to come!

21. Or do they have partners in religion who validate for them the things that Allah forbids? If it were not for the word regarding division at a specified time, it would surely have been concluded between them... As for the wrongdoers, there is intense suffering for them.

22. You will see the wrongdoers trembling in fear when it befalls them, of what they earned (the results of their deeds)! While those who believe and fulfill the requisites of faith are in the best parts of Paradise, having whatever they desire in the presence of their Rabb... This is it! This is the great bounty!

23. This is what Allah gives as good news to those who believe and fulfill the requisites of faith... Say, "I do not want anything in return for this message other than love of kinship"... Whoever earns a good deed We will increase its good for him! Indeed, Allah is the Ghafur, the Shakur.

24. Or do they say, "He has lied about Allah"? If Allah wills He can seal your heart (consciousness)! Allah destroys falsehood and establishes the Truth as His words! Indeed, He, as your absolute essence with His Names, is the Aleem.

25. It is He who accepts repentance from His servants, and pardons misdeeds and the One who knows what you do.

26. And He responds to the believers who fulfill the requisites of faith and increases (His blessings for them) with His bounty! As for

those who deny the knowledge of the reality, there is severe suffering for them.

27. Had Allah extended and expanded provision for His servants, they would surely have caused rampage on the earth! But He sends what He wills with measure... Indeed, He is Habir and Basir of His servants.

28. He is the One who sends down rain and spreads grace when they (His servants) are in despair... He is the Waliyy, the Hamid.

29. It is from among His signs that He creates the heavens, the earth and the creatures (biological forms) dispersed throughout them... HU is all Powerful (Qadir) to gather them when He wills.

30. And whatever strikes you of disaster, it is the result of what your hands have done! But (Allah) pardons much of it.

31. You cannot render (Allah) helpless on earth! You have no friend or helper besides Allah.

32. The (ships) that sail in the sea like mountains are also from His signs.

33. If He wills, He can make the wind still and they (the sailing ships) would remain motionless... Indeed, there are signs in this for those who are patient and grateful.

34. Or He could destroy them because of what they have earned... But (Allah) forgives much of it.

35. So that those who argue about Our signs can know that they have no place of escape.

36. The things you have been given are but the wealth of the worldly life (world = the lowest state of existence)! But that which is with Allah is better and more lasting for those who believe and place their trust in their Rabb.

37. They refrain from the great offence (duality; shirq, slander) and immoralities, and they forgive when they are angry...

38. And they respond to their Rabb and establish salat, and consult one another to resolve their affairs... And they give unrequitedly from the things with which We provide them...

39. They are those who, even when faced with tyranny, strive in unity and they prevail!

40. The retribution of a bad deed is a bad deed! But whoever forgives and reconciles, his rewards is with Allah... Indeed, He does not like the wrongdoers.

41. And whoever avenges himself after being wronged, for them, there is no blame!

42. Blame is upon those who wrong people and cause corruption on the earth without right! There is an intense suffering for them.

43. And whoever is patient and forgives, indeed, this is a matter that requires determination.

44. Whoever Allah leads astray, there is no friend (Waliyy) for him... You will see the wrongdoers say, "Is there any way to return (to the life of the biological body)?"

45. You will see them being exposed (to the Fire), in awe from humiliation (with their heads bent low) looking covertly from behind... The believers will say, "They are the very losers; they caused loss upon themselves and their close ones during Doomsday! Pay heed! Indeed, the wrongdoers are in an enduring suffering."

46. And they will have no guardian friend to help them besides Allah... For whoever Allah leads astray – for him there is no way.

47. So, respond to your Rabb before the time comes from Allah for which there is no repelling... At that time, you will have nowhere to seek refuge, nor will your denial (of your deeds) will be of any avail!

48. If they turn away (let them), We did not disclose you as their keeper! Your only responsibility is to inform! Indeed, when We make man taste a grace from Us, he rejoices with it... But if the bad consequence of his deeds afflicts him, then indeed, man is very ungrateful!

49. The sovereignty of the heavens and the earth is for Allah (who created them with His Names while they were inexistent)! He creates whatever He wills. He grants females to whom He wills and grants males to whom He wills.

50. Or He makes them both males and females... And renders whom He wills barren... Indeed, He is the Aleem, the Qadir.

51. It is not possible that Allah speaks to a man! Only through revelation, or from behind a veil, or by disclosing a Rasul (angel) to reveal, by His permission, what He wills! Indeed, He is the Aliy, the Hakim.

52. Thus We have revealed to you a spirit (the sensing of the meanings of the Names in your consciousness) by Our command... And you did not know what the knowledge of the reality and sunnatullah was, or what faith meant! But We formed it (the spirit) as Nur (knowledge) by which We guide to the reality whom We will among Our servants! And indeed, you guide to the reality (the straight path).

53. The path of Allah, to whom belongs everything in the heavens and the earth is for Him alone! Pay heed, all affairs return to Allah!

43

AZ-ZUKHRUF

By the one who is denoted by the name Allah (who created my being with His Names in accord with the meaning of the letter 'B'), the Rahman, the Rahim.

1. Ha, Meem.

2. By the knowledge that clearly discloses the reality...

3. Indeed, We have made it an Arabic Quran, so that you may use your intellect (understand and evaluate it)!

4. And indeed, it is in the Mother of Books (the knowledge of Allah) in Our presence, high in dignity (Aliy) and full of wisdom (Hakim).

5. Shall We forsake warning you because you are a people who transgress (squander your inherent essential forces)?

6. And many Nabis We have disclosed within previous peoples.

7. But whenever a Nabi came to them, they mocked what he brought.

8. So We destroyed many nations, mightier than them, because of it... The former people became history full of exemplary lessons!

9. Indeed, if you were to ask them, "Who created the heavens and the earth?" They would surely say, "The Aziz and Aleem One."

10. It is He who made the earth (body) a cradle for you (to grow in) and formed pathways (of thought) upon it that you may be guided to the reality.

11. It is He who sent down water (knowledge) from the sky in measured amounts... And with it, We revived a dead land (consciousness)! Thus will you be brought out (from your graves – bodies).

12. It is He who created the pairs (double helix DNA) **and formed ships** (consciousness) **and animals** (biological body) **upon which you ride.**

13. That you may settle yourselves upon their backs, and when you have settled upon them, remember the favor of your Rabb and say, "Exalted (Subhan) is He who has subjected this to us, otherwise we could not have evaluated it."

14. "We will surely reach our Rabb (through continuous transformation)**!"**

15. But they attributed a portion of His servants to Him (denied His Absolute Oneness and assuming Him to be made up of parts, claimed He had a son)**... Indeed, man is clearly ungrateful!**

16. Or has He taken the daughters for Himself, out of His creation, and left the sons for you?

17. When one of them is given the news of a daughter, which he attributes to the Rahman, his face becomes dark with grief!

18. Or do you attribute the one brought up in ornaments (daughters)**, who you consider is unable to engage in an argument** (to Allah)**!**

19. They defined the servant angels of Allah as females! Were they witnesses to their creation? Their testimony is recorded; they will be questioned!

20. They said, "Had Rahman willed, we would not have served them"... They have no knowledge (evidence, certainty) **of that... They only talk nonsense based on mere assumptions.**

21. Or did We give them the knowledge (Book) **before this on which they are basing their claims?**

22. On the contrary, they said, "We found our forefathers upon this religious understanding and we are guided to the reality upon their footsteps (conditionings – genes)**.**

23. Thus it is... To whichever people We disclosed a warner before you, its wealthy leaders said, "We found our forefathers upon this religious understanding and we follow their work (conditionings, genes)**."**

24. (The Rasul of Allah) **said, "Even if I brought you that which is more correct than what you found your forefathers upon?"** They said, "We reject the knowledge with which you have been disclosed!"

25. So we took revenge from them... Look at the end of those who denied!

26. And (mention) when Abraham said to his father and his people, "Indeed, I am disassociated from what that you idolize..."

27. "Except for He who created me (upon a natural disposition – creational program)! Indeed, it is He who will guide me to the reality!"

28. He made this word a lasting thought throughout later generations, that perhaps they will turn back to the Truth.

29. I made them and their forefathers enjoy of the world until there came to them the Truth and a clear Rasul.

30. But when the Truth came to them they said, "This is magic... We do not accept it!"

31. They said, "Why was this Quran not sent to one of the great men of these two cities?"

32. Do they distribute the grace of your Rabb? It is We who have apportioned among them their livelihood in the life of this world... We raised some over others (in terms of wealth and rank) so that some may subjugate others... The grace of your Rabb is better than the things they accumulate (of wealth).

33. And if it were not that the people would become a community of a single way (through wealth, as wealth exhilarates externalized living and deprives one from inner wealth) surely We would have made, for those who deny that Rahman comprises their essence, houses with silver ceilings and silver staircases upon which to climb...

34. And for their house, (silver) doors and couches to rest upon...

35. And ornaments of gold! But all that is nothing but the temporary pleasures of the worldly life! And the eternal life to come is for those who are protected in the sight of their Rabb.

36. And whoever is blinded (with external things) from the remembrance of Rahman (remembering that his essential reality is composed of the names of Allah and thus from living the requirements of this), We appoint for him a Satan (a delusion; the idea that he is only

the physical body and that life should be lived in pursuit of bodily pleasures) **and this** (belief) **will become his** (new) **identity!**

37. And indeed, these will avert them from the way (of the reality) **while they think they are on the right path!**

38. When finally he came to Us, he said (to his friend), **"I wish there was between you and I the distance between the two easts** (an unreachable distance)... **How wretched a friend you are!"**

39. And never will they (feelings of regret, excuses, the desire to compensate) **benefit you during this time! For you did wrong! You are partners** (consciousness and the spirit-body) **in suffering!**

40. Will you make the deaf hear? Or will you guide the blind and those who are in clear error?

41. Even if We were to take you (from the world) **We will surely take revenge from them.**

42. Or We will show you what We have promised them... We have the power to do whatever We will to them!

43. So adhere to that which has been revealed to you!

44. Indeed, it is a remembrance for you and your people! Soon you will be questioned for what you are responsible!

45. And ask those We disclosed before you among Our Rasuls (study the knowledge that was given to them)! **Have We formed gods to be served besides Rahman?**

46. Indeed, We disclosed Moses with Our signs to Pharaoh and his eminent ones, and (Moses) **said, "I am the Rasul of the Rabb of the worlds."**

47. But when he came to them with Our signs, at once they laughed at them!

48. Every miracle We showed was greater than the previous one... And We seized them with a suffering that perhaps they will turn to Us.

49. They said, "O magician! Pray to your Rabb by virtue of your contract with Him! We will be guided!"

50. But when We removed the suffering from them, they broke their word immediately!

51. Pharaoh called out among his people, "O my people! Does not the kingdom of Egypt and these rivers flowing beneath me belong to me? Do you still not see?"

52. "Or am I not better than this insignificant one who can hardly explain himself?"

53. "(If Moses is really as he claims to be) should there not have been placed upon him bracelets of gold or angels accompanying him?"

54. (Pharaoh) fooled his people and they obeyed him... Indeed, they were a people corrupt in faith!

55. And when they angered Us, We made them live the consequence of their deeds; We drowned them all.

56. We made them a precedent and an example for later generations!

57. When the son of Mary was presented as an example, immediately your people turned away...

58. They said, "Are our gods better or him?" They only presented this to dispute with you! They are a people fond of dispute!

59. He was a servant upon whom We bestowed favor and made an example for the Children of Israel that they may take a lesson.

60. Had We willed We could have formed angels from you to be the vicegerents on earth (but We made you humans containing angelic properties instead)!

61. Indeed, He has the knowledge of the Hour... So, do not be in doubt thereof and follow me! This is the right way!

62. Let not Satan prevent you! Indeed, he is to you a clear enemy!

63. When Jesus came out with clear proofs, he said, "I have indeed brought wisdom (the Truth about the system and order) to you and (came) to explain some of that over which you differ... So, protect yourselves from Allah (as He will subject you to the consequences of your actions) and follow me."

64. "Indeed, Allah, HU, is my Rabb and your Rabb! So serve him! This is the right way!"

65. But those who differed in understanding fell into opposition between themselves. Woe to those who wrong themselves from the suffering of a severe time!

66. Do they await something other than the Hour (of death – Doomsday) to come suddenly upon them while they are not aware!

67. Close friends (of worldly pleasures) at that time will become enemies to one another! Except those who protect themselves!

68. "O my servants... There is no fear for you at this time... Nor will you grieve!"

69. They believed in Our signs within their being, and became of those who accepted being in submission...

70. So enter Paradise, you and your partners (consciousness and spirit-bodies), with joy and pleasure!

71. Plates and jugs made of gold will be circulated above them... And therein is whatever they (their consciousness) desire and their eyes take delight in (pleasurable insightful observation of forces)! You will abide therein eternally!

72. This is the Paradise that you are made to inherit as a result of your deeds!

73. There are many varieties of fruits (gnosis) therein from which you will eat.

74. Indeed, the guilty (dualists) will abide eternally in the suffering of Hell.

75. Their suffering will not be lightened! They are in despair therein about the future!

76. And We did not wrong them... It was they who wronged themselves!

77. They will call out, "O Malik (keeper of Hell)! Let your Rabb pass judgment against us (kill us)!"... (Malik) will say, "Indeed, you are of those who will remain (here in this state)!"

78. Indeed, We came to you as the Truth! But most of you despised the Truth!

79. Or will they decide on what the Truth is! It is We who determine the Truth!

80. Or did they think We could not hear what they concealed and whispered? Yes (We hear)! And Our Rasuls with them are recording.

81. Say, "If Rahman had a child, I would have been the first to worship him!"

82. But the Rabb of the heavens and the earth, the Rabb of the Throne, is beyond their definitions of Him!

83. So, let them immerse (in their worlds) and amuse themselves until they meet the promised time!

84. It is HU who is (thought to be) the god of the heavens (with His Names) and the god of earth! HU, the Hakim, the Aleem.

85. Sublime and blessed is He to whom belongs the sovereignty of the heavens, the earth and everything between them! The knowledge of that Hour (of death – Doomsday) is with Him... To Him you will be returned!

86. Those to whom they turn besides Him have no (power of) intercession, except those who consciously testify to the Truth!

87. Indeed, if you were to ask them who created them they would surely say, "Allah"... So, how are they averted (from the Truth)?

88. His word is, "My Rabb, these are people who do not believe!"

89. (My Rasul!) Do not pay attention to them, and say, "Salam"! They will know (the reality of the matter) soon!

44

AD-DUKHAN

By the one who is denoted by the name Allah (who created my being with His Names in accord with the meaning of the letter 'B'), **the Rahman, the Rahim.**

1. **Ha** (life), **Meem** (knowledge – the reality of Muhammad);

2. **The Clear Book** (the apparent sunnatullah and the knowledge of the reality).

3. **We disclosed it during a blessed night** (an instance of the experience of non-existence)! **We are the warners!**

4. **The wisdom pertaining to all affairs are realized in it** (in that state of 'nonexistence');

5. **By a command from Us! We are the disclosers** (of the Rasuls)!

6. **As grace from the Rabb** (of those who are disclosed)! **Indeed, He is HU, the Sami, the Aleem.**

7. **The Rabb of the heavens, the earth and everything in between... If you are of those who have attained certainty!**

8. **There is no god, only HU, who gives life and takes life! He is your Rabb and the Rabb of your forefathers!**

9. **But no, they are in doubt, amusing themselves** (with the worldly life).

10. **Watch for the day** (the time when the reality of man will become apparent) **when the sky will bring a visible smoke** (dukhan).

11. **It will encompass the people! It is a severe suffering** (for not having realized and fulfilled the requisites of the reality)!

12. **"Our Rabb! Take us out of this state of suffering; we are indeed believers** (now)!"

13. **How is it possible for them to be contemplating and taking a lesson now? When a clear Rasul had already come to them...**

14. But they turned away from him and said, "He is a well instructed madman (possessed)."

15. Indeed, We will lighten the suffering a little... (But) you will return to your old state.

16. At that time (when the sky brings the visible smoke) We will seize with the greatest seizure... Indeed, We take retribution for all offences!

17. Indeed, We had tried the people of Pharaoh before them with difficulties... A karim (noble and generous) Rasul had come to them.

18. (Saying), "Deliver the servants of Allah to me... Indeed, I am a trustworthy Rasul..."

19. "Do not be arrogant towards Allah (do not defy the Rasul)... I have presented to you a clear and undeniable proof."

20. "And I have sought refuge in my Rabb (the Names comprising my essence) and your Rabb (your essence) from your desire to stone me to death."

21. "If you do not believe me then at least leave me alone!"

22. (Moses) turned to his Rabb, "These are guilty (dualist) people!"

23. (His Rabb said), "Set out with My servants in the night (take them away)... Indeed, you will be pursued."

24. "Leave the sea in its open state... Indeed, they are an army to be drowned."

25. They left behind many gardens and springs.

26. And many crops and beautiful sites...

27. And the many blessings with which they found comfort and pleasure!

28. Thus it is... And we left them for another people to inherit.

29. And the heaven and the earth did not weep for them (for those who drowned in corporeality) and nor were they looked upon (acknowledged).

30. Indeed, We saved the children of Israel from that humiliating suffering...

31. **From Pharaoh** (who symbolizes the ego)! **Indeed, he was arrogant and a squanderer** (who wasted his inherent essential forces).

32. **Indeed, We chose them** (the children of Israel) **over all the worlds** (people) **with the knowledge!**

33. **And We gave them signs in which there was a clear trial.**

34. **Indeed, they said:**

35. **"There is nothing further than the first death; we are not to be resurrected after death!"**

36. **"Then bring back our forefathers, if you are truthful!"**

37. **Are they better or the people of Tubba'** (the ruler of Yemen) **and those before them? We destroyed them! Indeed, they were guilty** (dualists).

38. **And We did not create the heavens, the earth and everything in between for play...**

39. **We created only as the Truth** (the manifestations of Our Names)! **But the majority of them do not know** (this Truth).

40. **They will all be gathered at the specified time of differentiation.**

41. **That is time when no friend will avail a friend! Nor will they be helped...**

42. **Except those upon who Allah bestows His grace... Indeed, He is HU, the Aziz, the Rahim.**

43. **Indeed, the tree of Zaqqum,**

44. **Is food for the denier** (who denies his essential reality)!

45. **It is like molten metal; it boils in their bellies.**

46. **Like the boiling of hot water.**

47. **"Seize him and drag him into the midst of Fire..."**

48. **"Then pour the suffering of that boiling water over his head!"**

49. **"Taste it! You considered yourself Aziz and Karim!"**

50. **"This is the thing you doubted** (and denied)!"

51. Indeed, those who protected themselves are in safety.

52. Among Paradises and springs!

53. Dressed in fine silk and brocade, facing one another.

54. **Thus it is... We partnered them** (the conscious humans manifesting the forces of the Names) **with houris** (bodies with superior and clear vision [heart])!

55. **They will ask therein for every kind of fruit** (expressions of gnosis) **– safe and secure.**

56. **They will not taste death therein except the first death** (they are immortal)**! And He will have protected them from the suffering of burning.**

57. **As bounty from your Rabb! This is the great attainment!**

58. **And We eased the Quran in your language, that perhaps they may reflect on it.**

59. **So, observe and wait! Indeed, they too are waiting.**

AL-JATHIYA

By the one who is denoted by the name Allah (who created my being with His Names in accord with the meaning of the letter 'B'), the Rahman, the Rahim.

1. Ha, Meem.

2. The disclosure of the knowledge (its detailed explanation) is from Allah, the Aziz, the Hakim!

3. There are signs in the heavens and the earth for those who believe.

4. And in your creation (humans – consciousness) and the variety of animals (races) are signs for those who have attained certainty.

5. In the alternation of night and day, and in Allah disclosing sustenance (knowledge) from the sky with which he gives life to the earth (enables conscious living in the body) after its death (unconscious state – thinking you are only the body), and in His directing of the winds (continuous thoughts and ideas) are signs for people who can use their intellects.

6. These are the signs of Allah... We inform you of them in Truth... Which statement will they believe after Allah and His signs?

7. Woe to he who lives in denial of his essential reality, deceiving himself with the impulses and instincts coming from his constructed illusory identity.

8. He hears the signs of Allah when he is informed of them, yet becomes arrogant as though he has not heard them and persists (in his duality)... Give him the news of an intense suffering.

9. When any of Our signs reach him, he mocks them! For them is the humiliating suffering.

10. Behind them is Hell! And neither what they earned nor the friends they took besides Allah can avail them from any suffering! There is severe suffering for them.

11. This is the guide to the reality! As for those who deny the signs of their Rabb within their being, for them is the worst of sufferings.

12. It is Allah who delegated for you (consciousness) the sea (knowledge) so that the ships (brains) may sail upon it by His command (sunnatullah) that you may seek His bounty and be grateful!

13. Whatever is in the heavens (levels of consciousness in the brain) and the earth (bodily life) He has delegated all of them to your service (your consciousness)! Indeed, there are (important) signs in this for a people who contemplate.

14. Tell the believers to forgive those who do not expect the 'Days of Allah' (when the disclosed knowledge is experienced) so that He (Allah) may recompense them with the consequences of their deeds!

15. Whoever does a deed of faith, it is for his own sake! And whoever does a bad deed, it is against his own self! To your Rabb you will be returned in the end!

16. Indeed, We gave the knowledge of the reality and sunnatullah, the Wisdom and Nubuwwah to the children of Israel and nourished them with clean sustenance and preferred them over the worlds (humans who are devoid of these).

17. We gave them clear proofs (the knowledge of sunnatullah) by Our command... but, after the knowledge had come to them, they fell into diversion out of jealousy (ego) between themselves! Your Rabb will judge between them during Doomsday over what they differed.

18. It is with the conditions under Our command that We formed you! So, follow it (the reality, religion) and do not follow the baseless desires (ideas and wants driven by corporeality) of those who do not know!

19. Indeed, those (ideas that are not based on the reality) will not give you (your consciousness) any benefit from Allah (His Names comprising your essence)! The wrongdoers are friends of one another! But Allah is the friend (Waliyy) of those who protect themselves!

20. This (Quran) is enlightenment (Truths to be grasped by mankind) and a guidance and grace for those who have attained certainty.

21. Or did those who earned bad deeds think We would make them equal, in life and death, to those who have believed and fulfilled the requisites of faith? What bad judgment!

22. Allah has created the heavens (consciousness) and the earth (the body) in Truth (with His Names), so that each person may live the consequences of what they have earned and they will not be wronged!

23. Did you see the one who deified his baseless desires and thus who Allah led astray in line with his knowledge (assumption) and sealed his ability to sense the reality and veiled his vision? So, who can lead him to the reality after (this application of) Allah! Do you still not think and evaluate?

24. They said, "Life comprises only the world! Death, life; all of it is here! Only time destroys us!" They have no proof in regards to this! They are only assuming!

25. And when Our signs are clearly explained to them, they have nothing to say except, "If you are truthful, then bring back our forefathers."

26. Say, "Allah gives you life! Then He will make you experience death! Then He will gather you during Doomsday, of which there is no doubt! But the majority of the people do not know (these Truths)!"

27. The sovereignty of the heavens and the earth is (to manifest the qualities denoted by the Names of) for Allah (who created them out of nonexistence for this specific function)! When that Hour comes, those who try to invalidate the reality will be in loss!

28. You will see every group of faith on their knees! Every group of faith will be called according to their knowledge. And it will be said, "This is the time to live the consequences of your deeds!"

29. This is our knowledge! It speaks to you in Truth... We were recording your deeds! (The universal memory of existence.)

30. As for those who believe and fulfill the requisites of their faith, their Rabb will include them into His grace! This is clear success!

31. But to those who deny the knowledge of the reality, it will be said, "Were you not informed of My signs? But you were arrogant and became of the guilty ones (dualists)!"

32. And when you were told, "The promise of Allah is true and that Hour (when the reality will become apparent) – there is no doubt about it," you said, "We do not know what that Hour is... We think it is only assumption; we are not certain of it!"

33. But the bad of their deeds became apparent and the very thing they mocked enveloped them!

34. They are told, "Just as you forgot the meeting of this time, We now forget you! Your abode is Fire and there is no one to help you either!"

35. "The reason for this is: You did not take the signs of Allah seriously and the pleasures of the world deceived you!"... Today, they will not be removed (from the Fire) and their apologies will not be accepted!

36. Hamd belongs to Allah, the Rabb of the heavens, the Rabb of the world, the Rabb of the worlds (He is the One who does Hamd)!

37. Majesty (the Absolute 'I') belongs to Him in the heavens and the earth! He is the Aziz, the Hakim.

46

AL-AHQAF

By the one who is denoted by the name Allah (who created my being with His Names in accord with the meaning of the letter 'B'), the Rahman, the Rahim.

1. Ha, Meem.

2. The revelation (detailed explanation) of the knowledge is from Allah, the Aziz, the Hakim.

3. We only created the heavens and the earth and everything between them in Truth and for a specified time... But those who deny the knowledge of the reality turn away from that of which they are warned.

4. Say, "(Consider this) have you seen those to whom you turn besides Allah? Show me what they have created of the earth? Or do they have a share in the creation of the heavens? If you are truthful, then bring me a remnant of knowledge or a scripture from the past in regards to this."

5. And who is more astray than the one who prays to things besides Allah, which cannot respond to him until Doomsday, which are not even aware of their prayer?

6. When the people are gathered (those to whom they turned besides Allah) will be enemies to them and they will deny their worship.

7. When Our signs were clearly explained to them, those who deny the knowledge of the reality said when the Truth came to them, "Clearly, this is magic."

8. Or do they say, "He made it up"? Say, "If I have made it up, you do not possess the power to protect me from Allah... HU knows well that you go to excess in His regard... He is sufficient as Witness between me and you... He is the Ghafur, the Rahim.

9. Say, "I am not forming a new thing that has not already manifested among previous Rasuls. I do not know what will

manifest through me or you! I do not follow anything other than what is revealed to me! I am only a clear warner!"

10. Say, "Did you see (consider) what if (the Quran) is from Allah and you have denied it (what will be your state)! A witness from the children of Israel had testified to something similar and believed, but you were arrogant (about this)! Indeed, Allah does not guide the tribe of the wrongdoers."

11. Those who deny the knowledge of the reality said to the believers, "If it was a good thing they could not have surpassed us in attaining it"... Just because they cannot find guidance by it, they say, "This is an old lie."

12. Before (the Quran) was the Book (knowledge) of Moses to lead and as grace... This (Quran) is a source of the knowledge, confirming those before it, in the Arabic language, to warn those who have wronged themselves, and as good news to the doers of good.

13. Indeed, those why say, "Our Rabb is Allah" and live their lives accordingly will have no fear, nor will they grieve.

14. They are the people of Paradise... They will abide therein eternally as the result of their deeds!

15. And We advised man to be kind to his parents. His mother has carried him in hardship and given birth to him in difficulty. His gestation and weaning period is thirty months... When he reaches maturity and reaches the age of forty years he says, "My Rabb... Enable me and my parents to be grateful for the blessings You have bestowed upon us from Your favor, and to engage in deeds that will please You... And make righteous my offspring. I have repented to You and indeed I am of the Muslims (those who are aware of their submission)!"

16. Those are the ones whose good deeds We will validate and whose bad deeds We will overlook... This promise is the reward of Truth!

17. But there is one who says to his parents, "Woe to you! Are you telling me I will be brought forth (resurrected) while so many generations have passed on before me?" While his parents ask Allah for help and say, "Woe to you! Believe! Indeed, the promise of Allah is true"... But he persists and says, "This is nothing but the fables of the past!"

18. Those are the ones, of jinn and men, upon whom the suffering of the past generations will also come into effect... Indeed, they were losers.

19. All of them have degrees (formed) as a result of what they have done, so they may be fully compensated for their deeds, without any injustice.

20. At the time when those who deny the knowledge of the reality are brought to the Fire (it will be said), "You exhausted your pleasures in the worldly life and wasted your life on transitory amusements! So, today you will be requited for being arrogant on the earth without right, and for living with a corrupt faith!"

21. And mention the brother of Aad (Hud)... When he, before and after whom many warners had passed on, warned his people in the sand dunes, "Do not worship anything besides Allah... I fear for you the suffering of a mighty time."

22. They said, "Did you come to avert us from our gods? Then bring the thing with which you warn us, if you are of the truthful!"

23. (Hud) said, "Its knowledge is with Allah! I (only) inform you of what has been disclosed to me... But I see that you are ignorant people!"

24. And when they saw the enormous cloud (the suffering of which they were warned) approaching their valley, they said, "This cloud brings us rain." No, that is the thing for which you were impatient! It is the wind containing severe suffering.

25. (That wind) completely destroys everything by the command of his Rabb! And they became such that nothing remained of them other than their dwellings! Thus We recompense the guilty people for their deeds!

26. Indeed, We gave opportunities to them, which We have not given you... We formed ears and eyes for them, and hearts with which they can comprehend the reality... But because they consciously denied the signs of Allah, neither their ears, nor eyes, nor their hearts (the reflectors of the Names to their consciousness – heart neurons) availed them from anything! They were enveloped by the very thing they mocked!

27. Indeed, We destroyed the cities surrounding you... We repeatedly explained the signs to them in various ways that perhaps they will turn back!

28. Were the gods, which they took besides Allah assuming they would bring them closer, of any help to them? On the contrary (their deities) vanished from them! This (their assumption of god) is a lie and a fabrication of their own making!

29. And We directed to you a group of the jinn (beings outside the human visible spectrum), so they may listen to the Quran... When they were ready for it, they said, "Be silent!" And when it was concluded, they went back to their people as warners.

30. They said, "O our people, indeed we have heard a knowledge revealed after Moses confirming what was before it, which guides to the Truth and to a straight path (tariq al-mustaqim; knowledge that leads to the realization of one's servitude to Allah, with or without their consent).

31. "O our people, respond to the DAI'ALLAH (the jinn perceived him as the Dai'Allah not the Rasulullah; misused words such as 'messenger' denoting a courier of information derive from this word) and believe in him; Allah will forgive for you some of your sins and protect you from a great suffering..."

Note: The jinn recognized the Rasuls as 'DAI'ALLAH,' which literally means the 'inviters of/to Allah.' The commonly used phrase 'Messenger of Allah,' which denotes a postman position to the Rasuls, also arises from this word.

32. And whoever does not respond to the caller of Allah (Dai'Allah) cannot render (Allah) helpless on earth! And they will have no friend besides Allah... They are in clear error.

33. Do they not see that Allah, who created the heavens and the earth without failing in their creation, is Qadir to give life to the dead... Yes! Indeed, He is Qadir over all things.

34. At that time when those who deny the knowledge of the reality are brought to the Fire it will be said, "So was it not the Truth?" And they will say, "Indeed, by our Rabb, yes!"... "Then taste the suffering now for denying the knowledge of the reality!"

35. Be patient, as were those of great determination among the Rasuls, and do not be impatient for them! When they see the thing

of which they have been warned (when they taste death) **they will be like as though they had not remained** (in the world) **for more than an hour of a day! This is enough** (notification)**! Will any be destroyed except those whose faith is corrupt!**

47

MUHAMMAD

By the one who is denoted by the name Allah (who created my being with His Names in accord with the meaning of the letter 'B'), **the Rahman, the Rahim.**

1. **Those who deny the knowledge of the reality and prevent from the way of Allah are those whose deeds are lost!**

2. **Those who believe and fulfill the requisites of faith and who believe in what has been revealed to Muhammad, which is the Truth from their Rabb,** (Allah) **has covered/concealed their bad deeds from them; He amended their conditions.**

3. **This is because those who deny the knowledge of the reality followed invalid ideas! But those who believed followed the Truth from their Rabb... Thus does Allah give the example** (of the two groups) **to people.**

4. **When you encounter those who deny the knowledge of the reality** (in battle), **strike their necks! And when you have overpowered them, secure their bonds** (take them as captives). **Thereafter, either free them out of favor or ransom them. Until the war is over. Thus it is! Had Allah willed He would surely have made them live** (suffer) **the consequence of their offences. But he tried some of you with some of them** (through war)**... As for those who are killed in the way of Allah, their works will never be lost!**

5. **He will guide them to the reality and amend their conditions!**

6. **He will include them into the Paradise that He has made known to them** (at the end of the period of battle)**!**

7. **O believers! If you help Allah, He will help you; He will keep your feet firm.**

8. **As for those who deny the knowledge of the reality, falling on to their faces in destruction is what they deserve! (Allah) has made their deeds amount to nothing!**

9. This is because they disliked what Allah disclosed... So, (Allah) made their deeds amount to nothing.

10. Did they not observe (travel throughout) the earth and see the end of those who came before them! Let them observe (with their mind's eye and take a lesson). Allah has destroyed them! And something similar awaits these deniers of the reality.

11. That is (the truth of the matter)! Allah is the protector over the believers. But those who deny the knowledge of the reality have no protector!

12. Indeed, Allah will include those who believe and fulfill the requisites of faith to Paradises underneath which rivers flow... But those who deny the knowledge of the reality will benefit (from the world only in terms of their body) and eat like cattle (animals)! The Fire is where they will abide.

13. There were many cities (people) stronger than your city, which drove you out! And We destroyed them (imagine)! And there was no one to help them.

14. Are those who are upon a clear proof from their Rabb like those to whom bad deeds have been made attractive (made to be perceived pleasurable) and who follow their baseless desires and amusements?

15. The allegoric description (metaphoric representation) of **Paradise,** promised for those who protect themselves, is as the following: There are rivers of fresh water there that never go stale, and rivers of milk the taste of which never goes bad, and rivers of wine delicious to its drinkers, and rivers of pure honey! There they will have all kinds of fruit and forgiveness (covering) from their Rabb! Can those (who live in this state of bliss) be like those who abide eternally in Hell in a state of burning, and who are given a drink of boiling water that tears their bowels?

16. And some of them will (come and) listen to you... And when they leave they will say to those to whom the knowledge has been given, "What did he just say?" (They will not understand!) They are the ones whose hearts Allah has sealed (locked their consciousness) who follow baseless desires and amusements.

17. But to those who attain the reality, He expands their ability to experience the reality and enables them to protect themselves (from behaviors that go against or impede the experience of the reality).

18. Are they awaiting the Hour (of death) to suddenly come upon them? Its signs have already come! But what can they do when (that Hour) actually comes to them?

19. So, know then that there is no god, there is only Allah; and ask forgiveness for your mistakes (inadequacies of your human nature) and the believing men and women (help them to understand the reality so they may be forgiven)! Allah knows of your movement (states) and the place of your eternal abode!

20. The believers say, "Why has a surah (chapter) not been disclosed (regarding the rules of battle)?" But when a surah with clear rules is disclosed and battle is mentioned therein, you will see those in whose hearts is sickness (duality, hypocrisy) looking at you like one who has fainted in fear of death! (Whereas) this is better for them!

21. (Their duty here is) obedience and a good word! And when the matter is settled, if they had been loyal to Allah, surely it would have been better for them.

22. If you turn back, would you not be causing corruption on the earth and severing your ties of relations?

23. They are those who Allah has cursed, deafened and whose vision (Allah) blinded.

24. Do they not contemplate on the Quran systematically and in depth? Or are there locks (incorrect conditionings) upon their hearts (consciousness)?

25. As for those (hypocrites) who turn away after the reality becomes clearly manifest, Satan (corruptive thoughts) has made this pleasing to them and amused them with wishful thinking.

26. The reason they are in this state is because they said, to those who were not pleased with what Allah disclosed, "We will follow you in part of the matter"... (Whereas) Allah knows what they conceal.

27. And how will it be when the angels take them in death (disconnect them from their bodies), striking their faces and backs?

28. It is thus! This is because they followed things that angered Allah; they did not like (the way of) His pleasure, and Allah made their deeds worthless!

29. Or did those with ill thoughts think Allah would not expose their (concealed) **hatred?**

30. **If We had willed, We could have shown them to you and you would have recognized them from their faces! Indeed, you will know them from the tone of their speech...** Allah knows what you do!

31. **Indeed, We will try you** (with afflictions) **until the strivers** (in the way of Allah) **and the patient ones among you become apparent... And We will spread your news!**

32. **Indeed, those who deny the knowledge of the reality, prevent from the way of Allah, and who oppose the Rasul** (of Allah) **after the knowledge of the reality is explained to them can never cause any harm to Allah! But their deeds will be rendered worthless.**

33. **O believers! Obey Allah and obey the Rasul; do not render your deeds worthless!**

34. **Indeed, those who deny the knowledge of the reality and prevent people from the way of Allah** (with physical or spiritual means) **and who die with their denial, Allah will never forgive them!**

35. **Do not weaken and call to peace** (merge the truth with falsehood) **while you are superior! Allah is 'One' with you! He will never lessen your deeds.**

36. **The life of the world is only play and amusement! If you believe and protect yourselves, He will give you your rewards and He will not ask you** (to give up) **all of your wealth** (for this cause)!

37. **If He had asked you** (for all of it) **and pressured you, you would have been stingy and** (thus) **He would have exposed your unwillingness.**

38. **Here you are, being invited to share unrequitedly in the way of Allah! But among you are some who are stingy! And whoever is stingy, is only stingy towards his own self! Allah is the Ghani; you are the needy! If you turn away, He will replace you with another people, and they will not be like you!**

48

AL-FATH

By the one who is denoted by the name Allah (who created my being with His Names in accord with the meaning of the letter 'B'), the Rahman, the Rahim.

1. Indeed, we have given you the Clear Conquest (fath; the clear observation of the system of the reality)!

2. That Allah may forgive (cover/conceal) your past and (in spite of the conquest – fath) future misdeeds (the veils resulting from corporeality) and complete His favor upon you and guide you to the experience of your reality (essence).

3. Allah will lead you to an unmatched mighty victory!

4. It is HU who sends tranquility (sense of security) to the hearts of the believers that they would increase in faith! The soldiers of the heavens and the earth belong to Allah! Allah is the Aleem, the Hakim.

5. And to admit the believing men and women to Paradises, underneath which rivers flow, in which they will abide eternally, in order to remove from them their bad deeds... This is the great attainment in the sight of Allah!

6. And that He may punish the hypocrite men and women and the dualist men and women who misperceive Allah who comprises their essential reality with His Names (as a god)! May the evil turn of fortune be upon them for their assumptions! Allah's wrath and curse is upon them (distanced them from the experience of the reality due to their denial) and prepared Hell for them! What a wretched place of return!

7. The soldiers (forces) of the heavens and the earth belong to Allah... Allah is the Aziz, the Hakim.

8. Indeed, we disclosed you as a witness, giver of good news and as a warner!

9. So, believe in Allah – your essential reality with His Names – and His Rasul; support him, exalt and respect him, and engage in glorifying Him (tasbih) by morning and night.

10. Indeed, (my Rasul) those who pledge allegiance to you have pledged allegiance to Allah. The hand of Allah is over their hands (the hand of Allah administers over the hands of those who pledge allegiance)! So, he who breaks his word has broken it against his own self, and he who keeps his word to Allah will be given a great reward!

11. Those who remained behind of the Bedouins say, "Our properties and children kept us occupied, so ask forgiveness for us"... But they say with their tongues what they do not actually mean! Say, "Who can go against the will of Allah if He intended to give you harm or if He willed to benefit you?"... No, Allah is aware of what you do (as the creator of your actions).

12. You thought the Rasul and the believers would not return to their families! This seemed pleasing to your consciousness, and thus you assumed a bad assumption and became a people worthy of suffering!

13. Whoever does not believe in Allah and His Rasul, as their essential reality with His Names, let them know that We have prepared a blaze (of fire – waves of radiation) for those who deny the knowledge of the reality.

14. The sovereignty of the heavens and the earth is for (the manifestation of the Names of) Allah! He forgives (covers the offensive state of) whom He wills and gives suffering (the consequence of corporeality) to whom He wills! Allah is the Ghafur, the Rahim.

15. Those who remained behind will say when you go to collect the spoils of war, "Let us come with you." They want to change the words of Allah. Say, "You can never follow us; for this is what Allah said (decreed) before"... Then they will say, "No, you envy us"... On the contrary, they are people devoid of understanding!

16. Say to the Bedouins who remained behind, "You will be called to battle with a people of great strength and might... Either you fight them or they will submit (to Islam). If you obey, Allah will give you a good reward... But if you turn away as you turned away before, then He will subject you to a great suffering."

17. There is no obligation upon the blind, the cripple and the one who is ill! If he obeys Allah and His Rasul He will admit him to Paradises underneath which rivers flow... But whoever turns away, He will punish him with a severe suffering.

18. Indeed, Allah was pleased with the believers when they pledged allegiance to you under the tree. He knew what was in their hearts, so He gave tranquility (serenity) to their hearts and rewarded them with an imminent conquest (certainty).

19. And He gave them many spoils of war... Allah is the Aziz, the Hakim.

20. Allah has promised many spoils of war to you... And He has hastened this for you and withheld the hands of people from you that this may be a sign for the believers and that He may guide you to a straight path.

21. And He promised other things to them, which you are not capable of, that Allah had already encompassed (internally and externally). Allah is Qadir over all things.

22. If those who deny the knowledge of the reality were to fight with you they would surely have turned their backs in flight... And then they would not have found a friend (protector) or a helper.

23. This is the established sunnatullah! And never will you find in the sunnatullah (the mechanics of Allah's system) any change!

24. It is HU who withheld their hands from you and your hands from them in the center of Mecca after He made you overcome them. Allah is Basir of your actions (as their creator).

25. They are those who deny the knowledge of the reality, obstruct you from the Masjid al-Haram, and prevent the offerings from reaching their places... If it was not for the believing men and women (among them), of whom you are unaware, and thus could inadvertently trample and then be upset by it (Allah would not have prevented the battle)... This was so that Allah may admit whom He wills to His grace... If the (believers and nonbelievers) had been separate from one another, surely We would have punished those who disbelieved with a severe suffering. (Suffering does not befall a place where there are righteous people... 8:33, 29:32)

26. The deniers of the knowledge of the reality had put patriotism (ethnocentricity, pride out of ignorance) and narrow-mindedness

(conservatism) **into their hearts... Allah gave tranquility** (serenity) **to those who believed in Allah and His Rasul and secured them upon the Truth: "There is no god, only Allah"** (La ilaha illaAllah)**... They were those who experienced this reality and were deserving of it... Allah is Aleem of all things.**

27. Indeed, Allah confirmed to His Rasul his vision in Truth... InshaAllah (with the manifestation of the Names of Allah comprising your essence)**, you will most definitely enter the Masjid al-Haram, in safety, with** (some of) **your heads shaved or shortened, without any fear!** (Allah) **knowing what you do not know, has arranged before this an imminent conquest** (of closeness/certainty).

28. He disclosed His Rasul as the articulator of the reality and upon the religion of Truth (the understanding of the reality of sunnatullah, which is the system and order manifesting the Names of Allah) **superior to all understanding of religion! And sufficient is Allah** (with His presence in their being) **as Shahid** (Witness).

29. Muhammad is the Rasul of Allah! Those with him are stern against the deniers of the reality, but compassionate among themselves... You will see them bowing (in awe of the observation of Allah's Names as the absolute administrator over existence at all times)**, prostrating** (with the awareness that existence comprises only the Names and thus experiencing their nonexistence with the realization of not having a separate independent being)**, seeking the bounty** (the awareness of the forces of the Names) **and the pleasure of Allah** (enlightenment to the reality and the ability to actualize its potentials)**... And on their faces** (consciousness) **is the mark of prostration** (the comprehension of their nonexistence)**! This is their metaphoric description in the Torah** (laws in regards to the identity-self)**... And their description** (similitude) **in the Gospel is that of a plant, which produces its offshoots and strengthens them so they grow firm and stand upon their stalks, giving delight to its sowers... Allah does this to enrage the deniers** (coverers) **of the reality with them** (the manifestations of His Names)**! Allah has promised those who believe and fulfill its requisites, forgiveness and a great reward.**

HUJURAT

By the one who is denoted by the name Allah (who created my being with His Names in accord with the meaning of the letter 'B'), the Rahman, the Rahim.

1. O believers... Do not forge ahead of Allah and His Rasul (with your identity based thoughts, comments and interpretations), and protect yourselves from Allah (for He will subject you to the consequences of your conditioned value judgments)! Indeed, Allah is the Sami, the Aleem.

2. O believers... Do not raise your voices (ideas and thoughts) over the voice (the teachings) of the Nabi! Do not address him loudly like the way you (recklessly) address each other! Or your deeds will become worthless without you even realizing!

3. Those who lower their voices in the presence of the Rasul of Allah, they are the ones whose level of understanding Allah has revealed... There is forgiveness for them and a great reward.

4. As for those who call out to you from (outside) your house, most of them cannot use their intellects! (Note that calling him out is looked upon as an unintellectual act. A noteworthy topic!)

5. Had they been patient until you went out to them, it would surely have been better for them. Allah is the Ghafur, the Rahim.

6. O believers... If someone with corrupt faith brings information to you, investigate it well... Lest you maltreat a people without knowing the truth of the matter and then become regretful over what you have done!

7. Understand well that the Rasul of Allah is within you! If he was to follow you in most affairs, surely you would be distressed! But Allah endeared faith (experiencing your essence) to you and made it pleasing to your perception and made denial (of the reality), defiance (acts that go against faith and which blind one's consciousness) and rebellion (ego-based ambitions) unpleasing to you... Those are the ones who have attained maturity!

8. As bounty and favor from Allah... Allah is the Aleem, the Hakim.

9. And if two groups among the believers fight against each other, make peace between them... If one goes to excess and oppresses the other, fight the oppressors until they return to the command of Allah! If they return, then make reconciliation between them with justice. Indeed, Allah likes those who give all things their due right.

10. Indeed, the believers are brothers! So, make peace between the two brothers and protect yourselves from Allah so that you may attain grace.

11. O believers... Let not one group mock the other! They (who they mock) may be better than them! And let not the women (ridicule) the women! Perhaps they (the others) are better than them! And do not criticize one another and do not call each other by offensive names! What a terrible label it is when faith gives way to non-belief. And whoever has not repented, they are the very wrongdoers!

12. O you who have believed, avoid most assumptions (guesswork about things of which you have no certain knowledge). Indeed, certain assumptions are an offence (lead to or are an outcome of duality). And do not spy on others (do not inspect or inquire into the private matters of others out of curiosity), and do not backbite. Would one of you like to eat the flesh of his dead brother? You would detest it! So, protect yourselves from Allah, the Tawwab, the Rahim.

13. O people... Indeed, We have (always) created you from a male and a female (no stated exception for Adam here); and made you into races-nations and communities so that you may come to know (and acquire different qualities and virtues from) each other... Indeed, the noblest of you in the sight of Allah are those who are true to themselves (their essential reality)! Indeed, Allah is the Aleem, the Habir.

14. The Bedouins (those who lived in ignorance as tribes and clans) said, "We have believed"... Say, "You did not believe! Say 'We have submitted (become Muslims)'! For faith is not yet clarified and established in your consciousness! If you obey Allah and His Rasul, (Allah) will not detract anything from your work... Indeed, Allah is the Ghafur, the Rahim."

15. The believers are those who have believed in Allah, who has created their being with His Names, and His Rasul, and did not fall into doubt thereof and fought in the way of Allah with their wealth

and their very beings (lives)! **They are the truthful ones** (who conform the reality with their very lives)!

16. Say, "Are you attempting to teach your understanding of religion to Allah! Allah knows what is in the heavens and the earth... Allah is Aleem over all things."

17. Do they think they are doing you a favor by becoming Muslims! Say, "Do not consider your Islam a favor to me (it is for your own sake)! **On the contrary, it Allah's favor to you that He has directed you to faith! If you are truthful** (to your faith, you will know this is true).**"**

18. Indeed, Allah knows the unperceivable within the heavens and the earth... Allah (within your very being) **is Basir over what you do.**

50

QAF

By the one who is denoted by the name Allah (who created my being with His Names in accord with the meaning of the letter 'B'), the Rahman, the Rahim.

1. **Qaf** (The Arabic letter Qaf symbolizes the ego, the first of the three reflections of the absolute essence of man [ego, oneness, identity] In Sufism, Mount Qaf is considered to be the symbol of the ego. Mountains often symbolize the ego)**, the Magnificent Quran** (the disclosure of magnificent Knowledge)!

2. **Surprised that the warner who came to them was someone from among themselves, the deniers of the knowledge of the reality said, "This is a strange thing, indeed..."**

3. **"Will we** (be resurrected) **once we have died and become dust? That is a distant return** (a far-fetched claim)."

4. **We know exactly what the earth detracts from them** (what is lost with old age)**... With us is the Book of Records** (the universal memory recorded within the essence of existence).

5. **No, they denied their essential reality when it came to them! They are in a confused state.**

6. (Assuming to be the body) **did they not look at the sky above them** (consciousness) **to see how We formed it and adorned it** (with senses)! **There is no flaw in it!**

7. **We developed the earth** (the body) **and formed upon it firmly set mountains** (organs)**! And produced therein from every beautiful pair** (double helix DNA) **the vegetal properties of the body.**

8. **To activate insight, to remind and give admonition to every servant** (who turns to his essence).

9. **We sent down water** (knowledge) **from the sky with which We made to grow gardens** (the experience of the beauteous inherent forces) **and grains that are harvested** (various abilities).

10. And lofty palm trees with clusters of fruit...

11. As sustenance of life for the servants... We gave life with it to a dead land... Thus is the resurrection (from one's cocoon world).

12. And before them, the people of Noah, the people of the well and Thamud also denied (the eternal life to come after death).

13. And Aad, and Pharaoh, and the brothers of Lot.

14. And the people of the wood and the people of Tubba... All of them denied and thus My punishment, of which they were notified, was fulfilled.

15. Were We inadequate in the first creation? No, they are in doubt of the new creation.

16. Indeed, it is We who created man... We know what his soul whispers to him (the idea of being only the body formed by his mind)... We are closer to him (within the dimensions of the brain) than his jugular vein!"

17. Two recording forces record from his right and from his left!

18. Every thought (of man) is observed (recorded) by an observer!

19. And the intoxication of death has come, revealing the Truth! This is the very thing you tried to escape!

20. And the Horn (body) is blown (the act of blowing occurs from the inside out – the spirit has left the body)! This is the time of which you were warned!

21. Every soul (consciousness) will come with an attendant (his constructed identity through corporeality) and a witness (the call of his conscience voicing the Truth)!

22. (It will be said), "You were certainly unaware of this (you were living in your cocoon), and We have removed from you your veil, so your sight, from this period on, is sharp."

23. His companion (body – jinn friend) will say, "Here it is, ready with me."

24. (It will be said), "Cast into Hell every persistent ungrateful denier of the reality!"

25. "The preventer of every good (pertaining to the Truth) and doubter."

26. Who made besides Allah another god! Throw him into severe suffering!"

27. His companion (while the word human/man is a reference to consciousness, the word companion denotes one's body or one's jinn friend) said, "My Rabb, it was not me who made him transgress, he himself was in an extreme error."

28. (Allah) said, "Do not bicker in my presence (there is no point in arguing in My presence)! I had already warned you about what was to come!"

29. "And My judgment shall not be changed! I am not unjust to the servants!"

30. At that time We will ask Hell, "Are you now full?"... (Hell will say), "Are there any more?"

31. And Paradise will be brought near to the protected ones... It was not far from them anyway.

32. "This is what you were promised," it will be said to those who turned to their essence and protected themselves.

33. The one who is in awe of the Rahman as his unknown, and who comes in a state of consciousness turned (to his essence).

34. Enter therein as salam (experiencing the meaning of the Name Salam)... This is the eternal life!

35. They will have whatever they desire therein, and even more with Us!

36. Many generations We have destroyed before them who were mightier than them in strength! And they sought a place (of refuge) because of this... Is there any place of escape?

37. Undoubtedly this reminder is for the conscious one or the one who listens attentively!

38. Indeed, We created the heavens, the earth and everything in between in six stages! And We were not touched by weariness!

39. So, be patient about what they say! And glorify (tasbih) your Rabb as His Hamd (fulfill your purpose) before sunrise and sunset!

40. And glorify Him in the night and after prostration!

41. And listen, in that time, when the Caller will call from within!

42. The time when they will hear the blast in Truth! That is the time of emergence (awakening to the reality outside the cocoon)!

43. Indeed, it is Us, yes Us, who gives life and takes life! And to Us is the return!

44. At that time, the earth (body) will hastily break away from them! That is, for Us, an easy gathering.

45. As We are present within them, We know better what they say! You cannot force them into anything! Remind (the reality) by the Quran to those who fear my warning of suffering.

51

ADH-DHARIYAT

By the one who is denoted by the name Allah (who created my being with His Names in accord with the meaning of the letter 'B'), the Rahman, the Rahim.

1. By the scattering and the dispersing (winds).

2. And the bearers of burden.

3. And those who flow with ease.

4. And those who apportion the command!

5. What you are promised is certainly true!

6. Indeed, religion (the system) is an absolute reality!

7. The heaven (consciousness) full of pathways (of various thoughts)!

8. Indeed, you are in differing views!

9. He who is turned away is turned away from it!

10. May the deniers perish!

11. Who are confused in ignorance and blindness!

12. "When is the time of religion (recompense)?" they ask.

13. They will thrash about in the fire at that time.

14. (They will be told by the creatures of Hell), "Taste your suffering! This is what you were impatient for!"

15. Indeed, those who protected themselves will be in Paradises and springs.

16. As receivers of the blessings of their Rabb (from within). Indeed, before this they were doers of good.

17. They would sleep in a small portion of the night.

18. And ask for forgiveness before dawn.

19. And there was a portion among their properties for the needy and the troubled.

20. There are signs on the earth (the body) for those who are certain!

21. Within your own selves (the essence of the self). Do you still not see (realize)?

22. Both your provision and what you are promised is in heaven (experienced from one's consciousness)!

23. By the Rabb of the heaven and the earth, it (what you are informed of in regards to the future) is true – as natural and true as your ability to speak.

24. Did you receive the news of Abraham's honored guests?

25. When they came to him they said, "Salam"... (And Abraham said), "Salam"... And thought, "Unusual people..."

26. Then He turned to his family and brought a (roasted) calf.

27. And offered it to them and said, "Will you not eat?"

28. (When he saw that they did not eat) he felt apprehensive! "Fear not" they said and gave him the good news of a learned son.

29. And his wife cried and returned to the guests, covering her face with her hands, and said, "But I am a barren old woman!"

30. (Abraham's guests, the angels) said, "Thus it will be! It is what your Rabb said... Indeed, He is the Hakim, the Aleem."

31. (Abraham) said, "O disclosed ones... What is your (real) business (purpose)?"

32. They said, "Indeed, we have been disclosed for a guilty people!"

33. "That we may send down stones of clay upon them."

34. "Marked (stones) in the sight of your Rabb for the transgressors (who waste the forces they are given to attain the reality)!"

35. So, We took all the believers out from there.

36. Not that we found any, except for a single household of those who have submitted (Muslims)!

37. And we left a sign therein for those who fear that severe suffering.

38. Like that in Moses... When We had disclosed him as a clear sign to Pharaoh.

39. But he turned away with his rulers and said, "A magician or a madman!"

40. So, We seized him and his army and cast them into the sea... And he beat himself up in regret!

41. And in Aad... How We had disclosed that wind within which there was no good or blessing (cyclone)...

42. It left nothing standing of whatever it came upon; disintegrated it into bits!

43. And in Thamud... How they were told, "Enjoy yourself for a time."

44. But they went against the command of their Rabb! So, a thunderbolt seized them while they were looking on.

45. And they were not able to survive, nor did they receive any help!

46. And the people of Noah before them... Indeed, they were a people of corrupt faith!

47. As for the heaven (the universe and the capacity of the brain), it is We who built it and We who expands it (via dimensional formations – beings – the expansion of the usable area within one's brain through the increase of comprehension)!

48. And We furnished the earth (energy lines – the nervous system of the body)... What excellent furnishers We are!

49. And We created everything in pairs (positive – negative energy; the double stranded DNA)... That perhaps you will remember and contemplate.

50. "Flee to Allah (from corporeality)! I am indeed a clear warner to you from Him!"

51. "Do not assume a god besides Allah! Indeed, I am a clear warner to you from Him!"

52. **This is** (the truth of the matter)**! There came not to those before them a Rasul** (calling them to Allah, their essential reality)**, except that they said, "A magician or a madman."**

53. **Did they** (genetically) **suggest this to one another? No, they are a people in transgression!**

54. **Turn away from them! You are not to be blamed** (for this).

55. **And remind! Indeed, reminding benefits the believers.**

56. <u>**I have created the jinn and men only so that they may serve Me**</u> <u>(by means of manifesting the qualities of My Names).</u>

57. **I do not ask for provision from them; nor do I want them to feed Me.**

58. **Indeed, Allah is HU, the Razzaq, the Dhu'l Quwwati'l Mateen** (Possessor of Enduring Strength).

59. **Indeed, the wrongdoers will have their share of that** (suffering) **that befell their friends** (those who came before them)**! Let them not rush.**

60. **Woe to those who deny the reality, from the suffering they are promised** (forewarned)**!**

52

AT-TUR

By the one who is denoted by the name Allah (who created my being with His Names in accord with the meaning of the letter 'B'), the Rahman, the Rahim.

1. By the Mount (Mount Sinai, on which Moses encountered the reality),

2. And the inscribed knowledge (encompassing every detail)!

3. By the evident (manifest) house (the perceivable dimension of acts).

4. And the prosperous house (the dimension of Names comprised of the knowledge pertaining to the Absolute Essence, the Reality of Muhammad, the perfectly constructed house – the human consciousness experiencing the quality of vicegerency generating from the Names of Allah);

5. And the raised ceiling (the knowledge that surpasses the dimension of acts),

6. And the overflowing ocean (waves of knowledge)!

7. Indeed, the punishment of your Rabb will occur!

8. There is no power to repel it!

9. At that time, the heaven (consciousness) will be bewildered!

10. And the mountains (egos) will depart! (Your Rabb is the Baqi!)

11. Woe to those who deny that time!

12. (Those deniers) who now amuse themselves with (worldly imaginary) indulgences!

13. They will be relentlessly dragged into the Hellfire at that time!

14. (And it will be said), "This is the Fire you denied!"

15. "So is this magic then, or do you not see?"

16. "Dwell in the Fire! Be patient or impatient; it makes no difference for you! You are living the consequences of your deeds!"

17. Indeed, the protected ones are in Paradises and among blessings.

18. They rejoice with what their Rabb manifests through them! Their Rabb (the Names comprising their being) has protected them from the suffering of Hell.

19. "Eat and drink the results of your deeds with pleasure!"

20. Resting on couches arranged in rows... We partnered them (the conscious humans manifesting the forces of the Names) with houris (bodies with superior and clear vision [heart])! (All expressions in the Quran of female houris are symbolic, allegoric expressions, like other metaphors pertaining to the life of Paradise. The statement 'Math'alul jannatillatiy' contained in various verses, which means, "The example [metaphor] of Paradise" [13:35] or "The allegoric description [metaphoric representation] of Paradise" [47:15] are indications of this truth. [Note that there is also a Hadith which states, "Allah says, 'I have prepared for My righteous servants things which no eye has ever seen, and no ear has ever heard, and no human heart/mind has ever perceived!'" Sahih Bukhari, Muslim, Tirmidhi])

21. Those who believe and whose descendants followed in faith, We shall unite them with their descendants and ascendants. And We did not detract anything from what they earned... Every person is bound by the consequences of his own deeds!

22. We provided them abundantly with fruits (of gnosis) and meat (bodily qualities with which to manifest these qualities) as they desire.

23. They will share cups of drinks therein, which does not cause intoxication!

24. Youthful servants (energetic forces) will circulate around them, like they are hidden pearls!

25. And they will turn to each other and discuss their previous states.

26. They will say, "Indeed, previously we were the terrified ones among our people."

27. "So Allah conferred favor upon us and protected us from the suffering of the (Hellfire; the state of burning) **samum** (an infusing microwave radiation)!"

28. "Indeed, we used to turn to Him before this! Indeed, He is the Barr, the Rahim."

29. So, remind (my Rasul)! By the favor of your Rabb, you have not been disclosed as a soothsayer or one that is possessed!

30. Or do they say, "He is a poet... Let us wait and see how his end will be"!

31. Say, "Then wait! Indeed, I too am of those who are waiting!"

32. Is it their minds that suggest this to them or are they an insolent people?

33. Or do they say, "He has made it up"? No, they do not believe!

34. If they are true to their word, let them bring a word like it!

35. Or were they created without a cause? Or are they the creators?

36. Or did they create the heavens and the earth? No, they are not certain.

37. Or are the treasures of your Rabb with them? Or are they the rulers over all things?

38. Or do they have a staircase upon which they climb and listen (to the divine mysteries)? (If that is the case) then let them bring a clear and undeniable proof.

39. Or are the daughters His and the sons yours?

40. Or do you ask of them a payment by which they are heavily indebted?

41. Or do they have (knowledge of) the unknown; is it them who determines (what is to transpire)?

42. Or do they intend to plan a trap? Yet they, who deny the knowledge of the reality, are the very ones who are entrapped!

43. Or do they have gods besides Allah? Allah is Subhan from what they associate with Him!

44. If they see an object falling from the sky, they will say, "It is but layers of clouds."

45. Leave them until they meet the day (death) in which they will be struck by horror!

46. That day, neither their traps will repel anything from them nor will there be anyone to help them!

47. Indeed, for the wrongdoers there is a suffering before that too! But the majority of them do not know.

48. Be patient for the command of your Rabb! Indeed, you are under Our supervision! And glorify (tasbih) your Rabb as His Hamd, when you get up (during the night)...

49. And glorify (tasbih) your Rabb (as His Hamd) in a part of the night and after the setting of the stars!

53

AN-NAJM

By the one who is denoted by the name Allah (who created my being with His Names in accord with the meaning of the letter 'B'), the Rahman, the Rahim.

1. By the star (Najm) (that describes all of the reality by disclosing it part by part),

2. Your friend has neither strayed nor has he erred!

3. Nor does he speak from his own inclinations (imagination)!

4. It is only a revealed revelation!

5. Taught to him by one whose forces are intense!

6. That (force) became apparent to him and thus he became open (to receiving revelation)!

7. While he was at the highest point of the horizon (covering all of externality)!

8. The he approached and descended (externality transformed into internality).

9. And was (as close as) the distance between two bow lengths or nearer!

10. Thus He revealed to His servant what He revealed.

11. The heart did not lie about what it saw (the incoming information coalesced with the Truth revealed by the neurons in the brain)!

12. Do you argue with him regarding what he saw?

13. And indeed, he saw Him again (became aware as the reality descended to his consciousness).

14. In the presence of the Lote Tree (the experience of eternity as pure universal consciousness).

15. Near it (the Lote Tree) **is the Paradise of Mawa!**

16. When there covered the Lote Tree that which covered it (the light of the reality covered his being as he lost his sense of being a body)!

17. His sight neither wavered (to the concept of an 'other') **nor did it transgress its limit** (the observation of the reality did not lead him to become Pharaoh-like and deify himself)!

18. Indeed, he saw the greatest signs of His Rabb (the Names comprising his essence)!

19. Did you see the Lat and the Uzza?

20. And Manat, the third (can they make you experience such an ascension)?

21. Is the male yours and the female His?

22. If so, that is an unjust division!

23. They are mere names that you and your forefathers gave, for which Allah has not disclosed any proof (baseless names that do not point to anything that actually exists)! **They follow only assumption and the illusory desires of their ego** (even though) **the knowledge of the reality has indeed come to them from their Rabb** (the reality of the Names comprising their essence).

24. Or is there a rule that man shall have whatever he desires?

25. Both the eternal life to come and the world are for (the manifestations of the Names of) **Allah!**

26. And how many angels are there in the heavens whose intercession will not be of any avail, except for those to whom Allah allows, those for whom He wills and with whom He is pleased?

27. Indeed, those who do not believe in their eternal life to come define the angels as females.

28. But they have no knowledge (proof) **thereof... They follow only unverifiable assumptions, and indeed, never can assumption reflect the Truth!**

29. So, turn away from those who turn their backs to our dhikr (to the reality We remind them) **and who desire nothing but the pleasures of the world!**

30. **This is the highest point of their knowledge** (to live in and die in pursuit of worldly pleasures; they cannot think beyond this)! **Indeed, your Rabb, HU, knows better who strays from His way! And HU knows better who is guided to the reality!**

31. **Whatever is in the heavens and whatever is on the earth is for** (the manifestation of the qualities denoted by the Names of) **Allah! That is so He may recompense those who do bad deeds with the consequences of their actions and requite those who do good deeds with the best reward.**

32. **They are those who refrain from major mistakes** (duality, slander, murder, etc.) **and immoralities** (fornication, adultery, etc.) **only committing small mistakes resulting from their human nature... Indeed, vast is the forgiveness of your Rabb! He knows you better as He comprises your being with His Names; when He produced you from the earth** (your body) **and while you were fetuses in the wombs of your mothers! So, do not try to exonerate yourselves! He knows better who protects themselves** (as their creator with His Names)!

33. **Did you see the one who turned away?**

34. **Who gave little, then refrained** (from giving)!

35. **Has he the knowledge of the unknown, so that he sees?**

36. **Or was he not informed of the pages** (knowledge – laws) **of Moses?**

37. **And the** (pages of) **Abraham, the faithful?**

38. **No bearer of burdens** (guilty one) **can bear the burden** (offence) **of another!**

39. <u>**And man will only accrue the results** (consequences) **of his own deeds** (what manifests through him; his thoughts and actions)!</u>

40. **And the results of his efforts will soon be seen!**

41. **Then he will live the full results** (of his deeds)!

42. **Indeed, the end of all things is to your Rabb!**

43. **Indeed, it is HU who makes one laugh and weep!**

44. Indeed, it is HU who causes death and gives life (resurrects one with knowledge and enlightenment)!

45. Indeed, it is HU who creates the two sexes, male and female...

46. From a drop of sperm ejected (into the womb – the Rahim)!

47. And upon Him is the second creation (second life)!

48. And indeed, it is HU who enriches and deprives.

49. And indeed, it is HU who is the Rabb of Sirius (the star)!

50. And indeed, it is HU who destroyed the former Aad.

51. And Thamud... (Of whom) **none remains!**

52. And before them the people of Noah... Indeed, they, yes they, were more unjust and worse in egocentric indulgences.

53. And He overthrew the cities (the destroyed cities: Sodom and Gomorrah)!

54. And thus covered them with their coverings (as the result of their deeds)!

55. So which of the favors of your Rabb will you doubt now!

56. This is a warner just like the previous warners!

57. That which nears (death) has neared!

58. There is none to avert (the hardship of death) besides Allah.

59. Do you find this (the commencement of an eternal life through death) to be strange?

60. And you laugh rather than weeping!

61. You amuse yourselves in heedlessness!

62. Prostrate (experience your nonexistence) in the sight of Allah (your essential reality with His Names) and continue your servitude. (This is a verse of prostration.)

54

AL-QAMAR

By the one who is denoted by the name Allah (who created my being with His Names in accord with the meaning of the letter 'B'), **the Rahman, the Rahim.**

1. **The Hour has neared and the Moon** (Qamar) **has split asunder!**

2. **Yet when they see a miracle they turn away and say, "Ordinary magic"!**

3. **They deny and follow their own baseless desires** (all that is pleasing to their egos)**! But every matter will be settled!**

4. **Indeed, there has come to them news in which there is deterrence.**

5. **Wisdom** (erudite knowledge with an accurate explanation of the purpose)**! Yet warning does not help** (the intellectually incapacitated)**!**

6. **So, turn away from them! At that time when the Caller calls to the terrifying event...**

7. **Their eyes will be cast down in terror, they will emerge from their graves** (cocoons) **as if they are locusts spreading about.**

8. **Those who deny the knowledge of the reality will run to the Caller saying, "This is an intense day!"**

9. **Before them the people of Noah had also denied. They denied Our servant and said, "He is possessed" and prevented him** (from his mission)**.**

10. **So, he** (Noah) **prayed to his Rabb, "Indeed, I am overpowered, help me."**

11. **And We opened the gates of heaven with pouring rain!**

12. **And caused the earth to burst with springs and the waters met for a purpose, which had been decreed!**

13. **We carried him** (Noah) **on** (the Ark) **made of planks and nails.**

14. (The Ark) **sailed under Our supervision. To requite the one who had been shown ingratitude** (Noah)!

15. **Indeed, We left it** (the Ark) **behind as a sign** (for the people)! **Is there not anyone who thinks?**

16. **Look at how My suffering and warning was fulfilled!**

17. **Indeed We have eased the Quran that the reality may be remembered and contemplated! Is there not anyone who thinks?**

18. **Aad also denied! And how was My suffering and warning fulfilled?**

19. **Indeed, We sent upon them a hurricane of continuous destruction on an unfortunate day.**

20. **Extracting the people as if they were uprooted trunks of palm trees.**

21. **And My suffering and warnings were fulfilled!**

22. **Indeed, We have simplified the Quran, that the reality may be remembered and contemplated! Is there not anyone who thinks?**

23. **And Thamud also denied.**

24. **They said, "Are we to follow a man like us? Indeed, we would then be astray from our faith and in foolishness."**

25. **"Has dhikr** (the reminder of the knowledge of the reality) **been sent to him from among all of us? Rather, he is an insolent liar!"**

26. **They will know who the insolent liar is soon!**

27. **Indeed, We disclosed to them a she-camel as an object of trial... So, observe them and be patient.**

28. **And give them the news that the water has been shared between them... Each group is to take their share in turn.**

29. **They called out to their friends. They took their share and then savagely hamstrung her!**

30. **And how was My suffering and warning fulfilled!**

31. Indeed, We disclosed upon them the single blast (an intense vibrant sound) and they became like crumbs and debris (which they give to their cattle).

32. Indeed, We have eased the Quran that the reality may be remembered and contemplated! So, is there not anyone who thinks?

33. The people of Lot also denied the warner.

34. Indeed, We sent upon them a storm of stones... Except for the family of Lot... We saved them at dawn.

35. As a favor from Us... Thus We requite the grateful!

36. Indeed, he (Lot) warned them of Our intense seizure, but they doubted the warners!

37. Indeed, they wanted to take advantage (lustfully) of his (Lot's) guests so We blinded their vision, saying, "Taste My suffering and warnings now!"

38. And indeed, the deserved suffering was effectuated upon them in the morning.

39. So, taste My suffering and My warnings now!

40. Indeed, We have simplified the Quran, that the reality may be remembered and contemplated! So, is there not anyone who thinks?

41. Indeed, warners came also to the family of Pharaoh.

42. But they denied all of Our signs! So We seized them with unchallengeable might!

43. Are your deniers of the knowledge of the reality better than these? Or have you been given news of immunity in the scriptures (the revealed knowledge of wisdom)?

44. Or do they say, "We are a community supporting each other"?

45. Soon that community will be defeated and they will turn their backs and flee!

46. No, the Hour (of death) is when they will meet the suffering! That hour is more intense and more painful (than being defeated in war).

47. Indeed, the guilty are in error and foolishness.

48. They will be dragged into the Fire on their faces that day! And it will be said, "Taste the burning of Saqar (Hell)!"

49. Indeed, We have created everything with its program (qadar – fate).

50. Our command (the order and the execution) **is one; like a glance of the eye** (everything transpires in a 'single instance' in the sight of Allah)!

51. Indeed, We destroyed many of your kinds... So, is there not anyone who will ponder on this?

52. The knowledge of everything they do is recorded in the Zabur (books of wisdom).

53. Small or big, everything is inscribed in detail!

54. Indeed, the protected ones are in Paradises and on the banks of rivers.

55. Living the reality through the forces of the Maleek, the Muqtadir!

55

AR-RAHMAN

By the one who is denoted by the name Allah (who created my being with His Names in accord with the meaning of the letter 'B'), the Rahman, the Rahim.

1. **Rahman** (the possessor of all of the qualities referenced by the Beautiful Names),

2. **Taught the Quran** (formed the qualities pertaining to the dimension of Names).

3. **Created man,**

4. **And taught him eloquence** (manifested the Names on man) (as Hadhrat Ali says, "Man became a talking Quran.");

5. **The Sun** (comprehension) **and the Moon** (emotion – feeling) **are with a measure** (in levels).

6. **The star** (ideas) **and the tree** (the body) **are in prostration** (in a state of nonexistence in the sight of the Names).

7. **He has raised the heaven** (consciousness; from the level of the self-accusing self [nafs-i lawwama] to the level of the pleasing self [nafs-i mardhiya]) **and established a balance** (the ability to live in balance of unity and multiplicity).

8. **That you do not do injustice to that balance** (so that you do not go to extreme in one and thus be deprived of the other).

9. **Evaluate justly** (according to the laws of Uluhiyyah) **and do not become losers by failing to live by that balance!**

10. **And upon the earth** (the body) **He formed the creatures** (the micro-universe)!

11. **Therein** (on earth) **is a fruit** (man), **like palm trees** (brain) **full of sheathed clusters** (ready and receptive)!

12. And sprouted grains (blossoming observations of the reality) **and pleasantly scented plants** (behaviors pertaining to the reality of man).

13. So, which of the favors of your Rabb (the Names comprising your essence – your consciousness and body) **will you deny?**

14. He created man (the body) **from processed dry clay** (the formation of the cellular structure).

15. And He created the jann (the invisible beings; the jinn) **from a smokeless flame of fire** (radiation, radiant energy, electromagnetic wave body).

16. So, which of the favors of your Rabb (the Names comprising your essence – your consciousness and body) **will you deny?**

17. He is the Rabb of the two easts (the world and the eternal life after death) **and the Rabb of the two wests** (the world and the dimension of the grave).

18. So, which of the favors of your Rabb (the Names comprising your essence – your consciousness and body) **will you deny?**

19. He let loose the two seas (angelic and animalistic tendencies; the universal consciousness and the individual consciousness)**; they meet together.**

20. Yet between them is a barrier; which they do not transgress (both fulfill their own functions within their own field).

21. So, which of the favors of your Rabb (the Names comprising your essence – your consciousness and body) **will you deny?**

22. From them comes forth the pearl and the coral (various qualities).

23. So, which of the favors of your Rabb (the Names comprising your essence – your consciousness and body) **will you deny?**

24. To Him belong the constructed ships (bodies) **that sail like mountains** (constructed identities – ego) **in the sea** (the knowledge of the reality)!

25. So, which of the favors of your Rabb (the Names comprising your essence – your consciousness and body) **will you deny?**

26. Everyone on the earth (corporeal life) **is transitory** (every sense of self - identity or individual consciousness will taste death).

27. **Baqi** (eternal, without being subject to the concept of time) **is the face** (the absolute reality) **of your Rabb** (the meanings of the Names comprising your essence)**, the Dhul-Jalali Wal-Ikram**

28. **So, which of the favors of your Rabb** (the Names comprising your essence – your consciousness and body) **will you deny?**

29. **Everything in the heavens and the earth asks from Him; at every instance HU** (the Absolute Essence of Existence) **manifests Himself in yet another way!**

30. **So, which of the favors of your Rabb** (the Names comprising your essence – your consciousness and body) **will you deny?**

31. **Soon We shall attend to you** (for account)**, O guilt laden community of man and jinn!**

32. **So, which of the favors of your Rabb** (the Names comprising your essence – your consciousness and body) **will you deny?**

33. **O communities of jinn and man, if you are able to pass beyond the regions of the heavens and the earth, then pass** (live without a body)**! But you cannot pass unless you possess the power** (the manifestation of Allah's attribute of Power [Qadir] on you).

34. **So, which of the favors of your Rabb** (the Names comprising your essence – your consciousness and body) **will you deny?**

35. **There will be sent upon** (both of) **you a flame of fire and smoke** (ambiguity and confusion in your consciousness)**, and you will not be successful!**

36. **So, which of the favors of your Rabb** (the Names comprising your essence – your consciousness and body) **will you deny?**

37. **And when** (during death) **the heaven** (the identity; ego) **is split asunder and** (the reality) **becomes** (undeniably clear and the ego-self disappears) **burnt oil colored, like a rose** (the reality is observed)**!**

38. **So, which of the favors of your Rabb** (the Names comprising your essence – your consciousness and body) **will you deny?**

39. **At that time none among men or jinn will be asked about his offences** (they will begin to live the natural consequences of their deeds)**!**

40. **So, which of the favors of your Rabb** (the Names comprising your essence – your consciousness and body) **will you deny?**

41. The guilty will be recognized by their faces (the reflection of their disposition) and seized by their foreheads and feet.

42. So, which of the favors of your Rabb (the Names comprising your essence – your consciousness and body) will you deny?

43. This is the Hell the guilty ones denied!

44. They will go around between it and boiling water (the burning value judgments brought by their conditionings).

45. So, which of the favors of your Rabb (the Names comprising your essence – your consciousness and body) will you deny?

46. There are two Paradises for the one who fears the position of His Rabb (action and sensation – Paradises of meaning).

47. So, which of the favors of your Rabb (the Names comprising your essence – your consciousness and body) will you deny?

48. With various branches (life qualities) spread out (in both Paradises).

49. So, which of the favors of your Rabb (the Names comprising your essence – your consciousness and body) will you deny?

50. In both of them are two springs, flowing!

51. So, which of the favors of your Rabb (the Names comprising your essence – your consciousness and body) will you deny?

52. In both (of those Paradises) are fruits (gnosis) of both kinds (extrinsic and intrinsic)!

53. So, which of the favors of your Rabb (the Names comprising your essence – your consciousness and body) will you deny?

54. They will rest upon beds whose linings are of silk brocade... The fruits of both Paradises will be so easy to pick!

55. So, which of the favors of your Rabb (the Names comprising your essence – your consciousness and body) will you deny?

56. There are those whose glances are directed only to their partners, untouched by any man or jinn before them (no impurities caused by identity/ego-based ideas and emotions)!

57. So, which of the favors of your Rabb (the Names comprising your essence – your consciousness and body) will you deny?

58. As if they are rubies or coral.

59. So, which of the favors of your Rabb (the Names comprising your essence – your consciousness and body) **will you deny?**

60. Is not good the reward for good (servitude done through the observation of the Truth)?

61. So, which of the favors of your Rabb (the Names comprising your essence – your consciousness and body) **will you deny?**

62. And besides these two Paradises are two more Paradises.

63. So, which of the favors of your Rabb (the Names comprising your essence – your consciousness and body) **will you deny?**

64. Both of them ever green!

65. So, which of the favors of your Rabb (the Names comprising your essence – your consciousness and body) **will you deny?**

66. In both of them are two springs (reflections of the Rahman), constantly spouting!

67. So, which of the favors of your Rabb (the Names comprising your essence – your consciousness and body) **will you deny?**

68. In both of them are fruits and palm trees (symbolic of consciousness manifesting the attributes of the Truth) **and pomegranates** (symbolic of the single consciousness administering the life of multiple forms)!

69. So, which of the favors of your Rabb (the Names comprising your essence – your consciousness and body) **will you deny?**

70. In (those Paradises) **are the most magnificent, the most beautiful.**

71. So, which of the favors of your Rabb (the Names comprising your essence – your consciousness and body) **will you deny?**

72. Houris reserved only for their partners (partners – bodies that are equipped and capacitated to fulfill all of the desires of the forms of consciousness that manifest the attributes of the Truth. Please see 13:35, 47:15)!

73. So, which of the favors of your Rabb (the Names comprising your essence – your consciousness and body) **will you deny?**

74. Untouched by no man or jinn before them (no impurities caused by identity/ego-based ideas and emotions)!

75. So, which of the favors of your Rabb (the Names comprising your essence – your consciousness and body) **will you deny?**

76. They rest upon green cushions and beautifully embroidered fine carpets.

77. So, which of the favors of your Rabb (the Names comprising your essence – your consciousness and body) **will you deny?**

78. Sublime is the name of your Rabb the Dhul-Jalali Wal-Ikram!

56

AL-WAQI'A

By the one who is denoted by the name Allah (who created my being with His Names in accord with the meaning of the letter 'B'), **the Rahman, the Rahim.**

1. When that truth (of the second life after death) **occurs.**

2. There will be none to deny its reality!

3. It brings down (some) **and raises** (some) **up!**

4. When the earth (the body) **is shaken with intensity,**

5. And the mountains (the organs in the body) **are crumbled,**

6. And become dust dispersing.

7. And you become divided into three kinds:

8. The people of the right (the fortunate-happy ones who have attained the Truth) **– and what people of the right?**

9. The people of the left (the unfortunate-unhappy ones who have lived their live cocooned from the Truth) **– and what people of the left?**

10. And the forerunners are the forerunners (of certainty);

11. They are the ones who have attained (the state of divine) **closeness.**

12. Within Paradises of Bliss.

13. Most of them of the former people.

14. And the minority of them of the later people.

15. On thrones embroidered with jewels. (The verses in regards to Paradise as of this verse should be read in light of the statement "The example [metaphoric representation] of Paradise" mentioned in various verses [13:35, 47:15]. All expressions are symbolic and should not be taken literally.)

16. Seated facing one another.

17. With eternally youthful servants around them...

18. With vessels filled from the source, pitchers and cups...

19. Neither headache nor intoxication caused by them!

20. Whatever fruit they prefer;

21. Whichever meat of fowl they desire;

22. And the houris (partner-bodies with superior and clear vision – unrestricted by the limitations of the biological body – enabling the conscious man to experience his essential qualities. The state of living with multiple forms [bodies] under the administration of a single consciousness).

23. Like hidden pearls (raised in the mother of pearl; formations of the Names of Allah [bodies] and the manifestations of their qualities through the human consciousness).

24. This is the reward (result) **of their deeds!**

25. They will neither hear any empty discourse therein, nor any concept of sin!

26. Only saying, "Salam, salam" (meaning; "may the experience of the quality denoted by this Name be continual").

27. And the people of the right (the believers) **– and what people of the right?**

28. Among the lote trees with their fruits,

29. And banana trees layered with fruit...

30. In extended (eternal) **shade,**

31. And flowing waterfalls,

32. Among many (varieties of) **fruits,**

33. (Fruits that) **neither run out nor are forbidden!**

34. (They are) **upon lounges raised high.**

35. Indeed, We designed them (the partners of consciousness; bodies) **with a** (new) **design.**

36. And formed them of a kind never used before!

37. In love with their partners (bodies that have never been seen or used before, who enable the peak experience of the qualities of the human consciousness, as opposed to the animalistic body that made man 'descend to the world as enemies,' directing him towards materialistic gains) **and who are equal in age** (came into existence with consciousness)!

38. (These are) **for the people of the right** (the fortunate ones).

39. A group of them (the people of the right) **are from the former people.**

40. And some from later people.

41. And the people of the left (the unfortunate ones who deny the reality and live in their cocoon worlds) – **and what people of the left?**

42. In samum (poisonous fire, radiation) **and hamim** (scalding water; unrealistic/baseless data and conditionings),

43. And a shade of black smoke (unable to see and experience the forces in their essence),

44. (That shade) **that is neither cool nor generous** (in what it brings)!

45. Indeed, before this they were rampaging in an abundance of worldly, lustful pleasures!

46. They used to persist in committing that great offence (denying their essential reality and its experience).

47. They used to say, "Will we really continue to live (be resurrected) **with another body once we have died and become dust and bones?"**

48. "Even our forefathers?"

49. Say, "Indeed, the former and the latter,"

50. "They will surely be gathered for the appointment of a known time!"

51. After which, O those astray deniers (of the reality)...

52. Indeed, (you) **will be eating from the trees of zaqqum** (the fruits/products of thinking you are only the body).

53. Filling your bellies with it.

54. And drinking scalding water on top of it.

55. And you will drink it like the drinking of thirsty camels that are unable to quench their thirsts due to their afflictions.

56. Thus shall be their state (what manifests through them) **on the day of the religion** (the system – the time when the reality of the sunnatullah is realized)!

57. We created you! So, will you not accept?

58. Have you seen the sperm that you emit?

59. Is it you who creates it or are We the creators?

60. We determined death among you and you cannot overpass Us!

61. (We determined death) **so that We may bring** (new bodies of) **your like and that We reconstruct you** (anew) **in a form which you do not know.**

62. Indeed, you have already known the first creation... So, should you not contemplate?

63. Did you see what you sowed?

64. Is it you who makes it grow or Us?

65. Had We willed, We could have made it a dry, weak plant, and you would be left in wonder!

66. "Indeed, we are in loss!"

67. "No, we are the deprived."

68. And have you seen the water that you drink?

69. Is it you who discloses that from the white clouds or are We the disclosers?

70. Had We willed, We could have made it bitter (water)... Should you not be grateful?

71. And have you seen the fire that you ignite (from the tree)?

72. Did you make that tree or are We the makers?

73. We made it a reminder and provision for the ignorant wayfarer!

74. So, glorify (tasbih) your Rabb whose name is Azim!

75. I swear by the universe full of stars (where the Names become manifest)!

76. If only you knew how great an oath this is!

77. Indeed, that (universe) is the noble Quran (for those who can 'READ' it).

78. Contained within the knowledge that cannot be seen! (The universal data in the form of an endless ocean of waves and the data within the brain based on the holographic principle.)

79. None but the purified (from the dirt of shirq – duality – animalistic nature) can touch it (i.e. become enlightened with the knowledge of the Absolute Reality).

80. A disclosure (detailed explanation) from the Rabb of the worlds.

81. Now, you take this lightly and make little of it!

82. But was your denial the means of your livelihood?

83. And when the soul reaches the throat (at the time of death)!

84. You will be left (helpless)!

85. We are closer to it than you are, but you do not see.

86. If you are not to be recompensed for your deeds,

87. And if you are truthful, then turn (death) away (if you think there is no sunnatullah)!

88. (Everyone shall taste death) but if he is of those who have attained divine closeness;

89. For him there will be a life with the Rahman qualities, the observation of the reflections of the Names and a Paradise of bliss.

90. If he is of the people of the right,

91. (It will be said), "Salam to you" by the people of the right.

92. But if he of is the deniers (of the reality) who are astray in faith,

93. Then scalding water will be spilled over him!

94. He will be subject to burning conditions!

95. Indeed, this is the very reality (that will be personally experienced)!

96. So, glorify (tasbih) **your Rabb whose name is Azim!**

57

AL-HADID

By the one who is denoted by the name **Allah** (who created my being with His Names in accord with the meaning of the letter 'B'), **the Rahman, the Rahim.**

1. **Everything in the heavens and the earth glorifies** (tasbih) **Allah** (through fulfilling their functions). **HU is the Aziz, the Hakim.**

2. **To Him belongs the sovereignty of the heavens and the earth... He gives life and takes life! He is Qadir over all things.**

3. **HU is the Awwal** (the first and initial state of existence) **and the Akhir** (the infinitely subsequent One, to all manifestation), **the Zahir** (the explicit, unequivocal and perceivable manifestation; the Absolute Reality beyond the illusion) **and the Batin** (the unperceivable reality within the perceivable manifestation, the source of the unknown; the Absolute Self beyond the illusory selves)**! He is Aleem over all things** (the Knower of all things as their creator with His Names)!

4. **He created the heavens and the earth in six periods and then established Himself on the Throne! He knows what goes into the earth and what come out from it; what is disclosed from the sky and what ascends to it... And He is with you** (the origin of your being) **wherever you are** (as your reality exists with His Names)... (This points to the unity of existence beyond the illusion of duality.) **Allah is Basir of what you do** (as their creator).

5. **To Him belongs the sovereignty of the heavens and the earth! All affairs are returned to Allah.**

6. **He transforms the night into the day and the day into the night! He, as their absolute essence** (with His Names), **knows what is in the hearts!**

7. **Believe in Allah and His Rasul, your essential reality with His Names... Give** (for His sake) **from that of which He has made you vicegerents! Those among you, who believe and give, there is a great reward for them.**

8. What is your reason for not believing in Allah, your essential reality with His Names? While the Rasul invites you to believe in your Rabb, who brought you into existence from nonexistence with His Names, and has even taken your word! If, indeed, you are true believers!

9. He discloses clear (detailed) signs to His servant to take you out of the darkness (of ignorance) into the Nur (light of knowledge)... Indeed, Allah is Ra'uf and Rahim to you.

10. What is wrong with you that you do not give unrequitedly in the way of Allah, when the heritage of the heavens and the earth belongs to Allah (you will eventually leave all of your seeming possessions behind in the world)? Those of you, who gave unrequitedly and fought before the conquest (fath), are not equal (to those who did not)! They are higher in degree than those who gave and fought after (the conquest)! Allah has promised a good reward to all of them. Allah is Habir of what you do.

11. He who gives a good loan to Allah, Allah multiplies it for him and gives him a generous return.

12. That day you will see the believing men and women with their light (Nur) running before them and on their right side... (And it will be said), "Your good news today is of Paradises underneath which rivers flow! This is the great attainment indeed!"

13. On that Day the (hypocrite) men and two-faced women will say to those who believed, "Wait for us that we may acquire some of your light (Nur; knowledge of the reality)." It will be said, "Go back and seek light." And an (unsurpassable) wall will be placed between them with a door, its interior (inner world) containing grace, but its exterior is torment (the condition of those who fail to experience the reality is suffering, whereas observing the qualities of the Names leads to a state of grace).

14. They (the hypocrites) will say (to the believers), "Were we not with you?" They will say, "Yes, but you succumbed to provocation (did not experience faith) until there came the command of Allah (death), and you continuously monitored and fell into doubt, and your delusions deceived you and the great deceiver (the conditioned mind) deceived you with Allah (deluded you with the idea that since you are of Him you are free to do whatever you desire)!"

15. So, no ransom will be accepted of you (hypocrites) or the deniers of the reality today! Your refuge is the Fire... That (Fire) is your protector... What a wretched place of return it is!

16. Has not the time come for the believers to be in awe of the remembrance of Allah and what has been disclosed in Truth? So that they may not be like those who were given a book before (that they do not reduce their worship to customs and traditions, and stop feeling and contemplating)! A long period had passed over them (the children of Israel; their worship had become customary practices), so their hearts hardened (they stopped contemplating and feeling their worship and only do it out of custom)! Most of them (the Jews) are corrupt in faith!

17. Know well that Allah will give life to the earth after its death! We have made the signs clear to you so that you may use your intellect and understand.

18. Indeed, men who give charity and women who give charity, and those who have given a good loan to Allah, it will be multiplied for them... They will have a generous reward.

19. As for those who believe in Allah and His Rasul as their essential reality with His Names, they are the very martyrs (referenced in 3:18) in the sight of the truthful and their Rabb! They have reward and Nur (light of the knowledge) (they have believed both in the Nabi and the Rasul)... Those who deny the knowledge of the reality and the signs of Our Names in their essence, they are the people of Hell.

20. Know well that the life of this world is but an amusement and diversion, and adornment and boasting to one another, and competition in increase of wealth and children... Like the example of the rain, which makes the crops grow, giving joy, but then it dries and turns yellow and becomes debris! And in the eternal life to come there is either severe suffering or forgiveness and the pleasure of Allah. The things pertaining to the worldly life are nothing but a delusion.

21. So, race towards forgiveness from your Rabb and a Paradise whose size is as big as the heaven and the earth, prepared for those who believe in Allah and His Rasul as their essential reality with His Names! Such is the bounty of Allah (the realization of the vastness of the qualities of the Names), which He grants unto whomever He wills. Allah is Dhul-Fadhlul Azim (possessor of great bounty).

22. No calamity befalls you on earth (on your physical body and outer world) **or among yourselves** (your inner world) **that has not already been recorded in a book** (formed in the dimension of the knowledge) **before We bring it into being! Indeed, for Allah, this is easy.**

23. We inform you of this in order that you do not despair over your losses or exult (in pride) **over what We have given you, for Allah does not like the boastful and the arrogant!**

24. Those stingy ones (who exult in their wealth) **and enjoin stinginess upon people! Whoever turns away** (from Allah), **indeed, Allah is the Ghani, the Hamid.**

25. Indeed, We have disclosed Our Rasuls as clear proofs and with them We disclosed the knowledge of the reality and the sunnatullah, and the balance (judgment-reasoning) **so that people may uphold justice. And We sent down iron** (Hadid) **wherein great power and benefit for the people** (the relation between magma and the iron in the human body) **that Allah and His Rasul may know who, although unknown to them, supports them. Certainly Allah is the Qawwi, the Aziz.**

26. Indeed, We also disclosed Noah and Abraham... We formed Nubuwwah and the Book (the knowledge of the reality and sunnatullah) **for their offspring! There are some among them who attain the reality... But the majority of them are corrupt in faith!**

27. Then We followed their work up with Our Rasuls and followed them with Jesus and gave him the Gospel (the knowledge containing good news)... **We formed in their hearts compassion, infinite tolerance and grace, and clergy** (the attainment of Allah), **but they innovated it** (and changed it into monasticism out of fear). **Whereas We had not made** (clergy) **compulsory upon them. They did so to seek the pleasure of Allah** (the blessings of Paradise)... **But they did not duly observe it! We gave the believers among them their rewards... But the majority of them are corrupt in faith!**

28. O believers! Protect yourselves from Allah and believe in the disclosure of His Names through His Rasul so that He may give you a double portion of His grace and form for you Nur (light of knowledge) **by which you walk, and forgive you... Allah is the Ghafur, the Rahim.**

29. This is so the people of the book (those to whom religion – knowledge of the reality have been given) **may know that they are not**

**able to obtain anything from the bounty of Allah, and that all
bounty is indeed by the hand of Allah** (not through their own
acquisition) **and He gives to whom he wills... Allah is Dhul-Fadhlul
Azim** (possessor of great bounty).

58

AL-MUJADILA

By the one who is denoted by the name Allah (who created my being with His Names in accord with the meaning of the letter 'B'), the Rahman, the Rahim.

1. Allah has indeed heard the words of the one who disputes with you about her husband and directs her complaint to Allah. Allah hears your discussion; indeed, Allah is the Sami, the Basir.

2. Those among you who separate themselves from their wives by pronouncing, "To me you are like my mother" (a pagan practice) should know that they (their wives) are not their mothers! Their mothers are only those who gave birth to them! Indeed, they utter an outrageous and baseless word! Indeed, Allah is the Afuw (infinitely forgiving) and the Ghafur.

3. And those who proclaim such things (and separate themselves from their wives) and then go back on what they have claimed (want to reunite with their wives) must free a slave before they can have relations with their wives! This is what you are advised to do... Allah is Habir of what you do (as their creator).

4. He who cannot find a slave to free, must fast for two months consecutively before he can have relations with his wife. And he who is unable (to fast for two months as atonement) must feed sixty needy people... These (laws) are for you to experience your faith in your essential reality, Allah and His Rasul; these are the limits set by Allah. And for those who deny the knowledge of the reality there is severe suffering.

5. Indeed, those who oppose Allah and His Rasul are debased as those before them were debased. Whereas We have indeed disclosed clear signs... There is a humiliating suffering for those who deny the knowledge of the reality.

6. The time will come for Allah to resurrect them all (bring them back to life in a new dimension with a new constitution) and inform them of what they did... Allah had recorded (what became manifest through them), but they have forgotten... Allah is Shahid over all things.

7. Do you not understand that Allah knows everything in the heavens and the earth! There is whispering (private conversation) **between three** (people) **where He is not the fourth of them...** If there were five of them (conversing in privacy) **He would be the sixth of them... And whether they are lesser than this or more, and wherever they may be, He is with them** (for He comprises their very being with His Names – the unity of existence – non-duality)! **Then during Doomsday Allah will inform them of what they did! Indeed, Allah knows all things** (as He comprises their essence with His Names).

8. Did you not see those who were forbidden from whispering (hypocrisy; two-facedness) **yet returned to that which they were forbidden? They whisper** (converse privately) **among themselves about villainy, animosity and disobedience to the Rasul... When they** (the Jews) **come to you, they greet you with what Allah does not greet you, but inside themselves they say, "If what we said was wrong, Allah would have punished us"... Sufficient is Hell for them, to which they will be subject... What a wretched place of return!**

Note: Due to the phonetic proximity in their speech, the Jews would deliberately mispronounce certain words and expressions, such as, "as salamu alayka" (salam be to you) as "as samu alayka" which means "death be to you"... To such greetings, the Rasul (saw) would only say "Alaykum" (to you) rather than "wa alaykum" (to you too), denoting that he did not take it upon himself. When Hadhrat Aisha (r.a.) once responded to such greetings by saying, "Death be to you, may the curse and wrath of Allah be upon you", the Rasul (saw) warned her, "O Aisha... Allah does not like those who say more than what is necessary", thereby restricting the permissible reaction to an action to the magnitude of that action (preventing reactive behavior).

9. O believers... When you whisper (privately converse) **among one another, do not whisper villainy, animosity and disobedience in regards to the Rasul... Whisper in regards to actions that will take you closer** (to Allah) **and provide protection. Protect yourselves from Allah to whom you will be gathered** (and who will subject you to the consequences of your deeds)!

10. Whispering (gossip) **is from Satan** (satanic/delusive thoughts) **to cause grief to the believers! But he** (satanic/delusive thoughts) **cannot cause any harm to them** (the believers), **except by the permission of Allah. Let the believers place their trust in Allah.**

11. O believers... When you are told, "Make space" in assemblies, make space so that Allah will expand your space! And when you are

told, "Arise", arise so that Allah may raise those who have believed among you and those who were given the knowledge, by degrees. Allah is Habir of what you do. (Habir: The All-aware – The One who is aware of the manifestations of His Names beyond the concept of time and space, as He is the One who brings them into existence from nonexistence with the qualities denoted by His Names.)

12. O believers! Give charity before you engage in a private consultation with the Rasul. This is better and purer for you... But if you do not have the means, then indeed Allah is the Ghafur, the Rahim.

13. You feared to give charity before consulting (the Rasul)... Though you did not do this (due to your stinginess), Allah has accepted your repentance – then establish salat and give alms and obey Allah and His Rasul! Allah is Habir of what you do.

14. Did you see those who befriended people who incurred the wrath of Allah? They are neither of you nor of them; and yet, knowing this, they swear upon a lie.

15. Allah has prepared severe suffering for them... Wretched is what they do!

16. They took their oaths as a cover and prevented from the way of Allah... There is a humiliating suffering for them.

17. Neither their wealth nor their children will avail them against what is to come to them from Allah! They are the people of Hell. And forever they will abide therein.

18. A time will come and Allah will resurrect them all, and they will swear to Allah like they swore to you, thinking they have some basis. Take heed, they are the very liars!

19. Satan (corporeality; the idea of being just the physical body) has overcome them and made them forget the remembrance of Allah (their own reality of which they have been reminded, and that they will abandon their bodies and live eternally as 'consciousness' comprised of Allah's Names!) Those (who are receptive to satanic impulses and think of themselves as only the physical body) are the acquaintances of Satan. Take heed, most assuredly, the partisans of Satan are the very losers!

20. Indeed, those who oppose Allah and His Rasul are among the most abased!

21. Allah has inscribed, "Indeed, I and my Rasuls are prevalent!" Indeed, Allah is the Qawwi, the Aziz.

22. You cannot find the believers in Allah, as their essential reality, and the eternal life to come, befriending those who oppose Allah and His Rasul. Even if they are their fathers, or sons, or brothers, or fellow tribesmen. They are the ones in whose hearts (consciousness) Allah has inscribed (enabled the experience of) faith and strengthened with a Spirit of His own. He will include them into Paradises underneath which rivers flow, where they shall abide forever. Allah is pleased with them and they are pleased with Allah. They are the partisans of Allah... Take heed, indeed, the partisans of Allah are the ones who have succeeded.

AL-HASHR

By the one who is denoted by the name Allah (who created my being with His Names in accord with the meaning of the letter 'B'), the Rahman, the Rahim.

1. **Whatever is in the heavens and the earth glorifies** (tasbih) **Allah** (effectuates their servitude by manifesting the Names through the functions they serve).

2. **It is He who drove out of their homes those among the people of the book who denied the knowledge of the reality, and who had gathered for war** (before the war even began)**... You never thought they would leave** (their homes)**... And they thought their fortresses would protect them against Allah! But Allah came to them from where they least expected and cast terror into their hearts! They pulled down their homes with their own hands and with the hands of the believers! Take a lesson from this, O you who have insight!**

3. **If Allah had not prescribed exile for them, He would surely have afflicted them with suffering in this world. But there is the suffering of the Fire for them in the eternal life.**

4. **For they separated themselves from Allah and His Rasul... And whoever severs his tie from Allah** (denies the Names comprising his essence – his spirit – and his eternal life to come, and confines his existence to his mortal physical body) **– then indeed, Allah is severe in retribution** (Shadid al-Iqab)**!**

5. **Whatever you have cut down of their** (those who wanted to go to war) **palm trees or left standing on their roots, it was by the permission of Allah** (B-iznillah) **for Him to disgrace and debase those with corrupt faith.**

6. **As for the spoils Allah gave to His Rasul from them, you neither spurred a horse nor rode a camel for them! But Allah directs His Rasuls upon whom He wills. Allah is Qadir over all things.**

7. **And the spoils Allah gave to His Rasul from the towns that were conquered without war are for the Rasul, his relatives, the orphans,**

the needy and the travelers... (Thus it has been decreed) **so that**
(wealth) **is not passed on only among the rich among you! Take**
whatever the Rasul gives you and refrain from what he forbids you...
Protect yourselves from Allah (for He will most definitely subject you
to the consequences of your deeds). **Indeed, Allah is severe in**
recompense.

8. (Those spoils) **are for the needy emigrants who have been expelled**
from their homes, seeking the bounty and pleasure of Allah and
supporting Allah and His Rasul... They are the truthful!

9. **And those who were settled in that city** (Medina) **and adopted the**
faith before them (the emigrants) **love those who migrate to them.**
They harbor no desire or need in their hearts for what has been
given (to the emigrants). **Even if they are needy themselves, they give**
them (the emigrants) **preference over themselves. Those who protect**
themselves from their own stinginess and ambitions, they are the
truly successful ones.

10. **Those who come after them say, "Our Rabb, forgive us and our**
brothers who preceded us in faith and leave no ill thought or
emotion in our hearts for the believers... Our Rabb! Indeed, you are
the Ra'uf, the Rahim."

11. **Did you not see those two-faced** (Jewish hypocrites) **who said to**
their disbelieving brothers from among the people of the book (the
Jews of the Banu Nadir tribe), **"If you are driven out** (of your homes),
we will indeed leave with you! And we will never listen to anyone
against you! And if they wage war against you, we will indeed help
you"... Allah bears witness that they are most certainly liars!

12. **If they are driven out** (from their homes), **they will not leave with**
them! Indeed, if war is waged against them, they will not help them!
And even if they were to help, they would turn their backs and flee!
Then they will not be helped.

13. **Their fear of you is greater than their fear of Allah! This is**
because they are a people devoid of understanding.

14. **They will fight with you only from within a fortified area and**
from behind walls... And they have serious problems and issues
between themselves... You think they are united, but they are of
differing views. This is because they are a people devoid of reason.

15. **The example of them** (these Jews) **is like those who recently tasted the consequences of their deeds** (at the Battle of Badr) **and for whom there is a severe suffering** (in the eternal life to come).

16. (The exemplary state of the Jewish hypocrites is) **like the exemplary state of Satan, who says to man, "Deny** (cover the reality and delight in the lowest states of corporeality)**!" But when** (man) **denies** (his essential reality and becomes blocked in that state) **he says, "Indeed, I am disassociated from you! I fear Allah, the Rabb of the worlds."**

17. **Thus, in the end, both will be in the Fire, wherein they will abide forever! This is the recompense of the wrongdoers.**

18. **O believers, protect yourselves from Allah! And let every soul look to what it has put forth for tomorrow** (the life after death)**! Protect yourselves from Allah! Indeed, Allah, as your creator, is Habir of what you do.**

19. **And do not be like those who forgot Allah, so He made them forget themselves** (their essential reality)**... They are the corrupt in faith!**

20. **Not equal are the people of the Fire and the people of Paradise... The people of Paradise are the attainers of success!**

21. **Had we revealed this Quran** (this truth) **upon a mountain** (the ego) **you would have seen it humbled and shattered to pieces in awe of Allah** (the realization of the nothingness of his ego or seeming 'self' in respect to the One denoted by the name Allah)**. And these examples** (symbolic language) **We present to mankind so that they will contemplate.**

22. **HU is Allah, there is no god, only HU** (as HU is the inner essence of the reality of everything that is perceived)**! The Knower of the unknown and the witnessed! HU is the Rahman** (the potential of the source of the entire creation; the quantum potential)**, the Rahim** (the One who manifests the infinite qualities denoted by the Names and experiences the world of acts with and through their observation).

23. **HU is Allah; there is no god, only HU!** (as HU is the inner essence of the reality of everything that is perceived)**! HU is the Maleek** (the Sovereign One who manifests His Names as he wishes and governs them in the world of acts as He pleases; the One who has providence over all things)**, the Quddus** (the One who is free and beyond being defined, conditioned and limited by His manifest qualities and concepts)**, the Salam** (the One who enables a state of emancipation from the conditions of nature and bodily life and endows the experience of 'certainty' [yakeen]), **the Mu'min** (the One who enables faith and guides individuals to observe their reality), **the Muhaymin** (the One who observes and protects the manifestations of His Names with His own system), **the Aziz** (the One whose will to do as He likes, nothing can oppose), **the Jabbar** (the One whose will is compelling), **the Mutakabbir** (the One to whom the word 'I' exclusively belongs; Absolute 'I'ness belongs only to Him)! **Allah is Subhan** (exalted and absolutely pure) **from the concepts of god they attribute to Him!**

24. **HU is Allah, the Khaliq** (the One Absolute Creator – the One who brings individuals into the existence from nothingness with His Names), **the Bari** (the One who fashions all of creation [from micro to macro] with unique functions and designs yet all in conformity with the whole), **the Musawwir** (the fashioner of forms; the One who exhibits 'meanings' as 'forms' and devises the mechanism in the perceiver to perceive them); **to Him belongs the beautiful Names. Whatever is in the heavens and earth glorify** (tasbih) **Allah** (by manifesting the qualities of the Names comprising their essence, i.e. by actualizing their servitude). **HU is the Aziz** (the One whose will to do as He likes, nothing can oppose), **the Hakim** (the One whose power of knowledge appears under the guise of 'causes', hence creating causality and leading to the perception of multiplicity).

60

AL-MUMTAHINA

By the one who is denoted by the name Allah (who created my being with His Names in accord with the meaning of the letter 'B'), the Rahman, the Rahim.

1. O believers! Do not befriend those who are My enemies and your enemies! You are offering them love even though they deny what has come to you of the Truth, and expelled you and the Rasul (from your homes) just because you believe in Allah, your Rabb who comprises your essence with His Names. If you have come out to fight in My cause and seeking My pleasure (then do not take them as friends); though you hide your love for them (within). I know what you hide and what you reveal! Whoever does this among you has indeed strayed from the balanced way.

2. If they gain dominance over you they will become enemies to you. They will extend their hands and tongues (speech) to you with bad intent and they will ardently long for you to deny the knowledge of the reality.

3. Neither your relatives nor your children will ever be of benefit to you! During Doomsday they will cause division! Allah is Basir of what you do.

4. There is an excellent example for you in Abraham and those who followed him. When they said to their people, "Indeed, we are far from you and those you serve besides Allah! We reject and refuse you until you believe in the Oneness of Allah." Except to his father, Abraham said, "I shall indeed ask forgiveness for you, but I do not possess the power for anything else from Allah (besides praying for you)." Then they prayed, "Our Rabb, in You we have placed our trust and to You we have turned, the final return is to You!"

5. "Our Rabb! Do not make us objects of trial for those who deny the knowledge of the reality. Forgive us, our Rabb! Indeed, You are the Aziz, the Hakim."

6. Surely there is a good example in them (Abraham and his people) for those who place their hopes in Allah and (the experience of) the

eternal life to come... Whoever turns away from Allah, indeed, Allah is the Ghani, the Hamid

7. Perhaps Allah will form love between you and your enemies. Allah is the Qadir... Allah is the Ghafur, the Rahim.

8. Allah does not prevent you from being kind and just to those who have not fought you on account of religion and who have not expelled you from your homes. Indeed, Allah loves those who are just (who give everything its due right).

9. Allah only forbids you to befriend those who have fought you on account of religion, who have expelled you from your homes and helped others to do so. And whoever takes them as friends, they are the very wrongdoers!

10. O believers... When the believing women come to you as refugees, question them. Their faith is best known to Allah. But if you find them to be true believers then do not return them to the deniers of the reality. Neither are they permissible for them (the deniers) nor they are permissible to them (the believing women). Give back to them (the deniers) what they gave them (as dowry). There is no blame upon you to marry them, provided you give them their dowry. But do not maintain your marriages with women who deny the knowledge of the reality... Ask back for what you have spent on them and let them also ask back for what they have spent. This is the judgment of Allah. He judges between you. Allah is the Aleem, the Hakim.

11. If any of your women leave you and go to the disbelievers, and if any of their wives come to you or you capture them, give to those who have been deserted by their wives the equivalent of the dowers they gave them. And protect yourselves from Allah in whom you believe.

12. O Nabi! When the believing women come to you and pledge not to associate anything to Allah, their essential reality, and pledge not to steal, commit adultery, kill their children or bring forth a slander they have invented between their arms and legs, and not to oppose you in what you enjoin upon them, accept their pledge and ask forgiveness for them of Allah... Indeed, Allah is the Ghafur, the Rahim.

13. O believers! Do not befriend those who have incurred the wrath of Allah, those who have no hope in the eternal life to come just as

the deniers of the Truth have lost all hope in the people of the grave.

61

AS-SAFF

By the one who is denoted by the name Allah (who created my being with His Names in accord with the meaning of the letter 'B'), the Rahman, the Rahim.

1. **Whatever is in the heavens and the earth glorify** (tasbih; effectuate their creational purpose through fulfilling their functions) **Allah! HU is the Aziz, the Hakim.**

2. **O believers... Why do you say what you do not do!**

3. **Saying things that you do not practice yourself incurs great hatred in the sight of Allah!**

4. **Allah loves those who fight in His cause, in rows like a single solid structure of steel.**

5. **And when Moses said to his people, "O my people... Why do you harm me when you know I am a Rasul of Allah** (disclosed) **for you?" But when they strayed** (from the Truth), **Allah turned their hearts away** (from the Truth, so they could no longer perceive it)! **Allah does not guide the corrupt in faith to the reality.**

6. **And when Jesus, the son of Mary said, "O children of Israel... Indeed, I am a Rasul of Allah to you! Confirming what came before me of the Torah and bringing the good news of a Rasul who is to come after me, whose name is Ahmad." But when they came as miracles they said, "Clearly, this is magic."**

Note: The Rasul of Allah (saw) says in regards to this: "My name in the Torah is 'Ahyad' (the one who distances), for I distance my people from the Fire... My name in the Zabur is 'Al Mahi' (the obliterator) for Allah has obliterated with me those who served idols... My name in the Gospel is 'Ahmad' (the One who does Hamd [evaluates] as the reflection of the Absolute Essence)... And my name in the Quran is 'Muhammad' (the One to whom Hamd is continually done), for I am the 'Mahmud' (the one who is evaluated) among the people of the heavens and the earth."

7. And who does more wrong than the one who slanders against Allah (assumes the existence of an 'other' than Allah), even though he is invited to Islam? Allah does not guide the wrongdoing people!

8. They want to extinguish the Nur (light of knowledge) of Allah with their mouths. But Allah is the perfector of His Nur. Even though those who deny the knowledge of the reality may not like it!

9. It is He who disclosed His Rasul by the Truth and the reality, with the religion of Truth (the absolute knowledge of the system and sunnatullah). Even though the dualists may not like it!

10. O believers... Let me show you a trade that will save you from a grave suffering.

11. Believe in Allah and His Rasul as your essential reality with His Names and strive in the way of Allah, without expecting any return, with your wealth and your lives! This is better for you, if only you can comprehend!

12. (Then) He will cover your mistakes arising from your egos and admit you to Paradises underneath which rivers flow and pure dwellings in Paradises of Bliss... This is the great attainment!

13. And there is more that you will love: Help from Allah and an imminent conquest (the experience of divine closeness)! So, give the good news to the believers!

14. O believers, be supporters of Allah; like when Jesus, the son of Mary said to his disciples, "Who are my supporters for Allah?" And his disciples said, "We are the supporters of Allah!" A group of the children of Israel believed and a group denied (the Truth). So We supported those who believed against their enemy, and they became prevalent.

62

AL-JUMU'A

By the one who is denoted by the name Allah (who created my being with His Names in accord with the meaning of the letter 'B'), the Rahman, the Rahim.

1. Whatever is in the heavens and whatever is on the earth glorify (tasbih, with their unique dispositions) Allah, the Maleek, the Quddus, the Aziz, the Hakim (to manifest whatever meanings He desires).

2. It is He who disclosed among the illiterates a Rasul from among themselves, so that he may recite His signs to them, purify them, and teach them the Book (knowledge of the reality and the sunnatullah) and Wisdom (knowledge of formations). Whereas before this they were corrupt in faith.

3. And (He disclosed the Rasul) to others besides them! He is the Aziz, the Hakim.

4. This is the bounty of Allah, which He gives to whom He wills! Allah is the possessor of great bounty.

5. The example of those who were entrusted with the Torah, yet who failed to uphold it, is like the example of a donkey carrying big books! Wretched is the state of those who deny the signs of Allah! Allah does not guide the wrongdoing people.

6. Say, "O you who are Jews! You think you are the only (protected) friends of Allah! Then wish for death if you are truthful!"

7. But they will never wish for it (death), because of what they have done with their own hands. Allah is Aleem of the wrongdoers.

8. Say, "Death, from which you try to flee, will most definitely reach you! Then you will be returned to the Knower of the unknown and the manifest, and He will inform you of the consequences of what you have been doing."

9. O believers... When you are called for the Friday prayer (salat) leave trade and race towards the remembrance of Allah (the call to

remember your essential reality)! **This is better for you, if only you can comprehend** (the Truth).

10. And when the prayer has been concluded, spread out within the land and seek the bounty of Allah (your essence with His Names) **and remember Allah often so that you may succeed!**

11. But when they saw an opportunity for trade or entertainment, they raced to it and left you standing (as the imam of the Friday prayer)! **Say, "That which is with Allah is better than entertainment and trade... Allah is the best of providers!"**

63

AL-MUNAFIQUN

By the one who is denoted by the name Allah (who created my being with His Names in accord with the meaning of the letter 'B'), the Rahman, the Rahim.

1. When the two-faced (hypocrites) came to you they said, "We testify that you are indeed the Rasul of Allah!" And Allah knows that you are His Rasul. And Allah testifies that the hypocrites are liars.

2. They took their oaths as a cover and prevented from the way of Allah... Wretched is what they do!

3. This is because they believed, and then they denied (the Truth in which they claimed to have believed)... Thus their hearts (understanding) were sealed (because of their denial), so they cannot comprehend (the function of Risalah)!

4. When you see them, their bodies (outward appearance) pleases you... And when they speak, you listen to what they say... But they are like pieces of wood (unconscious bodies) stacked together! They think that every shout is directed against them. They are the enemies, so beware of them! May Allah kill them (so they see what the reality is)! How they are deluded (from their reality)!

5. When they are told, "Come, let the Rasul of Allah ask forgiveness for you," you see them turn their heads away in arrogance.

6. It is all the same whether you ask forgiveness for them or not! Allah will never forgive them! Indeed, Allah does not guide the corrupt in faith to the reality.

7. They are the ones who say, "Do not spend on those who are with the Rasul of Allah, so they scatter." To Allah belong the treasures of the heavens and the earth! But the hypocrites cannot comprehend this.

8. (The hypocrites) said, "Indeed, if we return to Medina the most honored one will surely expel the most debased one!" But honor

belongs to Allah, to His Rasul and to the believers. But the hypocrites do not know.

9. O believers! Let not your worldly goods or your children prevent you from the remembrance of Allah (the remembrance of your essential self and the fulfillment of its requisites). And whoever does this – it is they who are the losers!"

10. And spend in the way of Allah from what We have provided you before death comes to one of you (and he becomes aware of the reality) and says, "My Rabb, if only You could grant me respite for a brief time so that I may give away my wealth and fulfill the requisites of my faith."

11. But Allah will not grant respite to any one when death comes! Allah is Habir of what you do.

64

AT-TAGHABUN

By the one who is denoted by the name Allah (who created my being with His Names in accord with the meaning of the letter 'B'), the Rahman, the Rahim.

1. Everything in the heavens and the earth (all manifestation of the Names of Allah) glorifies Allah (fulfill their servitude by carrying out their specific functions). To Him belongs the Sovereignty, to Him belongs Hamd. He is Qadir over all things.

2. It is HU who has created you. Some of you are deniers of the knowledge of the reality, and some of you are believers. Allah is Basir over what you do.

3. He created the heavens and the sky in Truth (as manifestations of the Truth, His Names) and gave them forms (different compositions of the Names), and gave you the best of forms. To Him is the return!

4. He knows whatever is in the heavens and the earth. He knows what you conceal and what you reveal. Allah, as the absolute essence of your being, is the Aleem.

5. Did you not receive the news of those (the people who came) before you who denied the knowledge of the reality and tasted its consequence? There is severe suffering for them.

6. That was because their Rasuls came to them as clear proofs, but they said, "Is a mortal going to guide us to the reality?" And so they denied the knowledge of the reality and turned away. Allah has no need for such people (or their faith)! Allah is the Ghani, the Hamid.

7. Those who deny the knowledge of the reality think they will never be resurrected! Say, "No (you are mistaken), by my Rabb, you will most definitely be resurrected, and then all the meanings of your actions will be disclosed through you! This is easy for Allah!"

8. Believe in Allah, your essential reality with His Names, his Rasul, and the Nur (light of knowledge) that We disclosed! Allah (by the mystery of the letter B) is Habir of what you do.

9. When He gathers you for the Time of Gathering. The time when deception is clearly realized and its consequences lived! Whoever believes in Allah as their essential reality with His Names and fulfills the requisites of their faith, He will erase their bad deeds and admit them to Paradises underneath which rivers flow to abide therein eternally... This is the great attainment!

10. As for those who deny Our signs inherent within their beings, they are the people of Hell, and they will abide therein eternally! A wretched place of return it is!

11. No harm can afflict you other than by the permission of Allah (the suitability of the Names comprising your essence)! Whoever believes that the Names of Allah comprises his essence, He will enable their consciousness to experience the reality! Allah, with His very presence within all things, is the Aleem.

12. Obey Allah and obey the Rasul! If you turn away, then upon Our Rasul is only the responsibility to convey.

13. Allah. There is no god. Only HU! Let the believers place their trust in Allah!

14. O believers! Indeed, you have enemies among (within) your wives and children, so beware of them! If you forgive, forego and pardon, indeed Allah is the Ghafur, the Rahim.

15. Your wealth and children are only objects of trial to you! And with Allah is the great reward.

16. So, protect yourselves from Allah as much as you can (for He will most definitely subject you to the consequences of your deeds); perceive and obey, and give unrequitedly for your own sake! Whoever protects himself against his own stinginess and ambitions, they are the ones who attain true success!

17. If you give a good loan to Allah (to the needy who are also manifestations of the Names of Allah), He will multiply it for you and forgive you... Allah is the Shakur, the Halim.

18. He is the Aleem of the unknown and the manifest realms. He is the Aziz, the Hakim.

65

AT-TALAQ

By the one who is denoted by the name Allah (who created my being with His Names in accord with the meaning of the letter 'B'), the Rahman, the Rahim.

1. O Nabi! When you want to divorce women, take heed of their waiting period (wait for the end of their menstruation cycle) then divorce them and keep count of the waiting period... Protect yourselves from Allah, your Rabb. Do not drive them out of their homes, and let not them leave their homes, unless they openly commit fornication... This is the limit set by Allah. And whoever transgresses the limit of Allah has indeed wronged himself. You never know, perhaps Allah will bring about a different situation after this.

2. And when their waiting period has come to an end, either keep them in marriage according to custom, or release them according to custom... And hold two just people as witnesses and establish testimony for Allah... This is what is advised to those who believe in Allah, their essential reality with His Names, and the eternal life to come... Whoever protects himself from Allah, He will open a way out for him.

3. And He will provide sustenance for him from where he does not expect. He who places his trust in Allah, Allah will be sufficient for him (he who believes in the forces pertaining to the qualities of the Names comprising his essence and complies with their requirements, those forces will be ever sufficient for him). Indeed, Allah will fulfill His word! And indeed, Allah has determined a measure (fate) for all things.

4. Those whose wives no longer menstruate (have gone into menopause), if you doubt (regarding their waiting period), their waiting period is three months. And it is the same for those who have not yet menstruated. As for pregnant women, their waiting period is until they deliver. Whoever protects themselves from Allah, He will ease their tasks for them.

5. These (applications) are the commands of Allah that He had disclosed to you... Whoever protects himself from Allah, He will erase his bad deeds from him and increase his reward.

6. Accommodate them (your ex-wives), according to your means, as you live yourselves, and do not harass them to make their lives difficult. If they are pregnant, give them alimony until they deliver. If they are breastfeeding (your children), give them payment. And discuss among yourselves (regarding these matters) in a pleasant way. But if you cannot come to an agreement, then let another woman breastfeed (the child).

7. Let the man of means give alimony according to his wealth, and let the man whose means are restricted give according to what Allah has provided him... Allah will not hold anyone accountable for more than what He has given him! Allah will bring about ease after hardship.

8. How many a nation rebelled against the commands of your Rabb and His Rasuls and We called them to severe account and subjected them to severe suffering.

9. Thus they tasted the consequence of their deeds and the result of their deeds was loss.

10. Allah has prepared severe suffering for them! Protect yourselves from Allah, o you who have believed, and who are the intimates of the reality through whom Allah hears, sees and speaks (Ulul albab)! Allah has indeed disclosed a reminder (dhikr) to you!

11. And a Rasul who informs you of the signs of Allah to bring those who believe and fulfill the requisites of faith out of the darkness into Nur (light of knowledge). Whoever believes in Allah and his essential reality with His Names, He will admit them to Paradises underneath which rivers flow to abide therein eternally. Allah has indeed provided sustenance for him.

12. It is Allah who created the seven heavens, and of the earth, the like of them. His command continually (without interruption) manifests between them (astrological [angelic] influences that are also manifestations of Allah's Names and their effect on creation). So that you may know that Allah is Qadir over all things and that He (as the creator) encompasses all things with His knowledge.

Note: In Ghazali's 'Ihya'u Ulumud'deen' it is narrated from Ibn Abbas (r.a.): "If I were to interpret the verse 'It is Allah who created the seven heavens, and of the earth, the like of them. His command continually manifests among them...' indeed, you would stone me", and in another narration, he says, "You would announce me a disbeliever!"

66

AT-TAHRIM

By the one who is denoted by the name Allah (who created my being with His Names in accord with the meaning of the letter 'B'), the Rahman, the Rahim.

1. O Nabi! Why do you forbid yourself from what Allah had made permissible to you, seeking to please your wives? Allah is the Ghafur, the Rahim.

2. Allah has ordained you to resolve your oaths (by paying compensation)! Allah is your protector. He is the Aleem, the Hakim.

3. And remember when the (final) Nabi confided a secret to one his wives (Hafsa [r.a.]) and she informed the other (Aisha [r.a.]) and Allah showed it to him (Rasulullah saw), he made known a part of it and avoided mentioning a part. Then when he told this to his wife (Hafsa [r.a.]), she said, "Who told you this?" and he said, "The One who is Aleem and Habir."

4. If you both (Aisha [r.a.] and Hafsa [r.a.]) repent to Allah (it is best), or your hearts will have deviated (from the Truth)... But if you cooperate against him, indeed Allah is his protector, and Gabriel, and the righteous among the believers (Aisha's father Abu Bakr [r.a.], Hafsa's father Omar [r.a.]) and the angels are also his helpers.

5. Were he to divorce you, his Rabb may well replace you with better wives, who have submitted, who believe, obey, repent, worship, who are given to fasting (from worldly things), both previously married and virgins.

6. O you who have believed! Protect yourselves (nafs) and your close ones (the correspondent of your body in the future) from the Fire whose fuel is people and stones (idols and other inanimate objects of worship), over which are appointed angels, who are powerful, harsh and severe and who do not disobey Allah in what He commands them, but do as they are commanded.

7. (The keepers of Hell will say), **"O you who have denied the knowledge of the reality! There is no room for excuse today! You are only living the consequences of your own doings!"**

8. **O believers! Repent to Allah with a sincere, genuine repentance. Perhaps your Rabb will cover your bad deeds and admit you to Paradises underneath which rivers flow. He will not disgrace the Nabi and those who believed with him at that time. Their Nur** (light of knowledge) **will race before them and on their right. They will say, "Our Rabb... Perfect our Nur** (increase the scope of our observation) **and forgive us... Indeed, you are Qadir over all things."**

9. **O Nabi! Strive with those who deny the knowledge of the reality and the two-faced** (hypocrites), **and be firm and uncompromising towards them. Their abode is Hell. What a wretched place of return!**

10. **Allah gives the example of the wives of Lot and Noah to those who deny the knowledge of the reality...** (Both those women) **were under** (the marriage of) **two of Our righteous servants. But they** (the wives) **betrayed them, so they** (Lot and Noah) **could not repel anything** (coming) **from Allah from them** (their wives). (Both those women were told), **"Enter the Fire along with the others!"**

11. **And Allah gives the example of Pharaoh's wife** (as a lesson). **She** (Asiya) **said, "My Rabb, build for me in Your sight a house in Paradise! Save me from Pharaoh and his deeds! Save me from the wrongdoing people!"**

12. **And** (the example of) **Mary, the daughter of Imran, who protected her chastity so We breathed** (manifested) **from Our spirit into her. She confirmed her Rabb's existence with His Names in His Words** (manifestations) **and His Books** (knowledge) **and was of those who submitted and obeyed.**

67

AL-MULK

By the one who is denoted by the name Allah (who created my being with His Names in accord with the meaning of the letter 'B'), **the Rahman, the Rahim.**

1. Supreme is He in whose hand is dominion (the dimension of acts, which He administers as He wills at every instance)! **He is Qadir over all things.**

2. It is HU who created life and death to reveal which of you is best in deed. He is the Aziz, the Ghafur.

3. It is HU who created the heavens as seven dimensions. You cannot see any inconsistency in the creation of the Rahman. So, turn your gaze and have a look! Can you see any conflict or discrepancy?

4. Then turn your gaze twice again and have a look! Your vision will return to you fatigued (unable to find what it was looking for) **and humbled!**

5. Indeed, We have adorned the nearest heaven (of earth – the thought processes) **with illuminants** (the knowledge of the reality). **We made them to stone and fend off the devils** (satanic ideas). **And We have prepared for them the suffering of the blazing Fire.**

6. There is the suffering of Hell for those who deny their Rabb who comprises their essence! What a wretched place of return!

7. When they are cast into it, they will hear it rumble as it boils up and gushes!

8. It almost bursts from rage. Every time a group is cast into it, its keepers will ask them, "Did no warner come to you?"

9. And they (the people of Hell) **will say, "Yes, indeed, a warner did come to us, but we denied him in disbelief! We told them, 'Allah did not reveal anything, and you are in gross error.'"**

10. They will say, "If only we had listened to them and used our reason, we would not be among the people of Hell now!"

11. Thus they will confess their mistakes. Let the people of the blazing Fire experience isolation!

12. As for those who are in awe of their Rabb as their unknown, there is forgiveness for them and a great reward.

13. Conceal your thoughts or reveal them! Indeed, He is Aleem of what is in the hearts (consciousness) as the absolute essence therein.

14. Will He not know what He created! He is the Latif, the Habir.

15. He made the earth (body) obedient (to your consciousness)! So, walk upon its slopes and eat of its provisions. To Him will be your resurrection!

16. Are you confident that that which is in the heaven will not cause you to be swallowed up by the earth, when suddenly it begins to shake!

17. Or are you confident that that which is in the heaven will not send upon you a cyclone? You will know how true My warning is!

18. Indeed, those before them also denied! And how was My recompense for their denial!

19. Do they not see the birds above them spreading their wings and ascending, then folding them in and descending! They do this with the forces of the Rahman. Indeed, He, as the essence of the all things, is the Basir.

20. Or do you have an army to help you against the Rahman? Those who deny the knowledge of the reality are in nothing but delusion!

21. If He was to cut your provision off, who will nourish you? No, they persist in their escapism, in rage and hatred!

22. Is one who blindly crawls on his face better guided or the one who walks upright upon the straight path?

23. Say, "It is HU who formed you and gave you the ability to perceive and comprehend (insight) and hearts (heart neurons that reflect the meanings of the Names to the brain). How little you thank (evaluate)!"

24. Say, "It is HU who created you on the earth. To Him you will be gathered!"

25. They say, "If you are truthful, when will your warning be fulfilled?"

26. Say, "Its knowledge is with Allah. I am only a clear warner!"

27. When they see it (death) approaching, the faces of those who deny the knowledge of the reality will darken. And it will said, "This is that which you impatiently wanted to experience!"

28. Say, "Think! If Allah were to destroy me and those with me or give grace to us, who can save the deniers of the reality from the severe suffering?"

29. Say, "He is the Rahman; we believe He comprises our essence and we have placed our trust in Him. Soon you will know who is in clear error!"

30. Say, "Think! If your water was to recede, who could bring you flowing water (knowledge)?

68

AL-QALAM

By the one who is denoted by the name Allah (who created my being with His Names in accord with the meaning of the letter 'B'), the Rahman, the Rahim.

1. **By Nun** (the knowledge of Uluhiyyah) **and the Pen** (Qalam; the discloser of the knowledge) **and everything it inscribes** (the creator of the detailed manifestation of the knowledge as the sunnatullah)...

2. **You are not, by the favor of your Rabb, possessed** (by invisible beings; the jinn)!

3. **Indeed, there is uninterrupted reward for you.**

4. **And indeed, you are of a great morality!**

5. **Soon you will see and they will see;**

6. **Who the possessed ones are!**

7. **Indeed, your Rabb knows well** (from their being) **who has gone astray from His way. And He knows well who has attained the reality** (as He is present within their being)!

8. **So do not follow the deniers!**

9. **They wished that you would soften in your approach** (compromise), **so they can show tolerance** (to you)!

10. **Do not conform to every base and imprudent habitual swearer** (as they are cocooned from Allah and the sunnatullah);

11. **Who mocks, reproaches and gossips;**

12. **Who prevents the experience of** (the reality) **and is guilty of transgression;**

13. **Stingy, ignorant and moreover branded with disbelief!**

14. (Will you obey him) **just because he has wealth and children!**

15. When he was informed of Our verses he said, "Legends of the former people."

16. Soon We shall brand him by his nose (he will not be able to overlook the Truth)!

17. Indeed, We afflicted them as We afflicted the people of the garden. When they vowed to harvest in the morning.

18. Without saying "If Allah wills"...

19. So a calamity befell the garden as they slept.

20. And it (the garden) dried and blackened!

21. (When they awoke) in the morning they called out to one another:

22. "Go early to the crops if you are going to cut and pick."

23. So they set out, whispering among themselves:

24. "There shall not enter (the garden) today any poor person!"

25. They set out, assuming they had the power to prevent the poor.

26. But when they saw the garden (destroyed), they said, "We must have come to the wrong place."

27. "No (this is the right place), but we have incurred loss!"

28. The most reasonable one among them said, "Did I not tell you to exalt (tasbih; fulfill your servitude to your Rabb)?"

29. They said, "Our Rabb is Subhan! Indeed, we have fallen short of giving your due!"

30. And they turned to each other and began to blame each other!

31. They said, "Woe to us! Indeed, we have been insolent!"

32. "Perhaps our Rabb will give in its stead one that is better! Indeed, we are (now) of those who turn to their Rabb."

33. Such is the suffering! And the suffering of the eternal life to come is even greater! If only they knew...

34. Indeed, for those who protect themselves there are Paradises of Bliss with their Rabb.

35. Will we treat those who have submitted (the Muslims) **like those guilty of denial?**

36. What is wrong with you! How do you judge?

37. Or do you have a book from which you learn?

38. By which you are given the commands that you like (and assume you are not in compliance with the sunnatullah)!

39. Or have you received a word from Us, valid until the Doomsday, that you are free to do what you like?

40. Ask them which of them takes responsibility for this (claim)?

41. Or do they have partners that they associate with Us? Let them bring their partners if they are truthful!

42. The time when the reality becomes manifest and they are invited to prostrate (confess the nonexistence of their assumed separate existence) they will be unable to do so!

43. Their eyes humbled with terror, humiliated! Whereas they used to be invited to prostrate while they were sound and in the world.

44. (My Rasul) leave Me to deal (alone) with those who deny! We shall gradually take them to ruin from where they know not!

45. And I give them time... But indeed, my trap is firm!

46. Or do you ask from them a return by which they feel indebted and burdened?

47. Or do they have (knowledge of) the unknown (the unperceivable) which they write?

48. Be patient for the judgment of your Rabb and do not be like the companion of the fish (Jonah, the Nabi)! How he had turned in distress.

49. If the favor of your Rabb had not reached him he would have been thrown onto the naked shore, debased!

50. But his Rabb chose him and made him of the righteous (the experiencers of the reality).

51. Indeed, those who deny the knowledge of the reality were about to knock you down with their looks when they heard the reminder (of their reality; dhikr) **saying, "Indeed, he is possessed** (under the influence of the jinn)."

52. Whereas it is only a reminder to the people (of their essential reality)!

AL-HAQQA

By the one who is denoted by the name Allah (who created my being with His Names in accord with the meaning of the letter 'B'), the Rahman, the Rahim.

1. The absolute reality (which will become evident with death)!

2. What is the absolute reality?

3. What informs you of the absolute reality?

4. Thamud and Aad denied the eternal life after death.

5. So, for Thamud, they were destroyed with the loud earthquake!

6. And Aad, they were destroyed with an intense hurricane!

7. He subjected them (to that hurricane) for seven nights and eight days! You will see them fallen therein like hollow trunks of palm trees!

8. What do you see of their remains?

9. Pharaoh, those before them, and the destroyed cities, they all made the same mistake!

10. They were disobedient to the Rasul of their Rabb and so (their Rabb) seized them with intensity!

11. Indeed, when the water overflowed it was Us who carried you in the sailing ship!

12. (We narrated it) so that We might make it a reminder for you and so that a perceptive ear can discern it well!

13. When the Horn (the forms – the bodies that are present at that time) is blown with a single blow (when the individual consciousnesses realize their essential reality without their body)...

14. When the earth (bodies) and the mountains (egos – identities) are crushed and destroyed with a single impact;

15. At that time the great event will have taken place (everyone will have become aware of the absolute reality)!

16. And the sky (the sense of self, identity) will be split apart, for at that time it will be frail!

17. And the angel will be around it! Eight (forces) above them, (the creation) will bear the Throne of your Rabb at that time.

18. And you will be brought forth that day with none of your secrets left concealed (fully exposed)!

19. He whose (life record) is formed from his right will say, "Here is my record, read it."

20. "Indeed, I knew I was going to meet the results of my deeds!"

21. So he will be in a state of bliss;

22. A high (sublime) Paradise!

23. The resulting fruits of his deeds will be within his reach!

24. Eat and drink with joy as the result of your past deeds!

25. As for he whose (book) life record is formed from his left, he will say, "I wish I had never been given my record!"

26. "I wish I had never known what is my account (the consequences of my deeds)!"

27. "I wish it ended (before it came to this point)!"

28. "My wealth has been of no avail to me!"

29. "All my power is lost and gone."

30. "Seize him and tie him!"

31. "Then cast him to the Hell!"

32. "Then insert him into a chain that is seventy cubits."

33. "For he did not believe in Allah the Azim, his essential reality with His Names!"

34. "Nor did he make any effort to feed the needy (he was stingy)!"

35. "So there is no devoted friend for him at this time."

36. "Nor any food for him except for pus."

37. "And the guilty will eat only that!"

38. So I swear by what you see,

39. And what you do not see!

40. Indeed, it is the word of a generous Rasul.

41. It is not the word of a poet... How limited is your faith!

42. Nor is it the word of a soothsayer... How little you remember and think!

43. It is a (detailed) disclosure from the Rabb of the worlds!

44. Had he made it up and attributed it to Us;

45. Surely We would have taken his right hand (power).

46. Then We would have cut his jugular vein (carotid artery)!

47. And none among you could have prevented it.

48. Indeed, it (the Quran) is a thought-provoking reminder for those who want to protect themselves!

49. Surely We know who among you are the deniers.

50. Indeed, it (Doomsday) will be a time of bitter regret for those who deny the knowledge of the reality!

51. Indeed, that (Doomsday period) is the (clear) experience of the Truth!

52. So glorify (tasbih) your Rabb by continuing to carry out your function (in servitude to His Names), whose name is Azim!

AL-MA'ARIJ

By the one who is denoted by the name Allah (who created my being with His Names in accord with the meaning of the letter 'B'), the Rahman, the Rahim.

1. The inquisitor asked about the suffering to occur!

2. It (the suffering of death) is for those who deny the knowledge of the reality! None can fight against it.

3. From Allah are the (many) Ways of Ascent (dhul ma'arij)!

4. The angels and the Spirit will return to their essence in a period (which will seem to be) of fifty thousand years (the period of time to reach Allah in their essence).

5. So be patient with a gracious patience.

6. Indeed, they see it (the day of suffering; death) as far!

7. But We see it as near!

8. That day the sky will be like molten metal.

9. And the mountains will be like colored wool.

10. And no friend will be in the state to call another!

11. When they are shown to each other... To save themselves from the punishment of that period, the guilty one will want to offer his children (to the Fire) in his stead as ransom...

12. And his wife and his brother;

13. And his nearest kin who shelter him;

14. And everything on earth so that it could save him!

15. Never! Indeed, it is the Laza (smokeless flame).

16. That peels and sears the skins!

17. It (the Laza) **invites he who turned his back and walked away** (when invited to his essential reality)!

18. And collected wealth and hoarded!

19. Indeed, man is created with ambition and greed!

20. When misfortune touches him he begins to cry and lament (he is intolerant)!

21. But when good touches him, he is stingy and selfish!

22. Except the observers of prayer (who actively experience salat)!

23. They are in a constant state of salat (they maintain their introspective turning to Allah, their essence)!

24. They are those within whose wealth there is a share;

25. For those who ask for help and the deprived.

26. They are those who confirm (believe without doubt in) **the day of religion** (the time of recompense)!

27. They are those who are anxious of the punishment of their Rabb.

28. Indeed, they have no assurance against the punishment of their Rabb!

29. They are those who guard their sexual organs from excessiveness.

30. Except from their wives or those their right hands possess, for which they are not to be blamed.

31. But those who desire more than this, they are the very transgressors!

32. They are those who are faithful to their trusts (entrusted upon man) **and to their pledges** (which they have given to Allah).

33. And who stand by their testimony. (A reference to verse 3:18.)

34. And who are steadfast in their salats (maintain their state of constant introspective turning to Allah, their essence).

35. And who will be honored in Paradises.

36. What is the matter with those who deny the knowledge of the reality that they rush bewildered toward you?

37. From the right and from the left, in groups!

38. Do they hope to enter the Paradise of Bliss?

39. No, never! Indeed, We created them from that which they know (sperm)!

40. By the Rabb of the easts and the wests, We are indeed powerful over all things!

41. To replace them with those better than them... We are the irrepressible power!

42. So, let them amuse themselves (in their worlds) until they meet the promised time!

43. That day, they will rapidly emerge from their graves! As though they are running towards erected idols.

44. Their eyes humbled with terror, covered by utter humiliation... This is the time that they have been promised!

71

NUH

By the one who is denoted by the name Allah (who created my being with His Names in accord with the meaning of the letter 'B'), the Rahman, the Rahim.

1. Indeed, We sent Noah to his people saying, "Warn your people before there comes to them a severe suffering."

2. (Noah) said, "O my people, I am indeed a clear warner to you!"

3. "Worship Allah, protect yourselves from Him and obey me..."

4. "So that He may forgive some of your mistakes and grant you life until the end of your appointed term. Indeed, when the time set by Allah comes, it will not be delayed. If only you knew!"

5. (Noah) said, "My Rabb... Indeed, I have invited my people by day and by night."

6. "But my invitation did not increase them in anything except flight."

7. "The more I invited them to your forgiveness, the more they put their fingers into their ears, covered themselves with their garments and persisted in their ways (beliefs) becoming more and more arrogant."

8. "Then I invited them openly."

9. "Then I invited them publicly, and I also explained it to them in private."

10. I said, "Ask forgiveness of your Rabb... Indeed, He is the Gaffar."

11. "He will send the sky (waves of data from space) upon you in abundance."

12. "And support you with wealth and sons, and form gardens and rivers for you."

13. "What is the matter with you that you despair the majesty of Allah?"

14. "When He has created you in stages."

15. "Did you not see how Allah created the heavens as seven layers?"

16. "And made the Moon therein Nur and the Sun a source of light – energy."

17. And Allah causes you to grow from the earth gradually like a plant (the body that comes from the earth continues its life as consciousness).

18. "Then He will return you into it and again extract you from it."

19. "And Allah has made for you the earth an exhibition (living environment)."

20. "So that you may traverse therein, on spacious ways."

21. Noah said, "My Rabb... Indeed, they have disobeyed me, and followed the one whose wealth and children increased him in nothing other than loss."

22. "And they conspired a mighty plot!"

23. They said, "Never leave your gods! Never leave Wadd, Suwa or Yaghuth and Yauq and Nasr (the names of their deities)!"

24. "And thus they lead many astray... So, increase the wrongdoers in their error!"

25. Because of their mistakes they drowned and were put into the Fire and they could not find any helper for themselves besides Allah.

26. And Noah said, "My Rabb... Do not leave upon earth anyone from among those who deny the knowledge of the reality!"

27. "For if you leave them, they will lead your servants astray and spawn no other than those who deny the knowledge of the reality and who disobey the commands (their genes will only reproduce their like!)."

28. "My Rabb... Forgive me, my parents, the one who enters my house as a believer, the believing men and the believing women! And do not increase the wrongdoers except in destruction!"

72

AL-JINN

By the one who is denoted by the name Allah (who created my being with His Names in accord with the meaning of the letter 'B'), **the Rahman, the Rahim.**

1. **Say: "It has been revealed to me that a group of the jinn listened** (to the Quran) **and said, 'Indeed, we have heard an amazing Quran.'"**

2. **"It guides to the right course** (maturity/perfection), **so we have believed in it. And we will never associate partners to our Rabb!"**

3. **"Indeed, exalted is the nobleness of our Rabb; He has not taken a wife or a son!"**

4. **"Our inadequate understanding has been making us claim foolish things about Allah!"**

5. **"We had thought that mankind and the jinn would never speak a lie about Allah."**

6. **"And yet there were men and women from mankind who sought refuge in men and women from the jinn, thereby increasing** (provoking each other) **in excessive** (carnal) **behavior."**

7. **"And they had thought, as you thought, that Allah would never resurrect** (ba'th) **anyone."** (This verse indicates that jinn, like humans, have no proficiency pertaining to life after death/resurrection.)

8. **"And we touched the heaven but found it filled with powerful guards** (forces) **and burning flames** (rays that impeded our judgment)."

9. **"And we used to take up positions therein to listen, but whoever listens now will find a burning flame lying in wait for him."**

10. **And we do not know whether evil is intended for those on earth** (body) **or whether their Rabb intends for them a right course** (the maturity to observe the reality). (This verse is a clear proof that the jinn have no knowledge of how people will live; how their essential

composition of Names will manifest in their lives and what their purpose of manifesting in the sight of Allah is.)

11. **"And among us are the righteous, and among us are those who are below** (the righteous state)**; we are of various ways** (different breeds/species/races; a cosmopolitan community of different make-up and understanding)**."**

12. **"And we have become certain that we can never invalidate Allah's command upon earth, nor can we escape Him by flight."**

13. **"When we heard the guidance** (Quran)**, we believed it was the reality. And whoever believes in his Rabb as his own reality, will not fear any deprivation** (of his rights) **or derogation."**

14. **"And among us are those in submission, and among us are wrongdoers who rebel against the commands. And those who submit are the aspirants of the fullness of the reality."**

15. **"But as for the wrongdoers who disobey the commands, they will be firewood for Hell!"**

16. **If they had walked upon the path** (to their reality)**, surely We would have watered them with the water** (of knowledge and gnosis)**.**

17. **We would have tried them with it, to reveal their true nature. And whoever turns away from the remembrance of his Rabb, He will subject him to an increasing suffering!**

18. **Indeed, the places of prostration are for Allah. So do not** (while in the state of prostration) **turn to things besides Allah!**

19. **Whenever Abdullah** (the servant of Allah – Muhammad [saw]) **stands to turn to Him, they crowd around and stifle him!**

20. **Say, "I turn only to** (and ask only from) **my Rabb! Never will I associate others to He who comprises my essence!"**

21. **Say, "I can neither give you harm nor form the maturity in you to experience the reality** (these are things for Allah to manifest through you)**!"**

22. **Say, "For none can save me from Allah and there is no place of refuge besides Him!"**

23. Except for what Allah reveals and His risalahs (the knowledge He discloses through His Rasuls)! So, whoever disobeys Allah and His Rasul, for him there is Fire in which he will abide forever!

24. But when they see the thing that they have been promised (death), they will understand who the minority and the helpless are!

25. Say, "I do not know whether what you have been promised is near or whether my Rabb has set for it a long period."

26. He knows the unknown! And He does not disclose His Unknown (Absolute Essence) to anyone;

27. Except for a chosen-purified Rasul! And indeed, He places guards in front and behind him (the Rasul)!

28. That they may know that they have conveyed the disclosed knowledge of their Rabb. He has encompassed whatever is with them and recorded everything in detail!

73

AL-MUZAMMIL

By the one who is denoted by the name Allah (who created my being with His Names in accord with the meaning of the letter 'B'), **the Rahman, the Rahim.**

1. O covered one (Muzammil)!

2. Arise in the night, except for a little;

3. Half of it or less,

4. Or increase it, and recite and contemplate upon the Quran!

5. Indeed, We will send upon you (make you experience in your consciousness) **a heavy word!**

6. Arising in the night gives greater perception and clarity in the evaluation of the call!

7. For during the day you are occupied.

8. Remember (dhikr) **the qualities of the Names comprising your essence; your Rabb, and seclude yourself to Him in complete devotion.**

9. He is the Rabb of the east (that which shines) **and the west** (that which extinguishes)! **There is no god, only HU! So take only him as the disposer of your affairs!**

10. Be patient about what they say and depart from them with a pleasant departure!

11. Leave me (to deal alone) **with those who deny in their abundance! Give them respite.**

12. Indeed, there are chains and Hellfire with us.

Note: Imam Razi, a renowned interpreter of the Quran, says the following about the symbolism used in regards to the suffering of Hell: "These four states may be seen as the spiritual results of what the person did in his life. 'Heavy irons' is symbolic of his former material interests and the continuation of his imprisonment to his bodily pleasures. The day when they are no longer able to actualize these irons and chains become the means to prevent the resurrected person (ego) from reaching the stations of sublimity and purity. Thereafter, these spiritual irons bring about 'spiritual fire', for when the person feels a strong desire for a bodily pleasure and is unable to attain it, a sense of severe burning takes place within his being. This is the meaning of the 'burning hellfire'. The sinner, in this state, feels in his throat the pain of separation from the things he desires and the suffocating sensation of being deprived of them. This is the meaning of the expression 'food that gets stuck in their throats'. And finally, because of being in this state, he is bereft of the company of those who are enlightened with the Nur of Allah and sanctified, thus the meaning of 'severe suffering'. But know that I am not asserting that the meaning of these Quranic expressions are confined only to what I say..."

13. And food that gets stuck in their throats and a severe suffering!

14. At that time the earth (body) **and the mountains** (ego-identities) **will be shaken... And the mountains will become a heap of dust!**

15. Indeed, just as We disclosed a Rasul (guider to the reality, purifier) **to Pharaoh, We have also sent a Rasul to you as a witness.**

16. Pharaoh disobeyed that Rasul and We seized him with a destructive seizure!

17. If you are ungrateful (to the disclosed reality)**, how will you be protected at that time which will make the children grey-haired and old?**

18. The heaven will split apart there from; His promise is fulfilled!

19. Indeed, this is a reminder! So whoever wills may take the way (that leads) **to his Rabb!**

20. Your Rabb knows that you arise in two-thirds of the night or half of it or a third of it, and so do a group of those with you. And it is Allah who determines the night and the day! (Allah) **knows you will never be able to evaluate it and accepted your repentance... So, recite** (comprehend) **what is easy for you of the Quran!** (Allah) **knows that there will be among you those who are ill, and those who travel throughout the land seeking the bounty of Allah, and those who fight in the way of Allah. So, recite what is easy from it and establish salat** (maintain your turning with observation)**, give alms and give a good loan to Allah... Whatever good you give for yourself you will**

find it much greater and better in the sight of Allah. Ask forgiveness of Allah! Indeed, Allah is the Ghafur, the Rahim.

AL-MUDDATHIR

By the one who is denoted by the name Allah (who created my being with His Names in accord with the meaning of the letter 'B'), the Rahman, the Rahim.

1. O wrapped one (Muddathir);

2. Arise and warn!

3. Realize the magnificence of your Rabb!

4. Purify your garments (consciousness – brain)!

5. Refrain from uncleanliness (duality, misevaluation)!

6. And do not engage in good to acquire more (with greed)!

7. Be patient for your Rabb!

8. When that trumpet is blown (death, resurrection);

9. It will be a difficult time, indeed!

10. Not easy at all for those who deny (cover) the knowledge of the reality!

11. So leave me (to deal) with the one I created alone;

12. The one whom I granted wealth;

13. And sons standing before him;

14. And enabled the experience of expansive abundance!

15. Yet he (greedily) wants me to increase it for him!

16. Never! Indeed, he is very stubborn against Our signs.

17. I will subject him to an arduous uphill climb.

18. Indeed, he reflected and decided!

19. May he die (and see the reality)! **How he decided!**

20. Again, may he die (and see the reality)! **How he decided!**

21. Then he looked.

22. Then he frowned and scowled!

23. Then he turned his back and became arrogant!

24. And he said, "This is nothing other than narrated words of magic!"

25. "It is no other than the words of a mortal!"

26. I will subject him to Saqar (painful tormenting fire).

27. And what informs you of Saqar?

28. (Saqar) **neither lets anything remain the same, nor does it let anything be!**

29. It burns and blackens the (flesh of) **mortals!**

30. Over it are nineteen!

31. We have appointed only (nineteen) **angels** (66:6) **to be the wardens of the Fire** (the hell of corporeality; not a breed of humans or the jinn)**... And We specified their number** (as if the number nineteen is meaningful) **as an** (object of) **trial for the disbelievers... So, those to whom a Book** (knowledge) **has been given can know with certainty** (what is referenced by these metaphors and thus confirm the revelation of Rasulullah [saw]) **and so those who believe** (in the nubuwwah and risalah of Rasulullah [saw]) **will increase in faith** (the knowledge of certainty; ilm al-yakeen) **and so those** (who acquire solid knowledge) **to whom a Book** (knowledge) **has been given** (and those who have attained certainty in faith) **do not fall into doubt! And so those in whose hearts there is sickness** (doubt, who are devoid of healthy thought) **and the disbelievers** (who are veiled from and thus deny the reality) **can say, "What did Allah intend to reference with this example?"... Thus Allah misguides whom He wills and guides whom He wills. Only HU knows the armies** (forces) **of your Rabb! This** (Saqar and other metaphors) **is only a reminder for people.**

32. No! I swear by the Moon,

33. And the night, when it returns,

34. And the morning, when it brightens.

35. Indeed, it is one of the greatest things!

36. A warning for the people;

37. For whoever wants to go forward or stay behind.

38. Everyone is bound by the results of their own deeds!

39. Except for the people of the right!

40. They are in Paradises... They ask,

41. The guilty ones:

42. "What has let you into the Saqar (the entwining fire with immense flames)?"

43. They say, "We were not of those who established (actively experienced) salat!"

44. "Nor did we feed the poor."

45. "And we indulged (in egotistic pleasures) with those who indulged!"

46. "And we denied the time of religion (sunnatullah – that recompense will definitely be experienced for all actions)!"

47. "Until finally there came to us certainty (confrontation of the reality)!"

48. Then the intercession of the intercessors will not avail them.

49. What is the matter with them that they turn away from the one who reminds them?

50. They are like wild donkeys running about in fear!

51. As though fleeing in fear from a lion!

52. Perhaps each one of them desires to be given pages (of revelation)!

53. No! They do not fear the eternal life to come!

54. No! Indeed, it is but a reminder!

55. Whoever wills will remember (and evaluate) **it!**

56. And they cannot remember (and evaluate) **unless Allah wills... He enables protection to whom He wills and forgives whom He wills.**

AL-QIYAMA

By the one who is denoted by the name Allah (who created my being with His Names in accord with the meaning of the letter 'B'), the Rahman, the Rahim.

1. By the reality of the Doomsday;

2. And the self-accusing self (nafs-i lawwama);

3. Does man think We will not assemble his bones?

4. Indeed! We even have the power to proportion his fingertips (produce a precise reformation of his fingerprints)!

5. But no! Man goes to excess despite what awaits him (life after death)!

6. They ask, "When is the time of Doomsday (the experience of death)?

7. When your vision is dazzled,

8. And the Moon is eclipsed,

9. And when the Sun and the Moon come together!

10. At that time, man will say, "Where can we escape?"

11. No, there is no place of refuge (outside)!

12. At that time, the permanent settlement (of every individual) is with his Rabb!

13. At that time, man will be told of all the things he put forward (accomplished) and left behind (postponed, failed to do).

14. (The truth is) man is the evaluator of his own self! (Remember 17:14 "Read your book [knowledge] of life! Sufficient for you is your individual consciousness at this stage to discern the consequences of your actions.")

15. Whatever excuse he presents (it will make no difference)!

16. Do not repeat it with your tongue to hasten (its memorization).

17. Indeed, upon Us is its compilation and its recitation.

18. So when We recite it, follow its recitation!

19. Then upon Us is its clarification (disclosure).

20. But no! You love the immediate (the world);

21. And leave the eternal life to come!

22. At that time faces will shine.

23. Looking at their Rabb.

24. And many faces at that time will be frowning!

25. They (with frowning faces) will feel their backs breaking...

26. No! When the life reaches the collarbones;

27. "Who will save him from death?"

28. He will know with certainty that it is the time of the known separation!

29. And the feet will be intertwined!

30. To your Rabb will be the dispatch at that time!

31. For he neither confirmed, nor established salat (turned to his Rabb)...

32. But denied and turned away!

33. And then went back to his people full of pride and arrogance.

34. Deserving you are, deserving you are!

35. Again, deserving you are, yes deserving you are!

36. Does man think he will be left to his own accord?

37. Was he not once a drop of sperm?

38. Which then became a clot (genetic structure), and (Allah) created him and proportioned him (according to his creational purpose).

39. And made of him two partners, the male (consciousness – active energy) **and the female** (the body – the receptive energy).

40. Is this (the system and order of Allah who made all of this) **not Qadir to give life to the dead?**

AL-INSAN

By the one who is denoted by the name Allah (who created my being with His Names in accord with the meaning of the letter 'B'), **the Rahman, the Rahim.**

1. Has there not been a time, when man was not a thing even mentioned? (Man was not yet manifest; he was the unmanifest within the dimension of the Names)!

2. Indeed, We created man from a mixture of (genetic heritage) **sperm and made him as one who perceives and evaluates.**

3. We showed him the way (to use his intellect and believe). **He will either be grateful** (and evaluate his Rabb) **or be a denier** (of the Truth)!

4. Indeed, We have prepared for those who deny the knowledge of the reality chains (environmental conditionings and value judgments) **and shackles** (the ties of corporeality) **and a blaze** (of fire – burning).

5. And indeed, the righteous will drink from a cup whose mixture is Kafur (a drink that strengthens the heart).

6. (That drink) **is an endless spring that they** (the servants of Allah) **will cause to gush forth and flow.**

7. They (the righteous) **keep their vows and they fear a day whose evil spreads far and wide!**

8. They feed the needy, the orphans and captives out of their love for Him.

9. Saying, "We feed you for the sake of Allah... We ask of you neither a return nor thanks."

10. "We fear from our Rabb a wrathful and intense time."

11. So Allah will protect them from the evil of that time and give them brightness and joy.

12. And the respite for their patience will be Paradise and silk.

13. They will lean on lounges therein and see neither the (burning) sun nor the (freezing) cold (meaning bodily senses will not be valid in that dimension of life).

14. The shades will be near above them, and its fruits (gnosis) will be lowered.

15. Silver cups and crystal vessels will circulate among them.

16. Silver and crystal cups of which they have determined the amount.

17. And they will be given a cup whose mixture is of ginger.

18. A fountain named 'Salsabeel'.

19. Young servants who are immortal will circulate among them... You will think they are scattered pearls when you see them!

20. And wherever you look you will (only) see bounty and a great sovereignty.

21. And they will be in garments made of fine silk and brocade, adorned with silver bracelets... And their Rabb will have given them pure wine (the euphoric state caused by the exposure to the reality...). (Note that all these descriptions pertaining to Paradise are similes and figurative representations as mentioned in the verses 13:35 and 47:15. This should not be forgotten.)

22. Indeed, this is your reward (the results of your deeds)! Your faithful practices have been duly appreciated!

23. Indeed, it is Us, yes Us, who revealed the Quran to you (manifested it through you part by part)!

24. So, be patient for the command of your Rabb and do not follow any from among them who rebels or covers the reality in persistent denial.

25. Remember (dhikr) the name of your Rabb by morning and by night!

26. And prostrate to him in a part of the night; glorify (tasbih) Him extensively during the night.

27. Indeed, these ones love the world in front of them without considering the intense hardship of the time that is to come after it.

28. We created them and strengthened their ties... And We will replace them with their like whenever We will.

29. Indeed, this is a reminder (of the reality)! So, whoever wills may take the path to his Rabb.

30. You cannot will unless Allah wills (your will is Allah's will)! Indeed, Allah is the Aleem, the Hakim.

31. He includes whom He wills to His grace. As for the wrongdoers, He has prepared an intense suffering for them.

AL-MURSALAT

By the one who is denoted by the name Allah (who created my being with His Names in accord with the meaning of the letter 'B'), **the Rahman, the Rahim.**

1. By those disclosed one after another;

2. That blow about violently;

3. Who bring to life and cause to rise;

4. Who choose and separate;

5. And those who disclose the reminder (the forces that manifest in consciousness; the Exalted Assembly [Mala-i Ala]. The word 'ilqa' or 'liqa' [disclosure] is like 'nafh' [breath] in that it goes outward from within; it is an explicit projection experienced in the consciousness. In the sequence: the Hidden [Reflection of Attributes], the Secret [Reflection of Names], the Spirit [Fuad: Reflectors of the Names], the Heart [Consciousness] and the Self [Identity – Individual consciousness]. It looks to the reflections from the spirit to the heart. 'Vicegerent' [Khalifa] – 'Man' is the totality of all of these states or one who incorporates all of these states is called a true 'Man').

6. To excuse (pardon misdeeds) **or to warn.**

7. What you are promised will definitely be fulfilled!

8. When the stars are extinguished,

9. And the sky is split open,

10. And the mountains are blown away,

11. And the Rasuls (not the Nabis) **take their new positions.**

12. For which day were they postponed?

13. For the time of sorting!

14. And do you know what the time of sorting is?

15. Woe to those who denied (life after death) at that time!

16. Did We not destroy the former people?

17. Then We will make the later ones follow them (they too will be destroyed).

18. Thus do We deal with the guilty!

19. Woe to the deniers at that time!

20. Did We not create you from a simple water?

21. We formed it in a safe place (the womb),

22. For a known time!

23. Thus We determined it! And excellent determiners We are!

24. Woe to the deniers at that time!

25. Did We not make the earth a place of gathering?

26. For the living and the dead!

27. We formed therein elevated (grand, majestic) mountains that are firm and made you drink sweet water.

28. Woe to the deniers at that time!

29. Proceed to that which you denied!

30. Proceed to the shadow of the trident (let your faith in the trinity [God-the Son and the Holy Spirit] save you now)!

31. It will neither shade you (from the Fire) nor save you from the blazing flame (different sensations of burning)!

32. Indeed, it shoots sparks as big as palaces!

33. Sparks like giant golden ropes!

34. Woe to the deniers at that time!

35. This is the day they shall not speak.

36. Nor will they be given permission to present excuses.

37. Woe to the deniers at that time!

38. This is the time of sorting! We have brought you and the former ones together.

39. So, if you have a trick, try your trick against Me now!

40. Woe to the deniers at that time!

41. Indeed, the protected ones will be among shades and springs.

42. With every fruit they desire.

43. "Eat and drink with joy as the result of your deeds!"

44. Thus We respite the doers of good (in whose observation there is none but the Truth).

45. Woe to the deniers at that time!

46. "Eat and enjoy yourself for a little (in this world)... Indeed, you are guilty!"

47. Woe to the deniers at that time!

48. And when they are told, "Bow," they do not bow!

49. Woe to the deniers at that time!

50. Then in what word will they believe after (this big news given by the Quran)?

78

AN-NABA

By the one who is denoted by the name Allah (who created my being with His Names in accord with the meaning of the letter 'B'), **the Rahman, the Rahim.**

1. What are they questioning?

2. **The mighty news** (regarding life after death)?

3. **Over this, they are in disagreement.**

4. **But no! Soon** (when they die) **they will know** (that it is not like what they think)**!**

5. **Again, no! Soon they will know** (it is not like what they think)**!**

6. **Did We not make the earth** (the body) **a cradle** (a temporary place in which you can grow and develop yourselves)**?**

7. **And the mountains** (the organs in the body) **as stakes.**

8. **And created you as partners** (consciousness – body).

9. **And made sleep a means for rest.**

10. **And the night a blanket.**

11. **And made the day for livelihood.**

12. **And constructed seven strong** (heavens) **above you** (the system with seven orbits – the dimension of consciousness).

13. **And a luminous lamp** (Sun – intellect).

14. **And disclosed pouring water from the rain clouds.**

15. **So that We may produce therein grain and vegetation.**

16. **Gardens within gardens!**

17. **Indeed, that time** (of sorting and separating) **is an appointed time.**

18. The Horn will be blown at that time and you will come forth in groups.

19. The heaven will open and become gateways (consciousness will be opened to perception without the bodily senses).

20. And mountains will be made to vanish as if they were a mirage (the limitations of the organs are removed).

21. Indeed, Hell has become a place of passage (everyone will pass from it).

22. A place of settlement for the transgressors (the wrongdoers who failed to protect themselves according to the sunnatullah).

23. To remain therein for a very long time!

24. They will not taste therein any coolness or a delightful drink!

25. Only boiling water and pus!

26. As the direct result of their deeds!

27. Indeed, they did not expect (to be called to) **account** (for their lives)!

28. They persistently denied Our signs within their beings!

29. But We have recorded everything in detail!

30. So taste it, never We will increase you in anything except suffering!

31. Indeed, there is an attainment for the protected ones.

32. Gardens and grapevines... (Remember that all descriptions pertaining to Paradise are metaphoric expressions.)

33. Magnificent partners of equal age! (Magnificently capacitated bodies bearing the qualities of that dimension of existence, without the concept of gender, formed to manifest the qualities of the Names emanating from the essence of the individual consciousness... Note again, without any differentiation of gender! Allah knows best.)

34. And cups that are full!

35. They will hear neither baseless speech therein nor any falsehood.

36. As respite from your Rabb, an endowment for their deeds!

37. He is the Rabb of the heavens, the earth and everything in between; He is the Rahman! The One of whom no one has the authority to speak.

38. At that time the **Spirit** (the single reality of the Names that manifests in the consciousness of all humans) **and the angels will stand in rows. None will be able to speak, except for whom the Rahman has given permission** (allowed his natural disposition). **And he will speak the truth.**

39. This is the time of the Truth! Then, whoever wills may take a way to his Rabb!

40. Indeed, we have warned you of a close suffering (caused by the realization of the Truth through the experience of death)! On that day, man will observe what his hands have put forth, and those who denied the knowledge of the reality will say "Oh, how I wish I was made of dust!"

AN-NAZI'AT

By the one who is denoted by the name Allah (who created my being with His Names in accord with the meaning of the letter 'B'), **the Rahman, the Rahim.**

1. By the intensely powerful (force; Mars),

2. And the (force) **that takes with ease** (Sun),

3. And the (forces) **that swim** (in their orbits; Saturn – Jupiter),

4. And the (forces) **that race ahead** (Mercury – Venus),

5. And the administrators of the command (the forces that reveal; the Moon). (That these verses denote the planets is the construal of Hasan al-Basri and Imam Razi, a perspective I also share.)

6. At that time the convulsion (of death; earthquake) **will convulse.**

7. Followed by a subsequent one (resurrection; commencement of a new life with the new spirit-body).

8. The minds (of some) **will be shocked at that time!**

9. Their vision will be confounded and crushed!

10. Yet still they say, "Will we really be returned to our former state (back to life, after having become dust)**; is resurrection really true?"**

11. "Even after we have become decayed and scattered bones?"

12. "That, then, (the continuation of life in this state) **will be a return in loss."**

13. Whereas, it is but one command!

14. And behold they will instantly find themselves on an open expanse!

15. Did the news of Moses reach you?

16. How his Rabb called out to him in the sacred valley of Tuwa:

17. "Go to Pharaoh! Indeed, he has transgressed!"

18. "And say, 'How about becoming cleansed and purified?'"

19. "How about I guide you to your Rabb? You will be in awe (of His might)!"

20. Then he showed him the great miracle!

21. But (Pharaoh) denied and rebelled.

22. Then turned his back and ran.

23. Then he gathered (his people) and called out:

24. "I am your Rabb, the most supreme!" (Pharaoh, who had attained the ancient knowledge of the reality, chose to use this in favor of his bodily existence and bodily pursuits rather than using it to observe the comprehensiveness of consciousness upon existence, and thus fell to the state of the inciting self. This is why, rather than conveying the knowledge of the reality to him and calling him to believe in Allah, Moses warns him by calling him to believe in the 'Rabb of the worlds.' In other words, he invites him to believe in the Names, which are manifest throughout, and administer the entire existence, rather than experiencing his understanding of this unity through his corporeality.)

25. So Allah seized him with an exemplary suffering of the eternal life to come and what is before it (the world).

26. Indeed, there is a lesson in this for those who are in awe!

27. Is your creation harder or the creation of the heaven? (Which Allah also) constructed!

28. He raised its ceiling and proportioned it (formed it with the qualities to fulfill its function).

29. He darkened its night and brightened its day.

30. Then He spread the earth and furnished it.

31. Then extracted its water and its pasture.

32. And the mountains, He set them firmly as if anchored.

33. So that you and your cattle (animals) may benefit from it.

34. But when the overwhelming calamity (the experience of death) begins,

35. Man will remember at that time the results of his deeds!

36. And Hell will be (openly) exposed to those who see (without the limitation of the eye)!

37. For he who transgressed without bounds,

38. And chose to live in pursuit of worldly pleasures;

39. Indeed, the place (state) of burning will be his abode!

40. But as for he who feared the position of his Rabb and protected himself from things whose results will be useless in the eternal life,

41. Indeed, Paradise will be his very abode.

42. They ask you about that Hour: when is its arrival?

43. But who are you to have this knowledge?

44. To your Rabb is its finality.

45. You are only a warner to those who are in awe of it!

46. The day they see it, it will be as though they had not remained (in the world), except for a time of sunset or twilight.

80

ABASA

By the one who is denoted by the name Allah (who created my being with His Names in accord with the meaning of the letter 'B'), **the Rahman, the Rahim.**

1. He frowned and turned away!

2. When the blind man approached him!

3. How do you know, perhaps he might be purified!

4. Or perhaps he is going to contemplate on the reminder and that remembrance is going to benefit him!

5. As for he who thinks himself without need...

6. You give attention to him!

7. But what is it to you if he is not purified!

8. Whereas the one who comes to you with a thirst for knowledge!

9. He is in awe!

10. Yet you do not give your attention to him!

11. No, indeed, it (the Quran) **is a reminder.**

12. So whoever wills shall remember it!

13. It is recorded in honored records,

14. And exalted and completely purified!

15. By the hands (forces) **of scribes** (recording angels).

16. Noble (dignified, supreme) **and dutiful,**

17. Woe to man! May he die (and see the reality)! **How he denies!**

18. From what did He create him?

19. He made him from a sperm-drop, and formed his nature!

20. Then eased his way.

21. Then killed and placed him in the grave (body).

22. Then, when He wills, He will resurrect him from his grave (body).

23. But no! He has not yet fulfilled what He commanded him (he has not duly fulfilled his vicegerency).

24. Let man look at what he eats!

25. We poured that water and made it flow in abundance.

26. And We split open the earth (and thus),

27. We caused sprouts to grow therein.

28. Grapes and fresh plants,

29. Olives and dates,

30. Dense gardens of large trees,

31. Fruits and pastures,

32. For the benefit of you and your cattle (animals).

33. When that frightening blast is heard,

34. At that time, man will flee from his brother,

35. And from his mother and father,

36. And from his wife and sons!

37. At that time, each will be to his own!

38. (Some) faces that day will be bright,

39. Laughing, rejoicing at the good news!

40. And (some) faces that day will be covered in dust!

41. Covered in darkness!

42. They, the falsifiers (who are inclined towards falsity), are the very deniers of the knowledge of the reality!

AT-TAKWIR

By the one who is denoted by the name Allah (who created my being with His Names in accord with the meaning of the letter 'B'), the Rahman, the Rahim.

1. When the Sun is wrapped up (when the mind loses its power in the sight of the reality),

2. And the stars are darkened (thought processes cease – ideas shed no light),

3. And the mountains are removed (the organs stop working),

4. And when the she-camels (objects of wealth and status) are neglected and (worldly values are) abandoned,

5. And when the beasts are gathered (animalistic senses lose their power),

6. And the seas begin to boil (information obtained via conditionings flame up and boil away in sight of the reality),

7. And when the souls are paired (individual consciousnesses are paired with their new spirit bodies),

8. And the female infant who was buried alive is asked,

9. "For what sin she was killed?"

10. And when the recorded pages are made public,

11. And the sky is ripped away (when the mind loses its reasoning power),

12. And Hell is ignited and set ablaze (the fire of remorse is flared up),

Note: These interpretations are in respect of Doomsday being the individual experience of the person, i.e. the person's own death.

13. And Paradise is brought near,

14. Every soul (individual consciousness) **will know what it has prepared** (apprehend the consequences of his deeds during his life in the biological body).

15. I swear by 'al-Hunnas' (the stars that are not observable during the day due to sunlight),

Note: Hadhrat Ali (ra) says the following in regards to 'al-Hunnas': "These are the stars (planets) that are invisible during the day, but visible in the night."

16. And by al-Jawar and al-Qunnas (the planets that run their course and those that orbit near the constellations),

17. And by the night as it closes in,

18. And by the morning that you breathe in,

19. Indeed, it is the word (conveyed by) **a noble Rasul;**

20. A powerful (Rasul)**! Secure in the sight of the owner of the Throne!**

21. Obeyed there (in the heaven) **and trustworthy.**

22. Your companion (Muhammad [saw]) **is not possessed!**

23. Indeed, he observed him in the clear horizon!

24. He does not withhold (the knowledge of) **the unseen!**

25. And it is not the word of Satan, the cursed (distanced from the reality)**!**

26. So, where are you going (by leaving the Quran)**?**

27. It is only a reminder to the worlds (humans)**!**

28. For those who want to live by the Truth!

29. You cannot will unless Allah, the Rabb of the worlds, wills!

82

AL-INFITAR

By the one who is denoted by the name Allah (who created my being with His Names in accord with the meaning of the letter 'B'), the Rahman, the Rahim.

1. And when the sky is split apart,

2. And the planets are scattered away,

3. And the seas boil and erupt,

4. And the spirits are removed from their worlds (realize the universal reality);

5. Every soul shall know what it has prepared (aforetime) and what it has failed to do (neglected, left for later).

6. O man! How did you dare to (be ungrateful to your essential reality) your Rabb, the Generous One?

7. Who created you (manifested you), formed you (with a brain, an individual consciousness and a spirit) and balanced you (the work process of your brain, consciousness and spirit)!

8. Whatever form (manifestation of Names) He willed for you, He configured your composition accordingly.

9. But no (it is not like what you think)! Rather, you are in denial of your religion (the system by which you live)!

10. Indeed, there are over you recorders (who record all of your thoughts from your brain to your spirit),

11. Magnificent noble scribes (forces)!

12. They know whatever you do.

13. Indeed, the righteous will be in Paradises of pleasure.

14. While the falsifiers (who strayed from the Truth) will be in Hell (Fire).

15. They will be subjected to it at the time when the commands of religion are applied!

16. They are in a state of constant observation of Hell!

17. Do you know what the Day of Religion is?

18. So then, do you know what the Day of Religion is?

19. A time when no one can do anything for another! The judgment at that time belongs to Allah (there is nothing the person can do other than live the consequences of his deeds)!

AL-MUTAFFIFIN

By the one who is denoted by the name Allah (who created my being with His Names in accord with the meaning of the letter 'B'), the Rahman, the Rahim.

1. Woe to those who do not measure and scale justly!

2. They take their right from the people in full;

3. Yet (when it comes to giving the right of others) they reduce the measure and give them less!

4. Do they not think they will be resurrected (immediately after death)?

5. For a tremendous time.

6. A time when mankind will stand before the Rabb of the worlds!

7. No (never)! Indeed, the record of the falsifiers (who have strayed from the Truth) is in the sijjeen!

8. And what informs you of the sijjeen?

9. It is a non-erasable record!

10. Woe to the deniers (of sunnatullah) at that time!

11. Who denied their time of religion (the time of recompense; when the consequences of all deeds are automatically experienced)!

12. It is only every guilty transgressor who denies it!

13. When he is informed of Our signs he says, "The legends of the old!"

14. No (never)! Rather, the products of their deeds have covered their consciousness (like rust).

15. No! Indeed, that day they are veiled from their Rabb!

16. Then, indeed, they will enter the Fire.

17. Then they will be told, "This is the thing you denied."

18. No... Indeed, the book of the righteous is in the iliyyun.

19. And what informs you of the iliyyun?

20. It is a non-erasable record!

21. Witnessed by the muqarriboon (those who have attained the state of divine closeness).

22. Indeed, the righteous will be in Paradises of pleasure.

23. On lounges, observing...

24. You will see the radiance of pleasure on their faces.

25. They will be made to drink from a sealed (protected) and purified wine.

26. The last of it is musk... So let those who compete, compete for this!

27. Its mixture is of Tasneem.

28. A spring from which those who have attained divine closeness (the muqarriboon) drink!

29. Indeed, the guilty used to laugh at the believers.

30. When they saw them they used to blink their eyes and mock them.

31. And when they returned to their people (families and friends) they used to return rejoicing.

32. And when they saw (the believers) they used to say, "Indeed, these ones have surely gone astray."

33. Whereas they (the believers) were not sent to be their guardians!

34. So, today the believers are laughing at the veiled ones who denied the Truth!

35. Upon lounges, observing...

36. So, are the deniers of the reality thus living the consequences of their deeds?

84

AL-INSHIQAQ

By the one who is denoted by the name Allah (who created my being with His Names in accord with the meaning of the letter 'B'), the Rahman, the Rahim.

1. When the heaven is split open,

2. And attends to its Rabb in submission – which is the Truth!

3. And when the earth is extended and spread out,

4. And it throws out what is within it and empties itself,

5. And attends to its Rabb in submission!

6. O man! Indeed, you are striving towards your Rabb! You will reach Him in the end!

7. Whoever is given his record, formed on his right side,

8. Will be called to an easy account,

9. And will transform into the composition of the people of Paradise!

10. But he who is given his book from behind,

11. Will call out, "Death be my savior!"

12. And will be subject to the (blazing) Fire!

13. Indeed, he used to rejoice among his like...

14. He thought he would never return (to his Rabb).

15. But no! Indeed, his Rabb was Basir within him!

16. I swear by the twilight,

17. And by the night and what it carries,

18. And by the full moon,

19. That you will certainly change dimensions and transform into bodies befitting those dimensions!

20. So, this being the case, what is the matter with them that they do not believe?

21. And when the Quran is recited to them, they do not prostrate? (This is a verse of prostration.)

22. And those who deny the knowledge of the reality further deny!

23. But Allah knows better what they collect and keep within themselves (their thoughts and beliefs).

24. So, give them the news of their severe suffering!

25. Except for those who believe and fulfill the requisites of faith! For them there is uninterrupted reward.

AL-BURUJ

By the one who is denoted by the name Allah (who created my being with His Names in accord with the meaning of the letter 'B'), the Rahman, the Rahim.

1. By the space containing the constellations!

2. And the promised time!

3. And by the witness and the witnessed!

4. Destroyed were the people of the trench...

5. In the fire full of fuel.

6. The fire around which they sat...

7. And they were witnesses to what they were doing to the believers!

8. And they avenged them (the believers) only because they believed in Allah, the Aziz, the Hamid.

9. To whom belongs the sovereignty of the heavens and the earth! Allah is witness to everything!

10. Indeed, those who torture the believing men and believing women and do not repent, there is the suffering of Hell for them, and there is a burning suffering for them.

11. Indeed, those who believe and fulfill the requisites of faith, there are Paradises for them underneath which rivers flow... This is the great attainment!

12. Indeed, the seizure of your Rabb is intense!

13. It is HU who originates (manifests) and then returns it (recreates)!

14. He is the Ghafur, the Wadud.

15. The owner of the Throne, the Majeed (the Majestic).

16. The doer of what He wills!

17. Did the news of those armies reach you?

18. Those (who destroyed) **Pharaoh and Thamud!**

19. No! Those who disbelieve in the knowledge of the reality are in denial.

20. But Allah encompassed them from (within their depths)!

21. Indeed, this is an honored Quran.

22. In a preserved tablet (Lawh-i Mahfuz; the unmanifest knowledge of Allah and sunnatullah)!

86

AT-TARIQ

By the one who is denoted by the name Allah (who created my being with His Names in accord with the meaning of the letter 'B'), the Rahman, the Rahim.

1. By the sky and the Tariq,

2. Do you know the Tariq?

3. It is the piercing star (pulsar)!

4. There is no soul over which there is no guardian (observer – protector).

5. So, let man look to see from what he was created!

6. He was created from an ejected fluid (sperm).

7. Emerging from between the hip (of the male) and the pelvis (of the female).

8. Indeed, He is Qadir to return him (to his origin)!

9. At that time all secrets will be exposed and known.

10. Then there will be no power or helper for him!

11. And by the sky with its orbiters,

12. And the earth cracked open,

13. Indeed, it (the Quran) is a word that separates falsity from the Truth;

14. It has not come as a joke!

15. Indeed, they are planning a plot.

16. And I am responding to their plot with My plot!

17. So, give respite to those who deny the knowledge of the reality; give them a little time.

87

AL-A'LA

By the one who is denoted by the name Allah (who created my being with His Names in accord with the meaning of the letter 'B'), the Rahman, the Rahim.

1. Glorify (tasbih) **the most exalted name of your Rabb** (experience the exaltedness of the reality that comprises your essence within your depths)!

2. **Who created** (the body) **and proportioned it,**

3. **And who determined and guided** (to manifest His perfection),

4. **And who formed the pasture** (as place of benefit for them),

5. **Then made it black stubble** (corpses to be cast into the earth).

6. **We will make you READ and you shall not forget!**

7. **Except for what Allah wills... Indeed, He knows what is manifest and what is concealed.**

8. **We are going to ease you toward ease!**

9. **So remind, if reminding benefits!**

10. **He who is in awe shall remember and contemplate!**

11. **While the most unfortunate one shall flee from it!**

12. **He** (the most unfortunate one) **will be subject to the greatest Fire** (falling eternally far from Allah)!

13. **Then he will neither die therein** (be saved) **nor live** (with the knowledge of the reality)!

14. **The purified and the refined have attained true success!**

15. **And he who remembers the name of his Rabb and establishes** (experiences) **salat has attained true success!**

16. **But you prefer the life of the world** (the lowest state of existence)!

17. When the life after (the dimension of power and consciousness) **is much better and more lasting.**

18. Indeed, this (knowledge of the reality) **was also in the previously disclosed knowledge.**

19. The knowledge disclosed by Abraham and Moses!

88

AL-GHASHIYA

By the one who is denoted by the name Allah (who created my being with His Names in accord with the meaning of the letter 'B'), the Rahman, the Rahim.

1. Did the news reach you of the Ghashiya (the overwhelming event – Doomsday)?

2. (Some) faces that day will look down in shame!

3. Having worked hard (complying with customs, traditions and customary practices of worship) and exhausted for nothing!

4. They (those faces) will be subject to an intense fire!

5. They will be made to drink from a boiling spring!

6. And there will be no food for them, except for a poisonous thorny plant,

7. Which will neither nourish them nor appease their hunger.

8. And many (faces) that day will show signs of pleasure.

9. They will be pleased with the results of their (duly spent) efforts!

10. In an elevated Paradise!

11. They will hear no baseless speech therein.

12. Within a (continually) flowing spring (of knowledge and power),

13. Couches raised high,

14. And cups put in place,

15. And cushions lined up (behind them),

16. And carpets spread (beneath them),

17. Do they not look at the camels (rain clouds), how they are created?

18. **And** (do they not look at) **the sky, how it has been raised** (how space has been formed)!

19. **And** (do they not look at) **the mountains, how they have been set!**

20. **And** (do they not look at) **the earth, how it has been furnished!**

21. **So remind! For you are a reminder** (you have been disclosed to remind them of their essential reality)!

22. **You are not a controller and imposer over them!**

23. **But whoever turns away and covers** (denies and refuses to see the reality),

24. **Allah will subject him to the greatest suffering!**

25. **Indeed, to Us is their return,**

26. **And it is up to Us to make them live the consequences of their deeds!**

89

AL-FAJR

By the one who is denoted by the name Allah (who created my being with His Names in accord with the meaning of the letter 'B'), the Rahman, the Rahim.

1. I swear by the dawn,

2. And by ten nights,

3. By the even and the odd,

4. And by the night when it passes...

5. Is there not in this a (sufficient) oath for a man of reason?

6. Did you not see how your Rabb dealt with Aad (the people of Hud),

7. And Iram, the (city) with lofty pillars?

8. The like of which has never been created in the land!

9. (What did your Rabb do) to Thamud (the people of Salih), who carved out the rocks in the valley?

10. And Pharaoh, the owner of the tall stakes (the pyramids).

11. They are those who lived egocentrically in the land and transgressed,

12. And increased corruption therein!

13. So your Rabb struck them the whip of suffering.

14. Indeed, your Rabb is in complete observation.

15. But as for man, when his Rabb tries him and is generous to him and bestows His bounties upon him, he says, "My Rabb has honored me, and preferred me (and becomes spoilt)."

16. But when He tries him with an affliction and restricts his provision, he (impatiently) says, "My Rabb has debased and humiliated me."

17. No! No, you do not honor the orphan!

18. And you do not encourage each other to feed the needy.

19. And you consume inheritance, devouring it all at once!

20. And you love wealth and you collect and hoard.

21. No (do not do this)! When the earth is crushed into pieces,

22. And (with death) the angels (forces) line up in ranks with (the command of your) Rabb,

23. It is then that Hell will be brought (to enclose the earth)! And man at that time will remember and think, but what benefit to him will the remembrance be (when he no longer has a body – brain with which he can develop his spirit)?

24. He will say "I wish I had done beneficial things (raised my consciousness level to observe the Names)."

25. And nothing can cause him more suffering at that time than the suffering by Him!

26. And nothing can bind him like the binding of Him!

27. "O the peaceful self (nafs-i mutmainna; one who has reached a state of contentment in experiencing the reality)!"

28. Turn to your Rabb (your essence) as the pleased self (nafs-i radhiya) and the pleasing self (nafs-i mardhiya) (as consciousness, experiencing the beauty of observation and providence)!"

29. "And enter among my servants (who continue their functions having annihilated their 'identities' – their assumed selves – to the bliss of nonexistence)!"

30. "And enter my Paradise!"

90

AL-BALAD

By the one who is denoted by the name Allah (who created my being with His Names in accord with the meaning of the letter 'B'), the Rahman, the Rahim.

1. I swear by this city (the world in which I live)...

2. That you are free of restriction herein!

3. And (I swear) by the One who gives birth (to man) and that which is born of him,

4. We have certainly created man in stages of difficulty!

5. Does he now think that none can overpower him?

6. He says, "I have spent much wealth."

7. Does he think nobody can see him?

8. Did We not form two eyes for him?

9. A tongue and two lips...

10. And showed him the two ways (of falsity and Truth)!

11. But he did not have (the courage) to climb that steep hill!

12. Do you know what that steep hill is?

13. It is to liberate from slavery (to free consciousness from its enslavement to the body)!

14. Or to feed another while hungry!

15. (To feed) an orphan of near relation.

16. Or to feed the impoverished one who is in distress.

17. And then to be of those who believe and advise patience and mercy to one another.

18. These are the people of the right (the fortunate ones).

19. But those who deny Our signs, they are the people of the left (the unfortunate ones).

20. They are enclosed and trapped in Fire!

91

AS-SHAMS

By the one who is denoted by the name Allah (who created my being with His Names in accord with the meaning of the letter 'B'), the Rahman, the Rahim.

1. By the Sun and its light (the time the sun starts to illuminate the earth);

2. And by the Moon when it follows it,

3. And by the day that reveals it,

4. And by the night that covers it,

5. And by the heaven and the One who constructed it,

6. And by the earth and the One who spread it,

7. By the self (the individual consciousness; identity) and the One who proportioned it (formed the brain);

8. Then inspired it as to what will lead it astray from the Truth and the system, and how to protect itself...

9. He who purifies (his consciousness) has succeeded.

10. And he who buries and hides (his consciousness by pursuing unconscious impulses) has lost.

11. Thamud (the people of Salih) denied (their reality and the system) by refusing the Nabi.

12. When the most unfortunate of them rose up,

13. The Rasul of Allah said, "Protect the she-camel of Allah, and her right to drink!"

14. But they denied (the Rasul of Allah) and savagely killed her (the she-camel). So their Rabb destroyed them for their sins and leveled their city to the ground.

15. The consequence of this does not frighten Allah!

92

AL-LAIL

By the one who is denoted by the name Allah (who created my being with His Names in accord with the meaning of the letter 'B'), **the Rahman, the Rahim.**

1. **I swear by the night when it covers over,**

2. **And by the day as it radiantly appears,**

3. **And by the One who created the male and the female** (active and receptive energies),

4. **Indeed, your efforts are of different intentions.**

5. **He who gives** (both of himself, i.e. his constructed identity, and from himself, i.e. from that which is valuable for him) **and protects himself,**

6. **And believes in** (confirms) **the Most Beautiful** (Names) (to be his essential reality),

7. **We will ease him towards ease.**

8. **But as for he who withholds and considers himself free of need** (for purification and protection),

9. **And denies the Most Beautiful** (to be his essential reality),

10. **We will ease him toward the most difficult** (to a life veiled from the knowledge of the reality and the sunnatullah)!

11. **And when he falls** (into Hell) **his wealth will be of no avail to him.**

12. **Upon Us is guidance to the reality.**

13. **And indeed, to Us belongs the eternal life to come and the present one!**

14. **I have warned you of a blazing Fire.**

15. **Only the most unfortunate will be subjected to it.**

16. **Who had denied and turned away** (from his essence)!

17. But the one who sought protection will be kept away from it.

18. The one who spends his wealth on others to become purified (rather than hoarding),

19. And he does this not for a return (nor as the return for anything)!

20. Only for the sake of the countenance of his Rabb, the Most High!

21. And indeed, he will be pleased!

93

AD-DHUHA

By the one who is denoted by the name Allah (who created my being with His Names in accord with the meaning of the letter 'B'), the Rahman, the Rahim.

1. I swear by the morning light (when the sun starts to illuminate the earth; ad-Dhuha),

2. And by the night, the time of tranquility.

3. Your Rabb has not forsaken you nor is He displeased with you!

4. Surely, the eternal life to come is better for you than the present one.

5. Your Rabb is going to give to you and you are going to be well pleased!

6. Did He not find you an orphan and gave you refuge?

7. Did He not find you lost (unaware of your essential reality) and guided you to the reality?

8. And did We not find you poor (faqr, in nothingness) and made you rich (with infinity – baqa, i.e.)? (Did we not make you a servant of the Ghani? Did we not enrich and emancipate you?)

9. So, do not look down on the orphan,

10. And do not scold the one who inquires and wants!

11. Express the blessings of your Rabb!

94

ASH-SHARH

By the one who is denoted by the name Allah (who created my being with His Names in accord with the meaning of the letter 'B'), the Rahman, the Rahim.

1. Did We not expand your breast (broaden your capabilities)?

2. Did We not remove your burden (of your identity) from you (by revealing the reality to you)?

3. Which had weighed (heavy) upon your back (overburdened you)!

4. Did We not exalt your remembrance (by reminding you of and making you live by the reality)?

5. So, surely with every hardship there is ease.

6. Yes, surely with every hardship there is ease.

7. So, when you are free (of your duties) labor (for your actual duty)!

8. And evaluate your Rabb!

95

AT-TIN

By the one who is denoted by the name Allah (who created my being with His Names in accord with the meaning of the letter 'B'), the Rahman, the Rahim.

1. By the fig and the olive,

2. And by Mount Sinai,

3. And by this secure city,

4. We have certainly created man in the best of forms (with the qualities of the Names).

5. Then We reduced him to the lowest of the low (to his world of conditionings).

6. Except for those who believe (in their essential reality) and fulfill the requisites of faith! For them there is an uninterrupted reward!

7. So what can cause you to deny the religion after this (when the reality and the sunnatullah are so evidently observable)?

8. Is Allah not the judge of all judges?

96

AL-ALAQ

By the one who is denoted by the name Allah (who created my being with His Names in accord with the meaning of the letter 'B'), the Rahman, the Rahim.

1. **READ with the Name of your Rabb** (with the knowledge that comprises your being) **who created.**

2. **Created man from alaq** (a clot of blood; genetic composition).

3. **READ! For your Rabb is Akram** (most generous).

4. **Who taught** (programmed the genes and the essential qualities) **by the Pen.**

5. **Taught man that which he knew not.**

6. **No** (it is not like what they think)**! Indeed, man transgresses** (pursues and indulges in his desires when he lives cocooned from his essence);

7. **Because he sees himself as self-sufficient** (the veil of his ego makes him think he is not in need of the reality).

8. **Indeed, to your Rabb is the return!**

9. **Did you see the one who prevents,**

10. **A servant at prayer!**

11. **Did you see** (have a think)**! What if he is living the reality?**

12. **Or demands protection!**

13. **Have a think! What if he denied** (his essence) **and turned away?**

14. **Does he not know that Allah sees?**

15. **No** (it is not like what they think)**! Indeed, if he does not desist, We will drag him by his forehead** (brain)**!**

16. **A lying, mistaken** (driven by corporeality) **forehead** (brain)**!**

17. Then let him call his council!

18. And We shall call the keepers of Hell (the degenerating forces of Fire)!

19. No, do not! Do not obey him! Prostrate and draw near! (This is a verse of prostration.)

97

AL-QADR

By the one who is denoted by the name Allah (who created my being with His Names in accord with the meaning of the letter 'B'), the Rahman, the Rahim.

1. **Indeed, We disclosed it** (the Quran) **during the Night of Power** (of Muhammad [saw])!

2. **Do you know** (the value, honor, magnificence of) **the Night of Power?**

3. **The Night of Power is better than a thousand months** (a lifetime of 80 years).

4. **The angels and the Spirit descend therein by permission of their Rabb** (Name composition) **for every matter** (that has manifested as Allah's decree).

5. **Salam** (the experience of the essence) **it is until the emergence of dawn** (until the consciousness recognizes the disclosure of the reality).

AL-BAYYINA

By the one who is denoted by the name Allah (who created my being with His Names in accord with the meaning of the letter 'B'), the Rahman, the Rahim.

1. **Those deniers of the reality, from among the people of the book and the dualists, were not to part** (from their excessive ways) **until there came to them clear evidence.**

2. **A Rasul from Allah, informing them of the pure pages** (knowledge pertaining to the reality, which those who are not purified from the filth of duality cannot touch).

3. **Within which are solid books** (solid – substantial – reliable information).

4. **But those to whom a Book was given fell into diversion after the clear evidence had come to them.**

5. **Whereas they were not commanded with anything other than to serve Allah by devoting their faith to Him as a Hanif** (without the concept of a deity; with the consciousness of being in servitude to Allah alone), **to establish salat and to give alms... This is the** (valid) **religion** (system)!

6. **Indeed, those who deny the knowledge of the reality, from among the people of the book and the dualists, are in the Fire, to abide therein eternally! They are the most evil of the people!**

7. **As for those who believe and fulfill the requisites of faith, they are the best of people!**

8. **The respite of their deeds in the sight of their Rabb is Paradises of Eden, underneath which rivers flow, to abide therein eternally...** Well-pleased is Allah with them, and well-pleased are they with Him** (the reflections of divine qualities)... **This is for he who is in awe of his Rabb!**

99

AL-ZALZALA

By the one who is denoted by the name Allah (who created my being with His Names in accord with the meaning of the letter 'B'), the Rahman, the Rahim.

1. When the earth (the body) is shaken with an intense quake,

2. And the earth discharges its burdens,

3. And man (consciousness panics and) asks, "What is wrong with it (the body)?"

4. That is the time it will report its news,

5. With a revelation from your Rabb.

6. That day the people will go forth in groups to see the results of their deeds!

7. Whoever does an iota's weight of good will see it,

8. And whoever does an iota's weight of evil will see it.

100

AL-ADIYAT

By the one who is denoted by the name Allah (who created my being with His Names in accord with the meaning of the letter 'B'), the Rahman, the Rahim.

1. By the racers (people who are like wild horses), panting (to collect worldly wealth),

2. Striking sparks of fire (out of their greed and anger),

3. And rising at dawn to make raids,

4. Who stir up clouds of dust with their greed,

5. And push and hustle their way among the people in that state... (woe to them)!

6. Indeed, man is very ungrateful to his Rabb!

7. And to this he bears witness!

8. Indeed, he has an intense desire for wealth!

9. Does he not know when that which is in the grave (the body) is dredged up and taken out,

10. And that which is in the hearts is made manifest,

11. That their Rabb, as the Names comprising their essence, is ever knowing (Habir) of them.

101

AL-QARIA

By the one who is denoted by the name Allah (who created my being with His Names in accord with the meaning of the letter 'B'), **the Rahman, the Rahim.**

1. The Qaria!

2. What a dreadful event, the Qaria!

3. Do you know what the Qaria is?

4. It is the time when the people will be like moths (propelling towards the fire).

5. And the mountains (egos) **like colorful soft wool** (depleted and weak)!

6. So the results of whomever weigh heavy (at that time),

7. He will be in a life well-pleasing!

8. And the results of whomever weigh light,

9. His mother (abode) **will be an abyss.**

10. Do you know what that is?

11. It is a fire that scorches at maximum intensity!

102

AL-TAKATHUR

By the one who is denoted by the name Allah (who created my being with His Names in accord with the meaning of the letter 'B'), **the Rahman, the Rahim.**

1. Greed (for wealth and offspring) **deceived and amused you!**

2. Even when you visited the graves...

3. But no! Soon (with death) **you will know.**

4. Again no! Soon you will know.

5. No! If only you had established your certainty through knowledge (before death)...

6. Indeed, you will definitely see the Hell!

7. Indeed, you will most certainly see it (Hell) **with the eye of certainty.**

8. Then indeed, at that time you will be asked about your blessings.

103

AL-ASR

By the one who is denoted by the name Allah (who created my being with His Names in accord with the meaning of the letter 'B'), **the Rahman, the Rahim.**

1. By that time (the life span of man),

2. Indeed, mankind is in loss!

3. Except for those who have believed (in their essential reality) **and fulfilled the requisites of faith, advised each other of the Truth and advised each other to patience!**

104

AL-HUMAZA

By the one who is denoted by the name Allah (who created my being with His Names in accord with the meaning of the letter 'B'), the Rahman, the Rahim.

1. Woe to every gossiper and abusive reprobate!

2. Who collects wealth and counts it and recounts it (constantly checking his bank account to see how much money he has)!

3. Thinking his wealth will make him immortal!

4. No, (it is not like what he thinks)! Indeed, he will surely be thrown into the Crusher (the crushing torment).

5. And what informs you of the Crusher?

6. It is the inflamed fire of Allah (ignited in the mind, deriving from his nature)!

7. Covering the hearts (the reflectors of the Names to consciousness).

8. Indeed, it closes in on them (they are eternally trapped in it),

9. In extended columns.

105

AL-FIL

By the one who is denoted by the name Allah (who created my being with His Names in accord with the meaning of the letter 'B'), the Rahman, the Rahim.

1. Did you not see how your Rabb dealt with the people of the elephant?

2. Did He not make their plan worthless?

3. And disclosed upon them the birds in flocks (the Common Swift),

4. Who threw upon them stones of hard clay,

5. Until they became like eaten straw.

106

QURAYSH

By the one who is denoted by the name Allah (who created my being with His Names in accord with the meaning of the letter 'B'), the Rahman, the Rahim.

1. In order to establish acquaintenceship and respect for the Quraysh,

2. For the safety and comfort of their winter and summer journeys.

3. Let them serve the Rabb of this city (as those who acknowledge the Truth of non-duality)!

4. Who fed them (saving them from hunger) and secured them from fear.

AL-MA'UN

By the one who is denoted by the name Allah (who created my being with His Names in accord with the meaning of the letter 'B'), **the Rahman, the Rahim.**

1. Did you see the one who denies his religion (the sunnatullah)?

2. Who scolds the orphan – pushing and shoving him,

3. And who does not encourage feeding the needy (stingy, selfish)!

4. So, woe to those who pray (out of custom),

5. Who are heedless (cocooned) **of** (the experience of the meaning of) **their salat** (which is an ascension [miraj] to their innermost essential reality; their Rabb).

6. They are the ones who make a show of their deeds,

7. And prevent good!

108

AL-KAWTHAR

By the one who is denoted by the name Allah (who created my being with His Names in accord with the meaning of the letter 'B'), the Rahman, the Rahim.

1. Indeed, We gave you the Kawthar!

2. So, experience salat for your Rabb and sacrifice (your ego)!

3. Indeed, it is the one who resents you that is cut off (whose progeny has been made discontinuous)!

109

AL-KAFIRUN

By the one who is denoted by the name Allah (who created my being with His Names in accord with the meaning of the letter 'B'), the Rahman, the Rahim.

1. Say, "O those who deny the knowledge of the reality!"

2. "I do not deify that which you deify (your Inciting Self [ego]- the second brain in your gut)."

3. "Nor are you worshippers of (in servitude to) what I worship."

4. "Nor will I worship (serve) that which you deify."

5. Nor will you worship (serve) what I serve."

6. "For you is your (understanding of) religion and for me is (my understanding of) religion!"

AN-NASR

By the one who is denoted by the name Allah (who created my being with His Names in accord with the meaning of the letter 'B'), **the Rahman, the Rahim.**

1. **When the help** (of Allah) **and the conquest** (absolute clarity – conscious observation) **has come,**

2. **And you see the people entering the religion of Allah in masses,**

3. **Glorify** (tasbih) **your Rabb as his Hamd and ask forgiveness of Him! Indeed, He is the Tawwab.**

111

AL-MASAD

By the one who is denoted by the name Allah (who created my being with His Names in accord with the meaning of the letter 'B'), **the Rahman, the Rahim.**

1. May the hands of Abu Lahab be ruined... And ruined he is!

2. Neither his wealth nor his earnings availed him!

3. He will be subject to a blazing Fire!

4. His wife as well... As a wood-carrier!

5. With a rope of palm-fiber around her neck!

112

AL-IKHLAS

By the one who is denoted by the name Allah (who created my being with His Names in accord with the meaning of the letter 'B'), **the Rahman, the Rahim.**

1. Say: "Allah is Ahad (One)." (Allah is the infinite, limitless and indivisible, non-dual ONENESS.)

2. "Allah is Samad." (Absolute Self-Sufficient One beyond any need or defect, free from the concept of multiplicity, and far from conceptualization and limitation. The one into whom nothing can enter, and the One from whom no other form of existence can come out!)

3. "He begets not. (No other form of existence has ever originated from Him, thus, there is no other.) **Nor was He begotten."** (There is no other god or form of existence from which He could have originated.)

4. "There is none like unto Him!" (Nothing – no conception – in the micro or macro planes of existence is equivalent to or in resemblance of Him.)

113

AL-FALAQ

By the one who is denoted by the name Allah (who created my being with His Names in accord with the meaning of the letter 'B'), **the Rahman, the Rahim.**

1. Say (recognize, realize, comprehend, experience): **"I seek refuge in the Rabb** (the reality of the Names comprising my essence) **of the Falaq** (the light that prevails over the darkness and brings enlightenment to me)."

2. "From the evil of His creation."

3. "From the evil of the darkness that settles in my mind preventing me from perceiving and comprehending..."

4. "From the evil of the women who blow on knots (those who manipulate brain waves to make black magic)."

5. "And from the evil eye of the envier when he envies!"

114

AN-NAS

By the one who is denoted by the name Allah (who created my being with His Names in accord with the meaning of the letter 'B'), **the Rahman, the Rahim.**

1. Say (recognize, realize, comprehend, experience): **"I seek refuge in the Rabb** (the reality of the Names comprising the essence) **of the Nas** (mankind)."

2. "The Sovereign of man," (The Malik, the One whose sovereignty and administration is absolute over Nas, mankind.)

3. "The God of man," (The reality of Uluhiyya that resides within the essence of every human, with which he subsists his existence, and mistakenly thinks this state pertains to a god outside of himself!)

4. "From the evil of the whisperer that covertly pervades then retreats, and reduces man to corporeality."

5. "That which whispers illusory thoughts into man's consciousness about man's essential reality."

6. "From among the jinni (invisible forces) **and man!"**

ABOUT THE AUTHOR

Ahmed Hulusi (Born January 21, 1945, Istanbul, Turkey) contemporary Islamic philosopher. From 1965 to this day he has written close to 30 books. His books are written based on Sufi wisdom and explain Islam through scientific principles. His established belief that the knowledge of Allah can only be properly shared without any expectation of return has led him to offer all of his works which include books, articles, and videos free of charge via his web-site. In 1970 he started examining the art of spirit evocation and linked these subjects parallel references in the Quran (smokeless flames and flames instilling pores). He found that these references were in fact pointing to luminous energy which led him to write *Spirit, Man, Jinn* while working as a journalist for the Aksam newspaper in Turkey. Published in 1985, his work called '*Mysteries of Man (Insan ve Sirlari)*' was Hulusi's first foray into decoding the messages of the Quran filled with metaphors and examples through a scientific backdrop. In 1991 he published *A Guide to Prayer and Dhikr (Dua and Zikir)*' where he explains how the repetition of certain prayers and words can lead to the realization of the divine attributes inherent within our essence through increased brain capacity. In 2009 he completed his final work, '*The Key to the Quran through reflections of the Knowledge of Allah*' which encompasses the understanding of leading Sufi scholars such as Abdulkarim al Jili, Abdul-Qadir Gilani, Muhyiddin Ibn al-Arabi, Imam Rabbani, Ahmed ar-Rifai, Imam Ghazali, and Razi, and which approached the messages of the Quran through the secret Key of the letter 'B'.